MARKETING 3e

James L. Burrow

Contributing Writer
Jim Bosiljevac
Associate Creative Director
DDB, San Francisco

SOUTH-WESTERN
CENGAGE Learning

Australia • Brazil • Canada • Mexico • Singapore • Spain • United Kingdom • United States

SOUTH-WESTERN
CENGAGE Learning™

Marketing, 3rd edition

James L. Burrow

Vice President of Editorial, Business: Jack W. Calhoun

Vice President/Editor-in-Chief: Karen Schmohe

Executive Editor: Eve Lewis

Senior Developmental Editor: Penny Shank

Consulting Editor: Peggy Shelton

Marketing Manager: Michael Cloran

Associate Marketing Manager: Linda Kuper

Content Project Manager: Jennifer A. Ziegler

Production Manager: Patricia Matthews Boies

Senior Technology Project Editor: Sally Nieman

Web site Project Manager: Edward Stubenrauch

Manufacturing Coordinator: Kevin Kluck

Production Service: Newgen

Senior Art Director: Tippy McIntosh

Internal Designer: Lou Ann Thesing

Cover Designer: Lou Ann Thesing

Cover Image: Atlantide Phototravel/Corbis

Photography Manager: Darren Wright

Photo Researcher: Peggy Shelton

Advertisement Researcher: Susan Van Etten Lawson

Student Edition ISBN 13: 978-0-538-44664-8
Student Edition ISBN 10: 0-538-44664-1

South-Western Cengage Learning
5191 Natorp Boulevard
Mason, OH 45040
USA

Cengage Learning products are represented in Canada by Nelson Education, Ltd.

For your course and learning solutions, visit **school.cengage.com**

Printed in the United States of America
2 3 4 5 6 7   11 10 09 08

Congratulations to the winners of the South-Western
Marketing 3e Marketing Message Contest

FIRST PLACE   *Marketing 3e*...It's More Than Essential

Vance High School, Charlotte, NC   Teacher: Vincent Esposito

FRONT ROW, Seated (L to R): Charles Carrouthers, Kyra Hoyle, Samantha Lehr, Farren Franklin, Bryan Plesz.
BACK ROW, Standing (L to R): Vince Esposito (Teacher/Advisor), Shawn Holyfield, John Palumbo (2007-2008 ZB Vance DECA President), Adam Mansour, Edoardo Agati, Wesley Cannon, Timothy Vernon, Justin Taylor.

SECOND PLACE   Your Guide to Marketing in the Fast Lane

Algonquin Regional High School, Northborough, MA
Teacher: Michele Tontodonato

THIRD PLACE

Marketing 3e:
Marketing on the Move

West Deptford High School
Westville, NJ
Teacher: Lauren Newman

Presenting the Most Comprehensive

DECA PREP –
Prepare for Performance

DECA Performance Indicators – core performance indicators and supporting performance indicators – are identified at the beginning of each chapter as a preview of chapter content, helping students prepare for competitive events.

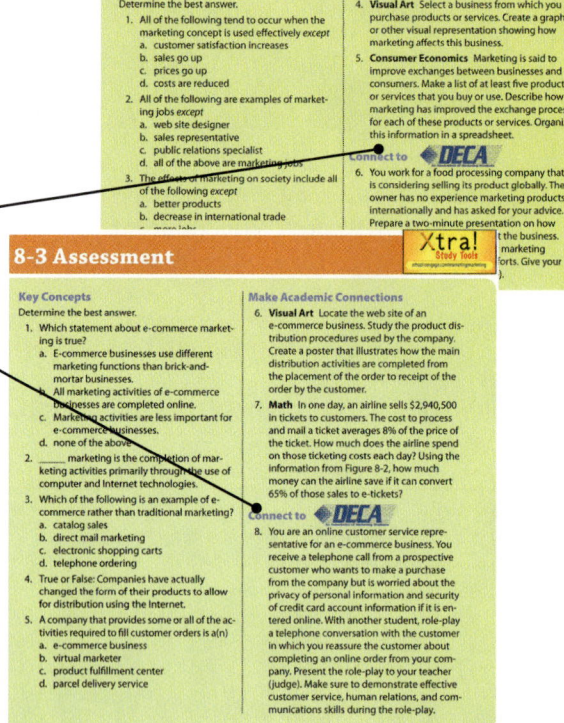

DECA PREP Assessment –
Connect to DECA

Connect to DECA activities at the end of each chapter are short case study activities which focus on DECA prep and require students to apply critical thinking and decision-making skills.

go to **school.cengage.com/marketing/marketing** and click on Connect to DECA

DECA Prep Available!

Creative Marketing Project Event

The Creative Marketing Project gives participants an analytical and creative approach to the marketing process by actively engaging students in the marketing activities of their community. It is designed to encourage students to recognize marketing as a force for the economic and social good of the community. Your project might concern itself with finding new markets for local products, promoting the community's resources, increasing the trading area of facilities, increasing local sales, increasing local employment, providing better shopping facilities, or solving marketing problems or challenges affecting the local community.

This project is limited to 30 numbered pages, including the appendix and excluding the title page and table of contents. Major parts of the written project include the Executive Summary, Introduction, Procedures and Research Methods Used, Findings and Conclusions, Recommendations, Bibliography, and Appendix.

You have been hired by your city to conduct research for attracting an appropriate company and additional business activity to your community. You must consider the population of your city, the available workforce, economic incentives, and the marketing and distribution of the products/services produced by the company you are trying to attract to your community. You will prepare a written entry for this project and an oral presentation to sell your research findings. The oral presentation must cover all performance indicators. You must present a compelling reason for a company to locate in your city.

PHOTOS: ©DECA INC.

Performance Indicators Evaluated

- Describe the project in an organized, clear, and effective presentation. (Communication)
- Identify the marketing information needs of this research project. (Marketing-Information Management)
- Interpret descriptive statistics used in the decision making process. (Marketing-Information Management)
- Explain the findings and recommendations. (Communication)
- Demonstrate professional appearance, poise, and confidence. (Communication)

Go to the DECA web site for more detailed information.

Think Critically

1. What are the greatest assets that your city has to offer a potential business?
2. Why must you describe the workforce in detail when trying to attract a business to a community?
3. How can tax incentives be used to attract business to a community?
4. Why is it important to describe the demographics of your community when presenting to a potential business?

www.deca.org

DECA PREP –
DECA event-prep projects

This **full page event-prep feature** is a project that assists students with competitive-event preparation and includes critical-thinking questions.

Real World Connections!

Visual Focus

Marketing involves a comprehensive set of activities needed to insure effective exchanges between a business and its customers. While we often think of promotion as an important marketing tool, it is no more important than many others. Companies must have a complete marketing strategy, including a quality product that is well priced, distributed, and promoted. This chapter introduces the basic concepts and principles of effective marketing.

Focus Questions:

What do you think is meant by the ad's headline? What role does Visa play in helping businesses market products and services to customers? How do credit and financial services such as the ones described in this ad make it easier for businesses to participate in international commerce?

Locate an advertisement that promotes a unique marketing activity that a company does well. Share your example in a class discussion.

Visual Focus features an actual advertisement that helps tie chapter content to the real world.

Text now includes even more **real-world examples,** making the content interesting, relevant, and tangible for students.

Planning a Career in... *Virtual Product Development*

Science, Technology, Engineering & Mathematics

"It's amazing how quickly new cell phone models are introduced. My stepbrother, who works in Virtual Product Development (VPD), says that VPD software allows companies to bring new products to market more quickly than ever before. To stay competitive, the mobile phone manufacturers keep developing phones with improved functions to meet customers' evolving needs."

Did you ever wonder how someone takes a great idea and makes it into a manufactured product? VPD utilizes state-of-the art software to streamline the development of manufactured items. By providing sophisticated software that integrates multiple planning modules, these software systems allow team members to quickly redesign products while working at different times and different locations.

Employment Outlook
- Computer Software Engineers who design the VPD software are expected to experience very rapid growth in their career fields.
- Industrial Designers who utilize VPD software to conceptualize new products are expected to experience average growth in their career field.

Job Titles
- Industrial Design Engineer
- Virtualization Program Manager
- Simulation Engineer
- Manager, Virtual Prototyping
- Product Development Manager

Needed Skills
- At minimum, a bachelor's degree is required. More complex positions may require a graduate degree, often with additional technology training.
- Strong, conceptual, problem-solving, analytical, and multitasking skills are necessary.

- Creativity, aesthetic sensibilities, and design principles training is needed.

What's it like to work in...
Virtual Product Development

Nitan, an industrial designer for a cell phone manufacturing company, is reviewing virtual customer feedback for two cell phone prototypes. This feedback was obtained without ever producing an actual physical product.

Nitan's VPD supplier developed an interactive, web-based game for consumers chosen by the company to test enhanced cell phone features found on the two prototypes. The game had built-in incentives for accuracy and thorough analysis.

The web site also provided users the opportunity to design their own prototypes. Users could select the most appealing combination of features when designing their ideal cell phone.

Using the combined results from the game and design modules, Nitan, in conjunction with the product engineering team, designed a final virtual prototype. To confirm that the features most important to customers have been properly incorporated, Nitan will have his VPD supplier prepare a 3-D virtual model that will be shown to people within the company, vendors, and consumers for final virtual feedback before a final production decision is confirmed.

By virtually fine-tuning the new cell phone, Nitan has provided his company with cost savings. He has spared his comp lead time and expense of manufactu tangible prototypes.

What About You

Would you like to participate in a vi development process to help your c develop customer-focused products

PHOTO: ©GETTY IMAGES/PHOTODISC

Career coverage is increased with the introduction of the Planning a Career in... feature, which incorporates **Career Clusters.**

SOS – Skills for Occupational Success is a full-page feature that introduces basic skills needed in everyday business and teaches students how to market themselves.

SOS — Skills for Occupational Success

Using Communications Technology Professionally

Gone are the days when people went to their mailboxes hoping for a long awaited letter from an old acquaintance. With 24/7 contact available, be it through e-mail, cell-phones, instant messaging (IM), text messaging, web sites, or blogs, individuals in modern society are accustomed to receiving information in a continuous, ongoing stream.

With the number of electronic communication tools available, it is easy to forget that communication is the objective. Communication devices are merely the tools that facilitate that goal.

Just as courtesy is necessary for face-to-face communication, it is also required for electronic communication. These courtesies are particularly important for business interactions.

Patience is important. Although a request for information can be delivered instantly, a response cannot necessarily be provided immediately. The recipient's schedule and the need to gather information before responding will affect response time.

During meetings, personal interactions take priority over anyone who might be available electronically. While meeting with others, communication devices that would cause distractions should be turned off.

Developing strong interpersonal relationships with coworkers is extremely important. These relationships are strengthened through face-to-face interactions. Therefore, although it may be tempting to IM or call your coworkers, it is often worthwhile to periodically walk down the hall and have a brief chat with them.

Texting and instant messaging use a form of abbreviated spelling designed to facilitate fast communication and to minimize key strokes. While these conventions are appropriate for electronic communications, they are not appropriate for written communications in the workplace. Utilize good grammar and standard English when preparing formal written documents.

E-mail signatures should include only pertinent contact information. Including political or religious quotes or symbols or links to web sites or blogs may violate your employer's e-mail policies.

Many employers monitor employees' use of e-mail and the Web. You should know and adhere to your employer's usage policies.

Keep in mind that the Web and its various components, such as web sites or blogs, are internationally accessible to most users. Use restraint when posting information on web sites. Confidential or negative information regarding an employer should not be posted on personal blogs.

As part of the background check for job applicants, many employers search the Web to see if information is available on the job applicant. Publicly recorded instances of bad behavior could impact your chances of getting hired.

Develop Your Skill

Consider some sensitive information you need to communicate to three people. Outline what your message is and why you need to share it. Define the goal you want to achieve by conveying your message.

Prepare three scripts for communicating the message—one for a phone conversation, one for an e-mail, and one for an IM. Using each type of technology only once, deliver the message to all three people.

Which type of delivery medium was most effective at conveying the message you intended? Which delivery method promoted ongoing, harmonious relationships with the people involved?

PHOTO: ©GETTY IMAGES/PHOTODISC

Engage Student Interest

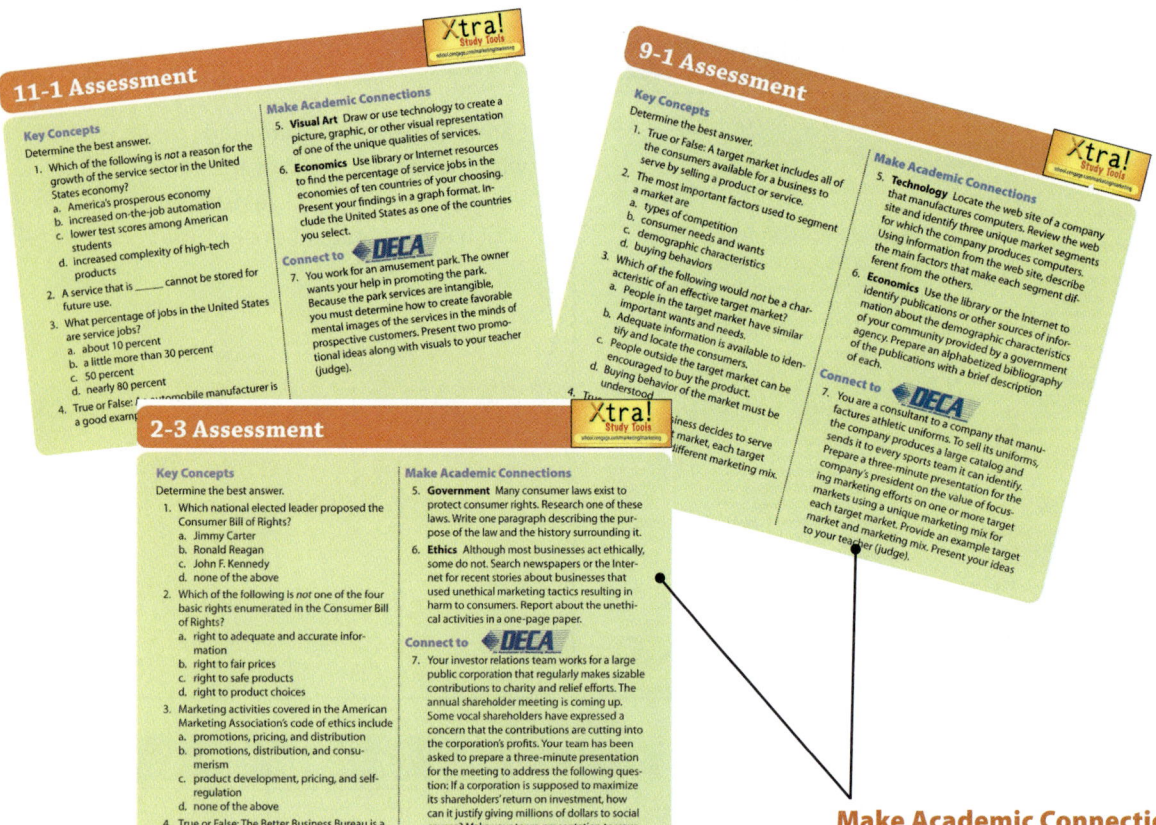

11-1 Assessment

Key Concepts

Determine the best answer.

1. Which of the following is *not* a reason for the growth of the service sector in the United States economy?
   a. America's prosperous economy
   b. increased on-the-job automation
   c. lower test scores among American students
   d. increased complexity of high-tech products
2. A service that is _____ cannot be stored for future use.
3. What percentage of jobs in the United States are service jobs?
   a. about 10 percent
   b. a little more than 30 percent
   c. 50 percent
   d. nearly 80 percent
4. True or False: [An] automobile manufacturer is a good example [...]

Make Academic Connections

5. **Visual Art** Draw or use technology to create a picture, graphic, or other visual representation of one of the unique qualities of services.
6. **Economics** Use library or Internet resources to find the percentage of service jobs in the economies of ten countries of your choosing. Present your findings in a graph format. Include the United States as one of the countries you select.

Connect to DECA

7. You work for an amusement park. The owner wants your help in promoting the park. Because the park services are intangible, you must determine how to create favorable mental images of the services in the minds of prospective customers. Present two promotional ideas along with visuals to your teacher (judge).

9-1 Assessment

Key Concepts

Determine the best answer.

1. True or False: A target market includes all of the consumers available for a business to serve by selling a product or service.
2. The most important factors used to segment a market are
   a. types of competition
   b. consumer needs and wants
   c. demographic characteristics
   d. buying behaviors
3. Which of the following would not be a characteristic of an effective target market?
   a. People in the target market have similar important wants and needs.
   b. Adequate information is available to identify and locate the consumers.
   c. People outside the target market can be encouraged to buy the product.
   d. Buying behavior of the market must be understood.
4. True [or False:] [...] business decides to serve [...] market, each target [...] different marketing mix.

Make Academic Connections

5. **Technology** Locate the web site of a company that manufactures computers. Review the web site and identify three unique market segments for which the company produces computers. Using information from the web site, describe the main factors that make each segment different from the others.
6. **Economics** Use the library or the Internet to identify publications or other sources of information about the demographic characteristics of your community provided by a government agency. Prepare an alphabetized bibliography of the publications with a brief description of each.

Connect to DECA

7. You are a consultant to a company that manufactures athletic uniforms. To sell its uniforms, the company produces a large catalog and sends it to every sports team it can identify. Prepare a three-minute presentation for the company's president on the value of focusing marketing efforts on one or more target markets using a unique marketing mix for each target market. Provide an example target market and marketing mix for each target market. Present your ideas to your teacher (judge).

2-3 Assessment

Key Concepts

Determine the best answer.

1. Which national elected leader proposed the Consumer Bill of Rights?
   a. Jimmy Carter
   b. Ronald Reagan
   c. John F. Kennedy
   d. none of the above
2. Which of the following is *not* one of the four basic rights enumerated in the Consumer Bill of Rights?
   a. right to adequate and accurate information
   b. right to fair prices
   c. right to safe products
   d. right to product choices
3. Marketing activities covered in the American Marketing Association's code of ethics include
   a. promotions, pricing, and distribution
   b. promotions, distribution, and consumerism
   c. product development, pricing, and self-regulation
   d. none of the above
4. True or False: The Better Business Bureau is a consumer protection organization sponsored by consumer groups.

Make Academic Connections

5. **Government** Many consumer laws exist to protect consumer rights. Research one of these laws. Write one paragraph describing the purpose of the law and the history surrounding it.
6. **Ethics** Although most businesses act ethically, some do not. Search newspapers or the Internet for recent stories about businesses that used unethical marketing tactics resulting in harm to consumers. Report about the unethical activities in a one-page paper.

Connect to DECA

7. Your investor relations team works for a large public corporation that regularly makes sizable contributions to charity and relief efforts. The annual shareholder meeting is coming up. Some vocal shareholders have expressed a concern that the contributions are cutting into the corporation's profits. Your team has been asked to prepare a three-minute presentation for the meeting to address the following question: If a corporation is supposed to maximize its shareholders' return on investment, how can it justify giving millions of dollars to social causes? Make your team presentation to your teacher (judge).

Make Academic Connections at the end of each lesson links chapter content to core-curricular areas and includes activities for:

- Career Planning
- Careers
- Civics
- Communication
- Consumer Economics
- Decision Making
- Economics
- English
- Entrepreneurship
- Ethics
- Finance
- Geography
- Government
- History
- Language Arts
- Management
- Math
- Psychology
- Reading
- Research
- Science
- Social Studies
- Sociology
- Statistics
- Success Skills
- Technology
- Visual Arts
- Writing

Channel Management
Marketing-Information Management
Market Planning
Pricing
Product/Service Management
Promotion
Selling
MARKETING
Marketing Core
Career Pathways™

Marketing Standards – The latest Marketing Standards identified by the Marketing Education Resource Center (MarkED) are covered and visually identified throughout the text where appropriate.

Special Features Enhance Learning!

World View

Online Music Stores Think Globally, Price Locally

The Internet has revolutionized the way people buy music. Downloading music has become the preferred method of purchase for many consumers. Online music stores, such as Apple's iTunes, allow customers to purchase music instantly and as individual songs if they don't want to buy an entire album. Albums are never sold out, and there are no shipping costs.

Just because people everywhere in the world have access to the Internet does not necessarily mean that they can all buy the same music at the same price. Music licensing agreements are complicated and usually stipulate in which countries certain music can be distributed. As a result, the same

music that is available in Japan, for example, may not be available to U.S. customers and vice versa.

The real benefit of segregated markets is to the online music stores. Keeping markets separate allows stores to better control the price of their music. Based on demand and what ~~~~~~~~~~~~~~~~~~~~~ may ~~~~~~~~~~~~~~~~~~ song ~~~~~~~~~~~

Thin~
1. ~~~~~~~~~~
2. ~~~~~~~~~~~~~

World View is a multi-cultural feature that discusses marketing techniques in the rest of the world.

Get the Message

Today's Fragmented Media

Fifty years ago, people got their information from a limited number of media outlets. Towns had one or two newspapers; there were only a few network television and radio stations; and there were a limited number of magazines.

~~~~~~~~~~~~~~~~~~~~~ sion
~~~~~~~~~~~~~~~~ res carry
~~~~~~~~~~~~~ est,
~~~~~~~~~~~~ M, and
~~~~~~~~~~~~ rowing
~~~~~~~~~~ e media
~~~~~~~~~ neral,
~~~~~~~~ because
~~~~~~~ media

outlets—a phenomenon known as media fragmentation.

What increasingly fragmented media mean to marketers is that they have to work harder to reach a broad audience. A TV commercial during the most popular show today will not reach as many people as one during the most popular show in 1980. Today, marketers might have to run the commercial on many different stations.

Think Critically
1. What are some advantages to consumers of media that is fragmented?
2. How do fragmented media make it easier for marketers to reach potential buyers?

Get the Message describes challenges, techniques, devices, and media used to convey product information to customers.

Digital Digest

Digital Photos Speed Products to Market

As the cost of digital photography declines and makes it affordable for more and more people, some businesses are cashing in on its advantages over film photography. PetSmart Inc., which sells pet products through stores, a web site, and a mail-order catalog, has used digital photography to slash the time it takes to bring new products to market. What used to take two or three months is now done in one month.

Digital photographs are transmitted over the Internet between the company's buyers and suppliers. Buyers show suppliers what colors they want or send sketches of new product ideas. Suppliers transmit images of products in development and get instantaneous approval to go ahead or instructions to make changes. The company

not only stays on top of its market but also saves lots of money by eliminating the need for much overseas travel.

The National Football League has also used digital photography to get products on the market quickly, taking maximum advantage of fans' Super Bowl enthusiasm before it cools off in the days after the game. Using digital photographs, it cuts at least one day off its production schedule for Super Bowl commemorative books. Those small but critical time savings can translate into a huge difference in profits.

Think Critically
1. What are the advantages of bringing products to market more quickly?
2. What do you think might be some drawbacks to using digital photography?

Digital Digest presents different technologies, software, hardware, and their computer-related issues useful to marketers.

Virtual Marketing

Interactivity Propels Kiosks

At one time, retailers thought video kiosks were going to revolutionize the way people shop. But aside from bank ATMs, kiosks were slow to catch on. The development of the World Wide Web and high-speed data transfers, however, may have supplied the missing ingredients needed for kiosks to take off.

Interactive kiosks can be networked and monitored from a central location through a retailer's web site. Instead of delivering the same information or promotions to every user, they can identify individuals and customize each presentation based on their buying habits or personal preferences.

Moreover, the enhanced capabilities of interactive kiosks arrived at the same time that the cost of hardware and software was coming down dramatically. For a fraction of the monthly cost of a minimum-wage

employee, a kiosk can supply customers with information, distribute coupons and other individualized promotions, or process orders and sales transactions.

For retailers and shoppers, kiosks can deliver the combined advantages of in-store ~~~~~~~~~~~~~~~~~~~~~ versa ~~~~~~~~~~~~~~~~~~~ larly ~~~~~~~~~~~~~~~~ reac ~~~~~~~~

Thi~
1. H~~~~~~~~~
    h~~~~~~~~~~~
    u~~~~~~~~~
2. U~~~~~~~~~~
    y~~~~~~~~~
3. D~~~~~~~~~
    f~~~~~~~~~~
    b~~~~~~~~

Virtual Marketing offers specific information about how the Internet is changing traditional ways of marketing.

Figure This

The Consumer Price Index (CPI)

Marketers are responsible for developing strategies to sell a company's products and services to consumers. Those consumers must decide how to spend the money they have available to get the greatest value and satisfaction from the purchases they make. Competition among businesses, improvements in technology and business procedures, and greater productivity from employees cause product prices to decrease over time. However, inflation results in increases in the prices customers pay. To measure the effect of inflation on consumer prices, the federal government calculates the Consumer Price Index (CPI). The CPI compares the cost of a group of products and services commonly purchased by consumers from year to year.

The base year, or a CPI of 100, was established as 1983. Years prior to the base year

have a CPI less than 100, and years after the base year have a CPI greater than 100. For example, the CPI for 1915 was 9.1, for 1950, 24.1, and for 1995, 152.4. If a consumer purchased $350 of goods and services in 1983, those same purchases would have cost $31.85 in 1915 ($350 × .091), $84.35 in 1950 ($350 × .241), and $533.40 in 1995 ($350 × 1.524).

Think Critically
1. If the cost of an automobile in 1983 was $15,580, how much could we expect the price to increase due to inflation by 2007 if the CPI for that year was 205.5?
2. If the actual cost of the automobile was less than what would be expected based on the CPI, what could account for the lower price?

Figure This teaches mathematical concepts important for successful marketers.

Judgment Call

Misuses of Marketing Affect Its Image

Consumers develop a negative view of marketing when they see companies use marketing practices that take advantage of customers or mislead them without satisfying their ~~~~~~~~~~~~~~~~~~~~~ business ~~~~~~~~~~~~~~~~~~~ le, not de- ~~~~~~~~~~~~~~~~ Common ~~~~~~~~~~~~~~~ or a price ~~~~~~~~~~~~~~ rice but ~~~~~~~~~~~ p it quickly

- Using misleading photos or descriptions of products in advertising.
- Asking people to participate in a survey but using the information to try to sell them something.

Think Critically
1. What other examples of misleading or inappropriate marketing have you experienced? How did you feel about the product and company?
2. What can people do to discourage misuse of marketing when they encounter it?

Judgment Call examines laws that control the marketing industry and ethical dilemmas faced by marketing professionals.

Integrated Technology Tools!

Instructor's Resource CD *includes:*

- DECA Competitive Events Guide
- DECA Prep PowerPoint Slides
- National MarkED Curriculum Correlation
- A*S*K Institute Competencies Correlation
- PowerPoint Slides
- Lesson Plans
- Marketing Planning Guide
- Activities & Study Guide, Student Edition
- Activities & Study Guide, Instructor's Edition
- Portfolio Forms
- Chapter Tests, Student Edition
- Chapter Tests, Instructor's Edition
- DVD Discussion Guide
- Teaching Tools

Exam*View*® CD– Save time while creating and grading quizzes, study guides, and tests easily and quickly with **Exam*View***. This computerized testing tool allows you to create paper and online tests and is ideal for building tests, worksheets, and study guides (practice tests).

New DVD – includes short, engaging video clips that motivate students to learn, while allowing teachers to easily add interest to the class and emphasize practical applications.

New Text/eBook Bundle – eBooks can be viewed on the computer and look exactly like the printed version, including content, photos, graphics, and rich fonts. Students can customize content by annotating text, highlighting key passages, inserting notes, and bookmarking pages.

Product Web Site –

school.cengage.com/marketing/marketing
Will include **DECA written event templates!**

Xtra! Study Tools provide an interactive review of every lesson with games such as Beat the Clock, First Things First, Labeler, Scenario, Sort it Out, etc.

Xtra! Quiz Prep provides an online review with immediate feedback.

NET Bookmark

Religious institutions, use marketing strategies to attract and keep members. Access school. cengage.com/marketing/marketing. Click on the link for Chapter 4, and visit the web site for Mustard Seed Studio, a leading church marketing company. What strategies does Mustard Seed Studio suggest churches use to create a "guest-friendly environment"? (Hint: Click the *Guestology* link.)

school.cengage.com/marketing/marketing

Net Bookmark encourages students to use the Internet for research. Product Web site provides a safe portal for students to gather real data for analysis.

Contents

DECA Prep Events

Features

Newsline

Visual Focus

Digital Digest

Figure This

Get the Message

Judgment Call

Planning a Career

SOS Skills for Occupational Success

Virtual Marketing

World View

Reviewers

Lisa Baynes
Marketing Teacher
Tunstall High School
Dry Fork, Virginia

James Belongia
Business Education Instructor
Green Bay East High School
Green Bay, Wisconsin

Patricia J. Bowie
Teacher, Fashion Merchandising
and Management
Warwick Area Career and Tech
Center
Warwick, Rhode Island

Madeline Cooper
Chair, Career and Technology
Marketing Education Teacher
Liberty-Eylau High School
Texarkana, Texas

Michael Crawford
Marketing/Advertising Instructor
GASC Technology Center
Flint, Michigan

Vincent Esposito
Marketing Teacher
DECA Advisor
Zebulon B. Vance High School
Charlotte, North Carolina

Tina L. Fulks
Department Chair
Business/Marketing Teacher
DECA Advisor
Sierra Vista High School
Las Vegas, Nevada

Deborah Hageman
Business Instructor
Northeast Iowa Community
College
Calmar, Iowa

Ryan Harrison
Marketing Education Teacher/
Coordinator
DECA Advisor
Rosemount High School
Rosemount, Minnesota

Kevin Hermann
Marketing Instructor/
Coordinator
CTE Department Chair
DECA Advisor
Mounds View High School
Arden Hills, Minnesota

Darrin L. Joines
Marketing Educator
Beech High School
Hendersonville, Tennessee

Joan M. Owen
Marketing/Business Instructor
Woods Cross High School
Woods Cross, Utah

Lynn Pitchford
Marketing Education
Coordinator
Tabb High School
Yorktown, Virginia

Elizabeth S. Pitts
Marketing Teacher
North Hall High School
Gainesville, Georgia

Michele Ray
Teacher
Blue Springs South High School
Blue Springs, Missouri

Bob Reinhardt
Business/Marketing Teacher
Cascade High School
Turner, Oregon

Kevin Reisenauer
State Supervisor, Marketing
Education
Career and Technical Education
Bismarck, North Dakota

Thomas A. Scharine
Marketing Teacher
Oregon High School
Oregon, Wisconsin

Jeffrey A. Schettino
Marketing Education
Coordinator
Turner High School
Kansas City, Kansas

Susan Schonauer
Marketing Research/
Management Instructor
Indian Hill High School
Great Oaks Institute of
Technology and Career
Development Satellite
Cincinnati, Ohio

Mark Steedly
Sports Marketing Instructor
Winton Woods High School
Great Oaks Institute of
Technology and Career
Development Satellite
Cincinnati, Ohio

Michael Vialpando
Department Chair
La Joya Community High School
Phoenix, Arizona

Marketing Today and Tomorrow

1-1 What Is Marketing?

1-2 Business Needs Marketing

1-3 Understanding the Marketing Concept

1-4 The Changing Role of Marketing

©GETTY IMAGES/PHOTODISC

Newsline

U.S. Exports Marketing Expertise

People around the world often look to the United States to determine what is the latest and hottest in consumer products, lifestyles, and trends. They are quick to adopt fashions, food, films, and the latest in technology. In much the same way, as developing countries adopt principles of capitalism and participate in international business, many look to the United States for expertise and leadership. They need help transforming their economies and organizing and managing their marketing systems. Many countries such as those that made up the former Soviet Union, African and Eastern European nations, and even China are changing from government controlled economies to free enterprise systems.

The capability of producing and manufacturing good products is not enough to guarantee the success of companies or economies. Marketing activities are also necessary. Companies and countries must understand consumer and customer needs and produce products that meet those needs. They must be able to move products efficiently, develop effective communications and promotion programs, assist with pricing and financing, and make sure products are useful, durable, and reliable.

Under government-controlled economies, companies were not as concerned about consumer needs or efficient business operations. Marketing was not well understood, making it difficult to apply the changes needed for new economic systems to succeed.

Hundreds of U.S. marketing experts went to work. They helped foreign governments and businesses redesign transportation systems, improve processes for handling and storing products, plan and use market research, and establish credit and financing procedures. They also assisted with many other activities needed for effective marketing. Those countries and their citizens are now reaping the rewards of U.S. marketing leadership.

Think Critically

1. Why is there often limited marketing expertise in government-controlled economies?

2. What advantages, if any, does the United States gain by providing marketing expertise and support to developing countries?

school.cengage.com/marketing/marketing

Prepare for Performance

This chapter develops the following Performance Indicators from the DECA Competitive Events program.

Core Performance Indicators

- Understand marketing's role and function in business to facilitate economic exchanges with customers
- Employ products/services to acquire desired business image
- Employ product-mix strategies to meet customer expectations
- Evaluate the effectiveness of the marketing-communications mix to make product-mix decisions

Supporting Performance Indicators

- Explain marketing and its importance in a global economy
- Describe marketing functions and related activities
- Explain the concept of product mix
- Plan product mix
- Identify product to fill customer need
- Explain the nature of product extension in services marketing

Go to **school.cengage.com/marketing/marketing** and click on Connect to DECA.

AD PROVIDED WITH PERMISSION BY CARGILL. ©2007 CARGILL, INCORPORATED.

Visual Focus

Marketing is often quite different than we expect. Often unique efforts are required to make sure that the products and services of a company are available to customers wherever they are located and at the time and in the form that satisfies customer needs. This chapter introduces you to marketing and its importance to businesses, other organizations, and consumers. You will learn how marketing has become a very important economic activity.

Focus Questions:

What marketing activities are being demonstrated by Cargill in the advertisement? Why do you believe a large international company like Cargill is concerned about how to get products to consumers living in Central America?

Locate another advertisement or visual example of a unique or unusual form of marketing used by a business to make sure its products are available to its customers. Share your example in a class discussion.

What Is Marketing?

GOALS

- Understand the importance of studying marketing.
- Explain what marketing is and describe important marketing functions.
- Define marketing.

KEY TERMS

marketing, *p. 9*

marketing matters

Marketing is one of the most important functions in today's American and international companies. It is estimated that companies worldwide spend over $250 billion on advertising each year. That amount is huge, but it is only a small piece of the large marketing pie. Many companies budget 50 percent of their expenses for marketing activities. For some e-commerce businesses, that amount can rise to nearly 90 percent of costs.

Work with team members to generate a list of ten different business activities that you feel are examples of marketing. What jobs and careers could be related to those activities? Discuss the differences among team members' views.

Why Study Marketing?

Marketing is exciting, important, and profitable. Businesses, individual consumers, and our economy benefit from effective marketing. This chapter introduces marketing in a way many people will not recognize. Even though *marketing* is a well-known word, it is often misused or misunderstood. Marketing activities and marketing jobs have changed a great deal in the past and will continue to change. Even though forms of marketing have been around for centuries, some businesses still do not understand marketing well or use it effectively.

Marketing is an important part of business operations and includes a number of different activities. Marketing is now seen as essential to the success not only of manufacturers, retailers, and other businesses but also of government agencies, hospitals, law offices, schools, and churches. Successful businesses and other organizations

Why is marketing an important part of a retail business?

©GETTY IMAGES/PHOTODISC

recognize the difference between effective and ineffective marketing. They develop an approach to marketing that responds to the needs of customers. They know that effective marketing leads to satisfied customers and a successful, profitable business.

Where Does Marketing Take Place?

Marketing is one of the most visible areas of business around you. You may not typically see products being manufactured, accountants maintaining the financial records of a business, or human resource employees hiring and training personnel. But you see marketing every day. Marketing includes advertisements in all types of media, products being transported by truck, train, and airplane, and marketing researchers surveying shoppers in shopping malls.

As a consumer, you are not involved in most business operations, but you make marketing decisions and participate in marketing activities every day. You are involved in marketing when you decide to make a purchase in a store or on the Internet, when you decide whether to pay for an item with cash or a debit card, and when you pay to transport a bulky item to your home rather than transport it yourself.

As you study marketing, you will learn how businesses use marketing effectively and profitably. You will see how you can use marketing skills in your personal life. Those skills can help you make better purchasing decisions as a consumer. They can help you as you complete an application for college or interview with a potential employer. They can help you be a more effective leader of an organization. They also are the skills needed for many exciting and well-paying business careers.

How Do Businesses Use Marketing?

Every business today is involved in marketing. Over four million companies in the United States have marketing as their primary business activity (see Figure 1-1). Most of the efforts of those businesses are directed at completing marketing activities rather than producing goods or providing other business services. Other companies, while not directly involved in marketing, devote a large part of their resources to marketing activities. Large businesses have marketing departments employing many types of marketing specialists. Even small companies employ people who can complete many marketing activities.

What Are Marketing Job Opportunities?

There are many types of marketing jobs, ranging from selling to inventory management. Careers in advertising, sales promotion, customer service, credit, insurance, transportation, and research require preparation in marketing. Marketers work

FIGURE 1-1
Some businesses are more actively involved in marketing than others, but all businesses complete many marketing activities.

All Types of Businesses Use Marketing

Businesses Directly Involved in Marketing	Businesses with Major Marketing Activities	Businesses with Limited Marketing Role
• advertising agencies	• retailers	• law offices
• marketing research firms	• manufacturers	• medical centers
• import/export offices	• banks	• accounting firms
• freight companies	• real estate agencies	• government agencies
• finance and credit firms	• insurance companies	• universities
• telemarketers	• automobile dealers	• construction businesses
• travel agencies	• farmers and ranchers	• public utilities

for manufacturers, law offices, hospitals, museums, professional sports teams, and symphonies.

Marketing jobs are available as you begin your career. These jobs include retail clerk, bank teller, stock person, telemarketing interviewer, and delivery person. You could advance to many marketing management jobs, some requiring a great deal of education and experience. Typically, marketing positions can be among the highest paid jobs in most companies. Because of the change and growth in marketing, many people view it as the most diverse and exciting career area of the twenty-first century.

Checkpoint ▶▶

Name three types of businesses whose activities are devoted almost entirely to marketing.

What Is Marketing?

When many people hear the word *marketing*, they think of only advertising and selling. However, many marketing activities need to be completed before a product or service is ready to be advertised and sold. Those many activities can be grouped within major marketing *functions* or related activities designed to accomplish an important marketing goal.

Fast FACTS

A large consumer products company may introduce as many as 100 new products a year. On average only five percent of new products are successful.

Marketing Functions

Many marketers recognize nine marketing functions. You will learn more about the functions and how each function is used as a part of effective marketing in later chapters. Here is a description of each.

Market Planning Identifying and understanding the markets a company wants to serve and developing effective marketing strategies for each market.

Product and Service Management Assisting in the design and development of products and services to meet the needs of prospective customers.

Distribution Determining the best methods and procedures to be used so prospective customers are able to locate, obtain, and use the products and services of an organization.

Pricing Establishing and communicating the value of products and services to prospective customers.

Promotion Communicating information to prospective customers through advertising and other promotional methods to encourage them to purchase the organization's products and services.

Selling Direct, personal communications with prospective customers in order to assess needs and satisfy those needs with appropriate products and services.

Marketing-Information Management Obtaining, managing, and using market information to improve decision making and the performance of marketing activities.

Financing Budgeting for necessary financing, and providing financial assistance to customers to assist them with purchasing products and services.

Risk Management Providing security for products, personnel, and customers and reducing the risk associated with marketing decisions and activities.

Each of these functions occurs every time a product or service is developed and sold. The performance of the activities described in the functions is the responsibility of marketers. So you can see that marketing is a very complex part of business and is very important to the success of businesses and to the satisfaction of customers.

How Companies Use the Marketing Functions

When you understand the marketing functions, you will be able to recognize the activities being performed by companies as they develop new products, improve marketing procedures, and respond to customer needs. You can find examples of these functions in hundreds of different forms.

Apple used *product/service management* by combining the technologies of a widescreen iPod, a cellular telephone, and an improved Internet browser to produce the iPhone.

Led by Hertz, most airport rental car companies now offer a convenient *distribution* strategy. Through a pre-arranged rental agreement completed online or by telephone, the customer's automobile is waiting with all paperwork completed to speed his or her departure.

Many professional firms are recognizing the importance of *personal selling.* Selected executives in law offices, accounting firms, and banks are completing professional sales training in order to effectively obtain new clients and handle their needs.

An example of *marketing-information management* is the use of electronic scanners at supermarket checkouts. They provide information about purchases so that managers can instantly determine what is being purchased, enabling them to keep the best assortment of products available.

To reduce their inventory of existing homes when there is a slump in housing sales, a major construction company offers customized decorating and new furnishings to customers who sign a purchase contract within 30 days. Rather than cutting the price of the home, this *pricing* incentive works to maintain sales levels while competitors continue to struggle.

Businesses selling expensive products, such as oceanfront condominiums, personal aircrafts, or yachts, prepare high-quality promotional CDs and brochures that provide detailed product information. The *promotion* materials are sent to selected customers to interest them in purchasing the product.

Major automobile manufacturers demonstrate the *financing* function when they maintain their own financing organizations to make loans or provide leases to consumers who purchase their products from local dealers.

©GETTY IMAGES/PHOTODISC

How might the information obtained from electronic scanners be used by store owners?

Marketing Core Standards for Employment

Marketing jobs exist in every industry and within most companies. Marketing jobs are found at the lowest and highest levels of a company and are available for people with varied amounts of education and experience. Job opportunities in marketing are available to match any interests.

Career programs in Marketing Education provide the most comprehensive preparation opportunities for high school students considering full-time employment in marketing after graduation or for those considering additional education after high school. A Marketing Education program incorporates complementary learning experiences—introductory and advanced courses in marketing, a student organization (DECA), and when appropriate, structured work experiences through internships and cooperative education.

To prepare for careers in marketing, you need a broad understanding of marketing functions and activities. You will also need to develop skills in one or more of the functions. In Marketing Education, seven curriculum areas have been identified as essential skills needed by marketers and are designated as Marketing Core Standards, as shown in Figure 1-2. Successful marketers must have a strong understanding of each core standard as described below.

 **Market Planning** Marketers must understand the concepts and strategies utilized to determine and target marketing strategies to a select audience.

 **Marketing-Information Management** Marketers must understand the concepts, systems, and tools needed to gather, access, synthesize, evaluate, and disseminate information for use in making business decisions.

FIGURE 1-2
Marketing Education identifies seven Core Standards for marketing employment.

 Judgment Call

Misuses of Marketing Affect Its Image

Consumers develop a negative view of marketing when they see companies use marketing practices that take advantage of customers or mislead them without satisfying their needs. That tends to occur when a business is concerned only with making a sale, not developing a long-term relationship. Common ways marketing is misused include:

- Stating that a product is on sale or a price is reduced when it really is not.
- Advertising a product at a low price but stocking only a small quantity so it quickly sells out.

- Using misleading photos or descriptions of products in advertising.
- Asking people to participate in a survey but using the information to try to sell them something.

Think Critically

1. What other examples of misleading or inappropriate marketing have you experienced? How did you feel about the product and company?

2. What can people do to discourage misuse of marketing when they encounter it?

Product and Service Management

Marketers must understand the concepts and processes needed to obtain, develop, maintain, and improve a product or service mix in response to market opportunities.

Channel Management
Marketers must understand the concepts and processes needed to identify, select, monitor, and evaluate sales channels.

Pricing
Marketers must understand concepts and strategies utilized in determining and adjusting prices to maximize return and meet customers' perceptions of value.

Promotion
Marketers must understand the concepts and strategies needed to communicate information about products, services, images, and/or ideas to achieve a desired outcome.

Selling
Marketers must understand the concepts and actions needed to determine client needs and wants and respond through planned, personalized communication that influences purchase decisions and enhances future business opportunities.

Checkpoint ▶▶▶

Which of the nine marketing functions occurs when a product is developed and sold?

Define Marketing

Because of the many functions and activities that are part of marketing, it is not easy to develop a definition that effectively describes it. A simple definition was presented in 1960 by the American Marketing Association (AMA). Marketing was described as "the performance of business activities that direct the flow of goods and services from producer to consumer or user." As marketing developed and was applied in a broad set of organizations, definitions became more complex. Marketing now includes customer research and product development activities. It applies to nonprofit businesses and to organizations not considered businesses (churches, schools, libraries). Not only is marketing used for products and services, it is also used for individuals (political candidates, artists, sports stars) and even to promote ideas (stop smoking, recycle, stay in school).

The most recent definition of marketing, accepted by the AMA in 2004, communicates how marketing has changed over the years. It defines marketing as "an organizational function and a set of processes for creating, communicating, and delivering value to customers and for managing customer relationships in ways that benefit the organization and its stakeholders."

Because marketing can be applied in different ways in various organizations, and because marketing needs to be easily understood, the following definition describes the value marketing offers to those who use it well. **Marketing** is the creation and maintenance of satisfying exchange relationships.

You need to carefully consider all parts of this definition in order to understand marketing. *Creation* suggests that marketing is involved from the beginning as products and services are being developed. *Maintenance* means that marketing must continue to be used as long as a business or organization is operating. *Satisfaction* of both the business and the customer is an important goal of marketing. When products and services are exchanged, the needs of everyone involved must be met as well as possible. *Exchange relationship* applies the definition to any exchange where people are giving and receiving something of value as shown in Figure 1-3. Marketing is needed by, but not limited to, businesses that are selling products and services.

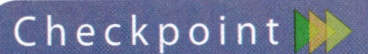

Checkpoint

What kinds of relationships exist when marketing is successful?

FIGURE 1-3
Marketing is a part of many types of exchanges.

Business/Organization	Exchange	Customer
• movie theater	• convenient and enjoyable access to entertainment	• moviegoers
• grain farmer	• high-quality wheat delivered for processing	• cereal manufacturer
• physician	• treatment for illnesses and injuries; health care	• patients
• college	• courses, degrees, professional development	• students
• commercial airline	• safe, on-time, and comfortable transportation between cities	• business travelers, individuals, and families
• city government	• clean and well-maintained streets, police and fire protection, enjoyable living	• citizens

1-1 Assessment

Key Concepts

Determine the best answer.

1. Marketing involves which of the following
   a. advertising
   b. transporting products
   c. taking surveys
   d. all of the above

2. A business with a limited marketing role is
   a. a retailer
   b. a farmer or rancher
   c. a physician's office
   d. none of the above has a limited marketing role

3. Which of the following is the best description of an important goal of marketing?
   a. satisfying exchanges
   b. profitable distribution
   c. creation of new products
   d. attention-getting promotions

Make Academic Connections

4. **Visual Art** Draw or use technology to create a picture, graphic, or other visual representation of the definition of marketing and common activities that are a part of marketing.

5. **Careers** Use the career center in your school or the Internet to identify a marketing job that would have major responsibilities for each of the nine marketing functions. Prepare a chart that lists the function, the job title, and a brief description of the work responsibilities that are a part of the job.

Connect to

6. Develop a two-minute presentation on the importance of marketing for businesses, other organizations, and consumers. Make sure to include an explanation of the definition of marketing. Prepare an outline of your presentation and one visual aid. Give your presentation to your teacher (judge).

Business Needs Marketing

GOALS

- Explain why businesses need marketing.
- Understand how marketing developed as a part of business.
- Describe the functions of business.

KEY TERMS

self-sufficient, *p. 12*

bartering, *p. 12*

specialization of labor, *p. 13*

money system, *p. 13*

central market, *p. 13*

production, *p. 14*

merchandising, *p. 15*

operations, *p. 15*

accounting and finance, *p. 15*

management, *p. 16*

marketing matters

Over time, marketing has developed into a sophisticated and complex business function. Several simple business activities that were taken for granted in the past have become important marketing tools today. For example, 100 years ago, providing credit to regular customers was common and was managed with a pen and paper to record customers' purchases. Today, providing financing options, including credit, is a complex process requiring computerized records and entire divisions of a business.

Working with team members, imagine that you are running a business 100 years ago. Think of a marketing activity that might have been common at that time. Discuss how that activity is performed today. Share your discussion results with the other teams.

The Need for Marketing

Ever since people began exchanging things with each other, there has been a need for marketing. In the past, marketing was viewed as a simple set of activities that helped a business sell its products to more customers. The first businesses developed ideas and activities designed to attract interest and sell their products.

Business executives know that marketing must be carefully planned and coordinated with other business activities. The approach to managing marketing activities changes as organizations understand what makes marketing effective.

Marketing is necessary in every business. Some people believe that if a business offers a good product, marketing is not necessary. However, if the customer does not know about the product, does not know where to purchase it, is unable to get to the place where it is sold, cannot afford the price being charged, or does not believe it is a good value, the product will not be purchased. A variety of marketing activities are required so that customers will be able to purchase the product and will be satisfied with their decision.

Marketing cannot be successful if the product is not what the customer wants or

Working in Teams

Form a team and discuss products you have purchased that you later found were not what you expected. Why did you make the purchase, and what did you do when you became dissatisfied? As a team, suggest how businesses could do a better job of satisfying customers.

if the quality is low. While a customer may be encouraged to buy a product through advertising, selling, or low pricing, the product must be viewed as satisfying a need. If the customer decides to buy the product but it is defective or does not work the way the customer was led to believe, the customer will likely return it for a refund. Even if the product is not returned, it is unlikely the customer will buy the same product again, and he or she may have a negative attitude about the business where the purchase was made.

Businesses and other organizations use effective marketing to provide satisfying exchanges of products and services with customers. The ways marketing is used have changed over the years, but the need for marketing has not changed.

Checkpoint ▶▶

Why does a business need marketing if it has a good product or service?

The Development of Marketing in Business

There have been times in history when people were self-sufficient. Being **self-sufficient** means you do not rely on others for the things you need to survive. People were able to find or produce the food and materials needed for themselves and their families. That type of lifestyle required hard work and was very risky. Self-sufficient people had to have good hunting, fishing, or farming skills as well as the capability to produce shelter, clothing, and other necessities. Often it was not possible to obtain everything needed to survive because of poor weather, competition with other people, sickness, or lack of skills.

Bartering

Some people who found they were not successful at being self-sufficient tried to find other ways to survive. They discovered that often when they did not have certain things they needed, other people did. If each person had something that the other person valued, they were able to make an exchange, so each would be better off than before. Exchanging products or services with others by agreeing on their values is known as **bartering**. A system of bartering was developed so that people could exchange with others to obtain the things they needed. For example, in an early bartering system, someone who was a good hunter but was not able to grow grain might exchange products with a person who had extra grain but needed meat. People who had developed skills in weaving

Why do you think people are not as self-sufficient as they once were historically?

cloth might barter with people who raised animals. Exchanging products through bartering was one of the first examples of marketing. Bartering still takes place today among individuals and businesses. Can you identify examples of bartering in your neighborhood or community or on the Internet?

Specialization of Labor

People discovered that they had particular interests or skills in certain kinds of work while they were not as good at or were uninterested in other types of work. When people concentrated on the work they did well, they were able to accomplish much more than when they tried to do a variety of things. Concentrating on one thing or a few related activities so that they can be done well is known as **specialization of labor**. Specialization of labor made it possible for people to produce larger quantities of a product rather than trying to produce many different products. Therefore, more of that product would be available to exchange with other people.

Money Systems

As specialization of labor became more common and a greater variety and quantity of products were available, bartering was not always possible. Not all people needed the products of others, and it was not always possible to reach agreement on what products were worth so that they could be exchanged directly. To assist with the exchange, a money system was developed. A **money system** established the use of currency as a recognized medium of exchange. With money, people could obtain products even if they did not always have something to exchange. Those with products to sell could do so for money, which could then be used for future purchases. The development of a money system is another example of marketing.

©GETTY IMAGES/PHOTODISC

How did people get the products and services they needed before a money system was developed?

Central Markets

With many people producing more types of products and with people having money to purchase the items they needed, the demand for products increased. Locating and gathering all of the products people wanted and needed was a difficult process. Much time was spent traveling to sell and purchase products. To solve that problem, central markets were developed. A **central market** is a location where people bring products to be conveniently exchanged. Central markets were often located at places where many people traveled, such as where rivers or roads met.

Towns and cities developed at those locations and became centers of trade. People brought the products they wanted to sell to the markets. When people needed things they could not produce, they would travel to the market to make purchases. Developing locations where products could be bought and sold was another step in the development of marketing.

Other Marketing Activities

As central markets expanded, other types of business services were created to make exchanges easier. It was not always possible for sellers and buyers to travel to the markets at the same time. Therefore, individuals often formed businesses to purchase products from producers and hold them for sale to purchasers as needed. Other businesses were started to loan money to buyers or sellers, to help with transportation of products, or to locate products that were not available in the market but that customers wanted. Each of those activities resulted in the development of another marketing activity and made the exchange process more effective for those who produced products and those who purchased and consumed the products. Soon marketing became a complex set of activities with some businesses specializing in marketing while others used the services of marketing businesses. Exchanges became easier as businesses added marketing services and improved the ones already provided.

Checkpoint ▶▶▶

How did the development of central markets aid in the growth of business?

The Functions of Business

From the previous discussion of the development and improvement of marketing activities, it is clear that marketing is an important part of business and that businesses cannot be effective without marketing. But marketing cannot be successful alone. Other important business functions are production, operations, accounting and finance, and management. These business functions are shown in Figure 1-4.

Production

The primary reason for a business to exist is to provide products or services to consumers and to earn a profit. The **production** function creates or obtains products or services for sale. Think of the variety of products and services available, and you can see that production can take various forms.

Raw Materials Production includes obtaining raw materials for sale to customers. Mining, logging, oil drilling, and similar activities are examples of this type of production.

FIGURE 1-4
Marketing is one of several important business functions.

Processing Other businesses take raw materials and change their form through processing so that they can be used in the production of other products or in the operation of businesses or equipment. Examples include oil refining and the production of steel, paper, plastics, and food products.

Agriculture A third example of production is agriculture. Food and other materials are grown for consumption or for processing into a variety of products.

Manufacturing Manufacturing businesses are also involved in production. Manufacturers use raw materials and other resources to produce products for sale to consumers or to other businesses. Most of the products consumed by you, your friends, your family, and businesses have been produced by manufacturers.

Services Creating and providing services is also an example of production. While a physical product is not provided to the customer, offering a service such as preparing tax returns, cutting hair, providing lawn care, or performing a concert meets customer needs in the same way that making consumable products does.

Merchandising Finally, some businesses do not produce or manufacture products. Instead, they accumulate products for resale to customers. Offering products produced or manufactured by others for sale to customers is known as **merchandising**. Retailers and wholesalers are examples of merchandising businesses. While merchandising is not production, it makes the products of other businesses available for sale.

Operations

The ongoing activities designed to support the primary function of a business and keep it operating efficiently are known as **operations**. Many things must occur for a business to successfully produce and market products and services. Buildings and equipment must be operated and maintained. Products must be obtained, transported, and stored. Paperwork and computerized records must be prepared and maintained. The ongoing operations or day-to-day activities of a business must be performed well in order for the business to be successful.

Accounting and Finance

Businesses are complex with a variety of activities occurring at once. Money is needed to finance those activities, and that money must be carefully monitored and managed. Many types of money, including cash, checks, and credit, are used in a business. The **accounting and finance** function plans and manages financial resources and maintains records and information related to a business's finances.

Finance begins by determining the amount of capital needed for the business and where that capital will be obtained. Budgets must be developed, monitored, and updated. Most businesses must borrow money for major purchases as well as for some day-to-day operations. Determining sources for borrowing, interest rates, and loan payback schedules are important responsibilities of accounting and finance personnel. Managers rely on accounting and finance personnel to provide the financial information they need to plan the activities of the business.

Management

Even in the smallest businesses, considerable time must be spent developing plans and organizing work. Someone must determine what the business will do, how it can best meet the needs of customers, and how to respond to competitors' actions. Problem-solving, managing employees,

Virtual Marketing

Basic Internet Business Models

Most businesses today use the Internet as a business tool. Many businesses have been challenged to find ways to generate profitable sales from the Internet because most consumers still expect information on the Internet to be free. The traditional way to use the Internet has been to offer online ordering for a company's products. However, traditional uses are now changing. New Internet business models are providing promise for new and existing businesses.

Online markets. Amazon.com is a classic example of this model. It sells everything online. It began by selling books and music, but it now provides a virtual mall for consumers by offering hundreds of businesses' products for sale. eBay is another example. It manages online auctions for individuals and businesses.

Access to an audience or a specialized service. Portals are places where people go on the Internet to access specialized content or to conduct searches. Portals may carry a subscription (AOL) or may offer a rich opportunity for advertisers to reach pre-selected audiences (Yahoo!, Google). Some portals collect listing fees (Monster.com).

Web site subscriptions. Specialized content providers (World Book Encyclopedia and NetFlix) require subscription payments for access to their product. Some providers offer basic information without a charge but require payment for advanced services, such as online investment research (MarketWatch) or complete magazine content (BusinessWeek).

Think Critically

1. Why are many people reluctant to pay for information and other services on the Internet?

2. What other ways can you identify that allow businesses to earn money via the Internet?

---

and evaluating the activities of the business are ongoing responsibilities of managers. The **management** function involves developing, implementing, and evaluating the plans and activities of a business.

Managers are responsible for everything that occurs in the business including the work of the employees. They must develop objectives and plans, make sure the appropriate resources are available, be responsible for buildings and equipment, and assign responsibilities to others. Managers are responsible for the performance of the company, including whether or not it is profitable.

Marketing

Marketing is also an important function of business. All businesses need to complete a variety of activities in order to make their products and services available to consumers and to ensure that satisfying exchanges occur.

Coordination of Business Functions

Each of the functions of an effective business depends on the other functions. Products can be produced, but if the company is not operated or managed well, adequate records are not maintained, or marketing is ineffective, the products will not be sold at a profit.

In the same way, operations maintains buildings and equipment and management plans and coordinates the work occurring in all parts of the business. Finance and accounting provides information to the other parts of the business to make sure that adequate funds are available and are used efficiently.

Some organizations have not been successful in coordinating business functions. Functions operate independently and often compete with each other. Products are produced that cannot be sold. Marketing activities are planned without considering costs. Managers concentrate on specific activities without considering if their decisions may have negative effects on other functions.

As a result, product quality and customer service decline while prices increase. Customers become unhappy about the declining product quality and service and rising prices. Competitors who are better organized can take advantage of those situations.

Checkpoint ▶▶▶

How can the lack of coordination among the business functions affect a company?

1-2 Assessment

Xtra!
Study Tools
school.cengage.com/marketing/marketing

Key Concepts

Determine the best answer.

1. In which business function are consumers most likely to be involved?
   a. production
   b. accounting
   c. marketing
   d. operations

2. Exchanging products or services with others by agreeing on their values is known as
   a. specialization of labor
   b. marketing
   c. developing a money system
   d. bartering

3. The ongoing activities designed to support the primary function of a business and to keep a business operating efficiently are known as
   a. operations
   b. management
   c. accounting and finance
   d. merchandising

4. The management function of business involves _____, _____, and _____ the plans and activities of a business.

Make Academic Connections

5. **Geography and History** Gather historical information about your state. Use the Internet to locate and print a state map. Mark the locations of five towns and cities that were central markets in the early years of your state's development. Identify why each town or city provided a good location for a central market.

6. **Economics** Most countries have their own money system and currency. However, international trade requires that currencies from different countries can be readily exchanged. Develop a table to identify ten countries other than the United States, the name of the main currency of each country, and the current exchange rate of that currency with the U.S. dollar.

Connect to ◆ DECA
An Association of Marketing Students

7. Your team members are the managers of a company in which expenses are increasing while sales and profits are declining. Each team member will assume the role of manager of one of the main business functions. Discuss how the function each manager represents can work with the other functions to identify the main problems facing the business and to develop a plan for improvement. Make a three-minute team presentation of your recommendations to your teacher (judge).

1-3 Understanding the Marketing Concept

GOALS

- Define the marketing concept.
- Determine how businesses implement the marketing concept.

KEY TERMS

marketing concept, *p. 19*

market, *p. 22*

marketing mix, *p. 22*

product, *p. 23*

distribution (place), *p. 23*

price, *p. 23*

promotion, *p. 23*

marketing matters

An important principle of effective marketing is to identify products and services that customers want and then provide them at an appropriate price. Companies spend many hours and hundreds of millions of dollars every year trying to identify new products that customers will buy. Often the new products are just improvements or changes to existing products. Other times, entirely new product categories are created that have not existed in the past.

Work with team members. You are a new product team in the marketing department of a company. Discuss ways that you can identify a product that customers would want to own. Once you have decided what the customers want and developed a product that responds to their needs, discuss how you are going to introduce the new product to them. Share your discussion results with the other teams.

The Marketing Concept

Marketing was not always viewed as an important part of business. Indeed, marketing was not even a term used in business until the last half of the twentieth century. In the early 1900s, businesses were mostly concerned about producing products that the business believed customers could afford and would purchase. Major efforts that today would be considered marketing were directed at one of the biggest challenges facing businesses—getting the products from the places where they were produced to the places where customers could purchase and use them. There were not many choices of transportation methods, and

Fast FACTS

In 1908, it took $280 to purchase one of the few available models of automobiles, the Model T Ford. It was a luxury few people could afford. In today's dollars, the same car would cost about $14,000, a more affordable price. However, few people today would be satisfied with the features and performance of the Model T.

roads and highways were not well developed. The primary challenge to the sale of more products was to be able to deliver them to a larger number of customers.

As consumers increased their standard of living and had more money to spend, their demand for newer and better products increased. Demand was usually greater than the available supply of products. Business people concentrated on production and seldom had to worry about marketing. Customers were often eager to buy new products and would seek out the manufacturer when they heard of a product they wanted.

Over time, production processes improved, there was more competition among producers and manufacturers, and consumers had more choices of products and services. Businesses had to compete with each other to get customers to buy their products. They began to increase their attention of basic marketing activities, such as advertising and selling, to persuade customers that their products were superior to those of competitors.

Satisfying Customer Needs

As it became more and more difficult and expensive for businesses to sell their products, some business people began to realize an important fact. Businesses could no longer be successful by just producing more products or increasing their advertising and selling efforts. They had to produce products that customers wanted. The most successful businesses were the ones that considered customers' needs and worked to satisfy those needs as they produced and marketed their products and services. That philosophy of business is now known as the marketing concept. The **marketing concept** is using the needs of customers as the primary focus during the planning, production, pricing, distribution, and promotion of a product or service.

Using the marketing concept is not as easy as it might sound. Three activities must be accomplished by businesses if they want to use it successfully. Those activities are illustrated in Figure 1-5.

ELEMENTS OF THE MARKETING CONCEPT

FIGURE 1-5
The marketing concept focuses on identifying and satisfying customer needs.

- First, the business must be able to identify what will satisfy customers' needs.

- Second, the business must be able to develop and market products or services that customers believe are better than other choices.

- Third, the business must be able to operate profitably.

Many businesses are successfully identifying and responding to needs of customers. Fast food restaurants provide breakfast menus and late night hours in order to make their products available when customers want them. Many banks provide services so that customers can pay bills, transfer money, and check account balances by using a telephone or a personal computer. Hospitals offer wellness programs, weight loss clinics, and fitness centers to attract clients and broaden their image. Colleges offer courses for area high school students to earn college credits prior to graduation and to interest students in enrolling full-time at the college.

When Customer Needs Are Not Satisfied

Businesses that do not use the marketing concept are more concerned about producing products than understanding customer needs. Once products are developed, they rely on traditional marketing activities to sell those products. Often when automobile

Get the Message

Getting the Word Out

Word-of-mouth promotion has been around since the beginning of business, but it is still an important promotional tool today. Stories of positive experiences spread by satisfied customers can be a powerful influence on family members, neighbors, and friends. On the other hand, there can often be no stronger negative influence than people talking about their negative experiences with a product or a business. Businesses have developed methods to try to influence word-of-mouth promotion. Some of those methods are:

After-sale follow-up. Making contact with purchasers in-person, on the telephone, and with letters and e-mails to make sure they are satisfied with their purchase.

Recognition and special services. Publicly recognizing purchasers in promotions and newsletters or at events.

Incentives. Offering purchasers small financial incentives, discounts, or special purchases for recommending the business and its products to prospective customers.

The Word of Mouth Marketing Association (WOMMA) describes several new methods to encourage positive messages from satisfied customers. They include:

Buzz Marketing. Using high-profile entertainment or news to get people to talk about your brand.

Product Seeding. Placing the right product in the right hands at the right time and providing information or samples to influential individuals.

Conversation Creation. Developing interesting or fun advertising, e-mails, catch phrases, entertainment, or promotions designed to start word-of-mouth activity.

Think Critically

1. Why is word-of-mouth information so influential for many consumers?

2. If you are the marketing manager for a new brand of sunglasses, what would you do to increase the positive word-of-mouth promotion by customers?

---

manufacturers have difficulty selling their cars it is because they are not producing the type, style, or quality of cars customers want. They then have to use advertising, price reductions, rebates, and pressure selling to persuade customers to buy a product the customers do not prefer.

Retail stores sometimes buy products that they believe will sell but then find that customers are not willing to buy them. The stores then have to cut prices, increase advertising, use special displays, and other strategies to persuade customers to buy the products. The extra expenses of marketing products that customers may not have a strong interest in buying can lead to reductions in profit or even losses for the

business. Also, after purchasing the product, customers may decide it is not what they wanted. They may return the product or become unhappy with the product and the company. They may be reluctant to buy from that company in the future and may express dissatisfaction to prospective customers, resulting in reduced sales for the company.

Checkpoint ▶▶

Under the marketing concept, what is a business's primary focus during planning, production, pricing, distribution, and promotion of a product?

Your Personal and Professional Image

Businesses are aware of the importance of the first impression—the image that is conveyed by a product and its package, the cleanliness and appearance of a store and its merchandise, and the impression made by the appearance, behavior, and language of its employees. If you walk into a law office, you expect a different image from one you might encounter in a supermarket or an auto repair shop. If that image does not meet your expectation, you may not feel comfortable or confident in becoming a client or customer.

Everyone makes decisions based on first impressions. As you walk down the halls of your school each day, you notice what other students are wearing. At the beginning of a new semester, the appearance and attitude of each teacher influence your initial feelings about them and the class.

You have your own personality and preferences, and that affects your dress and grooming choices. It would be a boring world if everyone looked, dressed, and acted alike. On the other hand, dress and grooming decisions have an effect on your success. Personal image, whether in business, school, or social situations, is formed by clothing, personal care and appearance, and language and voice tone.

Clothing

Don't overdress or underdress. Choose styles that reflect your personality and fit the setting in which they will be worn. Your clothing choices do not have to be expensive or exclusive, but they should be pleasing, not startling, to others. You do not have to be conservative, but you also should not dress so differently from others that the only thing people remember about you is how you dress.

Personal Care and Appearance

There are many elements to personal appearance, starting with cleanliness, skin and hair care, and personal hygiene. Regular bathing keeps you fresh. Brushing your teeth freshens your breath and maintains a healthy and beautiful smile. An easy-to-maintain and attractive hair style, clean and trimmed nails, and healthy skin increase personal attractiveness and self-confidence.

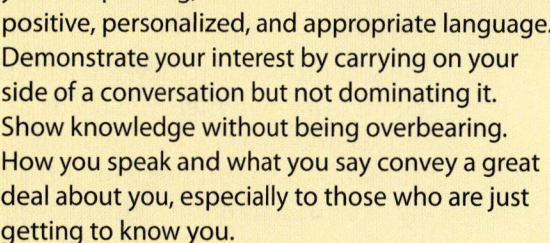

Language and Voice Tone

Your language and tone of voice are the final pieces of your successful image. No matter what the setting or with whom you are speaking, use positive, personalized, and appropriate language. Demonstrate your interest by carrying on your side of a conversation but not dominating it. Show knowledge without being overbearing. How you speak and what you say convey a great deal about you, especially to those who are just getting to know you.

Develop Your Skill

Use a digital camera to take a picture of yourself dressed for three situations.

1. Going to school
2. Going to work at a job you would like to have
3. Going to a social activity with your friends

Show the photos to three people—a close friend, a business person, and a teacher or other adult who knows you well. Ask them to provide honest feedback on whether the image you convey in each photo fits the situation. Ask each person to provide two positive comments and two recommendations for you that will help strengthen your image in the way you dress and your personal care and appearance. Use their feedback to set goals for personal improvement. Keep the pictures as a reminder of your goals and progress.

Implementing the Marketing Concept

Companies that believe in the marketing concept operate differently from those that do not. They follow a two-step process.

Identify the Market

The first step is to identify the market or markets the company wants to serve. A **market** is a description of a unique group of prospective customers a business wants to serve and their location. An example of a market for a bicycle manufacturer may be people who ride bicycles in the mountains for health and fitness. A potential market for a sports arena may be teens within 80 miles of the arena who attend concerts more than twice a year.

Develop a Marketing Mix

The second step is to develop a marketing mix that will meet the needs of the market and that the business can provide profitably. A **marketing mix** is the blending of four marketing elements—product, distribution, price, and promotion—by the business. The marketing mix is sometimes referred to as the *4 Ps of marketing*

Power Fusion

The Official Brand of Live Music has joined forces with the Official Brand of Mountain Bike Racing. Come by the Trek pit area between races and get your hair blown back by JBL Powervalve™ amplification and Grand Touring™ subwoofers. We'll be easy to find – just follow your ears!

The Official Brand of Live Music.

TREK
www.trekbikes.com

JBL

JBL Consumer Products, 250 Crossways Park Drive, Woodbury, NY 11797 USA
800.336.4JBL (4525) Fax 516.682.3523 ©2000 JBL, Incorporated. www.jbl.com
JBL is a registered trademark of JBL, Incorporated. H A Harman International Company

JBL and Trek offer products to the same unique market.

with *place* used as an alternate term for distribution.

Let's use the two markets described earlier to illustrate a possible marketing mix for each. The bicycle manufacturer may decide to offer three different types of mountain bikes. It can sell through a selected group of bicycle shops. The price can range from $280 to $550. It can be promoted by advertising in fitness magazines, on a cable sports channel, on travel and cycling Internet sites, and by salespeople in the bicycle shops.

The sports arena manager could choose a marketing mix for concerts that includes groups whose recent titles are among those most frequently downloaded from Internet music sites. Performances could be scheduled on Saturday or Sunday evenings and priced at $60 for reserved seating and $32 for open seating.

NETBookmark

Consumers communicate with others about their purchasing experiences using word-of-mouth promotion. Access school.cengage.com/marketing/marketing and click on the link for Chapter 1. Visit the web site for the Word of Mouth Marketing Association (WOMMA). Have you engaged in any of the word-of-mouth promotions described? Do you think the strategies listed on the site would work for all products or services?

school.cengage.com/marketing/marketing

The concerts could be promoted on the three area FM radio stations with the highest audience ratings for listeners age 15 to 25, by posters placed in local youth gathering places, and through word-of-mouth "buzz" marketing.

Each of the elements of the marketing mix provides many alternatives to better satisfy the market. The development and implementation of the marketing mix will be discussed in detail in other chapters. Basic definitions of each marketing mix element follow.

Product is anything offered to a market by the business to satisfy needs, including physical products, services, and ideas.

Distribution or *place* includes the locations and methods used to make the product available to customers.

Price is the amount that customers pay and the methods of increasing the value of the product to the customers.

Promotion includes the methods used and information communicated to encourage customers to purchase and to increase their satisfaction.

While each of the definitions is written to describe marketing of products by a business, the mix elements are also part of services and ideas. Non-business organizations and individuals can effectively develop marketing mixes.

Checkpoint ▶▶

What four marketing elements make up the marketing mix?

1-3 Assessment

Key Concepts

Determine the best answer.

1. True or False: Marketing has not always been viewed as an important part of business.

2. Which of the following is true about conditions facing businesses in the early 1900s?
   a. Transportation of products to consumers was quite easy.
   b. Consumers had many choices of products on which to spend money.
   c. Businesses were mostly concerned about producing products that customers could afford and would purchase.
   d. All are true.

3. Using the needs of customers as the primary focus during the planning, production, pricing, distribution, and promotion of a product or service is known as the marketing
   a. mix
   b. concept
   c. philosophy
   d. approach

4. Which of the following is *not* one of the marketing mix elements?
   a. product
   b. distribution
   c. price
   d. planning

Make Academic Connections

5. **Math** A company is considering two marketing mixes. With the first, it projects it can sell 8,500 units at a price of $23.50 per unit with total costs of $176,000. Unit sales for the second mix are projected at 9,875 at a price of $19.90 with total business costs of $158,500. What is the projected profit (total income – total costs) for each one?

6. **Management** Choose one of the businesses described in the lesson—the bicycle manufacturer or the sports arena. Identify a specific new market for the business. Then plan the marketing mix elements the business should offer to meet the needs of the identified market. Prepare a three-paragraph report explaining your decisions.

Connect to ◀ DECA
An Association of Marketing Students

7. You are a consultant working with the owner of a new restaurant who wants your advice on how to make effective marketing decisions. Meet with the new owner (judge) and describe the meaning and importance of the marketing concept to guide marketing planning.

The Changing Role of Marketing

GOALS

- Describe how businesses approach marketing differently today than they did in the past.
- Summarize how marketing is changing in businesses and other organizations.

KEY TERMS

relationship marketing, *p. 27*

employee empowerment, *p. 27*

marketing matters

Marketing is an important tool for businesses. In addition, many other organizations that are not businesses also find benefits in performing marketing activities. For example, colleges routinely send recruiters all over the United States and even to other countries to attempt to persuade students to attend their school.

Work in a team to identify a non-business organization with which team members are familiar. Discuss how the use of marketing can benefit the organization and help it achieve its goals. Describe several specific ways that marketing functions could be used by the organization. Share your results with the other groups.

The Changing Approach to Marketing

While marketing is necessary in all exchanges, businesses have not always believed marketing was important to their success. They expected customers to take most of the responsibility for completing marketing activities. It took many years before businesses began to realize the value of effective marketing. There are several changes in the role that marketing has played in U.S. businesses during the past century. The historical development of marketing is summarized in Figure 1-6.

Production Emphasis

In the early years of the last century (1900–1920), production processes were very

FIGURE 1-6

Businesses' approach to marketing has changed throughout history.

Production Era	Sales Era	Marketing Department Era	Marketing Concept Era
• 1900s–1920s	• 1930s–1940s	• 1950s–1960s	• 1970s–Today
• Emphasis on producing and distributing new products	• Emphasis on using advertising and salespeople to convince customers to buy a company's products	• Emphasis on developing many new marketing activities to sell products	• Emphasis on satisfying customers' needs with a carefully developed marketing mix

simple and few product choices were available. People had limited money to spend on products, and much of their purchasing was for basic necessities. Transportation systems were not well developed, so it was difficult to get products from where they were manufactured to people throughout the United States.

Businesses believed that if they could produce products, they would be able to sell them. They focused on developing new products and improving production. Their only marketing effort was devoted to distribution—moving products from the producer to locations where customers could buy them.

Sales Emphasis

During the 1930s and into the 1940s, businesses became more effective at producing products. Industrial improvements and modern methods of producing large numbers of products at a low cost, such as assembly lines, were introduced. Transportation systems, including the use of trains, boats, and trucks, improved, making it easier to get products to customers. At the same time, the standard of living of many Americans improved, so they had more money to spend on goods.

These changes resulted in increased competition among businesses. They could no longer rely on customers buying their products just because they were able to get the products to the customers. Companies began to rely on salespeople to convince customers that their products were better than the products of competitors. Good salespeople could introduce products that customers had not purchased before and demonstrate the advantages of ownership.

Marketing Department Emphasis

The sales emphasis continued into the 1950s for many businesses and well beyond that time for others. After World War II, the U.S. economy expanded rapidly, and wage levels increased for consumers as their hours of work declined. Consumers had more money to spend and more time to enjoy the use of many products. Companies increasingly found that consumers were not easily convinced to purchase products when they had many choices available to them. Therefore, businesses had to find different ways to be sure that consumers purchased their products. Companies began to organize marketing departments that were responsible for developing those new methods.

One of the first efforts of the new marketing departments was to expand the use of advertising. Advertising had an important role of informing consumers about a company's products, the reasons to buy the products, and where they could locate the products. The use of newspapers and magazines, the expanded use of radio, and the growth of television provided outlets to reach consumers with many forms of advertising.

New methods of getting products to customers were developed including

Throughout the history of business, advertising has introduced new products.

catalog sales with mail delivery to rural areas, expanded and improved truck and rail distribution, and even the use of airplanes to rapidly move perishable products. The expanding number of retail stores and the growth of city shopping centers gave customers easier access to product choices. Competition brought product prices down, and customers were offered credit to make purchases more affordable. As companies worked to find more ways to encourage customers to buy, they increasingly relied on marketing to find ways to expand markets and sell more products.

Marketing Concept Emphasis

The marketing department emphasis showed that marketing could be a very important tool for businesses. A number of activities were now available that had not been used in the past. However, just because more marketing activities were used, companies were not always more successful.

It was discovered that marketing was becoming quite expensive. Also, since the goal of the marketing department was to sell the products of the company, marketers began to misuse marketing activities. These inappropriate activities might have increased sales, but they also led to customer complaints. Examples included high-pressure sales, misleading advertising, and customer services that were not provided as promised. These past actions help explain why even today some people have a negative attitude toward marketers and some marketing activities.

Marketers also discovered that no matter how hard they tried, there were some products that customers did not want to buy. If customers did not believe that a product would satisfy their needs, marketing was not effective. Yet marketers were not involved in developing the products.

In the 1970s, some companies began to realize they could be more successful

Figure This

The Consumer Price Index (CPI)

Marketers are responsible for developing strategies to sell a company's products and services to consumers. Those consumers must decide how to spend the money they have available to get the greatest value and satisfaction from the purchases they make. Competition among businesses, improvements in technology and business procedures, and greater productivity from employees cause product prices to decrease over time. However, inflation results in increases in the prices customers pay. To measure the effect of inflation on consumer prices, the federal government calculates the Consumer Price Index (CPI). The CPI compares the cost of a group of products and services commonly purchased by consumers from year to year.

The base year, or a CPI of 100, was established as 1983. Years prior to the base year have a CPI less than 100, and years after the base year have a CPI greater than 100. For example, the CPI for 1915 was 9.1, for 1950, 24.1, and for 1995, 152.4. If a consumer purchased $350 of goods and services in 1983, those same purchases would have cost $31.85 in 1915 ($350 × .091), $84.35 in 1950 ($350 × .241), and $533.40 in 1995 ($350 × 1.524).

Think Critically

1. If the cost of an automobile in 1983 was $15,580, how much could we expect the price to increase due to inflation by 2007 if the CPI for that year was 205.5?

2. If the actual cost of the automobile was less than what would be expected based on the CPI, what could account for the lower price?

if they listened to consumers and considered customer needs as they developed products and services. The marketing concept uses the needs of customers as the primary focus during the planning, production, pricing, distribution, and promotion of a product or service.

When the marketing concept was adopted, marketing became more than the work of one department. It was now a major part of the business. Marketing personnel worked closely with people in other parts of the company. Activities were completed with customer satisfaction in mind. By coordinating the efforts of the departments in the company and by focusing on satisfying customers' needs, companies were able to develop and market products that customers wanted and that could be sold at a profit. Since its first use in the 1970s, the marketing concept has been proven as an effective method. It is now used by the majority of businesses and by other organizations.

Improving the Marketing Concept

The marketing concept has directed the efforts of many businesses for nearly 40 years, and it still achieves the desired goals—satisfied customers and profitable sales. You will learn in later chapters that even when the competitors of a business use the same philosophy, it is possible for each business to be successful because of its focus on satisfying the needs of its customers. However, the marketing concept continues to change as businesses become more effective marketers and find ways to improve the way they complete marketing activities. Two important improvements are an emphasis on relationship marketing and employee empowerment. A third improvement is attention to social responsibility, as discussed in the next chapter.

Relationship Marketing Businesses have learned that a one-time sale to a customer is not enough. It costs a great deal of money to identify new customers, inform them of a company's products, and convince them to purchase. Studies have found that retaining customers so that they continue to purchase from the company again and again can increase profits by 25 to 50 percent. The extra efforts required to replace a lost customer can reduce profits by the same amount or more.

Businesses are now implementing relationship marketing. **Relationship marketing** focuses on developing loyal customers who continue to purchase from the business for a long period of time. Customers prefer to shop and buy from businesses they trust and that they believe provide good products and great service. Companies that use relationship marketing stay in contact with customers, determine ways to provide better products and services, and immediately try to solve any problems the customers may have.

Employee Empowerment To most customers, a business is represented by the employees with whom they deal on a regular basis. If an employee has an uncaring or indifferent attitude, cannot answer customers' questions, appears unconcerned about a problem, or is unable to solve a problem, a customer will quickly become dissatisfied and will look for another place to shop.

Employee empowerment is an approach to customer service that gives employees the authority to solve many customer problems. Employee empowerment requires that businesses trust employees to make good decisions in the best interests

Working in **Teams**

Work with your team members to identify several businesses that you believe do a good job of relationship marketing. Discuss what the business does that demonstrates interest in customers and how those things encourage customers to return again and again.

of the company and the customer. Empowered employees are given training to understand the resources that are available to them when they work on a problem. They are also given guidelines to determine the appropriateness of possible solutions. Businesses have learned that empowered employees who understand the marketing concept make good decisions that satisfy customers.

Checkpoint ▶▶▶

Name the four major emphases in the development of marketing's role in business since 1900.

The Changing View of Marketing

Marketing is different today than it was even 15 or 20 years ago. If you look at the history of business, you can see that marketing played a role in even the simplest early businesses. But business people have not recognized the full value of marketing as a business tool until recently.

The role of marketing in business changed as did the business view of the importance of marketing. Previously, marketing was seen as a tool to help the business sell its products and services. It was not needed if sales were high. Today, business people see that marketing contributes in several important ways. It provides information about customers through market research. Marketing provides many ways to serve customers better and increase customer satisfaction. It can help businesses become more profitable by coordinating activities and controlling costs.

Marketing in Other Organizations

Because of the successful use of marketing in businesses, other organizations now look to marketing for help. Libraries, churches, government agencies, community organizations, and the military are using marketing activities. Some use marketing well while others do not understand marketing. They may view marketing only as advertising or selling and not as a way of satisfying their customers' or clients' needs.

You can evaluate organizations to decide if they understand the value of marketing. If they rely on promotion with brochures, advertisements, and public service announcements, they likely view marketing as a way to convince consumers of their organization's value. Without research to help them understand their clients, they are not able to respond to the clients' needs.

©UNITED STATES POSTAL SERVICE

The U.S. Postal Service uses marketing to improve customer service.

If they use marketing to determine what products and services to offer, where to make them available, how to help consumers determine the value of their services, and how to communicate effectively with consumers, they have adopted the marketing concept. The marketing concept works well for businesses and other organizations.

Marketers' Roles Today

Marketing managers are responsible for a large number and variety of activities. They must work with many people inside and outside of a company. Marketing managers are ultimately responsible for a large part of the company's budget. People involved in marketing need information about customers, competitors, and market conditions. This information helps marketers make decisions that will result in sales and profits for the business. Marketers have varied amounts of experience and education. Marketing is an exciting and challenging career area. If you are interested in marketing, you must be willing to develop the needed knowledge and skills. Marketing offers many opportunities for you now and in the future.

Checkpoint ▶▶▶

Why is marketing ultimately important to every business and organization?

1-4 Assessment

Key Concepts

Determine the best answer.

1. In the era in which the marketing efforts of a business were devoted to distribution, the business was said to have a
   a. marketing department emphasis
   b. sales emphasis
   c. production emphasis
   d. marketing concept emphasis

2. Relationship marketing is good for a business because it
   a. reduces costs
   b. increases profits
   c. develops long-term customers who continue to purchase from the company
   d. all of the above

3. An approach to customer service that gives employees the authority to solve many customer problems is
   a. the marketing concept
   b. relationship marketing
   c. employee empowerment
   d. social responsibility

4. True or False: Because businesses have become more concerned about profits and competition, marketing is less important today than it was in the past.

Make Academic Connections

5. **Technology** Use the library or Internet to identify a change in technology that you believe improved the way marketing activities were completed during four different times in history: 1900–1930, 1931–1950, 1951–1980, 1981–present. Use visuals or a written report to communicate your findings. Make sure you describe how the technology improved marketing.

6. **Communication** Compose a letter to the owner or manager of a business that you believe has a low level of customer service. Describe the reasons for your beliefs and explain how relationship marketing and employee empowerment might help the business.

Connect to

7. You have decided to run for the office of president of a student organization in your school. Prepare a two-minute speech you would deliver to the members of the organization in which you describe the importance of using marketing as a way to increase the number of new members in the organization. Deliver the speech to your teacher (judge).

Chapter 1 Assessment

Check Your Understanding

Now that you have completed the chapter, check your understanding of the lessons with these questions. Record the score that best represents your understanding of each marketing concept.

1 = not at all; 3 = somewhat; 5 = very well

If your score is 42–50, you are ready for the assessment activities that follow. If you score 33–41, you should review the lessons for the items you scored 1–3. If you score 32 or less, you will want to carefully reread the lessons and work with a study partner on the areas you do not understand.

Can you—

___ identify and define the nine marketing functions?

___ provide a simple definition of marketing that describes its value to those who use it?

___ offer reasons that marketing is needed by businesses, other organizations, and consumers?

___ discuss several ways marketing activities were first performed by businesses?

___ describe several functions of business in addition to the marketing function?

___ define the marketing concept and explain why businesses adopt it?

___ describe the two steps required to implement the marketing concept?

___ identify ways the approach to marketing has changed since the early 1900s?

___ provide examples of methods businesses are using to improve the marketing concept?

___ identify ways that marketing is being used effectively in non-business organizations?

Review Marketing Terms

Match the terms listed with the definitions. Some terms may not be used.

1. The creation and maintenance of satisfying exchange relationships
2. Using the needs of customers as the primary focus during planning, production, distribution, and promotion of a product or service
3. The prospective customers a business wants to serve and the location of those customers
4. Blending of the four marketing elements (product, distribution, price, and promotion) by the business
5. Anything offered to a market by the business to satisfy needs, including physical products, services, and ideas
6. The business function that creates or obtains products or services for sale
7. The actual amount customers pay and the methods of increasing the value of the product to the customers
8. Focuses on developing loyal customers who continue to purchase from the business for a long period of time
9. The locations and methods used to make the product available to customers
10. Exchanging products or services with others by agreeing on their values without using money

a. accounting and finance
b. bartering
c. central market
d. distribution (place)
e. employee empowerment
f. management
g. market
h. marketing
i. marketing concept
j. marketing mix
k. merchandising
l. money system
m. operations
n. price
o. product
p. production
q. promotion
r. relationship marketing
s. self-sufficient
t. specialization of labor

Review Marketing Concepts

11. Which marketing function involves designing and developing products and services?
    a. product/service management
    b. marketing-information management
    c. pricing
    d. selling

12. Which marketing function establishes the value of products and services?
    a. selling
    b. pricing
    c. product/service management
    d. marketing-information management

13. Which marketing function develops procedures so customers are able to locate, obtain, and use products and services?
    a. selling
    b. promotion
    c. distribution
    d. financing

14. Which business function involves activities that make products and services available to consumers and ensure that satisfying exchanges occur?
    a. management
    b. production
    c. marketing
    d. operations

15. Which business function involves developing, implementing, and evaluating the plans and activities of a business?
    a. management
    b. accounting and finance
    c. marketing
    d. operations

16. Which business function represents the ongoing activities designed to support the primary function of a business and keep it operating efficiently?
    a. management
    b. production
    c. marketing
    d. operations

17. Which marketing mix element includes the methods used and information communicated to encourage customers to purchase and to increase their satisfaction?
    a. product
    b. distribution
    c. price
    d. promotion

18. Which of the following is an approach to customer service that gives employees the authority to solve many customer problems?
    a. the marketing concept
    b. relationship marketing
    c. employee empowerment
    d. social responsibility

Marketing Research and Planning

19. Find an article from a current magazine or newspaper that describes how a company developed a new product or service, improved a marketing procedure, or responded to customer needs. Prepare a brief oral report describing the activity and how it does or does not illustrate the marketing concept.

20. Identify and record examples from your own experience for each of the following:
    a. Five marketing activities you have seen in the last week.
    b. Five businesses in your community that have marketing as an important activity.
    c. Five careers in marketing.
    d. Five examples of businesses performing marketing functions.
    e. Five descriptions of markets.

21. Identify ten people who vary in age, gender, occupation, and other personal characteristics. Ask each person the following three questions. Record their answers
    a. What do you believe "marketing" means?
    b. When you hear the word "marketing," are your feelings more positive, more negative, or neutral?
    c. Do you believe most people involved in marketing are attempting to meet your needs as a customer? Yes or no?

When you have completed the interview, write a summary of your findings for Part a using a word processing program. Then using a spreadsheet program, enter the gender, age, and occupation of each person you interview in the first three columns. In the fourth column, enter each interviewee's answer to Question b, and in the fifth column, enter their answers to Question c. Using the graphing function of the spreadsheet program, create several graphs or charts that illustrate the data you recorded.

22. Businesses may have problems when the business functions are not coordinated. An important way to increase customer satisfaction and make a profit is to organize the functions so that they cooperate rather than compete. For each of the following sets of functions, identify a problem that might result if the two functions compete with each other. Then identify a way that customer satisfaction or company profits could improve if the functions are coordinated.

Business Functions

production and marketing
finance and marketing
operations and production
management and finance

23. The two statements below express opinions often held by people who do not understand marketing. Using a word processing program, develop a paragraph of at least five sentences for each of the statements that demonstrates why the opinion is not correct.

"My business offers high-quality products, so it does not need marketing."

"Customers have been complaining that my products are not as good as they would like. I need to use marketing to be sure those poor products are sold."

Marketing Management and Decision Making

24. Managers regularly make decisions about the price of products to provide a good value for customers, make a profit for the business, and ensure that products are sold. Often the original product price is not the selling price. Collect information on price reductions for at least ten products. Gather the information from products you, your family, or friends have purchased by checking prices in stores in your community or in advertisements. Identify the original price and the reduced price for each product. Then complete the following activities:

a. Calculate the amount and percentage of decrease in price for each product. For example, if a compact disc (CD) player originally sold for $150 and is on sale for $125, the price reduction is $25 ($150 – $125). The percentage of decrease is the price reduction divided by the original price. For the CD player, the percentage of decrease in price is 16.7% ($25/$150).

b. Assuming the business makes 4% net profit on each sale, determine how much reduction in profit the store will have for each product.

For the CD player, at the original price, the profit would have been $6 ($150 × .04). At the reduced price, the profit is $5 ($125 × .04). The reduction in profit is $1.

c. Using the marketing concept, determine reasons why the manager of the business may have decided to reduce the price for each product you identified. Suggest other things the manager might have been able to do to avoid reducing each product's price.

25. Each of the marketing functions provides exciting career opportunities. There are marketing jobs available for people with varied levels of education, experience, interests, and talents. Use the classified section of a newspaper or a web site that lists jobs. For each of nine marketing functions, find two jobs that have duties related to it. One job should be open to people with a high school diploma and little or no experience. The other should require a college degree and several years of experience. Use the information to prepare a career poster or work with a team to develop a bulletin board to inform others about jobs available in the world of marketing.

Marketing Management Series Event

The Marketing Management Series Event consists of a 100-question multiple-choice comprehensive exam and role-plays. The role-play portion of the event requires participants to accomplish a task by translating what they have learned into effective, efficient, and spontaneous action. Students have ten minutes to prepare their strategy for the role-play and another ten minutes to explain it to the judge. The judge has five minutes to ask questions related to the presentation.

You are the marketing manager for a large national home builder (Solid Trust Homes) that builds homes around the country. Your company has earned numerous awards for building high-quality homes. However, the company's success is in jeopardy because of recent consumer complaints about faulty construction.

Most states have laws that require new homeowners to take cases not involving warranties to arbitration. Arbitration is an expensive process in which an agreed-upon third party hands down a decision that must be adhered to by the disputing parties. This strategy is very unpopular with home buyers because they have less money to spend on the legal process than large home builders.

There has been an alarming increase in the number of complaints filed by Solid Trust Home customers. Your company has a successful track record of defending itself in these cases because it has great attorneys and insurance to cover court costs. However, unhappy customers are now picketing at your large home design centers, using billboards to publicize complaints about the quality of work, and reporting problems with your new homes to the media. Solid Trust Homes has called upon you to help stop the unfavorable publicity. You must outline a strategy that includes steps to overcome all of the negative publicity that Solid Trust Homes has received. The goal is to create satisfied customers who, through word of mouth, will share positive comments with prospective customers.

Performance Indicators Evaluated

- Explain the nature of positive customer/client relations. (Emotional Intelligence)

- Demonstrate a customer-service mindset. (Emotional Intelligence)

- Explain management's role in customer relations. (Emotional Intelligence)

- Explain warranties and guarantees. (Product/Service Management)

- Evaluate customers' experiences. (Product/Service Management)

Go to the DECA web site for more detailed information.

Think Critically

1. Why should a home builder conduct follow-up with customers?

2. What is the problem that a company faces with one unhappy customer?

3. What may be the public's view of a company that has the finest lawyers to defend it?

4. Should Solid Trust Homes consider developing a Consumer's Bill of Rights or Customer Satisfaction Pledge? Why?

www.deca.org

Socially Responsive Marketing

©GETTY IMAGES/PHOTODISC

Newsline))))

Heeling Safely

In 2006, Heelys—the sneakers with wheels in the heels—became must-have items for millions of American kids. Almost 6.2 million pairs were sold that year, more than five times the number sold in 2005. With Heelys, wearers pop a wheel into the heel, transforming the sneaker into a skate and allowing them to roll or glide just about anywhere.

But not everyone loves Heelys. Citing safety concerns, many schools have prohibited students from wearing them on school property. Reports of broken bones and run-ins with cars have become common. A number of shopping malls have also banned the sneakers, claiming they damage flooring. They also fear lawsuits from injuries sustained from their use.

To date, information submitted to the Consumer Product Safety Commission from participating emergency rooms does not seem to bear out those worries. Heelys have not caused large numbers of hospital-treated injuries. But as their popularity grows, so does the fear that injuries will increase. "If sales are booming," says Dr. Steven Krug, a pediatrician at Chicago Children's Memorial Hospital, "we will see more injuries. The injuries that we fear most are head injuries."

Aware of the potential for injury, Heelys packages its shoes with a number of safety warnings. Visitors to Heelys' web site must read and accept a warning before they can watch any of the videos demonstrating the shoes. The site includes a list of Frequently Asked Questions about safety gear as well as a disclaimer that states, "We always recommend that anyone who attempts to use HEELYS in any capacity should ALWAYS wear full protective gear, including: helmets, wrist, elbow, and knee pads. . . . NEVER use HEELYS in an unsafe manner, and NEVER WITHOUT full protective gear."

In addition, Heelys commissioned an independent consultant to study the safety of its products. The study found that wheeled shoes have a lower injury rate than nearly all other popular sports. Still, parents need to be aware of the possible dangers. Kids need to heed Heelys' advice and wear protective gear whenever they wear the shoes.

Think Critically

1. Who is responsible if a child is injured while wearing Heelys—the manufacturer, the retail store, the parents, or all of them?

2. Do you think Heelys is being socially responsible by including safety warnings with the shoes and on its web site, or is the company just looking out for its own interests? Explain.

school.cengage.com/marketing/marketing

Prepare for Performance

This chapter develops the following Performance Indicators from the DECA Competitive Events program.

Core Performance Indicators

- Understand the nature of business to show its contributions to society
- Acquire knowledge of commerce laws and regulations to continue business operations
- Apply ethics to demonstrate trustworthiness
- Acquire foundational knowledge of business laws and regulations to understand their nature and scope

Supporting Performance Indicators

- Explain the role of business in society
- Explain the nature of trade regulations
- Describe the impact of anti-trust legislation
- Demonstrate honesty and integrity
- Explain the need for professional and ethical standards in marketing
- Describe the use of business ethics in marketing

Go to **school.cengage.com/marketing/marketing** and click on Connect to DECA.

©WASTE MANAGEMENT

Visual Focus

Marketing affects businesses, people, and society as a whole. If misused, marketing can have a negative impact. Because of this, there are some criticisms of marketing. Marketers must recognize the responsibility that goes along with their marketing efforts. Not only should marketers work to meet the needs of individual consumers, but they must also be responsive to the needs of society. Working under a code of ethics to increase public awareness and consumer safety will help combat the criticisms of marketing.

Focus Questions:

What message is being communicated by Waste Management in this advertisement? Do you think the message is effective? How does it demonstrate social responsibility? Find another example of marketing that demonstrates social responsibility to consumers or society as a whole and discuss it in class.

The Impact of Marketing

GOALS

- Explain how marketing affects businesses.
- Describe marketing's impact on individuals.
- Discuss ways marketing benefits society.

KEY TERMS

international trade, *p. 40*

marketing matters

There are a number of factors that go into making a purchasing decision. "Is the price right?" "Is the product what I need?" "Will the product perform as expected?" "Is there a guarantee or warranty in case it is defective?" People ask themselves these and many other questions when making most purchasing decisions.

Work with a group. Have each person in the group name a product he or she has purchased recently. Then list all the important questions that went into making the purchasing decision. Do the questions differ from product to product? Are there certain questions that were the same or similar for all or most of the products? What did the manufacturers and retailers do to help you answer these questions? Summarize your results and share them with the other groups.

Marketing Affects Businesses

Marketing helps businesses find customers and sell their products and services profitably. Many people question the value of marketing. Some people believe it adds to the cost of products. Others believe it encourages people to buy things they really do not want or need. Still others suggest that if businesses produce quality products and services, there is no need for marketing.

It is important to determine if marketing plays a positive or a negative role. What does marketing contribute to businesses, individuals, and society? If there are problems with marketing, what can be done to eliminate them?

Critical Business Function

Marketing is an important business function. Even though businesses have not always understood marketing and used it effectively, they could not have existed without it. Marketing is responsible for the activities leading to the exchange of a business's products and services for the customer's money. Distribution, financing, promotion, and the other marketing functions are needed to make the exchange possible.

Businesses that use the marketing concept benefit even more from marketing. In those businesses, marketing is used to identify and understand customers. Through the use of market research and marketing information systems, the business is able to determine customer needs, attitudes, likes, and dislikes. Then the business can carefully develop products and services that meet the needs of the customers and earn a profit.

Customer Satisfaction

Marketing helps a business satisfy customer wants and needs. Manufacturers developing a new brand of laundry detergent will make better decisions if they are aware of what consumers like and dislike about the current brand. Marketing also helps the business make better decisions about what to sell and how to sell it. The manager of a clothing store will want to know what consumers are expecting in terms of styles and prices before purchasing new items to sell. When customers' wants and needs are met, they are more likely to be loyal and continue to purchase from the business. So, effective marketing is important to the success of businesses.

Checkpoint ▶▶▶

Why do businesses that use the marketing concept benefit more from marketing?

Marketing Helps People

Individuals benefit from marketing because it improves the exchanges that occur between businesses and consumers. While many people do not easily recognize the benefits of marketing, there are numerous examples of its value.

Consider going to a supermarket to purchase party supplies. You want the store to be conveniently located. It should stock an adequate supply of your favorite brands of decorations, drinks, and snacks. When you get into the store, the products should be easy to locate. The prices should be clearly marked and affordable. Store employees should be able to answer your questions and help you check out and bag your purchases. The store should offer convenient methods of payment, including cash, check, and credit or debit card.

Each of the activities described for the purchase of your party supplies is an example of marketing. Those activities make it easier for you to shop. The business benefits because you purchase the products. You benefit because the business is able to satisfy your needs.

Better Products at a Lower Cost

Marketing provides other benefits to individuals that may not be as obvious. Marketing continually evaluates consumers' likes and dislikes and unmet needs. Based

Parents are attracted to products that respond to children's health concerns.

on this information, improvements are made to products and services, and new products are developed. As a result of marketing activities, more products are available to satisfy the needs of more customers. This results in higher sales. The increase in sales allows businesses to produce products more efficiently, and costs can decline.

The first personal computers were very basic and not very powerful, but they cost several thousand dollars. Today's personal computers are hundreds of times more powerful, have many features to make them easy to use, and can be purchased for less than $500. This is possible because of improved technology and marketing.

Expanded Opportunities

Another contribution of marketing to individuals is the large number of employment opportunities. Between one-fourth and one-third of all jobs in the United States are marketing jobs or have marketing as a major job responsibility. Salespeople, customer service representatives, warehouse managers, inventory specialists, marketing researchers, and many others have interesting, financially rewarding careers because of the need for marketing.

Marketing skills are also valuable to people who are not directly employed in the field of marketing. By understanding the marketing process and using the marketing concept, you will be able to

accomplish a number of your goals. Marketing skills can help you get elected to an office in a club, prepare for a job or for college, plan a fundraising activity for an organization, or start your own business.

As a result of marketing, people can choose from a wide variety of products and services, find businesses that respond to their needs, have access to good jobs, and develop skills that can help meet personal goals.

Checkpoint ▶▶

What percentage of jobs in the United States involves the performance of marketing activities as a major job responsibility?

Marketing Benefits Society

Does society benefit because of marketing? This question often is debated, but the evidence seems to indicate there are many positive effects of marketing for society, as shown in Figure 2-1.

New and Better Products

Marketing helps to identify and develop new and better products and services for consumers. Many of those products and services are beneficial to society in general.

More efficient automobiles use less gasoline and cause less pollution. Biodegradable products reduce the growing need for landfill space. Products like airbags and motorcycle helmets reduce the

FIGURE 2-1

All of the benefits of marketing are not obvious. However, those benefits are important to consumers, businesses, and society.

Benefits of Marketing
• Businesses meet consumer needs
• Consumers make better decisions
• Natural resources are used more effectively
• Standard of living is improved
• International trade increases

number and severity of injuries from accidents. All of these products were developed to meet the needs of consumers and society.

Digital Digest

Feedback for Sale

When marketers want quick feedback or additional research to supplement their data, they can turn to several Internet services. Many retail web sites such as Amazon.com and cnet.com allow consumers to review products. Other web sites such as planetfeedback.com, American Consumer Opinion (acop.com), and Epinions.com were created to give consumers a chance to voice their opinions about products and services.

These feedback services, in turn, are building databases that can complement companies' own marketing research. The web sites make money by selling the customer data they collect to businesses. The data can give businesses insight into their own products, services, and marketing efforts as well as those of their competitors. These Internet services can be quicker and more cost-effective in collecting data because they actively seek out consumers eager to review products and because they collect data on millions of products from consumers around the globe.

Think Critically

1. What kinds of useful information could a company obtain from data compiled by an Internet feedback service?

2. Why might dissatisfied customers vent their frustrations through an Internet feedback service rather than writing or calling a company directly themselves?

Marketing encourages businesses to provide products and services that consumers want. It also helps educate consumers to make better purchasing decisions. As a result, natural resources and raw materials can be used more efficiently rather than being wasted on products consumers will not buy.

Better Standards of Living

Market Planning

Marketing improves the standard of living in a country. The standard of living is based on the products and services available to consumers, the amount of resources consumers have to obtain the products and services, and the quality of life for consumers. Countries that have well-developed marketing systems are able to make more and better products available to consumers. Those countries also have more jobs for their citizens and higher wage scales as a result of marketing.

Marketing helps improve our standard of living. How is this demonstrated at your local supermarket?

©GETTY IMAGES/PHOTODISC

Improved International Trade

Marketing has been particularly effective in improving international trade. **International trade** is the sale of products and services to people in other countries. International trade has many benefits for the participating countries and for the consumers in those countries. Think of the number of products you buy that were produced in another country. Just as the United States is a large consumer of foreign products, many U.S. businesses sell products internationally. Without marketing, international trade would not be possible.

Marketing activities are essential for international trade. Marketers help to determine where products can be sold and how to sell them in countries that may have very different business procedures, money systems, and buying practices. Methods of shipping and product handling must be identified or developed. Decisions about customer service must be made. Promotional methods that are appropriate for the people in each country or region have to be developed to ensure that customers understand the products and their benefits.

How does marketing help the environment?

2-1 Assessment

Xtra! Study Tools
school.cengage.com/marketing/marketing

Key Concepts

Determine the best answer.

1. All of the following tend to occur when the marketing concept is used effectively *except*
   a. customer satisfaction increases
   b. sales go up
   c. prices go up
   d. costs are reduced

2. All of the following are examples of marketing jobs *except*
   a. web site designer
   b. sales representative
   c. public relations specialist
   d. all of the above are marketing jobs

3. The effects of marketing on society include all of the following *except*
   a. better products
   b. decrease in international trade
   c. more jobs
   d. improvements to the environment

Make Academic Connections

4. **Visual Art** Select a business from which you purchase products or services. Create a graphic or other visual representation showing how marketing affects this business.

5. **Consumer Economics** Marketing is said to improve exchanges between businesses and consumers. Make a list of at least five products or services that you buy or use. Describe how marketing has improved the exchange process for each of these products or services. Organize this information in a spreadsheet.

Connect to

6. You work for a food processing company that is considering selling its product globally. The owner has no experience marketing products internationally and has asked for your advice. Prepare a two-minute presentation on how international trade can benefit the business. Include two specific ways that marketing can support the company's efforts. Give your speech to your teacher (judge).

Criticisms of Marketing

GOALS

- Discuss three common criticisms of marketing.
- Explain how marketing can be used to solve social problems.

KEY TERMS

green (environmental) marketing, *p. 44*

marketing matters

The activities associated with marketing can sometimes cause customers and other people to get upset. Marketing has been accused of creating a false need for unnecessary products. Some people feel that marketing is a waste of money and only serves to increase the price customers pay. Others claim that high-quality products do not need any marketing because the products will sell themselves.

Work with a group. Discuss each of these complaints and reasons why they are valid. Then try to come up with reasons why these criticisms are wrong. Share your results with the other groups.

Common Complaints

It would be easy to say that marketing has only positive results. That is not always the case. If not used appropriately, marketing can have negative effects. The misuse of marketing has led to some criticisms and has created a negative image for some marketing activities. Business people must take criticisms of marketing seriously. If consumers have a negative opinion about an important part of a business, it can affect whether or not they will be customers.

Marketing Causes Unneeded Purchases

Because of marketing, consumers have many choices of products to purchase. Those products are readily available in many stores. They are displayed in ways that make them easy to purchase, and they are packaged to attract attention. Advertising is used extensively to encourage people to consider specific brands of products. Credit and special financing arrangements are often available for expensive products to make them seem more affordable. Marketing activities and the power of promotion can increase the sales of products and services.

Do you think credit cards are a positive outcome of marketing? Why or why not?

Businesses using the marketing concept should carefully consider the potential impact of marketing activities on consumers. While it might seem appropriate to use any tool that will result in more sales of a product, the long-term results of the sale should also be considered. If a customer buys a product because of marketing rather than because the product is really needed,

Borders Can Be Barriers

International borders can create challenges for companies marketing products overseas. Marketers must overcome cultural differences. Many countries also protect their local industries by regulating the number of foreign imports or by enacting high tariffs to make it easier for local businesses to compete with international companies.

It is particularly common for news and entertainment media to be regulated in foreign countries. Because most film markets cannot compete with the high budgets and marketing power of Hollywood studios, foreign governments sometimes require that a certain percentage of films shown be locally produced. France is particularly protective of its film and television industries, and the European Union tries to reserve at least half of its television programming for shows made in Europe.

The United States, on the other hand, has no formal barriers to entertainment imports. However, foreign films, especially foreign-language films with subtitles, typically only play in small theaters and enjoy modest success here. A foreign-made show occasionally crosses cultural barriers and finds success in the United States. *Teletubbies,* a children's program produced in the U.K., has been a smash hit here. But more often, U.S. studios will remake a foreign hit to be more relevant to American audiences, as they did with the British television comedy, *The Office.*

Think Critically

1. Why do you think foreign-language movies with English subtitles are not often successful in the United States?

2. How have the development of the Internet and the growth of cable TV helped to break down cultural barriers?

---

there is a good chance the customer will be dissatisfied. How many times have you purchased something and then quickly decided you really did not want or need the item? What actions did you take?

Many consumers simply return the item for a refund. The business has now lost the sale, and it also has a product that is worth much less than before and perhaps cannot be resold. Even if the consumers do not return the products, they are likely to be dissatisfied. Do you believe the consumers will buy that product again? The business is left with returned merchandise, a dissatisfied customer, and possibly a bad reputation among the customer's friends.

To respond to this criticism, business people must be sensitive to the needs and experiences of customers. Products and services should be carefully matched to customers' needs. Products that do not sell should be evaluated to determine why customers do not want them. In that way, the business can make better planning decisions in the future in order to offer products and services that customers want.

Marketing should start with good products. If a product is not meeting customer needs, business people should avoid using marketing strategies such as promotion

Working in Teams

Working with a team, select a product and list all of the marketing activities that must occur to accommodate the exchange between the business and the customer. Outline how the exchange would work without marketing. As a team, discuss why marketing is needed.

and price reductions to try to sell the product. This will often lead to dissatisfaction with both the product and the business.

Finally, the business must value long-term relationships with customers. One sale is not enough. The business will be successful only when customers return repeatedly because they are satisfied with the business and believe the business is concerned about their needs.

Marketing Wastes Money

As seen in Figure 2-2, the average cost of all marketing activities is about 50 percent of the price of products. For some products it is much higher, and for others, it is a very small percentage. Since many people think of marketing as only advertising and selling, they are upset when they believe those activities double the price of their purchases.

In reality, promotion and selling are a small part of the cost of marketing—typically about 2 to 10 percent of the product's price—and effective promotion and selling do increase the value to the customer. Advertising can provide product information so that you can make the best choice. It can inform you where a product can be purchased and when it is on sale. Advertising can even result in savings because of the information provided. A salesperson who helps you select the best product for your needs rather than sells you something you do not want helps you spend your money more effectively.

Economists who study the impact of marketing activities on product prices have demonstrated that marketing actually results in lower prices in the long run. Because of marketing, products can be sold to more customers. This, in turn, creates more competition among businesses. When consumers have more choices of products, they will usually buy those that are reasonably priced. That encourages businesses to keep prices as low as possible to be competitive. According to the economists, increased sales volume and competition result in lower prices for consumers.

Marketing Is Not Always Needed

There are many examples of businesses that rely on marketing to sell poor-quality products. Think of the used automobile with many mechanical problems that is sold because the salesperson convinced the unsuspecting customer that the car is in good condition. There are numerous tales of unsuspecting people buying land based on information in a brochure or video-tape only to discover that the land is in a swamp or on the side of a steep mountain. Marketing is misused in those situations to misrepresent poor products.

On the other hand, consider whether or not a high-quality product needs marketing. Without marketing, it would be the responsibility of the consumer to find out that the product exists and to gather information about it. The consumer would have to locate the product, pay cash for it, and transport it from where it was manufactured to where it would be used. The customer would assume all of the risk in moving the product. If it was damaged, the customer would be responsible.

These examples show that marketing is important even for quality products and

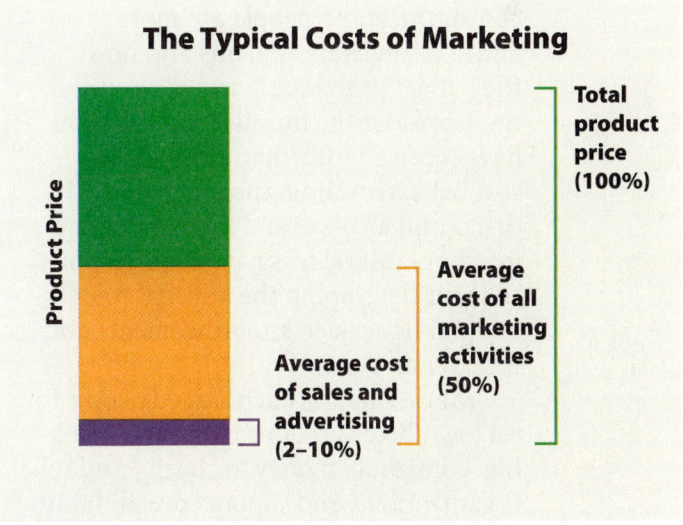

FIGURE 2-2

On average, total marketing expenses are about one-half of a product's price, while sales and advertising costs average about 2 to 10 percent of the price.

services. Marketing activities must be performed in every exchange. If the business is not responsible for marketing, consumers will have to complete the activities themselves in order to purchase the product or service.

Checkpoint ▶▶

Why is a business that is committed to long-term customer relationships less likely to use high-pressure sales tactics?

Marketing Solves Problems

Marketing, if misused, can have negative results. However, when it is used effectively, marketing can help to solve important problems and contribute to social improvement.

Marketing Increases Public Awareness

There are many serious problems facing our society. Concerns about health care, crime levels, poverty, diseases, racism, education, unemployment, drug use, teenage pregnancy, and the environment all require the attention of many people if solutions are to be found. Marketing contributes to the solutions in several ways. Through communication, people are more aware of societal problems and how they affect individuals and the country. Consider the number of times you have received information on using seat belts, recycling, the dangers of drugs and alcohol, and reasons to stay in school. Marketers have been responsible for developing the advertisements and public service announcements you have seen.

Marketing has encouraged people to eat low-cholesterol products, quit smoking, contribute money to charity and relief organizations, and support research into cures for diseases like AIDS and cancer. Marketing has encouraged people to vote and to avoid drinking and driving. Many important social issues are now receiving

Today, energy companies must work to demonstrate their commitment to a clean environment.

much attention because of effective marketing.

Many businesses now promote the use of green marketing. **Green (environmental) marketing** consists of marketing activities designed to satisfy customer needs without negatively impacting the environment. Businesses promote the importance of environmentally friendly products and encourage consumers to purchase such products.

Planning a Career in... *Community Relations*

Marketing, Sales & Service

"The fire engines that roared down our street last night woke up half the neighborhood. Our teenage neighbor had forgotten to extinguish a candle before going to bed. The smoke detector woke up the family. Their nine-year-old was a hero because he had reminded his parents to change the smoke detector batteries when the time changed."

Did you ever experience a positive outcome because you prepared for a potentially harmful event?

Public awareness campaigns reach out to communities to improve the quality of life within the community. Whether it is informing people about Lyme disease or reminding people to have cancer screening check-ups, these campaigns increase awareness on a number of vital issues.

Employment Outlook

- Although faster than average growth is expected, actual job opportunities will vary by industry.
- Related work experience and state-of-the-art Internet skills will increase a job candidate's competitiveness.

Job Titles

- Community Outreach Coordinator
- Public Relations Officer
- Community Relations Liaison
- Director of Media
- Social Service and Outreach Manager
- Programs Specialist
- Cancer Society Community Relations

Needed Skills

- A bachelor's degree is usually required.
- Excellent written and oral communication skills are helpful.

- A perpetual ability to stay abreast of current trends in your industry is required.

What's it like to work in... *Community Relations*

Jada arrives at her office at 9:00 A.M. As the Customer Communications Manager for her publicly funded city bus system, she will spend the next hour reviewing the print and radio "Ride the Bus" ad campaigns that will run for the rest of the summer. Reminding commuters how they can help reduce smog by riding the bus is an effective way to both increase ridership and minimize smog.

After lunch, Jada gives a presentation on the city's new "fare assistance" program to representatives from various social service agencies. Jada needs to inform the elderly, low-income city residents, and students about "fare assistance." The presentation feedback provided by the agency representatives will help her accomplish that goal. The bus system strives to provide economical transportation to as many citizens as possible.

At 4:00 P.M., representatives from a local advertising agency meet with Jada and her team to review the new posters designed to increase ridership. Featuring endorsements of riders from all walks of life, the posters are intended to increase ridership throughout the community.

What About **You**

What issues do you believe are important to a community's well-being, and how would you promote those ideas if you worked in community relations?

Marketing Helps Match Supply with Demand

Products and services are not always available where consumers most need them. For example, if there is a drought in one part of the country, farmers and ranchers in that area may not have enough hay and grain to feed their livestock. At the same time, there might be an excess supply in other areas. An effective distribution system can move the hay and grain quickly from one part of the country to another, matching supply and demand.

Oil products and gasoline can be distributed throughout the country using an extensive network of pipelines. If a greater supply of natural gas or heating oil is needed in the North during an especially cold winter, it can be routed away from areas that have less demand. Marketing helps to prevent or reduce the impact of problems that could otherwise result in serious outcomes for society.

Checkpoint ▶▶▶

If a heat wave in the West is causing electrical outages, how can marketing help alleviate the problem?

2-2 Assessment

Key Concepts

Determine the best answer.

1. On average, marketing costs represent what percentage of the price that a consumer pays for a product?
   a. 2%
   b. 10%
   c. 50%
   d. 75%

2. True or False: Marketing activities result in lower product prices in the long run.

3. Complaints about marketing include all of the following *except*
   a. Marketing leads to unneeded purchases.
   b. Marketing creates an imbalance in supply and demand.
   c. Marketing is a waste of money.
   d. Marketing is not necessary for all products.

4. Effective uses for marketing include
   a. contributing to social improvement
   b. matching supply with demand
   c. selling products that do not meet consumers' needs
   d. both a and b

Make Academic Connections

5. **Social Studies** Marketing is responsible for many successful public awareness campaigns, such as *Don't Drink and Drive, Buckle Up,* and *Just Say No.* Think of a problem that is prevalent in society today. Create a poster or some other visual aid that would contribute to a public awareness campaign for the problem.

6. **Economics** Explain the effects of marketing on the following business practices:
   • Competition
   • Pricing
   • Supply and demand

Connect to

7. You are a marketer working in the farming industry. Cranberry growers in your state are suffering from an oversupply of cranberries. This is forcing them to slash prices and is threatening to put them out of business. Develop a two-page written plan that outlines three specific ways marketing can help balance the supply and demand of cranberries. Present your plan to your teacher (judge).

Increasing Social Responsibility

GOALS

- Define consumerism.
- Explain ways by which businesses improve their own practices.
- Discuss how ethical issues affect marketers' professional responsibilities.

KEY TERMS

social responsibility, p. 47

consumerism, p. 48

boycott, p. 48

ethics, p. 50

code of ethics, p. 50

self-regulation, p. 50

marketing matters

Most consumers have at one time purchased a product that did not live up to their expectations. A shirt didn't fit right. A household cleanser didn't remove dirt well. A potted plant wilted and died in just a week. A new hairstyle didn't look very good.

Work with a group. Describe an occasion when a product or service you purchased didn't live up to your expectations. How did you handle the situation? Were you satisfied with the outcome? Would you have handled another group member's situation differently than he or she did? Share a summary of your discussion with the other groups.

Consumer Protection

Marketers cannot think only about selling products and making a profit. They must be aware of other effects of their activities. Marketing can have both positive and negative results. Marketers must be willing to pay attention to society's needs to determine how businesses can address those needs.

The trend today is a greater expectation for businesses to be socially responsible and to aid in solving the problems facing society. Concern about the consequences of actions on others is **social responsibility**. When making decisions, business people realize that they must consider factors beyond what their customers want and what is most profitable for the business. Most business people recognize that their businesses cannot be successful in the long run if society is facing major problems.

©GETTY IMAGES/PHOTODISC

How is a store that uses recycled bags being socially responsible?

Increasing the social responsibility of businesses is occurring in three major ways. The growth of consumerism, government regulation, and improving business practices are each playing a role, as shown in Figure 2-3 on the next page.

The Growth of Consumerism

Consumerism is the organized actions of groups of consumers seeking to increase their influence on business practices. Consumers as individuals can have only a small influence on the activities of a business. However, when organized as a group, consumers have a much greater impact. They can speak out and meet with business people to recommend changes. They can also use the money they spend on purchases to influence decisions.

While consumers have always attempted to influence business practices, consumerism became an important influence on business practices in the 1960s when President John F. Kennedy presented the Consumer Bill of Rights. The Consumer Bill of Rights identified four rights that all consumers should expect: the right to adequate and accurate information, the right to safe products, the right to product choices, and the right to communicate their ideas and opinions to business and government.

As a result of the attention focused on those rights, consumers have become very active in ensuring that their rights are protected. Some ways used to protect consumer rights are consumer education, consumer information, lobbying, and product boycotts. Consumer groups develop materials and educational programs to be used in schools and in other places to help people become better informed consumers. You may have used some of those materials to learn how to use banking services, purchase insurance, and apply for loans.

There are a number of consumer organizations that test products to determine whether they are safe and whether they provide a good value for the price. The organizations often publish the results in books, magazines, and on the Internet or have a telephone service so people can call for product information before making a

Social Responsibility Must Be Shared

FIGURE 2-3

Consumer groups, government, and business organizations all must play a role in improving society.

purchase. Consumer lobbyists work with national and state legislators to develop laws to protect consumer rights. Some important consumer laws are described in Figure 2-4 on the next page.

Finally, consumers have found that they can influence business practices by the way they spend their money, their consumer votes. If a group of consumers is dissatisfied with the actions or products of a business, they can organize a boycott. A **boycott** is an organized effort to influence a company by refusing to purchase its products. Consumer groups also reinforce positive business practices by encouraging their members to purchase products from businesses that respond to consumer needs.

Fast FACTS

The term *boycott* originated in 1880. It was named after Captain Charles Cunningham Boycott. As an English landlord in Ireland, he ruthlessly evicted his tenants, leading his employees to refuse all cooperation with him.

FIGURE 2-4
Federal legislation is one method of increasing the social responsibility of businesses.

Consumer Laws	
Legislation	**Purpose**
Sherman Antitrust Act, 1890	To increase competition among businesses by regulating monopolies
Food and Drug Act, 1906	To control the content and labeling of food and drug products by forming the Food and Drug Administration (FDA)
Federal Trade Commission Act, 1914	To form the Federal Trade Commission (FTC) to protect consumer rights
Robinson-Patman Act, 1936	To protect small businesses from unfair pricing practices between manufacturers and large businesses
Fair Packaging and Labeling Act, 1966	To require packages to be accurately labeled and fairly represent the contents
Consumer Credit Protection Act, 1968	To require disclosure of credit requirements and rates to loan applicants
Consumer Product Safety Act, 1972	To set safety standards and to form the Consumer Product Safety Commission (CPSC)
Americans with Disabilities Act, 1990	To prohibit discrimination and ensure equal opportunity for persons with disabilities
Telemarketing and Consumer Fraud and Abuse Prevention Act, 1994	To prohibit deceptive telemarketing practices and regulate calls made to consumers' homes
Millennium Digital Commerce Act, 1999	To regulate the use of electronic contracts and signatures for Internet business transactions
Gramm-Leach-Bliley Financial Modernization Act, 1999	To limit the sharing of consumer information by requiring financial services companies to inform consumers about how private information is handled

Government Regulation

The United States government plays an active role in business practices. The welfare of consumers is at the core of many of the laws and regulations enacted by government. These laws are designed to improve the social impact of business practices. Businesses must comply with consumer protection laws or risk fines and a loss of business.

Checkpoint ▶▶

What federal law is intended to protect consumers by requiring that packages be accurately labeled and contents fairly disclosed?

Improving Practices

Most businesses recognize their responsibility to consumers and to society. If consumers are dissatisfied with the business's practices, they will soon stop buying the company's products. If social problems exist, the government may increase regulation of business or increase taxes to pay for programs designed to solve the problems. Businesses do not want increased regulation or taxes.

Individual businesses and business organizations are working to improve business practices in several ways. Those ways include codes of ethics, self-regulation, and social action.

Codes of Ethics

Ethics are moral principles or values based on honesty and fairness. A **code of ethics** is a set of standards or rules that guide ethical business behavior. A code of ethics encourages honest and proper conduct. Business people recognize that the inappropriate or illegal behavior of one company can have a very negative effect on the whole industry. They attempt to influence that behavior by agreeing on standards of conduct. By agreeing to a code of ethics, business people encourage responsible behavior. In some groups, the codes of ethics are enforced by penalties established by the industry that are applied to businesses that violate the standards. The American Marketing Association (AMA) Code of Ethics describes specific responsibilities for marketers in the areas of product planning, promotion, pricing, distribution, and marketing research. A portion of the AMA's Code of Ethics is summarized in Figure 2-5.

Self-Regulation

Individual businesses and groups of businesses in the same industry have developed procedures to respond to consumer problems and to encourage customers to work directly with the businesses to solve problems. Taking personal responsibility for actions is known as **self-regulation**. The Better Business Bureau is a consumer protection organization sponsored by businesses. The purpose of the Better Business Bureau is to gather information from consumers about problems, provide information about improper business practices, and attempt to solve problems between businesses and their customers.

Many businesses have consumer service departments that work to solve consumer problems and to provide consumers with information about the company and its products. The Butterball Turkey Talk-Line has been in operation for 25 years. It is open through the months of November and December to answer consumers' questions about how to prepare a Butterball turkey for their holiday meals.

Some industries, such as homebuilders, developed procedures for consumers to use

FIGURE 2-5
Organizations and industries often develop a code of ethics to promote honest and proper standards of conduct.

Responsibilities of the Marketer
In Product Development and Management
• disclosing all substantial risks associated with a product or service
• identifying substitutions that change the product or impact buying decisions
• identifying extra cost-added features
In Promotions
• avoiding false and misleading advertising
• rejecting high-pressure or misleading sales tactics and promotions
In Distribution
• not exploiting customers by manipulating the availability of a product
• not using coercion
• not exerting undue influence over the reseller's choice to handle a product
In Pricing
• not engaging in price fixing
• not practicing predatory pricing
• disclosing the full price associated with any purchase
In Marketing Research
• prohibiting selling or fundraising disguised as conducting research
• avoiding misrepresentation and omission of pertinent research data
• treating clients and suppliers fairly

to resolve problems. Problems that cannot be resolved between the customer and the business are referred to an independent panel that can help determine a fair solution.

Social Action

Business people are concerned about the world in which they live. Many are active in helping to solve some of society's serious problems by investing time and money to help their communities. Recently, Microsoft and its employees reached a contribution milestone after donating more than $2.5 billion in cash, services, and software to nonprofit organizations around the world. McDonald's sponsors Ronald McDonald Houses for families with children who are hospitalized with serious illnesses.

NETBookmark

Marketers cannot think only about selling products and making a profit. They must be aware of other effects of their activities. Access school.cengage.com/marketing/marketing and click on the link for Chapter 2. Read the article about Burger King. What socially responsible action is the company taking? Why do you think Burger King has made this decision?

school.cengage.com/marketing/marketing

Checkpoint ▶▶▶

What is a code of ethics?

Ethics in Marketing

Each day you can see many examples of businesses that feel a social responsibility to help their community and its people. Business ethics has received a great deal of attention recently. Most business people behave ethically. However, the

Judgment Call

Should Marketers Target Kids?

While monetary profit is a goal of marketers, they must always consider what is ethical. The question of marketing to children is one such ethical dilemma. Because children represent an increasing amount of purchase power, they are an alluring target for marketers. But is it appropriate to target kids?

This issue was debated in 2000 when the in-school television educational program Channel One was introduced in more than 12,000 schools. Some people were appalled to learn that Channel One would carry commercials. Channel One, however, argued that the advertising income was funding the whole program.

Because marketing to children is such a hotly contested topic, children's advocacy watch groups and regulatory commissions such as the Children's Advertising Regulatory Unit (CARU) have been created to help determine what is appropriate and to set guidelines for marketers to follow when it comes to children.

Think Critically

1. Why might people oppose advertiser-supported TV in schools?

2. Is there an ethical difference between TV ads for children at home and TV ads for children in a program they are required to view in their schools?

actions of a few people can cause customers to wonder if ethical behavior is really valued in business.

Responsibility to Customers

Marketers deal directly with customers. They ask customers to spend money for products intended to satisfy needs and wants. Because of this relationship, marketers have a special responsibility to behave ethically. People place a high value on ethical business behavior. Business people are expected to be honest and fair in dealings with customers, employees, and other businesses.

Each marketer is responsible for ethical behavior. Decisions and actions should be evaluated to determine if they are honest and fair. Sometimes there will appear to be conflicts in what is best for the business, its employees, customers, competitors, and society in general. Some people suggest that the decision should be based on what is best for the most people. Others believe an action is right or wrong based on how it will affect the people directly involved.

In 2007, ConAgra Foods recalled all varieties of its Peter Pan Peanut Butter product because of a possible link to salmonella poisoning. Although initial product tests did not indicate the presence of salmonella, ConAgra voluntarily recalled the peanut butter and offered consumers a refund. ConAgra acted responsibly and ethically by making consumer health and safety a priority. Upon further investigation, ConAgra discovered that there was salmonella contamination caused by water damage experienced during a flood at one of its plants. ConAgra closed the plant to make renovations that would result in safer production processes.

Harm and Accountability

In some cases, it may appear there is no real harm in unethical behavior. If

Figure This

Ethical Marketing Pays Off

Not only is honest marketing the ethical thing to do, but it makes business sense as well. Ideally, a company wants to build brand loyalty and enter into long-term relationships with its customers. Loyal customers purchase repeatedly from the same company. Over a lifetime, these purchases can really add up. And when customers are happy with a product or service, they will recommend it to others.

It may be tempting for a company to try to increase sales through deceptive marketing that overstates the benefit of its product. This practice not only is unethical but also can be less profitable to the company in the long run.

Think Critically

1. Two car dealerships, Dealership A and Dealership B, both make an average of $1,000 profit for every car they sell. Through the use of deceptive sales and pricing, Dealership A sells 100 cars in May. However, none of those 100 customers ever buy from Dealership A again. Dealership B is honest with its customers but sells only 70 cars in May. However, 30 of those customers buy an average of three more cars from Dealership B throughout their lifetime. What is the difference in the monthly and long-term profit between Dealership A and Dealership B from those customers?

2. Dealership B's repeat customers also each recommend Dealership B to six friends. Fifty percent of those friends end up buying a car from Dealership B. How much profit does Dealership B make from this word-of-mouth promotion?

dishonesty results in a customer buying your product rather than your competitor's, or if you can conceal a mistake you made, you may believe that it does not matter. But marketers must remember that their emphasis must be on what is best for everyone in an exchange. Marketers' actions affect many others, both inside and outside the business.

In other cases, unethical behavior has negative consequences for individuals and businesses. Improper marketing can harm customers. Society is hurt by businesses that have no concern for the products and services they sell or how or to whom they are marketed. Senior citizens often fall prey to the unethical business practices of salespeople who sell them poor-quality or unneeded products or services. Finally, many unethical business practices are illegal. People have been fined and imprisoned as a result of unethical actions.

Some businesses are developing education programs and operating procedures to help employees understand how to make ethical decisions. They want to improve the ethical image of all businesses and ensure that customers believe they will be treated fairly.

Checkpoint ▶▶

Why do marketers have a special responsibility for ethical behavior?

2-3 Assessment

Key Concepts

Determine the best answer.

1. Which national elected leader proposed the Consumer Bill of Rights?
   a. Jimmy Carter
   b. Ronald Reagan
   c. John F. Kennedy
   d. none of the above

2. Which of the following is *not* one of the four basic rights enumerated in the Consumer Bill of Rights?
   a. right to adequate and accurate information
   b. right to fair prices
   c. right to safe products
   d. right to product choices

3. Marketing activities covered in the American Marketing Association's code of ethics include
   a. promotions, pricing, and distribution
   b. promotions, distribution, and consumerism
   c. product development, pricing, and self-regulation
   d. none of the above

4. True or False: The Better Business Bureau is a consumer protection organization sponsored by consumer groups.

Make Academic Connections

5. **Government** Many consumer laws exist to protect consumer rights. Research one of these laws. Write one paragraph describing the purpose of the law and the history surrounding it.

6. **Ethics** Although most businesses act ethically, some do not. Search newspapers or the Internet for recent stories about businesses that used unethical marketing tactics resulting in harm to consumers. Report about the unethical activities in a one-page paper.

Connect to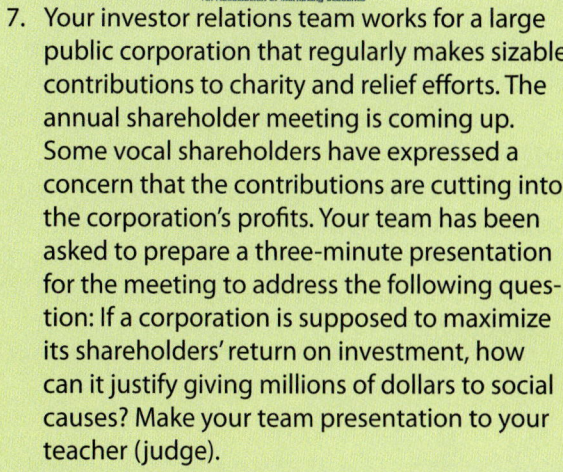

7. Your investor relations team works for a large public corporation that regularly makes sizable contributions to charity and relief efforts. The annual shareholder meeting is coming up. Some vocal shareholders have expressed a concern that the contributions are cutting into the corporation's profits. Your team has been asked to prepare a three-minute presentation for the meeting to address the following question: If a corporation is supposed to maximize its shareholders' return on investment, how can it justify giving millions of dollars to social causes? Make your team presentation to your teacher (judge).

Check Your Understanding

Now that you have completed the chapter, check your understanding of the lessons with these questions. Record the score that best represents your understanding of each marketing concept.

1 = not at all; 3 = somewhat; 5 = very well

If your score is 42–50, you are ready for the assessment activities that follow. If you score 33–41, you should review the lessons for the items you scored 1–3. If you score 32 or less, you will want to carefully reread the lessons and work with a study partner on the areas you do not understand.

Can you—

___ list various ways that marketing affects businesses?

___ identify how marketing affects individual consumers?

___ list the ways that marketing benefits society?

___ describe three common criticisms of marketing?

___ discuss how marketing can be used to solve social problems and raise public awareness?

___ discuss how marketing helps match supply with demand?

___ describe ways consumer action and government regulations are used to ensure businesses respect consumer rights?

___ explain why businesses adopt codes of ethics?

___ provide examples of how a business can use self-regulation to resolve customer problems?

___ explain why marketers have special ethical responsibilities to customers?

Review Marketing Terms

Match the terms listed with the definitions.

1. The organized actions of groups of consumers seeking to increase their influence on business practices

2. Taking personal responsibility for actions

3. An organized effort to influence a company by refusing to purchase its products

4. Concern about the consequences of actions on others

5. Moral principles or values based on honesty and fairness

6. A set of standards or rules that guide ethical business behavior

7. Marketing activities designed to satisfy customer needs without negatively impacting the environment

8. The sale of products and services to people in other countries

a. boycott
b. code of ethics
c. consumerism
d. ethics
e. green (environmental) marketing
f. international trade
g. self-regulation
h. social responsibility

Review Marketing Concepts

9. True or False: When marketing is effective, prices usually increase more than enough to cover the costs of marketing, so sellers make larger profits per unit sold.

10. Which of the following are involved in completing marketing functions?
    a. manufacturers
    b. consumers
    c. trucking companies
    d. all of the above

11. Effective marketing is used to encourage people to buy what kinds of things?
    a. things they otherwise would not buy
    b. things they need or want
    c. things that businesses cannot otherwise sell
    d. luxury items they cannot afford

12. Marketing can be an effective tool in helping society solve some serious problems when it is used by
    a. government
    b. business
    c. nonprofit groups
    d. all of the above

13. On average, the cost of all marketing activities is about _____ of the price of a product.

14. True or False: An important social problem created by marketing is that it tends to result in the misuse and waste of raw materials and natural resources.

15. Transporting water to an area where there is a severe drought is an example of
    a. self-regulation
    b. consumerism
    c. matching supply and demand
    d. public awareness

16. True or False: Individual consumers acting alone can usually be quite effective in influencing the activities of businesses.

17. True or False: Federal laws to improve business practices and protect consumers have been in existence only since 1960.

18. When a business practices environmentally friendly production processes, it is using _____ marketing.

Marketing Research and Planning

19. The four consumer products in the table below have undergone significant price decreases from the time they were first sold until now. Those price decreases occurred because of improved technology and effective marketing and resulted in higher sales. The prices listed for each product are typical of the prices charged when the products were first introduced and more recent prices.

Product	Introductory Price	Recent Price
Hand-held calculator	$ 138	$ 16
Quartz watch	320	50
Personal computer	2,800	599
Microwave oven	860	110

   a. For each product, find the price reduction and the percentage decrease from the introductory price to the recent price.

   b. Assume that you planned to buy all four of the items. Calculate the total cost of the purchases if all were purchased at the introductory price. Now calculate the total cost if all were purchased at the recent price. Calculate the percentage savings to you if you were able to make all purchases at the recent price.

   c. List four other products with large price decreases from the time they were first introduced until now.

20. Review the business section in five issues of a newspaper or five issues of a business magazine (*BusinessWeek, Fortune,* or *Money,* for example). Identify all articles that relate to the social responsibility of businesses. For each article, determine (a) the primary issue involved; (b) whether the problem is being addressed by consumer groups, government, businesses, or a combination; and (c) the type of action being proposed to solve the problem. After you have collected the information, summarize your findings in a

one-page written report. Before submission, check the document for correct grammar, spelling, punctuation, and format.

21. Using an Internet search engine and browser, find the FedStats home page, which is a gateway to statistics from more than 100 federal agencies. Select your state from the MapStats drop-down menu, and then locate the most recent population statistics for your state and county. What percentage of your state's total population resides in your county? Describe what other kinds of information are available on this web site. Identify several ways that marketers could use the data provided by FedStats.

22. The following statements describe marketing activities that may result in a problem for society. For each statement, describe a problem that may result from the practice and one way that consumers, government, and businesses could respond.

   a. Fast-food restaurants use a large amount of packaging.

   b. Credit card companies use advertising to encourage people to use credit for more of their purchases.

   c. A hospital cannot afford to admit patients who do not have health insurance.

   d. A market research organization asks a large number of personal questions during interviews.

23. a. For each of the following criticisms of marketing, describe with specific examples why each is not always accurate.

   Marketing causes people to purchase things they otherwise would not buy.

   Marketing adds to the cost of products without providing anything of value.

   Quality products and services do not need marketing.

   b. For each of the following positive results of marketing, provide specific examples demonstrating that those contributions do exist.

   Marketing increases public awareness of problems and solutions.

   Marketing helps match supply and demand to solve serious problems.

Marketing Management and Decision Making

24. Work in small groups to prepare a code of ethics for students and teachers. Pattern your code of ethics after the example in the chapter or another code of ethics you can locate. When you are finished, share your group's code of ethics with the other groups. Identify the areas of agreement and disagreement in the various codes of ethics. Discuss how the students in the class could enforce the code of ethics through self-regulation.

25. Both the Newsline on Heelys sneakers and the Judgment Call discussing Channel One News in schools present situations in which business people must decide how their decisions can be socially responsible. Choose one and answer the following questions:

   a. What is the social responsibility issue presented?

   b. Who is affected by the decisions of the business? How is each group affected?

   c. What is a possible action that can be taken by a concerned consumer group, government, or group of businesses? By the business involved?

   d. What do you believe is the most socially responsible action? Why?

26. Work with a partner to plan a fundraising campaign in your school or community. The purpose of the campaign may be to raise money for a school function, to fulfill a community need (such as cleaning up a local park), or to meet some other need. Consider how marketing can be used throughout the campaign process. Address questions such as:

   - What product or service are you offering, and how will it satisfy needs?
   - How can market research help you develop a successful campaign?
   - What kind of promotions will you use?
   - Do you need sponsors or investors to help finance the campaign?

   Give an oral presentation using visual aids to your class describing the purpose of the fundraising campaign. Communicate your marketing plans and the goals you want to accomplish.

Apparel and Accessories Marketing Series Event

In the fashion industry, what goes around comes around. Today's popular styles often are styles that were popular 20 to 30 years ago.

The manufacturer of a popular cotton tennis shirt with a reptile emblem has made an incredible comeback from its popularity 25 years ago. Twenty-five years ago, the well-constructed cotton tennis shirt sold for $35 to $42. Retro clothing has made an incredible comeback, and now the reptile tennis shirt commands a price ranging from $72 to $85.

The popular reptile-emblem shirt can once again be seen on college campuses, on tennis courts, at social gatherings, and in schools throughout the country. The shirt has not really changed from 25 years ago, but innovative marketing, selective merchandising, and high demand from other countries have caused the price of the shirt to soar. Only the top-end department stores and high-priced specialty stores currently are allowed to sell the retro tennis shirt. However, outlet stores have also been selling the popular reptile tennis shirt for only $60.

You have been asked by the CEO of the tennis shirt manufacturer to determine additional means to sell the very popular shirt without lowering the price. You must describe how the advertisements in the United States will vary from the advertisements in Mexico, where high-income individuals are purchasing many of the shirts from outlet malls.

Your marketing strategy must describe the target market, the advertising campaign, and the pricing strategy for the shirt manufacturer. You will have ten minutes to plan your marketing strategy, ten minutes to present the strategy to the shirt company's CEO,

and five minutes to answer questions about your plan. You will meet in the CEO's office to present your plan.

Performance Indicators Evaluated

- Defend your marketing strategy objectively. (Communication)

- Describe the concept of price. (Economics)

- Explain the concept of competition. (Economics)

- Explain the nature of international trade. (Economics)

- Explain marketing and its importance in a global economy. (Marketing)

Go to the DECA web site for more detailed information.

Think Critically

1. Why is it important to determine the target market(s) for the shirt?

2. What types of stores are the best outlets for the popular retro shirts?

3. What can the shirt company do to show responsibility to society?

4. Why should the company consider selling the shirts in other countries?

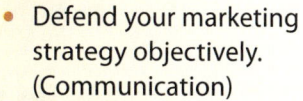

www.deca.org

Marketing Begins with Economics

©GETTY IMAGES/PHOTODISC

Newsline

Competition and Cable TV

In most areas of the United States, cable television service providers have traditionally operated as natural monopolies. To provide service to individual homes, a cable provider must obtain special permission (called a franchise agreement) to install cable lines along streets from the local government that owns the streets. Although some communities are served by multiple cable companies, almost all local governments issue franchise agreements to only one provider. As a result, most Americans who want cable TV must go to that one, single provider to get service.

Now, telephone companies are trying to compete with cable companies by offering customers programming through their phone lines without first applying to local authorities for a franchise. Legislation that would allow telephone companies like AT&T and Verizon to provide television service is being debated in California, Illinois, and many other states. Not surprisingly, the cable television industry is lobbying strongly against it.

Critics suggest that phone companies will "cherry-pick" service areas, choosing to operate only in higher-income communities and leaving lower-income households without similar choices. Others have raised concerns about consumer privacy and want assurances that telephone companies will not disclose customer information to other businesses.

However, phone company supporters argue that opening the cable market will increase competition and improve the quality of service television viewers receive from their providers.

Think Critically

1. Suppose telephone companies begin providing television service in your state. How do you think this would affect cable television prices? Explain.

2. In addition to telephone companies, what other businesses are direct or indirect competitors to cable television service providers?

school.cengage.com/marketing/marketing

Prepare for Performance

This chapter develops the following Performance Indicators from the DECA Competitive Events program.

Core Performance Indicators

- Understand the fundamental economic concepts to obtain a foundation for employment in business
- Understand economic systems to be able to recognize environments in which businesses function
- Explain the types of economic systems
- Explain the concept of competition

Supporting Performance Indicators

- Distinguish between economic goods and services
- Explain the concept of economic resources
- Describe the concepts of economics and economic activities
- Determine economic utilities created by business activities

Go to **school.cengage.com/marketing/marketing** and click on Connect to DECA.

小心碰头限高1.9米

Morgan Stanley
WORLD WISE

What it means to be World Wise. It means seeing the world as interconnected and flowing, and knowing how borderless economies affect the investment decisions you make. It means having the wherewithal to invest as confidently in Ningbo, China, as in Chicago or New York. At Morgan Stanley, World Wise is an understanding of the world as more complex and more dynamic than it has ever been. Which means that success is not only a matter of what you've invested in, but more importantly, whom you've invested with.

Ask a Financial Advisor today.
morganstanley.com/WORLDWISE

©MORGAN STANLEY

Visual Focus

An understanding of the economy is essential in order to make effective marketing decisions. Marketers know that economic factors have an effect on marketing planning. This chapter introduces you to the basic economic problem of scarcity and describes how different economic systems make decisions regarding this problem. It also discusses the effect of the laws of supply and demand and economic competition on businesses. Finally, economic utility and its role in marketing are introduced.

Focus Questions:

Does the use of a Chinese language headline increase or decrease your interest in the advertisement? What is the key message Morgan Stanley is trying to communicate? Offer examples of how the growth of the economies in other countries around the world affects U.S. businesses and consumers. Locate another advertisement that identifies the importance of the global economy. Share your ad with other students in a class discussion.

Scarcity and Private Enterprise

GOALS

- Identify the basic economic problem.
- Describe how America's private enterprise economy works.

KEY TERMS

scarcity, *p. 61*

controlled economy, *p. 62*

free economy, *p. 62*

mixed economy, *p. 62*

private enterprise, *p. 63*

profit motive, *p. 63*

value, *p. 63*

demand, *p. 64*

supply, *p. 64*

marketing matters

Knowledge of economics and how people make economic decisions improves marketers' ability to make marketing decisions. Unlimited needs and wants combined with limited resources produce scarcity. Scarcity is the basic economic problem. People always want more than they can buy, so they must make choices. The way those choices are made determines the type of economic system a society has.

The United States has a private enterprise economy, which has many of the characteristics of a free economy. America's economy is driven by consumers' independent decisions about what they want to purchase and by producers' decisions about what they will produce. The government's role in making economic choices is very limited.

Make a list of your ten most recent purchases. Identify how the availability of product choices and the amount of money you had to spend affected your purchasing decisions.

The Importance of Economic Understanding

Many people believe that effective marketing relies almost solely on creativity. In their view, people who can create a memorable image for a product or attract a customer's attention will increase sales. People who understand marketing, however, know that the marketing process is more scientific. Effective marketing relies on the principles and concepts of economics. Knowledge of economics and how economic decisions are made improves marketing decision making and

results in increased customer satisfaction and higher profits for the company.

An understanding of the types of competition that businesses face also contributes to better marketing decisions. Marketers need to manage based on the type of competition they face. They also must learn how to interpret economic information to improve marketing decisions. Marketers and other business people should recognize that the increased competition faced by most businesses places a whole new importance on understanding and using economic information.

The Basic Economic Problem

People's wants and needs are unlimited. They seldom feel that their wants and needs are completely satisfied. Conversely, resources are limited. There are never enough available to meet everyone's wants and needs. For example, producing a car requires a variety of resources, including glass, rubber, steel, and plastic. Yet each of those resources is in limited supply. They are also used to produce other items in addition to cars. So there may not be enough resources to make as many cars as people might want.

Unlimited wants and needs, combined with limited resources, result in **scarcity**.

Think of all the resources used to make a car. What other products require the use of these same resources?

Scarcity is the basic economic problem. Because of scarcity, choices must be made. How will limited resources be used to

Digital Digest

Database Marketing Made Easy

Many businesses create databases that contain huge amounts of data about their existing customers and potential customers. Their marketers use the data to generate computerized mailing lists and individualized promotions as well as research for product development efforts.

Database programs store, sort, and analyze large volumes of data. They are very useful for businesses with large customer bases or even those with relatively small customer bases but a large number of customer transactions.

To build a database, you first identify each relevant bit of information you want to keep track of, and then input that information into a database field. A business might want a separate field for the customer name,

phone number, e-mail address, each item ordered, price, the transaction date, and so forth. A collection of fields pertaining to a particular customer or order is called a record. All of the records combined make up the database.

The practice of using databases to make marketing decisions is called database marketing. Databases may also be purchased from outside vendors that specialize in compiling mailing lists or sales leads.

Think Critically

1. What is a database field?

2. Give an example of how a marketer might use a database's sorting capabilities to obtain useful information.

satisfy people's unlimited wants and needs? Because wants and needs will always be greater than the available resources, choices and tradeoffs must be made. The available resources will have to be allocated to satisfy some wants and needs but not others.

Scarcity creates difficult problems for a society. Some needs and wants are satisfied while others are not. Resources are used to produce certain products and services. Other products and services are not produced. What is produced and for whom it is produced must be determined. The way those decisions are made indicates the type of economic system a society has.

Who Makes the Decisions?

An economy is designed to facilitate the use of limited resources to satisfy the individual and group needs of people in the economy. All economies must answer three questions.

1. What goods and services will be produced?
2. How will they be produced?
3. For whom will they be produced?

Economies are organized into different economic systems based on how these three economic questions are answered. The type of economic system determines who owns the resources. It determines how decisions are made regarding the use of resources. Which needs are satisfied and how resources are distributed also depend on the type of economic system. Even the cost of resources depends on the economic system.

In a **controlled economy**, the government answers the three economic questions. It attempts to own and control

In a controlled economy, ads such as this one for Converse shoes may not be seen because the government limits the selection of products available to consumers.

important resources and to make the decisions about what will be produced and consumed. In a **free economy**, also known as a *market economy*, resources are owned by individuals rather than the government. The market provides answers to the three economic questions. Decisions are made independently with no attempt at government regulation or control. In a **mixed economy**, some goods and services are provided by the government and some by private enterprise.

Checkpoint ▶▶▶

What is the basic economic problem?

America's Private Enterprise Economy

The United States has many of the characteristics of a free economy. The U.S. economic system is often called a private enterprise or free enterprise economy. **Private enterprise** is based on independent decisions by businesses and consumers with only a limited government role regulating those relationships.

Characteristics

Several important characteristics define a private enterprise economy.

- Resources of production are owned and controlled by individual producers.
- Producers use the profit motive to decide what to produce. The **profit motive** is the use of resources to obtain the greatest profit.
- Individual consumers make decisions about what will be purchased to satisfy needs.
- Consumers use value in deciding what to consume. **Value** is an individual

view of the worth of a product or service. Consumers make decisions of worth by comparing the cost of something they are considering purchasing to other available alternatives.

- The government stays out of exchange activities between producers and consumers unless it is clear that individuals or society are harmed by the decisions.

Because businesses have a great deal of independence in a private enterprise economy, their decisions can determine whether they succeed or fail.

Virtual Marketing

The Emergence of Online Auctions

When auction web sites first appeared in the late 1990s, they appealed mostly to individual consumers. But as online auctions have grown and gained credibility, businesses, and even the government, have joined in on the action.

Retailers quickly realized that auction sites such as eBay would be a major source of competition. However, it was also an opportunity to reach a new market, and smart retailers got into the game early. Independent bike shops, bookstores, and clothing stores could easily add to their

customer base and compete with big online retailers.

Auctions also work well for commercial buyers. Companies looking to buy goods can attract a large number of suppliers and pick the best deal. Even the government has started using online auctions. Through the auction web site FedBid, government agencies purchase commercial items through pre-approved, competing suppliers.

Think Critically

1. What advantages do online auctions offer smaller retailers?
2. How can online auctions cut costs?

Why do retailers offer so many different choices of clothing?

Consumers Individuals who purchase products and services to satisfy needs are consumers. They have limited resources, or money, to satisfy their needs. Consumers select products that they believe will provide the greatest satisfaction for the price. **Demand** is a relationship between the quantity of a product consumers are willing and able to purchase and the price.

Consumers gather information about available products and services so they can select those that appear to satisfy their needs. For example, clothing is a basic consumer need. Some consumers will sew their own clothes. Some will buy basic and inexpensive clothing. Others will spend a great deal of money on a large and expensive wardrobe.

Producers Businesses that use their resources to develop products and services are producers. They hope to sell products and services to consumers for profit. **Supply** is a relationship between the quantity of a product that producers are willing and able to provide and the price.

Producers gather information about the types of products and services consumers want so they can provide those that are most likely to be purchased. An example of a producer's decision is the development of a day-care center. Many parents need someone to watch their children during the day while they are at work. There are opportunities to start businesses that respond to that need.

Government Under ideal circumstances, government allows consumers and producers to make decisions without any interference. However, there are times when some consumers or producers are at a disadvantage and will not receive fair treatment, or society will be harmed by the decisions made by producers or consumers. In those situations, the government enacts laws and regulations to help those who are treated unfairly.

Economic Forces

An example of decision making in a private enterprise economy illustrates how the system operates. Suppose a city has a variety of entertainment options but has no social club for teenagers. Many teenagers indicate a need for some type of club and suggest they would visit it and spend money there if one was developed. Even though it appears that the need for the new type of business exists, no one is required to open a teen social club. It will be developed only when someone recognizes the need, determines that a club could be opened and operated profitably, wants to operate that type of business, and has the resources to do so.

Members of city government might recognize the need for a teen club. They may see teenage crime rates increasing, have concerns expressed to them by teenagers and parents, or just want to meet important needs of city residents. Based on that concern, city leaders may encourage the development of a teen club through tax incentives or other economic assistance. They may even decide to develop and operate a teen center as a city service.

In a private enterprise economy, government would not typically get involved with the economic problem described. It would rely on the profit motive to encourage the development of a new business and on consumers to express their needs for products and services to businesses.

Checkpoint ▶▶

In a private enterprise economy, when does government get involved in exchange relationships?

3-1 Assessment

Xtra! Study Tools
school.cengage.com/marketing/marketing

Key Concepts

Determine the best answer.

1. The government exerts the greatest influence over economic decisions in a
   a. mixed economy
   b. controlled economy
   c. free economy
   d. private enterprise economy

2. Which of the following is *not* an important characteristic of a private enterprise economy?
   a. resources of production are owned and controlled by individual producers
   b. individual consumers make decisions about what will be purchased to satisfy needs
   c. government involvement in the economy is relatively limited
   d. businesses decide what to produce based on what is best for society as a whole

3. An individual view of the worth of a product or service is called
   a. scarcity
   b. the profit motive
   c. value
   d. demand

4. True or False: Unlimited wants and needs, combined with limited resources, result in scarcity.

Make Academic Connections

5. **Social Studies** Prepare a one-page paper describing the basic economic problem and include an example of it. Explain how this problem would be handled in different economic systems (controlled, free, mixed, and private enterprise).

6. **Consumer Economics** As your textbook explains, consumers gather information about available products and services so they can select those that appear to satisfy their needs. Compile a list of resources—either print or online—that consumers can use to do this, briefly describing each one.

Connect to ◆ DECA
An Association of Marketing Students

7. You work for a clothing manufacturer that would like to sell its products in China. You have been asked to explore the marketing opportunities in China. Conduct research to determine the key differences between the Chinese and American economic systems. Develop a two- to three-minute presentation on the key economic factors that would have an impact on marketing your clothing line in China and present it to your teacher (judge).

Observing the Law of Supply and Demand

marketing matters

Microeconomics analyzes the interaction of consumer demand with producer supply to predict how changes in one affect the other. Much depends on consumers' needs and wants and on the availability of alternatives. When the independent decisions of consumers and producers are combined, they can be illustrated as curved lines on a two-dimensional graph that intersect at the market price.

Make a list of the last article of clothing you purchased, the last restaurant menu item you bought, and your last transportation-related expense, along with the prices you paid for each. If each had cost 20% more, would you still have bought them? What if they were 50% more? Twice as much as you paid? What determines the point at which you decide not to buy something or to find an alternative?

Microeconomics and Consumer Demand

Economics attempts to understand and explain how consumers and producers make decisions concerning the allocation of their resources. That understanding helps consumers and producers use their resources more effectively. It also helps government decision makers determine if and when they should become involved in the economy as they work to maintain an even balance between producers and consumers and to maintain a strong economy that improves the standard of living for citizens.

Economics operates on two levels. The first level, **macroeconomics**, studies the economic behavior and relationships of an entire society. Macroeconomics looks at the big picture. It helps to determine if society's resources are being used as effectively and efficiently as possible. Macroeconomics studies the decisions of all consumers and producers and the effects of those decisions on the economy.

The second level, **microeconomics**, examines relationships between individual consumers and producers. Microeconomics looks at small parts of the total economy. Microeconomics studies how individuals make decisions about what to produce and what to consume.

While a broad understanding of economics is important to marketers, they are

How do the concepts of supply and demand apply to a farmers market?

most concerned about microeconomics. Information about how consumers make purchasing decisions and how much they are willing to pay can be very important in selecting target markets and developing effective marketing mixes. Marketers must also understand how a business's competitors make decisions about what they will produce and the prices they are likely to charge. Microeconomics looks at supply, demand, and the level of individual product prices. The relationship between supply and consumer demand is an important tool for marketers.

Factors Affecting Demand

A number of factors influence consumers' decisions regarding what to purchase and how much to pay. If a need or want is particularly important or strong, a consumer might be willing to spend more money to satisfy it. For example, if you are at a baseball game and your favorite player hits three home runs, obtaining a t-shirt with the player's name on it may seem very important to you. You may be willing to pay much more to buy a t-shirt right away

at the ballpark rather than waiting to make the purchase later at a sporting goods store.

Another factor that affects consumers' decisions is the available supply of products and services to satisfy their needs. If there is a very large supply of a product, consumers will usually place a lower value on it. Imagine walking through a farmers' market where a large number of producers are selling fresh fruits and vegetables. As a consumer, you see there are many choices of sellers and a large quantity of each product available. Therefore, you will probably be careful not to overpay for the fruits or vegetables you want. On the other hand, if a large number of customers are at the market and only a few farmers are there to sell their products, the customers may pay much higher prices to be sure they get the items they need.

A third factor is the availability of alternative products that consumers believe will satisfy their needs. If consumers believe there is only one product or brand that meets their needs, they are willing to pay a higher price. If several options seem to be equally satisfying, consumers are more careful about how much they pay.

An example of this factor is your choice of entertainment for an evening. If there are very few things from which you and your friends can choose, you will likely be willing to pay quite a bit for a specific activity. However, if you identify several options (a movie, bowling, an amusement park, renting a video game) and each seems enjoyable, you may consider the cost more carefully. You might select one that is inexpensive but which you and your friends will still enjoy.

Analyzing Demand Curves

Economists try to determine how much consumers are willing and able to pay for various quantities of products or services. The relationship between price and the quantity demanded is often illustrated in a graph known as a demand curve. Figure 3-1 shows a sample demand curve for movies. As the price of movies increases, fewer people buy tickets. As the price decreases, more tickets are sold. This relationship is known as the law of demand: When the price of a product is increased, less will be demanded. When the price is decreased, more will be demanded.

Just as in marketing, economists use the concept of markets. All of the consumers who will purchase a particular product or service comprise an economic market. Economists believe that the consumers in an economic market view the relationship of products and prices in the same way.

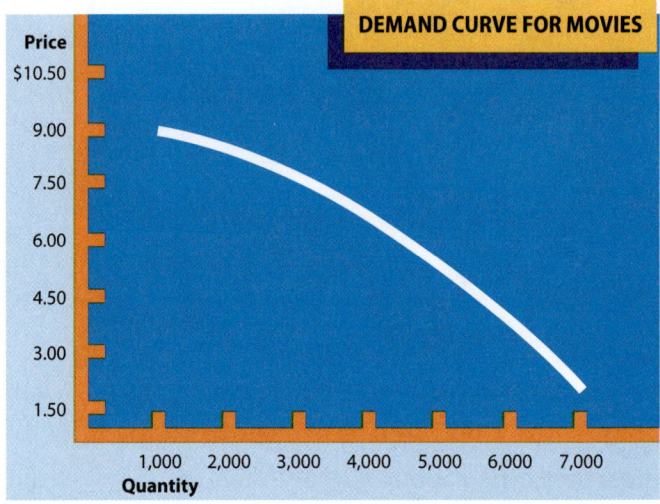

FIGURE 3-1

As the price of movies increases, the number of consumers willing and able to pay that price decreases.

Checkpoint ▶▶

How does microeconomics differ from macroeconomics?

Supplying the Product

There are several factors that influence what and how many products or services a business will produce. Factors include the possibility of profit, the amount of competition, and the capability of developing and marketing the products or services.

One of the most important reasons for businesses to operate in a private enterprise economy is to make a profit. Businesses will try to offer products and services that have a good chance of making a large profit, rather than products and services likely to yield either a small profit or the likelihood of a loss. Business managers carefully consider both the costs of producing and marketing products and the prices they will be able to charge for those products. That analysis helps in determining the most profitable choices to produce.

Handling the Competition

When looking for opportunities, businesses consider the amount and type of competition. When competition is intense—with many businesses offering the same types of products or services—there are fewer opportunities for success than when there is little competition. When possible, suppliers may choose to offer products and services that have few competitors. Another option when there is a lot of competition is to change the product to make it different from those offered by other businesses. For example, an owner of an apartment complex in a community where there are many vacant apartments may provide free cable TV for residents. The owner may extend short-term leases or may offer furnished apartments if those types of services are not available in other apartment complexes.

Finally, businesses use the resources available to develop products and services. **Economic resources** are classified as natural resources, capital, equipment, and labor. The specific types of resources a business has available will determine the types of products and services it can develop and sell. Some resources are very flexible, enabling a business to change and offer new products quickly. For example, if the owners of an electronics store found that equipment such as fax machines and scanners was not profitable, they could quickly change the products sold in that part of the store to some that are more profitable. Other businesses have more difficulty changing products. Companies that own oil wells or coal mines, for instance, have few options because the natural resources they own are their products. They must sell the oil and coal even if those products are not very profitable.

Analyzing a Supply Curve

Some economists predict how the quantity of products

NETBookmark

More and more Americans are becoming interested in eating organically grown food—that is, food that is produced without the use of artificial pesticides, herbicides, or genetically modified organisms (GMOs). Access school. cengage.com/marketing/marketing and click on the link for Chapter 3. After you read the article, explain whether you think a pound of organically grown carrots is likely to cost more or less than a pound of conventionally grown carrots. Explain your answer using the principle of supply and demand.

school.cengage.com/marketing/marketing

and services changes at various prices. The graph of the relationship between price and quantity supplied is known as a **supply curve**. An example supply curve for cell phones is shown in Figure 3-2. The graph shows that as the price increases, producers will manufacture more cell phones. As the price goes down, fewer will be manufactured. This relationship

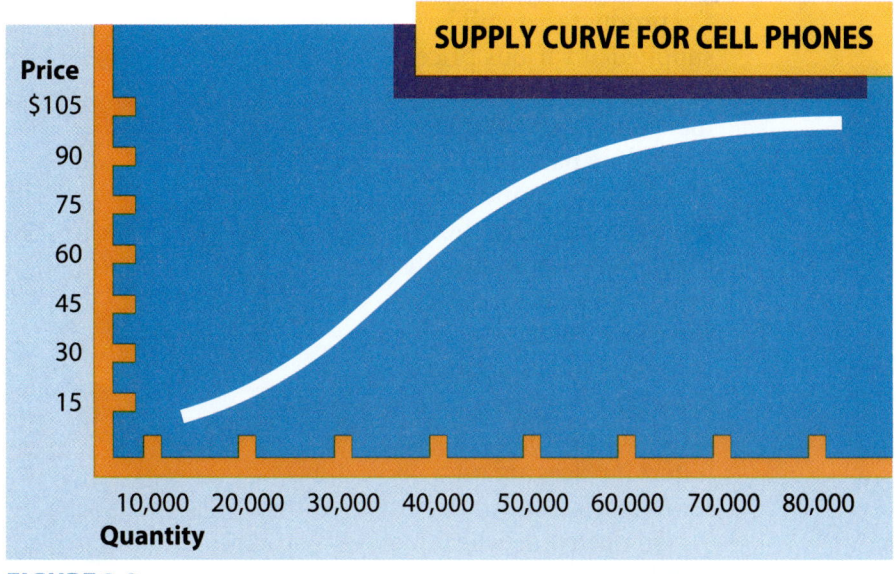

FIGURE 3-2
As the price for cell phones decreases, so does the quantity of phones that manufacturers will be willing to supply.

is known as the **law of supply**: When the price of a product is increased, more will be produced. When the price is decreased, less will be produced.

Whenever possible, producers use their resources to provide products and services that receive the highest prices. Just as with demand, economists believe that all producers in a market respond in similar ways when determining what to produce. Like consumers, producers see a relationship between products and prices.

Intersecting Supply and Demand

We learned that suppliers and consumers make independent decisions. When the decisions of many consumers of the same product are combined, they form a demand curve illustrating the quantity of a product or service that will be demanded at various prices. And when the decisions of all the suppliers of the same product or service are combined, they form a supply curve. That curve illustrates the quantity of the product that will be supplied at various prices.

Figure 3-3 shows a demand curve and a supply curve for a particular type of notebook computer. The demand curve shows that fewer computers will be purchased as the price increases. As expected, computer manufacturers are willing to supply a larger number of computers if prices are high, fewer if prices are low.

To determine the number of computers that will actually be produced and sold, the two curves

must be combined. The combined curves are shown in Figure 3-4 on the next page. Notice that the two lines cross or intersect at a price of $1,300 and a quantity of 450,000 computers. The point where supply and demand for a product are equal is

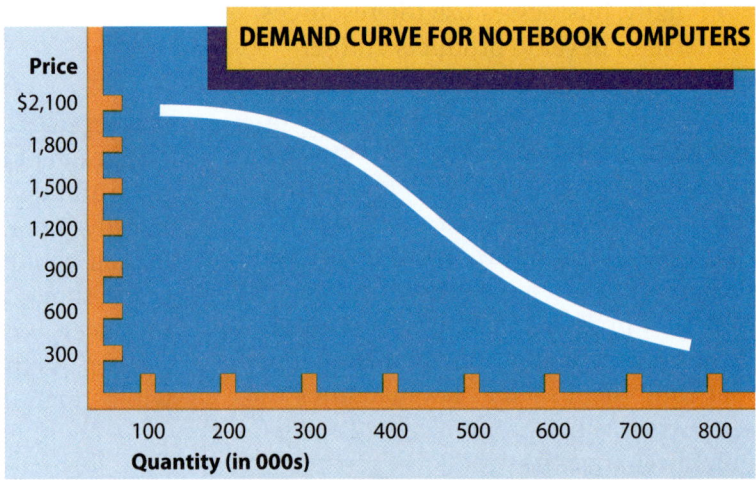

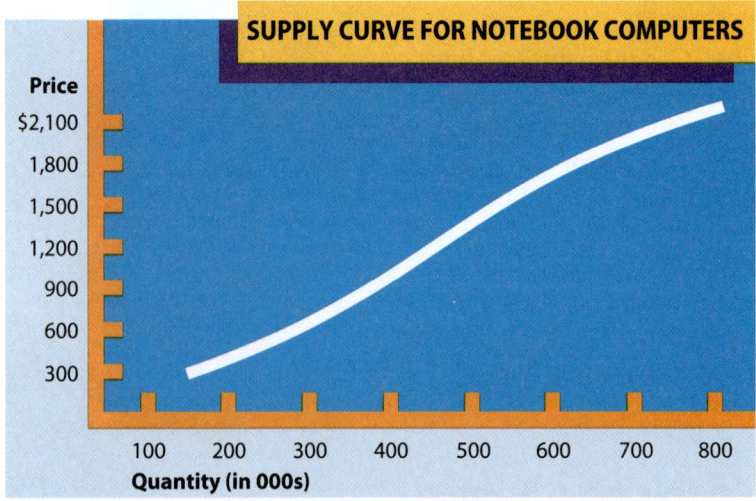

FIGURE 3-3

Consumers and suppliers respond very differently to price changes. The demand curve illustrates consumers' responses, and the supply curve illustrates suppliers' responses.

known as the **market price**. At that price, 450,000 computers will be manufactured and sold.

Each product in a specific market has its own supply and demand curves. And each market has price and quantity relationships that are unique and result in different curves on the graphs.

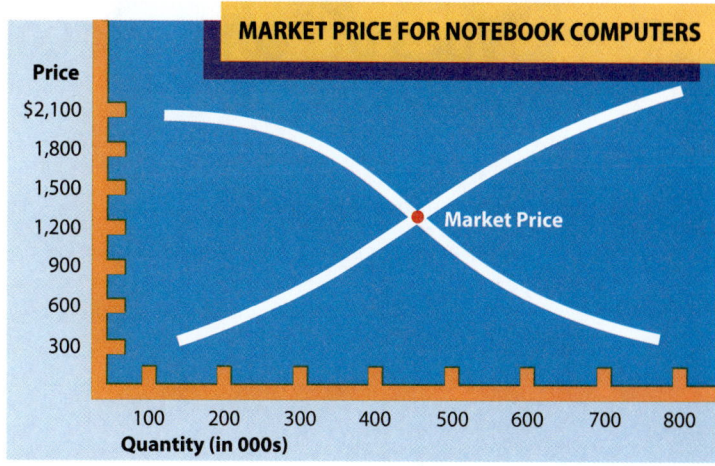

FIGURE 3-4

The point at which the demand curve and the supply curve for notebook computers intersect is the market price.

Checkpoint ▶▶▶

What are the main factors that businesses consider when deciding what and how much to produce?

3-2 Assessment

Key Concepts

Determine the best answer.

1. What can generally be expected to happen when the price of a product is increased?
   a. demand will increase
   b. demand will decrease
   c. supply will increase
   d. supply will remain constant

2. All of the consumers who will purchase a particular product or service are known as
   a. an economic market
   b. competitors
   c. producers
   d. a demographic

3. The point where supply and demand for a product are equal is known as the
   a. competitive price
   b. discount price
   c. market price
   d. fair value price

4. True or False: Most marketers are primarily concerned about macroeconomics.

Make Academic Connections

5. **Visual Art** Create a picture, poster, or other visual representation of macroeconomics and microeconomics.

6. **Economics** Use the following data to create supply and demand curves for cameras.

Quantity Demanded	Price	Quantity Supplied
100	$70	750
200	60	550
400	50	300
700	40	150

Connect to

7. You work for a party planning company that has declining sales and profits. Consider the factors that affect the demand for your services. Based on these factors, develop a plan to improve your business. Write a two-page report for your teacher (judge) describing possible reasons for the decline in business and your recommendations to increase demand for your services.

Types of Economic Competition

GOALS

- Define pure competition and monopoly.
- Explain the characteristics of oligopolies and monopolistic competition.

KEY TERMS

pure competition, *p. 73*

monopoly, *p. 73*

oligopoly, *p. 74*

monopolistic competition, *p. 74*

marketing matters

Businesses' responses to consumer demands are strongly influenced by the competitive structure of the industries they are in and the markets they serve. The type of competition, or in some extreme cases the lack of competition, determines how much control businesses have over pricing and what strategies they should follow to obtain the greatest long-term profits. Each type of competition produces a unique demand curve. Identifying the type of demand a business faces is important in developing marketing strategies.

Make a list of six businesses, large and small, that operate in your city or town. Now rate the businesses on a point scale of 1 to 10 based on how much market control you think they have over the prices they charge, with a rating of 10 indicating the greatest control.

All-Out Competition or No Competition at All

The type of competition found in a market affects consumer and supplier decisions alike. If consumers see a variety of products that seem to be very similar, they will be less willing to pay higher prices. If suppliers are in a market with many other businesses offering similar products, they will have difficulty raising their prices. Businesses must determine the type of competition they face and the amount of control they have over the prices they can charge to make effective marketing decisions.

Two characteristics are important to determine the type of economic competition in a specific market:

1. The number of firms competing in the market
2. The amount of similarity between the products of competing businesses

Economists use these characteristics to define four forms of economic competition—pure competition, monopoly, oligopoly, and monopolistic competition.

Pure Competition

A few markets contain a large number of suppliers with very similar products. In these markets, consumers have a great deal of control over choices and prices. Because the suppliers are unable to offer products that consumers view as unique, they must accept the prices that consumers are willing to pay, or the consumers will buy from another business. This market condition is known as pure competition. In **pure competition**, many suppliers offer very similar products.

The traditional examples of industries in pure competition are producers of agricultural products such as corn, rice, wheat, and livestock. Each producer's products are just like every other producer's. There are many producers, so customers have no difficulty finding a business that will sell the products. Because customers have so many choices of suppliers and the products of all suppliers are similar, prices will be very competitive. No single supplier will be able to raise the price. Other examples of markets in which businesses face something close to pure competition are those for many of the low-priced consumer products you purchase—milk, bread, paper clips, light bulbs, blank CDs and DVDs, and the like.

An example of the demand curve for a business in a purely competitive market is shown in Figure 3-5. In theory, it is a straight line at one price. That suggests that the supplier will receive the same price no matter how much of the product the supplier is willing to sell. Therefore, businesses have no control over price if they want to sell their products.

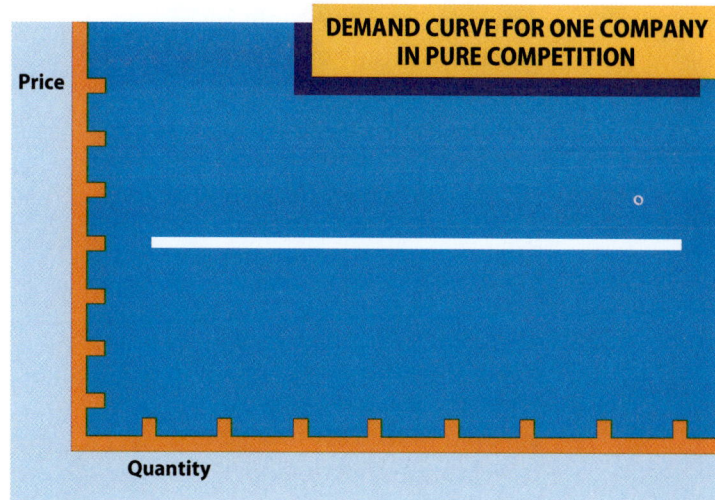

DEMAND CURVE FOR ONE COMPANY IN PURE COMPETITION

Price

Quantity

FIGURE 3-5
In pure competition, the seller must accept the market price no matter how much of the product is sold.

market in which one supplier offers a unique product. In this market, the supplier has almost total control, and the consumers will have to accept what the supplier offers at the price charged. This occurs because of the lack of competition.

Because of the obvious advantage a business has in monopoly markets, governments attempt to control them. Therefore, there are few examples of monopolies that actually dictate prices. Utility companies that supply communities with electricity, gas, or water are typically organized as monopolies. There is only one supplier of each product since it would be very inefficient to have several companies extending gas and water lines or electrical service to every home. Once a home is supplied with the utilities, it would be easy for the company to raise the price. The consumer would have no choice but to pay the higher price or go without the gas, water, or electricity. So government agencies regulate the prices that can be charged by the utility companies. Other examples of markets that can operate much like a monopoly are some local telephone and cable television services and businesses that are the only ones of their type in a particular geographic area where consumers have no choices. If you are driving

Working in **Teams**

Discuss with team members the last business you patronized and name as many of that business's competitors as you can. Then explain why you visited that business rather than one of its competitors. Discuss what the business does to help it stand out from its competition.

Monopoly

The opposite of pure competition is a monopoly. A **monopoly** is a type of down an interstate highway and there is only one gasoline station at a particular exit, that business can operate much like a monopoly for those customers who need gasoline or other automotive products. A pharmacy or other retail business in an area where there is no other similar business can also operate as a monopoly for those customers who are unable to travel to a competing business. In theory, the demand curve facing a business that has a monopoly would look like the one in Figure 3-6. There is a fixed demand for the product, since there are no other businesses offering a similar product. Therefore, if unregulated, the business can charge any price it chooses. The consumer either pays the price set by the business or goes without.

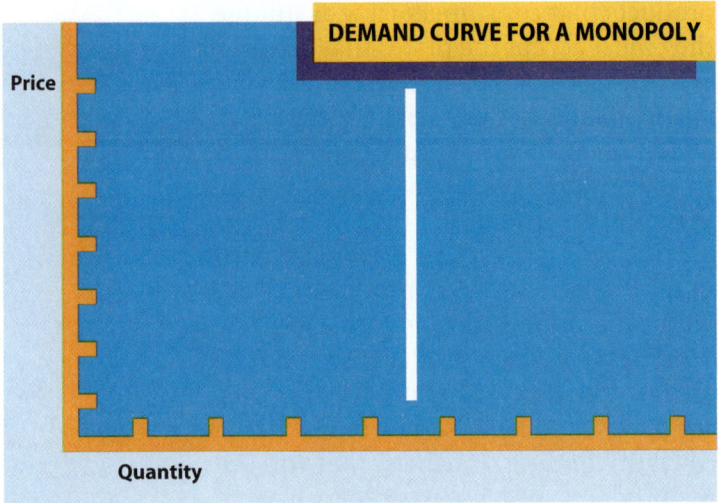

DEMAND CURVE FOR A MONOPOLY

Price

Quantity

FIGURE 3-6
In theory, a business in a monopoly can charge any price because it is selling a unique product.

Checkpoint ▶▶

Distinguish pure competition from monopoly based on the two characteristics that economists use to define types of competition.

Between the Extremes

Between the extremes of pure competition and monopoly are two other types of economic competition—oligopoly and monopolistic competition. In an **oligopoly** a few businesses offer very similar products or services. In **monopolistic competition**, there are many firms competing with products that are somewhat different.

Oligopolies

As you consider the difference between an oligopoly and the other types of markets, you might be able to see the problems and advantages facing businesses in this type of market. If the businesses work together, they will

What are the advantages and disadvantages of an oligopoly, such as the airline industry, to consumers?

be like a monopoly and have a great deal of control in the market. On the other hand, if they are very competitive, the

Measuring the Demand Curve

Economists have a way of quantifying demand curves so that businesses can use them to develop better marketing strategies. This method of quantifying is referred to as "elasticity of demand." In economics, elasticity means responsiveness to change. Elasticity of demand measures how much consumer demand for a product changes when the price is raised or lowered.

If demand is highly elastic, the demand curve is more horizontal, and a small change in price will have a big effect on consumer demand. If it is inelastic, the curve is more vertical, and demand remains relatively constant as prices change.

Elasticity is quantified by calculating the ratio of the percentage change in the quantity demanded over the percentage change in price. To illustrate, let's say a movie theater's research indicates that if it raises its ticket price from $6 to $8, the average number of tickets it sells will decrease from 300 to 250 per night. To calculate the elasticity of demand, first calculate the percentage of change in number of tickets sold: 50 ÷ 300 = 17%. Then calculate the percentage change in price: $2 ÷ $6 = 33%. Now calculate the ratio of the change in demand (17%) over the change in price (33%): 17 ÷ 33 = 0.52.

When the ratio is greater than 1, the demand is said to be elastic, and raising prices decreases overall revenue. When it is less than 1, demand is inelastic, and raising prices increases revenue. The theater's revenue should increase even if fewer tickets are sold.

Think Critically

1. Research for a bicycle shop indicates that if it lowers the price it charges for a tune-up from $30 to $20, it will sell twice as many tune-ups. Calculate its elasticity of demand.

2. Is its demand elastic or inelastic?

3. If the shop's costs per tune-up remain the same regardless of how many tune-ups it does, what should it do to maximize profits?

similarity of their products or services will give consumers choices, much like in pure competition. In that case, the consumers will have more control, and prices will be lower.

The airline industry is an example of an oligopoly. There are only a very few large airlines competing for national travel in the United States. It is difficult to see important differences between airlines that serve the same cities. Therefore, if one airline wants to increase its number of passengers, it will often do it by reducing prices. To counter that effort and to keep passengers from flying with the competitor, other airlines will reduce their prices as well.

One airline will not usually succeed in increasing prices alone. If the airline industry wants higher prices to cover operating expenses and contribute to profit, competing companies will need to cooperate in raising their prices as well. Depending on the industry, government agencies may attempt to regulate that type of activity, making it illegal for businesses to work together to control prices. Notice, however, that if one airline announces a price increase or decrease, competitors are usually very quick to match the change.

Other examples of industries with characteristics of an oligopoly are automobile manufacturers, greeting card companies, interstate delivery services, computer manufacturers, Internet service providers, and companies offering long-distance or wireless telephone services. On the local level, some businesses operate as oligopolies because there are only a few businesses offering almost identical products and services to the consumers in that market. Some examples in medium- to large-size communities are taxi services, movie theaters, banks, and hospitals.

The demand curve facing businesses in an oligopoly is difficult to describe. For an individual business, the demand curve will look like the demand in pure competition since one business cannot influence the price it can charge to any great extent. Figure 3-7 shows an example of a demand curve for one company in an oligopoly.

The demand curve for all of the businesses combined in an oligopoly will look much like that of a monopoly. Cooperatively, the businesses have a great deal of control over price. Consumers who want the product or service will have to purchase from one of the few companies in the market or go without. A demand curve for the entire industry in an oligopoly is shown in Figure 3-8.

Monopolistic Competition

By far the most common type of economic competition facing most businesses is monopolistic competition, where many firms compete with products that are somewhat different. The fewer the number of competitors and the greater the differences among the competitors' products or

services, the greater the control each firm will have in the market. With more competitors and only minor differences, businesses will have very limited control.

There are many examples of businesses in monopolistic competition. Most retail businesses in which you shop face this type of competition. Most of the products or services you buy fit the definition.

As a consumer, you typically have several choices of businesses or products. Among those choices, you can identify

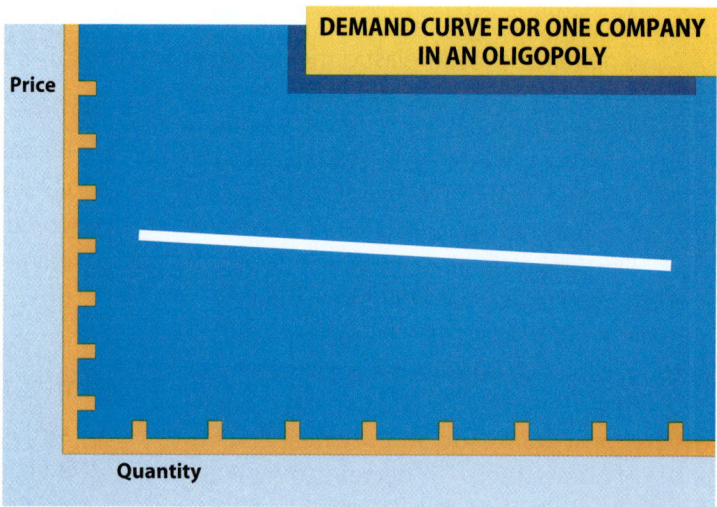

FIGURE 3-7
One business in an oligopoly will have little influence over the price it can charge.

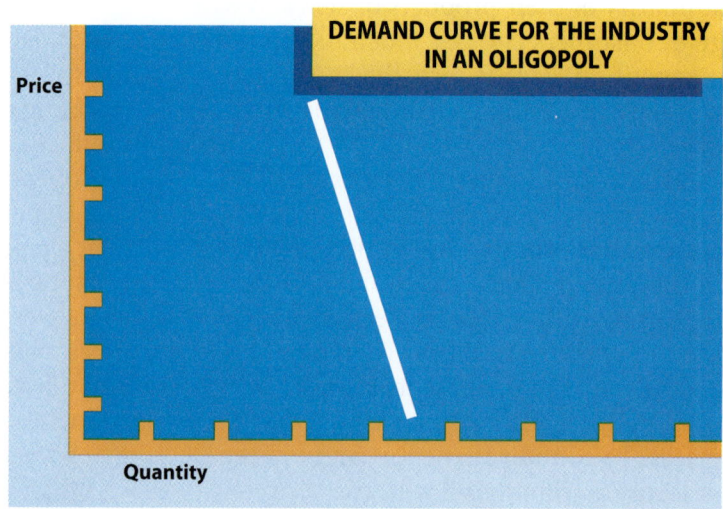

FIGURE 3-8
Because there are few firms in an oligopoly, the total industry has much more control over prices.

What kind of competition do retailers in a shopping mall face? Why?

differences. Some differences are very noticeable and important. Other differences are only minor. When you have choices as a consumer, you usually select the one providing the most satisfaction at the best value. Examples of businesses and products in monopolistic competition include restaurants, movie theaters, shopping malls, athletic shoes, consumer electronics equipment, and cosmetics.

The demand curve for businesses in monopolistic competition falls somewhere between that of pure competition and monopoly. If there are few differences, the business has less control, so the demand curve is more horizontal. An example of this type of demand curve is shown in Figure 3-9.

The greater the differences among products and services, the more control the business has, so the demand curve is more vertical. An example is shown in Figure 3-10.

Understanding the Competition

It is important for business people and especially marketers to know the type of economic competition they face and to act accordingly in order to maximize profits.

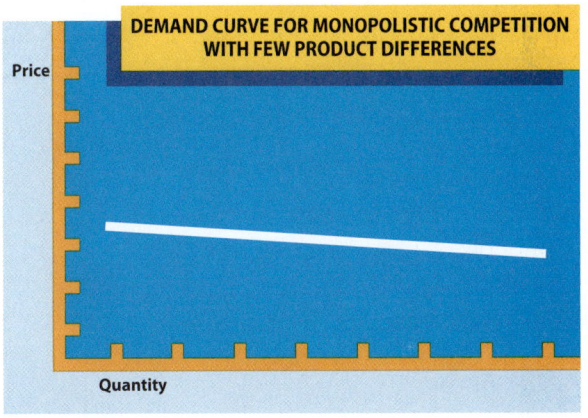

FIGURE 3-9
When there are few differences among products, businesses will have little price control.

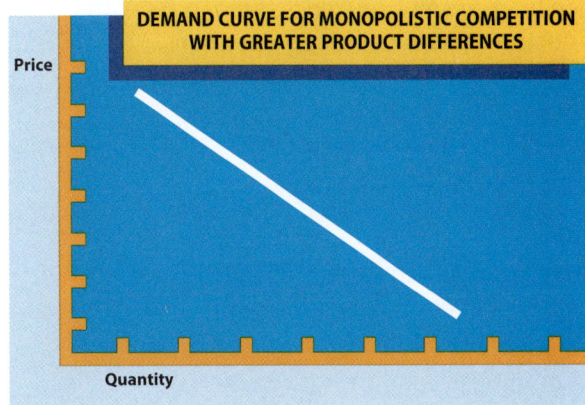

FIGURE 3-10
With greater product differences, businesses have more control over prices.

A business in pure competition will not be able to exercise much control in the market, while one in a monopoly will have almost total control. Businesses in an oligopoly must pay careful attention to the actions of competitors. For the largest number of businesses, those in monopolistic competition, the differences between competing products will be very important. Wherever possible, marketers will want to do things that result in products that are different and better than those of competitors. In that way they will have more control in the marketplace.

Checkpoint ▶▶▶

Contrast oligopolies and monopolistic competition.

3-3 Assessment

Key Concepts

Determine the best answer.

1. In this type of economic competition, a few businesses offer very similar products or services.
   a. pure competition
   b. monopolistic competition
   c. monopoly
   d. oligopoly

2. In theory, the demand curve for a business in this type of market is a straight line at one price.
   a. pure competition
   b. monopolistic competition
   c. monopoly
   d. oligopoly

3. When there are few differences among products in a monopolistic competition,
   a. the government will likely set limits on prices
   b. businesses will have little control over prices
   c. businesses will have total control over prices
   d. one business can greatly influence prices, since competitors will be forced to follow suit

4. True or False: By far the most common type of economic competition facing most businesses is oligopoly.

Make Academic Connections

5. **Management** Most restaurants operate in a monopolistic competition environment. Outline several changes a manager could make to increase profits in that type of competitive environment.

6. **Technology** Use the library or Internet to find a change in technology that you believe increased economic competition in the United States. Find another change that you believe reduced economic competition. Use visuals or a written report to communicate your findings. Make sure to describe how the technology affected competition.

Connect to DECA

7. You have been hired by the owner of a new ice cream shop in your community to analyze the competition. Create a list of questions you believe need to be answered to help you complete an effective analysis of the competitive environment. Present these questions to the owner (judge), and explain why each of them is important. You should also present a list of sources and/or techniques you will use to gather information for your analysis.

Enhancing Economic Utility

GOALS

- Define four types of economic utility.
- Explain how marketers use utility to increase customer satisfaction.

KEY TERMS

economic utility, *p. 79*

marketing matters

Although consumers rarely analyze precisely how they decide to buy products or services, they unconsciously make buying decisions based on the satisfaction they expect to receive from them. Businesses therefore try to increase consumers' satisfaction by making improvements to products and services.

Economists have developed a concept called economic utility and identified various types of utility to explain why consumers get more or less satisfaction from different products. For businesses, economic utility is important to help them develop better products.

Identify two products in your classroom and propose changes that you believe would increase the satisfaction they provide to users.

Utility Means Satisfaction

Most people would like to purchase more things than they can afford. Because of limited resources and unlimited needs, they have to choose among products and services. People select those that provide the greatest satisfaction for the money they are able or willing to spend. You may have to choose between attending a concert and purchasing a new video game, for example. Saving for college may be more important than buying a car.

To analyze how people make choices among competing products, economists use a concept called economic utility. **Economic utility** is the amount of satisfaction a consumer receives from the consumption of a particular product or service. Products that provide great satisfaction have a higher economic utility, while those providing less satisfaction have a lower utility.

Businesses use economic utility to increase the chances that consumers will buy their products or services. If a consumer believes that a particular product

©DIGITAL VISION

How could the economic utility of athletic shoes be improved?

The Changing Face of Radio

Although many people predicted the downfall of radio as more advanced technology emerged, that has not been the case. Every week, radio reaches approximately 95 percent of Americans over the age of 12, making it still a powerful way for marketers to reach consumers.

In 1996, the government passed the Telecommunications Act, which deregulated the radio industry and allowed large companies to buy many radio stations across the country. Today, ten companies own over two-thirds of the radio market. While some listeners complain that this decreases the diversity of radio programming, it also helps radio stations cut costs to become more profitable and makes it easier for advertisers to reach their audience.

With the advent of satellite radio, the format is changing once again. Satellite radio companies such as Sirius and XM beam a digital signal to receivers via satellite, so listeners have access to hundreds of stations anywhere in the country. Currently, satellite radio is a subscription service and boasts of being "commercial free" on many of its music stations, but it does allow "promos," or short product messages. It is too early to tell if satellite radio will be a success story, or a very expensive failure. Either way, radio in general will remain a valuable tool for marketers.

Think Critically

1. How do national radio broadcasts, like those via satellite, differ from local radio stations in terms of the types of advertisers they will attract?

2. What are the advantages of having hundreds of diverse radio stations? What are the disadvantages, if any?

will provide higher utility than other choices, that product will likely be purchased. The four primary ways businesses can increase the economic utility of a product or service are changes in form, time, place, and possession.

Form Utility

The physical product provided or the service offered is the primary way that consumer needs are satisfied. *Form utility* results from changes in the tangible parts of a product or service.

Some products and services are in a more usable form than others. One product may be constructed better or have more features that consumers want. One service provider—a hair stylist, for example—may be more skilled than another.

Time Utility

Even though a product is in the form a customer wants, it may not be available when the customer wants it. *Time utility* results from making the product or service available when the customer wants it. Examples include a bank that stays open in the evening and a dental office that accepts appointments on weekends.

Place Utility

Just as some consumers are concerned about when a product is available, others may want to purchase or consume the product at a particular place. Making products and services available where the consumer wants them is *place utility*.

Check-cashing outlets and businesses that provide mailing, photocopying, and printing services are successful if they are located where consumers and businesses that need those services reside. A convenient location for products and services is an important utility for people with busy lives.

Communicate with Charts and Graphs

The old adage "a picture is worth a thousand words" still holds true. With a highly scheduled, multitasking society, people want to get the information they need, quickly understand it, and move on.

Data analysis often begins with spreadsheets that help automate the analysis of raw data. The results of the data analysis can be presented in charts, graphs, and tables. Charts and graphs facilitate swift decision making by presenting relationships among variables in a visual, understandable form. Tables provide a concise method to summarize data. Effective data summaries do not overwhelm the target audience with an excessive amount of data.

Choosing a Data Summary Tool

When deciding which type of data summary tools to use, keep your audience in mind. Certain types of graphs are far more common, and therefore easier for the public to understand. Line graphs, bar charts, and pie charts are among the most frequently used.

A line graph is helpful for conveying changes over a period of time. The slope of the line indicates whether the variable has an increasing or decreasing trend. If the line goes up and down frequently, it may represent cyclical changes. A bar graph often conveys variations in quantity at specific points in time or among different elements or groups. Those quantity changes are usually displayed on the vertical axis.

Pie charts are effective for illustrating percentages of a whole. To insure that the pie chart is easy to interpret, try to limit pie slices to five or six variables.

Each chart or graph should be concise, presenting an important relationship. Start with a simple meaningful title. The graph axes and variables should be labeled. The unit of measurement as well as the item being studied should be easily distinguished. Using consistent units of measurement throughout a graph is important to avoid distortions when presenting information.

Presenting the Results

The analysis process may build a strong visual case to understand a relationship between two or more items. Likewise, data analysis may provide a startling "aha" moment that contradicts previous beliefs. Although it may be tempting to omit data or vary the way the information is presented, you must always maintain the integrity of your data and share important analyses. Your audience is relying on your objectivity to help guide their decision making.

Interpreting Data

Learning how to interpret the charts and graphs of others is also an important skill. Pay close attention to the units of measurement, the source of the data, and any possible bias in the presentation. Ask yourself whether the conclusions made from the analysis are reasonable. When you have doubts, ask to see the original data on which the analysis was based.

Develop Your Skill

Review local or national newspapers (*USA Today*, for example) for articles that present data in tables, charts, and graphs. Determine which present information in an understandable way and which seem to present a biased view or confuse the reader. Now use a computer and spreadsheet program to record numerical information about your class or school. Summarize important relationships in a chart and a graph. Review the results with fellow students or a teacher. Ask for feedback on how clearly your charts and graphs convey information and help them understand the information.

Possession Utility

A product may be in the form a consumer wants and be available at the right time in the right place, yet the consumer still may not be able to purchase the product because of a lack of resources. *Possession utility* results from the affordability of the product or service. It is usually not possible for a business to decrease the price just so a product can be sold. Yet there are other ways besides cutting the price to make a product more affordable.

Credit allows people to purchase things for which they do not have enough cash at the time. They can then pay for the product when the credit bill is received or pay gradually with monthly payments.

Few people want to spend money to purchase a movie just so they can watch it more than once. Video stores are very successful because they rent movies rather than sell them. With low-cost rentals, people can watch more movies. Likewise, automobile dealerships lease new automobiles. Leases make it possible for customers to drive new cars without having to make a huge down payment. You will probably rent rather than buy a tuxedo for formal occasions such as the prom.

Finding ways to finance, rent, or lease products has become an important business activity today. It is a valuable way to offer possession utility to customers.

Checkpoint ▶▶

What are the four types of economic utility?

How does possession utility affect auto sales?

©GETTY IMAGES/PHOTODISC

Utility as a Marketing Tool

Business people who use the marketing concept try to identify customer needs and develop marketing mixes to satisfy those needs. Economic utility supports the marketing concept. It identifies ways to add value to products and services through changes in form, time, place, and possession. Economic utility can be a particularly effective marketing tool when a business focuses on the unique needs and characteristics of each target market. When economic utility is improved, so is customer satisfaction. Marketers need to determine what changes customers would like to have in products and services in order to develop an effective marketing mix. There are many possible ways to improve products and, in turn, improve product demand.

Checkpoint ▶▶

How does the marketing concept relate to the concept of economic utility?

3-4 Assessment

Xtra!
Study Tools
school.cengage.com/marketing/marketing

Key Concepts

Determine the best answer.

1. The amount of satisfaction a consumer receives from the consumption of a particular product or service is called
   a. the profit motive
   b. economic value
   c. economic utility
   d. economic expenditure

2. Which type of economic utility results from changes in the tangible parts of a product or service?
   a. time utility
   b. possession utility
   c. place utility
   d. form utility

3. Marketers need to determine what changes customers would like to have in products and services in order to develop
   a. an effective marketing mix
   b. the law of supply and demand
   c. pure competition
   d. an economic market

4. True or False: Economic utility supports the marketing concept.

Make Academic Connections

5. **Creative Writing** Compose either a jingle or script for an advertisement for a local business, focusing on one type of economic utility—form, time, place, or possession.

6. **Geography** Use the Internet to locate and print a map of your neighborhood or community. On the map, mark as many locations of grocery stores/supermarkets as you can find. Then write an explanation of which store you would most likely patronize if place utility was the most important consideration. What about form utility? Possession utility? Time Utility?

Connect to ◀ DECA
An Association of Marketing Students

7. You are the manager of a medium-size appliance store, and you want to increase sales in your store. Consider the different types of economic utility. Prepare a two-minute presentation you would deliver to the store owner (judge) in which you describe at least three ways you can improve economic utility to accomplish your goal.

Chapter 3 Assessment

Check Your Understanding

Now that you have completed the chapter, check your understanding of the lessons with these questions. Record the score that best represents your understanding of each marketing concept.

1 = not at all; 3 = somewhat; 5 = very well

If your score is 42–50, you are ready for the assessment activities that follow. If you score 33–41, you should review the lessons for the items you scored 1–3. If you score 32 or less, you will want to carefully reread the lessons and work with a study partner on the areas you don't understand.

Can you—

___ explain why an understanding of economics is important to marketing?

___ identify the basic economic problem?

___ list the important characteristics of a private enterprise economy?

___ distinguish between microeconomics and macroeconomics?

___ identify factors affecting supply and demand?

___ explain what is meant by the laws of supply and demand?

___ identify the characteristics that determine the type of economic competition in a specific market?

___ define the four forms of economic competition and give an example of each?

___ name the four types of economic utility?

___ explain how economic utility supports the marketing concept?

Review Marketing Terms

Match the terms listed with the definitions. Some terms may not be used.

1. An economic system where the government attempts to own and control important resources and to make the decisions about what will be produced and consumed

2. The type of market in which there is only one supplier offering a unique product

3. The result of unlimited wants and needs combined with limited resources

4. The study of economic behavior and relationships for the entire society

5. The use of resources toward the greatest profit for the producer

6. The point where supply and demand for a product are equal

7. The type of market in which there are a large number of suppliers offering very similar products

8. An economic system in which resources are owned by individuals and decisions are made independently with no attempt at government regulation or control

9. A graph that illustrates the relationship between price and the quantity supplied

10. An economic system based on independent decisions by businesses and consumers with only a limited government role

a. controlled economy
b. demand curve
c. free economy
d. macroeconomics
e. market price
f. microeconomics
g. mixed economy
h. monopoly
i. private enterprise
j. profit motive
k. pure competition
l. scarcity
m. supply curve

Review Marketing Concepts

11. True or False: A private enterprise economy is heavily regulated by government.

12. True or False: Consumers have limited resources and unlimited needs and wants.

13. Changes in a product's physical features affect its _____ utility.

14. True or False: A larger supply of a product will usually cause consumers to place a lower value on it.

15. When the price of a product is increased, a smaller quantity will be purchased. That statement is known as which of the following?
    a. the law of supply
    b. the law of demand
    c. the law of the land
    d. the law of economic utility

16. True or False: Economic resources are classified as natural resources, capital, equipment, and consumers.

17. In pure competition, there are a large number of suppliers offering which of the following?
    a. very similar products
    b. somewhat different products
    c. unique products
    d. an unlimited supply of products

18. True or False: Economic utility is the amount of profit businesses make from selling a product.

19. True or False: The quantity of a product that producers are willing and able to provide at a specific price is known as demand.

20. Locating an automated teller machine in an airport is an example of improving the _____ utility for banking services.

21. _____ is a relationship between the quantity of a product that producers are willing and able to provide and the price.

22. True or False: Individuals who purchase products and services to satisfy needs are known as producers.

23. The relationship between price and the quantity demanded is often illustrated in a graph known as a(n) _____ curve.

24. True or False: In theory, a business in a monopoly can charge any price because it is selling a unique product.

Marketing Research and Planning

25. Businesses can be classified into the four types of competition—pure competition, monopoly, oligopoly, and monopolistic competition—based on two factors: the number of competitors in the market and the amount of similarity between the products of competing businesses.

    Use the advertising section of your local telephone directory, a business directory, or copies of newspapers or business magazines to identify two businesses that fit into each of those four categories. Explain each decision based on the two factors listed.

26. Select a popular food item that is sold in your school's cafeteria or in a vending machine in your school. Determine the current price for the item. Then construct a chart showing the following price increases and decreases for the product:

    +10%, +25%, +50%, +100%,

    −10%, −25%, −50%, −90%.

    Survey five people from your school. Ask each person how many of the items they typically purchase in one week at the current price. Then ask each person how many of the items they would purchase at each of the price increases and decreases. Based on the results, construct a demand curve to illustrate the effect of price changes on demand for the product.

27. When a marketer analyzes a demand curve, it is important to determine what effect changes in price and quantity demanded would have on the amount of money the business will receive from selling the product. The amount received is known as the total revenue and is determined by multiplying the price by the quantity demanded.

    For example, if the price of a product is $8.50 and the quantity demanded at that price is 1,550 items, the total revenue would be $13,175 ($8.50 × 1,550). The information in the table that follows was taken from the demand curves for two different products. Calculate the total revenue for each price listed. Then construct a demand curve for each product.

Product 1		Product 2	
Price	Quantity Demanded	Price	Quantity Demanded
$1.00	350,000	$250	1,125
$2.50	280,000	$325	950
$3.25	225,000	$400	600
$4.00	175,000	$500	425
$4.75	75,000	$850	250
$5.50	25,000	$1,000	200

28. You have been an economist for the United Nations for the past 15 years. Now, in the year 2028, a large industrial colony is being developed on the moon. It will be started by 2,000 people initially, and there are plans to expand it until nearly one million people are living in the colony by 2050. The United Nations is studying the best form of economic system to develop on the colony.

Prepare a two-page report in which you compare three types of economies—controlled, free, and private enterprise. Discuss the advantages and disadvantages of each for consumers, businesses, and the government. Make a recommendation on the most appropriate system for the colony. Consider factors like resources available, supply and demand, the amount of competition, and so forth.

Marketing Management and Decision Making

29. Marketing managers must be creative in determining ways that products and services can be improved to increase customer satisfaction. For each of the following three items, determine changes that could be made in form, time, place, and possession utility. Then recommend the one change for each product that you believe would be the most effective in improving customer satisfaction and explain why.
   a. Vending machine selling snacks
   b. MP3 Player
   c. A college recruiting high school seniors

30. Tasha Formby is a recent college graduate with a degree in Business Administration and extensive course work in computer information systems and marketing. She completed a summer internship with a computer manufacturer. She worked full time during another summer at a company that provides commercial printing services to small businesses. She was in charge of design work using computer software.

Tasha decides to open her own printing business. There are already three large printing companies in the city. Those businesses compete for the printing services of the large and small companies in the area. There are eight other small printing businesses, each of which serves individual consumers rather than businesses.

Tasha decides to compete with the larger companies rather than with the small printers. She believes there is more opportunity for larger printing jobs. She also believes her computer background could help her better serve the businesses' needs.

After operating the business for six months, Tasha is becoming concerned. The prospective customers she contacts are more concerned about her prices rather than the personalized service she provides. The larger printers are usually able to offer lower prices than her business can. It also seems that the larger printing businesses have much more control over the prices they charge, raising prices for some customers and lowering them for others.
   a. What type of competitive environment do you believe Tasha's business is facing? Why?
   b. Would she face the same type of competition if she sold to individual consumers? Why or why not?
   c. What do you believe Tasha can do to improve the chances of success for her new printing business? What economic concepts support your answer?

Internet Marketing Business Plan Event

Internet marketing involves the buying and selling of products and services by businesses and consumers over the Internet. Internet marketing sites are sometimes referred to as electronic storefronts. Internet marketing can also include the electronic transfer of funds.

This event requires you to research and design a plan to start or improve an existing Internet marketing business. Your business plan will be based upon research and conclusions that are supported by your findings.

This project consists of two major parts: the written document and the oral presentation. The project will be completed by one to three students. All participants must present the project and respond to questions asked by the judge/audience.

The oral presentation will include ten minutes for students to explain and describe the project followed by five minutes for the judge's question.

Parts of the written Internet marketing business plan include the following:

Executive Summary Write a one-page description of the project.
Introduction Describe the business and proposed product or service.
Analysis of the Business Situation Provide a trading area analysis and competitor analysis.
Planned Operation of the Proposed Business/Product/Service Describe the proposed organization, proposed business/product/service, and proposed strategies.
Planned Financing Include projected income and expenses and the proposed plan to meet capital needs.
Conclusion Include a specific request for financing and a summary of key points supporting the financial request.

Bibliography List all sources used.
Appendix Inclusion is optional.

Performance Indicators Evaluated

- Identify the potential for Internet marketing. (Marketing-Information Management)

- Design and conduct a marketing research study to identify the potential for Internet marketing. (Marketing-Information Management)

- Conduct marketing research. (Marketing-Information Management)

- Prepare a written proposal for an Internet marketing business based on the market research. (Communication Skills)

- Request financing for the proposal in a role-playing interview with a bank or venture capital official. (Financial Analysis)

Go to the DECA web site for more detailed information.

Think Critically

1. Why has Internet marketing become increasingly popular?

2. Why are some consumers hesitant to participate in Internet marketing?

3. What expenses are decreased or eliminated by a business that is based totally on Internet marketing?

4. What age group may be the most hesitant to purchase goods and services through Internet marketing?

www.deca.org

The Basics of Marketing

©STOCKBYTE

Newsline

Providing Quality with Differences

What do Ritz-Carlton Hotels and Microtel have in common? Very little except that they both received the highest ratings in consumer satisfaction surveys. Ritz-Carlton topped the ratings in the luxury hotel category. Consumers gave the exclusive hotel brand top marks for delivering consistently superior quality, exclusivity, and uniqueness. They rated it the brand most likely to be chosen by people who are admired and respected. It is a measure of social status. The survey participants were people who earned over $200,000 per year and had an average net worth of $2 million.

At the same time, Microtel Inns and Suites was the highest-ranked hotel chain in a survey of consumers who typically stay at economy hotels and spend less than $100 per night on a room. According to survey respondents, Microtel excelled in its reservations and check-in/check-out services. It also was highly rated for the comfort and cleanliness of its rooms and the value provided for the cost.

The travel market, like most markets, is very large. It is made up of people with different needs and expectations. Both the Ritz-Carlton and Microtel can be successful when they are devoted to providing the types of services that their customers want. The two businesses demonstrate that commitment to quality works in both the luxury and the value-conscious markets.

Think Critically

1. Name the brands of three different products that you think have a high-quality image. What do you think makes each of those brands different from and better than competing brands? Are all of the brands you identified expensive?

2. Is quality the most important factor for you in most of your purchases? Why or why not?

3. Why do many brands have difficulty developing and maintaining a quality image?

school.cengage.com/marketing/marketing

Prepare for Performance

DECA PREP

This chapter develops the following Performance Indicators from the DECA Competitive Events program.

Core Performance Indicators

- Acquire foundational knowledge of channel management to understand its role in marketing
- Discuss levers employees can use to motivate decision making
- Explain customer/client/business buying behavior

Supporting Performance Indicators

- Explain the nature and scope of channel management
- Explain the relationship between customer service and channel management
- Align marketing activities with business objectives

Go to **school.cengage.com/marketing/marketing** and click on Connect to DECA.

BUSINESS TAKES COMMERCE

COMMERCE TAKES **VISA**

Commerce—the age-old act of buying and selling—is the foundation of global business. Yet, the modest act of payment makes it all possible. Even small improvements in your company's payment process could add millions to the bottom line. Imagine what big improvements could do. Visit us at visa.com/commerce, or speak with your Commercial Banker, and learn how Visa can help your company cut costs, manage cash flow better, and turn payment into a whole new strategic advantage.

©VISA

Visual Focus

Marketing involves a comprehensive set of activities needed to insure effective exchanges between a business and its customers. While we often think of promotion as an important marketing tool, it is no more important than many others. Companies must have a complete marketing strategy, including a quality product that is well priced, distributed, and promoted. This chapter introduces the basic concepts and principles of effective marketing.

Focus Questions:

What do you think is meant by the ad's headline? What role does Visa play in helping businesses market products and services to customers? How do credit and financial services such as the ones described in this ad make it easier for businesses to participate in international commerce?

Locate an advertisement that promotes a unique marketing activity that a company does well. Share your example in a class discussion.

Changes in Today's Marketing

GOALS

- Explain how marketing today differs from marketing in the past.
- Show why understanding customers is crucial to applying the marketing concept.

KEY TERMS

integrated, *p. 92*

market opportunities, *p. 92*

marketing matters

Marketing as it is practiced today is much different from what it was just a few decades ago. It is more complex and more interconnected with other business functions. For those reasons, it is even more important that businesses focus on making the best marketing decision possible from the beginning. Today's businesses know that marketing must be planned carefully. Satisfying customer needs has to be their primary objective. Even the best products and services will fail if they do not fit the needs of their customers.

Make a list of four products or services that you have purchased recently that provided you with a high degree of satisfaction. What characteristics do these products or services and the companies that offer them have in common?

Marketing Has Changed

Camilla and Marcos are waiting for the start of their career seminar. As they look at the course outline, they see that they are beginning a study of marketing today. They begin to talk about their interest in marketing careers.

Camilla: Marketing seems to be an area where there are a lot of jobs. You hear about marketing all the time. Several of my friends are planning to major in marketing in college.

Marcos: I'm not sure I'm interested in a marketing job. It seems like you have to be a salesperson, and you know what people think of salespeople. It doesn't seem to take much to be a retail salesperson. Do you know how many people work long hours for no money in retail? What is your image of an automobile salesperson? What do you think about the telemarketer who calls you on the telephone at home to sell

Why do you think it is important to learn about marketing regardless of your career choice?

something? Even the good sales jobs in industry require you to travel all of the time. It seems like you have to be able to out-think and out-talk your customers to convince them to buy your products.

Camilla: It does seem that way, but there are other marketing jobs.

©GETTY IMAGES/PHOTODISC

Advertising is a part of marketing. Don't you think it would be exciting to create magazine or television commercials or even some of the new video ads we see on the Internet? Some ads are not very good, but the good ones are really creative. They get me interested in the products they are selling.

Marcos: I guess you're right. Still, it seems that marketing is used to get people to buy things they don't really need. I know companies need to sell their products to stay in business. I'm not sure, however, that I want to be the one who has to convince someone to spend their money on my business's product or service, whether it is with advertising or selling.

Camilla: Well, I'm going to be open-minded. I want to work in business, and everything I read now says that marketing is one of the fastest-growing and highest-paying career areas in business. I'll be interested to see what types of jobs are available and what it takes to be successful.

Marketing Experiences

Just like Camilla and Marcos, you may have started your study of marketing with limited understanding of this important business function. Much of your understanding comes from experience, and people have not always had positive experiences with marketing. They may not have recognized that some of their positive experiences with business occurred because of effective marketing.

Now that you have begun the study of marketing, you know that marketing is different than many consumers and business people realize. There are many marketing activities and many ways to improve exchanges between businesses and consumers.

Understanding the Differences

Marketing today is quite different from marketing only a few years ago. Understanding those differences will help you use marketing more effectively.

From Few to Many Marketing has expanded in scope from a few activities to a variety of activities. The earliest use of marketing was to move products from the producer to the consumer. Then promotion and sales were added to help persuade customers to buy a business's product. Today, businesses are able to complete a vast number of marketing activities ranging from research to offering customers credit. Effective marketers understand all of the marketing tools and know when and how to use them.

From Independence to Integration Marketing has changed from an activity that was an independent part of most businesses to one that is well integrated with other business functions. In

How can the integration of marketing into business planning benefit a company?

the past, marketing was not well understood by business people who did not have marketing backgrounds. Marketers often worked by themselves and had little contact with others in the business. Planning for marketing was done after other business planning was complete. Now, marketing is **integrated**, meaning it is considered an essential part of the business. It is involved in all important business decisions. Marketing strategies are developed as a part of the business plans.

From Problems to Opportunities
Marketing used to be handled as a problem-solving tool, but now it is regarded as an opportunity-creation tool. Businesses often called on marketing when they faced a problem. If inventory was too high or competitors were attracting customers away from a business, marketers were asked to increase sales and promotion efforts or to find weaknesses in the competitor's programs.

Today's businesses cannot afford to wait until problems occur. They are continuously looking for market opportunities. **Market opportunities** include new markets and ways to improve a company's offerings in current markets. Marketing is responsible for identifying and planning for opportunities.

From Expense to Investment
What used to be thought of as an expense is now prized as a critical investment. Marketing can be very expensive. In the past, when businesses have faced financial problems, some have viewed marketing as a place to cut costs. Most business people today recognize that companies will not be able to make a profit if products remain unsold. Effective marketing is an investment because it is responsible for matching a company's offerings with market needs. Spending money to improve marketing usually results in increased profits.

Get the Message

Pinpointing Promotion

Imagine you are walking down the street and pass a music store. Suddenly, your cell phone rings, and you receive an advertisement for the new CD of your favorite band. Wireless telephone and Internet services offer a new method of providing specific advertising messages to consumers. The message is targeted to those people who have an interest in the product. It can also be sent at a specific time when the consumer may be most interested in making a purchase.

This targeted advertising uses the new global positioning system (GPS) technology that is integrated into many of the newest cell phones. The GPS can identify where the user is at any time. If you are walking through a mall, a store could send you a digital coupon for 20 percent off of a purchase if you visit the business within the next 15 minutes. If you are driving down the interstate, ads from gas stations and restaurants may encourage you to stop.

Think Critically

1. Why is the targeted marketing used in GPS technology more likely to boost sales than traditional media advertising such as TV ads?

2. There are concerns that businesses and others will misuse the new technology to pinpoint your location at any time. Do you believe there should be restrictions on GPS technology?

3. Would you be willing to complete a survey from your cellular service provider that helps identify your interests? Why or why not?

Understanding and using marketing is an important business skill. Marketing is a valuable business asset in today's competitive world. People who understand the basics of marketing are in high demand in the business world. Those basics include understanding the marketing concept, planning a marketing strategy, responding to competition, and integrating marketing into the business.

Checkpoint ▶▶▶

What are the four ways that today's marketing differs from marketing practices in the past?

What Does Marketing Mean to a Business?

The marketing concept has changed the way businesses operate. It is more than just a new way to complete marketing activities. It requires a totally new approach to thinking and planning. The marketing concept keeps the main focus on customers' needs during the planning, production, distribution, and promotion of a product or service. That may seem simple, but some examples show how difficult it actually is.

Reliable Auto Service

Maria Santoz has always enjoyed repairing cars. As a teenager, she bought older cars, fixed them, and resold them at a profit. She studied auto mechanics in high school and became a certified mechanic at a local community college. She began working at a franchised auto repair center, but she became dissatisfied. She had to complete repairs as quickly as possible and use inexpensive repair parts rather than those specified by the manufacturer. Maria wanted to be able to spend more time with each car to make sure that all problems were identified and repaired with the best available parts.

After a few years, Maria decided to open her own auto repair business. She rented a small building on the edge of a large shopping center two miles from her home. She opened Reliable Auto Service and was pleased with the early response. She didn't spend a great deal on advertising, but the store's location and signs seemed to attract customers. Many people

©GETTY IMAGES/PHOTODISC

Why would the owner of an auto repair shop need to be concerned about marketing?

liked the convenience of being able to leave their car while they were shopping. They also said they had more confidence in a business where the owner worked on their car. Now that she owned the business, Maria knew she would be able to give each car special attention and the best possible service.

It didn't take long, however, for Maria's customers to start complaining. Many were upset when they had to leave cars overnight while Maria completed repairs. They were also concerned that repair costs were higher than they were used to paying. Maria told them that the price reflected the highest quality parts and that she guaranteed all repairs. Customers told her that other businesses also offered guarantees at much lower prices. Maria's business began declining. She was disappointed that customers did not value the quality of her work.

Dee's Designs

Dee Sloan combined her talents in art and sewing to work with the community theater. She designed and made the costumes for the theater's productions. Several of the actors and actresses were impressed with her unique designs. They asked her to create some items for their personal wardrobes.

Dee enjoyed the work, and word-of-mouth from her customers soon resulted in more orders than she could fill. Because of her success, she hired several people so that she could expand into a full-time business. She believed that she could sell her products through small businesses that would use the unique designs to compete with larger stores. She contacted several small retail chains hoping to find one that would agree to buy and distribute her fashions.

After three contacts, Dee was discouraged. Retailers agreed that the clothing was unique and well constructed. However, the first retailer felt the fashions did not fit the image of her stores. The second retailer was willing to buy one or two of the designs if Dee could produce a large volume of each in various sizes. Dee preferred to produce a variety of designs and styles. The last contact was willing to display Dee's fashions but required a full display for each store in the chain and was unwilling to pay until 60 percent of the original order was sold. Dee could not afford that investment.

Dee could not understand how her current customers could be so excited about her work, yet she could not interest people in the fashion business.

Working in **Teams**

As a team, select either Reliable Auto Service or Dee's Designs for analysis. What did the owner do right? What did she do wrong? As a team, suggest the changes that should be made in the marketing strategy to demonstrate understanding of the marketing concept.

How might marketing be used for a clothing design business?

Focus On Customer Needs

These experiences illustrate the difficulty of applying the marketing concept. These businesses both offered a quality product or service. Initial reactions from customers were positive, yet they were unable to develop a successful business strategy. They were unsuccessful for several reasons.

1. They were concerned only about the product or service.
2. They believed that they knew what customers wanted.
3. They did not study the market.
4. They failed to use a variety of marketing tools available to them.

It is not just new businesses that do not use marketing effectively. Car manufacturers, retailers, and restaurants fail, often after many years of successful operations. A business that is unwilling to study the needs of its customers when planning and marketing products and services is taking a big risk. Competitors who understand and use the marketing concept will turn that understanding into an advantage.

Checkpoint ▶▶▶

What different approach to marketing planning is required of businesses that use the marketing concept?

4-1 Assessment

school.cengage.com/marketing/marketing

Key Concepts

Determine the best answer.

1. The earliest use of marketing was to
   a. conduct marketing research
   b. move products from producer to consumer
   c. use advertising and selling to convince customers to buy
   d. identify new market opportunities

2. New markets and ways to improve a company's offerings in current markets are known as
   a. innovations
   b. the marketing concept
   c. market opportunities
   d. none of the above

3. When marketing is integrated, it is considered a(n) _____ part of the business, and it is _____ in all important business decisions.

4. Which of the following is evidence that a business is using the marketing concept?
   a. being concerned only about the product or service
   b. believing they know what the customer wants
   c. using only a few marketing tools
   d. studying the market

Make Academic Connections

5. **Math** Maria Santoz can purchase economy car batteries for $28 each and sell them for $42. She can buy heavy-duty batteries for $68 and sell them for $86. Research tells her that she can sell 38 economy batteries or 21 heavy-duty batteries per month. What will be the difference in monthly profit for her business based on selling the economy batteries instead of the heavy-duty batteries?

6. **Communication** Market opportunities consist of either totally new markets or ways to improve a company's offerings in existing markets. Choose a business in your community. Write a three-paragraph memo to the owner or manager identifying a possible market opportunity and the reasons you believe the company should consider the opportunity.

Connect to ◀ DECA
An Association of Marketing Students

7. Dee Sloan of Dee's Designs has asked you to help her use the marketing concept to improve her business. Develop a two-minute presentation explaining the changes you recommend in her approach to marketing. Give your presentation to your teacher (judge). Be prepared to answer questions about your recommendations.

Planning a Marketing Strategy

marketing matters

When businesses use the marketing concept, the planning process is in many ways turned on its head. Instead of starting with a product or service and then looking for customers who are willing and able to buy it, a business starts by researching potential customers and their needs. Only then does it move on to planning the product. Even then the product is not developed in isolation. It is planned as part of a comprehensive marketing mix. All elements of the marketing mix are focused on satisfying the needs of the target market customers that the company's research has identified.

For a company with which you are familiar, describe the marketing mix (product, distribution, price, and promotion) it uses for a specific group of customers. What needs does it appear to be trying to satisfy? How do you think the mix could be improved?

Putting Marketing Up Front

Every business decides how it will attempt to achieve its goals. Most businesses use carefully prepared plans to guide their operations. A plan that identifies how a company expects to achieve its goals is known as a **strategy**. A business's strategy provides the clearest indication of whether that business understands the marketing concept.

Without the marketing concept, a business first develops a product or service and then decides how it will be marketed. There will be little consideration of who the customers are or what their needs are until the product is completed. Marketing planning will occur only after the product has been designed. It will typically be done by marketing specialists working apart from others in the company. The business expects that most people are potential

Why is marketing research important in developing a marketing strategy?

©GETTY IMAGES/PHOTODISC

FIGURE 4-1
With the marketing concept, planning begins with customer needs.

How Does the Marketing Concept Affect Planning?

Without the Marketing Concept	With the Marketing Concept
1. Develop a product. 2. Decide on marketing activities. 3. Identify potential customers.	1. Conduct research to identify potential customers and their needs. 2. Develop a marketing mix (product, distribution, price, promotion) that meets specific customer needs.

customers for the product. It assumes that with adequate marketing those customers can be persuaded to buy the product.

With the marketing concept, a very different strategy will be used. The company believes it will be most successful if it can respond to the needs of customers. It recognizes that those needs may be different among various consumer groups. It also realizes that customer needs can change over time.

As shown in Figure 4-1, before doing anything else, the company will begin its planning by identifying potential customers and studying the needs of those customers. Marketers as well as others will be involved in the research and in using the results to plan the products and services to be developed. The company will attempt to develop products and services that respond to customers' needs rather than what the company thinks should be offered. Marketing and product planning will occur at the same time, involving many people in all parts of the company. Marketing will be directed at meeting the identified needs of the customers rather than developing ways to persuade people to buy something they may not need.

Checkpoint ▶▶

What is the initial focus of planning when the marketing concept is followed?

Understanding the Customer

Consumers have many choices of products and services they can purchase to meet their needs. Today, consumers are well informed and experienced in gathering information. They often spend time comparing products and services before they make decisions. Even if a hurried decision is made, if the buyer is dissatisfied with the purchase or finds a better choice later, the buyer will likely return the original product for a refund.

Bringing a new product to the marketplace is expensive. It takes time and money to develop, produce, distribute, and promote products. When a new product enters the market, it must compete with many products offered by other companies. These companies also have invested a great deal and do not want their products to fail. The competition among products is very intense.

Planning a Career in... *Marketing Research*

Marketing, Sales & Service

"Grandma finally agreed to move into a supportive living environment. Her new apartment has wide hallways that accommodate her walker. The bathtub has a door that swings open so she doesn't have to step in over a high edge. Her apartment key is mounted in an oversized holder that makes turning the key easier. Someone sure put a lot of thought into making this place easy for her to navigate."

How did the building owners know what features to include in apartments for the elderly? How do bathroom fixture manufacturers know that a growth in the elderly population warrants redesigning standard products for ease of use?

Marketing research enables companies to determine consumers' needs and wants. Products can then be developed or refined to meet consumers' needs.

Employment Outlook

- Faster than average growth is anticipated for the marketing research field.

- As international economies expand and create the opportunity for more purchases, demand for international marketing research will increase.

- Rapidly expanding media outlets are driving fiercer demand for consumers' attention. Marketing research will be used to plan effective strategies to reach consumers.

Job Titles

- Focus Group Facilitator
- Marketing Research Analyst
- Survey Sales Representative
- Marketing Research Account Executive
- Media Research Analyst
- Research and Development Manager

Needed Skills

- Depending on the type of research, educational requirements vary from a B.A. to an M.A. or Ph.D. degree.

- A blend of coursework in business, quantitative analysis, and information science is beneficial.

- Strong analytical skills and attention to detail are important.

What's it like to work in... *Marketing Research*

It's 7:15 A.M. and Dimetri, a marketing research associate at a consumer products company, is reviewing what consumers need most from a laundry detergent. The results, obtained from a recent focus group, indicate that effectiveness at stain removal, colorfastness, and value were the most important factors to consumers. Dimetri will incorporate questions on these attributes into the online survey he is developing for current and prospective customers.

Dimetri's afternoon team meeting focuses on the most effective way to deliver coupons to consumers. Six weeks ago, in three separate test markets, coupons for the laundry detergent were distributed via newspaper ads, by having retailers' cash registers print out coupons when a competing brand was purchased, and by making coupons available through the Internet. By comparing coupon distribution methods to recent sales in test markets, the group hopes to determine which method of coupon distribution was the most effective.

What About **You**

How would you like to contribute to product enhancements through marketing research projects?

Identifying Customer Needs

Successful companies are usually those that meet customer needs. Think of your favorite businesses or the products you purchase regularly. They are usually not the only choices you have, but they meet your needs in specific ways better than the other choices. The reasons may be higher quality, convenience, better prices, or a unique image. Satisfying exchanges occur when you spend your money for products and services that meet your needs, and the business is able to make a profit on the sale of its products.

Meeting customer needs is not easy. First, many customers are not sure of their needs or may have conflicting needs. Second, while consumers have many needs, they typically have limited amounts of money available to satisfy those needs. They may not have enough money to buy a specific product even though they believe it is the one that best meets their needs. Finally, the needs of individuals and groups of consumers can be quite different. Their perceptions of the products or services that will meet their needs are also quite different. Compare your feelings about specific products or services with those of your friends or family. You will find that there often are differences of opinion.

Businesses tend to deal with customer needs in one of two ways. Some businesses don't view the specific needs of consumers as important. They believe either that consumers don't understand their own needs or that businesses can influence consumer needs with well-designed products and effective prices and promotion. In other words, if they can effectively produce and market products, consumers will buy their products. These businesses feel that most consumers are similar in terms of their needs and purchase behavior.

Other businesses believe that an understanding of consumer needs is an important part of their business activities. They study needs and try to understand how consumers evaluate products and services to make decisions about what to purchase. The businesses recognize that consumer needs can be quite different, so they try to identify groups of consumers who have similar characteristics and needs. They feel that they can do a better job of satisfying consumers if they can develop products and services that respond to what the consumer wants and expects.

Satisfying Customer Needs

The business that is concerned about consumer needs believes in the marketing concept. Its activities begin with a focus on the customer and a belief that if it can satisfy customer needs better than its competitors, it will have the best chance for success. The business studies markets to identify groups of consumers with unsatisfied needs on which to focus its efforts. Through extensive marketing research, the business gathers and analyzes consumer information. It categorizes customers according to similar characteristics, needs, and purchasing behavior. Groups of similar consumers within a larger market are known as market segments.

After distinct market segments have been identified, the business analyzes each of them. It tries to determine which market segments can be served most effectively and which have the strongest needs, the most resources, and the least competition. It tries to identify other characteristics that can provide the business with opportunities for success. Studying and prioritizing market segments to locate the best potential based on demand and competition is known as **market opportunity analysis**.

Once segments have been identified and prioritized, the business selects those segments on which it will focus its efforts. The segments selected become the business's target market. A **target market** is a clearly defined segment of the market to which a business wants to appeal. The business can then use the information it has collected from the research to make production and marketing decisions specifically focused on that target market.

Checkpoint ▶▶▶

What is a market segment?

Planning the Offering

Much of the planning efforts of a company are used to determine what to sell and how it will be presented to the customer. Products and services to be offered need to be developed. Marketing strategies need to be planned in order to make the products and services available to the targeted customers.

A business that believes in the marketing concept bases the planning process on customer needs. It knows that product planning and marketing must work hand in hand. Therefore, it will carefully coordinate the development of the marketing mix.

The Marketing Mix

The marketing mix is a blend of the four marketing elements—product, distribution, price, and promotion. Many decisions are needed to insure that a satisfying product is made available to the selected markets at the time, in the location, at the price, and with the information that best meets customers' needs. An effective strategy will bring together many complex activities. A business will be able to control a large number of the activities, but it will usually have to rely on other businesses to help with its plans.

Creating the Right Mix

Some of the decisions in the marketing mix are obvious while others are not. The results of one decision affect others. For example, if an improvement is made to a product, then the company might need to increase the price. Developing the best marketing mix requires the cooperation of many people as well as careful planning and creativity.

A business uses the marketing concept because it believes that the best decisions can be made when the needs of consumers are an important focus of the planning. By combining the planning of product, distribution, pricing, and promotion, as shown in Figure 4-2, the company has the

FIGURE 4-2
Effective marketing strategies combine the parts of the marketing mix to satisfy customers.

best opportunity to develop a satisfying, competitive, and profitable mix. Business people need to understand each of the mix elements and all of the choices available in order to develop a good marketing mix.

Developing Products

When the term product is used, many people think of the basic offering of a company, such as an automobile, a desktop computer, or a meal at a restaurant. But there is much more to the product. Each competitor must make decisions that will make the product offered under its brand different from and better than the products offered by competitors.

Parts of the product decision that can improve customer satisfaction include special features such as a unique design, construction, size, color, or operation. Added accessories can make the product easier to operate and more efficient.

Products can be improved by offering services to customers. Services can be provided before or after the sale. They can be related to the purchase, delivery, installation, use, or maintenance of the product. Guarantees and warranties should be considered as a part of some products because they make customers more confident in the purchase of the product.

Another part of the product decision is the use of the product. Often products have more than one use. Customers may be dissatisfied if they are not able to use the product in the way they want. Packaging is needed not only to protect the product but also to make it easier to use and to provide customer information.

Making Distribution Decisions

Distribution is a critical part of a business's marketing decisions. It has an important impact on customer satisfaction by making the product available where and when the customer wants it. You can probably identify many examples of products that were

Hybrid car manufacturers found ready customers and rising profits while other auto companies struggled for sales.

not available when you needed them or were not found where you expected to find them. Products may have been damaged during shipment, poorly packaged, or assembled incorrectly. Poor distribution leads to customer dissatisfaction.

While some products and services are exchanged directly between the producer and the customer, usually other businesses must be involved in the distribution process. Manufacturers must rely on wholesalers and retailers to get products to the consumer. Similarly, a retailer must locate sources of the products its customers want and obtain them.

An interesting activity is to try to trace the distribution path for products you purchase. Sometimes it is almost impossible to identify the companies involved in some part of the distribution process or even the company that manufactured the product. Even though many of the businesses that are part of the distribution process are not obvious to the consumer, each business involved and the activities it performs are important. Activities such as order processing, product handling, transportation, and inventory control must be completed efficiently in order for companies to get the product to the customer. If one fails, the entire marketing effort may fail.

Pricing Products and Services

Price is probably the most difficult marketing decision to understand and plan. Theoretically, price is determined from the interaction of supply and demand. That relationship is important in setting the best price, but it is almost impossible to set the price of a specific product in a specific business using only supply and demand. Businesses must develop specific procedures to set prices that are competitive and allow the business to make a profit.

First the business needs to know its objectives in pricing its products and services. If the goal is to increase the sales volume of a particular product rather than make the most profit possible on each sale, a different price will be used. Many businesses set their prices the same or slightly lower than their major competitors. That pricing strategy may be necessary in some situations, but it can also create problems.

Virtual Marketing

Consumer Products Giant Taps Internet for New Product Launch

The Procter & Gamble Company is the world's leading marketer of consumer packaged goods. It knows how to use all types of advertising and how to manage distribution channels to get its products prominently displayed on store shelves around the globe. So why did it quietly roll out an innovative new product on an Internet web site months before it was made available to retailers?

P&G wanted to create word-of-mouth buzz for its new product, Crest Whitestrips teeth whitening treatments, by making the product available even before it hit store shelves. So even as it was completing product test marketing, P&G sold more than 250,000 units through dental offices and the Internet.

Dentists gave the product credibility, and the Internet was a good fit for the launch for several reasons. The price—$44 for two weeks' worth of applications—was high enough to overcome consumers' reluctance to pay shipping charges for inexpensive items, yet low enough that people would be willing to risk that amount of money on a completely new product.

P&G also used the web site to gather information for future marketing efforts. In addition to getting buyers' names and addresses, P&G offered free shipping if a buyer gave it the names of three other people who might want to try Whitestrips.

Think Critically

1. Why are consumers reluctant to pay shipping and handling charges for inexpensive items?

2. What do you think P&G hoped to gain by releasing Whitestrips months before it began retail distribution?

Why do some businesses offer special promotions such as double coupons or other discounts?

Calculating the price to be charged involves several elements. The price must be acceptable to customers, but it must cover all costs and allow for a reasonable profit. Production, marketing, and operating costs make up a large percentage of the final price of most products, so the net profit available is very small. If prices are not carefully calculated, businesses may not make a profit after expenses are tallied.

Another part of the pricing decision is how price is presented to customers. Normally, retailers use a price tag or sticker, and customers pay the price that is marked. Price may be communicated by manufacturers through catalogs or price sheets or by sales representatives.

It is common for businesses to offer discounts from their list prices to some or all of their customers. Prices can also be changed by markdowns, allowances, trade-ins, and coupons. Finally, credit is commonly used to allow customers to purchase a product without paying the full price at the time of purchase.

In pricing products and services, marketers must try to balance the cost of the product with customers' feelings about the value of the product. The goal is a fair price and a reasonable profit.

Planning Promotion

Promotion communicates the value and benefits of a product or service to help consumers make decisions. Advertising and other promotional methods are powerful tools if used to support effective marketing programs. However, they can easily be misused and can have no impact or even a negative effect on consumers.

Think of promotions you believe are particularly good. Now try to determine the impact of a specific promotion on your purchase behavior. It is difficult to determine the influence of just one promotion on a decision, even if it is memorable. There are more messages around us each day than we can ever notice or to which we can respond.

When planning promotion, business people select from a variety of methods. The most common methods are advertising, personal selling, sales promotion, visual display, and publicity. The choices will be based primarily on the objectives the company wants to accomplish and the audience it wants to reach. Each method varies in the cost per person, number of people reached, types of messages carried, and other factors. Careful planning needs to be done to reach the target markets with an understandable message that helps them make appropriate decisions.

Promotion is a unique type of marketing tool. It does not create economic utility by itself. It is used to communicate the value and benefits of other product and marketing decisions to the consumer. Promotion cannot do a great deal to help a company that has a poor product, excessively high prices, or ineffective distribution.

Checkpoint ▶▶

Why should marketing mix elements be planned together rather than separately?

4-2 Assessment

Xtra! Study Tools
school.cengage.com/marketing/marketing

Key Concepts

Determine the best answer.

1. When using the marketing concept, planning begins with
   a. determining customer needs
   b. identifying a product
   c. assessing competitors
   d. building a budget

2. Studying and prioritizing market segments to locate the best potential based on demand and competition is known as
   a. market research
   b. the marketing concept
   c. market opportunity analysis
   d. target marketing

3. True or False: In order to develop an effective marketing mix, the product needs to be well developed before planning other mix elements.

4. The marketing mix element that does not create economic utility by itself is
   a. product
   b. distribution
   c. price
   d. promotion

Make Academic Connections

5. **Visual Art** Draw or use technology to create a picture, graphic, or other visual representation of the marketing mix used by a company for one of its products. Make sure your visual includes each of the four elements of the marketing mix.

6. **Language Arts** Some companies have a specific target market for their products and services while others appear to be marketing to everyone. Locate an advertisement for a company that demonstrates a clear target marketing strategy and another that does not. Based on the purpose of the promotion mix element, determine how the language used in the two advertisements helps communicate the marketing strategy. Use the two ads to verbally describe your conclusions to other students.

Connect to ◀ **DECA**
An Association of Marketing Students

7. You are part of a team responsible for planning a marketing mix for a new fast-food breakfast item targeting health-conscious families. Develop a description of each mix element. Make a three-minute team presentation of your decisions and explain to your teacher (judge) how you applied the marketing concept.

Understanding Consumers and Competitors

GOALS

- Detail the stages of consumer decision making.
- Understand how business can use the marketing concept in various types of competition.

KEY TERMS

decision, *p. 105*

marketing matters

People follow a fairly predictable series of steps in making purchase decisions. They follow those steps to identify and evaluate various products and services that might satisfy their needs. By providing the right information at the right time when consumers are making a decision, businesses try to demonstrate to consumers that their products will deliver the best value. If that does not happen, consumers will likely choose another product. Much of a business's marketing strategy depends on the type of competition it faces from other businesses. The number and type of competing businesses affects the choices consumers have and how businesses will compete with each other.

Identify a major purchase you have made recently. How did you go about deciding what product to buy and how much to pay? Did you feel you had a number of good choices and adequate information to make the decision? Discuss your purchasing process with other students to see if it was similar to or different from theirs.

Consumer Decision Making

Consumers make decisions every day. A **decision** is a choice among alternatives. Decisions are made to satisfy a need or solve a problem. Consumers want to choose the alternative that provides the most satisfaction or the greatest value. Without choices, there would be no need for a decision.

If marketers want to satisfy customer needs, they must understand how consumers choose what they will buy. Researchers have developed a number of theories about what influences consumers to make decisions. However, there is general agreement that people follow a series of decision-making steps when making a commitment to purchase.

©DIGITAL VISION

If you were shopping for a computer, how would you decide which one to buy?

It is not always easy to recognize the stages as a person makes a decision. You may have to review several purchase decisions you have made in order to see a pattern. If you often buy the same product or service, you have probably formed a habit. In that case, you may not go through all of the steps that you would use when making a new decision. Purchase decisions become routine and simple when repeated. The decision-making process is more evident with an infrequent, important decision.

The Stages of a Decision

Figure 4-3 illustrates the five stages in consumer decision making. Consider an important decision you have made as you study each stage to help you understand it.

Stage 1—Recognize The typical purchasing process begins when the consumer recognizes that a need exists. Prior to that time, the consumer may have been aware of many products and services but took no action. Once a specific need is identified, the consumer moves through the stages of decision making. If the need is urgent, the process may occur quickly. If not, the consumer may take time before a decision is made.

Stage 2—Identify Once a need is recognized, the consumer becomes interested in finding a solution. That interest leads to identifying products or services that relate to the need and sources of information that can help the consumer make an effective decision.

Stage 3—Evaluate When several choices have been identified, the consumer then gathers information and uses it to evaluate the choices. An evaluation is done to determine if any one choice seems to be better, more available, or more affordable than other choices. Consumers must determine if one product or service meets their needs better than the other products and services being evaluated.

Some consumers spend very little time and use a small amount of information to evaluate choices. Others are very deliberate. Some people are careful and objective while others are much less rational.

Stage 4—Decide When the consumer is comfortable with the evaluation, a decision is made. The decision will be to select one of the available choices, to gather more information, or to do nothing at that time.

Stage 5—Assess The final step in the process is to determine whether or not the choice was correct. If the consumer tried a specific product, it will be evaluated to see if it satisfied the need. If it did, the decision will likely be repeated the next time the same need occurs. If it did not satisfy the need, the purchase decision will probably not be repeated.

Understanding the decision-making process is an important marketing skill. Knowing where consumers are in that process helps marketers offer the right information at the right time. The result should be a more effective exchange.

FIGURE 4-3
Consumers make a series of decisions when deciding on a purchase.

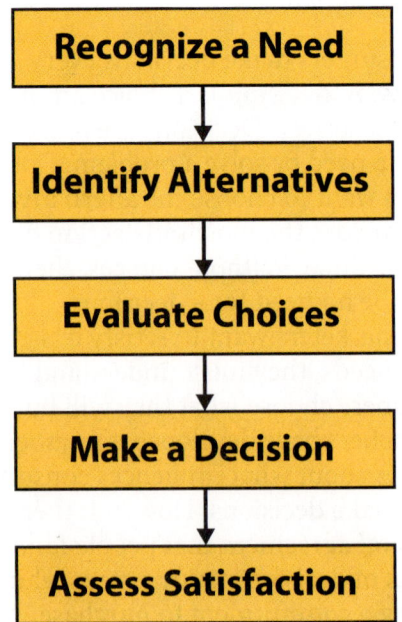

Recognize a Need

Identify Alternatives

Evaluate Choices

Make a Decision

Assess Satisfaction

Relying On Information

Marketers are often described as creative people. Indeed, a great deal of creativity is needed to plan a marketing mix. Developing new product features and uses, preparing promotional materials and activities, and demonstrating value to customers depend on the creativity of the people involved. Marketing is increasingly becoming a scientific process. Information is gathered to improve decisions, and alternative methods are studied to determine which are most effective.

Conducting research is an important marketing activity. Marketers need to be skilled in organizing research and using research results. The most important type of research for most businesses is the study of potential and current customers. Companies need to be able to clearly identify their customers, characteristics that make groups of customers different from others, their important needs, and how they make purchase decisions. Additionally, research about competitors will identify the type of competition and the strengths and weaknesses of competing companies. Finally, businesses study alternative marketing strategies to determine which ones are most effective and most profitable.

Marketers are using more and more information to make decisions. Most companies are developing marketing information systems that collect and store a variety of information. That information is readily available, often through the use of computer databases, when decisions need to be made.

Working in **Teams**

Have each team member in turn describe a recent purchase and how the purchase decision was made. As a team, discuss whether or not the decision seemed to follow the stages of the decision-making process. What types of decisions seem to follow the steps and what types do not?

Checkpoint ▶▶▶

Why are the stages of consumer decision making important in marketing planning?

Responding to Competition

The private enterprise economy offers many opportunities for businesses. A person who wants to start a business and has the necessary resources can probably do so. Our economy is also good for consumers. Because of the opportunities for people to operate businesses, consumers typically have many available products and services from which to choose.

Even though private enterprise offers many opportunities, it also presents challenges to business people. When there are many businesses in a market, competition is usually very intense. Consumers can select from among a number of products and services. They expect real value from businesses. Otherwise, they will purchase from a competitor. Value is not always the same for every consumer. It may mean higher quality, more service, or lower prices. Businesses that are unable to meet customer expectations better than their competitors may not be able to survive.

Marketers need to be able to identify the type of competition a company faces and develop an appropriate marketing strategy. Using the marketing concept provides direction for developing effective strategies.

Intense Competition

The most difficult type of competition businesses face is a market in which businesses compete with others offering very similar products. One example is *pure competition*, where there are many businesses offering the same product. Another example is an *oligopoly* where only a few companies compete in the same market but offer products in which consumers see few, if any, differences. Business people can study the customers in the market to determine if there are some groups who are not currently satisfied with the choices available.

In the past, businesses facing intense competition responded by emphasizing price or promotion. When they found that customers saw no important difference among competing products, they believed they had to reduce prices to make a sale. Companies that emphasized promotion tried to convince customers that their products were better than those of competitors. In some cases, they created minor differences and then promoted those differences as being important to consumers. In other cases, they attempted to create unique brand names and images so that customers would remember the brands and select them from the available choices.

Companies that face intense competition need to examine their marketing mix. With careful study of consumer needs and their experience with available products, businesses may be able to identify ways to change or improve products, features, or the services offered with the products. New product uses might be identified. The goal of any product change is to make the product different from that of competitors so that it is more satisfying to the target market.

There may also be opportunities in other parts of the marketing mix.

Distribution can focus on making the product available at better locations and times, with more careful handling, or greater customer service. Pricing can offer alternative methods of payments or greater ease of obtaining credit. It can provide extended time for payment or leasing rather than ownership. Promotion can provide more personalized or detailed information. It can use non-traditional methods or media. It can also communicate with the customer after the sale to aid in the use of the product.

Limited Competition

Some businesses have the advantage of offering a product or service with little or no direct competition. In economic terms, this situation is known as a *monopoly*. Businesses facing limited competition often operate in very different ways than those facing intense competition. They do not have to worry as much about price or even promotion since consumers are restricted in their choice of products. Therefore, a business will usually concentrate on maintaining its advantage in the market. It will try to keep competing businesses from entering the marketplace. It will protect its location and concentrate on keeping its product or service as unique as possible.

Customers using the products and services of a monopoly business often become dissatisfied with their lack of choice. They believe that without competition they pay higher prices and receive poorer service. They must also deal with a company that may be more concerned about protecting its market and making a profit than about meeting the needs of consumers.

Consider the only hospital in a community where the next closest hospital is 60 miles away. That hospital would be in a market much like a monopoly with no direct competition. It would be difficult for consumers to drive the 60 miles every time they needed health care. The hospital administrators would not have to be particularly concerned about the people who need hospital services. They could offer the

Digital Digest

Using Scanners to Collect Market Data

Most people are familiar with the devices cashiers use to scan purchases in grocery store checkout lanes. The scanners read bar codes from the products and automatically ring up the correct price for the item. But that is not all those electronic devices do. They also feed data into a computer that keeps track of inventory for the store. If the store runs low on a certain item, the computer can automatically order more from the supplier.

Scanners also provide useful information to marketers. When a purchase is made using a credit card or store discount card, the purchase information is logged into a database. That database shows who the customers are, what and when they buy, the price they pay, and whether they use coupons.

Marketers can use this information to determine if a certain promotion is successful. They can also make certain conclusions about their market and can better target future efforts. For example, if a customer buys diapers and baby formula, marketers might also send that customer information about other products and services for parents of young children. So while a grocery store's discount cards can save customers money, they are even more valuable to marketers.

Think Critically

1. How does good inventory management affect customer satisfaction?

2. How can detailed sales data help gauge the effectiveness of a sales promotion?

---

services that provided the highest level of profit. Customers might not be happy, but they would have little choice of an alternative.

While it may not be as profitable in the short run, the hospital administrators could adopt the marketing concept to make operating decisions. As a result, consumers will be more likely to use the local hospital and to encourage others to use it. They will be less likely to look for other places and other methods to meet their health care needs.

The same analysis could apply to the only convenience store, supermarket, or other retail business in a neighborhood. It could also apply to the only distributor of fuel or agricultural supplies in an area or to a government agency or school system. Each of these businesses has the characteristics of a monopoly and can decide whether or not to adopt the marketing concept.

Monopolistic Competition

Most businesses face competition somewhere between monopoly and intense competition. They have many competitors, but customers see some differences among the choices. The customers will attempt to determine which of the available products and services best meet their needs. It is important for the companies to have clearly identified differences that result in customers selecting their brands from among all of the available choices.

Companies in monopolistic competition find the marketing concept to be of most value. Since customers already recognize the unique choices available to them, they attempt to select the brands that are most satisfying. Companies that use the marketing concept focus on specific groups of customers and attempt to identify their needs. Then they will use the full range of decisions within the marketing mix to develop products and services for those customers. Changes and improvements can be made in the product, distribution, price, and promotion that make the brand not only different from its competitors but also more attractive to potential customers.

Here are some examples of the use of the marketing concept. A manufacturer of portable CD players makes its product smaller and more durable and offers the product in a variety of colors and styles. A day-care center keeps children overnight to meet the needs of parents who have evening jobs. A supermarket accepts orders and payments on its web site or by telephone and has the order ready at curbside for the customer at a convenient drive-up location. In each case, a change is made in the marketing mix that is designed to improve the mix, make it different from the competition, and respond to an important need of the target market.

Checkpoint ▶▶

Why is the marketing concept particularly useful for businesses facing monopolistic competition?

4-3 Assessment

Key Concepts

Determine the best answer.

1. A choice among alternatives is a(n) _____.

2. In order for the decision-making process to begin, a consumer must
   a. recognize a need
   b. have prior experience with products
   c. identify possible products that will satisfy the need
   d. all of the above

3. In the final stage of the decision-making process, the consumer
   a. makes a choice of the best alternative
   b. may decide not to make a purchase
   c. gathers information about the price
   d. assesses whether or not the choice made was correct

4. A strategy for a company in intense competition that uses the marketing concept is to
   a. reduce prices below their competitors' prices
   b. create a unique brand name for its products
   c. change the marketing mix to make it different and more satisfying to customers
   d. increase the amount of promotion

Make Academic Connections

5. **Technology** Using the drawing tools of a word processing program, create a flowchart that illustrates each of the stages of the decision-making process. Fill in the flowchart with information about an important purchasing decision you made.

6. **Management** For each of the three types of competition discussed in the lesson, identify a business in your community that you believe faces that type of competition. For each business, decide whether or not you believe the business is using the marketing concept in its response to competition. Act as the marketing manager for one of the businesses and write a paragraph explaining how the marketing concept could be used more effectively by the business.

Connect to  DECA
An Association of Marketing Students

7. Your marketing research team must prepare a short survey to determine the most important reasons consumers are loyal to a specific business or brand. Survey 15 people and analyze the results. Prepare a two-page research report with two supporting charts or graphs. Provide the report to your teacher (judge), and be prepared to answer questions about the research.

The Varied Role of Marketing

GOALS

- Explain how the role of marketing differs in various types of businesses.
- Identify ways marketing is used by non-business organizations.

KEY TERMS

channel of distribution, *p. 112*

channel members, *p. 112*

non-business organization, *p. 113*

marketing matters

Marketing activities must be performed every time an exchange of products and services occurs. That exchange may occur between businesses, a business and a consumer, or even between consumers. The same basic marketing functions and activities are used in all exchanges. Each exchange involves a supplier, a consumer, and a complete marketing mix. However, there are differences in the ways that various types of businesses use marketing tools. It may be surprising to learn that the same marketing tools are used by non-business organizations and even individuals. Marketing principles can apply to a variety of types of exchanges even when profit is not the ultimate motive.

Make a list of three products or services used in your classroom. Then investigate how each was marketed to the school by various businesses. Now identify three products or services your school provides to its consumers. Discuss how marketing activities are a part of those exchanges.

The Varied Uses of Marketing

There are many different types of businesses. The entire marketing mix and all marketing functions are important to all businesses. However, each type of business will need to place more emphasis on some of its marketing decisions than on others.

Producers and Manufacturers

Producers and manufacturers develop the products and services needed by other businesses and by consumers. Because of that role, the product element of the marketing mix usually receives the most attention. Distribution is also important as the companies must make sure the products get to their customers. Unless manufacturers and producers distribute products directly to the users, they must rely on other businesses to make good decisions about product distribution, prices charged to consumers, and even consumer promotion. Even if manufacturers and producers do not sell directly to the final consumers of their products, they still must understand and respond to the needs of consumers. In addition to the design of products, other marketing activities must meet consumer needs as well. Manufacturers and producers must also be able to satisfy the needs of the businesses involved in the marketing channels for the products.

Channel Members

A **channel of distribution** is made up of all of the businesses involved in completing marketing activities as products move from the producer to the consumer.

Channel members are the businesses used to provide many of the marketing functions during the distribution process. For those channel members, less emphasis will be placed on the product element of the marketing mix although they must have the products that customers want. If the product does not meet their customers' needs, the customers are likely to hold the channel member as responsible as the producer or manufacturer.

After decisions are made about what products and services to offer, channel members then focus their attention on the other mix elements. Wholesalers emphasize distribution planning. Many wholesalers help their customers with financing and provide marketing information.

Retailers are responsible for most final pricing decisions. They use a variety of promotional activities to encourage consumers to purchase their products. Channel members must work closely with both producers and their customers to make sure the entire marketing mix is satisfactory to everyone involved.

Service Businesses

Service businesses face unique marketing challenges. Most service businesses work directly with their customers rather than through a channel of distribution. Therefore, they are responsible for the entire marketing mix. Also, services are usually developed and delivered by people, making it more difficult to control the quality of the service.

Because of the characteristics of services and the expectations of customers, the product mix element is very important

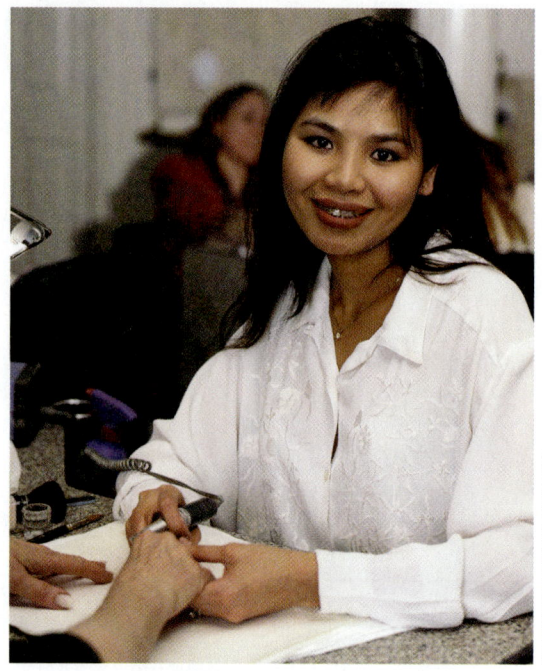

Does a service business need to develop a marketing mix? Why or why not?

for service businesses. The business must develop procedures to insure quality service every time.

Distribution planning is also important because the service must be available where and when the customer wants it. If the business is not conveniently located, sales may be lost. If the business offers more services than the customers want, expenses will be high.

Service businesses usually have more control over pricing than businesses that sell products. It is more difficult for customers to determine the appropriate price for a service or to compare prices since different businesses may offer the service in a different way. Services are difficult to promote since the customer may not be able to see or examine them. Services that customers are not familiar with may require a great deal of promotion.

Checkpoint ▶▶

What is the main way that marketing for service businesses differs from marketing for other types of businesses?

Gray Marketing

Controlling the channels through which a company's products are distributed and sold can be an important part of building a brand. That is particularly true for companies that sell their products internationally. Difficulties can arise if an unauthorized business imports products into a country and competes with the authorized distribution channel. This practice is called *gray marketing.* Unlike the "black market," the gray market is legal. Gray market products are simply sold outside the normal distribution channels by people or companies that have no relationship with the producers of the products. Someone may buy a product cheaply and then import it legally into another country where it is sold at a price below the normal market price.

Manufacturers commonly complain about gray marketers and try to stop them with legal action. They claim that gray marketers damage their products' reputations and confuse consumers. They also interfere with exclusive marketing contracts that manufacturers have made with authorized distributors. Gray marketers argue that manufacturers simply want to control prices and gouge consumers for as much as they can. They say their efforts provide consumers with the same products at lower prices.

Think Critically

1. How does the prohibition of gray marketing enhance a company's ability to maximize its profits?

2. Do you think gray marketing is an ethical business practice? Why or why not?

Marketing by Non-Business Organizations

The successful use of marketing has moved from the business world to other non-business organizations. A **non-business organization** has as its primary focus something other than providing products and services for a profit. Previously, many people who headed non-business organizations such as government agencies, churches, schools, museums, and even professional organizations viewed marketing in negative ways. Because of those views, they did not see how marketing applied to or could help their organizations. Today, people are more aware of marketing. They see many businesses using marketing effectively. Because of a better understanding of marketing and its goal of creating satisfying exchanges, non-businesses organizations have begun to recognize that marketing can help them achieve their goals.

It is not unusual today to see marketing being used by museums, libraries, symphonies, athletic teams, churches, and clubs. The unique characteristics of several types of non-business organizations suggest how they might approach marketing.

Government Agencies

Most government agencies have many of the characteristics of a monopoly. They seldom have competition for the services they provide. Citizens usually pay for fire and police protection, garbage collection, street repairs, and other city, state, and federal services through taxes. As a result, they have no choice but to pay the cost of those services established by the government.

American Red Cross
Together, we can save a life

Make a plan.

How your family reacts in an emergency can make all the difference. Develop a family disaster plan with help from your local Red Cross and learn what everyone in your family can do in the event of a fire or other disaster. When we come together, we become part of something bigger than us all. To learn what you can do, contact your local American Red Cross chapter or visit www.redcross.org

TOGETHERWE   Make a plan | Build a kit | Get trained | Volunteer | Give blood

A simple safety message reminds people of the importance of the Red Cross.

It becomes easy for those providing the services to feel they know what citizens want and how best to provide it. They may not be concerned about a high level of customer service. They may be more concerned about controlling costs to meet their budget.

Today, however, many government officials and employees recognize the importance of providing quality services and responding to customer questions and concerns in positive ways. They are making information and services available in more convenient and accessible ways. Many government agencies have begun using e-government, where information is readily available through a well-designed and secure web site. Citizens can transact much of their business with government using the Internet.

Government agencies have also worked with the pricing element of the marketing mix. While they cannot reduce the prices of services, they have made it possible to use credit or debit cards for payments or to spread payments over a period of time rather than requiring full payment all at one time. Promotion has also become a popular marketing tool for government agencies to inform customers of services and to build a positive image.

Nonprofit Organizations

Nonprofit organizations have a unique situation. They do not operate with a profit motive. However, they still need adequate resources to provide services to people in need. Often they must rely on fundraising from people who will not directly benefit from the organization's services. They must be able to convince people of the value of those services and the need to support the organization financially. Promotion is a very important marketing mix element for many nonprofit organizations.

Nonprofit organizations provide products and services for their clients. Therefore, the product mix element is important to make sure the products and services provided meet the clients' needs. Since many organizations serve clients across the country and even worldwide, distribution decisions are also important. Distribution may involve shipping food and clothing to impoverished parts of the country or transporting people to help with relief efforts.

Fast **FACTS**

According to a survey by the National League of Cities, 75 percent of U.S. cities have a web site. The survey also found that almost half of those cities offer their citizens online payment options for city services, utility bills, and even parking tickets and traffic citations.

©USED WITH PERMISSION OF THE AMERICAN RED CROSS

Supporting Non-Business Organizations

Many organizations seek help from people who understand marketing and know how to use the marketing concept to identify target markets and develop marketing mixes. With the help of marketers and increased understanding of and use of marketing tools, those organizations have seen positive results. They now view marketing as an important part of their efforts.

NETBookmark

Religious institutions, use marketing strategies to attract and keep members. Access school. cengage.com/marketing/marketing. Click on the link for Chapter 4, and visit the web site for Mustard Seed Studio, a leading church marketing company. What strategies does Mustard Seed Studio suggest churches use to create a "guest-friendly environment"? (Hint: Click the *Guestology* link.)

school.cengage.com/marketing/marketing

Checkpoint ▶▶

Why is marketing important to non-business organizations?

4-4 Assessment

Key Concepts

Determine the best answer.

1. The marketing mix element that usually receives the most attention from producers and manufacturers is _____.
   a. product
   b. distribution
   c. price
   d. promotion

2. Wholesalers emphasize _____ while retailers are responsible for most final _____ decisions.

3. Which marketing mix element do service businesses usually have greater control over than do businesses that sell products?
   a. product
   b. distribution
   c. price
   d. promotion

4. Non-business organizations have something other than _____ as their primary focus.
   a. customer needs
   b. profit
   c. marketing
   d. all of the above

Make Academic Connections

5. **Visual Art** Draw or use technology to create a visual representation of a channel of distribution involving three or more businesses that produce and distribute a product that you have purchased. The visual should show each business and the marketing activities that it performs as a part of the channel of distribution.

6. **Government** Locate the web site of a local, state, or federal government agency. Analyze the web site for evidence of the use of marketing. Based on the web site, do you believe the agency understands the marketing concept? Prepare a two-paragraph report describing your findings and conclusion.

Connect to

7. As the membership chairperson for your local DECA chapter, you are responsible for developing a marketing plan for increasing membership. Prepare three computer slides that summarize your decisions about a target market and marketing mix. Use the slides to present your ideas to your teacher (judge).

Chapter 4 Assessment

Check Your Understanding

Now that you have completed the chapter, check your understanding of the lessons with these questions. Record the score that best represents your understanding of each marketing concept.

1 = not at all; 3 = somewhat; 5 = very well

If your score is 42–50, you are ready for the assessment activities that follow. If you score 33–41, you should review the lessons for the items you scored 1–3. If you score 32 or less, you will want to carefully reread the lessons and work with a study partner on the areas you do not understand.

Can you—

___ identify four ways that marketing is different today than it was in the past?

___ explain why even successful businesses with superior products should still be concerned about customer needs?

___ describe how a marketing strategy is different when the marketing concept is used to develop it?

___ offer a definition of a market segment and market opportunity analysis?

___ explain why it is important for a business to define its target market?

___ explain why product planning and marketing planning must work together?

___ list and briefly describe each of the stages of consumer decision making?

___ provide examples of how the marketing concept can be used in intense, limited, and monopolistic competition?

___ identify and defend the marketing mix elements that are important to each of the major types of businesses?

___ explain why marketing is important to non-business organizations?

Review Marketing Terms

Match the terms listed with the definitions. Some terms may not be used.

1. Studying and prioritizing market segments to locate the best potential based on demand and competition

2. Occurs when marketing is considered an essential part of the business and is involved in all important business decisions

3. A plan that identifies how a company expects to achieve its goals

4. Has something other than providing products and services for a profit as its primary focus

5. New markets and ways to improve a company's offerings in current markets

6. Groups of similar consumers within a larger market

7. A choice among alternatives

a. channel members
b. channel of distribution
c. decision
d. integrated
e. market opportunities
f. market opportunity analysis
g. market segments
h. non-business organization
i. strategy
j. target market

Review Marketing Concepts

8. True or False: Marketing consists of only a few basic activities such as promotion and distribution.

9. True or False: In the past, marketing was used basically as a problem-solving tool, such as a way to reduce inventory.

10. True or False: Spending money to improve marketing usually results in increased profits for the company.

11. True or False: Following the marketing concept requires a total commitment to satisfying customers' needs.

12. True or False: Understanding and meeting consumer needs is relatively easy to do because most people have the same needs.

13. True or False: The marketing mix elements all act independently of each other.

14. True or False: Because of so many other variables, it is impossible to set a product or service price based strictly on the concepts of supply and demand.

15. True or False: The promotion element of the marketing mix is the communication link between the seller and the buyer.

16. True or False: Because effective marketing requires large amounts of information, most companies are now developing marketing information systems that collect and store information.

17. The first step in the consumer decision-making process is recognizing that a _____ exists.

18. True or False: In a limited-competition situation, it is not important for marketers to pay attention to the effectiveness of their mix elements.

19. In monopoly situations, businesses face which type of competition?
    a. intense
    b. limited or none
    c. monopolistic
    d. unlimited

20. Service businesses face unique marketing challenges because services are delivered by people, making it difficult to assure consistent _____ each time.

21. When businesses regard marketing as a provider of opportunities, they look for which of the following?
    a. new markets
    b. ways to improve existing products
    c. changing customer needs
    d. all of the above

Marketing Research and Planning

22. Marketing involves understanding customers and their wants and needs. To demonstrate two views on customers, draw two large circles on a piece of paper. Within each circle, create a collage of pictures. One should contain customers that are all alike and would respond to a mass-marketing approach. The other circle should contain pictures of customers who represent different market segments and would respond to target marketing.

23. The type of competition faced affects the type of marketing strategy a company will use. Locate an advertisement for a business from your community that faces intense competition (auto dealership, supermarket, cellular telephone service, etc.) and another advertisement for a company that faces limited competition (utility company such as electricity, natural gas, telephone, cable, etc.). Create a poster that compares the marketing strategies of each company by highlighting differences in the advertisements.

24. Brand names often have a significant impact on the consumer's perception of quality. Survey 10 people to find their perception of the quality of the products represented by the following brands: Nike, Chrysler, Microsoft, Sony, and Kellogg's. Ask them to use a rating scale where 1 is the worst quality and 10 is the highest quality. Use a computer spreadsheet program to create a chart. Record each person's responses in your chart and find an average quality rating for each product. Prepare three written conclusions from the data.

25. Develop a marketing strategy including a description of a target market and a complete

marketing mix for a house painting service. Make sure that you consult the textbook to include all of the variables of each mix element. Describe the decision-making process you believe the target market will follow to choose a painting service. Identify and justify the type of competition such a service would face in your community.

26. Use an Internet search engine, an online library research service, or a web site such as www.findarticles.com that searches magazines and professional journals to find a recent article on the use of marketing by non-business organizations. Then use a word processing program to compose a 150- to 200-word summary of the article's main points.

Marketing Management and Decision Making

27. A service that is gaining in popularity is a shuttle service for children whose parents work. These shuttle services provide rides to and from after-school activities such as dancing, gymnastics, music lessons, and sports practices. The service is gaining in popularity since more families are unable to transport their children because the activities occur while both parents are still at work.

You are responsible for completing a market opportunity analysis, determining the type of competition a children's shuttle service would face, reviewing the stages of decision making for a parent considering the service, and describing each of the marketing mix elements you would recommend.

To analyze the potential for a children's shuttle service in your community, prepare written answers to the following questions:

a. What individuals, groups, or organizations are potential customers for the service?

b. What type of information is needed to determine if there are enough potential customers for the business? What are some possible sources to determine the number of potential customers?

c. What are two possible market segments for the service, and what are the important needs of each segment?

d. What type of competition would exist for this service in your community—intense, limited, or monopolistic competition? Who are the major competitors?

e. What information would a customer need about the service at each stage of the decision-making process?

f. Based on your market analysis, what would be the most important factors to focus on to ensure you provide a satisfying product, effective distribution (place), a reasonable price, and effective promotion of the new business?

28. The study of customers and their wants and needs is primary for a successful business. As the needs and wants of customers change, marketers must be able to identify new markets or customer groups for old products or services. Pick-up trucks, fast food, and photo processing services are products that have been on the market for a long time. Traditional markets are changing, so marketers are looking for new markets for each of those products. For each product, prepare a table that describes and compares (a) a traditional market, (b) the marketing mix for the traditional market, (c) a new market, and (d) the marketing mix for the new market.

29. A markup is the difference between the price a business pays for a product and the price it sells the product for. It is usually expressed as a percentage of the price paid by the business. For example, if a retailer pays $1 for a box of laundry detergent and sells it to its customers for $1.50, its markup is 50 cents divided by $1, or 50%.

A bicycle shop buys six models of bikes for the following prices: $66, $99, $142, $180, $245, and $300. Determine the effect of various markups by designing an electronic spreadsheet that will calculate prices for the bicycle shop. Input the amounts the shop paid and develop formulas to calculate selling prices for the following markups—25%, 33 $1/3$%, 48%, and 60%. Then use the spreadsheet and each of the four markup percentages to calculate the total cost and total revenue for the bicycle shop if it purchased and sold three of each of the bicycle models.

Creative Marketing Project Event

The Creative Marketing Project gives participants an analytical and creative approach to the marketing process by actively engaging students in the marketing activities of their community. It is designed to encourage students to recognize marketing as a force for the economic and social good of the community. Your project might concern itself with finding new markets for local products, promoting the community's resources, increasing the trading area of facilities, increasing local sales, increasing local employment, providing better shopping facilities, or solving marketing problems or challenges affecting the local community.

This project is limited to 30 numbered pages, including the appendix and excluding the title page and table of contents. Major parts of the written project include the Executive Summary, Introduction, Procedures and Research Methods Used, Findings and Conclusions, Recommendations, Bibliography, and Appendix.

You have been hired by your city to conduct research for attracting an appropriate company and additional business activity to your community. You must consider the population of your city, the available workforce, economic incentives, and the marketing and distribution of the products/services produced by the company you are trying to attract to your community. You will prepare a written entry for this project and an oral presentation to sell your research findings. The oral presentation must cover all performance indicators. You must present a compelling reason for a company to locate in your city.

Performance Indicators Evaluated

- Describe the project in an organized, clear, and effective presentation. (Communication)

- Identify the marketing information needs of this research project. (Marketing-Information Management)

- Interpret descriptive statistics used in the decision making process. (Marketing-Information Management)

- Explain the findings and recommendations. (Communication)

- Demonstrate professional appearance, poise, and confidence. (Communication)

Go to the DECA web site for more detailed information.

Think Critically

1. What are the greatest assets that your city has to offer a potential business?

2. Why must you describe the workforce in detail when trying to attract a business to a community?

3. How can tax incentives be used to attract business to a community?

4. Why is it important to describe the demographics of your community when presenting to a potential business?

www.deca.org

Marketing Information and Research

©GETTY IMAGES/PHOTODISC

Newsline

The New American Restaurant

The increase in the choices and popularity of ethnic restaurants has been one of the most noticeable trends in the restaurant industry. In fact, three types of ethnic cuisines—Italian, Mexican, and Chinese—are so commonplace today that they are no longer considered ethnic. Today, the most popular categories of ethnic restaurants are Japanese, Thai, Caribbean, and Middle Eastern.

In the past, most of the ethnic restaurants were small, independent businesses owned and operated by immigrants to serve others with the same ethnic background. Today, large national and international restaurant chains are located in the shopping malls and entertainment districts of towns and cities. A study by the National Restaurant Association identified several segments of consumers that have different expectations and needs for ethnic meals.

- The *Basic Family* segment expects familiar foods, a great value, and a family dining atmosphere or carryout.

- The *Authentic and Mild* segment is composed of younger, upscale consumers who want well-prepared, pleasantly flavored ethnic foods.

- The *Adventurous and Spicy* segment wants a menu that is new and full of surprises. These consumers are willing to try flavors with which they are unfamiliar, and they insist that the menu be authentic ethnic food.

- The *Festive* segment is attracted by the atmosphere. A unique and enjoyable experience is as important as the food. They want a full menu, hearty portions, and entertainment.

Think Critically

1. Why have the variety and types of ethnic foods and restaurants increased in recent years in the United States?

2. Identify some restaurants in your community that have ethnic menus and themes. Do they seem to be directed at any of the segments identified?

school.cengage.com/marketing/marketing

Prepare for Performance

This chapter develops the following Performance Indicators from the DECA Competitive Events program.

Core Performance Indicators

- Acquire foundational knowledge of marketing information management to understand its nature and scope
- Understand marketing-research activities to show command of their nature and scope
- Understand data-collection methods to evaluate their appropriateness for the research problem/issue
- Evaluate marketing research procedures and findings to access their credibility

Supporting Performance Indicators

- Describe the need for marketing information
- Explain the nature of marketing research
- Explain types of primary marketing research
- Identify sources of primary and secondary data
- Explain research techniques
- Identify information monitored for marketing decision making

Go to **school.cengage.com/marketing/marketing** and click on Connect to DECA.

INNOVATIONS FOR THE mailstream

What will we put our stamp on next?

Pitney Bowes mailstream solutions use satellite imagery to let you see customers in unprecedented detail.

For the first time, business can see the big picture for what it really is: a composite of precise demographic, geographic and lifestyle snapshots of its customers. Our Geocoding Solution allows insurers to analyze data on a house by house basis, so they can structure premiums that accurately reflect differing levels of risk. This is just one of the ways Pitney Bowes is merging the boundaries of mail and data into mailstream solutions that are helping many Fortune 500 companies stay compliant, competitive, and profitable. What's next? **Visit pb.com/mailstream** and see for yourself.

Pitney Bowes
Engineering the flow of communication

©PITNEY BOWES

Visual Focus

Marketing information and marketing research are important marketing resources. With information, decisions are objective and accurate. Without information, past experiences and personal opinions will often influence those decisions. This chapter will help you recognize the types of information needed for marketing decision making, how the information is obtained and used, and effective research procedures.

Focus Questions:

What is your first impression when viewing the advertisement? Does the image encourage you to read the ad? What type of product or service is Pitney Bowes describing? Who does it appear the company wants to see the ad? Why do you believe that companies need precise information about their customers?

Locate an advertisement that includes research or other specific information about customers or competitors that was used by the business in developing and marketing its product or service. Share your choice in a class discussion.

Understanding the Need for Market Information

GOALS

- Explain the importance of information in making marketing decisions.
- Describe the categories of information needed by marketers.

KEY TERMS

discretionary purchases, *p. 123*

marketing matters

People who value the marketing concept understand why market information is important. When businesses use the production philosophy, they make decisions based on their own experiences and their ideas about what is needed. The marketing concept, in contrast, is based on satisfying customer needs, so it is essential to know and understand prospective customers. When implementing the marketing concept, businesses start with information to be able to identify customers and their needs, attitudes, and expectations. With information, marketers can confidently select the markets they will serve and plan effective marketing mixes tailored to those customers.

As a class, agree on several products and services that most students buy on a regular basis. Individually identify why you buy each product or service, what needs it satisfies, and the important factors you look for when you purchase each product. Compare your purchasing behavior with other students. Discuss similarities and differences and how that information could be helpful to marketers.

Starting with Information

Most businesses today do not have a production emphasis. They do not believe that customers will buy a product simply because they produce it. Important factors facing businesses today increase the need to gather and study information. They recognize that an understanding of consumers, expanding choices, competition, and the global marketplace will help them make better decisions.

Consumer Differences

Most businesses no longer believe that all consumers are alike and all want the same things. Instead, they recognize that various consumers have very different needs and wants and that they likely view product and service choices quite differently. Businesses know that if they are to meet the specific needs and expectations of consumers, they must have detailed and specific information about them. They must be able to determine the similarities and differences among market segments and decide how they can best meet the unique needs and wants of those segments.

Expanding Choices

Customer needs are changing, and so are the choices customers make to satisfy those needs. Many consumers are able to satisfy their basic needs much more easily than was possible in the past. Therefore, they have moved beyond basic needs and

Online Music Stores Think Globally, Price Locally

The Internet has revolutionized the way people buy music. Downloading music has become the preferred method of purchase for many consumers. Online music stores, such as Apple's iTunes, allow customers to purchase music instantly and as individual songs if they don't want to buy an entire album. Albums are never sold out, and there are no shipping costs.

Just because people everywhere in the world have access to the Internet does not necessarily mean that they can all buy the same music at the same price. Music licensing agreements are complicated and usually stipulate in which countries certain music can be distributed. As a result, the same music that is available in Japan, for example, may not be available to U.S. customers and vice versa.

The real benefit of segregated markets is to the online music stores. Keeping markets separate allows stores to better control the price of their music. Based on demand and what people are willing to pay, a music store may charge more to download the same song in one country than in another.

Think Critically

1. Do you think segregated markets are fair? Why or why not?

2. What would happen to the price of music if online music stores desegregated their markets and allowed customers to buy music from any country they wanted?

---

are devoting more resources to satisfying their wants with discretionary purchases. **Discretionary purchases** are not essential, so consumers can decide whether or not to purchase them.

Consumers have many choices of most products and services, and much more information about those choices, so their decisions are more informed. In order to develop a marketing mix that will satisfy consumer wants, businesses must have a clear understanding of expanding consumer choices and consumer purchasing decisions.

Competition

Competition is becoming much more intense for most businesses. It is more difficult to make marketing decisions that will ensure customers will prefer one company's products to those of competitors. Gathering information about competitors' products and marketing activities in order to determine their strengths and weaknesses will help businesses to be more competitive.

As consumers' wants and needs have expanded, products and services have changed as well. In the past, products may have been quite basic with few additional features or options available for consumers. When products have limited differences, businesses try to compete for sales by emphasizing such things as their brand name, availability, or price. Businesses also try to compete by developing unique designs, product improvements, or special features. However, such changes can be expensive and may not always meet customer needs.

The correct product design and marketing decisions can be very profitable, but the wrong choices can result in losses for the company. Decision makers want information so that the best and most profitable product and service choices that improve on competitors' offerings can be implemented.

The Global Marketplace

As businesses develop an international focus, the differences among customer groups and the number of distinct market segments can become even greater. Even if businesses believe that they understand the consumers in their own country quite well, they will not have as much confidence about consumer groups in other countries that they have never served. Gathering information about the country and its people as well as new competitors can help determine how to become an effective global business.

Checkpoint ▶▶▶

When a business uses the marketing concept, what is the first thing it needs to begin marketing planning?

Deciding on Information Needs

Many marketing decisions are made with too little information or the wrong types of information. It is also possible to become overwhelmed with too much information, making it difficult to use it to make good decisions. Consider the approaches of two apparel companies as they decide on their apparel lines for the upcoming year.

Approaches to Planning

J'Borg Apparel is deciding on next year's designs for its lines of shirts and shorts. The members of the design team meet and share their ideas about possible changes. Several of the designers suggest that J'Borg should keep its basic designs from this year because they have been so successful. They think the company should simply develop new colors and some additional accessories. Another group believes that customers may be tiring of the company's current casual offerings and will want more tailored styles. They argue that entirely new designs for its lines of apparel should be developed.

J'Borg's primary competitor is Dominique Designs. Dominique's designers are also meeting to consider changes in product lines. Before the meeting, they request information from the company's marketing manager. The marketing department provides records on each of the company's products. Those records identify the quantity sold by size and color for each week of the year. They also show the region of the country and the retail store in which sales were made. Original prices of products sold, markdowns, and the number of items returned or unsold are also recorded.

In addition, the marketing manager distributes copies of a report that was purchased from a national apparel manufacturing association. It presents information on total consumer apparel purchases in the United States for each of the past five years for ten major categories of apparel. Sales are broken out for four geographic regions of the country and are categorized by age and gender and by type of retail store where products are sold. The report also identifies the top six brands of apparel and shows the percentage of total sales contributed by each brand over the five-year period. The final section of the report discusses the anticipated changes in the economy and in customer expenditures for apparel for the next year.

Finally, the marketing manager shares the results of a marketing research study completed during the past month. Four groups of consumers from across the country were invited to a meeting to discuss their attitudes about apparel and their ideas about purchases they expected to make. The consumer groups discussed ten questions about designs, brands, and value. The results of the discussions are summarized in the research report. All of the designers for Dominique have studied the market information, and they discuss it before deciding on next year's designs.

How will each of the companies decide whether to make design changes and the types of designs to use for the next year? Which of the companies do you believe will make decisions that are most likely to be successful? What is the biggest difference in the way Dominique Designs makes decisions compared to J'Borg?

Categories of Information

Put yourself in the position of the marketing manager for a national chain of yogurt stores. It is your responsibility to collect information to help store managers decide what they can do to increase sales and profits. What information do you think is needed?

Each type of business needs specific information, but there are general categories of information that all businesses should consider. Those categories include consumers, the marketing mix and the business environment. Figure 5-1 provides examples of the types of information for each category.

As the marketing manager of the yogurt stores, you will need information

from each of the categories. You will want to help store managers determine who their customers are, where they live, how much they spend on desserts, how they make decisions on what and when to purchase, and how they feel about your store and its brand of yogurt.

You will want to know what new flavors to add, if other food products should be sold, whether specific locations or certain store layouts are more effective, the prices to charge, and the most effective promotional messages and methods. A study of internal operations such as costs of operations, training requirements for employees,

FIGURE 5-1
Marketers need information to make effective decisions

Types of Information Needed for Effective Marketing Decisions		
Consumers	**Marketing Mix**	**Business Environment**
• age • gender • income • education • family size • occupation • attitudes • primary needs • purchase frequency • brand preferences • information needs • media preferences • shopping behavior	• basic products • product features • services • product packaging • guarantees • after-sale customer service • product price • credit choices • discounts • location and method of sale • type of distribution used • promotion and sales methods • promotional message • promotional media	• type of competition • competitors' strengths • competitors' strategies • economic conditions • government regulations • new technology • consumer protection • ethical issues • tax policies • proposed laws • international markets

and management methods may help determine the best ways to operate the stores.

Your store managers will want to know if the economy will change in the next year, if there will be new competitors or if current competitors are making important changes, if taxes or government regulations will increase, and even specific information such as whether the city is planning to make street improvements in front of a store.

There are many reasons to collect information. However, all the reasons can be summarized in two statements. Effective marketing information improves the decisions of businesses, and effective marketing information reduces the risk of decision making. If a business can make better decisions that increase the likelihood of making a profit, the time and money spent gathering information is a good investment.

Checkpoint ▶▶▶

What are three general categories of information needed by businesses for effective marketing decisions?

5-1 Assessment

Key Concepts

Determine the best answer.

1. True or False: Most businesses no longer believe that all consumers are alike and all want the same things.

2. Most consumers have moved beyond basic needs and devote more resources to satisfying their wants with _____ purchases.

3. When products have limited differences, businesses try to compete for sales by emphasizing all of the following *except*
   a. their brand name
   b. availability
   c. price
   d. all of the above are emphasized

4. When moving into international markets, businesses are likely to face customers
   a. who are quite similar to existing customers
   b. who are already well satisfied by competitors
   c. for whom they have little information or experience
   d. with no need for the company's products

5. Effective marketing information _____ the decisions of businesses and _____ the risk of decision making.

Make Academic Connections

6. **Psychology** Businesses respond to differences in consumer needs by offering choices of the same product. Select a company that offers at least three choices of a product. Examine the product and product information to determine the differences and the customer characteristics or needs to which each appeals. Prepare a one-page report or a summary chart of your analysis.

7. **Economics** Review several recent issues of a local or statewide newspaper. From the news reports, identify five factors that could affect the economic environment for consumers and businesses in the next six months. Suggest how each factor might affect businesses in your community.

Connect to ◀ DECA
An Association of Marketing Students

8. Your marketing research team works for a local movie theater. Your goal is to increase the number of movie-goers and the average amount each customer spends on concessions. As a team, determine three specific types of information you will need for each category: consumers, marketing mix, and business environment. Decide why each type of information is needed. Make a team presentation of your ideas to your teacher (judge).

Finding and Managing Marketing Information

GOALS

- Describe common sources of internal and external market information.
- Explain the five critical elements of an effective marketing information system.

KEY TERMS

internal information, *p. 128*

external information, *p. 130*

marketing information system (MkIS), *p. 131*

input, *p. 132*

storage, *p. 132*

analysis, *p. 133*

output, *p. 134*

marketing matters

One of the functions of marketing is marketing-information management. In Chapter 1, marketing-information management was defined as obtaining, managing, and using market information to improve decision making and the performance of marketing activities. In order to use information effectively, businesses have to first know where to find it. Once they have it, they need to develop marketing information systems to get the most out of it.

If your class decided to operate a concession stand at school events, what market information would you need to start the business? Identify five sources you could use to locate needed information. Discuss your ideas with other students.

Sources of Market Information

Where do you go to find the titles of the most recent movies available on DVD or for download from the Internet? What is a good source of information to help you learn about careers or college choices? If you want to know the best price to pay for a specific model of automobile, where do you turn for help? Each of these decisions requires information. For most decisions, there is usually more than one information source. Factors that influence your choice of an information source may include its availability, how quickly it can be accessed, how complete or accurate you believe it to be, and your past experience with the source.

Business people need information to make marketing decisions. As they determine what information they need and where to obtain it, they go through a similar process. The process can be summarized in the following steps:

1. Identify the types of information needed.
2. Determine the available sources of each type of information.
3. Evaluate each source to determine if it meets the organization's needs in terms of accuracy, time, detail, and cost.
4. Select the sources that best meet the identified needs.
5. Enter the information into a marketing information system.

Marketing information can come from one of three sources: internal sources, external sources, and marketing research. Internal and external information sources are discussed next while marketing research will be discussed in Lesson 5-3.

Internal Information Sources

Internal information is information developed from activities that occur within the organization. A great deal of information flows through a business. Much of it is useful for marketing decision making. Often, however, the information is not recorded or is not available to the right people or at the time when it would be useful for decisions. For example, salespeople learn a great deal from current and prospective customers. They get information about needs, perceptions of price, satisfaction with services, or requested changes in products. That information may never be communicated back to the company. Even if it is, it may not be part of the information reviewed when marketing plans are being developed.

Most businesses keep detailed records on production schedules and inventory levels. If the people planning special promotions are expected to increase demand for particular products, they should study that production and inventory information to make sure the promotions match the available products. Three categories of important types of internal information are customer records and sales information, production and operations reports, and performance information.

Customer Records and Sales Information

Customer information is essential in order to plan marketing directed at those customers. Therefore, customer records are an important information source. Many companies keep a complete record of all transactions they have with a customer. They record what is purchased, the dates of purchase, and the quantities purchased. If the customer purchases accessory or related products, then or at a later time, the information is also recorded and matched with the original purchase. Detailed information on payments and credit is also recorded. If the customer requires service, a service record is prepared. Customer problems and complaints should also be a part of their records. When a customer stops

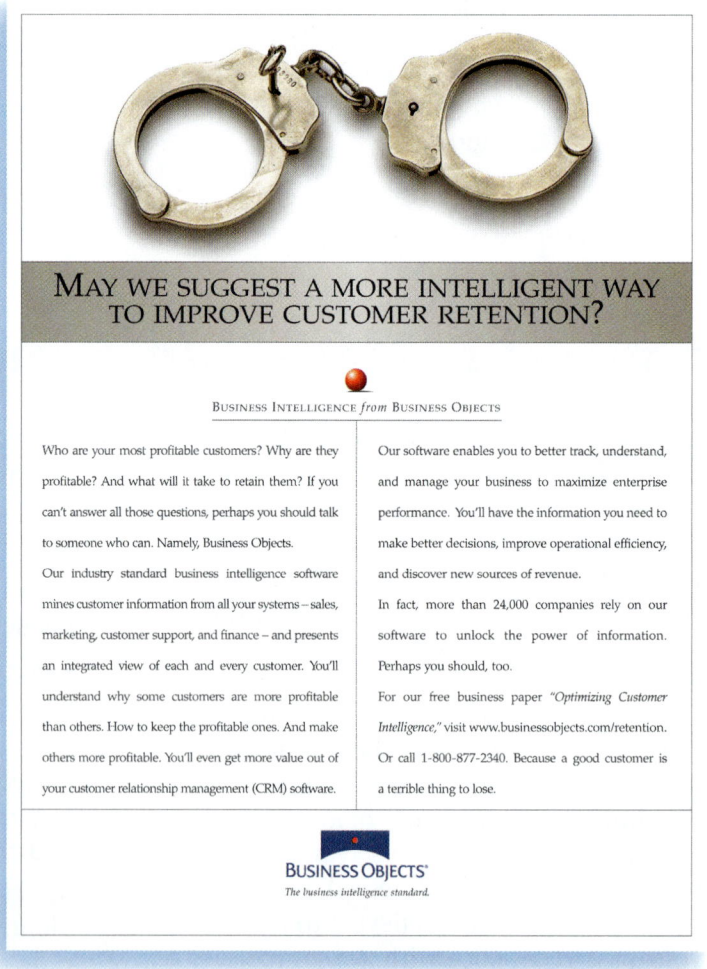

COURTESY BUSINESS OBJECTS

Detailed analysis of customer information can identify problems before customers are lost.

buying the product or service, the record should not be discarded. It should be analyzed to determine why the customer was lost.

To target products and marketing activities for specific customers, information more detailed than sales records is needed. That information includes demographic information such as age, family size, income, and mailing and e-mail addresses. Businesses need an understanding of customer needs, interests, and attitudes. They need to know how consumers make buying decisions, such as where they gather information, what choices are considered, where they decide to purchase, and when.

Customer information can be gathered through market research, but some businesses have discovered other ways to get it. Detailed profiles might be completed on a customer by the salesperson as a part of the selling process. Many realtors ask prospective buyers a great deal of information in order to locate the best possible home. Salespeople who work in clothing and apparel stores develop complete information on their regular customers' needs and preferences. Customers may be asked to provide profile information in response to an advertisement, special offer, or information request.

A relatively new information tool used by some businesses is a customer club. Prospective and current customers are provided with special incentives to join the club. In order to join, the consumer completes a detailed profile form. Based on that profile, each consumer is sent regular mailings or e-mail messages providing new product information, special purchase opportunities and discounts, and promotional information for products and services the company believes the customer will want to buy.

Some companies have used the consumer club or a similar tool to develop a consumer database of thousands of people. When that information is collected and maintained by the company, each individual must be informed of the recordkeeping and the company's privacy policies.

Effective security procedures must be put in place to protect the information from misuse, loss, or theft.

Production and Operations Reports

Production and operations activities are important to marketing. Products and services must be available when customers want them. Quality standards need to be met. Expenses need to be controlled in order to price products and services competitively. Information about production and operations activities is collected, but it might not be shared regularly with the people planning marketing activities.

When a business is a part of a distribution system working with a manufacturer, it is even more difficult to get needed information about production and operations. Often manufacturers do not believe channel members need that information, or they believe it is confidential and are unwilling to share it.

When companies that make up a channel of distribution work closely together and share operating information, they can meet customers' needs much better and can operate more efficiently. In that way all members of the channel benefit. Those companies have developed information systems that can share information about sales, costs, inventory levels, and production and delivery schedules.

Performance Information

The success of a business is judged by its performance. Some people believe the only important performance measure is profit, and managers certainly must pay attention to the bottom line. However, there are other performance measures that need to be watched along the way as well. The types of performance measures important to most businesses are sales, costs, quality, and customer satisfaction.

Performance is typically measured in one of three ways. For companies that have operated for a number of years, there are records of past performance. The current sales or costs can be compared to those of

How are a company's records of past performance useful to marketers?

a previous month or year to determine if performance is improving or declining.

A second method is to compare performance with that of similar businesses. Information on other businesses is available from external information sources.

The most important performance measure is the comparison of actual performance with expected or planned performance. When managers plan marketing activities, they develop goals, performance standards, and budgets. Those plans need to be compared frequently with actual performance to determine if the company is meeting expectations.

External Information Sources

External information provides an understanding of factors outside of the organization. Marketers cannot plan effectively without understanding consumers, competitors, the economy, and other changes going on around them. Marketing research is an important method of collecting and analyzing external information. In addition, there are many valuable sources of external information that businesses should be aware of and review regularly.

Government Reports People often think of regulation and taxation as the major roles of government in business. However, another important activity of federal, state, and local governments is to supply information that can be used by businesses and consumers. There are a number of agencies that regularly collect helpful marketing information.

Probably the best-known data-collection agency is the U.S. Bureau of the Census. Every ten years, the Census Bureau conducts a complete census of the country's population. The report of that census is very detailed and specific. It provides an excellent source to learn about the number of people and important characteristics of individuals and households in specific areas of the country. The Census of Population data is available in digital form for easier analysis. Some companies analyze census data and sell reports to businesses.

The population of the United States is not the only census completed by the federal government. Others include the Census of Manufacturers, Retail Trade, Wholesale Trade, Transportation, and County Business Patterns. Many of the studies are completed in full either every five years or every ten years. Moreover, the Census Bureau issues yearly updates of some data that are not as comprehensive.

There are literally thousands of other databases, reports, and information sources available from government offices. One of the most difficult parts of using government information is determining just what is available. Information is developed on agriculture, education, housing, health, and international trade as well as many other areas of interest to businesses. Much federal government data can now be accessed through links at its comprehensive information web site at FedStats.gov.

Trade and Professional Associations
Trade and professional associations are organized to serve people and businesses with common interests. Members of the association may be a part of the same industry, such as travel, retailing, exporting, or corn producers. Other associations, such as the American Management Association and the National Association of Professional and Executive Women, provide services for people in particular job categories.

Most associations provide information specific to the needs of their members. That information may be disseminated through web sites, journals, newsletters, or more detailed research reports. Some associations have research services, libraries, or data services that can be used by members.

Business Publications
Magazines and journals provide useful information for business people. Those publications include general business newspapers and magazines such as *The Wall Street Journal, Forbes,* and *BusinessWeek,* as well as more specialized publications such as *Black Enterprise, American Demographics,* or *E-Commerce Times.* Business publications are useful sources of current information on the economy, legislation, new technology, or business ideas. Often the publications devote specific issues or sections to analysis of special topics or data important to their subscribers.

Working in **Teams**

Discuss with your team members why both businesses and consumers must be concerned about the privacy of information that is used by businesses to make marketing decisions. Agree on three recommendations to make to consumers and three to make to business people about information privacy.

Commercial Data and Information Services
There are a number of businesses that collect, analyze, and sell data. Experian, Equifax, and TransUnion are the three major credit reporting agencies for consumer credit. Dun & Bradstreet maintains the largest worldwide business database and offers tailored reports to its customers. ACNielsen is one of the best known of many companies that conduct market research on a number of topics and sell the information to business customers.

Checkpoint ▶▶

What is the key difference between internal and external market information?

Marketing Information Systems

Businesses need a great deal of information to operate successfully. With all of the information needed, business people could spend most of their time gathering and studying information. A **marketing information system** (MkIS, pronounced M-K-I-S) is an organized method of collecting, storing, analyzing, and retrieving information to improve the effectiveness and efficiency of marketing decisions.

Managing Information

Each business develops its own marketing information system. In some new, small businesses, an MkIS may be as simple as a filing cabinet in which the owner collects, organizes, and stores customer information, business records, and other information important to the business. Even the smallest businesses are now usually maintaining computerized records as well. In large businesses, there may be an information management unit with a dedicated computer system and a staff of people who collect and analyze information and prepare reports. Marketing managers carefully design MkISs to provide important information to make decisions. The information has to be complete, accurate, easy to use, timely, affordable, and cost-effective.

All effective marketing information systems contain five elements. Those elements are input, storage, analysis, output, and decision making. They are illustrated in Figure 5-2.

Designing a Marketing Information System

In planning an MkIS, several questions need to be answered. The questions and their results are shown in Figure 5-3 on the next page.

Input How do you make decisions? If you want to be as objective as possible and make good decisions, you must gather information. **Input** is the information that goes into the system that is needed for decision making.

A great deal of routine information results from the regular operations of a business. Routine information about customers, competitors, and business operations is used for marketing decisions. Marketers need to know what customers purchase, in what quantities, and at what prices. They must know where customers buy their products and what factors influence them.

Marketing is influenced by the activities of competitors. Information is needed on which businesses are competing in specific markets, the marketing mixes they use, their strengths and weaknesses, their market share, and their profitability. Marketers can use information about business operations to determine what activities are effective or ineffective.

Occasionally, additional information that is not routinely collected by the business is needed for a decision. In that situation, a marketing research procedure is used to collect the information.

Storage Have you ever rushed to a class only to discover that your assignment was not in your notebook? Many of us are very good at collecting information. We may not be as good at storing it where we can locate it when needed. **Storage**

| Input | Storage | Analysis | Output | Decision Making |

FIGURE 5-2

An example of a computer-based MkIS.

FIGURE 5-3

A marketing information system (MkIS) is designed to help marketers obtain, store, organize, and use information to improve decisions.

Designing an MkIS	
Question	**MkIS Element**
What information is needed to develop and implement the marketing strategy?	Input
How should the information be maintained so it is in a usable form, secure, and easy to access when needed?	Storage
What methods should be used to organize and study the information in order to make effective marketing decisions?	Analysis
How and when should the information be made available for most effective use?	Output
What ways should the information be used to improve marketing?	Decision Making

involves the resources used to maintain information, including equipment and procedures, so that it can be used when needed.

A storage system in an MkIS has several characteristics. Most important, it must protect the information. If information is lost or damaged, it is not useful when a decision must be made. Some business information is very confidential. The storage system should be designed so that only authorized people can access the information. Finally, the storage system should be organized so that information is easy to locate when it is needed.

Most of the information storage in businesses today is done using computer technology. After data is entered into the computer, it is stored and maintained on a hard drive, recordable CD, flash medium, or other storage device. Careful planning is done to make sure that back-up copies of all data are maintained and that information is secure. Some information and records are still maintained on paper and must be organized and stored in filing cabinets.

Analysis Information in an MkIS is collected and maintained in order to improve decision making. **Analysis** is the process of summarizing, combining, or comparing information so that decisions can be made. In order to plan a promotional budget, a manager may examine the budgets for other products or for past years. The effectiveness of one retailer in a channel of distribution may not be apparent until that company's sales are compared with those of similar companies. The costs of marketing activities for national and international activities need to be combined to determine the total marketing costs.

The type of analysis needed is usually determined when planning the marketing information system. Procedures are developed to obtain needed information from storage, to organize it, and to complete the needed analysis. Specific computer programs are available that assist with those procedures. For example, database and spreadsheet programs have procedures for common types of business data analysis using pre-developed formulas and graphing tools. Companies that complete a large amount of data analysis usually employ people skilled in organizing and analyzing data.

Digital Photos Speed Products to Market

As the cost of digital photography declines and makes it affordable for more and more people, some businesses are cashing in on its advantages over film photography. PetSmart Inc., which sells pet products through stores, a web site, and a mail-order catalog, has used digital photography to slash the time it takes to bring new products to market. What used to take two or three months is now done in one month.

Digital photographs are transmitted over the Internet between the company's buyers and suppliers. Buyers show suppliers what colors they want or send sketches of new product ideas. Suppliers transmit images of products in development and get instantaneous approval to go ahead or instructions to make changes. The company not only stays on top of its market but also saves lots of money by eliminating the need for much overseas travel.

The National Football League has also used digital photography to get products on the market quickly, taking maximum advantage of fans' Super Bowl enthusiasm before it cools off in the days after the game. Using digital photographs, it cuts at least one day off its production schedule for Super Bowl commemorative books. Those small but critical time savings can translate into a huge difference in profits.

Think Critically

1. What are the advantages of bringing products to market more quickly?

2. What do you think might be some drawbacks to using digital photography?

Output For managers and other decision makers, the most important part of an MkIS is the output. Many people never see information being collected, stored, or analyzed. They are given only summaries or reports to use in decision making. **Output** is the result of analysis given to decision makers.

Output is usually written information or graphics. It is provided in print form or accessed by decision makers using a computer. If it is not well organized or if it uses language or data that is difficult to understand, it may be misused or not used at all.

People who need output to make decisions should have access to it. However, business output is often confidential, and access is restricted and secure. The use of the Internet to store and access information makes data security a bigger issue than it was in the past.

Decision Making The purpose of a marketing information system is to improve decision making. Decisions should be better and should be made more quickly if an MkIS is well designed. The decision-making process includes who is involved in the decision, when decisions need to be made, any policies or procedures that should be considered, and the information needed by the decision makers.

Some decisions are routine, and the result of the analysis will determine the decision that should be made. For example, information in the MkIS of an office supply store shows that inventory levels of computer paper have dropped to a level where it needs to be reordered. The analysis program in the computer determines that 200 cases of paper are needed. It searches the vendor list to determine which approved vendor has the lowest current price. The vendor is selected, the reorder quantity is identified, and a purchase order is sent to the vendor. This type of routine decision requires no management attention.

Other decisions are unique. A major credit card company considers whether to offer a money-back guarantee on all products consumers purchase using the card. The guarantee is viewed as an important service that will encourage people to use the credit card and could attract many more customers. The results will affect the company, the businesses that accept the credit card, and competing credit card companies. The decision to add the guarantee means important changes in the entire marketing mix. Once the company announces the new service, it will be difficult to end the service even if it proves to be too expensive to maintain. That decision requires a great deal of time and information, and many of the company's managers will be involved in making it.

Checkpoint ▶▶

What are the five elements of an effective marketing information system, or MkIS?

5-2 Assessment

Xtra!
Study Tools
school.cengage.com/marketing/marketing

Key Concepts

Determine the best answer.

1. Which of the following is *not* an example of an internal information source?
   a. customer records
   b. production reports
   c. census data
   d. sales, costs, and quality reports

2. True or False: There are a number of businesses that collect, analyze, and sell data that businesses can use to meet their information needs.

3. The resources used to maintain information, including equipment and procedures, so that it can be used when needed is
   a. input
   b. storage
   c. analysis
   d. output

4. With an effective MkIS, no management attention is needed for decisions that are
   a. internal
   b. external
   c. unique
   d. routine

Make Academic Connections

5. **Technology** Use the Internet to locate three sources of information you would recommend to a small business owner as an aid in planning. Use computer presentation software and develop three slides that describe the information sources and why you are recommending each one.

6. **Success Skills** Choose one of the following personal decisions—choosing a college or applying for a full-time job after graduation. Describe five types of information you will need for the decision and five information sources you will use. Now write a two-sentence description of each of the components of an MkIS that will help you make the decision.

Connect to ◀ DECA
An Association of Marketing Students

7. Some business people are concerned about the time and expense required to gather and analyze all of the information needed to make marketing decisions. Develop a two-minute persuasive speech to convince a business owner of the value of marketing information. Make sure to address both concerns of time and cost. Give your speech to your teacher (judge).

Using Marketing Research

GOALS

- Describe how to define and develop an understanding of a problem as the first steps toward solving it.
- Identify the steps needed to gather and study data relevant to a problem.
- Explain how to prepare reports and present proposed solutions.

KEY TERMS

marketing research, *p. 136*

secondary data, *p. 137*

primary data, *p. 138*

population, *p. 138*

sample, *p. 138*

random sampling, *p. 138*

marketing matters

A well-organized and efficient marketing information system should provide the information needed for regular and routine decisions. However, marketers are also required to make decisions that relate to one-time problems or new situations. That often presents the need for information that has not been anticipated or previously collected. Marketing research uses tried and tested problem-solving procedures to gather the information needed.

Suppose the number of students in your school is increasing so rapidly the current facilities are no longer adequate but more space is not available. The school board asks for alternatives for handling more students including alternative schedules, temporary facilities, or other possibilities. How could you use marketing research to help them gather information to aid them with the decision? Discuss your ideas with other students.

Seeing the Problem Clearly

Suppose a business is considering entering a new market in which it has no previous experience. Maybe a company's engineers have developed a prototype product that has never been sold before. In situations like that, the company's MkIS will likely not have adequate information to support the required marketing decisions. **Marketing research** is a procedure designed to identify solutions to a specific marketing problem through the use of scientific problem solving.

You have probably studied and used scientific problem solving in many other classes. If you have, you already know the steps involved in that process. Those steps are shown in Figure 5-4. The scientific

method is used to ensure that a careful and objective procedure is followed in order to develop the best possible solution.

FIGURE 5-4
Effective marketing research uses the scientific problem-solving procedure.

Implementing a Marketing Research Study
1. Define the Problem
2. Analyze the Situation
3. Develop a Data-Collection Procedure
4. Gather and Study Information
5. Propose a Solution

Define the Problem

Marketing research is used when a business needs to solve a specific and unique problem. The first step is to be certain that the problem is clearly and carefully defined. That is not always an easy step. Sometimes the problem is very clear— to identify the characteristics of a market or select a new advertising medium. In other cases, you may not know the real problem. If sales are declining, the problem might be that customers' needs are changing, they are dissatisfied with some part of the marketing mix, or a competitor may have introduced a new product choice. Consumers may believe the economy is not strong and may be less willing to spend money. Usually decision makers and researchers gather and study specific information before the problem becomes clear.

It is important to prepare a written statement of the problem and have several people review it to make sure it is understandable. The problem should be specific enough that researchers know what to study, whom to involve in the study, and the types of solutions or results that might be appropriate.

Analyze the Situation

An important part of scientific problem solving is to understand the circumstances surrounding the problem well enough to determine how to solve it. Analyzing the situation allows the researcher to identify what is already known about the problem, the information currently available, and even possible solutions that have already been attempted.

During the analysis step, the researcher reviews available information and gathers information from people who might have ideas or additional information. Reviewing similar problems or previous studies can help the researcher decide how to approach the current problem.

It is possible that a careful situation analysis by itself may result in the identification of a solution. If the decision maker is confident in the proposed solution and has limited time or money to study the problem further, the marketing research process will come to an end. A good marketing information system will frequently provide the necessary information so that further study is not needed.

Develop a Data-Collection Procedure

After thoroughly reviewing the situation and the available information, the researcher decides what additional information is needed and how it should be collected. In this step, the actual marketing research study is planned. The researcher needs to know where to obtain information and the best and most efficient ways to obtain the information. There are two types of data that can be collected—secondary data and primary data.

Secondary Data Information already collected for another purpose that can be used to solve the current problem is **secondary data**. Examples of secondary

NETBookmark

The Statistical Abstract of the United States is one of the best external sources to find information to use as part of marketing planning. Would information from the Abstract be considered primary data or secondary data? Explain. Access school.cengage.com/marketing/marketing and click on the link for Chapter 5. Suppose you manufacture a kosher food product that you think would be of interest to Jewish Americans. Use information found in the Abstract to find three states that might be good markets for your product. (Hint: Click the Population link at the left of the home page.) Explain your reasoning.

school.cengage.com/marketing/marketing

data include company records, government reports, studies completed by colleges and universities, information from industry trade associations and other business groups, and research reported in magazines.

Primary Data Information collected for the first time to solve the problem being studied is **primary data**. It is obtained through data collection designed specifically in response to current needs of the company.

Checkpoint ▶▶▶

Once a problem has been clearly defined, what three things should a marketer identify?

Gather Information

Have you ever participated in a marketing research study? A common research method is to question study participants. A great deal of specific information can be obtained using questionnaires presented online or sent through the mail, with telephone interviews, or by stopping people in shopping malls to ask questions. No matter what method is used to gather the information, procedures must be carefully developed and followed to be sure the results are accurate.

Select the Participants

The selection of participants in marketing research is one of the most important decisions to be made. In most situations, there are many more potential consumers than a company can afford to involve in the research. Researchers usually collect information from a small percentage of possible consumers. In order for the results to be accurate and the research to be useful, that smaller group must be representative so that its members will give responses similar to those of the larger group. Research results will be misleading if they do not reflect the views or behavior of the prospective customers.

Researchers use several terms to describe the people who are the focus of study. All of the people in the group the company is interested in studying are known as the **population**. A smaller group selected from the population is a **sample**. To make sure a sample is representative of the larger group, the researcher will use random sampling. With **random sampling**, everyone in the population has an equal chance of being selected in the sample.

Working in **Teams**

Work with a team. Discuss with your team members how you would go about identifying a random sample of the students in your school for a survey? For what types of student issues or concerns might a random sample of all students not be the best approach?

Collect the Data

Research procedures should be carefully planned in advance to ensure that needed information is obtained and that the collection and review of information is done objectively. Procedures for primary data collection are particularly important. When gathering information directly from other people, researchers must be careful to maintain the privacy of the individual and treat the person ethically. A great deal of consumer research is conducted by telephone calls to people's homes. The number of calls and the time of day when people are called may upset many people. Some businesses unethically tell consumers that they are conducting a research study when they are really collecting personal information or attempting to sell a product or service.

Analyze the Data

Once information is collected, it needs to be reviewed to determine whether it can aid in developing a solution to the problem. For small amounts of information or simple studies, the information may not be difficult to review. However, most marketing research studies collect a large amount of information that requires a great deal of analysis. Therefore, most research is analyzed using computers and statistical programs in order to increase the speed and accuracy of obtaining the results.

After the study is complete, researchers examine the information collected. That information may be in the form of answers to surveys, observations that have been recorded, or data collected from an experiment. The information needs to be organized so that it is meaningful and easy to study in order to solve the problem for which the research was conducted.

Numerical Data Numerical data are the easiest to organize. Researchers total the number of responses to each question or for each factor being observed. When more than one group is involved in the research, it is typical to compare the responses of the groups. The simplest form of comparison is done by calculating the percentage of responses or average response (mean, median) of each group. Advanced levels of comparison can be made to determine the relationships between two or more variables. For example, the researcher may want to study the relationship between the number of times an advertisement runs on a television station and the number of customers who call a business seeking information about a product. Another comparison could be to determine if there is a relationship between the price of a product and the level of customer satisfaction identified through a survey of recent purchasers.

Non-Numerical Data Some research information is not numerical, so it is much more difficult to analyze. When customers respond to open-ended

Completing business on the Internet provides ready access to important customer information.

questions or observers describe how a consumer acted in a specific situation, there is not a common set of specific answers recorded. There are special methods for people trained to analyze that type of information. Results can be classified into broad categories that are identified before the information is collected or categories that are determined by looking for similar ideas from the responses. That type of classification allows for summaries of the non-numerical information.

Prepare Results

The results of the study are usually organized into tables, charts, and graphs. Pie charts and bar graphs are common ways of summarizing information. This makes it easier for decision makers to analyze a great deal of information in a brief time and to make comparisons of information from different groups and sources.

The results of the research are often summarized and analyzed in more than one way. That allows marketers to consider several possible solutions. Studying and analyzing marketing research is an important marketing skill. Marketing research departments and companies employ research analysts to complete those tasks.

Checkpoint ▶▶

Why is it important to select the right participants from which to collect data?

Propose a Solution

The purpose of marketing research is to identify strategies for a company to follow in implementing and improving marketing activities. Scientific problem solving often begins with the development of a hypothesis (or possible solution) to the problem. After the research results have been organized, they need to be studied to determine if the findings support the proposed solution or suggest an alternative solution.

In most cases, the marketing researchers completing the study do not make the final decisions about solutions. Instead, they prepare a report of the research results that is presented to decision makers who carefully study the report. Since decision makers use the results to help them with decision making, the report needs to be accurate, understandable, and meaningful.

©GETTY IMAGES/PHOTODISC

How do marketing research reports help in the decision-making process?

Research Reports

Marketing research reports are usually presented orally and in writing. Effective communication is an important skill for all marketers, especially market researchers. When a report is being prepared, two items are very important. First, the people preparing the report must know who will be receiving and studying the report. Just as a marketing mix should respond to the needs of customers, the research report must be prepared to meet the needs of its users. Second, the report must clearly describe the purpose of the study and the research procedures followed to collect the information. Without an understanding of the problem being studied and the methods used, those receiving the report may misunderstand or misinterpret the results.

A research report, whether written or oral, is usually organized just like the study. A research report begins with a statement of the problem or the purpose of the research and includes a brief discussion of why the study was needed. Then it summarizes the secondary data that was collected.

The third part is a description of the procedures used in the study. This includes the population studied and the way a sample was obtained. It also describes the method used to collect information including surveys, observations, or experiments. The report continues by presenting the results of the research and concludes with a summary and recommendations.

Understand Basic Statistics

Numbers are important to marketers and to every business person. Business people are presented with a variety of numerical data and must be able to understand the information and use it to make decisions. Are sales, profits and expenses increasing or declining? Are products profitable or not? Do we have a greater share of a market than our competitors?

Consumers may not use numbers as frequently as business people but must also be able to understand numbers they encounter—"50% off"; "10.5% financing available." How do those numbers influence your decisions?

Statistics is a type of mathematics that analyzes and presents numerical data in understandable forms including tables, charts, and graphs. Statistics are used to describe the characteristics of a group of numbers so they can be interpreted, compared, and used for decision making.

Your teacher hands back a test, and you received a "B" for a grade. While you may feel good (unless you expected an "A"), you really don't know a lot about your performance. If you answered 86 of 100 items correctly, you know a bit more about your performance. If your teacher tells you the average score of the 40 students in the class was 83, you know even more and can compare your performance to others.

How would the additional information provided below affect your understanding of your performance and that of the other students?

- Student test scores ranged from 97 – 63.
- More students scored 85 than any other score.
- The distribution of grades was 4 A's, 13 B's, 20 C's, 2 D's and 1 F.

The statistics helps you better understand your performance because you recognize how your grade and score compare with other students like you who took the same test. To understand and use statistics you need the following information.

Do you have an adequate amount of information to make a decision? One or two test scores tell you little about your possible semester grade. Knowing how three or four students performed does not give a true indication of how you performed in a class of 40.

Is the information representative of all of the information available? If student scores on this test are very much higher or lower than typical tests, you won't know very much about your overall performance.

Is the information presented in a way to aid understanding or does it confuse or mislead? Tables, graphs, and charts may leave out important information or present it in such a way that it misrepresents the real meaning.

Develop Your Skill

Over a period of several weeks, collect ten examples of statistics used by businesses in news stories and advertisements. Classify each example in a 3-row × 2-column table according to the following categories.

Row 1—the statistics DO or DO NOT present an adequate amount of information to be understandable and useful.

Row 2—the statistics DO or DO NOT appear to be representative of all of the related information available.

Row 3—the statistics DO or DO NOT appear to be presented to confuse or mislead the reader.

Now, develop charts or graphs that communicate the results of your research in an understandable and meaningful way.

Today's Fragmented Media

Fifty years ago, people got their information from a limited number of media outlets. Towns had one or two newspapers; there were only a few network television and radio stations; and there were a limited number of magazines.

Today, cable and satellite television offer hundreds of stations; bookstores carry magazines that cater to every interest, lifestyle, and hobby; there is AM, FM, and satellite radio; and the Internet is growing exponentially. While there are more media sources from which to choose, in general, each one draws less of an audience because viewers are now spread over more media outlets—a phenomenon known as media fragmentation.

What increasingly fragmented media mean to marketers is that they have to work harder to reach a broad audience. A TV commercial during the most popular show today will not reach as many people as one during the most popular show in 1980. Today, marketers might have to run the commercial on many different stations.

Think Critically

1. What are some advantages to consumers of media that is fragmented?

2. How do fragmented media make it easier for marketers to reach potential buyers?

Presenting Research Results

The most important part of the research report is the presentation of the results of the research. In a written report, the results are presented in the form of tables, charts, and graphs with brief written explanations. In an oral presentation, the results are presented using visuals. Those visuals are usually presented as computer slides projected during the presentation. They often are supported with printed information with the presenter providing explanations and answering questions.

Finally, the research report concludes with a summary that emphasizes the most important information from the study. It may also contain recommendations for solutions if they have been requested. Sometimes the research will not completely demonstrate that a solution will be successful. Marketers will need to decide if they have enough information or if they need to continue to study the problem.

When to Use Marketing Research

Some business people think marketing research is too time consuming and expensive. These people believe they have enough knowledge and experience to make good decisions. Others rely too much on marketing research. They spend too much time and money trying to ensure they have as much information as possible before making decisions.

Although marketing research can be very expensive and time consuming, it can be a valuable tool. Deciding whether to use research is based on two factors. How much risk is the business facing from the problem being studied, and how much time and money will be required to gather the information?

If there is little risk or if possible solutions are not particularly expensive to implement, there is little need for research. However, if a business faces a complex issue that may substantially affect sales, costs, and profits, research will be very important.

Since many decisions must be made almost instantaneously, most businesses maintain research budgets and conduct ongoing studies to reduce the time needed to gather information. Businesses try to reduce the need for special research studies by building extensive information databases as a part of their MkIS. Today's marketers recognize the value of using information to support marketing planning.

Checkpoint ▶▶▶

What two things are important when preparing a research report?

5-3 Assessment

Key Concepts

Determine the best answer.

1. The first step in the marketing research process is to
   a. study secondary data
   b. select the sample to be studied
   c. identify the problem
   d. propose alternative solutions

2. Information already collected for another purpose that can be used to solve the current problem is
   a. primary data
   b. secondary data
   c. research results
   d. summary data

3. With _____, everyone in the population has an equal chance of being selected in the sample.

4. True or False: Numerical data are easier to organize for analysis than non-numerical data.

5. Which is *not* one of the factors that should be considered when deciding whether to use marketing research?
   a. How much risk is the business facing?
   b. How much time and money will be required to gather the information?
   c. Do decision makers believe they have enough knowledge and experience to make the decision?
   d. All are important factors.

Make Academic Connections

6. **Ethics** Use the Internet to locate information on the rights of research participants. Based on that information prepare a one-paragraph ethics statement that could be used by marketing researchers to make sure they respect and protect the rights of consumers who might be asked to participate in research studies.

7. **Technology** A company randomly surveyed 350 customers about their preferred method of receiving information about special promotions. The results were: 140, enclosed with the monthly credit statement; 102, an e-mail message; 68, a special mailing for each promotion; 40, don't want promotional information sent. Use computer software to develop a table and a pie chart or bar graph to present the results of the survey.

Connect to DECA

8. Your local DECA chapter has a large membership, but attendance at monthly after-school meetings is frequently low, and only about 30 percent of members participate in the competitive events programs. You have been asked to recommend marketing research that will help the chapter develop a solution to the problem. Develop a written outline of the study, making sure to follow the steps in scientific problem solving. Prepare a two-minute presentation of your marketing research plan and present it to your teacher (judge). Be prepared to answer questions about your plan.

Collecting Primary Data

GOALS

- Describe the purpose of marketing research surveys.
- Explain the reasons for and limitations of using observation.
- Define various types of marketing research experiments.

KEY TERMS

survey, *p. 144*

closed-ended questions, *p. 144*

open-ended questions, *p. 144*

focus group, *p. 145*

observation, *p. 146*

experiments, *p. 147*

test markets, *p. 148*

simulations, *p. 148*

marketing matters

When completing marketing research, the data-collection method chosen will depend on the type of information you need. To find out how people shop for a product, you might use a different method than you would if you wanted to know how they use the product. A different method would be used to determine consumers' attitudes toward advertising than to identify the quantity of a product they consumed during the year. The data-collection method should be as efficient as possible to collect accurate data.

Survey a dozen people, and ask them to tell you the current time without looking at a watch or a clock. Note the actual time of each observation, and make a chart of the differences between the responses you get and the actual times. Discuss with other students what the exercise tells you about appropriate data-collection procedures and accuracy.

Conducting Surveys

A **survey** is a planned set of questions to which individuals or groups of people respond. The survey can be completed orally or by recorded responses. People can be surveyed in person, through the mail, by telephone, by e-mail or online, or even by using interactive technologies. With some methods, consumers are presented with questions on a computer or television screen. They may key their responses on the computer keyboard, push buttons on a special keypad provided by the researcher, or enter information on a touch-tone telephone.

Most surveys use **closed-ended questions** that offer two or more choices as answers, such as:

- yes or no

- agree or disagree
- select a, b, c, or d
- rate this item on a scale of 1-10

Occasionally, researchers will use **open-ended questions** to allow respondents to develop their own answers without additional information about possible choices. Examples of open-ended questions include:

- What are the most important features of this product?
- How does the durability of brand A compare to brand B?
- How did you feel about your shopping experience at Z-Mart?

What are the advantages of conducting a survey in person?

Focusing on the Issues

Open-ended questions are often used when researchers are attempting to identify the problem or are completing a situational analysis. They may not be certain of which alternatives to include in a closed-ended survey. In that case, researchers may discuss the problems with consumers using open-ended questions to get more specific information.

A popular research method used to gather information using open-ended questions is a focus group. A **focus group** is a small number of people brought together to discuss identified elements of an issue or problem. Focus group participants are carefully selected to ensure that the group is representative of a larger group of people or because participants are experts about the topic being studied. A skilled moderator uses a planned set of open-ended questions to guide the discussion and gather ideas. The discussion is videotaped or recorded, and a summary is prepared for analysis.

Questioning with Clarity

It is important that survey questions are carefully written. Each question must aid in the collection of information that will help to solve the problem. They must be written in such a way that each respondent understands what is being asked, is encouraged to respond honestly, and is not directed toward one answer so that the results

Fast **FACTS**

Face-to-face interviews have been the most popular method of collecting marketing research information. However, in recent years, its use has declined from about one-third of all research to less than 20 percent. Telephone surveys are now the most popular data-collection method, with online surveys growing rapidly to be used almost as much as face-to-face.

are biased. Questions should be short, clear, and simple. Each question should deal with only one concept and use language that is easily understood by the respondent.

The survey should be organized in a way that makes it as easy as possible to complete. Directions should be given so that the respondent knows how to record answers and what to do with the survey when finished. The respondent should be assured that the answers will be treated confidentially.

Surveys should ask only those questions that are necessary to accomplish the objectives of the research. Many people will not answer surveys that appear to be too long or complex. Gathering unnecessary information can be both misleading and, in some cases, unethical. It may also provide confusion in solving the marketing problem by introducing information that is not relevant.

Checkpoint

What is a common reason to use open-ended survey questions?

Making Observations

A second method of gathering research information is by observation. **Observation** collects information by recording actions without interacting or communicating with the participant. The purpose of observation research is to see the actions of the participants rather than to have them recall or predict their actions. This usually results in greater accuracy and objectivity. However, using observations to gather data normally requires more time and expense than using surveys. It is difficult to gather information from a large number of participants using observation.

Observations must be carefully planned in order to keep from changing the participants' actions as a result of the observation. If people know they are being watched, they may do things very differently. Trained observers typically know what to observe and how to record information quickly and accurately. In some situations observations can be made using technology with video cameras, audio tape recordings, or with other types of equipment designed to gather information about the actions of people. A common example of the use of equipment is the bar code scanners used at the checkout counters of many retail stores. They can record the types and quantities of products purchased, the timing of purchases, how payment was made, whether coupons or other promotions were used, and what items were purchased at the same time. You can learn about purchasing behavior in that way without asking the consumer any questions.

Another unique equipment-based observation method is the use of eye-tracking photography. A retail store may be interested in how customers examine displays. Through the use of close-up photography, researchers record where the eyes look first, how long customers focus on certain products, how they search the entire display, and what they look at when making a product choice. This information can be very helpful in organizing displays and placing specific brands in the displays. The same type of equipment is used to study how consumers read magazine and newspaper advertisements or view web pages on the Internet.

Some observations are made without consumers even being aware that they are being observed. Researchers are interested in learning how participants behave in normal situations. In other cases, researchers may ask people to participate in a planned situation. In these cases, the researcher wants to learn how people respond to specific, controlled activities. For

Virtual Marketing

Interactivity Propels Kiosks

At one time, retailers thought video kiosks were going to revolutionize the way people shop. But aside from bank ATMs, kiosks were slow to catch on. The development of the World Wide Web and high-speed data transfers, however, may have supplied the missing ingredients needed for kiosks to take off.

Interactive kiosks can be networked and monitored from a central location through a retailer's web site. Instead of delivering the same information or promotions to every user, they can identify individuals and customize each presentation based on their buying habits or personal preferences.

Moreover, the enhanced capabilities of interactive kiosks arrived at the same time that the cost of hardware and software was coming down dramatically. For a fraction of the monthly cost of a minimum-wage employee, a kiosk can supply customers with information, distribute coupons and other individualized promotions, or process orders and sales transactions.

For retailers and shoppers, kiosks can deliver the combined advantages of in-store and online shopping. Because they are so versatile and inexpensive, they are particularly effective for small retail chains that can react quickly to changes in the market.

Think Critically

1. How many times in the past month have you used a kiosk? What did you use it for?

2. Name some applications for kiosks that you have seen recently.

3. Describe some new applications for kiosks that you think would be good marketing tools for retailers or other businesses.

---

example, a business might want to know how customers would react if a different type of sales presentation is used. Another example would be to study consumer responses to a new piece of equipment, such as the keypad layout on a cell phone.

Checkpoint ▶▶

Why are the results of observations generally considered more accurate than survey results?

Performing Experiments

The most precise and objective information is obtained through experimentation. **Experiments** are carefully designed and controlled situations in which all important factors are the same except the one being studied. Scientific research is done by planning and implementing experiments and then recording and analyzing the data. Marketers use experiments to determine whether changes in a single element of the marketing mix will affect customer behavior.

Experiments are not used as often in marketing research as surveys or observations. That may be because it is difficult to carefully control factors related to a marketing experiment while making them realistic for consumers. It also takes a great deal of time to organize an experiment and operate it long enough to determine if significant differences result. The actions of competitors can affect experiments undertaken in actual markets.

Marketers often conduct experiments where one group of participants is given different marketing mix information than other groups. What do you think marketers can learn from this kind of experiment?

Implementing the marketing concept suggests many opportunities for research to determine the best market segments to serve and the appropriate mix elements to provide. A company may want to determine if a customer's geographic location makes a difference in purchasing behavior. An experiment in which two groups of customers from different areas are provided the same marketing mix may help to answer the question. A business owner may be uncertain about the effect of a price increase on sales volume. An experiment can be developed in which everything except the price is held the same for two groups of customers. One group is given a discount while the other is not. The experiment can demonstrate changes in the amount of sales resulting from the price difference.

Test Markets

Because of the need for control over important conditions, experiments are difficult to manage. Some companies have developed test markets. **Test markets** are

specific cities or geographic areas in which marketing experiments are conducted. The test markets are selected because they reflect consumer and competitive characteristics important to the company.

To prepare for a test market, companies gather detailed information about consumers, competitors, and past marketing activities in the area. The companies try new product ideas or make marketing changes in the test markets. They collect data on the product performance for a period of several weeks or months and compare it with previously gathered information. In this way, they can attempt to predict the performance in their total market based on the results in the test market.

Simulations

Sometimes experiments are not possible in actual markets. **Simulations** are experiments where researchers create the situation to be studied. For example, a business may want to see how children respond when playing with a new toy. Rather than observing children playing in their homes or schools, the business may organize a play center. Then they bring groups of children into the center and observe them under more carefully controlled circumstances. An automobile maker trying to improve the driving experience can build a small area that duplicates the front seat and dashboard of a car. By changing the design and positions of the seat, steering wheel, and controls, the company can determine which is most satisfying.

Many simulations are now done on computers. Computer graphics allow research participants to visualize a change and react to it. Architects can use computer software to develop a complete external view of a proposed building from all sides. The software allows the viewer to enter all doors and immediately see the interior of a room. The software could be used to test consumers' attitudes about changes in the architectural plans of the building before final design decisions are made.

Checkpoint ▶▶▶

What is the main benefit of using experiments compared with other methods of collecting primary data?

5-4 Assessment

Key Concepts

Determine the best answer.

1. Examples of answers to closed-ended survey questions include all of the following *except*
   a. yes–no
   b. choose a, b, c, or d
   c. rate the items on a scale of 1–10
   d. all are examples

2. A small number of people brought together to discuss identified elements of an issue or problem are called a(n)
   a. focus group
   b. simulation
   c. test market
   d. experiment

3. True or False: To make surveys shorter, each question should try to incorporate several concepts that need to be tested.

4. An effective test market is one
   a. in which there is very little direct competition
   b. that is cheaper to reach than other markets
   c. where the business has never sold products
   d. that reflects important consumer and competitive characteristics

Make Academic Connections

5. **Communication** Join with five to eight students to form a marketing research focus group. Assign one member as the facilitator and one member as a recorder. The topic of the focus group is positive and negative customer service experiences. When you have finished, have the recorder summarize the results of the discussion.

6. **Science** Prepare a two-paragraph written comparison of the similarities and differences between conducting an experiment in a science laboratory and conducting a marketing experiment in a test market. Based on your understanding of the scientific process, make two recommendations of how to conduct effective marketing experiments.

Connect to ◆DECA
An Association of Marketing Students

7. Your marketing research team is responsible for surveying parents about the important factors they consider when choosing a restaurant for dining with their children. Prepare a written survey with three closed-ended and two open-ended questions that demonstrate principles of effective questions. Present your survey to your teacher (judge) and explain why each question was included and the value of the results of the research.

Chapter 5 Assessment

Check Your Understanding

Now that you have completed the chapter, check your understanding of the lessons with these questions. Record the score that best represents your understanding of each marketing concept.

1 = not at all; 3 = somewhat; 5 = very well

If your score is 42–50, you are ready for the assessment activities that follow. If you score 33–41, you should review the lessons for the items you scored 1–3. If you score 32 or less, you will want to carefully reread the lessons and work with a study partner on the areas you do not understand.

Can you—

___ explain why marketing decisions are better when decision makers gather and analyze information?

___ identify the three main categories of information needed for marketing planning?

___ differentiate between internal and external information and offer examples of each?

___ identify the five elements of a marketing information system and explain the purpose of each element?

___ explain the importance of correctly identifying a problem in order to solve it?

___ list the steps of the scientific problem-solving process?

___ outline the main sections of a research report?

___ identify several characteristics of effective survey questions?

___ provide an example of using observation as a marketing research method?

___ explain the advantages and disadvantages of using experiments for marketing research?

Review Marketing Terms

Match the terms listed on top of the next page with the definitions. Some terms may not be used.

1. A procedure in which everyone in the population has an equal chance of being selected in a sample

2. The result of analysis that is given to decision makers

3. Questions that allow respondents to develop their own answers without information about possible choices

4. Information that goes into the system that is needed for decision making

5. A planned set of questions to which individuals or groups of people respond

6. All of the people in the group that a company is interested in studying

7. An organized method of collecting, storing, analyzing, and retrieving information to improve the effectiveness and efficiency of marketing decisions

8. Specific cities or geographic areas in which marketing experiments are conducted

9. Information collected for the first time to solve the problem being studied

10. A procedure to identify solutions to a specific marketing problem through the use of scientific problem solving

11. The resources used to maintain information, including equipment and procedures, so that it can be used when needed

12. Information developed from activities that occur within the organization

13. The process of summarizing, combining, or comparing information so that decisions can be made

14. Information already collected for another purpose that can be used to solve current problems

15. A way to collect information by recording actions without interacting or communicating with the participant

16. Controlled situations in which all factors are the same except the one being studied

a. analysis
b. closed-ended questions
c. discretionary purchases
d. experiments
e. external information
f. focus group
g. input
h. internal information
i. marketing information system
j. marketing research
k. observation
l. open-ended questions
m. output
n. population
o. primary data
p. random sampling
q. sample
r. secondary data
s. simulations
t. storage
u. survey
v. test market

Review Marketing Concepts

17. True or False: Focus groups can be composed of participants who are experts on the topic rather than a random sample of the population.

18. True or False: Marketing research helps businesses that are involved in international competition.

19. True or False: Businesses that have effective marketing information systems do not need to use marketing research.

20. True or False: Surveys should only ask questions that are needed to accomplish the objectives of the research.

21. True or False: Whether or not to use marketing research depends solely on its cost.

22. True or False: Open-ended questions are often used while researchers are trying to identify a problem or are completing a situational analysis.

23. True or False: Marketing research follows the steps of scientific problem solving.

24. True or False: The most precise and objective information about a potential market segment is obtained through focus groups.

25. True or False: A great deal can be learned about purchase behavior by observing consumers.

26. True or False: Secondary data is usually less expensive to obtain than primary data.

Marketing Research and Planning

27. A marketing information system (MkIS) has five components: input, storage, analysis, output, and decision making. An MkIS can be developed for many different applications, but each should include the five components. You want to get a high grade on your next marketing test, so you decide to develop an effective system to organize and review the information you are learning. Plan an MkIS you could use. Using pictures or brief descriptions, identify your a) inputs, b) storage, c) analysis, d) outputs, and e) decision making that will result in a high grade on your test.

28. Categories of information for marketing researchers include business data, consumer information, economic information, government data, and information about specific industries. Use the library or Internet to identify two information sources for each of these categories. For each information source, prepare a note card that describes the publication name, publisher, copyright date or frequency of publication, and type of information included in the publication. If you can obtain a copy of the publication, select a small sample of the information it contains and summarize it on your note card.

29. Identify which of the five steps in scientific problem solving is described by each of the following marketing research activities.

    a. After receiving the surveys from the respondents, the analyst tabulates the results and prepares charts illustrating the survey results.

b. The manager reviews sales records for the past five years to see if there have been changes in the geographic location of customers during that time.

c. After considering several methods to collect information, researchers decide to organize two test markets using different distribution methods to determine which is most effective.

d. The managers listened to the report of the research results and decided to implement the top three recommendations of the research team.

e. In a discussion with salespeople, the marketing manager agrees that there has been an increase in the number of customer complaints about the cost of repair parts for the product.

Marketing Management and Decision Making

30. The band boosters at your school are planning a fundraising activity. They want to sell two-pocket folders that can hold full-size papers. The folders would be printed and assembled by a local company and sold to students and faculty. The boosters want your help in determining a design for the folder, the price to charge, and the best ways to promote the folder in school to achieve a high sales volume. Prepare a proposal of three to five pages describing a marketing research study that will help the boosters answer their questions. Include the following sections in your proposal: identify the problem, design the research method, select the participants, analyze the data, and report the research results. The proposal should identify ways that include all three types of data collection—survey, observation, and experiment.

31. An important part of the marketing research process is analyzing the data after it has been collected. The chart below shows the data collected from a study of store and brand choices for four age groups of consumers. One thousand people were surveyed, and the respondents indicated their preferred store and brand.

    Calculate the following information from the data and develop tables, charts, or graphs to illustrate the results.

a. Determine the total number of participants who prefer each store and each brand. (To determine the total, add the numbers in each column.)

b. Using the totals from Part a, calculate the percentage of the total number of participants who prefer each store and each brand. (To calculate the percentage, divide the total of each column by the total number of participants.)

c. For each of the age categories, calculate the percentage of respondents who prefer each store and each brand. (Divide the number of respondents in each preference category by the total number of participants in that age category.)

d. Illustrate the rank order of stores and the rank order of brands for each age category. (Rank order shows the store and brand that is most preferred, next most preferred, and so on.) Then illustrate the rank order of stores and brands when the responses of all age categories are combined.

e. Using the information you have summarized for parts a through d, develop two conclusions about store and brand preferences for the sample surveyed.

Age	Store Preference			Brand Preference		
	Bardoes	Kelvins	1-2-3	Motif	Astra	France
16–20	38	82	130	80	106	76
21–25	56	20	174	156	90	18
26–30	110	64	76	104	98	60
31–35	44	120	86	54	30	128

Retail Marketing Research Event

You have been hired by a major home improvement chain store to conduct customer research. The company's current advertising campaign emphasizes personalized customer service, using actual testimonials from satisfied customers. Now the company wants to survey a cross section of customers to determine if the store is delivering on its promises. The purpose of your research is to determine customer perception of the company, expectations for customer service, and level of customer satisfaction. You will analyze current media and its effectiveness and propose institutional promotion campaign activities for the home improvement store chain.

The written entry will consist of the following parts:

Executive Summary Write a one-page description of the project.

Introduction Describe the business or organization and the target market. This part of the written entry should include geographic, demographic, and socioeconomic factors about the community.

Research Methods Used in the Advertising Media Analysis Describe the design for the advertising media analysis and methods used to conduct the advertising media analysis.

Findings and Conclusions Describe the advertising media available and provide a cost analysis of it. Describe the advertising media's potential impact on the target market. Provide a rationale for the selection of the most cost-effective media.

Proposed Institutional Promotion Campaign Highlight the goals, objectives, and rationale of the institutional promotion campaign. Outline the proposed institutional promotion campaign activities, timelines, and the budget.

Bibliography and Appendix These are the last two sections of the report. The appendix is optional.

Performance Indicators Evaluated

- Describe the business and the geographic, demographic, and socioeconomic factors for the community where the business is located. (Economics)

- Describe the current product/service offered and the product/service offered by the competition. (Product/Service Management)

- Design the study and the instrument to conduct research. (Information Management)

- Analyze the preferred customer research. (Information Management)

- Describe the goals, objectives, rationale, activities, and timelines for a promotional campaign. (Promotion)

Go to the DECA web site for more detailed information.

Think Critically

1. Why should a popular national home improvement store conduct customer research?

2. What incentive could be offered to customers to make sure they respond to a survey?

3. Why is it important for a store to validate its level of customer service before highlighting the service in advertisements?

www.deca.org

Chapter 6

Marketing Starts with Customers

©GETTY IMAGES/STOCKBYTE

Newsline

Sony Builds a Consumer Shopping Experience

Many consumer electronics manufacturers are moving their sales to the Internet or reaching customers through giant consumer electronics stores such as Best Buy and Circuit City. The belief is that sophisticated purchasers know what they want and will use the Internet to get the best price or shop the large stores to be able to quickly compare several brands and models.

Sony is maintaining a third alternative, a retail store that sells only Sony products. Despite the failure of single-brand stores such as Gateway, Sony believes that many consumers want a place where they can comfortably examine and learn about the growing range of consumer electronics products. Thus the SonyStyle® retail stores were created. The stores focus on offering customers pleasurable and comfortable shopping experiences. The first Sony product gallery was opened on Michigan Avenue, Chicago's main shopping street for upscale purchasers. There are now over 50 SonyStyle® locations in 22 states. Sony has expansion plans for the retail concept in the United States as well as other countries around the world.

As customers enter the store, they are greeted by a concierge who quickly helps them identify their needs and directs them to the correct product displays. Rather than long lines of products on shelves that consumers typically find in other stores, Sony's products are displayed in lifestyle settings, such as a living room, bedroom, or home office. Employees encourage consumers to interact with the products in the open and inviting atmosphere.

While everyone is invited into the Sony stores, they are especially designed to cater to women. Recent consumer research found that women initiate nearly half of all purchases of consumer electronics products. The store and its employees help demystify technology through demonstrations, opportunities to try the technology in realistic environments, and a high level of customer support including customization, delivery, and in-home installation.

The stores have become a good source of information on consumer behavior. Employees can watch customers to see which products elicit "oohs" and "aahs" and which are ignored. They can see firsthand how customers make decisions and what questions they have.

Think Critically

1. Why would Sony want to appeal to women shoppers with the SonyStyle® stores?

2. What are the advantages and disadvantages of the unique store layout for customers? For consumer electronics manufacturers?

school.cengage.com/marketing/marketing

Prepare for Performance

This chapter develops the following Performance Indicators from the DECA Competitive Events program.

Core Performance Indicators

- Acquire foundational knowledge of customer/client/business behavior to understand what motivates decision making
- Foster positive relationships with customers to enhance company image
- Acquire product knowledge to communicate product benefits and to ensure appropriateness of product for the customer

Supporting Performance Indicators

- Explain customer/client/business buying behavior
- Discuss levers employees can use to motivate decision making
- Demonstrate a customer-service mindset
- Reinforce service orientation through communication
- Identify company's unique selling proposition
- Identify internal and external service standards

Go to **school.cengage.com/marketing/marketing** and click on Connect to DECA.

MOST KIDS' COLDS START IN THE NOSE. GOOD NEWS, THAT'S WHERE DIMETAPP STARTS TO WORK.

Dimetapp is specifically formulated to fight stuffy and runny noses to let kids breathe easier.

Dimetapp Helping kids breathe easier.

Wyeth
Use only as directed.
©2005 Wyeth Consumer Healthcare

www.dimetapp.com

©WYETH

Visual Focus

Consumers must be aware of a product and a specific brand before they will purchase it. Then they must recognize that it meets a specific need better than any other choices available to the consumer. Connecting consumers, their needs, and a company's product is an important role of marketing. So often, marketing starts with an important problem prospective customers are likely to face.

Focus Questions:

The medication featured in the Dimetapp ad is actually designed for children. Yet, parents will make the decision whether or not to buy it. Is the advertising appealing to children, parents, or both? In what ways? What is appealing about the product that would influence parents to purchase Dimetapp Cold & Allergy rather than another brand of medication?

Locate an advertisement that clearly identifies a customer problem or need. Share your example in a class discussion.

Understanding Consumer Behavior

GOALS

- Describe the importance of understanding consumer behavior.
- Demonstrate an understanding of consumers' wants and needs.

KEY TERMS

consumer behavior, *p. 156*

final consumers, *p. 157*

business consumers, *p. 157*

want, *p. 158*

need, *p. 158*

marketing matters

In order to apply the marketing concept effectively, marketers study consumer behavior. There are two basic types of consumers—final consumers who make purchases for their own consumption and business consumers who make purchases for their business or to resell to customers. Both final consumers and business consumers make purchases to satisfy their wants and needs. By understanding the reasons consumers buy and the needs and wants they are attempting to satisfy, marketers can make sure their products and services match what consumers are looking for.

Make a list of ten things you've bought recently and describe the most important want or need that each of those purchases was meant to satisfy. Are your wants and needs easy to identify or not?

Consumer Behavior

If there is one idea that is key to understanding marketing, it is that marketing begins with customers. The marketing concept states that marketers must be responsive to their customers. Successful businesses are those that continually consider the consumers' wants and needs as they plan and implement their marketing strategies.

You cannot implement the marketing concept without understanding customers. Understanding customers is not simple. The study of consumers and how they make decisions is called **consumer behavior**. Consumer behavior includes factors that influence how people purchase and use products and services.

It is important for marketers to understand consumers and their buying behavior. There are several ways to analyze customer needs and to use the information

©DIGITAL VISION

Why do marketers need to study consumer behavior?

Television Advertising Around the Globe

In the United States, television commercials are the most popular advertising medium in terms of dollars spent. In 2006, U.S. advertisers spent over $65 billion on television advertising. This number makes up over 40 percent of total advertising. Advertisers spent approximately $30 billion on magazine advertising, the second most popular medium. During one hour of network television, as much as 18 minutes may be devoted to commercials.

In other countries, though, the opportunities for television advertising can be limited. In the United Kingdom, for example, two of the largest national channels have no paid commercials at all. In other countries around the world, governments and television networks sometimes limit the amount of television time that can be dedicated to advertising. Or, as is the case in many countries, people just don't watch as much television as they do in the United States. In these places, advertisers must find alternative ways to reach customers.

Think Critically

1. In a country with limited TV advertising, what other techniques could you use to advertise? What factors might influence the type of advertising you use?

2. Internet advertising is growing each year. How is advertising on the Internet like TV advertising? How is it different?

---

to make wise marketing decisions. There are two types of consumers of interest to marketers—final consumers and business consumers.

Final Consumers

Final consumers buy products or services for personal use. The traditional view of a consumer is someone who enters a retail store, purchases a product, takes it home, and uses it. Today the shopping experiences of final consumers may be quite different from that view. Consumers purchase a mix of products and services and gather information and make purchases in many different ways, including the Internet. When you go to a local store to purchase a notebook for your marketing class, you are a final consumer. Family members taking a trip to a regional shopping center are final consumers. A homeowner contracting with a landscaping service to provide monthly lawn maintenance and a photography buff searching the Internet for a new camera lens are both final consumers.

Business Consumers

A second category of consumers does not make purchases for personal use. **Business consumers** buy goods and services to produce and market other goods and services or for resale. An example of a business consumer is the manufacturer of the notebook you purchased. The manufacturer buys paper, glue, ink, wire, and other materials to produce the notebook. It will

Working in **Teams**

Form a team and identify ten products and services that members believe are typically used by final consumers. Now review each product and service on the list and discuss whether it could be used by a business consumer. As a team, identify similarities and differences in how the products and services would be marketed to each of the groups.

also purchase the raw materials and other products it needs to produce other products it will sell or will use to package, store, ship, and promote its products. In each case, when the manufacturer purchases materials to produce products it will sell to its customers, it is a business consumer.

Businesses also buy products and services that are used in their daily operations. The company purchases paper, pencils, security services, cleaning services, computers, furniture, and all the items needed for business operations. Even though it consumes the products and services as a part of its operations, it is still a business consumer.

Checkpoint ▶▶

Why is it important to understand consumer behavior?

Consumers' Wants and Needs

All consumers have wants and needs. A **want** is an unfulfilled desire. Consumers want pizzas, BMWs, vacation trips to France, a different hair color, a new DVD player, or tickets to the Super Bowl. The products and services people purchase to satisfy wants are not essential for living but are important for maintaining a desired lifestyle.

A **need** is anything you require to live. Needs are considered to be the root of all human behavior. You need nutritious food, a good night's sleep, shelter from the weather, air to breathe, and clean water.

Hierarchy of Needs

Abraham Maslow's classic work on the motivation theory has helped marketers immensely in their study of needs. Maslow, a psychologist, identified five areas of needs that people have (see Figure 6-1). They are physiological, security, social, esteem, and self-actualization needs.

Maslow believed that these groups of needs are satisfied in a hierarchy and that other needs become important as they satisfy the needs at each level. Everyone must satisfy the physiological needs. They are not options. You must eat, sleep, and breathe to exist. After these needs are generally satisfied, you can start to satisfy security needs. While it is important to be secure, it is only important to be secure after you have satisfied your physiological needs. To go one level higher, social needs are certainly important, but only after you meet important physiological and security needs.

Gaining respect and recognition from others satisfies esteem needs. Running for student council might be an attempt to satisfy esteem needs. The need for self-actualization usually involves intellectual growth, creativity, and accomplishment. Attending college or taking music lessons might satisfy needs for self-actualization.

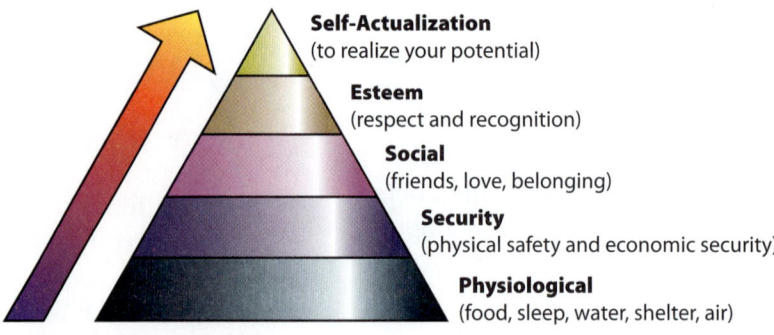

Self-Actualization
(to realize your potential)

Esteem
(respect and recognition)

Social
(friends, love, belonging)

Security
(physical safety and economic security)

Physiological
(food, sleep, water, shelter, air)

FIGURE 6-1
Maslow's hierarchy of needs illustrates the progression people follow in satisfying needs.

Different People, Different Levels

Marketers must recognize that people are at different levels on the hierarchy of needs. Some people are focusing on security needs while others are satisfying esteem needs.

Regardless of what needs individuals are attempting to satisfy, marketers must identify the important needs of their customers if they want to satisfy them. Housing provides a good example of how consumers' needs differ. The physiological need for housing is served by a home that provides protection from the weather. A house that is in a fairly safe neighborhood and has a security system would satisfy the need for security. For a family with young children, a house that is in a neighborhood with lots of young families might satisfy social needs. A house might satisfy esteem needs if it is well maintained and the yard is landscaped. Self-actualization needs might be satisfied by a home that is designed or even built by the owner.

Checkpoint ▶▶▶

What are the five levels of Maslow's hierarchy of needs?

6-1 Assessment

Xtra! Study Tools
school.cengage.com/marketing/marketing

Key Concepts

Determine the best answer.

1. The study of consumers and how they make decisions is called
   a. advertising
   b. consumer behavior
   c. psychology
   d. the marketing concept

2. _____ consumers buy goods and services to produce and market other goods and services or for resale.

3. An unfulfilled desire is a
   a. want
   b. need
   c. buying behavior
   d. purchasing factor

4. The level of needs identified by Maslow that everyone must satisfy is
   a. self-actualization
   b. social
   c. security
   d. physiological

5. True or False: Generally, most people are at the same level on the hierarchy of needs.

Make Academic Connections

6. **Visual Art** Use copies of old magazines and newspapers to locate and clip pictures and other illustrations that represent each of the levels of Maslow's hierarchy of needs. Use them to create a poster or other visual that illustrates the hierarchy in the correct order of needs satisfaction.

7. **Math** A building materials and supply store sells to business and final consumers. Last month the average sale to business consumers was $856.08, and the average sale to final consumers was $43.95. There were 128 business customers averaging 5 purchases during the month, and 2,593 final customers that averaged 2.3 purchases per month. Calculate the total monthly sales for each customer type, the overall total monthly sales, and the percentage of total sales for each customer category.

Connect to ◀ DECA
An Association of Marketing Students

8. Your advertising team must develop two 30-second radio advertisements for the new Xclaim automobile. The first should appeal to consumers' safety needs. The second should appeal to their self-esteem needs. Record the advertisements and present them to your teacher (judge).

What Motivates Buyers?

GOALS

- Distinguish the types of buying motives.
- Describe the five steps of the consumer decision-making process.

KEY TERMS

motivation, *p. 160*

buying motives, *p. 161*

emotional motives, *p. 161*

rational motives, *p. 162*

patronage motives, *p. 162*

buying behavior, *p. 163*

consumer decision-making process, *p. 163*

marketing matters

People have motives for the reasons they buy products and services. Motives can be emotional or quite rational. Often consumers don't think consciously about what motivates their decisions, but there are always important influences on a decision. Whatever the motivation, the consumer decision-making process generally involves a series of steps. Sometimes those steps are completed quickly with little consideration while at other times it is a long, thoughtful process. It is important for marketers to understand consumer motivation and decision making in order to be an effective influence in the final decision.

Think carefully about a recent major purchase you made. Describe the steps you went through from the time you began thinking about the need until you actually made the purchase. What was your initial motivation? Where did you find information on choices available to you? How many different alternatives did you consider? What was the main influence on your final choice? How happy were you with your decision? Discuss your purchasing process with other students to determine similarities and differences.

Motivation

All of our actions are influenced by motivation. **Motivation** is the set of positive or negative factors that direct individual behavior. People have both short- and long-term motivation. We are motivated to develop the knowledge and skills needed for a good career and salary. We are also motivated by happiness and enjoyment.

When you wake up in the morning, you may have a negative motivation to stay in bed for another hour of sleep. You also recognize that you should get out of bed and prepare for school. The

©DIGITAL VISION

What factors might motivate people to continue their education and obtain a college degree?

Judgment Call

The Scales are Tipping

Americans spend approximately $35 billion dollars a year on diet pills, books, clubs, and programs in an attempt to look good and stay fit. Because this is a relatively new trend, regulations have been lax. But there is a lot of money at stake, and a recent study found that 15 percent of ads for diet products were deceptive.

Diet companies often use doctored before-and-after photos as evidence of their effectiveness. And they sometimes claim that their products help people lose weight permanently, which is usually not the case. (Notice that the fine print on these ads almost always says "Results not typical.")

A series of lawsuits in recent years has led to new regulations by the Federal Trade Commission (FTC) in an attempt to crack down on deceptive marketing practices in the diet industry. While these regulations have not completely stopped deceptive advertising, they are working to make it a fairer market for consumers.

Think Critically

1. Use the Internet to find diet industry companies charged with deceptive advertising. How do you think those lawsuits have affected those companies?

2. How might a diet company ensure it is not engaging in deceptive advertising?

---

motivation for that choice may just be the chance to socialize with friends. There is also the longer-term motivation to complete the courses needed for your high school diploma, which will lead to college, a job, and your long-term career goals. The importance of the negative and positive influences will determine the choice you make each morning.

Motivation is an important factor in your behavior as a consumer. Your decisions to spend money on products and services are influenced by what marketers call buying motives. **Buying motives** are the reasons that you buy. There are three categories of buying motives that drive consumers to purchase products or services or respond to ideas: emotional motives, rational motives, and patronage motives.

Emotional Motives

Emotional motives are reasons to purchase based on feelings, beliefs, or attitudes. Forces of love, affection, guilt, fear, or passion often compel consumers to buy. Marketers realize that a person's emotional motives are frequently very strong and can be an important influence on decisions and behavior. For example, Hallmark advertisements encourage you to buy greeting cards based on the emotions of love and affection. Because of your feelings for others close to you or because of a special event such as Mother's Day, a birthday, or a friend's illness, you want to express your feelings with a card and a short note.

McDonald's appeals to the emotions of parents who may feel some guilt about the lack of time they have to spend with their children or the need for family meal times. They use their advertising to show busy young parents taking children to McDonald's restaurants on a Saturday morning or on the way to or from their child's activities. With that emotional appeal, a decision to stop at McDonald's may be influenced more by the thoughts of creating a happy family experience than by the actual items on the menu.

How might fear have an effect on consumer buying behavior?

Fear is also an emotional motivator that is used to encourage consumers to buy products. People who buy security systems for their home or automobile are motivated by the fear of having their home burglarized or their vehicle stolen. One of the appeals used to market organic foods is the fear of pesticides and other dangers in our food supply. With the recent outbreaks of illnesses and deaths from the consumption of tainted meats and vegetables, consumer motivation to make sure food purchases are safe to eat has increased. Marketers understand emotional motivation and use it to plan marketing mixes that appeal to those motives.

Rational Motives

Emotional motivation is not always appropriate or effective. Consumer behavior can be influenced by rational as well as emotional motivation. **Rational motives** are reasons to buy based on facts or logic.

Rational motives include factors such as saving time or money or obtaining the highest quality or greatest value. Rational buying motives may influence many purchases, but they are especially important for many expensive purchases. Even if emotions play a role in your purchase of a house or car or your selection of a college, you will still want to consider the quality and value of your choice.

How do you decide to buy a new computer system? While your current computer may work well, you may want to upgrade to get a more powerful or faster operating system, an upgraded sound or graphics card, or the latest software and Internet security. These are all attributes that affect the functioning of the computer.

Automobile purchases can be emotional but usually include a number of rational motives. As a prospective owner, you may consider the quality history of the car, the service and repair record of the dealership, and the maintenance costs. Fuel economy versus power may be an important factor. Do you want to purchase the additional safety options or the extended warranty? All of these are a part of the rational decision making that goes into most automobile purchases. But rational motives can be influenced by your emotions when you catch sight of that new Mercedes convertible!

Business consumers have both emotional and rational motives as well. However, they try to avoid basing purchases on emotions since it does not make good business sense. The emotions of fear, friendship, and enjoyment may result in poor purchase decisions for a business if those emotions are allowed to influence the process. Instead the business will evaluate choices, looking for the best price, fastest delivery, favorable credit terms, and highest quality products. Those are all rational motives.

Patronage Motives

The third type of buying motivation is the patronage motive. **Patronage motives** are based on loyalty. Patronage motives encourage consumers to purchase from a particular business or to buy a particular brand.

Loyalty is influenced by positive previous experiences or a close identification with the product or business. Consumers develop that loyalty for various reasons. They might like the low prices, high quality, friendly staff, great customer service or convenient location. They may be loyal because it is a business or brand name their family has used for years and years. People are often loyal to a local or neighborhood business. Some identify with the people who work in the business, who are featured in advertising for the product, or who appear to have the same beliefs and values as the customer.

Patronage purchasing is not limited to large, expensive purchases. It can involve a favorite restaurant, a brand of soda, a salesperson the customer feels comfortable with, or a regularly visited web site of a business. Business consumers can be influenced by patronage motives in the same way that final consumers are influenced. They may return to the same business time after time to purchase raw materials and supplies because they have been satisfied with the quality and service in the past. They may prefer a local supplier rather than risk working with a company that is located in another state or country. The important

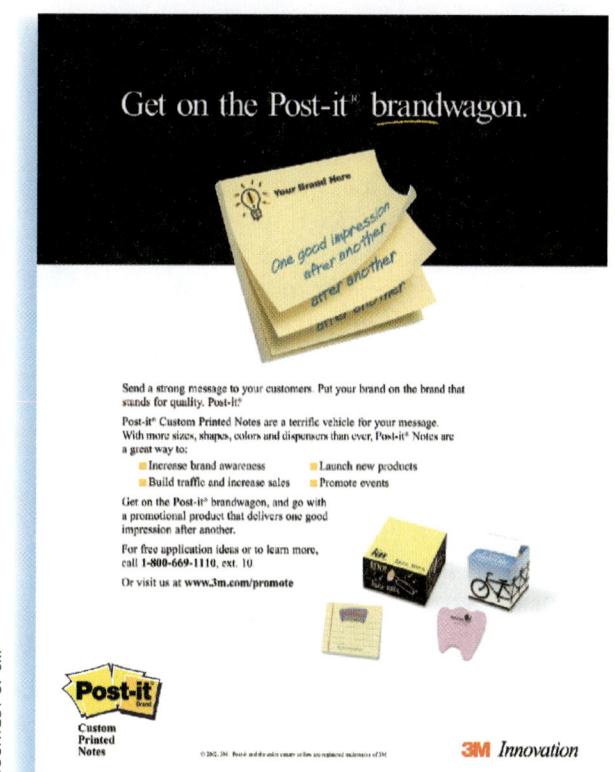

Loyalty and patronage motives can be strengthened by keeping your name in front of customers.

point to remember is that people who are motivated by patronage are very loyal to the product, service, or brand. Businesses encourage and cultivate patronage motives so that customers are less likely to consider the products of their competitors.

Checkpoint ▶▶▶

Describe the three different categories of buying motives.

The Consumer Decision-Making Process

The decision processes and actions of consumers as they buy services and products are known as **buying behavior**. Marketers know it is advantageous to understand the process customers go through when selecting goods or services so that they can assist the customers in making the best possible decisions.

A consumer goes through five steps when making a purchase decision, as shown in Figure 6-2 on the next page. The **consumer decision-making process** is the process by which consumers collect and analyze information to make choices among alternatives. Decision making as it applies to a specific purchase moves through problem recognition, information search, alternative evaluation, purchase, and postpurchase evaluation.

Problem Recognition

There is no reason for consumers to buy a product or service if they are currently satisfied. While we all have wants and needs, one or more must become important enough to us to influence our actions. The first step in the decision-making process then is when the consumer recognizes a need, desire, or problem. For example, unless you decide you want to learn to play the piano, there is no need to select a piano instructor. However, if that becomes an important goal, then you will begin the task of choosing the instructor who will give you lessons. Once you recognize the need, you are on the decision-making path to buy a product or service.

An important part of the first step is the strength of the need and the urgency to satisfy the need. We have many needs at any given time, but some become strong and even urgent at particular times. If you haven't eaten for most of the day, you will likely be quite hungry and look for food choices. If you have been working very hard for some time, you may try to identify ways you can relax and enjoy yourself. When a need is strong or urgent, it may result in a much faster decision with fewer choices. When a need is not as strong or urgent, you may delay the decision-making process or take more time to complete some of the steps.

Information Search

After a need or problem has been identified, the consumer gathers information about alternative solutions. The process you use to identify alternatives depends on your past experience. If the need is one you have satisfied before or that others you know have had experience with, you may

The Consumer Decision-Making Process

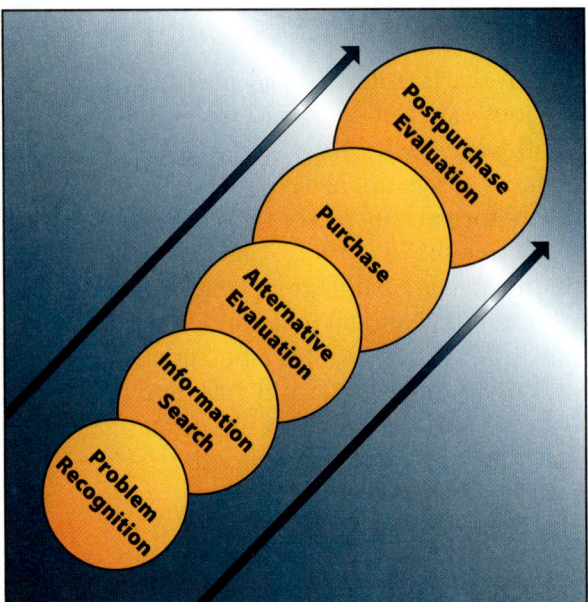

FIGURE 6-2
Consumers follow a series of steps each time they make a purchase decision.

already be able to identify choices. With a new problem you have not encountered in the past, identifying possible solutions may be quite difficult.

Satisfying a hunger need may be relatively easy because you can identify your favorite foods and restaurants, and you know how much money and time you have available. While the choice will not be the same each time, you will usually be able to identify a few businesses or products that

NET Bookmark

Consumers go through five steps when making purchasing decisions. Web sites such as Edmunds.com help consumers with some of those steps. Access school.cengage.com/marketing/marketing and click on the link for Chapter 6. Browse through the site, and then select two steps in the consumer decision-making process and explain how Edmunds.com might be helpful in completing each step.

school.cengage.com/marketing/marketing

seem appropriate based on your specific needs at the time. If you are in an unfamiliar location or decide you want to try something very different, you will need to use a different process to identify alternatives.

Choosing a piano teacher is an example of a unique problem. It is not likely you have gone through that decision-making process before. After you recognize the need to learn to play the piano, you will need to find ways to accomplish that goal, including locating a good teacher. You may talk to your parents or friends for advice and recommendations. You might look through the phone book or search the classified section of the newspaper or even use an Internet search hoping that piano instructors have developed web sites. You might ask for recommendations from a local business that sells pianos. Your goal, of course, is to identify choices of instructors so that you can work with the one that fits your level of experience, schedule, and resources.

When identifying alternatives, consumers also gather information about each alternative. The type and amount of information gathered will differ from situation to situation. It will depend on what information is readily available, the amount of time the consumer has to gather information, the importance of the need, and the type of information the consumer believes is needed to make an effective decision.

Consumers may not know what information is important at the time they are identifying alternatives. They may gather initial information only to learn later that they do not have the right type or amount of information they need. They may rely on others to help them determine the information they need if they are not well informed about the problem or have not experienced the problem previously. Over time and with experience, consumers become more effective in identifying alternatives and gathering information.

©GETTY IMAGES/PHOTODISC

If you were considering taking music lessons, how would the consumer decision-making process help you?

Evaluate Alternatives

After gathering information, the consumer evaluates the various alternatives to determine which is best. Sometimes this involves summarizing the information, comparing the pros and cons of each choice, making tradeoffs between price and various options, and ranking the alternatives. Evaluating piano instructors might involve determining whom you can afford, what hours the instructor is available, and the reputation of each instructor. Based on these evaluations, you will make a decision.

It is possible that you may decide you do not have adequate information to make a decision, that you do not have adequate resources to make a purchase, or that your need is not strong enough to justify the cost compared to other important needs. Depending on that information, the consumer may decide to forgo satisfying the need or to gather more information. The consumer may even decide to consider new alternatives.

After you make a purchase, why should you do a postpurchase evaluation?

Purchase

If a suitable choice is available that will satisfy the need or solve the problem, and if the consumer has enough money to pay for the choice, the purchase will be made. The purchase step involves agreeing with the business selling the product on what you will buy, the cost, payment method, and how you will receive the product or service. As you can see, the purchase decision involves agreement on the entire marketing mix.

In the case of your decision to take piano lessons, you choose to take lessons from a retired professor from the local university who comes highly recommended by several of your friends. She will give you a half-hour lesson each Saturday morning at your home at a price of $23 per lesson. You can pay cash each time, or if you want to pay for a full month of lessons in advance, you can save $3 per lesson.

Postpurchase Evaluation

Each time a purchase is made and the product or service is used, the consumer will begin to realize whether it met the need or solved the problem. The consumer will either be satisfied or dissatisfied with the purchase. After you have had several piano lessons, can play some simple songs, have worked with the instructor, and can tell how lessons are fitting into your schedule, you will have a better idea of whether or not you really are committed to the time and effort required to learn to play the piano well. If you are satisfied with your lessons and your decision, you will probably continue and may even recommend your instructor to your family and friends. If you are dissatisfied, you will probably find a new instructor or quit taking lessons altogether.

The postpurchase decision involves two parts. First you will determine whether the need or want was as important as you originally believed. You may decide the need was not important enough to warrant

Fast FACTS

A recent study from Cornell University found that Americans' favorite "comfort" foods are: potato chips (23%), ice cream (14%), cookies (12%), chocolate (11%), and pizza or pasta (11%).

the effort and expense, so it will not receive as much attention the next time it arises. You may decide the need was important to you, but the choice you made is not providing the satisfaction you believed it would. In that case, you will usually not make the same decision again. Instead, you will learn from your experience. The next time you recognize the same need or encounter a similar problem, you will choose a different alternative and evaluate the information more carefully.

Recently, marketers have been paying more attention to postpurchase satisfaction. They want to make sure that customers are satisfied with their purchase and will become regular customers. Toll-free telephone numbers for customer service departments let consumers easily call and ask questions or express concerns. Often the company will provide a follow-up telephone call or other contact or arrange for a free service visit or other after-sale service. The goal is to reassure customers that they made the right choice, resolve any customer problems and concerns immediately, and increase customer satisfaction with their decision.

Checkpoint ▶▶▶

What are the five steps in the consumer decision-making process?

6-2 Assessment

Key Concepts

Determine the best answer.

1. Reasons to purchase based on feelings, beliefs, or attitudes are _____ motives.
   a. emotional
   b. rational
   c. patronage
   d. consumer

2. True or False: Patronage motives are based on loyalty.

3. The decision processes and actions of consumers as they buy services and products are known as
   a. purchase decisions
   b. buying behavior
   c. the consumer decision-making process
   d. postpurchase evaluation

4. The first step in the consumer decision-making process is
   a. information search
   b. purchase decision
   c. alternative evaluation
   d. problem recognition

5. Recently marketers have been paying more attention to postpurchase _____.

Make Academic Connections

6. **Psychology** Work with a team to prepare a bulletin board display that demonstrates the use of the three types of buying motives by businesses. Provide examples of products and services that are effectively marketed using emotional, rational, and patronage motives.

7. **Language Arts** Compose a fictional story (humorous, mystery, or romance) about a person who encounters a major problem and solves that problem through the purchase and use of a product. Build the story around each of the steps of the consumer decision-making process.

Connect to ◀ **DECA**
An Association of Marketing Students

8. Your marketing research team has been identifying sources of information that students use most often when making purchase decisions. Prepare a short questionnaire (two to four questions) and distribute it to 15 students in your school. Analyze the results and develop a three-minute oral presentation of your results with two supporting charts or graphs. Present the report to your teacher (judge) and be prepared to answer questions about the research.

6-3 Influencing Consumer Decisions

GOALS

- Describe important influences on the consumer decision-making process.
- Explain how consumers and businesses use each of the three types of decision making.

KEY TERMS

personal identity, *p. 168*   lifestyle, *p. 169*

personality, *p. 169*   culture, *p. 170*

attitude, *p. 169*   reference group, *p. 171*

self-concept, *p. 169*

marketing matters

Purchase decisions by consumers are very complicated processes. It is not as simple as seeing a product and deciding to buy it. Many factors can influence consumers' buying decisions, including individual personality characteristics and personal image, the social and cultural environment of the consumer, and the influence and effect of others with whom the consumer identifies. How and which of those influences affect decisions depends in large part on the consumer's experience with the product or service being purchased and whether the consumer views the purchase decision as routine or complex. As marketers are able to analyze and understand the factors influencing purchase decisions, they can make decisions that influence and support their prospective customers.

List three products that you buy often and usually buy the same brand. What typically leads to the decision to buy the product? Why have you developed a preference for the particular brand? For each product, list three things that would make you switch to a competitive brand. Discuss with other students why brand names are important for some purchases and are less important for others.

Influences on Buying Decisions

In order to remain profitable, businesses must provide customers with products and services that meet their wants and needs. Knowing what influences a customer's buying decision is a key part of implementing the marketing concept. By understanding what motivates and influences customer purchases, businesses are able to provide the products and services at the right place and time.

Many internal and external factors influence purchase decisions. Two very important factors are individual characteristics and the cultural and social environment.

Individual Characteristics

Each consumer is different from all others. Even though a person is a member of a family, community, and other important personal, social, and career groups and organizations, a person's identity is a major influence on decisions and actions. **Personal identity** is the characteristics and character that make a person unique. Important factors that make up

Digital Digest

Direct Mail: More Than Just Junk

You have probably heard of "junk mail." You probably even get some of it, such as catalogs, coupons, promotional flyers, and free samples. Companies call this direct mail and spend millions of dollars a year to make sure it gets to you. A lot of technology goes into creating large databases that contain not only people's names and addresses but also demographic data such as age, sex, income, number of children, and purchase trends, such as what a person buys, when, where, and how much they pay. The data can then be sorted into mailing lists of people who fit certain profiles.

Companies pay a lot of money for these targeted mailing lists. For example, a store can buy a mailing list for men, age 18–25, living in a certain area, who own SUVs. Targeted lists like this ensure that companies reach the people most likely to buy their products and weed out those who might consider their mailings "junk."

Think Critically

1. Describe three pieces of direct mail sent to your home recently. What products were they promoting? Did the mailing affect your purchase decision?

2. Search the Internet for companies that provide direct mail database services. Describe the services each one provides.

---

personal identity are personality, gender, ethnicity, and age.

Personality The first individual characteristic that influences buying behavior is personality. **Personality** is an enduring pattern of emotions and behaviors that define an individual. How would you describe your personality? Are you outgoing, serious, or shy? How do you express your personality in the products and services you choose, including your clothing, hobbies, social activities, and even decisions about whether to save money for the future or spend it on immediate needs?

Personalities influence buying decisions because everyone has individual preferences based on attitude, self-concept and lifestyle choices. **Attitude** is a frame of mind developed from a person's values, beliefs, and feelings. You may already have formed attitudes about the value of education, the use of credit, or the need for conservation that shape your purchasing decisions. **Self-concept** is an individual's

belief about his or her identity, image, and capabilities. **Lifestyle** is the way a person lives as reflected by material goods, activities, and relationships. Decisions about type and location of jobs, housing, family size, leisure activities, and community involvement are all a part of a person's lifestyle.

Gender An individual's gender influences many decisions and actions. Dress, grooming, social relationships and activities, family roles, and career choices are frequently different for men and women. While gender roles and influences are changing over time and may be strongly influenced by family and culture, marketers identify differences in the product and service choices of each gender.

Ethnicity A set of characteristics uniting a group based on ancestry, country of origin, language, and traditions is known as *ethnicity*. The impact of ethnicity on a person's attitudes and actions varies based on individual identity and the views and values of others. Some individuals have a strong ethnic identification and demonstrate it in many lifestyle choices including dress, social activities, and food choices, among other factors.

Age A person's age has a major influence on consumer behavior. The age of a person generally indicates the types of products and services he or she will be interested in and the brands and features that are important. The evidence of the importance of age can easily be seen in television shows, movies, and magazines that are often developed for a specific age group. Not only are the shows, movies, and magazine articles different for adolescents, 20-somethings, and baby boomers, but the advertising that appears in each of the media is specifically targeted to the precise age range.

Cultural and Social Environment

The second important influence on buying decisions is a person's cultural and social environment. **Culture** is the history, beliefs, customs, and traditions of a group. A group's culture has a strong influence on values and behaviors. Traditionally, culture has been defined by the activities, relationships, and institutions shared by a group of people over many generations. A person's culture may place a high value on families, so a great deal of time is spent on family activities, and family members exert a strong influence on individual choices and decisions. In other cultures, individual independence is valued, and young people are prepared and encouraged to take personal responsibility for important decisions at an early age.

Today in the United States and some other parts of the world, due to the mobility of people and increasing diversity, culture is less important to many people than their social environment. A *social environment* is made up of the groups and organizations that people live and interact with on a regular basis. It has an influence on the values and behaviors of the people who are members of the group or organization.

Social environment may be defined by a community, a neighborhood, or even a social or business organization. Your school is a part of your social environment. In many parts of the United States, high school students have a car at their disposal.

Auto manufacturers try to establish an image that appeals to personal identities and social influences of prospective customers.

In other areas, high school students do not even expect to get a driver's license, much less own a car.

Some of the strongest influences on individual choices and behaviors are drawn from a person's reference groups. A **reference group** is a group of people or an organization that an individual admires, identifies with, and wants to be a part of. Reference groups might be clubs, social or civic organizations, business groups, or even informal groups of peers and others who have characteristics or lifestyles to which individuals aspire. If you are currently a member of a reference group or particularly if you want to identify with a group in which you are not a member, you will shape your behavior and your image around what you believe the group expects. Marketing that connects consumers with the images and actions of their reference group and encourages them to "join the group" by purchasing and using the products and services preferred by group members is often very effective.

Checkpoint ▶▶

What are the four factors that make up personal identity?

Figure This

Breakeven Point

The breakeven point is the number of unit sales a company must make to cover the expenses of a venture. Below the breakeven point, expenses exceed revenues, and a company will lose money. At the breakeven point, sales will exactly cover all expenses. Once the breakeven point is exceeded, a company will begin to make a profit.

To calculate the breakeven point, you must first find three different variables. You need to know the total fixed cost of an activity or process, the selling price per unit, and the variable cost per unit of a good or service. The breakeven point is the total fixed cost divided by the difference between the selling price and the variable cost per unit.

$$\text{Breakeven point} = \frac{\text{Total fixed cost}}{\text{Per unit price} - \text{per unit cost}}$$

For example, a clothing store at the mall wants to print and distribute flyers advertising its new line of sweaters. The fixed cost of the flyers is $2,400. The selling price of each sweater is $50, and the variable cost of each sweater is $10. The breakeven point for the flyer is 60 sweaters.

$$\frac{\$2,400}{\$50 - \$10} = \frac{\$2,400}{\$40} = 60$$

If the store sells fewer than 60 sweaters, the store will lose money on the flyer. If it sells exactly 60 sweaters, the cost of the flyer will be covered exactly. If it sells more than 60 sweaters, the store will make a profit from the use of the flyer.

Think Critically

1. At the same clothing store, a display unit for jeans costs $1,800. If the jeans sell for $45 with a variable cost of $9, what is the breakeven point for the display?

2. What would be the breakeven point if the store installs a second $1,800 display unit for a different brand of jeans that sell for $54 with a variable cost of $18 each?

Planning a Career in... *Customer Support*

Marketing, Sales & Service

"My stepmom is a stickler for food safety. If there's a product in the pantry that doesn't have an easily understood expiration code, she will call the company and ask how she can determine the expiration date. She says she just wants to serve us the freshest food possible. Sometimes she calls the food companies for cooking advice. She says it's never too late to learn a few new cooking tips."

Did you ever have a question about a product that required a call for help to a company's toll-free number? Has your family ever tried to get an inaccurate charge on a credit card bill adjusted?

Most corporations employ customer support representatives to answer product questions, resolve customer issues, and follow up with purchasers to make sure they are satisfied with the products. Customer support personnel may meet customers in person or respond by telephone, e-mail, or even live online chat sessions.

Employment Outlook

- Faster-than-average growth is expected in this field.
- About 20% of customer support jobs are part-time.
- Automated telephone systems, the Internet, and fewer barriers to locating call centers overseas will impact job availability in the United States.

Job Titles

- Customer Care Representative
- Bilingual Service Representative
- Account Coordinator
- Online Operations Associate
- Customer Support Administrator
- Order Expeditor

Needed Skills

- Most positions require at least a high school diploma.
- Complex or regulated products may require representatives to have a college degree.
- The ability to remain positive and composed is important when faced with concerned customers and supervisors who monitor some contacts.
- Bilingual skills will increase marketability.

What's it like to work in...
Customer Support

As a customer service representative for a hospital billing department, Vinnie often encounters emotionally draining situations. Vinnie just completed a conference call with two insurance companies and the parent of a young cancer patient. Midway through chemotherapy, the parent's insurance carrier changed. New authorizations were required, and a few bills were overdue because of the transition. In addition to caring for a very ill child, the exhausted parent had to spend time resolving the insurance issues. Vinnie was able to resolve the insurance issue and devise an affordable payment plan for the overdue bills.

During the afternoon, Vinnie had a conversation with the son of a new elderly patient. The son was trying to determine if his father had coverage for medical care. The changes in government insurance programs for the elderly often lead to confusion about benefits.

What About **You**

Do you have the patience and compassion required to assist customers with a variety of questions and problems?

PHOTO: ©GETTY IMAGES/PHOTODISC

Types of Decision Making

Consumers spend varying amounts of time and consider different factors when making decisions. It takes different decision-making skills to buy toothpaste for less than two dollars that you will use in the next month than it does to decide to borrow more than one hundred thousand dollars to buy a house that you plan to live in for ten years or more. The three types of decision making are routine, limited, and extensive decision making.

Routine Decision Making

Routine decision making is used for purchases that are made frequently and do not require much thought. For routine purchases, the consumer is familiar with the products available, often chooses the same brand repeatedly, or can make an easy substitution if the usual choice is not available.

Food and snacks, personal supplies, and basic necessities are most often purchased using routine decision making. You buy them regularly when you know you will need them or when you run out. You either choose your favorite brand if you have a strong preference or choose among two or three brands if you view them as similar. In that case you will buy the one that is most convenient or has the lowest price at the time. You basically give very little thought to the purchase since it has become a part of your routine and there is nothing that causes you to change that behavior.

Businesses use routine decision making when making regular purchases such as operating supplies or standardized raw materials that are needed continuously as a part of the production process. The business will often use one supplier and will reorder from that company whenever necessary. The business may have a backup supplier to maintain a reliable supply in case of problems with the preferred supplier.

Limited Decision Making

Limited decision making takes more time than routine decision making. Often, limited decision making is associated with a product that is more expensive or is purchased less frequently. When you go to the mall to buy a pair of jeans, you might try on several styles, compare prices, and consider the color and feel of the fabrics of a few selections before you make a decision. This is an example of limited decision making. You will usually identify and complete a reasonable comparison and evaluate a few alternatives before making a decision. You are not absolutely certain of the best choice, but you generally know what you are looking for and the important factors that will influence your decision.

However, limited decision making is not strictly for more expensive items.

©GETTY IMAGES/PHOTODISC

Does choosing a movie involve routine decision making or limited decision making? How might it involve both types of decision making?

Something as simple as buying a soft drink can involve limited decision making. If you are a Coke drinker and the store you stop at is out of Coke, what do you do? You may consider some other flavor choices that are Coke products, or you may decide that Pepsi is a reasonable alternative this time. Choosing a movie for an evening's entertainment with friends is another example of limited decision making. You may already have a preferred movie and theater, so the decision is routine. However, often you will spend time on the Internet reviewing the new releases and checking theater times and locations before making the final decision.

Businesses use limited decision making for many purchases, such as office equipment, furniture, and even selecting a parcel delivery service to use. The business knows generally what it needs, but it sees value in comparing several alternatives to determine if there are price or quality differences. Even for purchases that are usually routine, such as office supplies, limited decision making might be used if a new supplier offers substantially lower prices that the purchasing agent needs to evaluate or if a change in equipment or procedures requires the purchase of a new product that the current supplier does not carry.

Extensive Decision Making

The third type of decision making is extensive decision making. Extensive decision making occurs when the consumer methodically goes through all five steps of the decision making process. Normally, extensive decision making is for expensive purchases, like an automobile, home, or family vacation. Consumers do not make the decision lightly. They spend time and effort evaluating alternatives and arriving at a decision. They want to carefully review their needs and match them with the best choice possible. Differences among choices may not be evident or may involve a number of factors that need to be carefully analyzed by consumers in order for them to be comfortable with the decision.

Extensive decision making is used in business when a purchase has not been made before or when it involves a large investment. Perhaps a business needs a new mainframe computer or needs to order several new delivery vehicles. The purchasing agent will conduct an extensive search for the best deal before a purchase decision is reached. The company may require suppliers to prepare a written proposal with complete descriptions of the product being offered for review by several people in the business who have special expertise about the type of product being selected. Extensive negotiations may occur with the vendors before a final decision is made.

Working in **Teams**

Form a team and identify a product that the team agrees would typically be purchased using each of the three types of decision making. Now compare where each product is usually purchased, what factors are most important in deciding what to purchase, and what information consumers need in order to decide what product or brand to purchase.

Marketers' Role in Decision Making

Why do marketers need to understand the decision-making process used by prospective customers? Marketers want to match their products and services to the needs and expectations of customers. They want to be able to provide the information customers want in order to make the best choice. If consumers choose a product using routine decision making, they do not want to be overwhelmed with information. On the other hand, if they are making a difficult choice using extensive decision making, they will want more information related to the factors they view as most important.

Marketers want the opportunity to explain the benefits of their products and services and to demonstrate how they can satisfy consumer needs. By studying consumers, businesses should be able to develop products and services that match the needs and expectations of their customers. When those customers are taking the time to consider alternatives, marketers have the opportunity to explain their products through appropriate communication channels. The customer may want only a limited amount of information or may expect extensive communication with the business. Without the needed information, the customer will likely move on to another choice. On the other hand, if customers routinely buy the same thing because they are brand loyal, the business will focus on making the product available and reminding customers of the value of the brand.

Checkpoint ▶▶

Rank the types of decision making according to the time and research typically devoted to each by the consumer.

6-3 Assessment

school.cengage.com/marketing/marketing

Key Concepts

Determine the best answer.

1. Which of the following is not one of the important factors that make up personal identity?
   a. gender
   b. age
   c. personality
   d. all of the above are important factors

2. _____ is a frame of mind developed from a person's values, beliefs, and feelings.
   a. Attitude
   b. Self-concept
   c. Lifestyle
   d. Culture

3. Which of the following is most likely to be one of your reference groups?
   a. your ancestors
   b. your teachers for the current school year
   c. the members of a local business organization
   d. a student organization to which you would like to belong

4. True or False: Routine decision making is used for purchases that are made frequently and do not require much thought.

5. Marketers will have the greatest opportunity to explain the benefits of their products and services and how they can satisfy consumer needs when customers use _____ decision making.

Make Academic Connections

6. **Sociology** Ask a parent, an older relative, or a leader of a community cultural organization to discuss the influence that culture or ethnicity has had on his or her life. Prepare a written summary of the person's views. Compare those views and attitudes with your own and describe the differences and similarities.

7. **Technology** Use the Internet to locate detailed information on three different brands of a digital camera. Use a word processing, database, or spreadsheet program to prepare a table that compares the three brands based on at least five features of the cameras, noting differences and similarities among the brands. Also identify the price of each brand. Based on the analysis, which brand would you choose? Why?

Connect to DECA

8. A shoe manufacturer is introducing a new moderately priced athletic shoe targeted at females between the ages of 12 and 15. The company wants to use a strong reference group appeal to promote the shoe. Develop a unique brand name and sketch a simple print advertisement to introduce the shoe. Make sure the reference group appeal is evident in the ad. Present your ideas to your teacher (judge) and explain why you believe the advertisement will be effective.

Check Your Understanding

Now that you have completed the chapter, check your understanding of the lessons with these questions. Record the score that best represents your understanding of each marketing concept.

1 = not at all; 3 = somewhat; 5 = very well

If your score is 42–50, you are ready for the assessment activities that follow. If you score 33–41, you should review the lessons for the items you scored 1–3. If you score 32 or less, you will want to carefully reread the lessons and work with a study partner on the areas you don't understand.

Can you—

___ explain why an understanding of consumer behavior is important to businesses that believe in the marketing concept?

___ differentiate between final and business consumers?

___ explain the difference between a want and a need?

___ list the five levels of Maslow's hierarchy of needs in order?

___ provide examples of rational, emotional, and patronage buying motives?

___ explain what occurs in each of the stages of consumer decision making?

___ describe how factors that make up personal identity affect buying behavior?

___ explain the differences between culture, social environment, and reference groups?

___ explain why and when consumers use routine, limited, and extensive decision making?

___ describe what a marketer should do when consumers use limited or extensive decision making and when they use routine decision making?

Review Marketing Terms

Match the terms listed with the definitions. Some terms may not be used.

1. The study of consumers and how they make decisions
2. Those who buy a product or service for personal use
3. An unfulfilled desire
4. The characteristics and character that make a person unique
5. The reasons that people buy
6. The forces of love, affection, guilt, fear, or passion that compel consumers to buy
7. An individual's belief about his or her identity, image, and capabilities
8. The process by which consumers collect information and choose among alternatives
9. An enduring pattern of emotions and behavior that define an individual
10. A group of people or an organization that an individual admires, identifies with, and wants to be a part of

a. attitude
b. business consumers
c. buying behavior
d. buying motives
e. consumer behavior
f. consumer decision-making process
g. culture
h. emotional motives
i. final consumers
j. lifestyle
k. motivation
l. need
m. patronage motives
n. personal identity
o. personality
p. rational motives
q. reference group
r. self-concept
s. want

Review Marketing Concepts

11. Marketing begins with
    a. selling a good product
    b. understanding customers
    c. pricing the product correctly
    d. developing a consumer survey

12. Dinner in an exclusive restaurant and the newest model cell phone are usually classified as
    a. wants
    b. needs
    c. motives
    d. buying decisions

13. Maslow classified esteem needs as
    a. physical and economic safety
    b. realizing your potential
    c. friends, love, and belonging
    d. respect and recognition

14. Business people and purchasing agents are usually motivated by
    a. rational motives
    b. emotional motives
    c. buying motives
    d. objective motives

15. In the decision-making process, when the consumer gathers information about various products or services, it is called
    a. problem recognition
    b. information search
    c. alternative evaluation
    d. purchase evaluation

16. Gender, ethnicity, age, and personality are factors that make up
    a. personal identity
    b. attitude
    c. culture
    d. social class

17. Encouraging consumers to "join the group" through the purchase of products and services is based on
    a. rational buying motives
    b. personality
    c. reference groups
    d. routine decision making

18. When a business investigates new vendors or locates a supplier for a new component part, it uses what type of decision making?
    a. routine decision making
    b. limited decision making
    c. extensive decision making
    d. repeated decision making

Marketing Research and Planning

19. Some products are sold to both business consumers and final consumers. Name at least one business consumer use and one final consumer use for each of the following items: pencils, balloons, rubber bands, radio, sofa, all-terrain vehicle, bagels, pesticide, suitcase, blankets. Here is an example:

Item	Business Use	Final Consumer Use
banana	restaurant	family lunches

20. Marketers strive to capture your attention with advertisements that use meaningful buying motives. Choose an advertisement from each of the following media: magazines, Internet, television, and radio. Select ads that demonstrate each of the three types of buying motives—emotional, rational, and patronage. Make copies of the magazine and Internet ads. Prepare a written description of the television and radio ads. Classify the type of buying motive used in each advertisement.

21. You are the manager of a new furniture store that is opening in three days. You believe strongly in the marketing concept and want your salespeople to pay attention to customers' needs as they help perform their sales duties. Write an e-mail to them to remind them of the elements of the marketing concept, why it is important, and what they can do to put it into action with each customer. Use the following words or phrases: customers, buying behavior, consumer decision-making process, needs, wants, buying motives, lifestyle, and extensive decision-making process.

22. Using Internet news services, find a corporate announcement of a new product or service. Analyze the announcement to identify the personal, cultural, social, and reference group influences to which the product or service appears to appeal. Cite specific language in the announcement that provides evidence of the appeal being used.

23. Some consumer advocates believe that marketers use research on consumer motivation and buying behavior to exploit them with emotional appeals and social pressures. What are your thoughts? Is identifying buying motives and using them in a marketing campaign an ethical or unethical practice? Write an essay that takes a position on this ethical question and defends your viewpoint.

Marketing Management and Decision Making

24. In order to learn more about customers, many organizations use customer feedback cards like the one shown below for a restaurant. The organizations use the information to improve their products and services and increase customer satisfaction.

   In an effort to help your school provide better service, work with other students to develop a customer feedback card to give to students at your school. The customer feedback card should be designed to find out from students what they like and dislike about your school. You may wish to ask questions about the curriculum, classes, teachers, atmosphere, spirit, extracurricular activities, grades, homework, facilities, and any other items relevant to your school. Survey at least 15 students.

   After the surveys have been completed and collected, use a computer spreadsheet program to record and tabulate the responses. Then determine the mean, median, and mode for each question. (As you will recall, the mean is the average of all the responses to a question, the median is the middle value when all responses are arranged in order, and the mode is the response that was given most frequently.) Prepare tables, charts, and graphs to display the survey results. Based on the results, draw several conclusions about student attitudes. Make recommendations for improvements to your school.

Fine Foods and More

We value your opinions and strive to meet your expectations. Tell us how you like us by circling the rating that best represents your view of our restaurant.

What did you think of our:

	Poor				Excellent
Menu	1	2	3	4	5
Portion size	1	2	3	4	5
Atmosphere	1	2	3	4	5
Service	1	2	3	4	5
Cleanliness	1	2	3	4	5
Prices	1	2	3	4	5

Thank you for sharing your views with us!

---

25. Companies that provide cellular telephone services are now marketing telephones equipped with a digital camera and audio recorder. The owner can take a picture or short video clip, record an audio message, and forward them to one or more recipients using the Internet. To use the new features, the customer must purchase a more expensive wireless plan or pay an additional charge for each video message sent. Many consumers like the new features but not the high cost of the service.

   Assume you are a marketing specialist for a cellular telephone company. Identify a target market for the new phones and service. As a part of the target market description, identify important needs, personal identity characteristics, and the personal and social influences for the prospective customers. Then describe the consumer decision-making process customers would follow and the buying motives to which you would appeal. Use a computer to design a one-page product brochure you would use to introduce the new cell phone and service to the target market.

Automotive Services Marketing Individual Series Event

Quick Stop is a busy gas station/convenience store. You are the assistant manager for this popular service station. The recently added pumps that allow customers to pay with credit cards at the pump are very popular. Unfortunately, the pumps often need repair because they do not read the credit cards correctly, and/or they do not print a receipt.

Recently, you have listened to many angry customers complain about high gas prices. Customers become increasingly frustrated when they have to go inside the store/station to pay for or obtain a receipt for their gas purchase or when pumps are covered with plastic bags, indicating that they are not operational. Frustrated customers have indicated that they will take their business to a competitor.

Your task is two-fold—you must convince the owner of the station to repair the gas pumps immediately, and you must create a special promotion to bring back customers to your service station. You will present your proposal to the owner of the service station.

Description of the Proposal

Write down the main points that you want to emphasize to the owner of the service station.

Description of Promotion Plan

Outline your plan for a promotion to keep loyal customers coming to your service station. Remember, they are upset about high gas prices and problems with the "pay at the pump" service and inoperable gas pumps.

Role-Play

Translate what you have learned into effective, efficient, and spontaneous action, demonstrated in a role-play.

Performance Indicators Evaluated

- Explain the nature and scope of the product/service management function. (Product/Service Management)

- Identify routine activities for maintaining business facilities and equipment. (Operations)

- Describe the product mix that will be used to meet customer expectations. (Product/Service Management)

- Explain the nature of positive customer/client relations. (Emotional Intelligence)

- Evaluate the customer experience. (Product/Service Management)

Go to the DECA web site for more detailed information.

Think Critically

1. Why must self-service stations carefully maintain their pumps?

2. What type of incentive would be good for loyal customers of the service station?

3. How will improved customer service affect the number of employees needed to work each shift at the service station?

4. How do rising gas prices affect customer satisfaction at a service station?

www.deca.org

Competition Is Everywhere

©GETTY IMAGES/PHOTODISC

Newsline)))

New Cars for New Buyers

One of the most successful automobile manufacturers is not satisfied with the status quo. In 2003, Toyota introduced Scion, a new brand of automobiles, to U.S. consumers. Toyota says that Scion is aimed at "trend-setters." In reality, the goal of Toyota is to provide a unique automobile for the next generation of automobile buyers. Scion is designed for the 65 million 8-to-22-year-olds who are projected to buy four million cars by 2010.

Toyota and its luxury brand Lexus have become brands of choice for many baby boomers. However, the average age of Toyota purchasers is getting older. Toyota has a well-established image of quality, but it is sometimes viewed as having stodgy, middle-of-the-road designs. Enter Scion, a boxy, funky, brightly colored design with basic models priced below $16,000. A choice of options that appeal to the Y-generation can be added using personal design kiosks located in shopping malls, at street festivals, and concerts, as well as in auto showrooms and on the Internet.

Toyota's research shows that young customers make purchases in different ways than their parents do. They don't trust auto salespeople, want to be on the cutting edge, look to their peers for information, and like offbeat promotions. Scion has successfully gained attention by using young promotional representatives who set up displays in shopping center parking lots and other open spaces where people gather. Banners, kiosks, and blaring music attract attention. The reps give away gifts and recruit people to test-drive the new models. The Internet is being used heavily to promote the new cars. Scion ads and product information now appear on many of the targeted audience's favorite web sites.

Think Critically

1. What are the advantages and disadvantages to Toyota of developing a new line of automobiles under a different brand name?

2. Why would Toyota target people under the age of 16 who cannot even drive an automobile yet?

3. Now that the Scion models have been available for several years, do you believe Toyota's marketing strategy was effective? Why or why not?

school.cengage.com/marketing/marketing

Prepare for Performance

This chapter develops the following Performance Indicators from the DECA Competitive Events program.

Core Performance Indicators

- Understand the concept and strategies utilized to determine and target marketing strategies to a select audience
- Employ marketing information to plan marketing activities
- Describe the use of target marketing in professional selling

Supporting Performance Indicators

- Identify ways to segment markets
- Describe the nature of target marketing
- Develop customer/client profile
- Identify market segments
- Employ marketing information to determine and meet customer needs

Go to **school.cengage.com/marketing/marketing** and click on Connect to DECA.

Visual Focus

ORGANIC
Bourbon Vanilla
Made with Madagasgar Bourbon Vanilla
~ the finest vanilla on earth

PJ Mad
Organic Super-P
ONE PINT 473 ML

What do you get when you blend the best of American ice cream with the best of Italian ice cream using only the finest organic ingredients? Better ice cream.

PJ Madison's
Organic Super-Premium Gelato Style Ice Cream

PJ Madison's encourages every American to Donate Life through organ, eye and tissue donation. For more information and inspiring stories, visit www.donatelife.net.

COURTESY OF PJ MADISON'S. USED WITH PERMISSION.

Most products and services compete with other similar brands. Each company must find ways to make its brand different and more desirable to its customers. This chapter will help you learn how businesses use information about customers and competitors to develop successful marketing strategies for their product and services.

Focus Questions:

Ice cream is a commonly purchased product, and consumers have many choices of brands, flavors, and prices. In what ways is PJ Madison's trying to suggest its ice cream is different and better than other brands? What types of consumers do you believe will be attracted to the advertisement? In your view, is the ad effective at encouraging customers to try PJ Madison's ice cream? Why or why not?

Locate an ad for ice cream or another dessert that might compete with PJ Madison's. In a class discussion, share your ideas about the similarities and differences in the products and the customers to which each product seems to be appealing.

Focusing on Market Segments

GOALS

- Describe how markets can be segmented by geographic location, demographic characteristics, psychographics, product usage, and benefits derived.
- Explain how to evaluate market potential and calculate market share.

KEY TERMS

market segmentation, *p. 183*

mass marketing, *p. 183*

geographic segmentation, *p. 184*

demographics, *p. 184*

psychographics, *p. 184*

product usage, *p. 184*

benefit segmentation, *p. 185*

market opportunity, *p. 187*

market potential, *p. 187*

market share, *p. 188*

marketing matters

Businesses focus their marketing efforts on potential customers who are most likely to buy their products and services. They identify market segments or groups of consumers that share certain characteristics. Those characteristics may be personal factors such as age, education, income, or gender, or they may identify where consumers live, their lifestyles, needs, interests, or other factors that influence what they might want to purchase.

Make a list of six personal characteristics that describe who you are and what you think would be important factors if you were shopping for a new car. How would each of those characteristics affect your purchasing decision?

Market Segmentation

In order to compete in a free enterprise economy, businesses direct all of their efforts and resources toward achieving specific goals. As an important part of their efforts, they devise marketing strategies to compete for sales dollars, customers, market share, or whatever goal they have set. Marketing segmentation has become an important part of the marketing efforts of many companies.

Is it possible for this group of teenagers to represent more than one market segment? Explain why.

One Brand or Many?

One of the decisions global marketers must make is whether they are going to market their product under one brand name internationally or create smaller brands specific to each country or region. The Coca-Cola Company sells Coca-Cola using the first approach. This allows them to concentrate their money and efforts on building one global brand name. Although the marketing approach may vary from country to country, a Coke will be a Coke, whether it's served in Los Angeles or Hong Kong.

The drawback to the one-brand approach is that it limits the degree to which products can be tailored to each market. By creating different brands, a company can better meet the demands of specific markets. A laundry detergent, for instance, may sell better in one country if it has green flakes and is called Swift, and better in another country if it has blue flakes and is called Whizz. Creating separate brands gives companies the flexibility to do both. That's why, if you walk through a grocery store in a foreign country, you may find products with unfamiliar names made by companies you recognize.

Think Critically

Pick a well-known international brand. Use the Internet to research how it is marketed in another country. How does it differ from the way it is marketed in the United States?

The Benefits of Segmentation

A *market segment* is a group of individuals or organizations within a larger market that share one or more important characteristics. These shared characteristics result in similar product or service needs. Everyone belongs to many market segments. For example, you may belong to one segment of the population that enjoys rock music and another segment that drinks a certain brand of cola.

Businesses use marketing information and market research to complete market segmentation. **Market segmentation** is the process of dividing a large group of consumers into subgroups based on specific characteristics and common needs. Recognizing the needs of a group of prospective customers enables a business to develop marketing strategies that match those needs.

Some businesses may be unwilling to spend the extra time and money required to gather and analyze information in order to segment a market. Instead they use mass marketing. While market segmentation directs a company's efforts at a specific group of consumers with unique needs, **mass marketing** directs a company's marketing mix at a large and heterogeneous group of consumers. With market segmentation, the company views its competition as only those businesses that have products and services appealing to the selected market segment. Mass marketing considers all of the consumers in a market as potential customers and every other business competing in that market as a competitor. By appealing to a more diverse group of customers with different needs and competing with many more businesses, success may be more difficult. However, advantages of mass marketing include higher potential sales volumes and efficiencies of scale in a much larger market. Large companies with high-volume production and vast distribution networks reaching many national and international markets can be quite effective using mass marketing. Smaller or more specialized businesses have found that type of strategy difficult to maintain.

Companies that believe in the marketing concept recognize that the increased time and expense of market segmentation will enable them to identify groups of customers and understand their needs.

Segmentation Categories

Using market segmentation, consumers can be divided into groups based on geographic location, demographic characteristics, psychographics, product usage, and expected benefits.

Geographic Segmentation
Dividing consumers into markets based on where they live is referred to as **geographic segmentation**. These markets might be as large as a country or as small as a ZIP code. Companies vary in size and scope, and, therefore, the group of customers they want to reach can also vary in size.

Geographic segmentation is based on the concept that people who live in the same geographic area might have the same wants and needs. Consumers who live in Minnesota are more likely to have an interest in cold weather sports than people who live in Oklahoma. A political party may want to send newsletters on a particular issue to voters in specific congressional districts.

Demographic Characteristics
The descriptive characteristics of a market such as age, gender, race, income, and educational level are referred to as **demographics**. Figure 7-1 illustrates how the population of the United States can be described using two demographic characteristics— education and income. Often marketers want to serve a market segment that has similar demographic characteristics. Types of music, cable TV channels, magazines, and restaurant menus may be developed to appeal to different ages, education levels, or ethnic groups. You belong to many demographic market segments. Marketers may segment you according to your age, gender, ethnicity, religious affiliation, and even your body type.

Psychographics
People's interests and values are referred to as **psychographics**. Examples of psychographics are the way you spend your time and make your lifestyle choices. Lifestyle research has been particularly valuable in establishing market segments. People's lifestyles and social interests combine to influence the type of housing and transportation they prefer, where they choose to live, how they spend their time, and even how often they eat away from home.

Psychographic segmentation is responsible for book stores, coffee shops, sports venues, home decor, and health care products because businesses have found segments with wants and needs unique from the mass market.

Product Usage
Marketing strategies can differ based on **product usage**, meaning how frequently consumers use products and the quantity of product used. How frequently do the people you know consume particular types of beverages such as milk, soft drinks, coffee, or tea? Some people have a preferred beverage and drink it several times a day. Others vary their beverages at meals but

FIGURE 7-1

In the U.S. population, the demographic characteristics of education and income are closely linked.

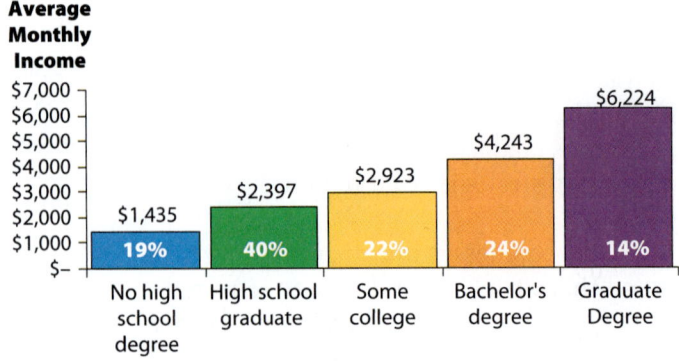

may have a particular choice for breaks or when exercising.

The quantity of a beverage consumed at one time varies and accounts for the range of container sizes used for beverages. Some people consume only a few ounces of a drink at one time. They may want to purchase a small container or want a resealable container to maintain the freshness of the beverage. However, with the popularity of the 32-ounce or larger soft drinks at convenience stores and fast-food restaurants, it is evident that some people expect to drink a large quantity at one time. By segmenting the market based on usage, business people can make sure each group has the preferred size and type of container to meet their consumption needs.

Other examples of marketing products based on product usage include planning hotel services for frequent business travelers and offering cellular telephone plans suited to the number of phones in a family and the amount of minutes used in one month.

A part of product usage is customer experience. Experience ranges from none to extensive. Of experienced users, some have tried the product and don't like it. Others believe it is one of several appropriate alternatives, but they have no preference. Still other customers purchase and use it regularly as their preferred choice. The type of experience will help determine whether a market segment represents a valuable group of potential customers and what type of marketing effort is needed.

Benefit Expectations As you learned earlier, each product or service on the market has a value or utility to the consumer. Consumers have specific benefits they expect to receive when using a particular product or service. **Benefit segmentation** divides consumers into groups depending on specific values or benefits they expect or require from the use of a product or service. An example of using benefit segmentation can be seen with shampoo. There are many market segments for a product as simple as shampoo based on the expectations

How can market segmentation be used to devise a marketing strategy for a hotel?

and requirements of consumers. There are shampoos for consumers with oily hair, dry hair, or normal hair. There are also shampoos for people with dandruff. Those who shampoo daily have different needs from those who use the product once a week or less. There are even shampoos with conditioners added for people who want one-step hair care. Add the various scents and additives and you can see the infinite number of segments that are created by benefits derived.

Segmenting the Business Market

Just as marketers segment the consumer markets, they also segment business markets. Business markets are segmented by the type of company and the major activities and operations of the business. The size of the business and its geographic location, including whether the company operates in multiple states and even internationally, may be important segmenting criteria. Finally the types of products and services purchased, the volume and frequency of purchasing, and the type of buying procedures used help to segment business customers.

Checkpoint ▶▶

Why do businesses that believe in the marketing concept use market segmentation rather than mass marketing?

Be an Effective Listener

There are a number of areas in your life where listening is required. How well you listen can affect your success in many ways.

Academically, it is important to listen during class. Focused listening and careful note taking will help you prepare for homework, projects, and tests.

Listening in social situations is also important. A friend may need you to listen to a problem and provide emotional support. When you are at a party, listening to the conversation of people around you may give you clues about their interests. By mentioning one of their interests, you can start or participate in a conversation.

In business, listening can mean the difference between success and failure. Businesses must listen to employees' and customers' opinions in order to be effective.

In all situations, it is important to use "active listening." Active listening goes beyond simply hearing what the speaker has said. It involves recognizing the emotions behind what was said. Suppose your friend, who is trying to qualify for a college scholarship, says, "That calculus test was hard. I got only a C+." Using the active listening technique, you might reply by saying "It sounds like you are worried about how that grade will impact your chance to get a scholarship. Do you want to talk about it?"

Being a good listener requires patience and generosity. You should give the speaker your full attention and stay focused on the topic.

Components of Effective Listening

There are several specific components to effective listening. They are decoding, comprehension, drawing a conclusion, and feedback.

Decoding a message involves translating what the speaker said into the real meaning of the message. Comprehension involves determining how the message relates to the overall topic. When the listener decides how to respond to the message, the listener is drawing a conclusion.

Feedback is given to the speaker by a verbal or non-verbal response.

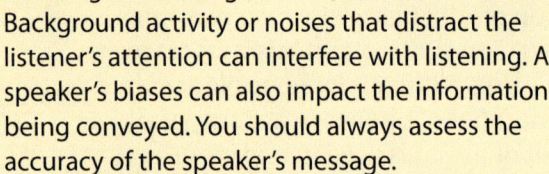

Improving Your Listening Skills

Some listeners are unaware of barriers to effective listening. The listener's preconceived attitudes about the speaker or the topic can interfere with understanding the message. Background activity or noises that distract the listener's attention can interfere with listening. A speaker's biases can also impact the information being conveyed. You should always assess the accuracy of the speaker's message.

Body language should convey that you are interested in what is being said. Maintaining eye contact, smiling, and leaning toward the speaker all signal that you are listening attentively.

Listening can be improved with practice. Techniques to improve listening skills include being prepared to listen, reducing distractions, asking questions to clarify main points, refraining from judgment, and paraphrasing what was said to confirm your understanding. In complicated or prolonged listening situations, consider taking notes.

Develop Your Skill

Let your parents know that for one week you are going to try to improve your listening skills. Whenever your parents talk to you, give them your full attention. Eliminate any background noise, including TVs, computers, or iPods. If they are outlining family plans for the week or giving instructions, take notes on what they say to capture the main points. See how smoothly the next day flows. Continue this practice through Friday. On Saturday, ask your parents for feedback on whether they have observed an improvement in your listening skills.

PHOTO: ©GETTY IMAGES/PHOTODISC

Identifying and Analyzing Market Segments

There are two reasons to segment a market. First, by carefully analyzing a market based on segmenting characteristics, a business has a better understanding of the market and the potential customers. Second, with detailed information on market segments, a business can identify the best market opportunities. A **market opportunity** is an identified market with excellent potential based on careful research.

Identifying Possible Segments

To successfully segment a market, a business must recognize possible factors that affect consumer purchasing and collect information to determine if market segments are alike or different in their purchasing behaviors and consumption patterns. Identifying market segments involves the following steps:

1. Select a market or product category to study. The market will be a large group of consumers who have similar but broad needs, such as entertainment or transportation, or who are likely to purchase a category of products such as computers or sporting goods. The market or product category is often one in which the business has experience, or it may be new. The business may be looking for new product ideas, new customers, or new opportunities for both customers and products.
2. Choose a basis for segmenting the market. Determine what factors seem to lead to the greatest differences among customers and may affect their expectations and choices.
3. Gather information for analysis. This step will usually involve a combination of reviewing current customer information, identifying and collecting information needed, and completing marketing research.

4. Identify the segments that exist in the market. Based on the information collected, several potential segments are identified and described based on unique characteristics that influence the market potential, such as geographic location or product usage.
5. Use market information to choose the markets that present the greatest and least amount of potential. Those with the greatest potential will be analyzed further to select the target markets that will be the focus for the company's marketing efforts.

Determining Market Potential

Once market segments have been identified, they must be analyzed. To be an effective market segment, it has to have the potential to be profitable with needs that the company can satisfy through its marketing efforts. Each segment should be evaluated on the following criteria:

1. Number of potential customers
2. Customers' interest in the product or service and other mix elements
3. Amount of money customers have available to make the purchase
4. Business's ability to communicate with and distribute the product to consumers.

Since businesses operate to make a profit, it is important to estimate the market potential. The **market potential** is the total revenue that can be obtained

Fast FACTS

According to a study of U.S. consumers and their interest in green marketing, 11% have made green purchasing and recycling a part of their lifestyle while 31% don't know or don't care about green products.

from the market segment. Since it is unlikely that one company will attract all customers in a given market, businesses also calculate their market share. **Market share** is the portion of the total market potential that each company expects in relation to its competitors.

For example, the total market potential for disposable cameras in one city is estimated at $1,850,000 per year. One manufacturer that is introducing a new disposable digital camera in the city expects to capture 12 percent of the total market in the first year. To calculate the company's planned market share in dollars, multiply $1,850,000 by 0.12 for a total of $222,000.

The company can also determine the market potential and market share in units instead of dollars. If the average price of a disposable camera is $9.25, the market potential in units is $1,850,000 divided by $9.25, or 200,000 units. The company's planned market share is 12 percent of 200,000 units, or 24,000 cameras (200,000 $\times$ 0.12). The company has the potential of selling 24,000 cameras in this market segment in this city.

Checkpoint ▶▶▶

What is the difference between market potential and market share?

7-1 Assessment

Key Concepts

Determine the best answer.

1. A mass market is _____ than a market segment.
   a. larger
   b. more homogeneous
   c. more profitable
   d. all of the above

2. Age, income, education, and gender are examples of
   a. geographic factors
   b. demographics
   c. psychographics
   d. lifestyles

3. _____ segmentation is based on the value customers expect to receive from using a product or service.
   a. Economic
   b. Market
   c. Benefit
   d. Consumer

4. True or False: All market segments present a market opportunity.

5. The market _____ is the total revenue that can be obtained from the market segment.

Make Academic Connections

6. **Visual Art** Draw a large circle that represents the mass market of all television viewers. Now draw and label five smaller circles within the large circle that represent a television show or a cable television channel that has a particular focus (example: The Food Network). For each small circle, identify several characteristics of a market segment that enjoys the shows or channels.

7. **Math** Sales of MP3 players in 2006 were 34 million units. Apple had a market share of 74%, followed by SanDisk with 9%, Creative with 4%, Microsoft with 3%, and Samsung with 2%. How many MP3 players did each company sell? How many players were sold by all other companies, and what market share did those sales represent?

Connect to

8. Your team members are the managers of a new jewelry store opening in your community. Identify a specific market segment based on demographic and psychographic characteristics to which you will direct your marketing efforts. Prepare two visuals that describe your market segment. Make a three-minute presentation to your teacher (judge) justifying your decisions.

Positioning for Competitive Advantage

GOALS

- Explain the various bases for positioning a product to distinguish it from the competition.
- Describe the three common positioning strategies.

KEY TERMS

market position, *p. 189*

consumer perceptions, *p. 192*

marketing matters

Businesses know that people usually consider a number of products or services as alternatives when they try to satisfy specific needs. Marketers carefully plan marketing mix elements to influence how a product or service is perceived. When planning a marketing mix, they should consider how it affects consumer perceptions, how it compares to the mixes of competitors, and how it will be affected by the business and economic environment.

Make a list containing a brand name for a model of automobile, a line of apparel, a national restaurant chain, a well-known retailer, and a line of consumer electronics. For each brand, write a one-line description that identifies its main appeal to consumers and its uniqueness in comparison to competitors.

Basis for Positioning

In order to influence consumers' purchases, businesses position their products and services to highlight their differences from those of competitors. **Market position** refers to the unique image of a product or service in a consumer's mind relative to similar competitive offerings. Companies use a variety of methods for positioning. An example of how the various positioning methods can be used for a product as simple as laundry detergent is shown in Figure 7-2.

FIGURE 7-2

Competitors develop marketing mixes that emphasize the market positions of their products. These laundry products are positioned to appeal to different target markets.

	Laundry Product A	Laundry Product B
Attribute	Cleans quickly and easily	Leaves fresh scent
Price and Quality	Low price, good value	Higher price for highest quality
Use or Application	Use as pre-wash on tough stains	Use for hand-washing delicates
Product User	Homemaker's reliable friend	New generation's discovery
Product Classification	Used by Olympic athletes	Used by professional laundries
Competitor	Gets out dirt Product B can't	Gentler on clothing than Product A

Attribute

One way to position a product is to highlight a product feature or attribute. For example, certain toothpastes have ingredients that whiten teeth. The manufacturer says "Our toothpaste does everything every other toothpaste does, and in addition, it helps make your teeth white." The positioning is accomplished with the specific product attribute and related promotion that identifies the attribute and its value for the consumer.

Price and Quality

This position strategy may stress a higher price as a sign of quality, or it may emphasize a lower price as an indication of value. Mercedes Benz does not apologize for the high price of its automobiles. Instead, it suggests that because they are high-priced they offer a unique, high-quality image. Wal-Mart implies that its products are well suited for consumers' needs with the advantage of being priced lower than competitors' products. While Wal-Mart's image and marketing strategy are much different from Mercedes Benz, its positioning goal is accomplished by convincing customers they are getting a good value when they shop at that store.

Use or Application

Stressing unique uses or applications can be an effective means of positioning a product. Arm & Hammer used to be a staple for homemakers who regularly baked bread. As more and more families began purchasing bread rather than making it at home, the market for Arm & Hammer declined dramatically. The company changed its positioning strategy by developing and promoting new uses and applications for its products. Today, few customers actually purchase Arm & Hammer baking soda as an ingredient in baking recipes.

Now, they view it as an effective product with uses ranging from deodorizing the refrigerator to brushing teeth.

Product User

This positioning strategy encourages use of a product or service by associating a personality or type of user with the product. For a time, Pepsi Cola suggested that Pepsi products were consumed by a young, active "Pepsi Generation." Athletic apparel manufacturers use images and obtain endorsements of popular professional athletes. Some cruise lines, such as Disney Cruises, position themselves as a family-oriented vacation line.

Product Classification

When positioning according to product class, the objective is to associate the product with a particular category of products. For example, Amtrak, which offers rail passenger service, uses a number of strategies that model the look, service, and scheduling associated with airlines. Pork, marketed as "the other white meat," is positioned along with turkey and chicken to create an image of a healthier product. The positioning strategy was selected to change the view that many customers may hold of pork products and to increase demand.

Outdoorsmen have always been challenged to find a way to stay warm and dry in winter weather. Access school.cengage.com/marketing/ marketing and click on the link for Chapter 7. SmartWool was founded by New England ski instructors. What type of product is sold by SmartWool? Who do you think is the target market for the products sold by SmartWool? How does SmartWool position itself in the market?

school.cengage.com/marketing/marketing

Digital Digest

Marketers Reap New Data

The compilation of huge databases of household purchasing data is having a big impact on the way manufacturers of consumer goods plan their marketing budgets. While it has long been easy to evaluate the short-term effectiveness of marketing campaigns by analyzing data from checkout scanners, the ability to access household data now gives marketers a keen insight into long-term effects.

Household purchasing information is collected every time someone uses a frequent shopper or loyalty card. Supermarkets and discount stores make extensive use of them to encourage repeat shopping with discounts, rebates, and other promotions tied to use of the cards. With transactions identifiable by household, marketers can now piece together strings of household purchases over time.

For example, when people buy a product in response to a promotional campaign, marketers can determine how many of them were first-time buyers, how many people continue to buy the product after trying it, how much time elapses before people buy again, and what other products the households buy or stop buying.

Marketers have long known that promotions have both short- and long-term effects on consumer buying, but until recently they could only guess at the long-term impact.

Think Critically

1. If a business finds that an ad campaign boosts sales by 5% over the following three months, but that 90% of new buyers continue to buy the product over the next 12 months, how might that affect its marketing strategy?

2. If $2-off coupons increase monthly sales by 50%, but only one out of ten coupon users buys the product again in the next 12 months, how might that affect a business's marketing strategy?

Competitor

Sometimes marketers make an effort to demonstrate how they are positioned against competitors that hold a strong market position. As the Korean automobile manufacturer Hyundai introduces new, larger and more luxurious models, it has begun to compare itself to the well-known luxury brands sold in the United States. It does not believe that consumers will immediately begin to believe that Hyundai has the most luxurious products, but it wants consumers to consider its models when they are considering the purchase of a luxury automobile. Ford recently ran a campaign in which consumers favorably compared the style and handling of the Ford Fusion with that of market leaders Toyota and Honda.

7UP used to promote itself as the "uncola" to offer a comparison with and unique position from the two leading brands of colas—Coke and Pepsi. Avis developed a marketing strategy identifying the company as "Number 2" among car rental brands but trying harder. The strategy was aimed at positioning itself against Hertz, the leading brand at the time. Anytime you see an ad comparing one product with a well-known competitor's products, you can assume that a competitor positioning strategy is being used.

Checkpoint ▶▶

What are six common bases for positioning?

Selecting a Positioning Strategy

All businesses need to develop a positioning strategy. A positioning strategy will outline how a company is going to present its product or service to the consumer and how it will compete in the marketplace with other businesses offering similar products and services. Positioning strategies usually revolve around three major areas:

1. Consumer perceptions
2. Competitors in the marketplace
3. Changes in the business environment

Consumer Perceptions

Consumer perceptions are the images consumers have of competing goods and services in the marketplace. The objective is for marketers to position their products to appeal to the desires and perceptions of a target market. A group of consumers that has a distinct idea of the image desired for a product or service might represent a target market. A business will do well with a target market when those consumers perceive the attributes of its products as being close to their ideal image.

Over the years, Hershey has done an excellent job of responding to consumer perceptions. For years, its product was perceived by many consumers as the ideal chocolate bar. However, in recent years, several competitors have entered the premium chocolate market, forcing Hershey to expand its product line and increase its promotional efforts.

©GETTY IMAGES/PHOTODISC

Why is consumer perception important for a restaurant?

Competition

Businesses are concerned about the perception consumers have of the company and its products in relation to those of competitors. The ideal situation is when consumers perceive a business's products to be superior to its competitors' products or services based on the attributes the company emphasizes in its marketing strategy.

A great deal of marketing effort is used in competitive positioning. The pricing, promotion, product development, and distribution strategies are all planned with an eye toward the competition. Certain products, such as soft drinks, must be carefully positioned in relation to competition because image is important to consumers as they choose a brand. Coca-Cola and Pepsi Cola have staged a very fierce and competitive promotional battle in recent years to gain a stronger competitive position. This competition has been referred to as the "Cola Wars."

Companies must be careful not to base their positioning decisions solely on the actions of their competitors.

Working in **Teams**

As a team, list three well-known brands of consumer products. Each team member should write a statement describing the image of each brand as he or she perceives it. Compare the statements for each brand and determine the amount of agreement on the image. Discuss the reasons for similarities and differences in perceptions.

Each company has unique strengths and weaknesses as well as specific goals. A competitor's new marketing strategy should be watched carefully, and information should be collected on the effect it has on a company's customers and its market share.

Business Environment

Organizations should continually pay attention to possible changes in the business environment that might affect the position of their products or services. These include new products entering the market, changing consumer needs, new technology, negative publicity, and resource availability. Manufacturers of golf clubs have been significantly affected by the introduction of new materials used in shaft construction as well as new club head designs.

Restaurants and food processing companies have had to respond to the concerns about trans fats and their negative effects on diet and health. Colleges have discovered that they must respond to the needs of non-traditional students, including more part-time and older students. Colleges have responded by offering convenient schedules, adding more parking, and expanding courses offered via the Internet. In each case, these business environment changes have affected marketing strategies and even the types of products and services offered.

Checkpoint ▶▶

Why should businesses be cautious when using competitive positioning?

7-2 Assessment

Xtra!
Study Tools
school.cengage.com/marketing/marketing

Key Concepts

Determine the best answer.

1. Another name for a product feature is a(n)
   a. marketing mix element
   b. positioning strategy
   c. attribute
   d. image

2. When pork developed an image as "the other white meat," the method of positioning was
   a. price and quality
   b. product user
   c. product classification
   d. competitor

3. Which of the following is *not* one of the areas that typically affects the selection of a positioning strategy?
   a. pricing
   b. consumer perceptions
   c. competitors in the marketplace
   d. changes in the business environment

4. True or False: The most important influence on a company's positioning decision should be the actions of competitors.

Make Academic Connections

5. **Communications** Use print, Internet, radio, or television advertisements to prepare an exhibit of the six methods of positioning described in the lesson. The exhibit can be in the form of a poster, audio or video recordings, or another medium.

6. **History** Use Internet or library research to identify and study a company that has operated for more than 50 years and has made a major change in the market position of a key product. Write a one-page report that describes the reasons for the change, including responses to consumer perceptions, competitors' actions, or changes in the business environment.

Connect to ◆ DECA
An Association of Marketing Students

7. A new bank in your community has asked your marketing team to propose an idea for a successful market position. Prepare a print advertisement that clearly communicates the image you have selected. Present the advertisement to your teacher (judge). Identify the basis for the market position chosen and explain why your team believes it will be effective.

Competing for Market Segments

GOALS

- Explain direct vs. indirect competition and price vs. non-price competition.
- Describe the benefits of competition to consumers.

KEY TERMS

direct competition, *p.195*

indirect competition, *p. 195*

price competition, *p. 196*

non-price competition, *p. 196*

marketing matters

Markets are important because they contain the potential customers for marketers' products. Competition is the rivalry between two or more businesses to secure a dominant position in a market. The products of some businesses are almost identical, resulting in stiff competition and pressures to reduce prices in order to attract customers. Other businesses have products that have notable differences, making competition less intense.

List two products that you buy that have recently undergone important changes and improvements. Identify the businesses you believe are the major competitors in that market and identify how those businesses compete with each other. Now list two products you buy that have not changed in any important ways for several years. Again, identify the businesses that are the major competitors offering that product and note how those businesses compete. Which of the products has more or less competition? Discuss with other students the effect competition has on changes and improvements to products.

Types of Competition for Positioning Decisions

Just as there are different types of market segments and positioning strategies, there are different types of competition that businesses face when positioning their products. To be able to compete successfully, businesses must be able to identify and reach a market segment that has a need for their product or service and position itself effectively against its competitors.

The type of competition faced by a business will affect its positioning. There are two major types of competition that businesses must recognize and address—direct versus indirect competition and price versus non-price competition.

What positioning strategy might a small neighborhood grocery store use to compete against larger, national supermarket chains?

©GETTY IMAGES/PHOTODISC

The Power of Word-of-Mouth Marketing

When a friend recommends a movie to you, you are more likely to go see it than if you just saw a movie preview. That's because you trust your friends more than you trust an ad for the movie. Of course the movie preview will say the movie is great—that's the job of a movie preview. But your friends have nothing to gain by you seeing the movie, so they'll give you their honest opinion.

The idea behind word-of-mouth marketing is to get people who like a product or service to tell others about it. When people are talking positively about a company's products, it is sometimes referred to as "buzz." A company can create buzz in several ways. It will sometimes target influencers, or people whom others look to for advice or recommendations. For example, a shoe company might send shoes to a celebrity to wear, or a pharmaceutical company might try to get a doctor to recommend a certain medication.

When Google launched Gmail, its e-mail service, it gave free accounts to key influencers. Individuals could not get a Gmail account unless they were invited by a current member. Limiting the supply created buzz and drove up demand, and Gmail, through word-of-mouth marketing, quickly became a major player in the world of e-mail providers.

Think Critically

1. For what types of products might word-of-mouth marketing be effective?

2. How has e-mail affected word-of-mouth marketing?

Direct and Indirect Competition

Direct competition is competition in a market with businesses that offer the same type of product or service. This is a common form of competition. For example, Holiday Inn and Ramada Inn compete with each other for travelers' dollars. Nike, Adidas, Reebok, and other sport shoe manufacturers compete head-to-head.

Businesses that compete directly must know who their competitors are. McDonald's has obvious competitors such as Hardee's, Burger King, and Wendy's. It also competes against other fast-food restaurants such as KFC, Taco Bell, and locally owned fast-food restaurants. These are all direct competitors even though they may offer different menu items. McDonald's competes head-to-head with these businesses. It tells consumers why its menu items taste better and are a better value.

McDonald's goal is to convince every customer that it offers the best choice among all competing brands.

Indirect competition occurs when a business competes with other companies offering products that are not in the same product category but that satisfy similar customer needs. A movie theaters competes directly with other area theaters, but it competes indirectly with video rental stores, the on-demand feature of many cable television services, and even more broadly with other entertainment choices.

If McDonald's promotes its products as easy and convenient to obtain, then it might be in indirect competition with meals offered at the deli counters of many supermarkets and convenience stores. McDonald's might also find itself competing with easy-to-prepare frozen meals that can be popped into the microwave for a quick and easy individual or family meal.

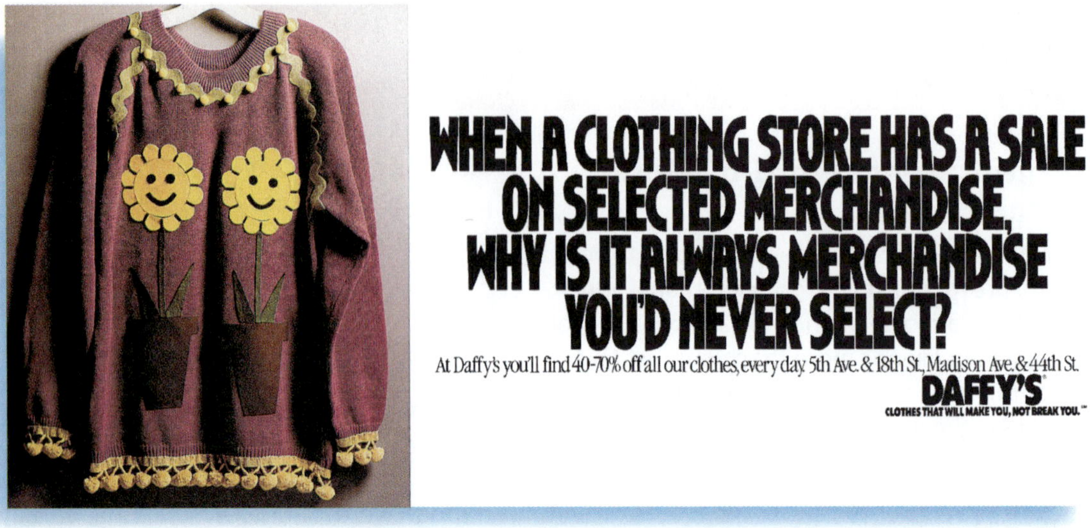
WHEN A CLOTHING STORE HAS A SALE ON SELECTED MERCHANDISE, WHY IS IT ALWAYS MERCHANDISE YOU'D NEVER SELECT?
At Daffy's you'll find 40-70% off all our clothes, every day. 5th Ave. & 18th St., Madison Ave. & 44th St.
DAFFY'S
CLOTHES THAT WILL MAKE YOU, NOT BREAK YOU.
COURTESY OF DAFFY'S

A low price is often not enough to convince customers to purchase a company's products.

Remember that you have limited dollars to spend on a meal, and there are many factors that can affect your choice of the type of meal and the place to purchase it. How does McDonald's compete with all of the indirect competitors available to consumers in the marketplace?

The marketing managers at McDonald's have some important decisions to make. One decision they must make involves what features of their products they will highlight or what benefits they will emphasize. Will it be quality, variety, price, convenience, or a friendly family atmosphere? Each market segment places value on different things, and each business must appeal to the characteristics of that segment or segments on which it focuses. McDonald's will compete differently for a market segment that wants a fast breakfast before school or work than it does for the young family segment that wants affordable and nutritious menu choices for both adults and children.

Price and Non-Price Competition

Since many consumers have limited dollars to spend on each of their purchases and are looking for the best value, some marketers decide to emphasize price when they compete. Rivalry among businesses on the basis of price and value is called **price competition**. Look in your local newspaper at the various grocery store advertisements and you will see an excellent example of price competition. Restaurants use price competition with their lunch or early evening dinner specials. Another example of price competition is airfares. If a new airline enters a market, it will often offer very low fares for the first weeks or months. In response, usually the competing airlines offering flights between the same cities will also lower their fares.

The opposite of price competition is **non-price competition**, which occurs when businesses decide to emphasize factors of their marketing mix other than price. Those factors might include product

Fast FACTS

In a recent survey of consumers considering the purchase of a high-definition television, 16% said screen size would be the most important factor in their decision while 24% valued the brand name over other factors. However, 60% reported the main influence in their purchase decision would be price.

quality, brand name, location, or special customer service. Non-price competition occurs for several reasons. First of all, some businesses do not have a great deal of control over their price in relation to competitors. Insurance companies may not have much control over the price they can charge for policies because a state government agency regulates the industry's prices. Therefore, they focus on non-price issues, such as an easy-to-complete application, personalized services from an insurance agency, and prompt claims service when the policyholder suffers a loss.

Another reason a company might choose to use non-price competition is because its product is higher priced. A small business may not be able to compete with large companies due to higher costs and lower volume. The small business may want to identify a specific market segment that is looking for factors other than price when making a purchase. The small business could emphasize individualized attention, delivery, set-up, and after-sale service, or even the long history of the business owners in the community as a balance for higher prices.

Non-price competition is effective when the market segment values something other than price. The consumers must recognize a unique quality in the product that leads to a product preference regardless of the price. These qualities might be service, quality, credit, location, guarantees, or a unique image.

Checkpoint ▶▶

What are the two major types of competitive strategies employed by businesses?

Benefits of Competition

Consumers benefit in many ways from competition. One benefit is that the consumer receives the best price for products. Competition forces businesses to offer reasonable prices for the products and services that consumers use. If businesses want to be successful, they must price their products in line with others in the same classification. As a result, the consumer is given the most value for the least amount of money.

A second benefit of competition is that it encourages improvements in products with the addition of unique features and benefits. Each company is looking for a way to make its product distinctive so that it attracts the attention of the market segment. The benefit to the consumers is that they continue to see changes and improvements in product features and quality, often at little additional cost.

Third, to match their competition, businesses must continuously search for new product ideas. Bicycle manufacturers saw a need for a bicycle that was a cross between a traditional racing bike and a mountain bike, and they created a new cycling product known as a cross-bike.

How can cyclists benefit from competition among bicycle manufacturers?

Rugged, lightweight, and easier to pedal and maneuver, the cross-bike is popular among weekend bikers and avid members of bicycle clubs. The model now makes up about 10 percent of all bicycle sales.

Finally, competition offers consumers the benefit of a wide variety of products from which to choose. The market segments are so diverse that businesses make sure that there are products to meet consumers' wants and needs. An example of this is the range of television channels available to viewers. Today, with cable or satellite television services, viewers can access more than 200 television channels as well as music channels and premium movies. Each channel competes with the other channels for viewership, and cable and satellite services compete to provide these services. The market is so large that major telephone companies are now seeking changes in laws to be able to offer television services via the telephone lines they already run into neighborhood homes. Viewers benefit from that type of competition by gaining more entertainment choices.

Checkpoint ▶▶

What benefits do consumers derive from competition among businesses?

7-3 Assessment

Key Concepts

Determine the best answer.

1. When a supermarket offers prepared meals for consumers to purchase on the way home from work, restaurants would view that as
   a. direct competition
   b. indirect competition
   c. price competition
   d. non-price competition

2. The newspaper ads featuring weekly specials at supermarkets are examples of
   a. indirect competition
   b. price competition
   c. brand preference
   d. none of the above

3. True or False: A negative effect of competition is that consumers usually end up paying higher prices for products and services.

4. Which of the following is *not* a typical business response to competition?
   a. reduce the variety of product choices
   b. search for new product ideas
   c. improve product quality and customer service
   d. identify additional market segments

Make Academic Connections

5. **Geography** Use an Internet mapping program such as Google Maps to prepare a map of a large shopping area in your community or a larger city close to you. Use the mapping feature to locate several businesses in direct competition with each other. Then locate several other businesses that offer indirect competition. Print a copy of the map and use it to mark the business locations and type of competition offered by each business.

6. **Consumer Economics** Visit a large electronics store or use the Internet to identify three competitive brands of a popular electronic product. Gather the following comparative information: (1) brand name, (2) current list price and current sale price, (3) three features that are similar to those of competitors, (4) two features that are different from competitors. Develop a table to compare the brands using your findings.

Connect to DECA

7. Develop a two-minute informative speech on how principles of the free enterprise economy contribute to the benefits that consumers receive from competition described in the lesson. Deliver your speech to your teacher (judge).

Learning about the Competition

GOALS

- Discuss the types of information businesses need to know about their competitors.
- Describe the kinds of activities businesses engage in to gain marketing intelligence.

KEY TERMS

market intelligence, *p. 202*

trade shows, *p. 202*

marketing matters

In order to compete with other businesses, a company needs to find out all it can about those competitors. Athletic teams have used scouts for many years. They attend the competitors' games to analyze their strategies, tactics, strengths, and weaknesses. The information is used to prepare their own teams to be more effective competitors. The same is true in business. In order to compete effectively, businesses take a number of steps to learn as much as they can about their competitors. Instead of scouting, the process is called gathering market intelligence.

Let's say you work for an automobile dealership and are given the assignment to gather market intelligence on competing dealerships. What type of information do you believe you would need to obtain? What are some information sources and data collection methods you would use? Are there any intelligence gathering methods you would not use based on ethics?

Types of Competitive Information

Marketers want to develop each element of the marketing mix for their products and services to best meet the wants and needs of their consumers. But understanding wants and needs of market segments is not enough. In order to make sure the company's offerings will be the best available, a business must be aware of the strategies that will be used by competitors. A company needs to gather information on each of the competitors' marketing mix elements.

Pricing Strategies

When businesses are in direct competition, competitors' pricing strategies are very important. Are competitors planning a sale, or are they going to raise the price and add features, options, or additional services? For example, if Chrysler reduces the price of all of its cars and trucks as part of an end-of-year promotion, there will be a significant difference between its prices and the prices of its competitors if the competitors do not offer similar price incentives. Even though Toyota may believe that it has established a brand preference in the minds of many consumers, will Chrysler's price cuts be enough to influence consumers? For some people, the answer would be yes because for that segment, price is the most significant factor when making a final choice between competing Toyota and Chrysler models. For others, the answer would be no because they value other factors, such as quality, more than price.

Virtual Marketing

The Effect of the Internet on Television

Back when television was introduced, many people thought it would be the end of radio. Before television, families crowded together in their homes at night to listen to the network programs on the radio. So when people started watching their shows on television, it seemed like radio was on the way out. Instead, radio was transformed by television. It shifted from carrying live programs and radio dramas to focusing more on music, news, and sports, the mainstays of radio today.

Similarly, we can expect that the introduction of the Internet will forever change television as we know it. We're already seeing it with on-demand television shows offered through many cable providers. Experts predict that in the near future, viewers will have the ability to watch whatever they want, whenever they want, with the click of a mouse. Every show, movie, and music video will be available to download and watch in an instant. But like radio, television won't become obsolete. It will just be very different from what we're used to now.

Think Critically

1. What effect will the ability to download shows have on television commercials? Will it make it easier or more difficult for advertisers to reach viewers?

2. What types of television programs might still be broadcast and watched in real time by by most people?

Distribution Decisions

The second area to gain information about is competitors' distribution systems. Are products conveniently available to customers in a large number of locations or is distribution selective? Are competitors making products available via the Internet or catalog sales, making it more convenient for customers to order and obtain the products?

An important part of satisfying the wants and needs of the consumer is to have the product in the right place at the time the customer wants to purchase it. If the competition is planning on distribution changes, its products might be more convenient to purchase than yours. However, making products available at more locations adds to the cost, which usually must be passed on to the customer, or it will result in lower profits for the company. Making distribution changes usually requires a great deal of time and may involve other businesses, so they need to be planned carefully.

Product/Service Planning

The third type of competitive information needed involves changes to the products and services offered. One of the greatest challenges to a business is anticipating the introduction of a new product or service by a competitor. A new product usually will result in at least a temporary shift in consumer purchases until customers decide whether or not they like the new product. If customers prefer the new product, it may be difficult for a business to attract them back even when it is able to obtain and offer a similar product choice.

When Pepsi introduced a clear cola, Coke did not put a comparable product on the market to compete. Coke may have decided that the clear cola was not significant competition, or it may have believed that the product would not succeed. However, if it had been successful, Coke would have had to scramble to develop a competing brand, or it would have risked losing market share.

Promotional Efforts

More attention may be focused on competitors' promotional efforts than on any of the other mix elements. Promotional strategies can be changed quickly. A unique promotional activity can grab consumers' attention. A well-timed promotion can have a direct effect on the sales of the business running the promotion and on its competitors.

If a furniture store runs a promotion offering discount prices and special financing for an upcoming weekend, how should competitors respond? Will they have time to plan and promote a similar sale? Should they allow the competitor's plans to influence their marketing strategy if it has already been determined? What effect will the promotion likely have on the competitors' sales during that weekend and for several weeks if the promotion results in high sales volume for the business?

Most promotions are designed to support other changes in a business's marketing mix—a new product introduction, opening a new location, or a special sale or price incentive. Competitors need to consider how to respond not only to the promotion but also to the other changes in the marketing mix.

Competitive Market Position

There are other factors that affect each business's competitive edge. Is a new competitor entering the market? If so, what has that competitor's success been in similar markets? Has your business identified a new market segment it wants to serve? If so, is the competition for that segment the same as or different from your current markets? What will be the effect of entering the new market on your existing customers?

How does the financial strength of your competitors compare to your own? Do they have the money available to develop new products and improve old ones? Do they have the financial flexibility to respond to pricing changes?

(MUSIC)   SEINFELD: Hot, hot, hot, hot, hot, hot. Pheu. (MUSIC)   (MUSIC) Um.   (MUSIC)

(MUSIC)   (MUSIC)   I was on a cruise ship, I slipped and ··right overboard.   Hi, boys.

2nd MAN: Ocean view?   SEINFELD: I don't think so.   I'm in a bit of a hurry.   (MUSIC/SFX)

That is so true.   So where was I?   ANNCR: The American Express Card, it's a life saver.   To apply look for this in your mailbox. (MUSIC/SFX OUT)

Effective promotion can reinforce the image of a well-known brand.

What are the competitive strengths and weaknesses of the other companies? Do they emphasize customer relationships and service, or do they appear to be more focused on mass markets and low prices? Do they have well-known brands with strong customer loyalty? Do they have flexible and efficient distribution strategies? Are they viewed as innovative market leaders, or are they more traditional and conservative in their business practices?

Factors such as these can make the difference between success and failure of

Working in **Teams**

As a team, identify a new consumer product that has recently been introduced which is of interest to team members. Discuss the marketing mix being used to market the product. What would it take to get you to try the new product? Why might you decide to continue with your current product choice rather than switch to the new product?

a product or service in the marketplace. Studying competitors to understand the strengths and weaknesses and to be able to anticipate and be prepared for competitors' actions is essential for the future success of a business.

Checkpoint ▶▶

What are the five types of information that businesses need to know about their competitors?

Collecting Competitive Information

The process of gaining competitive market information is called **market intelligence**. As a part of their marketing information systems and marketing research procedures, businesses determine the types of competitive information they need, the best sources for each type of information, and the procedures they will use to obtain and analyze the information for marketing planning.

Information Sources

Businesses engage in the following activities to gain information about the competition:

1. Direct salespeople and other employees to be alert to information about competitors' products, prices, and anticipated changes.

2. Purchase and analyze competitors' products. The information can be used to make product changes and recognize the areas where the competitive products have advantages and disadvantages.

3. Collect and study newspaper and magazine articles, government and university research reports, and other public information on competitors, new product research, and marketing trends. Companies may use employees or hire information services to collect the latest industry news.

4. Subscribe to professional association and trade group publications and special research reports.

5. Study customers and customer records to learn about the competition.

6. Attend trade shows. **Trade shows** are exhibitions where companies associated with an industry gather to showcase their products. You can gather information on what your competitors are displaying and hear customer views of the latest products.

7. Use the Internet. The Internet is becoming one of the best sources of current competitive information. Company web sites provide a great deal of information intended for customers and investors but useful to competitors.

Businesses do not collect competitive information randomly. Large businesses have staffs responsible for working with market intelligence and conducting marketing research, including research on competitors. Their objectives are to identify the strengths and weaknesses of key competitors, assess their current marketing strategies, and predict their future actions.

Ethics in Information Gathering

Some individuals and companies have used unethical methods to obtain information. It is not always easy to clearly determine whether or not a method is ethical. However, the usual standard is that if a competitor has information it considers to be private and does not disclose to people outside the business, obtaining and using that information would be unethical. In the same way, obtaining information through false pretenses or misleading information or by accessing data from restricted locations is unethical. In some instances, it may also be illegal.

Unethical actions might involve coercing a customer or supplier to provide competitive information. More complex and illegal activities are dumpster diving (sorting through a competitor's trash) and attempting to bribe an employee for access to private information.

Companies should communicate their expectations about the confidentiality of information to employees, suppliers, and customers. Many companies include guidelines in their codes of ethics about sharing information with others and obtaining and using competitive information.

Checkpoint ▶▶

What are some of the best information sources of market intelligence?

7-4 Assessment

Key Concepts

Determine the best answer.

1. True or False: Because businesses using the marketing concept thoroughly understand the needs of a target market, there is little need to gather information about competitors.

2. Which of the following mix elements can be changed very quickly by a competitor?
   a. product features
   b. distribution
   c. promotion
   d. all can be changed very quickly

3. True or False: An example of a change in competitive position is the entry of a new competitor into the market.

4. Marketing _____ is the process of gaining competitive market information.

5. Which of the following is an unethical source of competitive information?
   a. information gathered from searching the trash of a competitor
   b. information gathered by purchasing and analyzing a competitor's product
   c. information gathered from a survey of a competitor's customers
   d. all are unethical sources of information

Make Academic Connections

6. **Writing** You are the marketing manager of a local supermarket. Prepare a list of 20 questions (4 questions about each of the marketing mix elements and 4 questions about the supermarket's competitive market position) that you need to answer in order to understand the business's competitors. Compare your questions with other students' questions.

7. **Language Arts** You and a colleague are gathering information from a competitor's public web site when you access a link to a confidential report on a new product under development. It is obvious that the report was intended to be confidential, but the link had not been protected. Role-play with another student what you would do with the report, what you would say to your boss, and whether you would inform the competitor about the unprotected report.

Connect to

8. You are responsible for market intelligence for the Scion division of Toyota. Locate advertisements or other product information on the Honda Element. Prepare a one-page written competitive analysis describing the strengths and weaknesses of each of the mix elements for the Honda Element. Present your report to your teacher (judge) and be prepared to answer questions.

Check Your Understanding

Now that you have completed the chapter, check your understanding of the lessons with these questions. Record the score that best represents your understanding of each marketing concept.

1 = not at all; 3 = somewhat; 5 = very well

If your score is 42–50, you are ready for the assessment activities that follow. If you score 33–41, you should review the lessons for the items you scored 1–3. If you score 32 or less, you will want to carefully reread the lessons and work with a study partner on the areas you do not understand.

Can you—

— provide reasons why it is important of a business to complete market segmentation for its prospective customers?

— list examples of each type of segmentation: demographic, psychographic, product usage, and expected benefits?

— offer examples of three methods to position a company's products and services?

— suggest how consumer perceptions, competition, and the business environment can affect positioning decisions?

— identify examples of direct and indirect competitors for a business?

— suggest how a business can use non-price rather than price competition?

— discuss several ways that consumers benefit from the competition among businesses?

— provide examples of competitive information a business should collect for each marketing mix element?

— define market intelligence and identify useful sources of intelligence?

— explain why ethics is important in collecting and using market intelligence?

Review Marketing Terms

Match the terms listed with the definitions. Some terms may not be used.

1. The process of dividing a large group of consumers into subgroups based on specific characteristics and common important needs

2. Dividing consumers into markets based on where they live

3. People's interests and values

4. An identified market with excellent potential based on careful research

5. The total revenue that can be obtained from the market segment

6. The unique image of a product or service in a consumer's mind relative to similar competitive offerings

7. The images consumers have of competing goods and services in the marketplace

8. Occurs when a business competes with other companies offering products that are not in the same product category but satisfy similar customer needs

9. Rivalry among businesses on the basis of price and value

10. Directs a company's marketing mix at a large and heterogeneous group of consumers

a. benefit segmentation
b. consumer perceptions
d. demographics
e. direct competition
f. geographic segmentation
g. indirect competition
h. market intelligence
i. market opportunity
j. market position
k. market potential
l. market segmentation
m. market share
n. mass marketing
o. non-price competition
p. price competition
q. product usage
r. psychographics
s. trade shows

Review Marketing Concepts

11. True or False: A market segment must be defined by its demographic characteristics.

12. True or False: Each segment of a market presents a viable market opportunity for a business.

13. True or False: In order to compete effectively with other businesses, marketers must create a unique image of their product or service in the consumer's mind.

14. True or False: In today's economy, price competition must be used with direct competitors.

15. True or False: Marketers do not need to know how consumers are using their products, as long as they are using them.

16. True or False: An example of indirect competition would be competition between a bowling alley and a video arcade.

17. True or False: The type of competition that stresses convenient location or ample parking is called attribute competition.

18. True or False: There are relatively few consumer benefits from competition compared to the benefits businesses receive from increased sales and higher profits.

19. True or False: In order to compete effectively, it is important to learn as much as possible about your competitors' marketing strategies.

20. True or False: It is illegal for businesses to use trade shows to gather competitive information.

21. True or False: A publication of a trade or professional association is an example of an information source that a business could use to gain information about competitors.

22. True or False: Companies should communicate their expectations about the confidentiality of information to employees, suppliers, and customers.

Marketing Research and Planning

23. Use the Internet to access the Census Bureau's Statistical Abstract of the United States and use the data to identify distinct market segments based on the types of characteristics listed below. List the segments and the relevant population data from the Statistical Abstract. For each group of segments, name a product or service for which the segmentation you identify would be significant. For example, if you segmented people by region of the country, the segments would be significant if you were marketing heating and air-conditioning equipment.
    a. geography
    b. age
    c. education
    d. income

24. Businesses decide to compete using price or non-price competition. Locate two newspaper advertisements that clearly demonstrate a strategy of price competition and two advertisements that stress non-price competition. Cut and paste each advertisement onto separate sheets of paper. For each ad, highlight and use margin notes to describe how the businesses using price competition characterize or draw attention to the price and

how the businesses using non-price competition emphasize other factors that customers should consider.

25. It is important to position a product or service in relation to your competitors. The objective of positioning is to cause your product or service to occupy a prominent position in your customer's mind in comparison to the competition. Using the list below, decide which of the six positioning methods would be most important for each product or service. After you have made your selection, give a reason why you selected that technique.
    a. urgent care medical centers
    b. imported perfume or cologne
    c. home office furniture
    d. personal fitness classes
    e. farm tractors
    f. environmentally safe laundry detergent

26. A medium-size rural community has three major grocery stores that have 94 percent of the total market. The remaining 6 percent is shared by small, locally owned stores. It is estimated that the total market potential for grocery items for this town is $37.5 million. There are

approximately 25,000 potential customers in this town.
  a. What is the total market share in dollars for the three major grocery stores?
  b. What is the total market share in dollars for the small, locally owned stores?
  c. What is the market share in dollars for each major grocery store if they all have an equal share of the market?
  d. One of the major grocery stores has recently remodeled and expanded and has begun to stay open 24 hours. As a result of these changes, this store has increased its market share to 45 percent of the total market. What is its new market share in dollars?
  e. Assuming that the locally owned stores still have 6 percent of the market, what market share is left for the other two major stores (in dollars)?

27. An important part of competitive success is gathering market intelligence on competitors. Select one of the types of businesses below. Make a list of five types of market intelligence needed by the business and identify why it is valuable in planning a marketing strategy. For each type of business listed, identify one possible source of that information.
  a. pizza delivery
  b. intercity bus line
  c. travel agency
  d. furniture rental store
  e. radio station in a large city

Marketing Management and Decision Making

28. You are a marketing consultant in your local community. There is an association of downtown business people called the Business Improvement Bureau. It is an organization that is interested in improving the marketing practices of the individual businesses as well as improving the business economy of the entire community. Members have lunch together once a month and usually invite a guest speaker. Assume you have been invited to speak to the organization this month about positioning in the market. Prepare a presentation, including visual aids, for a speech to the Business Improvement Bureau. The talk and discussion are scheduled to last approximately ten minutes. Your presentation could include a discussion of positioning, the results the members could expect with effective positioning, and a discussion and examples of the six positioning techniques. Make sure to explain how positioning can work for the entire business community as well as for individual businesses. Your visual aids should emphasize the important aspects of your speech.

29. Because of a recession, you have become aware of an intense interest in your area in pricing. You think there is a business opportunity in this phenomenon. Specifically, you think that businesses and organizations in your area would pay to receive up-to-date competitive price information. You have decided to open a business with several classmates called Partners In Pricing. PIP will use various methods to determine the prices of an assortment of products and services sold by area businesses. It will also collect consumer perceptions of competitors' prices.

You will offer the service of finding out what competitors' current prices are for products and services. You will comparison shop in stores; call for prices on the telephone; read advertisements in newspapers, magazines, and circulars; and visit with business and organization owners directly to acquire this information. You will also conduct frequent consumer surveys via telephone and interviews in area shopping malls.

Prepare for marketing your business by describing how you would use each of the positioning techniques for PIP. That is, what attributes would you claim to have, what is unique about your price and quality, and how will your customers be able to use the information you provide them? Also, who are your competitors, how would you classify yourself in the larger arena of business, and who will be your most prominent users? Use your answers to these questions to prepare a threefold brochure or a promotional web site that you will use to recruit your first customers.

Sports and Entertainment Marketing Management Team Decision Making Event

The Dynamos are a new professional soccer franchise located in Houston, Texas. A new stadium for the team is being planned. Sugar Land and Pearland are Houston suburbs that have made serious bids for the soccer field to be built in their communities.

Downtown Houston has Minute Maid Park for professional baseball, Toyota Center for professional basketball, and Reliant Stadium for professional football. The light rail system transports fans to all three sporting venues. New restaurants and hotels have located near Minute Maid Park. The city of Houston has a piece of property near Minute Maid Park that it proposes be used to build a professional soccer field for the Dynamos. The city will give the Dynamos a property tax break.

Houston is a diverse city with a large Hispanic/Latino population. Sugar Land is an upscale planned community with a population of 100,000 located 30 minutes from downtown Houston. Pearland is a rapidly growing suburb also located 30 minutes from downtown Houston.

Your team will meet with the general manager for the Dynamos to discuss the pros/cons of all proposed locations for the soccer stadium. You must convince the GM to locate the stadium in downtown Houston. Your presentation must describe the target market for soccer, the product/service offered, potential corporate sponsors, proposed publicity for the team, multiple uses for the new soccer stadium, and the economic impact of locating in downtown Houston.

You have 30 minutes to prepare your presentation, 10 minutes to present it to the judge, and 5 minutes to answer the judge's questions about your proposal.

Performance Indicators Evaluated

- Determine the relationship between government and business. (Economics)
- Identify factors affecting a business's profit. (Economics)
- Identify information monitored for marketing decision making. (Marketing-Information Management)
- Explain the need for sport/event marketing information. (Marketing-Information Management)
- Describe the nature of target marketing in sport/event marketing. (Marketing-Information Management)
- Develop sport/event product positioning strategies. (Product/Service Management)
- Sell sport/event sponsorships. (Selling)

Go to the DECA web site for more detailed information.

Think Critically

1. Why must a sports venue have the versatility to house other entertainment events?

2. Why do cities compete for professional sporting venues?

3. Why are government incentives important when deciding where to locate?

4. Who are the target markets? What promotions can be used to attract the target markets to the stadium?

www.deca.org

E-Commerce and Virtual Marketing

©DIGITAL VISION

Newsline

Consumers Say No to Pets.Com

It seemed like the ideal e-commerce business. With millions of pet owners spending money on pet supplies, toys, and food, an online business where those consumers could conveniently make purchases could not fail. Pets.com had the financial backing of Amazon and Disney. It invested heavily in advertising featuring the famous "singing dog" hand puppet. Pets.com got worldwide attention and name recognition by spending over $1 million for advertising during Super Bowl XXXIV to introduce the puppet. The advertisement was so popular that the company was able to sell hundreds of thousands of the hand puppets. Yet late that same year, Pets.com announced it was closing its web site, laying off its employees, and ending business.

Why did a company that appeared to have everything needed for success come to such an unfortunate end? The company's owners blamed the Internet economy, pointing to a large number of e-commerce businesses that also failed at about the same time. However, it was a classic misunderstanding of marketing. The company's failure pointed out that customer needs and choices affect the success of a product. While pet owners spend millions of dollars each year buying a variety of products, there are thousands of businesses selling those products, including local supermarkets, discount stores, and corner convenience stores. Most pet owners don't need to and don't want to go online to order pet food or pet supplies and then wait a week or longer for delivery. They want to be assured of the quality of the products they purchase for their pets and are more likely to trust

the businesses they shop regularly rather than a new Internet company. Even though most people knew the company's name and loved the advertising, they weren't willing to make online purchases for their pets.

Think Critically

1. Why is the purchase of pet products less convenient using the Internet than shopping at a local business?

2. If you were the marketing manager of Pets.com, what would you have done differently to attract customers and sell your products?

3. Search the Internet to find news reports of other Internet companies that have failed and try to determine the reasons for their failure.

school.cengage.com/marketing/marketing

Prepare for Performance

This chapter develops the following Performance Indicators from the DECA Competitive Events program.

Core Performance Indicators

- Use communication skills to foster communications in e-business
- Foster positive relationships with customers to enhance company image in e-business
- Utilize sales processes and techniques to determine and satisfy customer needs in e-business
- Manage channel activities to minimize costs and to determine distribution strategies in e-business

Supporting Performance Indicators

- Explain the nature of effective communications in e-business
- Demonstrate a customer-service mindset in e-business
- Reinforce service orientation through communication in e-business
- Explain the nature of channel strategies in e-business

Go to **school.cengage.com/marketing/marketing** and click on Connect to DECA.

"The Clique," Nathan Phillips Square, Toronto. Image courtesy of the human network.

On the human network, you subscribe to people, not magazines. Welcome to a place where business and social networking are changing the way we work and play. Where colleagues and friends can subscribe to both your opinions and schedules or your playlists and photos. And you can be reached the way you want to be reached. Or not. Welcome to your life. On your terms. All it takes is a network. The story continues at cisco.com/humannetwork.

welcome to the human network.

Visual Focus

In many ways, the Internet has become the new shopping mall. It is the place where people go to shop for things they need, to socialize through online interactions, and to form virtual communities. The Internet provides both opportunities and challenges. This chapter describes the development and growth of e-commerce. It shows how businesses are improving their use of virtual marketing to support their traditional marketing methods and are increasingly using it as their primary method to reach customers.

Focus Questions:

Do you agree that using the Internet is the same as socializing and shopping with your friends at the mall? What problems might a business encounter if it tries to use the Internet only to sell products without realizing the other ways people use the Internet?

Use the Internet to find an example of how businesses are using social networking and communication tools to reach a target audience as suggested in the Cisco ad. Share your example in a class discussion.

What Is E-Commerce?

GOALS

- Describe the three stages of development for e-commerce businesses.

- Discuss the importance of the marketing concept to successful e-commerce.

KEY TERMS

e-commerce, *p. 210*

click-only businesses, *p. 211*

brick-and-mortar businesses, *p. 211*

brick-and-click businesses, *p. 211*

marketing matters

The beginning of e-commerce in the 1990s threatened to change the way businesses operate. After only a few years, though, many of the new companies operating solely on the Internet went out of business or were struggling to make a profit. They learned quickly that just providing easy access to their business through the Internet was not enough to ensure success. Consumers want assurance that they will get a quality product, they can make a payment with security, the product will be delivered quickly, and they can count on customer service if needed.

Make a list of the advantages and disadvantages of using the Internet to buy products and services. Discuss with other students how businesses that use the Internet can increase customers' confidence in making online purchases.

The Expanding World of E-Commerce

It is hard to believe that the use of the Internet to buy and sell products had its beginnings just over ten years ago. Today, many people use a computer daily to gather product information, locate businesses, compare prices, and make purchases. The Internet has become an important way for businesses to reach both final consumers and other businesses. But e-commerce is still a relatively new way of doing business, and companies continue to learn how to use the Internet effectively.

E-commerce involves business activities, including the exchange of goods, services, and information, completed electronically via the Internet. It includes purchasing and selling products online, providing and exchanging business information, and offering customer service and support. In a very short time, e-commerce has become a multibillion-dollar part of our economy.

The introduction of the personal computer in the late 1970s made it possible for people to have an important tool available at home and at work. Electronic communication between computers became realistic with the introduction of the World Wide Web in 1991. Since that time, with improved and

© GETTY IMAGES/PHOTODISC

Why do you think e-commerce has become so popular?

lower-cost computer technology and growing access to the Internet, millions of people around the world can instantly access information and communicate with each other.

By 2007, more than 200 million people in the United States or about 70 percent of the population had Internet access. Internet access has grown rapidly worldwide with over one billion users in 2007. That is a 209 percent increase since 2000. Those connections give businesses and individuals instantaneous global access. Almost all businesses of significant size use computers and the Internet in their daily operations. In a relatively short time, e-commerce has become a vital part of the business economy.

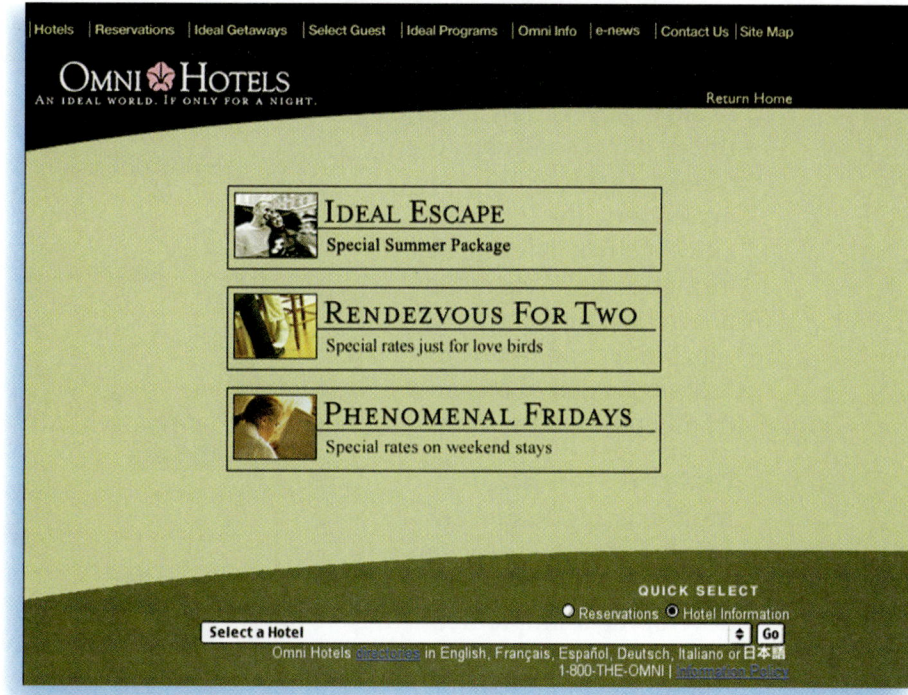

COURTESY OF OMNI HOTELS

Using the Internet to advertise enables hotels like Omni to communicate with travelers worldwide.

Business on the Net

Not all businesses can complete all of their activities using the Internet, but the Internet can be used for many activities. An automobile manufacturer uses video conferencing to bring designers from several countries together to work on new models of cars and trucks. A company headquartered in the United States transmits data overnight to Ireland where accounting specialists maintain many of the company's financial records. A Canadian telecommunications equipment producer trains technicians worldwide by connecting the desktop computers of trainees and trainers using a sophisticated audio-video system. A chemical company in Ohio has sensors installed in the chemical tanks of customers. When the level drops to a certain point, the sensors trigger a computer program that automatically orders a new supply of the specific chemical.

From Bricks to Clicks

Businesses can use the Internet for only a few activities, and some can operate their entire business using the Net. Companies that complete almost all of their business activities through the Internet are known as **click-only businesses**. Click-only businesses were first known as *dot. com businesses,* which came from the end of the web address for a commercial business—.com. While click-only businesses have received most of the publicity for moving business to the Internet, many other businesses have developed ways to use the Internet to support their business activities. Companies that complete most of their business activities by means other than the Internet are called **brick-and-mortar businesses**. The name "brick-and-mortar" suggests that the company relies on actual buildings such as retail stores, offices, or factories to conduct its business. Companies that combine traditional business operations with the use of the Internet are known as **brick-and-click businesses**.

Stages of Development

Businesses generally progress through three stages as they develop their e-commerce presence on the Internet. They begin by offering information only. Then they progress to interactive capabilities and finally to full integration of business transactions on the Web.

Information Stage

Most existing businesses first begin using the Internet for e-commerce by developing a simple web site. This form of one-way communication through the Web is known as the *information* stage. The web site provides basic information to help prospective customers as they gather information about products and companies. As the business gains more experience with the Internet, it will add additional information, including complete product descriptions, payment methods, customer services, and even product manuals.

The limitation of the information stage is that customers cannot use the web site to interact with the business. They must still visit the business in person or use the telephone or mail to obtain information that is not on the web site or to make a purchase.

Interaction Stage

The second stage of e-commerce development is *interaction*. In addition to providing information, the company uses its web site to interact with consumers. The simplest form of interaction is the use of e-mail. People viewing the company's web site can click on a link to bring up an e-mail form that they can use to request information, ask questions, or contact specific people in the company. In addition to e-mail, companies can add a database where customers can search for specific information about available products, features, and services. They can check product availability, calculate product costs and shipping charges, and determine how long it will take to have an order delivered. An order form may be included on the site along with a product catalog. Customers can complete, print, and then e-mail, fax, or mail the form to the company, but they cannot place an order directly from the web site.

REPRODUCED WITH PERMISSION OF YAHOO! INC. ©2005 BY YAHOO! INC.

Yahoo's web site demonstrates all three stages of e-commerce development—information, interaction, and full integration.

Get the Message

The Closing of the Digital Divide

Back in 2000, there was much talk of the "digital divide"—the disparity between the high percentage of whites who used computers compared to the lower percentage of minorities. Some said the digital divide could be attributed to the high cost of computers, but it was viewed by many education, business, and community leaders as a big problem. Knowledge of computers was becoming more critical in educational success and in the business world, and minority students could not afford to be left out.

But according to a 2006 study, 74 percent of white adults go online, compared with 61 percent of African-Americans and 56 percent of Hispanic-Americans. It seems as if the "digital divide" has begun to close.

Think Critically

1. What factors might have contributed to the closing of the digital divide?

2. How would this information impact marketers hoping to target minorities? What approach might such marketers take now that they would not have taken in 2000?

Full Integration Stage Companies that want to take full advantage of the Internet in their business move to *full integration*. With all of the Internet tools available, an entire business transaction can be completed on an integrated site. Customers can get necessary product, pricing, and shipping information. They can place an order and pay for it, track their shipment until it is delivered, and obtain customer, assistance before and after the sale—all using the Internet. Companies with integrated use of the Internet do not have to be click-only companies. Many customers will still prefer to complete some or all of their business in traditional ways. But full integration gives customers the option to use the Internet for part or all of their business transactions.

Checkpoint ▶▶

What is the main difference between a company in the interaction stage and one in the full integration stage of e-commerce development?

Success in E-Commerce

Many of the first Internet businesses were very much like the early production-oriented businesses. They did not understand the importance of marketing. They believed that if they had an attractive web site and advertised their products extensively to prospective customers, they would be successful. They soon learned an important lesson. If customers are uncertain of the quality of a company's products, do not receive merchandise they order in a timely fashion, or are concerned about the security of using a credit card on the Internet, they will not make purchases online.

Many e-businesses were not successful because they did not apply the marketing concept. Businesses that have been effective in e-commerce know that they must identify target markets and develop a marketing mix that meets the target market needs. They must also provide a high level of service in the operation of their web site and completion of all marketing activities.

Advantages of E-Commerce

Businesses that use the Internet have several advantages over those that do not. They have immediate access to prospective customers all over the world. They can introduce new products or update product information instantaneously. Internet access and communications are no longer confined to desktop computers but can be accomplished through mobile wireless devices such as wireless notebook computers, PDAs, and cell phones.

The Internet has become an important marketing research tool. It allows businesses to gather detailed and specific information about prospective and current customers that can be used to tailor a satisfying marketing mix.

Customers' concerns and questions can be sent to a company at any time, and a response can be delivered immediately. Customers can order products day or night, 365 days a year. They can review operations manuals and other product information that have been placed online.

The Internet has resulted in the development of products that can be delivered from computer to computer. E-tickets are replacing paper tickets for air travel. You can purchase postage or concert tickets online and print them at home rather than visiting the post office or box office.

The Internet has expanded competition. Small businesses can more easily compete with larger businesses because of the lower costs needed to start and operate an e-business and the ability to access customers easily with less promotion. Companies can enter international markets by translating the Internet site into the language of the country in which it wants to sell its products.

Disadvantages of E-Commerce

Not everything about the development of the Internet as a business tool has been positive. It provides an easy way for people to start a new business without understanding what is necessary for success. Customers who placed orders with new businesses often found that products were not

What are some of the advantages of e-commerce to consumers?

as described on the web site, not delivered on time, or damaged when received. Errors were made in order processing. Customer service was difficult to obtain. Returning an unwanted or defective product was often difficult.

Businesses learned that it is much more difficult to predict demand for products when product information is available worldwide on the Web. Customers expect to be able to obtain answers to questions and receive support any time of the day, seven days a week, putting pressure on the business to expand those services. Distribution channels, warranty and repair services, methods for accepting returns, and secure web sites for accepting credit card payments need to be developed to serve customers who order online.

One of the greatest disadvantages of e-commerce is the changing nature of competition and the purchasing behavior of customers. A brick-and-mortar company generally competes with similar businesses in the same geographic area. Internet businesses face competition from all other businesses offering similar products on the Web. Many consumers use the Web to gather information and compare prices and then go to a local business to make the purchase. In this way, Internet businesses aid local businesses without getting the benefit of actually selling a product.

The Marketing Concept Applied to E-Commerce

E-commerce has demonstrated the importance of the marketing concept to successful businesses. When information about a company's products and services can be viewed by people in many locations, it is especially important for the business to understand who its target market customers are, what their needs and wants are, and how those needs and wants can be satisfied with a marketing mix. The business must be able to offer the products and services that customers want. It must also be able to distribute them effectively, make purchases affordable, make ordering and payment of products easy, and provide information in the form of descriptions and pictures to answer important customer questions. The business must also answer questions, provide expected services, and solve problems after the sale. All parts of the marketing mix—not just selling a product online—are important for successful e-commerce.

Checkpoint ▶▶

How does competition change for businesses involved in e-commerce?

8-1 Assessment

school.cengage.com/marketing/marketing

Key Concepts

Determine the best answer.

1. True or False: To be involved in e-commerce, a business must sell products and services using the Internet.

2. By 2007, the percentage of the U.S. population with Internet access was about
   a. 25 percent
   b. 50 percent
   c. 70 percent
   d. 95 percent

3. Companies that combine traditional business operations with the use of the Internet are known as brick-and-_____ businesses.

4. The stage of e-commerce development in which customers can gather information and communicate with the company but not place an order online is
   a. information
   b. interaction
   c. limited integration
   d. full integration

5. True or False: Most of the early e-commerce businesses were successful because they understood and used the marketing concept.

Make Academic Connections

6. **Social Studies** Use of the Internet in the United States varies based on several demographic characteristics including age, gender, education, income levels, and ethnicity. Use the Internet to locate information on differences in the level of U.S. Internet usage based on three demographic factors. Prepare a table and a chart or graph that presents the information.

7. **Foreign Language** Locate the web site of a U.S. business that provides an alternate site in a language other than English. Locate the web site of a company in a non-English speaking country that provides an alternate site in English. Study the web sites and identify any differences other than the language in the organization of the alternate web sites of each country.

Connect to DECA

8. Your team is conducting research on customer satisfaction with e-commerce. Develop a four-item questionnaire to determine what customers like and dislike about online shopping. Survey at least 15 people of different ages. Summarize the data and prepare a two-page report of your findings. Present the written report to your teacher (judge) and be prepared to answer questions.

The Growing Importance of E-Commerce

GOALS

- Identify evidence of the growth of the Internet.
- Describe the various business uses of the Internet for e-commerce.

KEY TERMS

B2C, *p. 217*

B2B, *p. 217*

marketing matters

Consumers are most familiar with the businesses from which they make regular purchases or that advertise regularly. But not all businesses sell to final consumers. Many businesses serve other businesses, so consumers are less familiar with them. Business-to-business marketing is an important part of the economy. Just as businesses that sell to final consumers are adapting to the use of the Internet, e-commerce is becoming an important part of business-to-business marketing as well.

Use a business or telephone directory or the Internet to identify three businesses that sell directly to final consumers, three businesses that sell to other businesses, and three businesses that sell to both final consumers and other businesses. Determine which appear to use the Internet as a part of their marketing efforts and which do not.

Growth of the Internet

No one recognized the potential of the Internet when it was first developed in the 1950s as a military and research tool. It developed slowly until businesses and consumers accepted and used personal computers and technology allowed for the rapid exchange of information using specially designed software and modems.

The Internet has grown rapidly in the last decade of the 1900s and during the first years of the twenty-first century. Today, more people around the world have access to computers and Internet connections. Over 120 million business, organization, and individual registered web sites were active worldwide in 2007, with millions more being added each year.

An estimated one billion people worldwide can access the Internet for business or personal use. As shown in Figure 8-1, the United States leads the world in

FIGURE 8-1

Countries with the highest number of Internet users in 2007 (in millions).

Country	No. of Users
United States	211
China	137
Japan	86
Germany	51
India	40
United Kingdom	37
South Korea	34
Brazil	32
France	31
Italy	31
Russia	24
Canada	22

Internet use with approximately 21 percent of all users. However, that percentage has dropped from 50 percent in less than ten years as other countries expand their Internet access at a faster rate than in the United States. For example, China's Internet use has more than tripled in just four years but still reaches only 10 percent of its population.

Business use of the Internet is also increasing. While there are many other business uses of the Internet, an important measure of Internet usage by business is the sale of products and services. Because e-commerce is quite new, estimates of the volume of products and services sold vary greatly. According to the Census Bureau, **B2C** (business-to-consumer) Internet sales in the United States were approximately $110 billion in 2006, growing at a rate of 24 percent in just one year. That seems like a large amount, but it represents only 2.8 percent of all retail sales. In comparison, U.S. **B2B** (business-to-business) Internet sales for 2007 topped $800 billion. Many people and businesses around the world do not yet purchase online or make only a small percentage of their total purchases online. Even more are not yet connected to the Internet, so B2C and B2B sales likely will increase by millions and even billions of dollars in future years.

Checkpoint ▶▶▶

Why is it likely that B2C and B2B sales on the Internet will continue to grow in future years?

Business Uses of the Internet

Some companies are reluctant to use the Internet because they do not believe it is useful for their type of business activities. They assume that the Internet can be used only for selling products. But many other business activities can be completed online that benefit both the business and its customers.

Communicating

The Internet is a very efficient and effective communications tool for both individuals and businesses. From the beginning of the Internet, the primary way people have communicated is through e-mail. But many tools are currently available, and new ones are being developed to aid in person-to-person and business-to-business communications. Examples include chat rooms, bulletin boards, personal messengers, webcams, and online whiteboards that allow several people to share application software and collaborate using text and graphics tools. Businesses use the Internet to quickly and inexpensively distribute newsletters, reports, and other information to employees and investors.

Improved communications with current and prospective customers can occur using the Internet. Consumers use the Web to locate products and businesses. Companies can provide more detailed information than is possible with traditional methods. They can post their hours, identify contacts for information, and even provide a map and driving directions to the business. Today, if a business has not posted information about its business, location, products, and services on the Internet, it will miss many prospective customers.

Fast FACTS

Each day that they are online, Internet users are exposed to more than 1,000 ads on average. That is more than double the number of ads users were exposed to in 2000.

E-Readiness

Which country is best prepared for the growth of the Internet? It may surprise you that it is not the United States. *The Economist* developed an e-readiness index that measures a country's technology infrastructure, government support and policies, personnel prepared to work in Internet-related jobs, and the computer literacy and technology access of the country's citizens.

The country with the highest e-readiness rating in 2006 was Denmark, followed by the United States, Switzerland, Sweden, and the U.K. The United States had led the rankings until 2002 when reduced investments due to recession dropped it to third at that time.

Government leaders and business people watch the rankings to make sure their countries remain competitive in e-readiness and to determine the other countries that will make good technology partners and e-commerce markets.

Think Critically

1. What does e-readiness mean in relation to the growth of e-commerce?

2. Should U.S. government and business leaders be concerned about the country's ranking in the e-readiness index? Why or why not?

The Internet has become a common way for businesses to communicate with other businesses to place orders, provide product information, or share data. Business people send e-mail messages, exchange documents, offer training, and update records online.

Gathering Information

Businesses also use the Internet to obtain information to make decisions. Much information is free and is provided by government agencies, colleges and universities, libraries, and even private businesses. Other information can be purchased from research companies, professional and trade associations, and businesses that gather and publish information. It then can be accessed directly from the company's web site or downloaded in a research report.

The Internet has improved the capability to gather information on current and prospective customers. Customers who have purchased products are encouraged to submit product registration and warranty cards. The registration process allows the company to collect information about the customer, including an e-mail address. That information is valuable in future communications and promotional activities.

Information can be obtained on where customers purchase their products, reasons for purchasing, and whether the customer owns or plans to purchase related products. The information can help the company provide improved marketing mixes in the future.

Many web sites include a place to request information, be placed on a mailing list, or obtain answers to questions. That capability allows the company to develop a list of prospective customers and their specific interests.

Information about competitors is easier to obtain using the Internet. Businesses put a great deal of information about their products and operations on the Web. It is relatively easy to learn about competitors' products, prices, credit terms, distribution policies, and the types of customer services offered.

Planning a Career in... *E-Marketing*

Marketing, Sales & Service

"While doing my Earth Day homework, I took an online quiz about the environment. I noticed all of these environmentally friendly products and non-profit organizations advertised on the quiz web site. After learning about threats to the environment, I was glad to see organizations and products designed to help the environment."

Have you ever gone to a web site and been intrigued by the links to other sites that have similar information? Have you followed a link and decided to make a purchase from that site?

E-marketing is a rapidly evolving means for businesses to reach consumers. Whether visiting a web site of a company selling products, an information site of an organization, an online advertisement linked to a web search, or an individual blog, you have probably been affected by e-marketing. A growing number of exciting careers are part of the e-marketing industry.

Employment Outlook

- Faster than average growth is expected.
- As the number of uses of the Internet and access by consumers increase, demand for professionals who can optimize the effectiveness of e-commerce will increase.

Job Titles

- Interactive Marketing Manager
- Marketing Web Master
- E-commerce Project Manager
- Search Marketing Specialist
- Online Marketing Manager
- E-commerce Marketing Analyst

Needed Skills

- Varying educational levels from high school diploma to Ph.D. are needed in the broad range of e-marketing careers.

- A solid business background, strong analytical abilities, and effective written communications skills are needed.
- A technical background in computer hardware and software, including database software, open sourcing, web application programming, and search engine design, is a requirement for some jobs.

What's it like to work in...
E-Marketing

Evelyn, a digital marketing manager for a professional baseball team, was reviewing a report of the number of visits to the team's web site. Of particular interest was the amount of traffic resulting from a link from a sports memorabilia web site on which the team had purchased advertising space.

A phone call interrupted the report review. The electronic team newsletter, available to fans either by signing up to be added to a distribution list or by clicking a link on the team web site, was scheduled for release the next day. Confirmation was needed regarding which product promotions would be included in the newsletter.

In the afternoon, Evelyn ran an Internet sales review meeting. Sales of tickets, clothing, and memorabilia were correlated to variations in web site traffic. To determine the most effective advertising methods, the group reviewed the relationship between banners, sponsored sports web sites, and keyword advertising links from other sites to increased web site traffic and resulting sales.

What About **You**

Would you like to help increase online revenue through the creative use of Internet marketing? Are you interested in being part of a new and exciting career area?

Improving Operations

The performance of business and marketing activities has been improved as a result of business use of the Internet. Salespeople can log on to the company's web site and determine the availability of products to ensure that an order can be filled immediately. A production manager can access the records of a transportation company to see when an expected shipment will be delivered. Engineers in three locations can collaborate on a product design by examining a three-dimensional drawing online and making changes that each of them can see instantly.

A small business usually does not have the resources to reach customers located in other states or countries using traditional sales and promotion methods. The Internet makes it possible for the business to compete nationally and internationally without the cost of salespeople. The small business can use the Internet to identify other businesses that can assist with distribution, customer service, and even billing and collecting payments when making sales to customers located long distances away.

Checkpoint ▶▶▶

How can a business use the Internet to improve operations?

8-2 Assessment

Key Concepts

Determine the best answer.

1. True or False: The number of U.S. Internet users as a percentage of all users worldwide is actually declining.

2. Following the United States, the country with the largest number of Internet users is
   a. England
   b. Germany
   c. Canada
   d. China

3. The dollar value of business-to-business (B2B) sales in the United States is _____ that of business-to-consumer (B2C) sales.
   a. larger than
   b. smaller than
   c. about the same as
   d. Data on Internet sales are not collected.

4. True or False: To use the Internet effectively, businesses must be able to sell products online.

5. True or False: Small businesses are less able to compete with larger businesses as a result of the growth of the Internet.

Make Academic Connections

6. **Math** Assume there are one billion Internet users worldwide. Use the information from Figure 8-1 to calculate the percentage of total users for each country. Calculate the number and percentage of users represented by all other countries combined. Prepare a pie chart to show your results.

7. **Communication** Locate the web site of a business that provides several ways for users to communicate with it. Print a copy of the web page(s) and use a marker or pen to identify each of the communication methods. Write a one-paragraph description of each method and indicate whether you believe it is a useful and easy-to-use form of communication for the user.

Connect to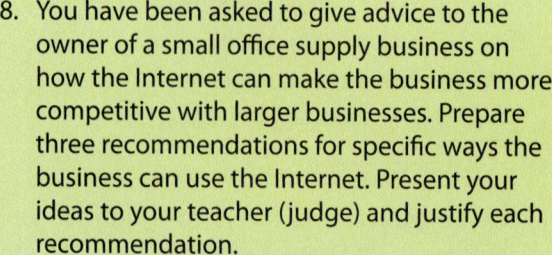

8. You have been asked to give advice to the owner of a small office supply business on how the Internet can make the business more competitive with larger businesses. Prepare three recommendations for specific ways the business can use the Internet. Present your ideas to your teacher (judge) and justify each recommendation.

GOALS

- Differentiate virtual marketing from traditional marketing.
- Describe distribution methods used in e-commerce.
- Identify distribution problems experienced by e-businesses and how they can be resolved.

KEY TERMS

virtual marketing, *p. 221*

product fulfillment center, *p. 225*

marketing matters

When customers place an order for a product using the Internet, they want to be assured that the order is correct, that payment has been received, that the products have been shipped, and that they will be received in a reasonable amount of time. They also want to be able to easily and inexpensively return the product if it does not meet their expectations.

Work with a group. Using the Internet, identify a company that accepts product orders online. Identify the ways the company provides information to the customer about how the product will be shipped, the status of the order, and return and refund procedures. Compare your findings with those of other groups and discuss the online procedures that seem to be effective.

Marketing Via the Internet

While marketing is an important function for all businesses, it is especially important for e-commerce businesses. The functions and activities of marketing are the same for click-only and brick-and-mortar businesses. However, with e-commerce, the importance of certain marketing functions and the way some marketing activities need to be completed may change. E-commerce usually requires a combination of traditional marketing and virtual marketing.

Virtual marketing is the completion of marketing activities primarily through the use of computer and Internet technologies. Examples include:

- market research using online surveys and other electronic data-collection methods

- distribution of electronic versions of products and services such as e-tickets and e-books

- processes for making electronic payments and managing finances such as secure credit card transactions and online banking and bill payments

- communication and promotion strategies such as Internet advertising, e-mail, live chats, blogs, and virtual communities where people with similar interests can exchange information

While virtual alternatives have been developed for many marketing activities, most e-commerce businesses also need to be able to use more traditional forms of marketing. Companies that sell products online will need effective order processing, product storage, and transportation

Working in **Teams**

As a team, discuss the advantages to consumers and businesses of virtual products such as e-tickets for airlines, online postage, and digital music and movie downloads. Why might consumers or businesses choose not to use these products even if they result in cost savings?

systems. For customers who are not comfortable with electronic payments, companies need to have alternative payment procedures. Some customers may not yet search for product information on the computer, requiring the use of traditional media for advertising and promotion.

Rather than simplifying marketing, e-commerce requires even more attention to marketing planning. Not only are the needs and wants of customers important, but their experience with technology and use of the Internet must also be considered when deciding whether to engage in e-commerce or how to effectively use virtual marketing.

Checkpoint ▶▶▶

Why does e-commerce make marketing more complex?

Distribution for E-Commerce

Effective distribution is an important part of satisfying customer needs. Customers want to locate products and services easily and conveniently. When they purchase a product, they want it delivered quickly and undamaged. If they experience problems, customers expect prompt, reliable service.

Distribution is the marketing function that can determine success or failure for a company engaged in e-commerce. Major distribution changes in e-commerce have occurred involving access to products and services, order processing, and distribution methods.

Finding and Buying Products

Before the development of the Internet, customers were limited to making most of their purchases from nearby businesses or from companies that sold their products through catalogs, telephone sales, or direct mail advertising.

With Internet access, customers can locate and purchase products from any company that has a web site. While it has opened up new markets for businesses, the Internet has also dramatically increased the competition they face.

More and more companies are integrating product purchasing into their web sites. Online shopping carts are designed to easily complete an order, make immediate payment, and securely submit the order. Order confirmation occurs almost instantly to assure the customer that the order has been received. Even for businesses that do not offer online purchasing, a web site can provide information on completing an order by telephone or provide an order form that can be printed and faxed or mailed to the company with payment.

Order Processing

Completing a sales transaction can be a complicated process within a company. When a customer purchases a product, the order must be submitted to the company. The departments responsible for filling, packing, and shipping the order must receive the order information. Information must also be sent to the accounting department for billing and processing of payments. It may be necessary for the production department to be notified of the order so that the products are available to fill the order or to replace the inventory sold.

Judgment Call

The Trouble with Cookies

Cookies are small files that a web server sends to your web browser when you access a site. They then transmit information from your computer back to the site. These files identify you to the web site server and can log which pages you visit and what links you connect to. Ideally, cookies benefit consumers by saving frequently entered information, allowing improved web design for easier use, and customizing products.

Because cookies are often invisible to users, and the transmitted information varies, some users regard them as an invasion of privacy and disable them in their browsers. But some sites bar visitors who do not permit cookies on their browsers. Businesses have a legitimate desire for information about customers, but to whom does such information belong? Privacy issues will increasingly be public-relations issues for businesses, and in some cases, legal ones if data are not carefully used.

Think Critically

1. Should a company be required to get consent if it sends and receives cookies from the person's computer?

2. If you operated an e-commerce business, would you favor the use of cookies with your customers?

In the past, the process for filling customer orders required many pieces of paper to be sent to every department and person involved. The Internet has streamlined order processing. An order can be placed online by the customer, a company salesperson, or another business that sells the company's products. Even before the order is placed, the customer or salesperson can determine if the product is in stock and how long it will take to fill and ship the order. The customer can also choose a faster shipping method and will know the additional cost of that choice.

When the order is submitted electronically, the necessary information is sent via computer to each of the departments involved. The customer or salesperson can check on the status of the order as it is processed, filled, and shipped.

The use of the Internet for order processing reduces the number of errors since the accuracy of the order can be more easily checked. There is also a large savings in order processing and distribution costs for many companies when the Internet is used. Example savings are shown in Figure 8-2.

Product Distribution

It may be difficult to see how the Internet can improve the physical handling and distribution of products. Many products will continue to be shipped in the same ways they have in the past. Automobiles will travel from the manufacturer to dealers by ships, trains, and trucks. Express packages, fresh flowers, and gourmet foods will be transported on airplanes to insure rapid shipment. It is not possible for those types of products to be distributed using the Internet.

FIGURE 8-2

Average cost savings for businesses when customers use the Internet to make purchases.

Product	Savings
Computer software	99%
Banking services	89%
Airline tickets	87%
Stocks	78%
Books	56%
Toys and gifts	48%

In the case of some other services and products, the use of the Internet makes distribution easier and much less expensive. Computer software companies do not have to produce diskettes or CDs. Instead, customers can download the software from the company's web site. The federal and state governments do not have to print and mail tax forms and instruction booklets for those taxpayers willing to go online and access the forms and instructions. They can print the forms or complete them online and submit the completed forms and even any payments due electronically.

Some companies have changed the form of their products for distribution using the Internet. Newspapers and magazines have created online editions. Film processors now offer to burn customers' photos onto a CD or transfer them to a web site. As customers become more comfortable with the Internet, more products will be purchased and distributed online.

Checkpoint ▶▶▶

What are the three major areas of change in distribution resulting from e-commerce?

Distribution Problems and Solutions

Today, one of the concerns that keep many people from buying products online is uncertainty about product distribution. The key distribution problems facing many e-commerce businesses are the security of transactions, expanded distribution requirements, and customer service demands.

Transaction Security

Almost all people with Internet access use it to gather information about possible purchases. They use search engines to compare and locate products and find the lowest prices. Over half of all Internet consumers make at least one online purchase every three months. But nearly two-thirds of all purchases started by customers are ended before the customer submits the order. In that case, the business not only loses the sale but probably has lost the customer due to problems with the purchasing procedure.

One of the greatest concerns of customers is the security of the information they provide when placing an order, such as their name, address, telephone number, and credit card number. Consumers have two security concerns. The most important is that their personal information will be stolen and misused while it is being transmitted or while it is stored on their computer or the business's computer. The second concern is that the business will misuse the information after the order has been processed. Many businesses sell customer information to other companies that intend to contact those consumers about their products.

E-commerce companies have gone to great lengths to provide security for customer information. They use security technology that makes it almost impossible for information to fall into the wrong hands. They also offer customers the option of transmitting information by fax or phone.

Companies have developed services that allow customers to prearrange transfers of

©GETTY IMAGES/PHOTODISC

What security concerns do customers have when shopping online?

payments from their bank account to the company's account so a credit card number does not have to be entered online. Credit card companies offer insurance so that they will be responsible for any losses if others misuse credit card information as a result of Internet purchases. Businesses are now required to provide privacy policies to customers and usually allow customers to choose whether they want to receive e-mails and promotions from the company, whether the company can share the customer's e-mail address with partnering businesses, and whether the customer wants the company to store personal information in its databases.

Expanded Distribution and Customer Service

When the Internet revolution hit in the late 1990s, many people opened e-businesses. Even experienced brick-and-mortar businesses tried to take advantage of e-commerce by creating a web site to sell their products and services.

Many of the e-businesses soon ran into trouble, however. If customers placed an order online, the product still needed to be packed and shipped. When an order was received, customers often had questions or needed help with assembly. If the product was damaged or was not exactly what customers wanted, they wanted to be able to return it easily for an exchange or refund.

The new e-businesses often were not prepared to handle the many necessary distribution activities. Even experienced businesses found that they had to distribute products in different ways to many more locations than before. As brick-and-mortar businesses, they were used to customers coming to them with problems or to return and exchange merchandise. However, their usual distribution methods no longer worked for Internet customers. Customers became dissatisfied when they could not get the service they expected, so they would stop using the e-business.

Successful e-businesses have found ways to improve distribution. Companies such as UPS and FedEx offer pickup and delivery services to meet the needs of e-commerce. Shipments can be tracked instantly, and customers can go online to determine when they will be delivered. Those companies make it easy for customers to return a product by providing preprinted labels, return instructions, and free pickup service.

Some e-businesses have now made arrangements for customers to return unwanted merchandise to local businesses. That arrangement is easier for a company that is also a brick-and-mortar business, but it is more difficult for a company that is click-only.

Customer service centers have been set up to respond to Internet customer questions and to offer help around the clock. Most web sites have links to frequently asked questions so that customers can get an immediate answer to common problems. Instruction manuals, product warranties and registrations, and places to order replacement parts are all online.

New types of businesses have been developed to serve the distribution needs of e-commerce businesses. A **product fulfillment center** provides some or all of the activities required to fill customer orders. Amazon.com is an example of a successful product fulfillment business. It does not produce products. Instead, it sells the products of other businesses by completing order processing, product storage, order filling and packing, transportation, payment processing, and customer service. Its distribution system uses regional warehouses and efficient computerized order processing systems to offer quick delivery to customers' homes and effective customer service policies including payment processing and easy returns.

Checkpoint ▶▶▶

What are the main distribution problems facing businesses using e-commerce?

8-3 Assessment

Xtra! Study Tools
school.cengage.com/marketing/marketing

Key Concepts

Determine the best answer.

1. Which statement about e-commerce marketing is true?
   a. E-commerce businesses use different marketing functions than brick-and-mortar businesses.
   b. All marketing activities of e-commerce businesses are completed online.
   c. Marketing activities are less important for e-commerce businesses.
   d. none of the above

2. _____ marketing is the completion of marketing activities primarily through the use of computer and Internet technologies.

3. Which of the following is an example of e-commerce rather than traditional marketing?
   a. catalog sales
   b. direct mail marketing
   c. electronic shopping carts
   d. telephone ordering

4. True or False: Companies have actually changed the form of their products to allow for distribution using the Internet.

5. A company that provides some or all of the activities required to fill customer orders is a(n)
   a. e-commerce business
   b. virtual marketer
   c. product fulfillment center
   d. parcel delivery service

Make Academic Connections

6. **Visual Art** Locate the web site of an e-commerce business. Study the product distribution procedures used by the company. Create a poster that illustrates how the main distribution activities are completed from the placement of the order to receipt of the order by the customer.

7. **Math** In one day, an airline sells $2,940,500 in tickets to customers. The cost to process and mail a ticket averages 8% of the price of the ticket. How much does the airline spend on those ticketing costs each day? Using the information from Figure 8-2, how much money can the airline save if it can convert 65% of those sales to e-tickets?

Connect to DECA

8. You are an online customer service representative for an e-commerce business. You receive a telephone call from a prospective customer who wants to make a purchase from the company but is worried about the privacy of personal information and security of credit card account information if it is entered online. With another student, role-play a telephone conversation with the customer in which you reassure the customer about completing an online order from your company. Present the role-play to your teacher (judge). Make sure to demonstrate effective customer service, human relations, and communications skills during the role-play.

The Role of Promotion for E-Commerce

GOALS

- Describe how companies use promotion on the Internet.
- Identify ways to increase the effectiveness of online promotion.

KEY TERMS

pop-up, *p. 228*

rich media, *p. 228*

business blogs, *p. 229*

marketing matters

The Internet was supposed to provide businesses with an inexpensive way to reach millions of prospective customers. A business could place an advertisement with an eye-catching product image in hundreds of places on the Web. Consumers would see it as they browsed, and it would cost much less than a comparable newspaper or magazine ad. With that promise, many companies switched some of their advertising budget from more traditional media to the Internet. Today businesses are rethinking how to advertise on the Internet. Many web sites and search engines are overrun with advertisements. A study found that less than one percent of the advertisements resulted in customers visiting a company's web site. The cost of putting an ad on the Web has dropped sharply.

Work with a group. Look through several different types of web sites. Identify a variety of ways that companies advertise their businesses and products online other than with their own web site. Discuss which methods seem to be effective and which do not.

Communicating with Internet Users

Most people today are not using the Internet to purchase products when they are online. In fact, only two percent of Internet users say they go online with the intention of making a purchase. Over 80 percent say their primary reason for going online is communication. Consumers are more likely to use the Internet to gather information on products and compare alternatives.

The purpose of promotion as part of a company's marketing mix is to communicate information to encourage customers to buy the business's products and services. Since consumers are using the Internet for communication, promotion can be an effective use of the Internet.

Both brick-and-click and click-only businesses can benefit from using the Internet for promotion. Even brick-and-mortar businesses are developing informational web sites that allow prospective customers to easily gather information and make purchasing decisions before visiting the store.

Advertising Expenditures

Many companies are turning to Internet advertising to promote their products and services. In 1998, U.S. businesses spent less than $2 billion for online advertising. By 2007, that amount had grown to $9.7 billion just for the use of actual advertisements. Newer forms of promotion are constantly being developed that call attention to a company's name and products, provide specific information in non-ad formats, or link information to a company's web site.

Figure This

Reach and Frequency

It is very important for companies to know how many people they are reaching with their TV advertising. Two numbers help them figure this out.

The first measure is the reach. Reach is how many people see the ad. It may be expressed as a total number or, more often, as a percentage of overall households with TVs. Nielsen ratings are the reach expressed as a percentage. If a TV show had a Nielsen rating of 10, then 10% of households with televisions were tuned to that show.

Another measure, frequency, is the number of times the average person sees a commercial. A frequency of 3 means that, on average, people saw the ad three times.

Companies are often interested in an ad's GRP, or gross rating point. To calculate the GRP, multiply the reach times the frequency.

Think Critically

1. A company sets a goal of achieving a GRP of 210. It feels that for its TV commercial to sink in, people need to see it three times. To achieve its GRP goal, what does the company's reach need to be?

2. There are 110 million television households in the United States. Forty-five million of those television households watched the Super Bowl game. During the game, Pepsi ran a commercial three times. Figure the GRP for that commercial.

Internet advertisers have become cautious with advertising expenditures. They are looking for ways to measure the effectiveness of online advertising methods before increasing spending.

Promotion Methods

Companies involved in e-commerce use several commonly used promotion methods to reach customers and promote products. Four primary methods include online advertisements, web site sponsorship, priority placement in web search engines and comparison shopping services, and informational web sites.

Online Advertising Companies compete on the Web for the attention of Internet users. They place their ads on pages that prospective customers are most likely to visit and use creative ad designs. Varied sizes, colors, and placements of ads encourage Internet users to pay attention to the information.

For many years, online advertisements were placed on web pages. They appeared as banners (across the top or bottom),

skyscrapers (vertically on the page margins), small boxes within the text, or buttons that opened links to full-page advertisements. Today, advertisers use the latest technology including pop-ups, short video clips, and rich media. A **pop-up** is an advertisement that opens in a new window when a web page is being viewed. **Rich media** include a variety of digital technologies that provide interactive multimedia experiences for users.

The Internet Advertising Bureau has established standards for the size, appearance, and use of Internet advertising methods. They recommend that users should be exposed to only one pop-up for each visit to a web site, and the pop-up should be labeled with the sponsor's name. Advertising videos should be limited to 30 seconds, and users should be able to control both video and audio.

Web Sponsorship An effective way to build recognition of a company's name and products with prospective customers is to sponsor a related informational web site. The sponsor's name is included on the web site so that visitors see the name each time they access the site. For example, a bank could sponsor a web site that helps consumers understand how to lease or finance the purchase of an automobile.

Priority Placement

When you use a search engine such as Google or Yahoo! to find information, you might believe that the list presented is in random order or in the order of popularity of the web sites. However, most search engines allow companies to pay to have their web site appear at the top of the list when the search results are shown. Some search engines make it clear when links are sponsored while others do not. Rather than displaying paid sponsors at the top of a search list, some search engines display the sponsor's name, a link to its web site, and a brief description or promotional message in a column beside the search results. This technique is sometimes called *classified advertising.*

Several web sites have been developed to help consumers identify sources for products they want to purchase and compare product features and prices (NexTag, mySimon, Buy.com). While some of those web sites are independent, others feature the products of companies that have paid to be listed. Those companies' products will appear at the top of the list, but the customer will still be able to compare the features and prices of all products.

Information Web Sites

The Internet is a vast source of information on almost any topic. Companies and organizations develop free web sites on topics of interest to their prospective customers. They believe that as customers become better informed, they are more likely to purchase related products and services. An example of a consumer information web site maintained by a company is Petersons.com, which provides information on choosing a college or university.

Other Types of Promotion

Businesses have developed many other ways to promote their products and services to Internet users. Companies develop e-mail lists using the addresses of people who have previously purchased products or sent inquiries to the company and by purchasing e-mail lists from other companies. They can then e-mail those consumers with special offers or new product information.

You may have seen online coupons similar to the coupons you receive in the mail or in newspapers and magazines. The coupons are used either by printing and mailing the coupon with an order or by entering a special code on the order form when purchasing online.

Internet promotions are used to encourage consumers to request free samples, send for CDs that provide detailed product information, or visit a local store where the company's products are sold. New audio-visual technology allows businesses to provide three-dimensional views of their products online so that customers can examine them as if they were actually handling the products.

Companies are increasingly using more informal and personalized methods of Internet communication. They include online newsletters, e-mail messages sent to regular customers, and business blogs. **Business blogs** are regularly updated online journals written by company experts. Businesses also communicate through established online interest or social groups or by establishing their own discussion and news groups that customers can join.

Checkpoint ▶▶▶

What four methods can a company use to promote its products online?

Preparing for E-Commerce Marketing

Most consumers are satisfied with their shopping experience when they make purchases using the Internet. In fact, as shown in Figure 8-3, Internet shoppers are more satisfied with the online shopping experience than with the other ways they make purchases.

The reasons for the higher level of satisfaction include convenience, saving time, and getting everything from one source. They also value the competitive prices they often find on the Internet.

Planning the Shopping Experience

Marketing using the Internet is quite different from marketing to customers who actually visit a store. When a consumer shops using the Internet, the business typically does not have direct contact with the person. The design of the web site and effective communication principles are needed to attract consumers to the business and to help them make a purchase. In order for promotions to result in a sale and a satisfied customer, the company must address the following questions.

1. How does the customer typically use the Internet to gather information? What search engines are used?

2. Is the information customers need to place an order easy to locate and understand?

3. Are the web pages well organized? Is it easy to move forward and backward? Is it easy to locate product information and prices, purchase products, and make payments?

4. Are web pages attractively designed? Do pictures and graphics effectively show products and how they are used?

5. Is it easy to get common questions answered? Can customers contact the company for assistance in selecting and purchasing products?

FIGURE 8-3
Customer satisfaction with types of shopping.

Type	% Satisfied
Shopping online	73%
Shopping in stores	60%
Shopping with catalogs	56%

6. Is there a secure method for customers to buy products online? Is there an alternative method for customers who don't want to buy online?

7. Are product delivery methods and costs clearly explained?

8. Are customers given information on how they can return products that don't meet their needs?

When companies carefully plan the shopping experience for Internet customers, provide needed information, and make shopping easy and enjoyable, customers will be willing to buy online.

Effective Promotion Methods

Customers are clear about the features that are helpful when shopping online. Those features are listed in Figure 8-4. You can see that almost all of the features customers identified involve communication between the business and the customer. So promotion needs to be more than just

FIGURE 8-4
Features likely to increase online purchasing.

- Close-up images of products
- Information on product availability
- Product comparison guides
- Easy-to-use search function
- Toll-free customer service number
- Consumer reviews and product evaluations
- Easy-to-use "shopping cart" and check out feature

advertising that creates customer awareness of the business and its web site. Promotion should strive to meet consumers' communication needs.

Effective promotional tools for e-commerce include the following:

- An easy-to-remember, meaningful Internet address

- Well-designed online advertisements

- Advertisements in other media such as newspapers and television

- Registration with search engines to identify the company to people gathering information about its products

- Customer service personnel to help customers and answer questions

- Information collected about who visits the company's web site, when they visit, how much time they spend, which pages and links are most popular, and what information influences them to make a purchase

- Online chat rooms, discussions, and clubs to exchange information with customers

- E-mail promotions and announcements to customers to encourage regular visits to the web site

Checkpoint ▶▶▶

Why are customers generally more satisfied with online shopping than with shopping in stores?

8-4 Assessment

Xtra! Study Tools
school.cengage.com/marketing/marketing

Key Concepts

Determine the best answer.

1. True or False: The main reason most people go online is to gather product information and make purchases.

2. Which of the following is not a method of e-commerce promotion?
   a. online advertisements
   b. web site sponsorship
   c. information web sites
   d. all are promotional methods

3. A _____ is an advertisement that opens in a new window when a web page is being viewed.

4. Customers have the highest level of satisfaction with which type of shopping?
   a. online
   b. retail store
   c. catalog
   d. none of the above

5. True or False: A meaningful, easy-to-remember Internet address is actually an effective promotional tool for e-commerce businesses.

Make Academic Connections

6. **Ethics** Write a three-paragraph analysis of the following statement: "Presenting sponsored business links as the first entries in an Internet search without disclosing that the companies paid for that placement is unethical."

7. **Economics** The final price of a product from an e-commerce business is often not the listed price. Choose a product that costs at least $50. Gather information from several companies that sell the product using a price comparison web site. Prepare a table that compares the companies offering the three highest-priced and three lowest-priced products. Show the initial product price, shipping charges, taxes, and total price to be paid.

Connect to DECA
An Association of Marketing Students

8. Your team members must prepare an e-commerce promotional plan for a farm that sells organic fruits and vegetables. Identify three different promotional methods that will be used and prepare a visual example of each. Present your plan and examples to your teacher (judge) with reasons for your decisions.

Chapter 8 Assessment

Check Your Understanding

Now that you have completed the chapter, check your understanding of the lessons with these questions. Record the score that best represents your understanding of each marketing concept.

1 = not at all; 3 = somewhat; 5 = very well

If your score is 42–50, you are ready for the assessment activities that follow. If you score 33–41, you should review the lessons for the items you scored 1–3. If you score 32 or less, you will want to carefully reread the lessons and work with a study partner on the areas you don't understand.

Can you—

___ identify the meaning of click-only, brick-and-click, and brick-and-mortar?

___ describe the differences among the three stages of development for an e-commerce business?

___ identify reasons why e-commerce businesses that don't understand the marketing concept often fail?

___ identify several factors that contributed to the growth of e-commerce in the past 20 years?

___ offer examples of several business uses of the Internet other than selling products?

___ discuss how virtual marketing is different from and similar to traditional marketing?

___ explain why distribution can be the marketing function that determines success or failure for an e-commerce business?

___ identify the three key distribution problems that face many e-commerce businesses?

___ describe the four primary promotional methods used in e-commerce?

___ provide examples of how e-commerce businesses can increase the effectiveness of their online promotions?

Review Marketing Terms

Match the terms listed with the definitions. Some terms may not be used.

1. The completion of marketing activities primarily through the use of computer and Internet technologies

2. Business-to-consumer

3. A variety of digital technologies that provide interactive multimedia experiences for users

4. Companies that complete almost all of their business activities through the Internet

5. Involves business activities, including the exchange of goods, services, and information, completed electronically via the Internet

6. Regularly updated online journals written by company experts

7. Companies that complete most of their business activities by means other than the Internet

8. Provides some or all of the activities required to fill customer orders

9. An advertisement that opens in a new window when a web page is being viewed

10. Companies that combine traditional business operations with the use of the Internet

a. B2B
b. B2C
c. brick-and-click businesses
d. brick-and-mortar businesses
e. business blogs
f. click-only businesses
g. e-commerce
h. pop-up
i. product fulfillment center
j. rich media
k. virtual marketing

Review Marketing Concepts

11. The use of the Internet as a place to buy and sell products had its beginnings
    a. just after World War II
    b. in the early 1970s
    c. about 1985
    d. in the mid-1990s

12. E-commerce includes all of the following except
    a. in-store sales
    b. online product purchases
    c. exchange of business information
    d. customer service

13. Which of the following is not one of the stages of e-commerce development?
    a. incorporation
    b. integration
    c. information
    d. interaction

14. Many of the first e-commerce companies were unsuccessful because they
    a. had poor web site designs
    b. didn't promote their products
    c. didn't understand the marketing concept
    d. set prices too low

15. True or False: The United States leads the world in the number of Internet users.

16. True or False: The total amount of business-to-consumer Internet sales is much larger than business-to-business sales.

17. True or False: Some products can actually be distributed directly to consumers' homes using the Internet.

18. True or False: While being able to process an order using the Internet is an important customer service, it actually costs more than a traditional sale.

19. True or False: Most Internet shoppers go online for the purpose of gathering information rather than to make an online purchase.

20. True or False: Today, most consumers are satisfied with their shopping experience when they purchase a product on the Internet.

Marketing Research and Planning

21. Some companies are well suited to be click-only businesses, and others are better suited to remain brick-and-mortar businesses. Use a business directory for your community and identify five businesses that you believe could be effective click-only businesses and five others that you believe should operate as brick-and-mortar businesses. Write a rationale for each business you selected. Share your lists with other students and compare your answers.

22. Businesses can move through three stages of Internet use as they develop e-commerce strategies. Use the Internet to find an example of a business web site for each of the three stages. Print the company's home page. Show each example to the class and explain why it illustrates the stage you selected.

23. Some business web sites ask customers to complete an online registration form before they purchase from the company's web site. As a part of the registration process, the company asks customers to provide specific information such as their education and income levels, interests and hobbies, and other information that would help the company understand and meet the customers' needs. Assume you are in charge of designing an online registration form for a travel agency. Using a computer, develop ten questions that would help you plan travel services for the customer. Explain why each of the questions is important.

24. The growth of the Internet has been remarkable as more and more people gain access to it and businesses move into e-commerce. Statistics for Internet use are reported on many web sites. Use the Internet to locate two different web sites that report data on the amount of Internet sales in several countries, including the United States, for several years. Prepare a bar chart that presents data from both web sites. It is likely that the data will not be the same on each web site. Why do you believe it is difficult to obtain accurate data on the use of the Internet?

Marketing Management and Decision Making

25. You are the advertising copywriter for PetSit, a company that provides pet care/boarding services. You have been asked to develop a series of Internet advertisements. Use the Internet to identify three different styles and sizes of Internet advertisements frequently used by businesses. Using a computer graphics program, design ads for the PetSit company using each of the ad styles you identified.

26. Package distribution companies such as FedEx and UPS now provide online tracking services. With that service, a shipper or customer can obtain up-to-date information on the location of a package being shipped and the expected delivery date. Using the Internet or by arranging an interview (face-to-face, telephone, or e-mail) with a representative of a package distribution company, learn about the technology and

equipment used to be able to instantly track each package, how and when the information is entered into the computer system, and how the company provides security for the information. Use a word processing program to prepare a written report on your findings.

27. In Lesson 8-4, eight questions were posed that businesses should use to evaluate the effectiveness of their web sites. Use the Internet to locate two business web sites that allow customers to make purchases online. Use a computer spreadsheet program to design a table like the example below. Use the table to compare the two web sites. For each question, provide a rating of 1 to 5 with 1 being a low rating and 5 a high rating. After completing all questions, total the points to give each business an overall rating.

Business 1	Business 2	Questions
		1. Is it easy to locate the web site using search engines?
		2. Is the information customers need to place an order easy to locate and understand?
		3. Are the web pages well organized? Is it easy to move forward and backward? Is it easy to locate product information and prices, purchase products, and make payments?
		4. Are web pages attractively designed? Do pictures and graphics effectively show products and how they are used?
		5. Is it easy to get common questions answered? Can customers contact the company for assistance in selecting and purchasing products?
		6. Is there a secure method for customers to buy products online? Is there an alternative method for customers who don't want to buy online?
		7. Are product delivery methods and costs clearly explained?
		8. Are customers given information on how they can return products that don't meet their needs?
		Total Points

Internet Marketing Management Team Decision Making Event

Holiday Joy is an online specialty store offering gifts, ranging from $5 to $50, for nationally recognized holidays. Customers who order gifts online can use all major credit cards to pay for their purchases. Females, aged 55-70, make up 70 percent of the customer base for Holiday Joy. Many of the customers prefer shopping at home instead of going to the store or mall. Follow-up customer surveys indicate that high-quality gifts are the main reason for repeat business at Holiday Joy. Customers also like the reliable, speedy delivery of orders.

Holiday Joy would like to expand its target market to attract younger consumers aged 25-54. The vice president of Holiday Joy has asked your team to develop a fundraising strategy to increase Internet sales for the company. The fundraising activity is to be implemented by student organizations such as DECA. You must develop a plan to be used by student organizations that describes how to distribute information to the expanded target market (females aged 25-54) and assist customers in placing their orders online. You must also develop a system to ensure the sale is credited to the appropriate school organization.

In addition, Holiday Joy wants your suggestion for a reasonably priced gift to give customers who purchase more than $50 of merchandise. The vice president would also like your suggestions on how to update the web site to promote products more effectively.

You will present your recommendations to the vice president. You will have ten minutes for your presentation, and the judge has five minutes to ask questions.

Performance Indicators Evaluated

- Describe the unique aspects of Internet sales. (Selling)
- Explain online sales strategies. (Selling)
- Discuss the features of an online sales campaign. (Promotion)
- Conceptualize web site design. (Promotion)
- Explain the relationship between customer service and distribution. (Distribution)
- Explain the nature of positive customer/client relations. (Emotional Intelligence)
- Explain the nature of online advertisements. (Promotion)

Go to the DECA web site for more detailed information.

Think Critically

1. Why must the web site for Holiday Joy be easy to use?
2. What is the benefit of having students assist customers with the online ordering process?
3. How does ordering online make the sales process simpler?
4. What incentives could Holiday Joy use to increase sales within its new target market?

www.deca.org

Chapter 9

Developing a Marketing Strategy and Marketing Plan

©GETTY IMAGES/PHOTODISC

Newsline

Refocusing on Customers

Croemers department store opened in 1917. Over the years, the store concentrated on serving an upper middle-class market segment. It offered clothing, jewelry, appliances, furniture, linens, and home accessories, with an emphasis on customer service. Croemers developed a loyal group of customers and achieved high sales and profits. But the business almost went bankrupt learning about the importance of a marketing plan.

Two large national chain discount stores opened in the same city, offering some of the same products as Croemers. Croemers saw an immediate impact on profits as many of its customers were attracted to these businesses by extensive promotion and lower-priced products.

The company turned to a marketing consultant who helped it complete a marketing study.

Croemers learned that its primary customers viewed it as their source of unique products that they couldn't easily find in competing stores. These customers said that if Croemers met their expectations for quality and service, they wouldn't switch to competitors just based on price.

Croemers prepared a detailed marketing plan using the results of the research. The company's buyers worked with selected manufacturers to develop a smaller but more profitable line of quality products that were not carried in the discount stores. They added a new line of high-end products under their own brand name, Croemers Exclusive. The company implemented a comprehensive training program for all employees to build a commitment to customer service. A new promotional program was

instituted that focused on a direct appeal to its target market rather than the broad-based mass media approach used by the discounters. Croemers was soon able to regain control over costs, increase profit margins, and reestablish strong ties with its target market. Its new success was the result of careful planning and responding to customers' needs.

Think Critically

1. Why is it that Croemers was able to succeed for years without a marketing plan but then suddenly found itself losing its customer base?

2. How is it possible for Croemers to increase profits while the discount stores are taking a big portion of the sales it used to make?

school.cengage.com/marketing/marketing

Prepare for Performance

This chapter develops the following Performance Indicators from the DECA Competitive Events program.

Core Performance Indicators

- Generate product ideas to contribute to ongoing business success
- Employ marketing information to develop a marketing plan
- Determine strategic marketing planning structure

Supporting Performance Indicators

- Identify product opportunities
- Explain the concept of marketing strategies
- Explain the nature of marketing planning
- Define business mission
- Set marketing policies

Go to **school.cengage.com/marketing/marketing** and click on Connect to DECA.

nabiscoworld.com/triscuit
Diets rich in whole grain foods and low in saturated fat and cholesterol may help reduce the risk of heart disease.

© 2005 KF Holdings

Heart healthy.

Triscuit
Original

Baked with 100% whole grain. 0g trans fat.   Crunch to your health.

©KRAFT

Visual Focus

An effective ad combines an attention-getting image and a brief written message to leave a memorable impression. It should communicate a unique appeal to a specific group of customers. This chapter will help you understand the importance of a clearly developed marketing strategy focused on the needs of a target market as well as how to develop a comprehensive marketing plan to implement the strategy.

Focus Questions:

What memorable impression is Nabisco trying to leave with consumers who view this ad? How are the words and images in the ad used effectively? What consumer needs are the focus of the ad? Do you believe Nabisco has clearly demonstrated how the product appeals to those needs?

Locate two examples of ads—one that has an effective, memorable focus directed at a specific customer need and one that does not. Discuss your choices in class.

Elements of a Marketing Strategy

marketing matters

Marketing requires much more than advertising and selling. In fact, marketing is even more complex than the major marketing functions. Effective marketing develops satisfying exchange relationships between businesses and their customers. In order to accomplish that, businesses need to develop a marketing strategy. The process begins with identifying a target market or markets, first by carefully studying several market segments and then by choosing a target that provides the best opportunity for the company to offer a satisfying marketing mix.

Make a list of five personal characteristics that affect your wants and needs. Identify the personal characteristics that you believe are similar to and those that are different from the characteristics of most of your family members, friends, and classmates. Do you believe the differences affect your wants and needs as well as the choices of products and services that interest you? Discuss your views with other students.

Differentiating Market Segments

A **marketing strategy** is the way marketing activities are planned and coordinated to achieve an organization's goals. An organization that believes in the marketing concept develops marketing strategies to profitably satisfy customer needs. In most instances, those organizations follow a two-step process. First they carefully select a target market. Then they develop a marketing mix for that target market.

Start with a Market

A market includes all of the consumers available for a business to serve by selling a product or service. However, because the people in a market can be so different, it is nearly impossible for a business to serve all customers well. What if a business came into your classroom to sell items for students who will be graduating next spring? It is likely that not everyone in the room is a senior, so some would automatically not be customers. Each person has different plans for graduation. Some students have no plans yet and will not have any for several months. Others probably made plans as early as last summer and may have already purchased many of the things they will need. In some families, graduation ceremonies are an important tradition with specific procedures to be followed. In other families, it is up to each graduate to determine his or her plans.

Recognize Differences and Similarities

Your class is a very small market. It is likely that the business visiting your class will be interested in all prospective graduates from your school and from other schools in your city and state. It might want to serve graduating students from colleges and universities as well as from high schools. Some companies offer products for graduates from adult education programs, junior high schools, and even "graduates" from preschools. The differences among all of the people who buy graduation products will affect purchasing decisions and the information they need.

Segmenting Factors

Markets are made up of many segments. *Segments* are components of a market in which people have one or more similar characteristics. Characteristics used to segment markets are shown in Figure 9-1. The most important factors used to segment a market are the wants and needs of consumers. People make purchases to satisfy wants and needs. If a product does not appeal to an important consumer want or need, it will remain unsold. People in a market segment have one or more strong wants or needs in common.

A second identifying factor is demographic characteristics such as age, income, location, and educational level.

Important Factors Used to Segment a Market

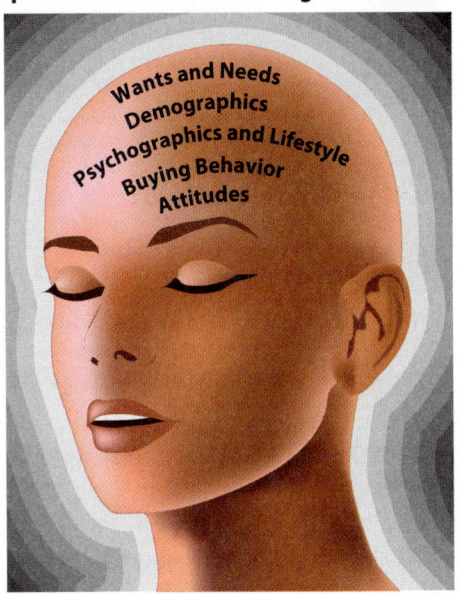

FIGURE 9-1
Businesses study a variety of information to identify unique market segments.

Markets can also be described by psychographic or lifestyle characteristics including activities, attitudes, customs, and traditions. The attitudes of potential consumers are especially important in segmenting markets. How do consumers feel about the type of products and specific brands of the products?

Another way to segment is by identifying the way consumers make their purchase decisions or their *buying behavior.* These factors could include their previous experience with products, what sources of information they use, whether decisions are more rational or emotional, and how much time they take in gathering and evaluating information before a decision is made. Marketing information systems and marketing research are used to gather information in order to divide markets into segments.

Working in **Teams**

Work with your team members to complete a demographic analysis of all of the students in your class. Identify five or more demographic characteristics and two or three categories for each characteristic. For example, the characteristic could be "age" and the categories could be "14–15," "16–17," and "18 and older." Develop a table that shows each of the characteristics and the number of students from your class that fit within each of the categories.

Checkpoint ▶▶▶

Why are people's wants and needs an important basis for identifying market segments?

Using Communications Technology Professionally

Gone are the days when people went to their mailboxes hoping for a long awaited letter from an old acquaintance. With 24/7 contact available, be it through e-mail, cell-phones, instant messaging (IM), text messaging, web sites, or blogs, individuals in modern society are accustomed to receiving information in a continuous, ongoing stream.

With the number of electronic communication tools available, it is easy to forget that communication is the objective. Communication devices are merely the tools that facilitate that goal.

Just as courtesy is necessary for face-to-face communication, it is also required for electronic communication. These courtesies are particularly important for business interactions.

Patience is important. Although a request for information can be delivered instantly, a response cannot necessarily be provided immediately. The recipient's schedule and the need to gather information before responding will affect response time.

During meetings, personal interactions take priority over anyone who might be available electronically. While meeting with others, communication devices that would cause distractions should be turned off.

Developing strong interpersonal relationships with coworkers is extremely important. These relationships are strengthened through face-to-face interactions. Therefore, although it may be tempting to IM or call your coworkers, it is often worthwhile to periodically walk down the hall and have a brief chat with them.

Texting and instant messaging use a form of abbreviated spelling designed to facilitate fast communication and to minimize key strokes. While these conventions are appropriate for electronic communications, they are not appropriate for written communications in the workplace. Utilize good grammar and standard English when preparing formal written documents.

E-mail signatures should include only pertinent contact information. Including political or religious quotes or symbols or links to web sites or blogs may violate your employer's e-mail policies.

Many employers monitor employees' use of e-mail and the Web. You should know and adhere to your employer's usage policies.

Keep in mind that the Web and its various components, such as web sites or blogs, are internationally accessible to most users. Use restraint when posting information on web sites. Confidential or negative information regarding an employer should not be posted on personal blogs.

As part of the background check for job applicants, many employers search the Web to see if information is available on the job applicant. Publicly recorded instances of bad behavior could impact your chances of getting hired.

Develop Your Skill

Consider some sensitive information you need to communicate to three people. Outline what your message is and why you need to share it. Define the goal you want to achieve by conveying your message.

Prepare three scripts for communicating the message—one for a phone conversation, one for an e-mail, and one for an IM. Using each type of technology only once, deliver the message to all three people.

Which type of delivery medium was most effective at conveying the message you intended? Which delivery method promoted ongoing, harmonious relationships with the people involved?

Selecting Target Markets

Rather than trying to satisfy every person in a market, a business will be more successful in meeting customer needs by concentrating its attention on a specific target market. A *target market* is a clearly identified segment of the market to which the company wants to appeal. In order to be an effective target market, it must meet four criteria:

1. The people in the target market must have common, important needs and must respond in a similar way to marketing activities designed to satisfy those needs.

2. The people outside of the target market should have enough differences from those in the market that they will not find the marketing mix satisfying.

3. The company needs adequate information about the people in the target market so that they can be identified and located.

4. The important wants and needs of the target market and their buying behavior must be understood well enough that an effective marketing mix can be developed.

In the earlier example of a business selling graduation products, the market of all students who will be graduating should be studied. Segments can then be identified based on the type of school, its location, and when the graduation will occur. Other segments could be based on factors such as the age, gender, or even income of the graduate.

After identifying several segments, the company would study needs, attitudes, and family customs to see if they are similar or different among various segments. Also, information will be collected to see when and how each segment makes purchase decisions about graduation products. Then, the business will identify which segment offers the best marketing opportunity. That will become the target market.

It is possible for the company to select more than one segment for a target market. To be successful, the segments must have enough common needs that they respond in the same way to marketing efforts. For example, males and females from the same school may be a part of one target market. Or all graduating seniors from

©GETTY IMAGES/PHOTODISC

Do these graduates meet the four criteria for being an effective target market? Why or why not?

high schools in the Midwest may be similar enough to be considered one target market. Larger companies often work with several target markets at the same time. Each of the target markets requires unique marketing mixes that respond to the differences between the target markets.

What four criteria must be satisfied in order to have an effective target market?

How many different market segments can you think of for this group of students?

9-1 Assessment

school.cengage.com/marketing/marketing

Key Concepts

Determine the best answer.

1. True or False: A target market includes all of the consumers available for a business to serve by selling a product or service.

2. The most important factors used to segment a market are
   a. types of competition
   b. consumer needs and wants
   c. demographic characteristics
   d. buying behaviors

3. Which of the following would *not* be a characteristic of an effective target market?
   a. People in the target market have similar important wants and needs.
   b. Adequate information is available to identify and locate the consumers.
   c. People outside the target market can be encouraged to buy the product.
   d. Buying behavior of the market must be understood.

4. True or False: If a business decides to serve more than one target market, each target market will require a different marketing mix.

Make Academic Connections

5. **Technology** Locate the web site of a company that manufactures computers. Review the web site and identify three unique market segments for which the company produces computers. Using information from the web site, describe the main factors that make each segment different from the others.

6. **Economics** Use the library or the Internet to identify publications or other sources of information about the demographic characteristics of your community provided by a government agency. Prepare an alphabetized bibliography of the publications with a brief description of each.

Connect to

7. You are a consultant to a company that manufactures athletic uniforms. To sell its uniforms, the company produces a large catalog and sends it to every sports team it can identify. Prepare a three-minute presentation for the company's president on the value of focusing marketing efforts on one or more target markets using a unique marketing mix for each target market. Provide an example target market and marketing mix. Present your ideas to your teacher (judge).

Marketing Mix Alternatives

GOALS

- Describe aspects of a basic product that can be altered to improve its market appeal.
- Discuss important influences on distribution, pricing, and promotion.
- Define four stages of a product life cycle.

KEY TERMS

brand, *p. 245*

image, *p. 245*

guarantee, *p. 245*

warranty, *p. 245*

product life cycle, *p. 248*

marketing matters

The most important work of marketers is to design and implement the marketing mix. The four elements of the marketing mix include all of the activities that marketers will complete to satisfy the target market. Marketers recognize that there are many ways to make a product more appealing to customers in addition to making changes in the product itself. Effective marketing involves careful study of each of the marketing mix elements to determine what can be changed and to identify the effect of the changes on the target market and on company profits.

List three products you have purchased recently that you believe met your needs and expectations. Describe the marketing mix of each product and identify what parts of the marketing mix made the choice better than other products you could have selected.

Fine-Tuning the Product

Have you ever shopped for an item only to find that you really have very few choices? While there may be two or three brands available, each of the brands is almost identical to the others. This problem often occurs when businesses try to sell products to a large market. They have to offer a product that will appeal to the average consumer. If you are not average, you probably won't find the resulting product particularly satisfying.

It is very difficult for a business to compete when its products are almost identical to those of its competitors. When customers see few differences, they will often look for the lowest price, which reduces the profit margin for businesses. To avoid this situation, businesses can try to make their products different from the competition

and more satisfying to the customers. But that means they will probably not be able to focus on a large market.

The product or service as a marketing mix element includes anything offered to the customer by the business that will be used to satisfy needs. Even for very simple products, there are many choices businesses can make when developing the product element of the marketing mix. In addition to the basic product, other components include features, options, services, brand names, guarantees, packaging, and alternative uses. The goal is to create a product that is quite different from competitors' products and that responds to the specific needs of the target market.

Not all of the components will be used with every product or service. In some cases, all the target market wants is the basic product. At other times, services and a guarantee are important. Both research and creativity are needed to develop an effective product. Marketers need to be familiar with all of the possible changes that can be made in a product and select the most satisfying combination to serve a target market.

Basic Product

The most important part of this mix element is the basic product offered. The basic product is a computer, an automobile, a pair of jeans, or a box of breakfast cereal. It is the first factor considered by the consumer in deciding whether or not to purchase. If the basic product does not meet an important need, the consumer will not consider it. A service can also be the basic part of a marketing mix. Movie theaters, child care, home cleaning, and tax preparation businesses all offer a basic service.

Product Features

Businesses can add features to a basic product to make it different from and better than competitors' products and services. Most basic products are sold with many additional features. Consider the product offerings of automobile dealers. Every automobile today has hundreds of features. Some, such as seat belts, outside rearview mirrors, safety bumpers, and emission control equipment, are required by law. Others—carpeted floor mats, heated seats, locking gasoline covers, and multi-speaker music systems—are included to satisfy the common needs of automobile purchasers.

Examples of features on other products include a shirt that offers tailoring, easy-care fabric, double-sewn buttons, and multiple color choices. A telephone may have voice mail capabilities, 50-number memory, redial, and a volume control. A shampoo may contain special

A computer is a basic product. How could each of the product mix elements be used to ensure the computer meets the needs of various target markets?

©GETTY IMAGES/PHOTODISC

moisturizers, a conditioner, and a pleasant scent. Consumers expect many of these features, and they will not buy products that do not include them.

Options

Features are added to improve the basic product. Some businesses make decisions about the features they offer to customers. Customers are not given choices. They must accept the features the company offers. Other companies give customers choices of the features to be included on the product they purchase. Those choices are known as options. When you order telephone service, you are given choices such as call waiting, call forwarding, and three-way calling. Some customers choose one or more of these options, while others choose just the basic service.

Associated Services

If your family has purchased a major appliance such as a washer or refrigerator, you were probably offered a maintenance contract by the salesperson. The maintenance contract is an associated service that will pay for repair work if the appliance fails to operate properly. There are many cases where services provided with a product make the product easier to use for consumers. If you purchase a computer system, you might want someone to set it up and test it to make sure it works properly. When purchasing or leasing a car, you may have the option of purchasing a service package that provides basic maintenance for a set number of miles or years.

Brand/Image

A **brand** is a unique name, symbol, or design that identifies a product, service, or company. At first, the brand may not seem to be an important part of a product or service. However, you can probably identify products that you buy where the brand name is one of the most important factors in your decision. In fact, you may refuse to buy a pair of jeans, athletic shoes, or even a can of soda unless it is a specific brand. The brand of certain products is an important factor in making a purchase decision for many people.

Your parents may not always understand why you want to buy specific brands of certain products, but they are probably just as loyal to particular brands of automobiles, foods, office equipment, or magazines.

One of the important reasons for brand loyalty is the image of the brand. The **image** is a unique, memorable quality of a brand. Some brands have an image of quality, others of low price, and still others of innovation. To be effective, the image must match the important needs of the consumer.

Guarantee/Warranty

When customers purchase products or services, they want to receive a good value. If they are concerned the product is poorly constructed, will not work properly, or may wear out quickly, they may be unwilling to purchase it. Companies offer guarantees or warranties with products as

©2004 HOYU CO., LTD.

Products that offer features to meet consumer needs are likely to have a higher rate of success.

assurance that the product will be repaired or replaced if there are problems. A **guarantee** is a general promise or assurance of quality while a **warranty** is a specific written statement of the seller's responsibilities related to the guarantee.

Packaging

An often-overlooked part of the marketing mix is the package. Packaging provides protection and security for the product until the consumer can use it. It has other purposes as well. The package can provide information that helps the customer make a better purchasing decision. It can be

Uses

The final part of the product element of the marketing mix is the use of the product. It is possible that products and services can be more satisfying to customers or can appeal to new markets if other uses are found. A classic example of expanding markets through new product uses is baking soda. Because very few consumers bake their own bread today in the United States, sales at a baking soda manufacturer began to decline. In a study of consumer behavior, it was discovered that consumers use the product for many purposes other than baking. Some use it to freshen refrigerators, garbage disposals, and litter boxes for pets. Others use it to brush their teeth. Through promoting those and other uses and actually creating some new products, the company has increased its sales dramatically.

useful in promoting the product by attracting attention and illustrating the product in use. Packaging can even make the product more useful for the consumer. Producers of orange juice found that sales increased when a plastic spout with a cap that could be screwed on and off was added to their cardboard carton.

Checkpoint ▶▶

Name the seven aspects of a product that can be changed to improve its appeal.

Distribution, Price, and Promotion

The complete product or service offered by a company is certainly an important element of the marketing mix. However, unless the product is known to consumers in the target market, is available when they want it, and sells for a satisfactory price, the company will not be successful.

Distribution

Distribution is the marketing mix element that facilitates the physical exchange of products and services between businesses and their customers. Just as with product/service planning, there are many possible distribution decisions. Some important questions that should be answered in planning distribution include:

- Where will the customer be best able to obtain the product?
- Where will the customer use it?
- Are there special requirements to transport, store, or display the product?
- When should distribution occur?
- Who should be responsible for each type of distribution activity?

In addition to these general distribution decisions, many products require specific attention to physical distribution factors including the type of transportation, inventory control, product handling, protective packaging, order processing, and customer service.

Price

Price as a marketing mix element is defined as the amount a buyer pays as well as the methods of increasing the value of the product to the customers. There are several decisions about how to develop and present the price that can affect the customer's perception of value. They include:

- Does the business want to increase sales, increase profits, or enhance the image of the product?
- Should price be based on cost, what customers are willing to pay, or what competitors are charging?
- Will there be one price for all customers?
- Will customers be allowed to negotiate price? Will discounts or sales be used?
- Will the price be clearly communicated through a price tag or catalog?
- Are there things that clearly satisfy the customer and make the product a better value than alternatives?

Promotion

Consumers need information about product and service choices and help in making the best purchasing decisions. Businesses use the promotion element of the marketing mix to provide that information and assistance. Promotion includes the methods and information communicated to customers to encourage purchases and increase their satisfaction.

Maybe more than any of the other mix elements, it is easy to see a variety of promotional choices businesses have. Decisions to be made include:

- Will promotions be directed at a general market or specific segments? Who is the decision maker? Where are the customers in the decision-making process?
- Is the specific goal of promotion to increase knowledge, to change attitudes, or to influence behavior?
- What specific information does the audience need to make a decision?
- Will promotion be most effective through advertising, personal selling, sales promotion, publicity, or some other form of communication?
- What is the total amount of money needed for effective promotion? When should the money be spent, on what activities, and for which media?
- When and how can feedback be obtained to determine if customers understood the message?

Checkpoint ▶▶

Besides the total product or service being offered, what other elements must marketers consider in developing a marketing mix?

Analyzing the Product Life Cycle

With all of the choices available to businesses, it may seem that it will be difficult to determine the best combination of product, distribution, price, and promotion to use. Think of the graduation products company. If you were helping the company selling graduation products plan its marketing mix, how would you determine the mix it should use?

There are three factors to be considered each time a business plans its marketing mix. Those factors are:

- the type of competition
- the purchase behavior of consumers
- the strengths and weaknesses of the business

An important marketing tool to identify the type of competition faced by a business is life cycle analysis. A **product life cycle** identifies the stages a product goes through from the time it enters the market until it is no longer sold.

Products go through four stages in their life cycle, as shown in Figure 9-2. The stages of the life cycle are determined by changes in the amount and type of competition. By studying the competition, a business can determine the type of marketing mix needed in each stage of the product life cycle.

Introduction

In the first stage of the product life cycle, a new product is introduced into the market. It is quite different from existing products,

so customers are not aware of it or don't realize how it can satisfy their needs. Because it is new, there are no other products that are direct competitors. It will be competing with older, established products.

As with many new things, few people will want to be the first to try the product. The business needs to identify those consumers who are very dissatisfied with current products and those who are most likely to want to experiment with something new. These people are the target market for the new product.

The product itself will be very basic since it has just been developed. There will not likely be many features or options. To assure the customers of the quality of the new product, the company may offer a guarantee or warranty. A well-known brand name may also encourage people to buy the new product.

The product will not have to be widely distributed in the market since only a small number of customers will buy it initially. It would be too risky and too expensive for the company to try to get widespread distribution. The company will select those locations where the target market will be most likely to buy this type of product.

The price will be high at first since the company has many expenses in developing the product and expects fewer early sales. People who are the first to buy a new product will often pay a higher price. They have no other similar products to use in comparing the price.

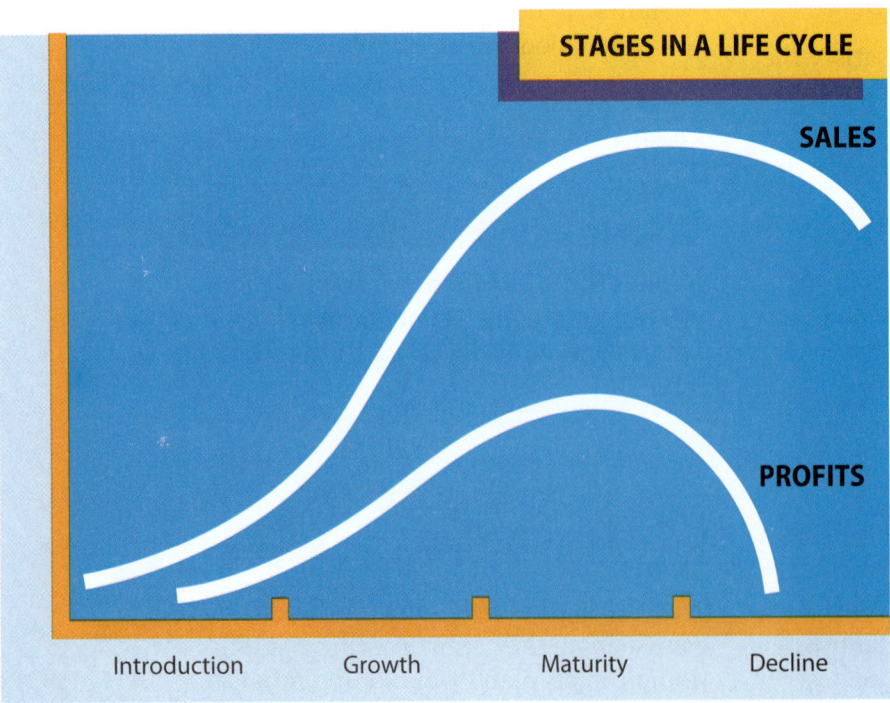

STAGES IN A LIFE CYCLE

SALES

PROFITS

Introduction | Growth | Maturity | Decline

FIGURE 9-2
Competition affects sales and profits in each stage of the product life cycle.

The Emerging Chinese Market

While trailing much of the rest of the world for years, e-commerce in China is now on the upswing. In 2006, China's economy was sixth in the world in rate of growth, and the Internet in China is growing even faster. Between 2000 and 2007, the number of Internet users in China grew from 10 million to nearly 140 million.

Insightful business owners took advantage of the growing Internet market in China by getting in early. Peggy Yu was one such person. She started dangdang.com, the Chinese equivalent of Amazon.com. Dangdang was able to meld traditional purchasing methods with Internet shopping. Dangdang used couriers to deliver products and collect cash payments from customers, because credit cards were not widely used.

Many American companies have taken notice of China and entered the market. Amazon.com bought one of Dangdang's rivals in 2004 and now competes directly with Dangdang, and Google launched a version of its web site specifically designed for the Chinese market. Many experts believe China will be an e-commerce powerhouse in the decades to come.

Think Critically

1. What advantages would a local company like Dangdang have over a foreign competitor like Amazon in the Chinese market?

2. Why might a company like Amazon buy a local competitor when entering a new market rather than just entering the market with its own name?

Promotion needs to inform the target market that a new product is available and show how it will satisfy an important need. Customers need to know where they can purchase the product. Often promotion in the introductory stage of the life cycle will emphasize that the product is new and exciting to encourage people who want to be the first to own something.

Growth

If a new product is successfully introduced, it eventually attracts more customers, and sales begin to grow rapidly. Competitors see that the new product offers opportunities for sales and profits, so they enter the market with their own brands of the product as soon as they can. With this growing market and increasing competition, the marketing mix must change.

Competitors need to offer something different from the first brand in order to attract customers. They will add features and options to make their brand better than the first one. They may also provide customer services that customers want. Brand name will be very important as each business tries to show consumers that its choice is best.

Because more consumers are now buying the product, it must be distributed more widely. To be as efficient as possible, manufacturers will often use other businesses to distribute and sell their products. Since customers now have choices, each business tries to be sure its brand is available where and when the customer wants it. They concentrate on improving their order processing and handling, transportation, and customer service activities.

Customers see a range of prices during the growth stage. They have more choices of brands, features, options, and services. Brands with a quality image charge higher prices. Those just entering the market or presenting an economical image have lower prices. Businesses emphasize the value customers receive from their brand.

Promotion in the growth stage becomes more competitive. It is focused on attracting customers who have not yet tried the product, as well as demonstrating the advantages of specific brands. More money is spent on promotion. Unique messages are directed at specific segments of the market. The messages aim to inform prospective customers, persuade those who are making decisions, and remind those who have already purchased about the effectiveness of their decision.

Maturity

During the maturity stage of the life cycle, sales peak and profits begin to decline. Consumers are aware of the product and either buy it or not based on their needs. Many businesses now offer their own brand of the product. Therefore, the level of competition is more intense as businesses compete for sales.

The products of competing companies have become very similar in the maturity stage. The features and options that were successful have been adopted by all of the companies while those that were not successful have been eliminated.

Since customers view the products in this stage as very similar, they pay much more attention to price. Prices will be very competitive, and businesses will regularly offer discounts or sale prices to encourage customers to purchase their brands.

Companies will increase the availability of products to make sure customers can easily obtain them. The products will be sold through many locations.

Promotion is very important in the maturity stage. Companies continually remind customers of their brand name and try to persuade them that their company's brand is the best. Because of the large number of customers in the market, mass media and advertising are emphasized. A great deal of money is spent on promotion to try to persuade customers. Because sales have peaked and yet costs continue to

increase, profits in the market start to go down. A few companies may still be profitable, but many struggle, and some will be unable to survive.

Decline

A market declines when consumers decide that a product is no longer satisfying or when they discover new and better products. Sales begin to drop rapidly, and there is little or no profit available to companies with products still in the market. When a market declines, businesses try to get out as quickly as possible unless they have a group of loyal customers.

For products in the decline stage of the life cycle, there is little opportunity for product improvement. Because sales and profits are declining, companies are not willing to invest in product changes. Some companies may try to identify other uses

©GETTY IMAGES/PHOTODISC

During which stage(s) of the product life cycle are you likely to find products on sale regularly?

of the product to broaden the market and retain customers.

Distribution will be cut back to only the profitable locations. Companies may save money in distribution by keeping inventory levels low and cutting back on customer service.

Price is a difficult mix element to manage in this stage of the life cycle. Since profits are declining, businesses want to keep prices high. Only the most loyal customers will pay that high price, however. In most cases, prices have to be reduced to continue to sell the product, and even that may not be enough to keep customers.

Since promotion is expensive, companies reduce the amount of promotion during this stage. They choose less expensive media and promote much less frequently. Since there are fewer customers interested in this product, companies can use more direct methods of communication to keep their loyal customers as long as possible.

Checkpoint ▶▶▶

What are the four stages of a product life cycle?

9-2 Assessment

Key Concepts

Determine the best answer.

1. True or False: When customers see few differences among competing products, they will usually look for the most well-known brand.

2. Choices companies give customers of the features to be included on the products they purchase are known as _____.

3. A unique, memorable quality of a brand is its
   a. brand name
   b. image
   c. guarantee
   d. warranty

4. The stage of the product life cycle where both sales and profits increase rapidly as new customers and competitors enter the market is
   a. introduction
   b. growth
   c. maturity
   d. decline

5. When consumers decide that a product is no longer satisfying or when they discover new and better products, the marketing is in the _____ stage of the product life cycle.

Make Academic Connections

6. **Visual Art** Cut and paste or draw an illustration of a product on poster paper. Identify each of the components of the product discussed in the lesson by placing a label and drawing a line to that part of the product. Label those components that are not visible on the product and write a brief explanation of each.

7. **Economics** Create a 4 × 3 table (four rows × 3 columns) using computer software. Identify a product that represents each of the four stages of the product life cycle and write the name of the product in the first column. Use the second column to describe the type of competition facing businesses selling that product. In the third column, describe the most important marketing mix element(s) being used by businesses to compete with each other.

Connect to DECA
An Association of Marketing Students

8. Your team is responsible for proposing a marketing mix for the company that is selling graduation items to the seniors in your school. Prepare a one-page brochure that identifies the target market and describes each of the marketing mix elements your team recommends. Use the brochure to make a team presentation to your teacher (judge).

Analyzing Consumer Purchase Classifications

GOALS

- Describe the four consumer purchase classifications.
- Explain how the purchase classifications affect marketing planning.

KEY TERMS

staple goods, *p. 253*

impulse goods, *p. 253*

emergency goods, *p. 254*

attribute-based goods, *p. 254*

price-based goods, *p. 255*

specialty goods, *p. 255*

unsought goods, *p. 255*

marketing matters

By observing and analyzing the way consumers shop, marketers have identified four basic groups into which products and services fall based on consumers' perception of their need for them. These consumer purchase classifications—convenience goods, shopping goods, specialty goods, and unsought goods—can be used as keys to developing effective marketing mixes. Each purchase classification requires a different mix in order to effectively respond to consumers' needs and wants.

Name four things that you bought in the past month and consider the process that you went through in making each purchase. What factors influenced your decision? Did you shop around for alternatives? How long did you take to make the decision? Do you always buy the same brand, or do you buy whatever brand is readily available when the need arises? Compare your purchase decision with those of other students.

How Consumers Shop

Consumer purchase classifications describe the ways consumers shop for products based on their needs and perception of products. The classifications are shown in Figure 9-3.

You do not purchase all products in the same way. For some purchases you are very careful, spending a great deal of time and comparing several brands before deciding on the one to buy. For others, you know what you want and will buy it as quickly and conveniently as possible. Finally, there are some products you would not consider buying. Through careful study of the ways consumers purchase products, marketers have developed the consumer purchase classification system to help plan marketing strategies. The categories are based on two important factors:

1. The importance of the purchase to the consumer.
2. The willingness of the consumer to shop and compare products before making the purchase.

Convenience Goods

Consumers want to make many of their purchases as conveniently as possible. The reason for that purchase decision determines whether the product or service is a staple, impulse, or emergency good. All three are convenience goods but for different reasons.

CONVENIENCE GOODS

Staple   Impulse   Emergency

SPECIALTY GOODS

SHOPPING GOODS

Attribute-based   Price-based

UNSOUGHT GOODS

Consumer Purchase Classification System

FIGURE 9-3
Marketers develop better marketing mixes by understanding how consumers shop for a product.

Staple Goods Products that are regular, routine purchases are **staple goods**. You need to buy them frequently, are aware of the needs they satisfy, and probably have a preference of brands. These are products you routinely pick up when you go to a store. Staple goods include bread, milk, toothpaste, snack foods, and many other regularly purchased products.

Since you know you will need them, you make regular purchases. You will typically purchase them at a convenient location or when you make a routine shopping trip. It is not likely you will shop around in order to buy a staple good. If the store you are in does not have your favorite brand, you may buy another brand, or you may wait to buy it until the next time you go shopping.

Impulse Goods How many times have you walked into a store to buy one or two items and left with several more purchases than you planned? Items purchased on the spur of the moment without advance planning are **impulse goods**. Some examples are candy, magazines, low-cost jewelry,

unique items of clothing, and inexpensive new products. Impulse goods are often the items you see displayed near checkout counters in retail stores.

Consumers do not actively shop for impulse goods. They purchase them when they see the product displayed or advertised. At that point they identify an important need that they believe can be satisfied by the product. Because of the strong need and a belief that there is no real value to be gained in comparing other products or brands, the consumer makes the purchase immediately.

Emergency Goods You may have a favorite brand of gasoline or soft drink. When given a choice, you select those brands and may even go out of your way to find them. But when the fuel gauge on your car is on empty, you will probably pull into the most convenient gasoline station and buy that brand of gas. If you are very thirsty, you may be willing to buy another brand of soft drink or even a different beverage if your favorite drink is not available. Products or services that are

Judgment Call

Market Intelligence

Kelvin Gardner is a sales representative for Agri-Gro, an agricultural chemical producer. He sells to farm supply businesses. For four years, Kelvin has been number one in company sales. However, this year, because the economy is slowing, customers are delaying purchases, and Kelvin has fallen to 10th place in sales.

One company in Kelvin's territory, Farmmore, has never purchased chemicals from Agri-Gro. It has businesses in three of the four states where Kelvin works and purchases 8 percent of all chemicals sold in those states. Kelvin thinks that if he can gain Farmmore's business, he'll be back on top.

Kelvin is meeting with Farmmore's vice-president when the VP is called away.

While he waits, Kelvin notices Farmmore's marketing plan on the desk. If Kelvin knew more about its plans, he could show how Agri-Gro's products would help Farmmore be more effective. But he realizes that the marketing plan is a confidential document.

Think Critically

1. Should Kelvin look at the plan, or should he respect its confidentiality?

2. What would be the likely result if he picked up the marketing plan and the VP returned and caught him looking through it?

3. What tactic might Kelvin use to try to gain some insights into the company's plans without violating its confidentiality?

---

purchased as a result of an urgent need are **emergency goods**. Common examples of emergency goods are automobile towing services, umbrellas, ambulance services, and plumbing repair services.

As with impulse goods, consumers do not actively shop for emergency goods. They decide to purchase only because the situation creates an urgent, important need. Because of the emergency, the consumer is unable or unwilling to shop and compare products before purchasing.

Shopping Goods

Most of the major purchases made by consumers are shopping goods. These products and services are typically more expensive than convenience goods. Consumers believe that the need is important, the amount of money to be spent on the purchase is significant, and real differences exist among the choices of products and brands. Therefore, they are willing to spend time shopping and comparing alternatives before making a final purchase

decision. Examples of shopping goods include clothing, cars, houses and apartments, stereo equipment, major appliances, colleges, dentists, and vacation locations.

Attribute-Based Goods For most shopping goods, consumers see a number of different choices. Each brand may have a different set of features or services. Prices may vary or some brands may be purchased on sale or using credit. When a variety of differences exist and the consumer considers a number of factors to determine the best value, the product is an **attribute-based good**.

Price-Based Goods Some people evaluate major purchases and decide that several products or brands are basically alike. They will each provide the same level of satisfaction. Yet the consumer believes the price is likely to be quite different among the choices. Because the need is important and the cost is high, it is worth the time needed to shop for the best possible price. Products that consumers believe are similar but have significant price differences are **price-based goods**.

Specialty Goods

There are some products and services consumers purchase that are so satisfying that the consumer will not consider buying anything else as a substitute. Products that have this strong brand loyalty are known as **specialty goods**. People often think of very well-known and expensive products as specialty goods. Automobiles such as Rolls Royce, Porsche, or Lamborghini fit this description. Lear jets and Rolex watches also are specialty goods.

Inexpensive and regularly purchased products are also treated as specialty goods by some customers. Do you have a favorite brand of blue jeans? Do you shop for DVDs and CDs at the same store every time? Do you and your friends usually go to the same restaurant or other business? If you do and you would not typically consider another choice, then they would be specialty products and businesses. Even such things as chewing gum and toothpaste can be specialty goods if the customer will not buy a different brand.

The two factors that determine if a product is a specialty good are its importance in satisfying an individual's need and the willingness of the customer to delay a purchase until the specific product or brand is located. In the case of specialty goods, consumers believe the brand is the only thing that will provide satisfaction. That belief is usually based on very positive past experiences with the brand and less positive experiences with others. Because of the strong belief in the brand, customers will not compare brands when shopping. They will not make a purchase until they can find their

©ROLEX WATCH USA, INC.

Consumers seek out brands of certain products, such as Rolex, and won't consider purchasing a different brand.

choice. If that means waiting or traveling to another store, the customer is willing to do so. This type of customer loyalty is very valuable to businesses.

Unsought Goods

While consumers go to great lengths to find specialty goods, **unsought goods**

Working in **Teams**

As a team, identify a product for each of the consumer purchase classifications. Discuss why the products fit the classification and whether they might be considered as another classification by some consumers.

are those products that consumers do not want to buy. If you were choosing things to purchase in the next year, would the choices include life insurance or legal services to prepare a will? Those are typically not considered important needs for young people, so they would currently be unsought goods in that market. Nevertheless, when you get older and have a career and a family, either or both of those items may become much more important and could become shopping goods or even specialty goods.

When a product or a specific brand of a product is first introduced into the market, consumers are not aware it exists, so it is unsought. As soon as they become aware of the product, they decide if it is something that might meet a need. If a product or service does not fill a customer need, it remains unsought and unsold. Even if the business makes it easy to buy through telephone or Internet sales or a salesperson visiting the person at home, consumers will not purchase an unsought product.

Checkpoint ▶▶▶

What are the four consumer purchase classifications?

Using Purchase Classifications in Marketing

Just as life cycle stages provide important information about competition, consumer purchase classifications help marketers better understand consumer behavior. That understanding is important in planning the best marketing mix. Each purchase classification requires a different mix in order to effectively respond to consumer needs.

Convenience Goods

Consumers want to purchase convenience goods as easily as possible. They do not see important differences among products and brands that make it worth their time to shop and compare. Therefore, businesses need to emphasize product location (convenience) in the marketing mix. The product mix element will focus on brand, packaging, and image.

Price is important for staple goods. Prices cannot be set higher than similar products in the same location, or the consumer will switch brands. For impulse goods, price is less important, and for emergency goods, price is only a minor consideration. Promotion is used to remind people of brand and image for staple goods, the need to be satisfied for impulse goods, and location and availability for emergency goods.

Shopping Goods

Because consumers are willing to shop and compare, the marketing mix for shopping goods is different from convenience goods. Products and services no longer have to

What part of the marketing mix is most important for shopping goods, such as furniture?

be available in the most convenient locations. Promotion emphasizes the qualities of the product or service that consumers believe are most important. Promotion often helps consumers compare products or brands.

Consumers are interested in the best combination of features, options, services, and uses. For attribute-based shopping goods, the product mix element is very important. For price-based shopping goods, price is the most important. While customers want a quality product, they believe that several products are very similar. They search for the best possible price. Businesses must demonstrate that they have the lowest price or the best possible financial terms. They also need to emphasize price in promotional activities.

What are some of the best ways for an owner of a local delicatessen to market his products?

Specialty Goods

Specialty goods are in some ways the easiest to market. In other ways, they are somewhat difficult. The emphasis in the marketing mix will depend on why consumers believe the product or service is a specialty good. Typically, that status results from a unique or quality product. In that case, the business wants to emphasize the product in marketing planning to insure that the quality or uniqueness is maintained. Promotion reminds consumers of the reasons they prefer the product.

It is possible that consumers prefer a product or service because of its location. Some people select a bank, a physician, or even a college because it is close to home or work. Therefore, marketing activities for that product would emphasize location more than product features. There are some instances where price is the reason for specialty status. Consumers may buy only one brand because they believe it has the best price. Again, marketing would maintain that price so that consumers remain satisfied. Promotion that is able to create excitement, a unique image, or a belief that one product is far superior to others may result in the product being treated as a specialty good for at least a short time.

Unsought Goods

The marketing mix developed for unsought goods is particularly important. If a product is not well marketed, there will be no demand, and the product will fail. If a product is new, the marketing mix will emphasize promotion and distribution. Consumers must be aware of the product, how it satisfies needs, and where they can purchase it. If a business is successful with those two mix elements, the product will quickly become a convenience, shopping, or specialty good.

If customers are aware of the product or service and it remains unsought, the mix must be very carefully developed. The product is most important. The business must evaluate the product to determine why consumers do not want it. The product must be redesigned to make it more appealing to consumers and to relate to their important needs. Promotion can then be used to show consumers how the product will meet their needs.

Businesses must market unsought goods very carefully. Consumers may become quite upset if they believe a business is trying to sell them something they do not need. If consumers develop a negative attitude toward a product or a business, it will be difficult to sell them products in the future. Businesses that successfully sell unsought goods use a target market strategy. They identify the specific segments of the market that have needs related to the product or service. They then develop very personalized marketing mixes to work with those target markets at times and locations where there is a good chance for success. Some businesses are so effective with their marketing that an unsought good becomes a specialty good for customers.

For example, people who had never purchased life insurance may be impressed by the personal attention and knowledge of one insurance agent. They buy not only one insurance policy but also additional products from the same agent without considering other companies.

Checkpoint ▶▶

The product location generally is most important for which consumer purchase classification?

9-3 Assessment

Key Concepts

Determine the best answer.

1. Regular, routine purchases are classified as
   a. staple goods
   b. impulse goods
   c. emergency goods
   d. shopping goods

2. Consumers who see few differences among several products but will still take the time to shop and compare are looking for
   a. impulse goods
   b. emergency goods
   c. attribute-based goods
   d. price-based goods

3. True or False: If a product is an unsought good, consumers are not aware that it exists.

4. Consumers want to purchase _____ goods as easily as possible.

5. Which of the following is the *least* appropriate marketing strategy for an attribute-based shopping good?
   a. creating a promotion to emphasize the important qualities that satisfy customer needs
   b. charging a higher price than competitors because more features are offered
   c. distributing the product in the most convenient locations
   d. making the product the most important marketing mix element

Make Academic Connections

6. **Writing** Tour a retail store or supermarket and identify one product that fits each of the four major categories of the consumer purchase classifications. Write a one-paragraph report on each product describing how it is marketed in the store.

7. **Ethics** Promotion can be a powerful marketing tool to persuade people to purchase something they otherwise might not buy. However, when misused, it might result in dissatisfied customers and a poor image for the company. Write five guidelines for marketers describing the ethical use of promotion when marketing impulse goods and unsought goods.

Connect to ◀ DECA
An Association of Marketing Students

8. You are introducing a new unsought good—an insurance policy that provides protection for damages suffered from personal identity theft that occurs when a person is using the Internet. It will cost $5 a month added to the customer's Internet bill and will only be promoted via the Internet. Use presentation software to prepare three slides that outline the marketing mix you propose for the unsought good. Present your slides to your teacher (judge).

Marketing Planning

GOALS

- Understand the benefits of marketing planning.
- Describe the steps in developing a marketing plan.

KEY TERMS

marketing plan, *p. 260*

marketing matters

Developing a marketing plan is one of the most important steps businesses take to market their products and services. The marketing plan serves as a guide for coordinating marketing activities. Today, almost all successful businesses have a written marketing plan. Developing an effective marketing plan requires the commitment of time and attention by top marketing managers and the gathering of information about the company, competition, changes in the business environment, and current and prospective customers.

Write a description of the planning process you went through to prepare for a recent exam or important assignment. How could you have applied better organization and planning to improve the results?

The Benefits of Planning

When a group of friends decides to take a one-week travel vacation, they can simply start driving and choose what to see as they go along. They might use their time effectively and have a good vacation, or they might not. A better method may be for the group to agree on the destination, travel time, and activities. Then they can gather information about the planned destinations and activities. Using that information, they can develop a schedule to make the best use of their time and money.

A business person might try to get by without any planning before deciding what products to sell, how to promote them, what prices to charge, or how to respond to competition. In this case, each decision will be made when it seems important or when a problem occurs. The result might be that some decisions are made too late, without enough information, or without considering the impact on other parts of the business. To improve decision making,

©GETTY IMAGES/PHOTODISC

Why is planning an important part of almost any activity?

Virtual Marketing

E-commerce Accommodation

The Internet has improved the capability of businesses to market to unique customer groups. However, one market segment has been largely ignored—the estimated 500 million people worldwide with disabilities.

The Web may not be accessible to the visually impaired. Colorblindness may render web text unreadable on various background page colors. People without use of arms or hands cannot manipulate keyboards or use touch-screen technology. If companies do not recognize physical limitations, those consumers will not have access to company web sites.

Advances in hardware and software can make the Internet accessible to all. Businesses and government agencies are working together to increase Web accessibility for the disabled. Laws have been passed to support these actions. E-commerce businesses that respond to the accessibility needs of disabled persons will find new customers for many of their products and services.

Think Critically

1. Why should an e-commerce business be concerned about special technology needed to serve disabled consumers?

2. Should a business treat people with disabilities as a unique market or as a part of a larger market of consumers?

---

the business person gathers information about customers and competition, decides on the profit and sales goals the business can achieve, and then carefully develops a specific plan to guide the purchase, distribution, pricing, and promotion of products and services.

With careful planning, the group taking a trip and the business person managing the sale of products have a much better idea of what they want to accomplish, the best ways to reach their objectives, and the likelihood that they will be able to accomplish what they planned.

What Is a Marketing Plan?

Marketing in most businesses involves a large number of very complex activities. To be successful, the activities need to be coordinated with each other and with the activities occurring in other parts of the business. A great many decisions must be made, and often a large amount of money and other resources must be committed by

the business from the time of production until the sale of the product. Coordination of decisions and resources will be needed in order for the business to make a profit once the products have been sold. Many people are involved in carrying out the marketing activities. To make the best use of the time and efforts of those people, their activities should be coordinated as well.

To aid in decision making and the coordination of the many people, activities, and resources involved in successful marketing, businesses develop a marketing plan. A **marketing plan** is a clear written description of the marketing strategies of a business and the way the business will operate to accomplish each strategy.

From Strategy to Plan

In a marketing strategy, the business identifies the target market to be served and develops a marketing mix. The marketing plan is based on a marketing strategy.

Marketing strategies must be developed very carefully. They need to be based on a complete study of a market and the possible ways the business can serve the market. If marketers are not careful in developing the strategy, they will be no better off than the companies with a production orientation. They will likely make decisions based on their own opinions rather than the target market's needs.

A marketing plan is an organized, objective method of planning each part of a marketing strategy and determining how the business should operate to make sure the strategy is successful. The process of developing a marketing plan encourages the marketer to gather and analyze information, consider alternatives, determine what competitors are likely to do, and study possible responses of customers.

Based on that study, procedures can be planned to achieve the marketing strategy. It is possible to determine in advance whether the strategy can be implemented as planned. If not, the strategy can be modified to avoid mistakes. The marketing

©GETTY IMAGES/PHOTODISC

Why are so many business people involved in developing the marketing plan?

strategy describes what the business wants to do, and the marketing plan details how the strategy will be implemented and evaluated.

Checkpoint ▶▶▶

What are the benefits of developing a written marketing plan?

Preparing for Marketing Planning

Marketing planning is not easy. It requires time, information, and people who understand marketing planning procedures. Because of these requirements, some business people believe they do not need or cannot afford to develop marketing plans. They feel their past experience has prepared them to make marketing decisions. That attitude gives an advantage to the business people who carefully prepare marketing plans. They will know when changes are occurring in the market, how customers are likely to respond to new marketing strategies, and what competitors are likely to do. They will know in advance what needs to be done to accomplish their objectives rather than having to wait for problems to occur.

Fast **FACTS**

According to a survey by Accenture, middle managers spend more than a quarter of their time searching for information necessary to perform their jobs. When they find it, it is often not useful or is even wrong. More than 50 percent of managers believe that their companies do a poor job of determining the information each manager needs.

Planning to Plan

Marketing plans are developed for a specific time period, often six months to one year. Companies may have an overall marketing plan, but they usually develop a specific plan for each major product. The preparation of the plan is usually coordinated by the top marketing manager with input and assistance from many other people. Usually, large companies have a number of researchers, analysts, and support staff working continuously on preparing and updating marketing plans.

Plans Require Information

The work needed to develop a marketing plan begins long before the plan is actually written. A great deal of information is necessary, so the people responsible for marketing planning must make sure needed information is collected, analyzed, and ready for use in the planning process.

Each business uses somewhat different information for its marketing plan. The following types of information are usually a part of marketing planning.

Performance of the Company In
order to plan for the future, marketers must know what has happened in the past and what is expected to happen in the future. Information on sales and profits, effective and ineffective marketing activities, and the company's strengths and weaknesses needs to be collected and reviewed. Marketers need to know what new products are being developed, if others are being eliminated, and if resources are likely to change in the future.

Performance of Competitors

Customers usually have several brands of products or services from which to choose. In order to develop marketing strategies that will be successful, marketers must evaluate the products and marketing efforts of those competing businesses. They must also understand each company's strengths and weaknesses and what competitors are likely to do in the future.

Changes Outside the Company

Many things occur that affect the potential success of a product but are outside of the immediate control of the business or its competitors. The economy can decline or improve. Laws can be passed by state and local governments that affect business activities. Additional taxes or licenses can increase costs. Newly developed technology can result in improved products or innovative production and marketing procedures. Businesses that regularly collect information to determine if changes are likely to occur are in a better position to respond to changes than businesses that do not pay attention to change.

Information about Current and Prospective Customers Understanding customers makes it possible for businesses to develop marketing plans to satisfy their needs. Businesses must continually gather and study information about their customers, including who their customers are and what their needs are. How do customers perceive the business and its competitors? Would they like to see changes and improvements in products and services? It is also important for businesses to continue to identify prospective customers and new target markets to help the business grow.

Why is it important for a business to gather information from its customers?

Gathering Needed Information

Companies that successfully prepare and use marketing plans have developed procedures to gather and analyze information. Business moves rapidly, and companies cannot wait until the time they are ready to develop a marketing plan to gather the needed information.

Much of the information used in developing marketing plans is already available in the company's marketing information system (MkIS). Records of production, operations, and sales are maintained. Detailed information on specific customers and their purchasing history is available. In addition, most businesses regularly gather and study information about competitors, business trends, and the economy. In addition to the information in the MkIS, the business should be aware of other groups and organizations that provide planning information, such as government agencies, trade associations, and private research firms. Finally businesses must be prepared to complete needed marketing research when adequate information is not available.

Checkpoint ▶▶

What four types of information are usually needed for effective marketing planning?

9-4 Assessment

Key Concepts

Determine the best answer.

1. True or False: As long as a company effectively communicates marketing plans to everyone involved, the plan does not have to be in writing.

2. True or False: A company's marketing plan is based on its marketing strategy.

3. True or False: A marketing plan is developed to last for the entire life cycle of a product.

4. Which of the following types of information is usually a part of marketing planning?
   a. performance of the company
   b. performance of competitors
   c. information outside the control of the company
   d. all of the above

5. The majority of information a company needs to develop a marketing plan should be obtained from
   a. specific marketing research studies
   b. information available from government agencies and universities
   c. information purchased from private research companies
   d. information maintained in the company's MkIS

Make Academic Connections

6. **Research** You are a member of the marketing planning team for a large electronics retailer. Use the Internet to locate current information that you believe should be considered by planners on performance of competitors, consumers of electronic products, and changes occurring outside the company. Write a memo to your marketing manager summarizing the information you located.

7. **Communication** Identify a local business person to interview either in person, by telephone, or by e-mail. Ask the person about the importance of marketing planning and the procedures he or she follows to prepare a marketing plan. Prepare a written report as an article for a newspaper.

Connect to DECA
An Association of Marketing Students

8. As the top marketing executive, you are meeting with all of the managers with responsibilities for marketing activities in your company. Prepare a three-minute persuasive speech that describes the value of a marketing plan and the need for managers to follow the plan and coordinate their efforts with each other. Make sure the speech incorporates the importance of customer satisfaction and company profitability. Present your speech to your teacher (judge).

Developing a Marketing Plan

GOALS

- Identify the five types of market analysis used in developing a marketing plan.
- Explain how a marketing strategy is incorporated within a marketing plan.
- Explain the need for activity schedules and evaluation procedures in the marketing plan.

KEY TERMS

market analysis, *p. 264*

mission, *p. 265*

positioning statement, *p. 268*

marketing matters

Marketing plans take many forms and can contain different types of information. They are developed to assist a specific business, so they are written in a way that is most useful for the people in that business.

Work with a group. If you were asked to develop a marketing plan, what steps would you need to take to complete your work? What type of information would you include in the plan? How would you determine if the marketing plan was effective or not? Share your ideas with others in a class discussion.

Analyzing the Market

A marketing plan is a complex and detailed document that provides guidance for the implementation of a marketing strategy. It needs to be carefully prepared, clearly written, and effectively communicated to everyone who has a role in implementing the marketing strategy. Marketing plans are developed in three stages—market analysis, marketing strategy, and action plans. The results of each stage are described in the written plan. Figure 9-4 provides a sample outline of a marketing plan. Each section of the marketing plan is discussed in this lesson. More detailed descriptions of each section of the marketing plan as well as questions that should be answered to develop each section can be found in the *Marketing Planning Guide* on the textbook web site at school.cengage.com/marketing/marketing.

Before developing a marketing strategy, a careful analysis of the market should be completed. That analysis will provide information to help develop a marketing strategy that is competitive, that meets customer needs, and that can be effectively implemented. A **market analysis** identifies a business's strengths and weaknesses and the opportunities and threats it faces. Because of those four factors, a marketing analysis is often referred to as a SWOT (strengths, weaknesses, opportunities, and threats) analysis.

An effective marketing strategy builds on what a company does well, its strengths. It recognizes and attempts to improve on any weaknesses that can interfere with the strategy. A market analysis uncovers opportunities for new customers and new products. It identifies possible threats to the company posed by competition or changes occurring in the economy, laws, and technology. A summary of the market analysis is usually the first section of a marketing plan to provide the objective information on which the marketing strategy is based.

Company Mission

The **mission** or purpose of the company identifies the nature of the business or the reasons the business exists. It is most often developed to describe broad categories of products or services the business provides (transportation, health care, legal services) or the types of customers the company wants to serve (business travelers, resorts in the Sun Belt, single parents with children under 18). By identifying the mission or purpose, marketing planners concentrate their efforts in areas where the company is known and works best. An example of a mission statement for an auto dealership is "to offer quality automobiles at fair prices, to provide fast and effective service, and to treat all customers with courtesy and respect."

Current Markets and Strategies

After identifying the mission, the planners briefly review the current marketing efforts of the company. The review identifies the markets in which the company is operating and the marketing strategies currently being used and provides a summary of current results and effectiveness. This reminds the planners and readers about activities underway in the business.

Determining the activities that are working well and those that are not helps planners decide whether to continue with the same strategies or to plan changes. A company might discover that

Marketing Plan Outline

I. **Market Analysis**
  A. Purpose and Mission of the Business
  B. Description of Current Markets and Strategies
  C. Primary Competitors and Their Strengths/Weaknesses
  D. External Environment Analysis
    1. Economy
    2. Laws and Regulations
    3. Costs
    4. Competition
    5. Technology
    6. Social Factors
  E. Internal Analysis
    1. Strengths
    2. Weaknesses
    3. Anticipated Changes

II. **Marketing Strategy**
  A. Marketing Goals/Expected Outcomes
  B. Target Market Description
    1. Identifying Characteristics
    2. Unique Needs, Attitudes, Behaviors
  C. Marketing Mix Description
    1. Product/Service
    2. Distribution
    3. Pricing
    4. Promotion
  D. Positioning Statement

III. **Action Plans**
  A. Activity Schedule
    1. Responsibilities
    2. Schedule
    3. Budget
  B. Evaluation Procedures
    1. Evidence of Success
    2. Method of Collecting Evidence

its advertising costs are increasing at a rate much faster than its sales. In that case, it needs to determine if the costs can be controlled or if the increased advertising might pay off in the long term with faster sales growth. Some products or markets might be outperforming others. Recognizing why those strategies are working well while others are not helps determine where to direct resources in the future.

Seeing Is Believing

Marketers have long used eye-tracking research to gauge the effectiveness of advertisements and displays. They refine ads based on what research subjects tend to look at, the sequence in which they look at various elements of an ad, and how long various images hold their attention.

Previously, researchers used expensive gaze-tracking equipment that required subjects to hold their heads steady by biting down on a bar so that movements could be captured accurately. Unfortunately for marketers, that created a very unnatural testing environment that could not help but affect results.

With the development of wearable eye-tracking devices, researchers now have the ability to see how subjects view things in a much more natural setting. They still know their actions are being watched, but aside from wearing a headset that records what they are looking at, subjects can be observed in an otherwise undisturbed setting. The result is research that more closely reflects real-life reactions to ads and displays.

Think Critically

1. Why are natural settings usually better for market research than artificial settings?

2. How can product development be improved by using eye-tracking technology?

Primary Competitors

An analysis of the competitors in the same product categories and serving similar customer groups is an important part of the marketing plan. In addition to identifying each competitor, an objective evaluation of the important strengths and weaknesses of each competitor is completed. This evaluation helps decide how to compete with each of those businesses. For example, if a competitor is known for keeping prices very low, it may be difficult for another company to develop a strategy that emphasizes price. On the other hand, if a competitor is having difficulty providing repair services for the products it sells, another company may be able to attract new customers by emphasizing its customer service department.

External Environment

The market analysis section identifies any factors outside of the company, called the *external environment*, that may affect its performance. Those factors include the economy, competition, laws affecting the business, technology, changes in costs, and the expectations and needs of society. An example of the effect of technology on businesses was the introduction and acceptance of transmitting legal documents with electronic signatures. That change required the development of new technology to create and transmit secure and identifiable electronic signatures for letters, orders, contracts, and other legal documents. It also required new laws that recognized the new electronically signed documents as legal business transactions. With those changes, many official business communications could be prepared and transferred almost instantly rather than waiting for delivery through the mail.

Internal Analysis

The final part of the market analysis should be a thorough and objective review of the current operating and financial performance of the company. This process is known as an *internal analysis*. The company's strengths and weaknesses are determined by reviewing and comparing current and past performance with company goals. Analyzing products and production methods, marketing activities, personnel, and financial performance can point out areas where the company is meeting expectations and where it is not. The internal analysis can be compared with competitive data to determine where the company has advantages and disadvantages. If a company has a unique production process that competitors have been unable to duplicate, it should be emphasized. If customers believe the company has a better customer service record, it will be important to use it in the next marketing plan. On the other hand, if the company is having difficulty competing on the basis of price, strategies should be developed to avoid direct price competition. If distribution costs are consistently higher than planned or if inventory levels cannot be maintained to achieve needed sales, those operations can be reviewed and changed.

Checkpoint ▶▶

What are the five types of market analysis used in developing a marketing plan?

Developing the Marketing Strategy

In terms of the company's success, the most important part of the marketing plan is the development of a marketing strategy. The *marketing strategy* is the description of the way marketing will be used to accomplish the company's objectives. The marketing strategy begins with the company goals on which the strategy is based. The goals are followed by a full description of the marketing strategy, including the target market, the marketing mix, and a specific positioning statement.

©GETTY IMAGES/PHOTODISC

How can setting a specific sales goal help a business determine the effectiveness of its marketing strategy?

Determining Goals and Outcomes

The marketing strategy is based on a specific statement of the goals the company plans to achieve or the expected outcomes of the marketing efforts. In that way, the company is able to determine whether the marketing strategy is effective. Marketing goals include such things as increasing sales or profits for certain products, increasing the market share for a product in a particular geographic area or target market, increasing the effectiveness of particular parts of the marketing mix such as distribution or customer service, or other specific results.

Defining a Target Market

The marketing strategy will clearly identify the target market to be served. The target market will be defined completely so it can be located, so people in the business understand the market's characteristics and its needs and wants, and so it is clear that the marketing mix is appropriate for that target market.

While each target market is unique, it is possible for an organization to serve several target markets at the same time. When more than one market is identified, marketing planners must remember that each market requires a specific marketing mix. A specific product or target market may have its own marketing plan or a specific section of the overall company marketing plan devoted to it.

Specifying the Marketing Mix

A complete description of each mix element is included in the marketing plan. Product, distribution (place), price, and promotion are described specifically and completely so that everyone involved in implementing the mix understands what the company plans to do. A description of the marketing mix is presented in the marketing strategy section of the marketing plan, and the activities and budgets needed to implement each element of the mix are developed in later sections.

Developing a Positioning Statement

One of the most interesting parts of the marketing strategy is the positioning statement. A **positioning statement** is a specific description of the unique qualities of the marketing mix that make it different from the competition and satisfying to the target market. For example, a discount store positions itself as the one-stop place

to shop for all home products needed by a family on a budget. A home improvement service specializes in working with realtors and homeowners who are planning to sell their homes. Its positioning statement describes how it can help secure a higher selling price for the home as a result of cleaning, repair work, and an improved visual presentation of the interior and exterior of the home.

Checkpoint ▶▶

What are the four elements needed in a marketing plan to describe the marketing strategy?

Planning for Action

The marketing strategy will not be successful just because it is described in a marketing plan. The activities of many people must be planned, and procedures must be set up to evaluate the activities. The final section of the marketing plan identifies actions needed to accomplish and evaluate the marketing strategy.

Activity Schedule

Completing each part of the marketing strategy requires a series of activities. The needed activities must be determined along with a description of how and when the activities will be completed. Responsibility for completing each activity must be assigned.

Many people both inside and outside the company are involved in marketing. Their activities must be coordinated in order to be successful. For example, if a manufacturer is introducing a new laptop computer, the production schedule must be coordinated with distribution to retailers, the development of printed product information for salespeople, and the advertising schedule. If the computer is advertised to consumers before the retailer has the product or before salespeople are prepared to provide product information, both the consumer and retailer will be unhappy with the manufacturer.

In addition to assigning responsibilities and developing schedules, planners must determine budgets for the various marketing activities. Without a budget, overspending can easily occur.

Evaluation Procedures

Evaluation procedures must be developed to determine if the action plan is effective. The evaluation procedures measure whether the marketing activities were completed correctly and on time. They will also determine if the marketing objectives identified earlier in the marketing plan were accomplished.

Information can be collected to determine if target markets are responding to the marketing mix and if their needs are satisfied. Each of the mix elements should be studied. Specific marketing activities should be evaluated to determine if the quality is acceptable and if they were accomplished within the established budget for the activity.

Information collected in the evaluation is used to make improvements in marketing activities while the plan is being implemented. As soon as problems are identified, actions should be taken to correct those problems. Evaluation information is also essential when developing the next marketing plan.

Checkpoint ▶▶▶

Why is an action plan needed once other parts of a marketing plan are developed?

9-5 Assessment

Xtra! Study Tools
school.cengage.com/marketing/marketing

Key Concepts

Determine the best answer.

1. A marketing strategy should be based on
   a. a careful analysis of the market
   b. the previous experience of managers
   c. the strategies of main competitors
   d. none of the above

2. A(n) _____ identifies a business's strengths and weaknesses and the opportunities and threats it faces.

3. A statement that identifies the nature of the business or the reasons the business exists is the company's
   a. positioning statement
   b. marketing strategy
   c. mission
   d. goals

4. True or False: The final section of a marketing plan includes a description of marketing activities and evaluation procedures.

5. True of False: Even if evaluation shows problems, a business should not take corrective action until the end of the time period identified in the marketing plan.

Make Academic Connections

6. **Communication** Review advertising or web sites of three well-known companies that you believe have unique images. Identify information that you believe provides an effective positioning statement for the company. Write each positioning statement on a note card. See if other students can guess the company from the statement.

7. **Math** A retailer had six-month sales of $83.6 million, with $18.2 million of that amount from the Internet. It set a goal to increase the percentage of total sales coming from the Internet by 4 percent in the next six months. The results were total sales of $87.3 million, with $23.1 million from the Internet. What was the percentage of Internet sales? What amount of Internet sales was needed to achieve the goal?

Connect to ◀ DECA
An Association of Marketing Students

8. Your marketing team is advising a new fitness center, FastFit, which offers 30-minute, high-intensity, aerobic workouts for people with busy schedules. Develop a marketing strategy for the business, including a positioning statement. Present your ideas to your teacher (judge).

Check Your Understanding

Now that you have completed the chapter, check your understanding of the lessons with these questions. Record the score that best represents your understanding of each marketing concept.

1 = not at all; 3 = somewhat; 5 = very well

If your score is 42–50, you are ready for the assessment activities that follow. If you score 33–41, you should review the lessons for the items you scored 1–3. If you score 32 or less, you will want to carefully reread the lessons and work with a study partner on the areas you do not understand.

Can you—

___ justify why a business should identify a number of market segments as a part of selecting a target market?

___ describe the four criteria of an effective target market?

___ identify several components of the product mix element in addition to the basic product?

___ discuss ways that each element of the marketing mix can be changed and improved to meet customer needs?

___ explain how competition changes in each stage of the product life cycle?

___ describe differences among convenience, shopping, specialty, and unsought goods that affect how they are marketed?

___ justify the importance of developing and following a written marketing plan?

___ list five types of information that are analyzed as a part of marketing planning?

___ identify the three major sections of a marketing plan?

___ explain the importance of activity planning and evaluation for effective marketing?

Review Marketing Terms

Match the terms listed with the definitions. Some terms may not be used.

1. A general promise or assurance of quality
2. Products in which a variety of differences exist, and the consumer considers a number of factors to determine the best value
3. A clear written description of the marketing strategies of a business and the way the business will operate to accomplish each strategy
4. The way marketing activities are planned and coordinated to achieve an organization's goals
5. Products that consumers do not want to buy
6. Items purchased on the spur of the moment without advance planning
7. Identifies the stages a product goes through from the time it enters the market until it is no longer sold
8. Products or services that are purchased as a result of an urgent need
9. A unique name, symbol, or design that identifies a product, service, or company
10. A specific description of the unique qualities of the marketing mix that make it different from the competition and satisfying to the target market

a. attribute-based goods
b. brand
c. emergency goods
d. guarantee
e. image
f. impulse goods
g. market analysis
h. marketing plan
i. marketing strategy
j. mission
k. positioning statement
l. price-based goods
m. product life cycle
n. specialty goods
o. staple goods
p. unsought goods
q. warranty

Review Marketing Concepts

The following items describe competitive situations faced by businesses. For each of the following situations, identify the stage of the product life cycle being described.

11. There is little profit in the market, and only the most loyal customers continue to buy.

_____

12. Many companies offer a service that consumers view as quite similar. Because of the intense competition, the businesses emphasize promotion and often give customers price discounts.

_____

13. As profits begin to increase in the market, several new companies decide to offer similar products for sale.

_____

14. A company invents a coating material for automobile windows that melts ice and snow at low temperatures. It learns that another company is developing a similar product, so it begins selling the product immediately to beat the other business into the market.

_____

These items describe examples of customer purchase behavior. For each of the following situations, identify the consumer purchase classification category being described.

15. Jai needs to replace his lost calculator. He goes to several stores but cannot find the TD Model 28 that he prefers. He finally locates one at the college bookstore and purchases it.

_____

16. Driving home from work, Arthur remembers that he forgot to plan something to cook for the evening meal. Since his family will be home when he arrives, he quickly turns into the deli and purchases the evening's special to take home.

_____

17. A telemarketer calls to describe a new product to a consumer. The consumer is not interested and hangs up the telephone.

_____

18. The customer carefully compares product features and price at several stores before making a decision.

_____

Marketing Research and Planning

19. People have different needs and different ways of shopping for products and services. Therefore, it is likely that the same product or service can fit into several of the product/service purchase classification categories. For the following products, describe the consumer purchase behavior that would be used for each of the categories in the classification system.
    a. movie   c. gasoline
    b. groceries   d. hotel room

20. Use the Internet to search for announcements and articles about a large public corporation's plans for a new business venture. Describe the product or service of the new venture and the marketing strategy, including target markets, the marketing mix, and the positioning statement. What types of information did the company gather about the external environment and prospective customers in planning for the venture?

21. Select one of the following products or services to use for your work on this activity: a professional music group, athletic/running shoes, or a magazine. Identify four people to interview. Determine the information you need to obtain from each person in order to develop a target market description and to classify his/her purchase behavior in the consumer purchase classification system. Conduct the interviews and complete the following activities:
    a. Develop market segment descriptions of each person.
    b. Determine whether the four people would be part of one target market or more than one.
    c. Identify the appropriate consumer purchase classification for each person interviewed and provide a brief statement describing why you selected that classification.

Marketing Management and Decision Making

22. The mature stage of the product life cycle is very difficult, especially for smaller businesses. There are many competitors appealing to a large market. They have very similar products and are increasing their distribution and promotion. Many businesses are starting to decrease their prices to encourage consumers to switch to their business. Since most businesses (and especially large businesses) are appealing to the mass market, smaller businesses may have the opportunity to be successful by using the marketing concept when planning a marketing strategy.

    You are a marketing consultant for a small hotel. The business is finding it increasingly difficult to compete with the national chains that have large advertising budgets, can offer a variety of services, and are willing to cut their prices to attract business people and weekend travelers. Prepare a four-page report for the hotel owner that briefly describes the meaning of the marketing concept and why it can help the hotel develop a marketing strategy. Describe an example marketing strategy that could be implemented to help the hotel compete with the large chains. Provide a rationale to support the strategy.

23. For 30 years, a national association of homebuilders has collected data on the sales of various styles of manufactured windows. One window style presents an interesting example of a product life cycle. It was introduced in 1984 and remained on the market until 2006. The table below summarizes its market performance during that time. Develop a table that illustrates the following information for each of the years listed:

    a. average dollar sales per manufacturer
    b. average sale price of each window
    c. average cost of each window
    d. total profit or loss for the industry

    Input the window data from the table into a spreadsheet program. Construct a graph of the life cycle for the window, illustrating total industry dollar sales and the industry's profit or loss for each year.

Year	Number of Manufacturers	Total Units Sold	Total Sales in Dollars	Total Product Cost
1984	1	800	$ 36,000	$ 38,400
1986	3	2,800	123,200	126,000
1988	5	4,500	193,500	189,000
1990	6	5,700	245,100	228,000
1992	9	10,800	464,400	410,400
1994	15	22,500	945,000	787,500
1996	15	23,000	954,500	828,000
1998	13	23,000	943,000	851,000
2000	12	22,500	877,500	855,000
2002	8	18,000	684,000	693,000
2004	4	10,500	393,750	404,250
2006	2	4,800	177,600	182,400

International Business Plan Event

The International Business Plan Event provides an opportunity to apply marketing skills in an international setting. You will prepare a written proposal for a new business venture (a new business or new product or service of an existing business) for a foreign country.

This project will be completed by one to three members. Participants will choose a product or service to introduce to a foreign country. Each individual or group must conduct thorough research to determine the trade area, economics, culture, and political climate of the chosen country. The demographics and psychographics for your selected country must be a good match for your idea. After you have determined the best international market for your product or service, you must persuade an international banker (judge) to grant the loan needed for your business idea.

This project consists of a written document and the oral presentation. The oral presentation may be a maximum of 15 minutes in length. The first 10 minutes will include an explanation of the project followed by 5 minutes for the judge's questions.

The body of your international business plan will consist of the following parts:

Executive Summary Write a one-page description of the project.
Introduction Include a brief description of proposed business, product, or service.
Analysis of the International Business Situation Provide an economic, political, and legal analysis of the trading country; provide trade area and cultural analysis.
Planned Operation of the Proposed Business/Product/Service Describe the proposed organization, proposed product/service, and proposed strategies.

Planned Financing Provide projected income and expenses.
Bibliography List all resources used.
Appendix Inclusion is optional.

Performance Indicators Evaluated

- Exchange information and ideas with others through writing and speaking. (Communication Skills)
- Participate as a productive team member. (Emotional Intelligence)
- Conduct international research to determine the feasibility of a business idea. (Information Management)
- Analyze research data to derive facts and other information needed to make international business decisions. (Information Management)
- Determine factors affecting business risk. (Economics)

Go to the DECA web site for more detailed information.

Think Critically

1. Why have more companies expanded operations to include international business?

2. Why is it important to understand the culture before conducting business with a foreign country?

3. What risks are involved in conducting international business?

4. What resources can the international entrepreneur use to be successful when conducting business in another country?

www.deca.org

Developing Successful Products

©BLEND IMAGES/JUPITER IMAGES

Newsline)))))

What Can We Learn from Labels?

Light. High-fiber. No cholesterol. Zero trans fats. What do these terms mean? Given their use in promotions, it appears as if some companies are more concerned about sales than about providing accurate information. For example, one company used the word "light" to promote a high-calorie product. When questioned, the company said that "light" referred to the product's color rather than the amount of calories. Others have promoted their product as "now cholesterol free" to influence health-conscious customers. However, the type of product was never made with ingredients that contain cholesterol, so the companies had done nothing to reduce cholesterol.

Many business people, consumer groups, and government officials are concerned about misleading or false nutritional labeling on products. The federal government has issued food-labeling rules that apply to most packaged foods sold to consumers. Nutritional information must appear on packaging for prepared foods such as breads, cereals, canned and frozen foods, snacks, desserts, and beverages. All food producers must use a standard label with specific information that allows consumers to compare products and determine the impact of the products on their diets.

The information on each label must be based on a standard serving size and a daily consumption of 2,000 calories. The label must report the number of calories in each serving and the amount of saturated fat, cholesterol, trans fat, sodium, carbohydrates, and protein in both grams and percentage of the total daily dietary requirements.

Specific meanings have also been established for nutritional words like *healthy*, *lean*, *low-fat*, *high-fiber*, and *light*. As an example, companies cannot label their products as light unless calories and fat are at least 30 to 50 percent lower than the original product.

The labeling requirements are not viewed positively by everyone. Some believe it is too costly. Others think the rules are not totally effective since they apply only to the information on product packages and not to advertising. The information is not required on fresh foods or on restaurant menus, although many restaurants are now voluntarily providing dietary and nutritional information for consumers.

Think Critically

1. Examine three "light" products and compare the number of calories and grams of fat they contain to corresponding regular products. Do they meet the labeling requirements?

2. Do you believe restaurants should be required to provide nutritional information similar to the information provided on packaged foods? Why or why not?

school.cengage.com/marketing/marketing

Prepare for Performance

This chapter develops the following Performance Indicators from the DECA Competitive Events program.

Core Performance Indicators

- Acquire a foundational knowledge of product management to understand its nature and scope
- Generate product ideas to contribute to ongoing business success
- Position products to acquire desired business image

Supporting Performance Indicators

- Generate product ideas
- Determine feasibility of product idea
- Identify the impact of product life cycles on marketing decisions
- Develop positioning concept for a new product idea

Go to **school.cengage.com/marketing/marketing** and click on Connect to DECA.

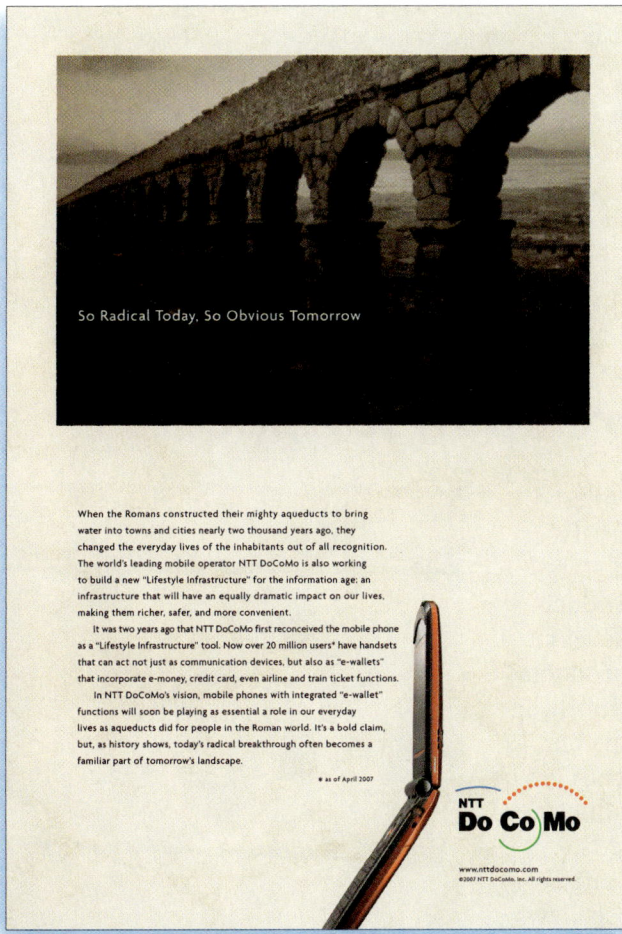

Visual Focus

Contrasting the old and the new often leaves a powerful impression in the mind of a customer. Many consumers are reluctant to try brand new products unless they are confident the product is superior to what they already use and is a good value. In this chapter, you will learn how companies plan and market their products in ways to make sure they meet consumer needs. Products can be simple or complex, new or well-known. Each requires careful planning and an effective marketing mix to be successful.

Focus Questions:

What is your initial impression when first seeing this advertisement? Why do you believe NTT Do Co Mo chose to use the image of the Roman aqueducts to introduce its new cell phone technologies? After studying the advertisement, do you understand the product being advertised? What additional information would you need to help you determine if you are interested in the company's products?

Locate an advertisement for a new product. In a class discussion, compare its effectiveness with the example ads from other students.

Starting with a Product

GOALS

- Explain how customers view products.
- Describe how marketers keep a consumer focus during product development.

KEY TERMS

product, *p. 276*

marketing matters

Businesses tend to view products as merely the physical items they produce and sell while consumers see products as ways to satisfy their wants and needs. Marketers play an important role in bridging that gap. They must make sure businesses stay focused on consumers' needs as products are being developed. During product development, marketers need to serve as the customers' representative by gathering information, suggesting product improvements, and testing marketing mixes. By doing so, they help others in the business develop products that satisfy needs better than existing or competing products. That should result in products customers want as well as profitable sales for the company.

Think about a product in your home that is no longer used because it failed to satisfy the needs for which it was purchased. If you were going to purchase a product to replace it, would you look for a similar but better designed competitive product, or would you try to find a new product that is quite different from the product that was purchased? Discuss your response with other students.

A Product Is More Than It Appears

A **product** is anything tangible offered to a market by a business to satisfy needs. It is important for marketers to realize that consumers view a product differently than the business that develops it. Business people often see their products as the first part of the definition—anything offered to a market. Businesses focus on what they offer—the tangible objects. Consumers have a different view of products. They are concerned about their needs, and they view products as ways to satisfy those needs. The differences in those views can result in problems when businesses develop and market products.

What are your motives when you decide you need to make a purchase? While you may plan to purchase a pair of shoes,

How do businesses and consumers view products differently?

©DIGITAL VISION

What's on Your Pizza?

Pizza is a staple food in the United States, with nearly 70,000 pizza shops grossing more than $31 billion in pizza sales annually. But U.S. pizza restaurants are also expanding rapidly into European, Asian, and South American markets.

Franchise restaurants are successful when they balance their need for set procedures and menu items with the ability to adapt to local tastes and customs. As a customer, you can expect the same store layout, menu, and level of service at all locations, but you might find unique menu items depending on your location.

For instance, Domino's requires franchisees to use the same dough, sauce, and cheese, but toppings can vary. You might order squid on your Domino's pizza in Tokyo or pickled ginger in Bombay. This balancing act has led to great success for Domino's. There are now more than 8,000 Domino's restaurants in 54 countries, with more than $1.4 billion in revenue.

Think Critically

1. Why would Domino's Pizza require international franchisees to use the same dough, sauce, and cheese while allowing changes in pizza toppings?

2. Should a franchisor encourage businesses in other countries to experiment with new product ideas? Why or why not?

---

a hamburger, or a book, you have reasons for each purchase that go beyond simply owning the product. People buy shoes for an important basic need, the protection of their feet. However, few people think only of protection when shopping. More often, they are focused on more specific reasons for the purchase such as to convey a certain style and image, to be able to play a sport, or to get durable footwear at a reasonable price. The purchase of a hamburger is typically a response to hunger. Additionally, taste, cost, and a social experience may be a more important part of your decision to choose the hamburger rather than another food item. When you purchase a book, you are probably more interested in entertainment or education than the physical appearance of the book.

More Than a Physical Product

A product is more than a tangible item for consumers. The physical characteristics of the product are important. It must be durable, attractive, and safe. But beyond those qualities, the product must be useful to the consumer and meet the consumer's needs. If not, the consumer will be uninterested in buying the product no matter what its physical characteristics.

Business people make a mistake when they don't think seriously about consumer needs or when they believe that the needs are so obvious that they are not particularly important to consumers when making a purchase. Some restaurant owners believe they offer great food and that people come to their restaurant mainly to satisfy their hunger. They fail to realize that hunger is a very basic need and that few people who eat in restaurants are so hungry that it is the only factor they consider. Instead, consumers decide on a restaurant on the basis of a large number of factors including menu variety, taste, speed and quality of service, atmosphere, location, and price. If a restaurant owner is not aware of how consumers make choices on the basis of those needs, the business will probably not be successful. Few products are so good that consumers will not consider alternatives, and few consumer needs are so basic or so obvious that business people can afford to ignore them.

Consumers Know Best

A second mistake of some business people is believing that they are better able than consumers to define the types of needs their products satisfy. U.S. automobile manufacturers made that mistake years ago when they were convinced that consumers were much more interested in style and design than in safety and economy. They recognized their mistake only after automobiles from other countries were designed to respond to the most important consumer needs and took away a large part of the U.S. automobile market. U.S. manufacturers have continued to struggle to maintain profitability and to change their approach to the design and production of automobiles that customers will view as superior to foreign competitors.

The teenage market is one that is often misunderstood by businesses. You can probably identify many businesses that try to sell products to you but make mistakes in trying to match their products with your needs and interests.

Another mistaken approach is to believe that products sold by a business will satisfy many different people. Some businesses believe that the same products and same approach to marketing will work the same with teenagers as it does with older adults.

When business people have been successful for a long time or with one group of customers, they often believe they know what types of products all customers want. Customer needs can change, and different consumer groups have unique needs and experiences. Careful study of markets before making decisions about new products or changes in existing products will pay off for businesses that follow that strategy.

Checkpoint ▶▶

How does a consumer's view of a product tend to differ from that of business people?

What is the advantage of selling products that can be custom ordered, such as furniture?

©GETTY IMAGES/PHOTODISC

Planning a Career in... *Virtual Product Development*

"It's amazing how quickly new cell phone models are introduced. My stepbrother, who works in Virtual Product Development (VPD), says that VPD software allows companies to bring new products to market more quickly than ever before. To stay competitive, the mobile phone manufacturers keep developing phones with improved functions to meet customers' evolving needs."

Did you ever wonder how someone takes a great idea and makes it into a manufactured product? VPD utilizes state-of-the art software to streamline the development of manufactured items. By providing sophisticated software that integrates multiple planning modules, these software systems allow team members to quickly redesign products while working at different times and different locations.

Employment Outlook

- Computer Software Engineers who design the VPD software are expected to experience very rapid growth in their career fields.

- Industrial Designers who utilize VPD software to conceptualize new products are expected to experience average growth in their career field.

Job Titles

- Industrial Design Engineer
- Virtualization Program Manager
- Simulation Engineer
- Manager, Virtual Prototyping
- Product Development Manager

Needed Skills

- At minimum, a bachelor's degree is required. More complex positions may require a graduate degree , often with additional technology training.

- Strong, conceptual, problem-solving, analytical, and multitasking skills are necessary.

Science, Technology, Engineering & Mathematics

- Creativity, aesthetic sensibilities, and design principles training is needed.

What's it like to work in...
Virtual Product Development

Nitan, an industrial designer for a cell phone manufacturing company, is reviewing virtual customer feedback for two cell phone prototypes. This feedback was obtained without ever producing an actual physical product.

Nitan's VPD supplier developed an interactive, web-based game for consumers chosen by the company to test enhanced cell phone features found on the two prototypes. The game had built-in incentives for accuracy and thorough analysis.

The web site also provided users the opportunity to design their own prototypes. Users could select the most appealing combination of features when designing their ideal cell phone.

Using the combined results from the game and design modules, Nitan, in conjunction with the product engineering team, designed a final virtual prototype. To confirm that the features most important to customers have been properly incorporated, Nitan will have his VPD supplier prepare a 3-D virtual model that will be shown to people within the company, vendors, and consumers for final virtual feedback before a final production decision is confirmed.

By virtually fine-tuning the new cell phone, Nitan has provided his company with significant cost savings. He has spared his company the long lead time and expense of manufacturing multiple tangible prototypes.

What About **You**

Would you like to participate in a virtual development process to help your company develop customer-focused products?

Product Development as a Marketing Function

Who should be responsible for product development in a business? When thinking of new products, people often have an image of inventors, engineers, or scientists working in research labs to create something new. Certainly those people are actively involved in most manufacturing businesses in developing new product ideas, but they can no longer afford to work alone.

The failure rate for new products is very high and very expensive. While the figures vary by the type of product, on average five of every ten new product ideas will not be successful. The cost to a company for the development and introduction of a new product is typically at least several hundred thousand dollars and could be as high as several million dollars. Those figures mean that the time and money spent on developing new products that fail are lost and can only be recovered from successful products. Those successful products have to be very profitable in order to recover the large losses. The cost of a high rate of new product failure has to be passed on to the consumer in the form of higher prices on the successful products.

Why do products fail? Economic studies and consumer behavior indicate that products will be successful if they meet consumer needs better than other choices. Therefore, failed products are those that do not meet consumer needs or are not superior to competing products. Companies should be able to reduce the rate of product failure by improving their understanding of consumer needs and competition.

The Role of Marketing

In the past, marketers were asked to sell the products that a business developed. That task was easy if consumers needed the product, but it was difficult if the product did not meet consumer needs well. Put yourself in the position of a salesperson of a product for which the consumer does not see a need or a product that does not appear to be better than competing products. Yet, your success depends on selling the product.

You can see why salespeople sometimes have a poor image. In this situation, the salesperson must try to convince the customer that the product is needed or that it is better than the competitor's product even if it is not. That certainly is not easy, and it probably is not the right thing to do. The salesperson who successfully sells the product may still have problems. The customer may discover that the product did not meet the needs described by the salesperson and may return it for a refund. Even if the product is not returned, the consumer may be upset with the salesperson and will not buy from the company again.

The role of marketing in product development has changed. A company that believes in the marketing concept uses the needs of customers as the primary focus during the planning, production, distribution, and promotion of a product or service. With that philosophy, marketers

©DIGITAL VISION

Why do you think new product development is so important in the fashion industry?

should not be in the position of having to sell products that do not meet customer needs. Marketers should be actively involved with others in the business in the design and development of new products.

Marketing Activities in Product Development

Marketing is the eyes, ears, and mouth of the customer in a business. Marketing is the direct link between a business and its customers. Marketers work with customers every day, whether in selling, promotion, product distribution, marketing research, or the many other marketing activities that occur in a business. Because of that close contact, marketers are in a good position to understand customers—what they like and do not like, how they view competing products, and whether they are satisfied with current products. Marketers must represent the consumer in the business as products are designed and developed.

There are three important roles for marketers in the product development process. Marketers gather information, design marketing strategies, and conduct market tests.

Gather Information
The obvious role for marketers in product development is market research. Gathering and studying market information and using the results to assist in product planning keeps the focus on consumer needs and competition rather than on the views of those involved in planning.

Information can be collected in many ways and from many different sources. Feedback from salespeople is very important in understanding both customers and competitors. Analysis of sales data will determine items that have sold well in the past and those that have not. It will identify the areas of customer complaints and product returns. The marketing department might meet regularly with consumer panels to discuss new product ideas and customer experiences. Those discussions provide important information for product changes and improvements.

©GETTY IMAGES/PHOTODISC

How can marketers gather information to aid in the product development process?

Marketers who are actively involved in product planning usually develop a marketing information system. It allows the information from many sources to be collected, stored, and analyzed to improve new product decisions.

Design Strategies
A new product is developed to meet company objectives. If the company's goal is to increase its share of a specific market, it might develop a different product than if the goal is to enter a market it has never competed in before. A new company that cannot risk failure with a new product may approach product development in a very different way than an experienced and profitable company.

A marketing strategy combines decisions about a target market and an appropriate marketing mix. The actual product is only one part of the strategy. Marketers participate in developing an effective strategy by identifying target markets, determining company strengths and weaknesses, and evaluating existing and potential competitors. They use that information to propose alternative marketing mixes.

Conduct Market Tests
After a product and the remaining parts of the marketing mix have been designed, most companies conduct tests to determine if the new product will be successful. Testing is a way to reduce product failures and to avoid spending money on products and in markets that will not be successful.

In the past, many companies used test markets. Test marketing has become increasingly expensive and can tip off competitors to new marketing strategies. Competitors may try to influence the test market results. Companies are constantly looking for new ways to conduct market tests. There are now sophisticated computer programs that allow companies to simulate the marketing of products and determine expected levels of sales and profits.

The Product Planning Function

Businesses that are marketing oriented involve marketing personnel in product planning. Therefore, an important marketing function is product/service planning—assisting in the design and development of products and services that will meet the needs of prospective customers. The key parts of the definition are *assisting*, meaning that marketers work cooperatively with others in product development, and *meet the needs*, meaning that the products are designed to satisfy customers.

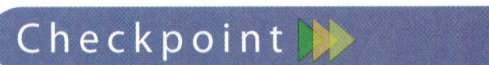

Checkpoint

What are the three important roles for marketers in the product development process?

10-1 Assessment

Xtra! Study Tools
school.cengage.com/marketing/marketing

Key Concepts

Determine the best answer.

1. True or False: Consumers view a product differently than the business that develops it.

2. A product is anything _____ offered to a market by the business to satisfy needs.

3. Which of the following is *not* a role for marketers in the product development process?
   a. gather information
   b. sell products after the business develops them
   c. design marketing strategies
   d. conduct marketing tests

4. A key part of the product development process for businesses is to
   a. keep costs as low as possible
   b. rely on engineers and scientists to identify new product ideas
   c. depend on marketers to lead the product development process
   d. ensure that product design responds to customer needs

Make Academic Connections

5. **Writing** Choose a product you have purchased that did not meet your needs. Write a positive one-page letter to the customer service department identifying the reasons for your dissatisfaction with the product and describing how you believe the product could be improved.

6. **History** Choose a company or a product that you believe is a good example of innovation. Use the library or Internet to learn more about the company or product, its history, and the factors that contributed to it being innovative. Prepare an oral report with visuals summarizing what you learned.

Connect to ◆ DECA
An Association of Marketing Students

7. Your team has been asked to gather consumer information for the local cable television company. Prepare a five-item questionnaire to determine the attitudes of subscribers about the cable television service and the improvements they would like to see. Give the questionnaire to ten people and summarize the results using tables and charts. Give a team presentation of the questionnaire and results to your teacher (judge).

Components of the Product Mix Element

GOALS

- Describe the parts of the product mix element.
- Outline the three steps of the product design process.
- Explain the importance of product lines, packaging, and brand development.

KEY TERMS

product line, *p. 287*

product assortment, *p. 287*

trademark, *p. 289*

licensed brand, *p. 290*

marketing matters

When a new product is developed, many decisions have to be made about its final form and the total product mix. Marketers start with a basic product, whether it is a toothbrush, an automobile, or a software program. Then they add enhancements to make it more satisfying to a target market. Finally, they decide on a brand name, packaging, and accessories that may make the use of the product more satisfying.

Find a product in your home that is more than a basic physical product. What features, enhancements, and accessories are included? If there is a package, what purposes does it appear to serve? Discuss how all the parts of the product mix element combine to offer greater satisfaction than would be possible with just the basic product itself.

Parts of the Product Mix Element

Even a product that seems very simple is made up of many parts. Think of the toothbrush you used this morning. Is it like every other toothbrush you could have purchased? What makes it unique? Why did you purchase it rather than one of the many other brands of toothbrushes available?

The basic product for a toothbrush is easy to describe—typically a plastic handle and head with bristles. Even with that basic product, there are choices. The handle may be long or short, contoured for an easier grip, bent to allow the head to fit comfortably inside your mouth, and manufactured in several colors. It may have a hole drilled through it so that you can hang the toothbrush when you are not using it, or it may have a rubber pick to massage your gums. The head also comes

©GETTY IMAGES/PHOTODISC

How can common consumer products like school supplies be differentiated from competitors' products?

in various shapes and sizes. The bristles can be firm, medium, or soft. They can be short, long, or varied with shorter bristles in the middle. One manufacturer even includes a strip of colored bristles that indicate when the toothbrush needs to be replaced. Bristles can be manufactured from several different materials.

Even with all of the possible variations, many people believe that all toothbrushes are quite similar. Yet there are still more features to choose from. There are compact toothbrushes that collapse into a small case that you can carry with you. There are disposable toothbrushes that come with toothpaste already applied. And there are electric toothbrushes in many varieties. One electric toothbrush is part of a complete dental care system. The rechargeable handle can be used with the toothbrush, a tooth polisher, a water pick, and a flossing tool.

Most toothbrushes are sold with a brand name. Some are well-known brands under which many products are sold, such as Colgate. Others are brands specifically associated with tooth care, such as Oral-B.

Offering a guarantee is another way to differentiate products. It may be especially important to persuade customers to switch to a more expensive electric toothbrush.

A manufacturer may guarantee replacement if the product is defective or may refund the purchase price to consumers who are not satisfied. A testimonial is similar to a guarantee. It is a recommendation from a professional group, such as the American Dental Association, about the quality of the product.

The toothbrush example demonstrates that every product can be quite complex and unique. Businesses have many choices in the development of new products.

©GETTY IMAGES/PHOTODISC

Why is product planning important for all products, even simple ones such as a toaster?

Checkpoint ▶▶▶

Why does developing even a simple product like a toothbrush involve so many decisions?

The Levels of Product Design

Product design moves through three levels. It begins with the basic product. Then, the basic product is modified and improved by adding features and options. Finally, services and complementary products are planned to make it as useful as possible to consumers.

Basic Product

The most important part of the product is the basic physical product. It is a readily recognizable product in its simplest form. Consumers should be able to easily identify the important need to which the product responds and how to use it. The basic product will be much like that of competitors. Examples of basic products include a house, computer, shampoo, bicycle, or automobile.

Enhanced Product

The basic product responds to an important need of consumers. However, we know that consumers are usually trying to satisfy several needs with one purchase. They evaluate products to see which one provides the best and most specific satisfaction. Companies add enhancements to their basic products to meet those needs.

Enhancements include features and options. For example, a bicycle can be manufactured in several frame sizes, in models ranging from mountain bikes to racing bikes, and with a single gear ratio of up to 27 speeds. Choices of materials used in manufacturing, seat design, and tire construction are available. Some bicycles have shock absorbers built into the frame. If you go to a large bicycle shop or a manufacturer's Internet site, you may be able to select from several hundred different bicycles or even customize a bike unlike that of any other purchaser. Other types of enhancements to a basic product are levels of quality, styling differences, colors, brand names, and packaging.

Each enhancement changes the basic product. The change is likely to be viewed as an improvement by some customers, increasing the satisfaction they receive from the product. Other customers may view the change as unneeded or even dissatisfying. Enhanced products make it possible for companies to satisfy several target markets with one basic product. Different combinations of features, options, and even brand names are developed with the needs of one target market in mind.

NETBookmark

Marketers often start with a basic product and then choose enhancements and extensions to make the basic product more satisfying to a target market. An article in the online edition of *Dairy Foods* magazine spotlighted the best new products of a recent year. Access school.cengage.com/marketing/marketing and click on the link for Chapter 10. Pick one of the products described in the article and identify the basic product. Then, identify the enhancements/extensions that were added to the basic product. Finally, determine the features most of these "best products" have in common.

school.cengage.com/marketing/marketing

Extended Product

Businesses can improve the satisfaction provided by a product in ways other than product enhancements. Customer satisfaction can be improved if the business offers services, guarantees, information on effective use of the product, and even additional products that improve the use of the primary product.

©GETTY IMAGES/PHOTODISC

Why do some businesses offer home delivery of their products?

Services are an effective way to meet additional customer needs beyond those directly related to the use of the product. Examples of important customer services that could influence product choice are credit, delivery, installation, repair services, and technical support.

Suggesting additional products that should be purchased so that the primary product can be used more effectively is often an important method of improving customer satisfaction. Would you like to purchase a new camera only to discover when you use it that you need a large memory card to store your pictures or that a tripod and flash attachment are needed for certain types of pictures? A skilled photography equipment salesperson will discuss with you how you will use the camera and the types of pictures you plan to take. Based on that information, a recommendation of additional products will be made so that you can get the greatest enjoyment and value from your purchase.

Checkpoint ▶▶▶

What are the three levels of product design?

Product Mix Components

When consumers evaluate products to determine the one that is most satisfying, they are interested in more than just the physical product. Four important considerations in planning the product mix are the product line, product assortments, packaging, and brand development.

Judgment Call

Whose Interests Are Being Served?

When a product injures people either because it fails or because it was poorly designed, those injured have a right to seek damages from the manufacturer. Corporations spend billions of dollars annually to protect themselves financially from these product liability lawsuits, both actual and potential. These costs inevitably inflate the prices that companies charge consumers, so consumers end up paying on both ends— whenever they buy something as well as when products cause injury.

Businesses say the situation has gotten out of hand and blame the legal system and trial lawyers. They contend that the lure of multimillion-dollar damage awards and lucrative contingency fees gives lawyers an incentive to pursue claims whether or not they are legitimate. Some of the reforms sought by businesses include requiring the losing party to pay the prevailing party's legal expenses, limiting contingency fees, and limiting punitive damage awards.

Consumer groups and trial lawyers say large damage awards are needed to counterbalance the huge sums of money that corporations use to defend faulty products and tie up injured consumers in court.

Think Critically

1. Search the Internet for news of a case where product liability lawsuits forced a business into bankruptcy. What was the problem with the product? What has happened since consumers became aware of the problem?

2. If the possibilities of large damage awards and lawyers' contingency fees were removed, how would it affect consumers' ability to bring product liability suits?

Product Line

New or small companies often offer only one product to a target market. With more experience and as a company grows, it is possible to expand into other markets and develop a product line. A **product line** is a group of similar products with slight variations in the product mix to satisfy different needs in a market. A company that manufacturers bath towels may offer various colors, sizes, and levels of quality to give customers choices. A soft drink bottler not only offers different sizes and types of containers for a flavor of soda but usually has many flavors in its product line. It may even sell fruit juices and flavored waters in addition to soft drinks.

As companies add items to their product line, they usually increase the number of potential customers and the satisfaction of individual consumers. However, the company is also adding to the costs of manufacturing, distribution, inventory control, and other related marketing activities. An expanded product line also requires additional display space for retailers. The retailer must make a decision whether to stock items from the complete product line of the manufacturer or use the space for the products of competing companies or even entirely different products. In a supermarket display of soft drinks, snacks, or cereal, you can see examples of companies' extensive product lines and the competition they have for display space.

Variation in Quantity

Product lines can be developed in several ways. One of the easiest ways to expand from one product into several is to vary the product size. The identical food item may be packaged in three sizes—single serving, 4 servings, and 10 servings. Facial tissue may be sold in a pocket-sized cellophane wrapper, a box of 250 tissues, or a multiple-box pack. Another type of quantity variation is to have different sizes for the same basic product. For example, bed sheets are sold in twin, full, queen, or king size. In this case, the product itself is manufactured in

Why would a shoe manufacturer want to offer more than one style and quality of shoe?

varied sizes rather than just changing the quantity in a package.

Variation in Quality

Differences in quality can also be used to develop a product line. Items such as paintbrushes, carpenter or mechanic tools, lawn mowers, computers, and even clothing often are sold in two or three varying levels of quality. Consumers who use the products infrequently may not need the best possible quality and would prefer to save money in exchange for accepting a slightly lower quality. Adding features to the basic product may produce several levels of product choices that vary in quality. Automobile and appliance manufacturers often have a very basic model at a low price and several other models with selected features and options at higher prices.

Product Assortments

In addition to product line decisions, companies plan product assortments. A **product assortment** is the complete set of all products a business offers to its market. Retail stores provide the best example of product assortments. Some specialty retailers, lawn and garden centers for example, have a very complete assortment of products homeowners need in one category. Other general merchandise retailers, such as discount and department stores, stock products in many different categories. They probably will not have as complete an assortment in one line as the specialty store, but they respond to a broader set of customers' product needs.

Some manufacturers specialize in one product category, mattresses for example, and have a full assortment of products in that line. Other manufacturers may have a product assortment in many different product categories, such as a full assortment of camping products or many types of home furniture.

Packaging

Most products are sold in a package. The package serves the dual purpose of protection and promotion. In addition, some packaging improves the use of the product. Containers with pour spouts built into the package, resealable liners, and handles for carrying are developed to solve customer problems related to the use of the product.

Ease of Use When designing the package, manufacturers must carefully consider the ways customers use a product. For example, if a cereal box is taller than the shelves on which it will be stored in the customer's home, it will not be purchased. A manufacturer of a liquid cleaner found that people would not buy a large economy size because the container could not be lifted and poured with one hand in the way people were used to handling the product. Products that consumers use in a microwave oven must not have metal in the package.

Safety Safety and protection are important concerns when planning the packaging of products. Products used by children certainly need to have safe packaging. A manufacturer of individual servings of puddings and fruits learned that children would lick the lid of the container when it was removed. As a result, the metal lid was covered with a plastic coating. Glass and other fragile products need well-designed packages to ensure that they are not broken during shipment and display.

Attraction The promotional value of packaging is also important for many products. Impulse items are often purchased because of an attractive package that clearly shows the use of the product. Perfumes and colognes usually have very expensive and uniquely designed containers to convey a certain image.

Skechers has become a shoe brand that many teenagers prefer over other brands.

Individually make a list of ten well-known brand names. Then, compare team members' lists and make a second list of the brands that were listed by more than one team member. For the three brands listed most frequently, identify two other brands that compete with each of those three brands. Discuss differences in the images team members have of the brands identified.

Handling Packaging can also be helpful in the display and security of products. In stores where products are displayed for customer self-service, the package may need to be designed to hang from a hook or to lie flat on a shelf. Small or expensive items are often packaged in large containers to reduce the chance of theft.

Environment There is growing concern about the type and quantity of materials used for packaging. Manufacturers are increasingly using recycled materials for packaging and developing materials that are biodegradable. Many retailers are reducing the amount of packaging used or are helping consumers reuse or recycle packages.

Brand Development

Do you know the brand names of the shoes and clothing you are wearing? Do you have a favorite brand of pizza or automobile? In what stores do you prefer to shop? Each of these questions demonstrates that the brand of products can be very important to consumers as they make purchase decisions. A *brand* is a name, symbol, word, or design that identifies a product, service, or company. A brand is important to a company because it provides a unique identification for the company and its offerings. To ensure that others cannot use a brand, a company registers a trademark with the federal government. A **trademark** is the legal protection of the words or symbols for use by a company.

Consider how difficult it would be to shop if there were no brand names. While some products are purchased without considering the brand (think of the paper you use for writing in school), in most cases consumers consider the brand as part of the purchase decision. Positive or negative experience with a brand will influence your future purchases. Business people know that brand recognition resulting from advertising often increases a product's sales.

The goal of a business in using branding is to gain customer recognition of the brand in order to increase the likelihood of a sale. Businesses want brands that convey a particular image and that can be recalled to encourage repeat purchases. There are several levels of consumer brand awareness as shown in Figure 10-1.

FIGURE 10-1

Businesses use brands to help consumers make choices. Branding is effective when consumers prefer or insist on a specific brand.

Levels of Brand Recognition	
Non-recognition	Consumers are unable to identify the brand.
Rejection	Consumers will not purchase the product because of the brand.
Recognition	Consumers can recall the brand name, but it has little influence on purchases.
Preference	Consumers view the brand as valuable and will choose it if it is available.
Insistence	Consumers value the brand to the extent that they reject other brands.

Brands can be developed by manufacturers, wholesalers, or retailers. Individual products can have their own brands, or groups of products can carry an identical or *family brand*. Breakfast cereals are often sold under a family brand, such as Kellogg's. Some companies offer licensed brands to add prestige or a unique image to products. A **licensed brand** is a well-known name or symbol established by one company and sold for use by another company to promote its products. Disney and Sesame Street are examples of companies that license the use of character names and images for products ranging from toys to clothing. Professional and college sports teams license their names and mascot images for use on many products. Some people prefer to purchase products with those brands rather than similar products that do not carry the licensed brand. Professional athletes such as Tiger Woods and Tony Hawk license their names for use on sporting goods, apparel, and computer games.

Checkpoint ▶▶

Why would a company want a trademark for its brand names?

10-2 Assessment

Xtra! Study Tools
school.cengage.com/marketing/marketing

Key Concepts

Determine the best answer.

1. True or False: The brands of most low-cost consumer products are very basic and quite similar to the other brands of the same product.

2. _____ to a product include(s) features and options.

3. A group of similar products with slight variations in the marketing mix to satisfy different needs in a market is a(n)
   a. product line
   b. brand
   c. product assortment
   d. extended product

4. The dual purposes of packaging are protection and
   a. competition
   b. safety
   c. promotion
   d. none of these

5. A _____ is the legal protection of the words or symbols for use by a company.

Make Academic Connections

6. **Visual Art** Use an advertisement or product catalog to locate a picture of a consumer product. Copy or cut the picture and paste it on poster paper. Using different colors, highlight the basic product, enhanced product, and extended product. Identify each of the components. Provide a legend to identify the meaning of each color.

7. **Research** Popular movies and movie characters such as Spiderman are often licensed for use by other companies to promote their products. For a current or recent movie, identify as many licensed users of the movie or its characters as you can find. Create a table that lists the company, the product, and a brief description of how the licensed movie or character is used in promotion.

Connect to ◀ DECA
An Association of Marketing Students

8. A company has created a new product that combines sunscreen and insect repellant on individually packaged moist tissues for convenient use. It has asked you to create a unique brand name and a supporting image or other visual for the new product. Complete the project and present it to your teacher (judge) with a brief discussion of why you believe it will be effective.

Products for Consumers and Businesses

GOALS

- Define consumer markets and describe what is meant by direct demand.
- Explain the importance of the business product classification system.
- Provide examples of how product classifications are used in product planning.

KEY TERMS

consumer markets, *p. 291*

direct demand, *p. 291*

business markets, *p. 292*

derived demand, *p. 292*

marketing matters

Product planning should be based on an understanding of the market in which the product will be sold. Knowing who will use the product, the purpose for which it will be used, and the needs customers are attempting to satisfy with the product will result in a product that is better designed for that consumer. Two broad market categories exist based on very different reasons for buying products—consumer markets and business markets.

Name five businesses in your area whose primary customers are other businesses and five businesses whose primary customers are individual consumers. How would the businesses have to change if each type was targeting the opposite category?

Consumer Markets

Individuals or socially related groups who purchase products for personal consumption are known as **consumer markets**. When you, your family, or your friends buy products for your own use or for others to use, you are part of the consumer market. You make purchase decisions on the basis of the satisfaction you receive from using the product. If you are buying the product for a friend or family member, you are interested in buying something that person will find to be satisfying. The demand for consumer products is known as direct demand. **Direct demand** is the quantity of a product or service needed to meet the needs of the consumer.

Because final consumers or their family and friends will use the products they purchase, they have a clear idea of the reasons for a purchase. They locate and purchase the products that best meet

©GETTY IMAGES/PHOTODISC

What factors might affect direct demand for a cell phone?

their important needs. To satisfy the direct demand, business people must be aware of consumers' needs and how they choose products to satisfy those needs. The consumer purchase classification system is reviewed in Figure 10-2. The system is based on two factors:

CONVENIENCE GOODS

Staple

Impulse

Emergency

SPECIALTY GOODS

SHOPPING GOODS

Attribute-based

Price-based

UNSOUGHT GOODS

Consumer Purchase Classification System

FIGURE 10-2
Marketers develop more effective products when they understand how consumers shop for them.

1. The importance of the purchase to the consumer
2. The willingness of the consumer to shop and compare products before making the purchase

Businesses can use the classifications when planning products and deciding how to market each category of product in consumer markets.

Checkpoint ▶▶

What is the connection between direct demand and consumer markets?

Business Markets

Companies and organizations that purchase products for the operation of a business or the completion of a business activity are known as **business markets**. Business markets include producers, manufacturers, retail businesses, nonprofit organizations, government agencies, schools, and others that provide products or services for consumption by others. Business markets make purchase decisions based on what is needed to effectively operate the business, to meet the needs of employees and customers, and to produce the products and services of the business.

Business markets make purchase decisions on the basis of derived demand. **Derived demand** is the quantity of a product or service needed by a business in order to operate at a level that will meet the demand of its customers. A movie theater needs to buy enough popcorn, oil, and boxes to meet its customers' needs for popcorn during the showing of movies. If the theater purchases too much, some of the product will not be sold, and money will be lost. If the theater purchases too little, customers will be dissatisfied, and sales will be lost.

Developing products for the business market requires an understanding of how the products are used by the business. A business product classification system has been developed to aid in understanding the business market. The categories are shown in Figure 10-3.

Capital Equipment

Capital equipment includes a business's land, buildings, and major pieces of equipment. They are usually the most expensive and most important products purchased.

They must meet the specific needs of the business so that it operates effectively. Often they are custom designed, so they will have little value to other businesses. A large office building, commercial airplane, and sophisticated computer system are examples of capital equipment. Most companies purchase the products using long-term loans from finance companies or the manufacturers. Some capital equipment is leased rather than purchased.

Operating Equipment

Smaller, less-expensive equipment used in the operation of the business or in the production and sale of products and services is known as *operating equipment*. This type of equipment makes production or operations more efficient and effective. Examples of operating equipment are tools, small machines, and furniture. They usually have a shorter life than capital equipment and must be replaced from time to time. They are also more standardized, meaning

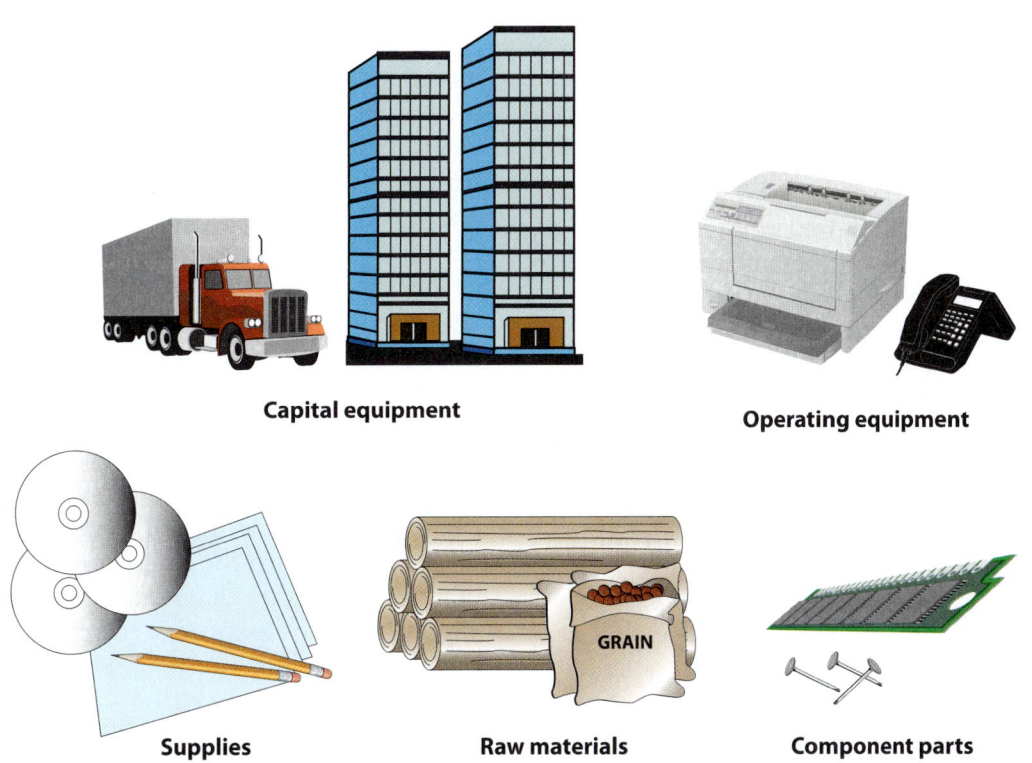

Capital equipment

Operating equipment

Supplies

Raw materials

Component parts

Business Product Classification System

FIGURE 10-3
Business products are marketed based on how they will be used by business customers.

Sales Tax on the Internet

One benefit of purchasing goods over the Internet is that out-of-state buyers usually do not have to pay sales taxes. Typically, the seller only charges sales tax to residents in states where the seller has a physical presence, such as a store, warehouse, or office.

Because sales tax contributes $150 billion to the states' income per year, states stand to lose a lot if Internet sales are not taxed. Therefore, any buyer who lives in a state that charges sales tax is expected to pay a "use tax" on all items bought over the Internet. States have tried to increase awareness of this use tax by adding it to tax forms and even campaigning to educate consumers, but it is difficult to enforce. In addition to lost revenue, states contend that not taxing Internet purchases gives an unfair advantage to out-of-state sellers over local businesses—yet another reason for the use tax. But to date, states have had success enforcing use taxes only on big-ticket items, such as cars and boats.

Think Critically

1. What problems do you think states encounter in trying to persuade their residents to declare what they bought online?

2. Pick an item on the Internet that costs more than $100. Figure how much it would cost to buy it from out of state, paying shipping costs but no sales tax. Compare that amount to how much it would cost to buy it at a local store, paying no shipping costs but paying a 7% sales tax.

---

that the same type of operating equipment may be used in many different businesses.

Supplies

The products and materials consumed in the operation of the business are *supplies*. A business needs paper, pencils, and paper clips, as well as cleaning supplies and parts for routine repairs of equipment. Some supplies are purchased and used in small quantities and are quite inexpensive. Others, such as fuel, electricity, or packing materials, may be needed in large quantities and are a major expense for the company. Most supplies are standardized, meaning they are not uniquely developed for one business. They are available from many suppliers and are used in a large number of different businesses.

Raw Materials

Producers and manufacturers buy many products that become part of the products they make. Often they purchase *raw materials*, which are unprocessed products used as basic materials for the products to be produced. Logs are purchased by lumber producers, oil by plastics manufacturers, and grain by cereal processors.

Purchasers of raw materials need to have an adequate supply and a standardized quality of raw materials in order to maintain a planned level and quality of production. The price of the raw materials is also important since the cost has a big influence on what the company needs to charge for its finished products. The purchasing company will want to sign a long-term contract with the supplier of the raw materials to ensure that it has a continuing supply and to be assured of the cost.

Component Parts

Component parts are also incorporated into the products that a business makes. However, *component parts* have been either partially or totally processed by another company. For example, a computer manufacturer will buy computer chips from a chip manufacturer. These chips have already been carefully developed and are simply installed as a part of the computer assembly. The same manufacturer buys parts for a disk drive from another company. Those parts must be assembled as part of the final assembly of the computers.

Component parts can be designed for the needs of one company, or they can be standardized for use by many companies.

As with raw materials, the purchasing company is concerned that a dependable source of supply is available when needed, that the component parts meet the quality standards of the company, and that costs are reasonable.

Checkpoint ▷▷▷

What are the five types of products in business product classification system?

Planning Products for Consumer and Business Markets

The classification systems for consumer and business markets are useful to marketers as they complete product planning. Knowing whether the customer is a final consumer or a business consumer determines whether the product is being developed to meet a direct demand or a derived demand. For consumer markets, products treated as convenience goods require different planning from those treated as specialty goods. The product is less important than the location for convenience goods, so the company needs to develop a basic product at a reasonable cost. A specialty good is very important to consumers, so care and attention must go into the product. It will probably require an enhanced and extended product to meet the consumers' needs.

For business customers, the type of product and its use are important factors to consider when planning products. Capital equipment is a major investment and an important decision for the customer. The business will usually spend time and involve several people when planning the purchase. It will work closely with the supplier in planning a product that will meet the company's

needs. Supplies, on the other hand, may involve routine purchases where the

Intel wants both consumers and businesses to know that its Pentium 4 processor is a key component of many brands of computers.

customer gives little thought to anything other than price as long as the supply is the type needed by the company. The same type of supply may be purchased over and over with one person determining when to reorder.

Some products are sold to both consumer markets and business markets. Consumers buy automobile tires for replacements when the original tires on their car become worn. Automobile manufacturers purchase thousands of tires to mount on the vehicles they produce. Consumers purchase bottles of shampoo for personal care. Hotels buy large quantities of shampoo packaged in small bottles or packets to place in rooms as a service to their guests. With both examples, you can see that while the basic product is the same, the extended and enhanced products may be quite different. Also, the reasons and methods of purchasing will not be the same. Marketers need to understand the differences in purchases between the two types of markets in order to develop effective products and marketing mixes for each.

Checkpoint ▶▶

Why is it important to understand product classifications during product development?

10-3 Assessment

Key Concepts

Determine the best answer.

1. The correct match of market and demand is
   a. consumer market, indirect demand
   b. consumer market, direct demand
   c. business market, direct demand
   d. none are correct

2. Which of the following is an example of a consumer market rather than a business market?
   a. a government agency
   b. a non-profit hospital
   c. a retailer
   d. a social club

3. True or False: Operating equipment is usually the most expensive and most important type of products purchased by a business.

4. _____ have been either partially or totally processed by another company and are incorporated into products a business makes.
   a. Raw materials
   b. Component parts
   c. Supplies
   d. Operating equipment

5. True or False: The same product can be sold to both consumer markets and business markets.

Make Academic Connections

6. **Technology** Identify five relatively new products that are examples of the use of new technology. Using the Internet, locate a picture of the use of each technology by consumers and another picture of its use in businesses. Create a visual that illustrates the consumer markets and the business markets.

7. **Math** A movie theater has determined that 34% of all moviegoers will purchase popcorn and 52% will purchase a soft drink. The average popcorn sale is $3.75, and the average soft drink sale is $2.50. The theater expects to sell 895 movie tickets on Saturday. Calculate the amount of popcorn and soft drink sales the theater can expect.

Connect to

8. You are the fundraising manager for your DECA chapter. Each year the club works with a water bottling company to sell contracts for weekly home delivery service to consumers in your community. You believe the chapter can make more money if you also sell contracts to business customers. Prepare a three-minute persuasive presentation of the benefits of selling to both consumer and business markets. Present your ideas to your teacher (judge).

New Product Development

GOALS

- Explain what businesses mean by "new" products.
- Describe the six steps in new product development.

KEY TERMS

new product, *p. 297*

marketing matters

Without new products, companies have a hard time keeping customers satisfied and matching competition. Yet it is not easy to develop successful new products. The risk of failure is high, and development and testing costs are great.

Describe a new product that you have tried in the past year. What did you like about it? What did you not like about it? Was the product highly successful, somewhat successful, or a failure in the market? Describe what you imagine the business had to do to bring the new product to market. Compare your ideas with those of other students.

What Is a New Product?

Few products are really brand new in the sense that no other product like it has been available before. Many "new" products are changes and improvements to existing products. Others are new to a particular market but have been sold previously in other markets.

When the personal computer was first designed in the 1970s, it was completely new. Computers were not available for individual purchase and use before the development of the personal computer. Today, there are hundreds of choices of personal computers as features are added and technology allows machines to be developed that are smaller, faster, and easier to use.

You are probably familiar with companies that promote products as new and improved. Brands of laundry detergent, toothpaste, diapers, and potato chips often use the words "new" and "improved" to attract attention in a competitive market. In many cases, it is difficult to see what really is new or better about the product. Because some companies have misused the term "new" for products that really were not new, the Federal Trade Commission regulates how and when the term can be used. A company can call something "new" for only six months after the introduction or change of a product. A **new product** must be entirely new or changed in an important and noticeable way.

Fashions, music, ethnic foods, and other specialized products may be new in some markets but well known in others. A product or service may become popular in one part of the country and then spread to other parts. Some companies enter

Working in Teams

As a team, choose a commonly used, inexpensive consumer product. Use creative brainstorming to identify ten new uses for the product. Agree on three that are most likely to be successful and identify a possible target market for each.

international trade with products that are already successful in their home country.

A new use for a product can be discovered, leading to new markets. Video cameras were first installed on large commercial vehicles to allow drivers to see when backing up. Now cameras are installed on private automobiles to alert drivers if children or obstacles are behind the car.

Checkpoint ▶▶

Who decides if a product is really new or merely improved?

The Steps in New Product Development

Companies use a very careful process to identify and develop new products. The process is used to screen out products that are not likely to be successful before too much money is spent for production and marketing. The process assures that the products meet an important market need, can be produced well and at a reasonable price, and will be competitive with other products in the market. The following steps are part of most companies' procedures for new product development.

Idea Development

The most difficult step in new product development is usually finding ideas for new products. You may see a new product on the market and say, "I could have thought of that." But few people have successful new product ideas. Since products are developed to meet consumer needs, gathering information from consumers may generate ideas for new products. Many companies have consumer panels that meet regularly to discuss ideas for new products.

Important sources of new product ideas are problems customers have that do not seem to be solved with current products. Often, salespeople who work with customers every day have ideas for new products or product improvements based on what they see and hear.

Developing new product ideas can be a very creative process. Some people

What are some ways that companies can develop ideas for new products?

seem to be more creative than others, and those people are often involved in the new product planning process. Tools such as brainstorming, creative thinking exercises, and problem solving are used to identify product ideas for testing.

Idea Screening

To encourage a large number of new product ideas, companies do not evaluate ideas in the initial idea development stage. Once a number of ideas has been identified, the second step is to carefully screen them to select those that have the greatest chance for success. Businesses develop criteria for selecting the best ideas, such as:

Why is it important to perform a financial analysis during the product development process?

- Is there an identified market for the product with a strong need?
- Is the competition in the market reasonable?
- Do we have or can we obtain the resources to produce the product?
- Is the product legal and safe?
- Can we produce a quality product at a reasonable cost?

Other criteria are not as straightforward and may be tailored to company circumstances. For example, some companies will not want to develop products that compete with their current products. Others will select products that can be developed with current equipment and personnel to control costs. Some companies are seeking opportunities to move into new markets, so they want product ideas that meet the new market needs. The initial investment required to produce the new product may be an important factor for some companies but may be unimportant to others.

Strategy Development

After determining that the product idea seems reasonable, the business will create and test a sample marketing strategy as a first step in developing a business proposal.

In this step, research is done to clearly identify an appropriate target market and ensure that customers exist with the need and money for the product.

Next, alternative marketing mixes are planned and analyzed to determine the possible combinations of product, distribution, price, and promotion. Again, each choice is carefully studied to determine if it is appropriate for the target market and if the company can effectively implement that mix. Based on that study, the best possible mix is selected. It is possible that the research in this step will determine that an effective mix cannot be developed, in which case the product idea would be dropped.

Financial Analysis

If it is determined that a new product idea meets a market need and can be developed, the company will complete a financial analysis. Costs of production and marketing, sales projections for the target market, and resulting profits will be carefully calculated. Usually companies have computer models that help with the financial analysis. Several levels of analysis are completed to determine the best-case and worst-case possibilities. An understanding of the type of competition (ranging from pure

Digital Digest

Debugging New Products

For manufacturers, prototypes represent the Catch-22 of new product development. Building them is very expensive, takes lots of time, and requires the collaboration of many people who are rarely in the same place at the same time. That last factor inevitably causes misinterpretation and miscommunication errors. Not building prototypes or building fewer of them, on the other hand, often means that errors are not caught until later in the development process, resulting in late-stage design changes.

Innovations in computer-aided modeling systems are helping manufacturers address the dilemma. New systems allow various people at different sites to view and examine a three-dimensional computer model simultaneously. Proposed changes can be experimented with and tested if necessary, and everyone can examine the results to make sure that errors haven't been introduced inadvertently.

As a result, less-error-prone prototypes can be built early in the product development cycle. They can be built more quickly and at a lower cost. Since more errors are eliminated with the modeling software, fewer expensive prototypes are needed before a product reaches the production stage.

Think Critically

1. Why are prototypes so critical in developing new products, particularly machinery?

2. Why is it more expensive to incorporate design changes to a new product late in the development process?

---

competition to monopoly) and the level of demand is important in determining what prices can be charged and the amount of sales to expect. The results of the analysis are matched against company goals and profit objectives.

Product Development and Testing

After careful research and planning, the decision may be made to move forward. For a manufacturer, that means designing the production process, obtaining the needed equipment and materials, and training personnel. For a retailer, it involves identifying a producer or manufacturer to supply the products and negotiating a contract for the production.

For very expensive or risky products, the company may decide to develop a prototype, or model. The prototype can be used to test quality and costs before beginning full-scale production. Another testing strategy is a test market. A limited quantity of the new product is developed, and the marketing mix is implemented in a small part of the market to determine if it will be successful. If the market test is not successful, the company can end production or change the product before a large amount of money is spent.

Product Marketing

The last step in product development is full-scale introduction into the market. A great deal of preparation is needed for this step. All of the marketing mix elements must be planned. Cooperating companies such as wholesalers, retailers, transportation companies, and advertising agencies need to be involved. Production levels must be high enough to have an adequate supply of the product available to meet sales requirements. Marketing personnel need to be prepared for their responsibilities. All activities and schedules must be coordinated.

If all of the steps in the new product planning process have been carefully completed, the opportunity for success is very high. However, marketers still need to continue to study the market carefully. It is possible that conditions will change, competitors may anticipate the new product, or consumers will not respond as predicted. Adjustments in the marketing strategy may be needed as the market develops.

©GETTY IMAGES/PHOTODISC

Checkpoint ▶▶▶

Name the six specific activities that are part of the new product development process.

How can changes in the market affect new product development in the auto industry?

10-4 Assessment

Xtra! Study Tools
school.cengage.com/marketing/marketing

Key Concepts

Determine the best answer.

1. True or False: A company can continue to label a product as new for up to 12 months after it is introduced.

2. The first step in the new product development process is
   a. strategy development
   b. idea screening
   c. idea development
   d. none of the above

3. A _____ of a product can be used to test quality and costs before beginning full-scale production.

4. When using a _____, a limited quantity of the new product is developed, and the marketing mix is implemented in a small part of the market to determine if it will be successful.
   a. target market
   b. test market
   c. simulated market
   d. financial analysis

5. True or False: Once the product marketing stage begins, a company should not make adjustments in the marketing strategy.

Make Academic Connections

6. **Science** Many new products and changes to existing products are being introduced by companies in response to environmental concerns. The effort is referred to as *green marketing*. Select a *green* product and compare it to existing products that are less environmentally friendly. Describe the differences in ingredients, product design, or packaging and the benefits they provide.

7. **Entrepreneurship** Conduct research on a young entrepreneur whose business resulted from a new product or service idea. Find out how the person came up with the idea and then developed it into a successful business. Prepare a short oral report on your research.

Connect to 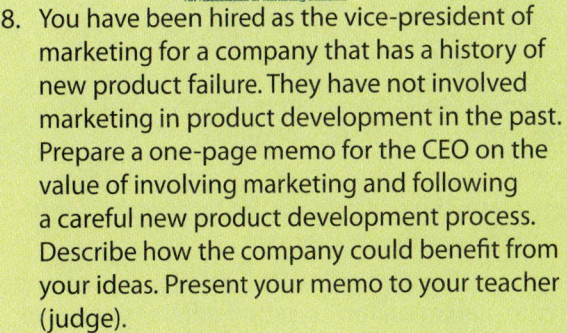 DECA
An Association of Marketing Students

8. You have been hired as the vice-president of marketing for a company that has a history of new product failure. They have not involved marketing in product development in the past. Prepare a one-page memo for the CEO on the value of involving marketing and following a careful new product development process. Describe how the company could benefit from your ideas. Present your memo to your teacher (judge).

Chapter 10 Assessment

Xtra!
Quiz Prep
school.cengage.com/marketing/marketing

Check Your Understanding

Now that you have completed the chapter, check your understanding of the lessons with these questions. Record the score that best represents your understanding of each marketing concept.

1 = not at all; 3 = somewhat; 5 = very well

If your score is 42–50, you are ready for the assessment activities that follow. If you score 33–41, you should review the lessons for the items you scored 1–3. If you score 32 or less, you will want to carefully reread the lessons and work with a study partner on the areas you do not understand.

Can you—

— describe the differences in how business people and consumers view products?

— identify the three important roles for marketers in the product development process?

— explain the three levels of product design: basic product, enhanced product, and extended product?

— describe differences between a product line and a product assortment?

— provide examples of ways packaging is used for protection and promotion?

— differentiate between consumer and business markets and between direct and derived demand?

— name the consumer purchase classifications and business product classifications?

— offer examples of how the same product can be marketed to both consumer and business markets?

— describe several ways that existing products can be considered to be new?

— list the steps in the new product development process?

Review Marketing Terms

Match the terms listed with the definitions.

1. Companies and organizations that purchase products for the operation of a business or the completion of a business activity

2. Something that is entirely new or changed in an important and noticeable way

3. Individuals or socially related groups who purchase products for personal consumption

4. The legal protection of the words or symbols for use by a company

5. The complete set of all products a business offers to its market

6. The quantity of a product or service needed to meet the needs of the consumer

7. A well-known name or symbol established by one company and sold for use by another company to promote its products

8. A group of similar products with slight variations in the marketing mix to satisfy different needs in a market

9. Anything tangible offered to a market by a business to satisfy needs

10. The quantity of a product or service needed by a business in order to operate at a level that will meet the demand of its customers

a. business markets
b. consumer markets
c. derived demand
d. direct demand
e. licensed brand
f. new product
g. product
h. product assortment
i. product line
j. trademark

Review Marketing Concepts

Match each of the products listed in the product column below with the correct product category.

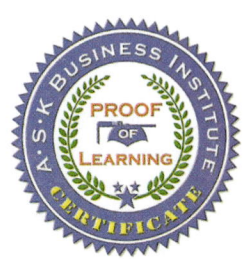

Product Category	Product
___ 11. Convenience good	a. $10,000 diamond ring
___ 12. Shopping good	b. Boeing 787 airplane
___ 13. Specialty good	c. One car battery
___ 14. Capital equipment	d. 500 gallons of window cleaner
___ 15. Operating equipment	e. Loaf of bread
___ 16. Supplies	f. 50 automobile tires
___ 17. Raw materials	g. Railroad car full of wheat
___ 18. Component parts	h. Cash register

19. True or False: A preference level of brand recognition exists when a consumer values a brand and chooses it if it is available.

20. True or False: When a consumer refuses to buy a brand, it is an example of the insistence level of brand recognition.

21. True or False: A trademark protects a brand by prohibiting its use by unauthorized companies.

22. True or False: If a product is purchased both by consumers and businesses, it makes sense to use the same marketing mix for each market.

23. True or False: Marketers who try to represent consumers during product planning will usually jeopardize their positions within the company.

24. True or False: The Federal Trade Commission requires that new products be clearly labeled as such for no more than nine months after they are introduced.

25. True or False: As part of the financial analysis of a proposed new product, businesses look at best-case and worst-case scenarios.

Marketing Research and Planning

26. Study advertisements, product catalogs, and merchandise available for sale in stores in your community. Identify at least three products that fit into each of the following categories:
    a. Products that are completely new
    b. Products that have significant changes or improvements
    c. Products that have been sold elsewhere but are new to this market

    Using those products, create a poster or a display that illustrates the concept of new products.

27. Business people often describe their products in terms of the physical characteristics and features. Consumers evaluate products on the basis of the needs that can be satisfied. For each of the following product descriptions, identify the consumer needs that can be satisfied or the benefits consumers will receive as a result of using the product.

Product Descriptions
a. cellular telephone with camera and MP3 player
b. online personal banking services
c. fax-ahead takeout restaurant menu
d. computerized tax preparation software
e. stationary bicycle with fitness monitor

28. Identify any consumer product that has been on the market for at least five years. On a large sheet of paper or poster board, draw three concentric circles to look like a practice target. Label the innermost circle BASIC PRODUCT. Label the middle circle ENHANCED PRODUCT. Label the outer circle EXTENDED PRODUCT. Study several brands of the product you selected to identify the components that are basic, enhanced, and extended parts of the product. Based on that analysis, use words or drawings to illustrate each part of the product in the appropriate circle.

29. Products are planned to respond to consumer needs. Those that best meet consumer needs are likely to be successful. For each of the common consumer needs listed, identify a product that has been successful for several years because it meets the need very well.

a. health
b. beauty
c. education
d. friendship
e. safety
f. economy
g. excitement
h. hunger
i. convenience
j. status

Marketing Management and Decision Making

30. Companies use product lines to be able to serve several target markets with the same basic product. Variations in the product's size, quality, features, etc., are used to meet specific needs of a market. Identify a consumer product that has a product line of at least four specific and different products. Prepare a chart that describes each of the specific products in the product line. For each one, identify the factors that make the specific product unique from the others in the product line. Then, describe the characteristics of the target market to which you believe each product is designed to appeal.

31. The Games & U Company is planning to update the marketing strategy for its line of children's swing sets. The products are sold to families through toy stores and discount stores and to daycare centers and community centers through the company's salespeople. To assist with planning, the company conducted a telephone survey of 360 previous purchasers of the swing sets. One-third of those surveyed were business customers, and the remainder were final consumers. The survey asked the respondents to identify what they liked most and what they liked least about the product. The results are shown in the table below.

a. Calculate the percentage of responses by business customers, final consumers, and total purchasers for each of the items listed. Prepare a bar graph that compares the responses in all three categories (business, final, and total).

b. Develop three specific recommendations for new product development based on the data. Make sure you apply the marketing concept when developing your recommendations.

	Business Customers	Final Customers
Liked Most		
A. Rapid delivery	15	0
B. Durability	50	28
C. Salesperson's product knowledge	30	12
D. Optional equipment	0	50
E. Safety features	20	110
F. Price	5	40
Liked Least		
G. Difficulty of assembly	10	95
H. Lack of credit terms	45	0
I. Limited product information when buying	0	40
J. Cost of replacement parts	60	35
K. Customer service	5	70

32. A new company has started to take advantage of people's interest in nature and the environment. It sells individual flowers that are no more than four inches tall and are planted in two-inch square plastic pots. The flowers are blooming and with proper care should live for several months or longer. They will be sold through supermarkets, gift shops, and even vending machines. Design a package that will protect the flower, provide an appropriate display, and provide information on the care of the flower. Also develop a brand name for the product.

Learn and Earn Project

The Learn and Earn Project is a chapter project that develops business and marketing skills. This project applies entrepreneurial skills to a single sales/service activity to be run as a real business venture.

Your group has earned a large sum of money baking cookies every Tuesday to sell in the school cafeteria. The school administration has given you permission to expand your business operation in school and throughout the community. You may consider opening a school store, taking custom orders from the community, and/or diversifying your product line. You must present a business plan for your extended operation. The main body of your plan consists of the following parts:

Executive Summary Write a one-page description of the project.

Introduction Explain the type of project proposed, a brief description of the major product/service involved, sources of information (resource materials, presentations, etc.), and a brief description of advisors and their involvement.

Analysis of the Business Situation Describe the trading area, market segment, and customer buying behavior.

Planned Operation of the Proposed Project Define the proposed organization, product/service, marketing strategies, and projected budget for the project.

Outcomes Describe the project implementation, unusual or unforeseen challenges or successes, and methods of handling them. Define the learning and earning outcomes of the project. Recommend improvements for the project. Describe plans for improving the learning and earning outcomes of the project.

Bibliography List all resources used.

Appendix The appendix is optional. Include in the appendix any exhibits appropriate to the written entry, but not important enough to include in the body. Items to include in the appendix may include sample questionnaires used, letters sent and received, general background data, and minutes of meetings.

Performance Indicators Evaluated

- Plan, organize, and conduct a sales/service project. (Strategic Management)
- Develop a business plan. (Strategic Management)
- Implement a promotional plan. (Promotion)
- Evaluate the planning, implementation, and outcome of the project. (Strategic Management)
- Demonstrate team communication, analytical and critical thinking, and production and time management skills. (Emotional Intelligence)

Go to the DECA web site for more detailed information.

Think Critically

1. Why must a successful business conduct research before expanding its operation?
2. What is the advantage of custom cookie orders?
3. What is the best means for taking custom cookie orders?
4. What special distribution considerations must be made for the product being sold?

www.deca.org

Services Need Marketing

©GETTY IMAGES/STOCKBYTE

Newsline

Celebrity Endorsements

Service marketers have long used celebrities to sell their companies' services. And they have often relied on their "gut instinct" to determine who to choose as a spokesperson: which actors have starred in the most popular movies, which singers are topping the charts, which athletes are having good years, who the gossip tabloids are (and are not) talking about. But how can a marketer be certain that a celebrity spokesperson is influencing the consumer in the desired manner? Davie-Brown Entertainment thinks it has the answer: a celebrity-evaluation index for brand marketers and their ad agencies. According to the company, the Davie-Brown Index, or DBI, is "an unbiased index that determines a celebrity's ability to influence brand affinity, consumer buying behavior and purchase intent."

The DBI is based on surveys of 1.5 million Americans, who scored more than 1,500 celebrities on eight key attributes: appeal, notice, trend-setting (their status in pop culture), influence (do they have any?), trust, endorsement (appropriateness as a spokesperson), aspiration (would we like to live like this person?), and awareness.

The raw scores are tweaked for various factors, such as the race, age, and sex of the survey participants, and then cross-referenced in a database that promises to help marketers decide which celebrity spokesperson can best help them sell their services. Marketers gain access to all the scores and rankings for a $20,000 annual fee.

Many advertisers and marketers have been sold themselves on the DBI's value. Major advertising agency BBDO New York is one of many already subscribing to the service. "I think it will be incredibly valuable when we look to marry various celebrities with various brands," says BBDO president John Osborn. Remember that the next time you see your favorite singer or ballplayer on TV, telling you to buy something.

Think Critically

1. Think of some celebrities who currently endorse services. Who seems to be an especially good match for the service and target market? Explain your reasoning.

2. Which of the eight key attributes of the DBI do you think a service marketer would value most highly? In what ways might the marketer's view depend on the particular service being sold?

school.cengage.com/marketing/marketing

Prepare for Performance

This chapter develops the following Performance Indicators from the DECA Competitive Events program.

Core Performance Indicators

- Acquire a knowledge of promotion of services to understand its nature and scope
- Position services to acquire desired image
- Understand the concepts needed to communicate information about services to achieve a desired outcome

Supporting Performance Indicators

- Explain the role of promotion in services as a marketing function
- Describe factors used by marketers to position services
- Explain the nature of service branding
- Build service brand

Go to **school.cengage.com/marketing/marketing** and click on Connect to DECA.

©BRITISH AIRWAYS

Visual Focus

Businesses that offer services are finding that there is an increased demand from consumers of all kinds. Marketing services is just as critical as marketing products. But creating the right marketing mix for services is not easy because a service cannot be seen or touched. Marketers must understand the unique qualities of services in order to create the right promotional strategies. Price and distribution strategies for services also offer unique challenges. Service marketers must stay focused on the marketing concept and the needs of the customer.

Focus Questions:

After reviewing the advertisement, who do you think British Airways is targeting? How is it promoting its services? Do you think the visual image used in the advertisement is effective? Why or why not?

Locate another advertisement for a service. Share your example with other students and discuss the impact of the message and the visual images used.

What Are Services?

GOALS

- Explain the growing importance of services to the U.S. economy.
- Describe four important qualities of services that are not shared by products.

KEY TERMS

service, *p. 308*

discretionary income, *p. 309*

intangible, *p. 310*

inseparable, *p. 311*

perishable, *p. 311*

heterogeneous, *p. 312*

marketing matters

Services are the biggest and fastest-growing part of the U.S. economy. By the beginning of the century, they accounted for four out of every five jobs, excluding agriculture. New services are continually being created in industries that didn't exist a few years ago, even as jobs in manufacturing are shrinking due to automation and competition from foreign competitors. Marketing services pose different challenges than marketing products because services possess four key characteristics that products do not share: They are intangible, inseparable, perishable, and heterogeneous.

Make a list of the jobs currently held by ten people you know. How many of them are in businesses that produce goods? How many of them are in businesses that provide services?

Growth and Importance of Service Industries

Marketing can be applied to both products and services. Products are tangible objects such as cars, DVDs, tables, and hamburgers. They are usually easy to see and understand. Services are more difficult to define, in part because the term is used in different ways.

In one sense, services are simply the support activities that are attached to the sale of a product, such as delivery, gift wrapping, and installation. In marketing, however, there is a second definition of the term. A **service** is an activity that is intangible, exchanged directly from producer to consumer, and consumed at the time of production. Services cover a broad range of activities, such as banking, entertainment, and computer repair.

The service sector is the largest and fastest-growing employment area of our economy. In 2006, nearly 79 percent of jobs in the United States were service jobs. Service jobs are found in industries such as communication, entertainment, information technology, recreation, and of course, marketing. According to the Bureau of Labor Statistics, the 18.9 million new jobs generated in the United States from 2004 to 2014 will be concentrated in service-providing industries.

Fast **FACTS**

In 1900, fewer than 30 percent of American workers had jobs in the service sector. Nearly half of all Americans worked in agriculture.

An example of a new service employment area with numerous job opportunities is health care. The gradual aging of the population will place the health care sector as a dominant source of overall projected employment growth. Health care employment—ranging from home health care and nursing to physical therapy—is projected to account for almost 1 out of every 5 new jobs by 2014. Figure 11-1 describes projected job growth in several service industries.

There are more services available today than ever before. People pay for child care, carpet cleaning, and security services. Businesses hire the services of landscapers, interior designers, electricians, and accountants. Services marketing is big business. There are many reasons for the growth of the service sector in our country.

Prosperity

The increased prosperity of our economy is one reason for the growth in the U.S. service sector. Today, people have more discretionary income to spend on services. **Discretionary income** is the amount of income left after paying basic living expenses and taxes. Americans are spending a greater percentage of their income on services and less on manufactured goods.

Automation

A second reason why the service industry is growing faster than the goods-producing industry is that the goods-producing industry is becoming more automated and less labor intensive. That means that companies use fewer people to produce their goods because of the increasing use of technology. Former manufacturing workers turn to the service industry for continued employment.

Complexity

A third reason that the service industry is growing is because many high-technology products require complex installation, repair, and training. Entire new service areas have opened up around the computer industry. Firms specialize in training, consulting groups specialize in applications, and other companies do nothing but service equipment. The rapid growth of the Internet and its use for communication and e-commerce have led to many new service jobs.

Foreign Competition

Finally, another contributing factor to the growth in the U.S. service industry is the expansion of international trade. The gains from international trade arise when businesses can produce goods and services more efficiently than other countries. In an effort to be more cost-efficient, manufacturers are shifting jobs that require less skilled labor to other countries where labor costs are lower. Cutting costs helps

FIGURE 11-1

Service-producing industries are projected to be the fastest growing in terms of job growth in the United States from 2004 through 2014.

Industry	10-Year Growth Rate	Number of Jobs Added
Education and Health Services	30.6%	5.19 million
Professional and Business Services	27.8%	4.57 million
Leisure and Hospitality	17.7%	2.22 million
Information Services	11.6%	0.36 million
Financial Activities	10.5%	0.85 million
Trade, Transportation, Utilities	10.3%	2.62 million

businesses stay competitive in an international market. U.S. workers who have lost manufacturing jobs due to this shift in labor often seek employment in the service sector.

Checkpoint ▶▶

What are four reasons for the growth of service employment in the United States?

Unique Qualities of Services

Four important characteristics distinguish services from products. Services are intangible, inseparable, perishable, and heterogeneous.

Intangible

The most important difference between goods and services is that services are intangible. **Intangible** means that the service cannot be touched, seen, tasted, heard, or felt. Examples of intangible services include haircuts, vision examinations, and vacation planning. Unlike products, they do not have a physical form.

The intangibility of services presents special challenges for marketers. Because people cannot see or handle a service, marketers must focus on the benefits customers will receive. Promotional activities need to be carefully conceived so consumers can visualize the benefits provided by the services. Tourism, for example, relies heavily on photos, posters, videos, and travelogues to entice customers to select vacation destinations. The objective and challenge of tourism marketing is to get customers to imagine what it is like to be at a particular tourist location.

World View

The World's Most Popular Sport

Baseball is said to be America's favorite pastime. Football is up there too. The most widely watched American sporting event in history was Super Bowl XXX, with 95 million viewers. But consider this: The 2006 soccer World Cup final game drew 284 million viewers worldwide.

In the United States, soccer is popular among kids, but by age 10, approximately 88 percent of them have moved on to baseball, football, basketball, and other sports. Internationally, however, soccer remains the biggest sport on the strength of incredibly passionate fans, nationalistic pride, and widespread media coverage. Marketers use the celebrity of famous international soccer players because they translate across many cultures and languages.

Soccer is growing in popularity in the United States, with a professional league and growing World Cup viewership, but it has a long way to go before it reaches the frenzied fan base it has overseas.

Think Critically

1. Internationally, soccer is called "football," and what NFL teams play in the United States is called "American football." How might this simple language difference concern marketers?

2. What types of brands might benefit from associating themselves with soccer in the United States? Which types might be better off associating themselves with "American football"?

Services Devise Unique Ways to Measure Performance

Service businesses that deal in highly perishable assets often develop industry-specific measures to track their performance from one time period to another. The lodging industry, for example, tracks "revPAR," which stands for "revenue per available room," to gauge how effectively hotel managers fill their rooms. Without such a measure, managers might be tempted to make their occupancy numbers look good by offering deep discounts on room rates. Or they might make their room rates look good (for hotel operators, higher rates are better) at the expense of high occupancy. With revPAR, room rates and occupancy percentages are combined in one easy-to-compare operating measure.

The airline industry uses similar performance measures such as "available seat miles," "revenue passenger miles," and "load factors." Available seat miles (ASMs) are equal to the total number of seats on all scheduled flights multiplied by the number of miles between the point of departure and the point of arrival for each flight. Revenue passenger miles (RPMs) are similar, except they include only seats that are occupied by paying passengers. Load factor is RPM divided by ASM, expressed as a percentage.

Think Critically

1. If a hotel manager's goal is to increase revPAR by 20% next month (and assuming he doesn't add more rooms), what are the different ways he can accomplish this?

2. If an airline's RPMs increase by 20% while its load factor declines, what is the likely explanation?

Inseparable

A second characteristic of services is that their production and consumption are inseparable. **Inseparable** means that the service is produced and consumed at the same time. Services such as a college class, a facial, or a car repair are produced and consumed simultaneously. In many cases, the customer is actually involved in the production of the service. When you drop money in a video game or pay for a ticket to a concert, you are demonstrating the inseparability of production and consumption in a service business.

This simultaneous production and consumption of services requires marketers to pay special attention to the distribution component of the marketing mix. Distribution involves having the service available where and when it is needed or wanted by the consumer. An example of ineffective distribution would be to locate a child day-care center in a retirement community. Because of its location, it probably would not attract many customers. On the other hand, a hotel limousine service located at the airport would be a good distribution strategy.

Perishable

Another characteristic of services is their perishability. **Perishable** means that services unused in one time period cannot be stored for use in the future. An example of this is a lawn care service. You cannot buy more than one grass cutting at a time. Though the person who cuts your grass might want to cut it ten times in the spring when the weather is cool, the service cannot be purchased that way.

Because of perishability, marketers are concerned about lost opportunity. An empty seat on an airplane cannot be sold later. After the plane has departed, the revenue that could have been earned from a paying customer is lost.

Airlines recognize that money is lost on each empty seat and can never be retrieved. That is why airlines offer discounted fares and special promotions when they know there will be empty seats. This is the airlines' attempt to overcome the perishability of their service.

The pricing component of the marketing mix is crucial in the sale of perishable services. Prices must be set to assure the business the greatest number of sales while covering expenses and allowing for a profit.

Heterogeneous

A final characteristic of services is heterogeneity. **Heterogeneous** means there are differences between services. Services are usually performed by people. Since people differ in their skill level or even their enthusiasm for a job, the service is often not consistent. One baseball game might be extremely different from another baseball game. The entertainment value of a baseball game in which your team wins may be different from a game in which your team loses. People who use a tax preparation service or an appliance repair business expect high-quality service. If customers cannot count on the type and quality of service, they are not likely to use that business.

Marketers who sell services need to pay particular attention to the marketing concept and satisfying the wants and needs of the consumer through the marketing mix. The heterogeneity of services allows marketers an opportunity to design services to meet the unique needs of a market segment.

Checkpoint ▶▶

What are the four important characteristics that distinguish services from products?

11-1 Assessment

Key Concepts

Determine the best answer.

1. Which of the following is *not* a reason for the growth of the service sector in the United States economy?
   a. America's prosperous economy
   b. increased on-the-job automation
   c. lower test scores among American students
   d. increased complexity of high-tech products

2. A service that is _____ cannot be stored for future use.

3. What percentage of jobs in the United States are service jobs?
   a. about 10 percent
   b. a little more than 30 percent
   c. 50 percent
   d. nearly 80 percent

4. True or False: An automobile manufacturer is a good example of a service business.

Make Academic Connections

5. **Visual Art** Draw or use technology to create a picture, graphic, or other visual representation of one of the unique qualities of services.

6. **Economics** Use library or Internet resources to find the percentage of service jobs in the economies of ten countries of your choosing. Present your findings in a graph format. Include the United States as one of the countries you select.

Connect to ◀ DECA
An Association of Marketing Students

7. You work for an amusement park. The owner wants your help in promoting the park. Because the park services are intangible, you must determine how to create favorable mental images of the services in the minds of prospective customers. Present two promotional ideas along with visuals to your teacher (judge).

Classifying Types and Evaluating Quality

GOALS

- Describe the various ways marketers categorize service businesses in order to develop effective marketing mixes.

- Identify the three types of service standards that are used to evaluate service quality.

KEY TERMS

labor intensiveness, *p. 314*

service quality, *p. 317*

marketing matters

Marketers classify service organizations in a variety of ways as they develop marketing plans. Businesses and other service organizations may be alike in some ways and quite different in others. A better marketing mix can be developed using a profile of an organization based on whether it targets businesses or consumers, whether it is profit-oriented or non-profit, whether it is labor intensive or relies more on equipment, how much contact service providers have with customers, and how much skill is required.

Maintaining a high level of customer satisfaction requires a high level of service quality. Marketers can evaluate service quality by comparing it to the services provided by competitors, by establishing objective standards, and by studying customer feedback.

Describe three different ways in which academic performance is measured at your school. What types of standards are used to measure effective performance?

Service Organization Classifications

A variety of organizations and businesses provide services to the public. Such diverse organizations as churches, dry cleaners, painters, day-care facilities, basketball teams, health clubs, barbers, law offices, and insurance companies are all service providers. The development and marketing of services can be quite different for various types of services.

It is helpful for marketers to classify services to develop viable and appropriate marketing plans. Service organizations can be classified by the type of markets they target, their organizational goals, their degree of labor intensiveness, the amount of contact they have with customers, and the level of skill they require.

Type of Market

Just as with products, there are two types of markets for services—business consumers and individual consumers. A business consumer might employ a cleaning service, a grounds service, a maintenance service, and an equipment repair service. Businesses that provide these services to other businesses must offer services tailored to business needs that are available where and when the business wants them.

An individual consumer, like you or your parents, might also employ a cleaning service, a lawn service, an auto maintenance service, and a computer repair service. For these consumer-oriented services, the target market and marketing mix will be quite different.

A marketing mix designed to reach business customers might stress personal selling and quantity price discounts. In contrast, a marketing mix designed to reach individual customers might stress personalized attention, advertising through print and broadcast media, and more standardized pricing. As a marketer, you need to know your market and its specific wants and needs in order to satisfy it.

Goals of the Organization

Some organizations have profit-making as a goal, while others operate as not-for-profit organizations. Most businesses that compete with one another in providing the variety of services for which people pay are profit-making organizations.

There are many not-for-profit organizations that also offer services. Examples of these types of organizations are universities, libraries, museums, government programs, churches, and social agencies. These organizations have goals and motives that are different from profit-making organizations. Their goals might be serving the community, making the public aware of a message or idea, increasing knowledge, or changing attitudes. Money is not normally a significant motivating factor for not-for-profit service organizations. Still, they are equally interested in delivering high-quality services that consumers need and want.

Labor Intenseness

Labor intensiveness refers to the amount of human effort required to deliver a service. Services range from those that are extremely labor intensive to those that are totally reliant on equipment. Most combine labor and equipment and fall somewhere in between.

Working in **Teams**

As a team, make a list of ten businesses from which you or your family recently purchased services. Then rank the businesses in three different ways: (1) most to least labor intensive; (2) highest to least amount of customer contact; and (3) highest to least skill level required. Write one or two paragraphs analyzing the different rankings.

Equipment-based services are provided with the use of machinery. These services require few people to deliver the services. Examples include automated car washes, dry cleaning, and vending machines. People-based services are provided through the work of people. Guitar lessons, manicures, teeth cleaning, and guided tours are examples of people-based services. These services are more labor intensive.

As a marketer, you will emphasize different parts of the marketing mix depending on whether your service is labor or equipment intensive. When marketing equipment-based services, you will pay special attention to the distribution or location of your services. Locating an automatic car wash on a busy avenue is more appropriate than on a quiet residential street. Placing an automatic bank teller machine in a safe, well-lighted place for a drive-through location gives customers a greater sense of security. You will also want to make sure the equipment is properly maintained.

With people-based services you will want to pay careful attention to the training of your personnel. You will train them in how to provide the service to satisfy your customers' wants and needs. A courteous, attentive, and efficient waiter is a good example of well-trained personnel.

Customer Contact

The amount of customer contact a service provider has is another way to classify services. Some services, such as barbers,

Judgment Call

Wireless Devices Raise Client Billing Issues

With the proliferation of wireless communications, providers of professional services such as lawyers and business consultants have the opportunity to drastically reduce down time. Now they can work—and bill clients for the time they spend doing it—virtually wherever and whenever they want. The troubling issue for clients is making sure they are getting their money's worth, because their business or affairs might not get a professional's undivided attention.

Internet-enabled phones and personal digital assistants (PDAs) allow a consultant to cruise down the highway while researching a client matter on the Internet or talking with clients on the phone. Safety issues not-withstanding, is it fair to bill a client for that time when the consultant simultaneously has to keep at least a few other things on her mind—such as the bridge abutments whizzing past and the semi in front of her that just hit its brakes?

Professional ethical standards aren't much help. Neither is the law. As long as a professional is providing something of value to a client, it's permissible to bill that time. And as one lawyer noted, it's possible to be just as distracted while sitting behind a desk as it is behind the wheel of a car.

Think Critically

1. If a lawyer is driving to a court appearance for client A and, while en route, takes a phone call from client B about an unrelated matter, do you think it would be fair to bill both clients for that time?

2. Do you think it would be feasible to bill clients at a reduced rate for time during which the professional's attention is divided?

---

doctors, schools, hotels, and restaurants, have high customer contact. Other services, such as equipment repair, lawn maintenance, and cable TV providers, have low customer contact.

Recognizing and responding to the level of customer contact is important if you are a service marketer. In general, the higher the contact, the more you must rely on personal selling as a promotional activity. With low-customer-contact businesses, it is important to stress planning to provide maximum customer satisfaction since there is not much opportunity to interact with customers.

Level of Skill

Another way to categorize services is by the level of skill the provider possesses. The most common way to categorize based on skill levels is to divide the providers into professional and nonprofessional groups. Professionals include providers whose services tend to be more complex and more highly regulated than nonprofessional services. The professional category would include accountants, pharmacists, teachers, physicians, therapists, and others who are required to have a combination of high-level skill, education, and a license to practice. The nonprofessional service group would include providers such as pet sitters, personal shoppers, hotel clerks, and bus drivers, whose jobs require less prescribed preparation.

Checkpoint ▶▶▶

Identify the various ways marketers categorize service businesses and organizations in order to develop effective marketing mixes.

Dealing with Rude and Discourteous People

How do you feel when someone cuts in front of you in line? What is your response to someone who drives aggressively?

There are a multitude of reasons for rude behavior. Fatigue, stress, insecurity, or ignorance may cause someone to behave badly.

Uncivil behavior has multiple ramifications. It angers people and diverts their energy from positive goals. Relationships are damaged when people behave badly.

Common courtesies help societies function peacefully and efficiently. Courteous behavior signals that you understand and respect the needs of the people around you. Courtesies soften daily interaction. People are more inclined to respond kindly when they have been treated kindly.

Most workplaces have explicit policies regarding expected behavior. Your behavior should conform to corporate expectations. Asking others about their political views or financial status is often taboo. You should refrain from revealing this type of information about yourself.

Define your personal boundaries. If anyone asks personal information that intrudes upon these boundaries, try to deflect the question. Saying "I prefer not to discuss that topic at work" is one method.

If you interact with customers who are behaving badly, you need to consider what has made them angry. Whether it is a perceived product failure or service error, keep in mind that they have a financial stake in the outcome of your discussion. Although it is fine to acknowledge their frustration or anger, try to focus the interaction on problem resolution. Keep your own emotions in check as you work with the customer.

You should never feel threatened because of someone's rude behavior. If their behavior has deteriorated to a level where safety becomes a concern, stop the conversation and leave the area.

There are a number of non-confrontational ways to deflect the disrespectful behavior of others. First, try to rely on yourself to handle the situation. As kindly as possible, point out the rude behavior to the person and its impact upon you. Jointly define the underlying concern that caused the behavior. Establish ground rules that will be used to maintain a respectful tone while discussing the issue. If the person violates these rules, remind them of the ground rules and ask for their agreement to comply with the rules before proceeding with the discussion. If the person continues to be rude or confrontational, you have the right to stop the conversation. Tell the person you will not participate in a conversation with a destructive tone.

Model the behavior you would like those around you to emulate. Proactively thank people as much as possible. It is harder for people to be nasty to someone who's shown them kindness and appreciation.

Develop Your Skill

Think of three examples where you have encountered rude behavior. For example, someone may have interrupted you during a conversation. Prepare a deflective, non-confrontational response for each of these situations. "Please let me finish what I was saying," could be used when interrupted.

Role-play positive responses to rude behavior with a friend or an adult. Evaluate which non-confrontational responses seem the most effective.

PHOTO: ©GETTY IMAGES/PHOTODISC

What factors would you use to rate the service quality of a restaurant?

© GETTY IMAGES/PHOTODISC

Evaluating Service Quality

The United States is becoming a service-oriented country. People are continually finding new services to offer, and consumers have more discretionary income to purchase these services.

With the large number of service businesses in the market today, a deciding factor for whether or not a company prospers is the quality of the service provided. **Service quality** is defined as the degree to which the service meets customers' needs and expectations.

Quality can be measured in a number of ways. It is controlled by the provider of the service. It might be measured by the qualifications of the provider or by the speed of service. It might also be based on cleanliness, efficiency, safety, comfort, or any number of variables.

To improve quality, an organization must first understand how customers decide which service they want and how they will judge the quality of the service. Three types of service standards can be used to evaluate service quality—competition,

performance standards, and customer satisfaction.

Competition

Marketers of services need to be aware of the nature and level of services their competitors are offering. Organizations must provide services that are at least equal in quality to what their competitors offer for the same price. Services must be positioned in a way that makes them unique and sets the business apart from its competition.

Performance Standards

A service organization should set its own service standards and communicate them to customers. Promotions should reinforce the commitment to quality service.

Just saying that the company is committed to quality isn't enough. An organization should have standards that support its advertising slogan. The standards should be measurable, such as: "Eighty-five percent of our arrivals will be on time" or "We will have no more than three customer complaints per month." The service should be evaluated regularly to see if it is meeting the standard. If not, the company should take corrective action.

Customer Satisfaction

The real test of service quality is customers' assessment of it. Firms use market research to find out exactly what customers think. One of the most important and useful indicators of customer satisfaction is repeat business. Do customers continue to come back to buy the service? If they do, it is a strong indication that they are satisfied with the service offered and that the organization is achieving its service standards.

Checkpoint ▶▶

What are the three types of service standards used to evaluate service quality?

11-2 Assessment

Xtra! Study Tools
school.cengage.com/marketing/marketing

Key Concepts

Determine the best answer.

1. Service organizations can be classified by
   a. the type of markets they target
   b. their organizational goals
   c. the amount of contact they have with customers
   d. all of the above

2. The amount of human effort required to deliver a service is called
   a. intangibility
   b. labor intensiveness
   c. heterogeneity
   d. service quality

3. Which of the following is *not* a type of service standard used to evaluate service quality?
   a. competition
   b. customer satisfaction
   c. professional or nonprofessional status
   d. performance standards

4. True or False: All service organizations are for-profit businesses.

Make Academic Connections

5. **Language Arts** Select a not-for-profit service organization in your community and write a two-page report about it, focusing primarily on the goals of the organization. Use library/Internet resources to help you prepare your report.

6. **Management** Create a brief survey that an owner of a child-care facility could use to measure customer satisfaction. Your survey should have no more than ten questions and should focus on topics important to customers of this particular service.

Connect to

7. Your team members manage a landscaping company that hopes to acquire jobs from both business and individual consumers. As a team, discuss the factors in your marketing mix that will be different for these two potential markets. Discuss how these factors will appeal to the different markets you seek. Make a three-minute team presentation to your teacher (judge) of your recommended marketing mix for each type of consumer.

Developing a Service Marketing Mix

GOALS

- Explain how businesses plan and promote services.
- Describe the importance of pricing and distribution of services.

KEY TERMS

endorsement, *p. 321*

bundling, *p. 322*

marketing matters

The unique characteristics of services make developing a marketing mix very challenging. A customer's ability to make a buying decision about a product is enhanced by the tangible nature of products. The purchase decision is easier because customers can see the products, smell them, touch them, or taste them. Because services are intangible, service marketers must help their customers visualize them. They do so by applying the principles of product/service planning, pricing, promotion, and distribution in ways that are suited to the nature of the services they provide. As with products, the objective is to satisfy their customers.

Make a list of five services that you have used in the past 24 hours, and describe how you arrived at your decision to use each of those services rather than competitive services or other alternatives.

Service Planning and Promotion

When dealing with services, businesses need to plan them carefully, keeping in mind the differences between services and products. Businesses also need to identify effective strategies for promoting their services.

Service Planning

When developing the service to be provided, service marketers must recognize that the services cannot be defined in terms of physical attributes. Instead, companies need to shape the attributes of the service to meet the needs and wants of consumers in the most satisfactory way possible.

UPS sells a service and communicates the attributes of its service: fast and reliable

©GETTY IMAGES/PHOTODISC

What mental image do you form about a bank's services when looking at this photo?

delivery. Banks also sell their services such as checking accounts, savings accounts, and loans. The attributes of bank services are dependability, convenience, low interest rates on loans, and high yields on savings. Both UPS and a bank must develop favorable mental images of their services by communicating their benefits.

Services are intangible, but businesses also recognize that customers pay attention to certain tangible elements associated with the service. The delivery trucks for UPS are a distinctive brown color, clean, and in good repair. Banks are typically quiet, low-key offices located in well-kept buildings to reinforce the idea that they are safe and responsible. Imagine the image you would have of your bank if the building needed major repairs, or if loud music blared at you as you entered.

Recognizing that tangible products are important, many service organizations provide physical items for customers to take along with them. Many times these items become a piece of specialty advertising as well. Dentists give patients toothbrushes, coffee shops give out mugs, and travel agencies may give away duffel bags. Banks provide checkbook covers, bands give out T-shirts at concerts, and professional hockey teams distribute pucks stamped with the team logo. In each case, the service organization is attempting to provide a tangible symbol and reminder of the service it provides.

Promotion

Services are sometimes considered difficult to promote. Something that cannot be touched is not as easily described in promotional strategies like print advertising or broadcast media. Services are also difficult to promote through personal selling since they are difficult to demonstrate. It is important to remember that, whether you are promoting a product or a service, you need to appeal to the buying motives of the target market and stress the benefits derived by use of the service.

Virtual Marketing

One-Stop Convenience

Personal computers liberated individuals and businesses from mainframes and computer operators by allowing them to process information from their desks. The Internet allowed people and businesses to buy and sell products online. Now application service providers, or ASPs, give service businesses the ability to provide highly personalized services over the Internet.

Financial consultants can subscribe to Internet-based planning services that allow them to merge clients' financial records in real time from multiple sources. Up-to-the-minute account data from banks, insurance companies, stockbrokers, mortgage lenders, and retirement plans are downloaded into a consolidated financial planning program with a few keystrokes.

With ASPs, clients and consultants no longer have to worry about working with outdated or incomplete information. Moreover, they can each view and analyze current data simultaneously from their own offices. So if someone wants to jump at a hot investment opportunity, the investor can run it by an adviser to see what overall effect it could have without either of them leaving their desks.

Think Critically

1. How are Internet-based ASPs superior to software programs that are installed on stand-alone personal computers?

2. What kinds of concerns might arise from having highly personal and confidential data floating around cyberspace?

One effective promotional strategy for services is to stress the tangible elements of the service. The well-dressed waiter, clean and undamaged late-model rental cars, and high-quality furnishings in a law office are all tangible elements associated with intangible services.

The last part of the promotion strategy is the nature and the timing of the message. The nature of the message should be such that it creates a mental image of the performance of the service. It must also foster the idea of satisfied needs in the customer. The timing of the promotional message must also be right. It must be close enough to the potential need and use for the service to be memorable and influence a decision.

©GETTY IMAGES/PHOTODISC

Would you be more likely to go see a movie if a friend recommends it? Why or why not?

Endorsements Many services use endorsements as a promotional strategy. An **endorsement** is an advertisement in which a satisfied user publicly expresses approval of a product or service. Sometimes endorsers are well-known role models for a target market. Celebrities and athletes often endorse products. Customers must identify with the endorser in order for the endorsement to be effective.

Word of Mouth Service organizations rely heavily on publicity and word-of-mouth promotion. People often consider information from friends to be very credible. Service sellers encourage word-of-mouth promotion. They ask satisfied customers to "tell a friend about us." They offer incentives to consumers who refer

new customers. They also develop publicity activities and even Internet "buzz" that encourage people to talk about their business.

Personal Selling Many marketers believe that personal selling is the most powerful promotional tool available. A well-trained sales staff can interact with customers to reduce their uncertainty, give reassurance, reduce doubts, and promote the reputation of the service provider. Careful training and management of customer-contact personnel is crucial to the success of a service organization.

Checkpoint ▶▶

What are the various strategies that marketers have found to be effective in promoting services?

Price and Distribution

Price and distribution of services each play a role in meeting customer expectations. Each needs to be carefully considered when developing marketing plans for services.

Price

In the past, pricing was not viewed as particularly important among service providers. Services were perceived to be unique, much like a monopoly. With increased competition and government deregulation of many industries, businesses began to see pricing strategies as a way to improve their market positions and to differentiate themselves from their competition.

Service businesses are in a good position to alter their pricing strategies because they can change prices fairly easily. A hair salon in your neighborhood can change its pricing schedule to meet competition or to create a new image. The amount or complexity of a service can be increased or decreased with the pricing strategy. For example, the hair salon can add styling specialists or additional services to justify price increases.

One interesting pricing strategy that many service providers use is called bundling. **Bundling** is the practice of combining several related services for one price. If you are planning a trip to Chicago, Illinois, the airline may attempt to bundle the price of a ticket, a rental car, a hotel, and two tickets to a Cubs game into one package for which you would pay one price. Another example of bundling is a college charging one price for a student's room, board, tuition, and fees.

Bundling is a type of quantity discount. A customer can purchase more services for a lower price than if they were purchased individually. This has advantages for both the customers and the sellers of services. The customer pays a reduced price and has the advantage of one-stop shopping. The service marketer forms mutually beneficial relationships with other service marketers to provide an appealing package for customers. The marketers are usually able to increase sales of their services by using effective bundling.

American Express bundles its credit services with FedEx Express shipping services in an attempt to meet the pricing and distribution needs of customers.

Distribution

The distribution of services is primarily concerned with having the service in a location and at a time that are convenient for the consumer. Many services for which people once had to travel to obtain are now provided in their homes. Pet grooming, computer maintenance, and tax preparation are examples of services that you can get at home if you prefer.

An important point to remember in marketing services is that the production and consumption of services happen simultaneously. That is, the service is performed, and you receive it at the same time. Therefore, the channels of distribution for a service are very short. In many cases, the channel is the producer and provider all rolled into one. A restaurant is a good example of this. The food is cooked and served at one site.

Fast FACTS

House calls were the norm for physicians until the end of the 19th century, but by 1971, only 1 percent of U.S. doctors were making home visits to patients. However, demand from America's aging population—many of whom have trouble getting to a physician's office—appears to be reviving the practice.

Some types of services, however, make use of intermediaries. For example, you might purchase an appliance from a large appliance store. However, if your appliance needs to be repaired, the store may contract with a local appliance repair business that will come to your home to make the repairs.

In planning a distribution strategy for a service, the most important element should be convenience for the consumers. Travel agents and airlines now use the Internet, making it easier for you to buy airline tickets and make other travel plans. Automated teller machines offer convenient locations and convenient hours. Video stores offer extended rental periods so people don't have to worry about returning movies the next day.

Checkpoint ►►

What is the key to effective distribution of services?

11-3 Assessment

Key Concepts

Determine the best answer.

1. In planning a distribution strategy for a service, the most important element should be
   a. providing the best possible price
   b. convenience for the consumers
   c. increasing the complexity of the service
   d. providing a tangible symbol of the service

2. A type of promotional strategy in which customers of a business recommend it to others is called
   a. endorsement
   b. word of mouth
   c. personal selling
   d. service planning

3. When promoting a service, marketers should
   a. stress the benefits derived from the service
   b. stress the tangible elements of the service
   c. time the promotion close to the potential need for the service
   d. all of the above

4. True or False: Service businesses are in a good position to alter their pricing strategies because they can change prices fairly easily.

Make Academic Connections

5. **Ethics** Celebrities often endorse services. The Federal Trade Commission (FTC) has several guidelines that must be followed by the endorser and the business being endorsed. Research the legal restrictions on endorsements and describe them in a two-page paper. Also, express your views on whether or not celebrities should actually use and like the services they endorse.

6. **Civics** List and briefly describe five tangible elements that are associated with services provided by your local government.

Connect to

7. You have been hired by a local optometrist to provide ideas for a physical item customers can take along with them after they have had their eyes examined. The optometrist hopes this item can serve as a piece of specialty advertising as well. Prepare a two-minute presentation with visual aids for the optometrist to describe at least three ideas for such an item. Deliver the presentation to your teacher (judge).

Check Your Understanding

Now that you have completed the chapter, check your understanding of the lessons with these questions. Record the score that best represents your understanding of each marketing concept.

1 = not at all; 3 = somewhat; 5 = very well

If your score is 42–50, you are ready for the assessment activities that follow. If you score 33–41, you should review the lessons for the items you scored 1–3. If you score 32 or less, you will want to carefully reread the lessons and work with a study partner on the areas you do not understand.

Can you—

___ describe what a service business is?

___ explain the growing importance of services to the U.S. economy?

___ identify four contributing factors to the growth of the service sector in the United States?

___ describe four important qualities of services that are not shared by products?

___ describe the various ways marketers classify service businesses in order to develop effective marketing mixes?

___ identify the three types of service standards that are used to evaluate service quality?

___ explain how businesses plan and promote services?

___ name three effective promotional strategies for services?

___ describe how businesses can use pricing strategies to improve their market position?

___ explain the importance of distribution of services?

Review Marketing Terms

Match the terms listed with the definitions. Some terms may not be used.

1. Incapable of being touched, seen, tasted, heard, or felt

2. The amount of human effort required

3. Produced and consumed at the same time

4. An activity that is intangible, exchanged directly from producer to consumer, and consumed at the time of production

5. The practice of combining several related services for one price

6. The degree to which a service meets customers' needs and expectations

7. Incapable of being stored for use at a future time

8. An advertisement in which a satisfied user publicly expresses approval of the product or service

a. bundling
b. discretionary income
c. endorsement
d. heterogeneous
e. inseparable
f. intangible
g. labor intensiveness
h. perishable
i. service
j. service quality

Review Marketing Concepts

9. _____ are tangible objects that can be purchased and resold.

10. True or False: Services unused in one time period can be stored for use in another.

11. True or False: A portion of the long-term decline in employment in some manufacturing industries can be linked to the expansion of trade.

12. True or False: Not all services require the same level of skill.

13. By 2014, health care employment is projected to account for nearly _____ of all new jobs created in the United States.
    a. 10 percent   c. 50 percent
    b. 20 percent   d. 80 percent

14. There are two types of markets for services: _____ and _____ .

15. Which of the following is *not* an equipment-based service?
    a. automated car washes
    b. teller machines
    c. a haircut
    d. telephone calling cards

16. Many marketers believe that personal _____ is the most powerful promotional tool available.

17. With increased competition and government deregulation, businesses now use _____ strategies as a way to improve their market positions and to differentiate themselves from their competitors.

18. True or False: Because services are heterogeneous, it is more difficult for marketers to design services to meet unique market needs.

19. True or False: Services characteristically have short distribution channels.

20. The service sector is growing faster because manufacturers are becoming more _____ and less labor intensive.

21. True or False: The real test of service quality is customers' assessment of it.

Marketing Research and Planning

22. On a separate sheet of paper create a table with three columns. Title the columns: Business Consumer Market, Final Consumer Market, and Combination of Both Markets. Use the telephone directory to identify service businesses that appeal to each of these markets. Write the names of the businesses in the appropriate column. Find at least three businesses for each column. Compare your results with your classmates' tables.

23. A dry cleaning business handed out a questionnaire to all customers who brought in or picked up clothes during the month of October. Of the 1,435 questionnaires distributed, 705 were returned with the following results.
    i. How often do you take items to a dry cleaning business?
    Results: At least once a week: 178; Twice a month: 199; Once a month: 200; Less than once a month: 128

    ii. Rate the factors shown in the table for this business.
    Results: Shown in table below.
    a. What percentage of the surveys were returned?
    b. What percentage of the customers use dry cleaning services at least once a week? Twice a month? Once a month? Less than once a month?
    c. Based on the rating of the store features and service quality, make three recommendations that management can implement to improve customer service.

24. Developing an appropriate marketing mix for a service is as important as developing the appropriate mix for a product. Develop a marketing mix for a service business that includes a description of the service, the pricing strategy, the promotional strategy, and a plan for distribution. Choose from one of the following service businesses:
    - Tutoring and study skills
    - Video arcade
    - Chimney cleaning service
    - Hot air balloon rides
    - Golf lessons
    - Coin-operated laundry

	Very Satisfied	Satisfied	Not Satisfied
Location of the store	599	100	6
Hours of operation	200	300	205
Turnaround time	351	257	97
Friendliness of staff	264	254	187
Quality of service	532	101	72

25. Bundling is an effort by service industries to sell related services in one location and for one price. Identify at least five services that can be bundled for each of the following service businesses:
    - Evening entertainment
    - Insurance
    - Automobile upkeep
    - Home appliance repair
    - Lawn maintenance

26. Search the Internet to find web sites of ten service businesses. Make a list of the businesses, what services they produce, their major target markets, and their major channels of distribution. How do they use their web sites to market their businesses?

27. Search the newspaper and magazine ads or the Internet and find an advertisement for bundled services of some sort. How much is the advertised price, and what services or products are included in the package deal? How much would each of the component services and products cost if they were bought individually? How much of a savings, if any, does the bundled price represent?

Marketing Management and Decision Making

28. As the owner of an automobile washing and detailing business, you have noticed that although the population of your community is growing, your business is not. You believe that you provide a quality service, but you are concerned about your business volume. You decide to evaluate your service quality. Using the service quality evaluation criteria, develop at least four specific things you can do to determine your level of quality.

29. As a marketing specialist, you have been asked to speak to a group of service providers about the future of the service industry and how service providers can effectively market their services. In order to do this, you have developed the following topics on which to speak:
    1. Future of services
    2. Differences between products and services
    3. Different types of services
    4. Importance of the marketing mix

    Using these topics, prepare a speech describing each of the items. Use as many examples as possible.

30. Services can be classified based on the following criteria:
    Type of market (business or individual)
    Labor intensiveness (low, medium, high)
    Customer contact (low, medium, high)
    Level of skill (low, medium, high)
    Organizational goals (profit or not-for-profit)

    Classify each of the following services by these criteria and create a chart as shown below to illustrate their appropriate classification. As an example, item a is shown in the table.
    a. An insurance policy protecting a professional volleyball team from loss of the team's star player
    b. A new paint job for an old car
    c. Three empty horses on a circus carousel
    d. A manicure while the customer's hair is styled
    e. A heart bypass operation performed at the Mayo Clinic
    f. An opera performed by a local community group
    g. Clean uniforms provided by the employer
    h. A long-distance telephone call
    i. Renting a motel room
    j. A golf course
    k. A high school education
    l. Cable television installed in a new neighborhood

Type of Market	Labor Intensiveness	Customer Contact	Level of Skill	Organizational Goal
a. Business	low	low	high	profit

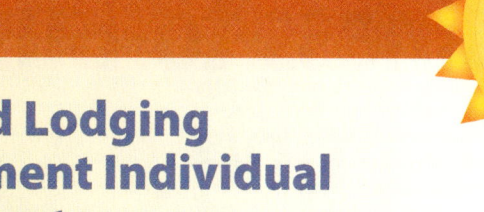

Hotel and Lodging Management Individual Series Event

The Hotel and Lodging Management Individual Series Event consists of a 100-question multiple-choice comprehensive exam and role-plays. The role-play portion of the event requires participants to accomplish a task by translating what they have learned into effective, efficient, and spontaneous action. The five performance indicators specify the distinct tasks the participant must accomplish during the role-play. Students have ten minutes to prepare their strategy for the role-play and another ten minutes to explain their strategy to the judge. The judge can ask questions during or after the presentation.

Hotel guests have always craved pampering. Upscale hotels have catered to guests by offering club-members-only floors. Now, many hotels are turning club floors into retreats where members choose their pillow and have access to a free iPod and cappuccino day or night. Because most hotels are trying to boost their revenue by raising room rates 5 to 25 percent, they are raising the customer service bar to justify the higher room rates.

Hotels must be aware of the current trends. More business travelers are bringing their families to business meetings. These travelers demand club lounges where their families can eat free breakfast. Women business travelers are requesting restricted-access floors and more exclusive lounges in place of bustling lobby bars.

The Towers Hotel chain has decided to increase its customer service efforts. The hotel chain has added fireplaces to rooms. Free wireless Internet service and new computers included in the hotel rooms allow guests to download music. The hotels have also added Starbucks single-serve coffee machines in all hotel rooms. Self-service refrigerators allow guests to help themselves to drinks or yogurt. In addition, the hotel offers a free delicious lunch (sandwiches and salads) to all guests.

To counter the additional costs of the new services, the Towers Hotel has increased room rates by 20 percent. You must create a promotional strategy that emphasizes all of the new amenities and downplays the increased room rates.

Performance Indicators Evaluated

- Determine services to provide to customers. (Product/Service Management)
- Demonstrate a customer-service mindset. (Emotional Intelligence)
- Explain the role of customer service in creating an image. (Product/Service Management)
- Explain factors affecting pricing decisions. (Pricing)
- Explain the types of promotion to be used. (Promotion)

Go to the DECA web site for more detailed information.

Think Critically

1. Why are some complimentary hotel amenities not actually free?
2. Why should the Towers Hotel consider using different promotions for different target markets?
3. Will all hotel guests want the extra perks?
4. What type of frequent guest program could the hotel consider implementing?

www.deca.org

Business-to-Business Marketing

©GETTY IMAGES/PHOTODISC

Newsline

Coding System Unlocks Business Markets

The U.S. business market includes nearly 7.5 million firms and over 116 million employees. Each business purchases goods and services, with some spending millions of dollars each day. The largest businesses will budget several billion dollars each year to buy products and services. The business market consists of producers, manufacturers, retailers, wholesalers, and service providers.

Selling to businesses can be very complex. Sorting through all of the differences among businesses to find the best target markets requires careful study and a great deal of information. But help is available in the form of a tool known as the North American Industry Classification System (NAICS). It was created to identify organizations in similar industries and to identify their primary activities, size, location, and other important descriptive information.

NAICS uses a six-digit code. It replaced the previous Standard Industrial Code (SIC) classification system in the late 1990s. The SIC system used four-digit codes and had become outdated with the creation of many new industries that didn't even exist when the system was designed by the U.S. government in the 1930s. The NAICS system is also used in Canada and Mexico, facilitating trade between those countries and U.S. businesses. The NAICS was updated in 2007 to clarify and provide additional classifications in the telecommunication and information industries. In addition, a new North American Product Classification System (NAPCS) was introduced that focuses on the products produced by the service industry.

To target business customers, most companies start with NAICS information. In that way, they can identify businesses with similar purchasing needs. They can track increases and decreases in the numbers of businesses, the volume of sales in the industry, and even changes in levels of employment. It is an important tool for marketing planning. Reports on industry information using NAICS codes are prepared by government agencies as well as business, trade, and professional organizations.

Think Critically

1. Using the Internet or library, find a NAICS code for a business that makes engines for farm equipment. What do the component numbers of the code mean?

2. How do businesses use the NAICS to find markets for their products or services?

school.cengage.com/marketing/marketing

Prepare for Performance

This chapter develops the following Performance Indicators from the DECA Competitive Events program.

Core Performance Indicators

- Understand the concepts and processes needed to obtain, develop, maintain, and improve a product or service mix in response to a market
- Employ product mix strategies to meet business-to-business customer expectations
- Describe the use of target marketing

Supporting Performance Indicators

- Determine product development objectives
- Employ sales techniques to enhance customer relationships
- Determine customer needs
- Evaluate market opportunities
- Facilitate customer buying decisions

Go to **school.cengage.com/marketing/marketing** and click on Connect to DECA.

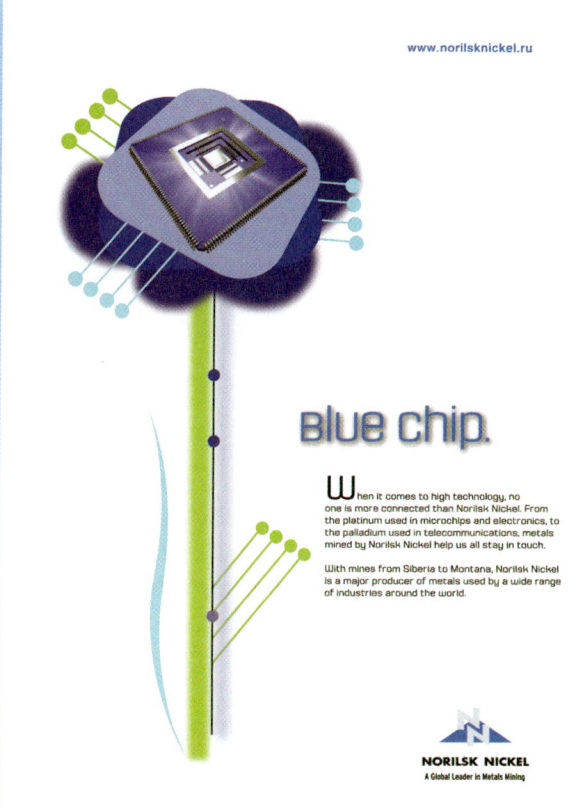

COURTESY, NORILSK NICKEL

Visual Focus

Most consumers are unaware of the many products and services that businesses sell to other businesses. There are many opportunities in the business-to-business market. Marketing strategies must be as carefully developed for business customers as for final consumers. Business-to-business marketing begins with identifying target markets and their needs in order to develop an effective marketing mix.

Focus Questions:

After reviewing the advertisement, what types of products do you believe Norilsk Nickel sells? Who might be some of its customers? Why would a company that sells to other businesses benefit from advertising? If you were a business customer, would the advertisement interest you in Norilsk Nickel? Why or why not?

Locate another advertisement for a product or service that is being marketed to business customers. Share your example with other students and discuss how business-to-business advertising is similar to or different from consumer advertising.

Business-to-Business Exchanges

GOALS

- Explain the reasons businesses buy things from other businesses.
- Define the five major classifications of business consumers.
- Describe the common characteristics typical of business markets.

KEY TERMS

business-to-business marketing, *p. 330*

purchasing, *p. 331*

marketing matters

Any exchange of products and services involves a buyer and a seller. People most often think about businesses as sellers and individual consumers as buyers. Actually, the majority of exchanges do not involve the final consumer. Instead, most exchanges take place between businesses. One business buys products and services from another business. Business-to-business marketing is a very important part of our economy.

Marketers should be aware that businesses buy products and services from other businesses for several distinct reasons. While there are five major types of business consumers, purchasing decisions of business customers tend to share a number of characteristics.

Every time a consumer buys a car, that one purchase is the culmination of hundreds of business-to-business exchanges that had to take place in order for that car to be available at that time and place. List ten business-to-business exchanges that had to be completed in order for a consumer to be able to purchase an automobile.

Reasons for Business Purchases

Businesses need a variety of products and services to be able to carry out their day-to-day operations. The various types of products and services bought and sold by businesses are identified in the business product classification system shown in Figure 12-1. The exchange of products and services between businesses is known as **business-to-business marketing**.

There are many reasons why businesses purchase products and services from other businesses. A producer or manufacturer usually does not own everything it needs to develop the products it sells. Some companies do not have the raw materials used

in production. Many of the component parts that are used in manufacturing products are produced by other companies. Purchasing products to be incorporated into a production process and then resold is an important part of business-to-business marketing.

Some businesses purchase products for direct resale to other customers. It is not efficient to sell every product or service directly from the producer to the final consumer. Therefore, other businesses facilitate the marketing and sale of products. Typically, those businesses do not change the physical form of the product, but they may repackage it. They will also provide a

FIGURE 12-1
Several types of products and services are bought and sold by businesses.

Categories of the Business Product Classification System	
Capital Goods	The building and major equipment of business
Operating Equipment	Equipment used in the daily operation of the business
Supplies	Consumable materials used in the operation of the business
Raw Materials	Unprocessed materials that are incorporated into the products by the business
Component Parts	Partially or completely processed items that become a part of the products produced by the business
Services	Tasks performed in the operation of the business or to support the production, sale, or maintenance of the business's products and services

number of the marketing functions as they complete the selling process.

A third reason for business purchasing is to obtain products and services needed to operate the business. Buildings and equipment are produced by one company for sale to others. Companies need a variety of supplies for their day-to-day operations. Many businesses purchase professional services from attorneys and accountants, business services from advertising agencies and printing companies, and services that support the products they sell such as delivery and repair services.

Checkpoint ▶▶

Name three reasons that businesses purchase products and services from other businesses.

Purchasing as a Marketing Activity

Purchasing is an important activity of marketing. **Purchasing** includes determining the products and services needed, identifying the best sources to obtain them, and completing the activities necessary to obtain and use them. Businesses must do an effective job of purchasing the products and services they need if they are to be successful. If a business purchases the wrong products or products that are of poor quality, if it pays too much for the products it purchases, or if a supplier is not able to deliver products as promised, the business will be unable to operate effectively and serve its customers well.

Types of Business Purchasers

Do you think marketing to businesses and organizations should be done in a different way than marketing to final consumers? If you just picture the two types of customers in your mind, you might believe the answer is yes. Consider selling radios to an automobile manufacturer compared to selling a radio to a consumer to be installed in that person's car. You see a large business purchasing hundreds and thousands of radios versus one person buying a single radio. You can expect that the business has very different reasons for purchasing the radios than does the individual. It is reasonable to believe that different procedures would be used to gather information and make a decision about the radio that will be purchased.

Even though those differences are great, the basic marketing process is not different. It is necessary to identify the target markets, determine their characteristics and needs, and develop a marketing mix that meets their needs better than other companies. Just as all final consumers are not the same, businesses also have important differences that require different marketing strategies.

Business Customer Classifications

One way of classifying business customers is by the type of organization. The major categories of businesses are producers, resellers, service businesses, government, and nonprofit organizations. All businesses and other organizations purchase the products and services they need to operate, including capital equipment, operating equipment, and supplies. They make purchases that are appropriate for the types of activities they perform.

Producers About 1.2 million businesses in the United States are involved in production. Those businesses range from farms and ranches, mining companies, and oil refiners to manufacturers of business and consumer products. The largest production category is construction with over 700,000 companies. Producers can be very small businesses that employ only a few people and spend less than $10,000 a year on purchases or companies as large as General Motors Corp. or Procter & Gamble that employ several hundred thousand people worldwide and may easily spend $10 million in one day on purchases. Producers are customers for raw materials and component parts as well as the other products and services needed for business operations.

What are the considerations for a reseller, such as a supermarket, when making purchasing decisions?

Resellers Wholesale and retail businesses are a part of the product distribution system connecting producers with consumers. They purchase products for resale and typically complete other marketing activities as a part of the distribution channel. They might offer distribution and storage services, promote products through advertising and personal selling, extend credit to consumers, and complete a variety of other marketing activities to meet customer needs. Over 1.1 million retailers and 430,000 wholesalers operate as resellers in the U.S. economy.

Service Businesses More companies in the United States produce services than produce products for resale. More than five million service businesses were operating in the United States in 2005. That number is growing faster than any other category of business.

Most of the purchases made by a service provider are used in the operation of the business and to develop the services it sells. Some service businesses, such as rental firms, actually purchase products that are used by final consumers. Rather than selling the products to those consumers, they retain title and allow the consumer to use the product. Some types of rental businesses are well known, like video stores, apartments, and stores that rent formal wear for proms and weddings. Other types of rental businesses are not as well known. Businesses leased automobiles to other businesses for many years, but it has only recently become a popular option for individual consumers. When you go to an amusement park, you can rent a video camera for the day. Investors build huge office buildings and then lease the space to companies.

Government Federal, state, and local government agencies provide services to citizens and develop and enforce laws and regulations. The total purchases made by the U.S. government make it the largest single customer in the world. From a supplier's viewpoint, the government is made up of thousands of separate customers with different needs and purchasing procedures.

Government agencies and institutions purchase the full range of products, from raw materials to supplies and services. Some government organizations, such as city utilities, purchase raw materials and operate very much like privately owned producers. Part of the military operates like wholesalers and retailers when it purchases products for distribution and sale to military personnel and their families through commissaries and stores on military bases.

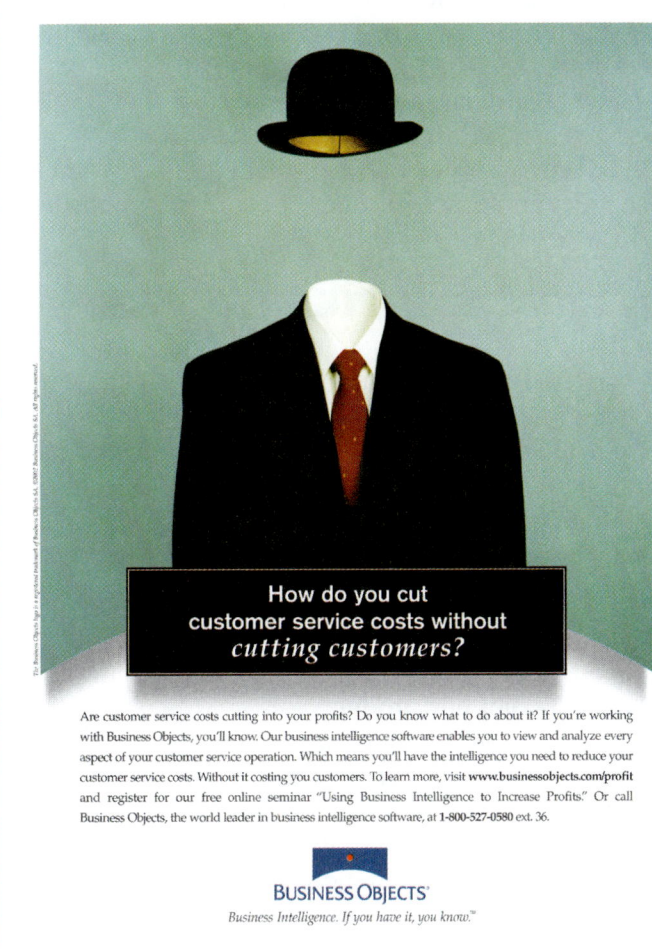

Business Objects is marketing a product that could meet the business needs of all types of organizations because all businesses have customer service concerns.

Nonprofit Organizations Many organizations in our communities do not operate in the same way as private businesses. They have specific goals or clients to serve, and that service is the primary reason for their operations. While they need an adequate budget to operate, profit is not their primary motive. Most have a nonprofit designation from the U.S. Department of Treasury so that they are tax-exempt. Common examples of these organizations are schools, museums, churches, social service organizations such as shelters and community centers, colleges and universities, professional organizations, and some social clubs.

As with government agencies, non-profit organizations operate to provide services to specific client groups. Therefore, they need to purchase those things necessary to offer the services. Those purchases could be only a limited number of operating supplies and products, or they could be the full range of products and services in the business products classification system.

Checkpoint ▶▶▶

What are the five major classifications of business consumers?

Characteristics of Business Markets

Businesses that sell to other businesses need to understand how those markets are different from final consumer markets. There are some common demographic characteristics and purchasing behaviors that are typical of business markets.

Derived Demand

Businesses do not buy products for final consumption. Instead, they make purchases to be used directly or indirectly in meeting the needs of final consumers. Therefore, the types and quantities of products and services demanded by the business are based on the level of demand of their customers. In other words, the business's demand is derived from its customers' demand.

Purchase Volume

Business customers usually purchase in much greater quantities than final consumers. While final consumers may buy the same product again, their needs change much more frequently than business purchasers. Because businesses are making purchases to be incorporated into other products or for operations, they usually purchase large quantities of those products. They are less likely to make major changes in the items purchased unless their customers' needs change dramatically.

Similar Purchases

Businesses that produce or resell similar products and services usually have common purchasing needs. Consider two furniture stores serving the same market. They will likely purchase the same types of furniture and home accessories for resale and will buy similar capital and operating equipment for their stores. In most communities, there will be several companies that mix concrete for use in construction projects. They need to purchase the same raw materials, such as cement, sand, and stone, as well as similar equipment, such as mixing facilities, trucks, and concrete pumps to operate the business.

Number of Businesses

The number of business customers for specific products is usually smaller than the number of final consumers who will purchase a product. That is typically an advantage for those who sell to the business market. Having fewer customers means that it should be easier to maintain contact with the customers and understand their needs. Because purchase volume for each customer is high, having fewer customers should not restrict the amount of total sales a company can make in the business market.

Working in Teams

As a team, identify five manufacturers and one product each of the manufacturers would purchase and use as a part of its operations. Now identify an important customer group each business serves and discuss how the demand by that group affects the derived demand for the product purchased by the manufacturer.

Buyer/Seller Relationship

Businesses that produce products for sale to final consumers often have little contact with the customer. Because customers are located throughout the country and sometimes throughout the world, it would be difficult to distribute products directly from the seller to the buyer. Retailers and wholesalers are usually a part of the distribution system for consumer products. The retailer is responsible for selling the product and often for responding to any customer problems and even some service needs.

In business-to-business selling, distributing the product directly to the business customer is more typical. The selling business is responsible for contacting prospective customers, selling the product, and providing follow-up support and service as well as solving customer problems. Those activities are possible because of the lower number of customers. Also, in some business markets, the businesses that purchase similar products are in the same industry and may be located in the same geographic area of a country.

Checkpoint ▶▶

What are common characteristics typical of business markets?

12-1 Assessment

Xtra!
Study Tools
school.cengage.com/marketing/marketing

Key Concepts

Determine the best answer.

1. Consumable materials used in the operation of the business are
   a. operating equipment
   b. supplies
   c. raw materials
   d. services

2. The largest category of business customers in the United States is
   a. producers
   b. wholesalers
   c. retailers
   d. service businesses

3. True or False: The total purchases made by the U.S. government make it the largest single customer in the world.

4. Compared to final consumers, business customers
   a. purchase in larger quantities
   b. base their purchases on derived demand
   c. more frequently buy directly from the producer
   d. all of the above

Make Academic Connections

5. **Economics** Visit the web site of the U.S. Census Bureau (www.census.gov). Enter "county business patterns" in the search box and locate census data on the number of businesses in your county. Prepare a pie chart that compares the number of manufacturers, wholesalers, and retailers in your county.

6. **Research** Use a business or telephone directory for your community. Identify two businesses or organizations that represent each of the types of business customers discussed in the lesson. For each, identify an important product or service it provides and one that it purchases. Prepare a table to present the information.

Connect to ◀DECA
An Association of Marketing Students

7. A local home-cleaning business is considering expanding and focusing on business customers. Develop a two-minute presentation to be presented to the owner of the business on the similarities and differences between its current market and the new business customers. Give your presentation to your teacher (judge). Be prepared to answer questions about your ideas.

Making Business Purchase Decisions

GOALS

- Describe how businesses make new purchase, modified purchase, and repeat purchase decisions.
- Explain the roles played by purchasing specialists.
- Identify issues that often arise in international purchasing.

KEY TERMS

purchase specifications, *p. 337*

reorder point, *p. 338*

reciprocal trading, *p. 340*

marketing matters

Effective marketing requires that the seller understand the buyer and how the buyer makes purchase decisions. Individual consumers go through a careful process of gathering information and evaluating choices before making a decision. Business consumers also use a careful decision-making procedure, but that procedure has some important differences from the one used by final consumers. Business buying decisions tend to be more rational and directly related to business needs. Purchasing activities frequently require the hiring of purchasing specialists and the involvement of top managers. International purchasing procedures present an additional set of issues.

Select a product or service that will be used by a business as a part of its operations or will be incorporated into another product. Describe the important factors you believe the business will consider when planning to purchase the product or service. Compare your list of factors with those of other students.

The Buying Decision

In business purchasing, the decision to buy is based on an identified business need. While the decisions of individual consumers are also based on needs, they are frequently influenced by emotion. Business purchasing is usually a rational process. The product or service purchased will be the one that best meets the needs of the business at a reasonable price. Purchases must improve the business or be resold to customers. Purchases must be cost-effective in order to contribute to profits. Therefore, business purchasing is done very carefully.

Make or Buy

Businesses, especially manufacturers, do not always purchase the products and services they need. They may first decide if they are able to make the product or provide the service with their own resources. For example, most businesses have a variety of printing needs. A company may want to send catalogs to customers or use direct mail advertising. It may use a large number of forms and other printed materials in the business. The company may be able to find several printing companies to produce the materials needed. It may also be able to establish its own internal printing department. If the volume of printing is large enough and printing is needed regularly, the company may save money by doing its own printing.

Incremental Cost Decisions

Whenever there is an opportunity for a business-to-business exchange of products or services, both the buyer and the seller need to be aware of two measurements of cost in addition to the total cost of the exchange. Average cost is the cost per unit. It is derived by dividing the total cost by the number of units being exchanged. If you buy 100 units for $2,500, that is $25 per unit. Average cost can be calculated for components, raw materials, or services.

Incremental cost is a decision-making tool. It differs from average cost in that it is calculated by examining the costs of an exchange in increments. If 100 units cost $2,500, but 200 units cost $4,000, the average cost would be $25 or $20, respectively. More significantly, perhaps, the incremental cost

of the second hundred units is only $15 each ($4,000 − $2,500 = $1,500 ÷ 100). A buyer might decide that at $15 it is better to buy a larger quantity, even if it means tying up cash in inventory.

Conversely, if a seller's incremental production costs decline for larger quantities, it might propose a long-term supply contract that benefits both parties.

Think Critically

1. If 1,000 units cost $50,000 and 2,000 units cost $80,000, what is the incremental cost per unit of the second 1,000 units?

2. If the cost per unit up to 10,000 units is $1, and unit cost is progressively reduced by 10% for each additional 10,000-unit increment, what is the incremental cost of the last unit if a buyer orders 40,000 units?

Types of Purchases

When a business decides to buy rather than make the products it needs, it develops specific purchasing procedures. Three different types of purchasing situations determine the procedure that will be followed. Those situations are a new purchase, a modified purchase, and a repeat purchase.

New Purchase The most difficult purchasing situation is when a business buys a product or service for the first time. Examples of new purchases for many companies are buildings, major pieces of equipment, and the raw materials and component parts needed when manufacturers develop a new product.

Because the product has never been purchased before, the business has no experience with it and may have no experience with the companies that sell the product. The business must carefully determine the needs it must meet with the purchase,

decide on the types of products that can meet those needs, and identify the companies that offer the products.

Often the company takes a great deal of time planning for the purchase. The company may develop purchase specifications that the selling companies must meet. **Purchase specifications** are detailed requirements for construction or performance of a product. The buyer will also have expectations in terms of the supply needed, delivery methods and schedules, and technical support required for use of the product.

Modified Purchase A company may find that the products purchased in the past do not totally meet current needs and so require some changes. The company will identify the changes or improvements needed. The modifications will be communicated to the company that has been selling the original product, and the company will have the opportunity to meet the new requirements. Other companies may be given the chance to supply the modified product if major changes are planned or if the buyer is not satisfied with the current supplier.

Retailers use modified purchasing when they have had success with a basic product and want to offer additional features and options to customers. Companies that have purchased computer systems may want to purchase additional computers but may want them upgraded with current technology. A company may have contracted with an accounting firm for bookkeeping services and now may want to extend the contract to include tax preparation.

Repeat Purchase Most business purchases are very routine. The same products and services are purchased over and over. The buyer is very aware of the needs that are being met with the purchase and has identified the product that meets those needs. In many cases, the buyer has developed a good relationship with a seller and does not even consider buying from another company. When a new supply of the product is needed, the company just reorders from the same seller.

The purchasing process may become so routine that it is handled by a computer. The computer maintains the inventory level of the product. As the product is used or sold, the inventory level decreases until it reaches the reorder point. The **reorder point** is the level of inventory needed to meet the usage needs of the business until the product can be resupplied. When the reorder point is reached, the computer issues a purchase order to the supplier, and the product is shipped.

When the product being purchased is not unique, with many companies offering the same product for sale, repeat purchasing becomes very competitive. Since the buyer realizes that the same product can be purchased from several sellers, price may become an important factor. The purchasing company may pressure the suppliers to reduce the price. This situation happens regularly with companies that sell to large retailers and companies that sell common operating equipment and supplies to businesses.

Checkpoint ▶▶

How do new purchases, modified purchases, and repeat purchases differ?

Purchasing Requires Specialists

Purchasing in businesses occurs continuously and involves thousands and even millions of dollars each day in many businesses. Many of the products purchased are unique and very complex and technical. The purchasing process involves negotiating on product specifications and costs and arranging delivery and payment schedules. Often lengthy and complex contracts are prepared between the buyer and seller.

Because the process is so important and complicated, many businesses have departments and personnel that specialize in

©DIGITAL VISION

Why is negotiating an important part of the purchasing process for a business?

purchasing. The person or persons responsible for managing the purchasing procedure are members of the purchasing department. Job titles of purchasing specialists include buyer, product manager, merchandise manager, and purchasing agent. They work with the purchasing department, identify possible suppliers, communicate needs and specifications, gather needed information, and manage the paperwork. They are usually responsible for negotiating the price and terms of the sale.

Usually several people are involved in the buying decision the first time a product or service is purchased or for particularly complex or expensive products. The department using the product plays an important role in the purchase decision. The manager and often experienced employees from that department will help prepare specifications. For a very technical product or a new product, engineers or others with technical expertise may be involved to review the specifications and evaluate and test the products of suppliers.

Financial personnel participate in purchases when the purchase is very expensive or the prices of competing products are quite different. Lawyers may help develop

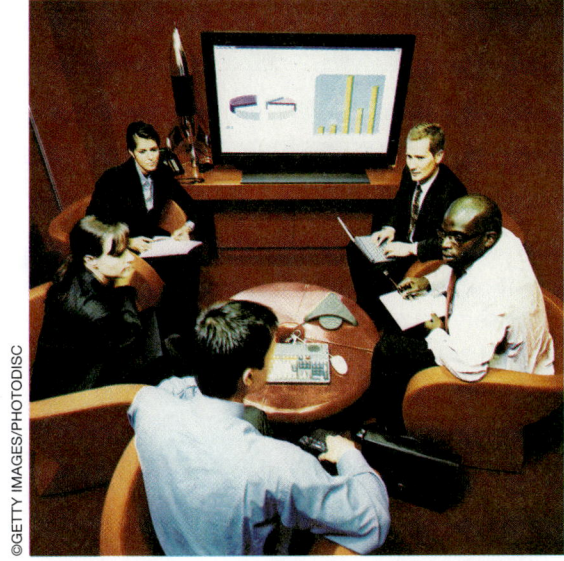

©GETTY IMAGES/PHOTODISC

Why should members of various departments be involved in the purchasing decision?

contracts and review all of the documents involved in the purchase. Finally, for the most important or expensive purchases, one or more members of top management will participate in the purchasing process.

Checkpoint ▶▶

What is the role of purchasing specialists in the purchasing process?

International Purchasing

As more companies become involved in international marketing, the importance of understanding the unique purchasing procedures of international trade increases. There can be advantages to purchasing products from international suppliers. They may offer unique products or manufacturing procedures, better availability, lower prices, or higher quality. Those advantages are lost if products are not supplied as expected or if costs are much higher than anticipated. Companies purchasing internationally must be aware of the unique customs and business practices of each country and must develop effective relationships with their suppliers.

Locating products from international businesses is easier today than at any time in the past. Many businesses have foreign buying offices or purchasing representatives in other countries. Manufacturers wanting to sell to other countries will be represented at international trade shows or in foreign trading offices and trade directories. Most states and many large cities now have international trade centers where buyers and sellers can meet to exchange information and negotiate purchases.

Selecting products and suppliers from other countries is based on factors other than just the product to be purchased. The product and its characteristics are important, and the purchaser must be assured of the product's quality. The purchaser should be able to inspect a sample of the product and talk to other businesses that have purchased or used the product.

Supplier Qualifications

The seller's qualifications are an important consideration. Problems result when the company is not reliable or financially stable. Often the purchaser's bank can help obtain financial information about the company. It is also important to consider the stability and economic conditions of the country in which the supplier is located. It can be risky to work with a business from a country that has a weak economy or is having political difficulties.

Pricing Considerations

One of the most important factors in international buying is negotiating price. Most countries have their own monetary system, and it may be difficult to accurately calculate rates of exchange. The exchange rate of money can change a great deal in the time it takes to negotiate a purchase and make delivery of a product. Also the countries of the supplier or buyer may impose tariffs or duties on the product, which can drastically change the price.

Reciprocal Trading

One procedure some businesses use in international trade is reciprocal trading. **Reciprocal trading** is a form of bartering in which the products or services of one company are used as payment for the products or services of another company. Reciprocal trading is used when an unsatisfactory exchange rate exists or when one of the companies does not have an adequate amount of cash to finance the purchase. As an example of a reciprocal trade agreement, a U.S. company that produces robots for use in automobile manufacturing sold a large order of equipment to a new company in Europe. Since the new company did not have enough cash to pay for the equipment, the companies negotiated a contract in which the U.S. business received a percentage of the sales of automobiles produced by the European company.

Financing

Banks that have experience in international business can provide a great deal of help in arranging financing of purchases. They can give advice on exchange rates, terms of payment, and methods of paying for purchases. Many banks that have experience in international finance have established working relationships with financial institutions in other countries. Those contacts make it

When conducting business in another country, why is it best to work with banks that have international experience?

easier to gather financial information and complete financial transactions with businesses in those countries.

Transportation

Transportation decisions include determining the method of shipment, selecting the transportation company, preparing the necessary transportation documents, and meeting each company's requirements for shipping, handling, and inspecting products. The time needed for transporting products between countries may be no longer than domestic shipments in some cases. However, the timing and reliability of international shipments is often a major concern. Careful transportation planning should be done before a decision is made to purchase from an international supplier. Some companies make a small purchase or require a sample shipment before committing to a large order.

Checkpoint ▶▶

What are important factors to consider when making international purchases?

12-2 Assessment

school.cengage.com/marketing/marketing

Key Concepts

Determine the best answer.

1. True or False: The purchase decisions of businesses are usually more rational than the purchase decisions of final consumers.

2. Detailed requirements for construction or performance of a product are known as
   a. a purchase contract
   b. an invoice
   c. purchase specifications
   d. derived demand

3. The _____ is the level of inventory needed to meet the usage needs of the business until the product can be resupplied.

4. Which of the following would *not* typically be involved in a complex and expensive purchasing decision for a business?
   a. an experienced employee from the department making the purchase
   b. a company lawyer
   c. a top company executive
   d. a customer of the business

5. Using the products or services of one company to pay for purchases from another company is known as
   a. business purchasing
   b. currency exchange
   c. reciprocal trading
   d. international trade

Make Academic Connections

6. **Communication** Locate magazine advertisements for three products or services directed at business customers. Using two colors of markers, highlight information in the ad that is an emotional appeal with one color and information that is a rational appeal with the other color.

7. **Government** Agencies of the U.S. and state governments provide assistance to businesses wanting to participate in international trade. Use the Internet to locate a government agency that helps with (a) identifying international suppliers or customers, (b) financing international sales and purchases, and (c) arranging transportation services. Prepare a one-paragraph summary of the agency and the type of assistance it provides.

Connect to DECA

8. Your team members are responsible for developing a procedure for your school to follow in purchasing a new bus to be used to transport students on field trips and club activities and to athletic events. Outline the steps that should be followed, the people who should be involved, and the main factors that should be considered when choosing the company from which the bus will be purchased. Make a three-minute team presentation of your recommendations to your teacher (judge).

Business Purchasing Procedures

GOALS

- Identify the steps in the business purchasing process.
- Explain why purchasing decisions need to take into consideration more than just the direct cost of products and services.
- Describe the importance of keeping accurate inventory and purchasing records.

KEY TERMS

vendors, *p. 343*

vendor analysis, *p. 344*

request for proposal (RFP), *p. 344*

bidding, *p. 344*

supply chain, *p. 348*

just-in-time (JIT), *p. 348*

total quality management (TQM), *p. 348*

inventory, *p. 349*

physical inventory system, *p. 349*

perpetual inventory system, *p. 349*

purchase order, *p. 349*

packing list, *p. 350*

invoice, *p. 350*

receiving record, *p. 350*

marketing matters

The procedures that businesses use to make purchase decisions are similar to the procedures used by final consumers, except that business processes tend to be more detailed and systematic. Also, they usually involve a number of people rather than just a single individual. Like the process used by final consumers, the steps begin with identifying needs and include a postpurchase evaluation to gauge how well those needs have been met. When making purchasing decisions, businesses need to consider all of the costs that might be affected and the impact they will have on profits. Important records that are needed to determine what and when to purchase include inventory and purchasing records.

List all of your personal expenses that would be affected by a decision to buy or not buy a car. What costs would be affected by the model you choose? How would you determine which car is the best value considering all of the expenses in addition to the cost of the car? Who would you consult to help you make that decision?

Steps in the Purchasing Process

The general process that business customers use in making a purchasing decision looks very much like that used by final consumers. The steps in the process are shown on the right side of Figure 12-2. For new or very expensive purchases, the business purchasing process will typically be more detailed and involve more people.

Identify Needs

Even the first step in the decision-making process, need identification, is complex. Remember that the demand for business products is derived from the needs of the business's customers. In addition, the needs of many parts of the business must be considered. Those needs may not always

FIGURE 12-2

The decision-making process used by businesses is similar but more detailed than that used by final consumers.

Purchasing by Final Consumers and Business Consumers

Final Consumers	Business Consumers
1. Identify needs	1. Identify purchasing needs
2. Gather information	2. Determine alternatives
3. Evaluate alternatives	3. Search for vendors
4. Make purchase decision	4. Select appropriate vendors
5. Evaluate decision	5. Negotiate a purchase
	6. Make purchase decision
	7. Evaluate purchase

be the same and might even conflict with each other. For example, a company with declining sales may experience an internal conflict regarding the purchase of training services. The sales department believes that additional training will help salespeople more effectively serve customers and increase sales. The human resources department needs to reduce expenses because of lower revenues and wants to cut back on the amount spent for training. This conflict must be resolved before a purchase decision can be made.

Determine Alternatives

In the second step, the business attempts to determine the types of products or services that will meet its needs. Here the business decides whether an existing product meets the needs best or whether a new product will be better. Money can probably be saved if suppliers do not have to develop a unique product, but that product may not be the ideal product. The business will develop product specifications in order to clearly describe the product needed.

Search for Vendors

Next the business begins the search for the products and services it needs to purchase. Companies that offer products for sale to other businesses are known as **vendors** or *suppliers.* In some businesses, the purchasing department is responsible for maintaining vendor lists for various types of products and services. Vendors are selected for consideration based on criteria established by the purchasing business. Those factors include availability of products, quality, reliability, delivery, service, and price. Organizations such as ISO (International Organization for Standardization) have been formed to certify businesses that meet specific standards. Purchasers can use the list of certified businesses to be sure the supplier has met the high standards of the certifying organization.

©GETTY IMAGES/PHOTODISC

How could ISO certification benefit a computer component manufacturer?

Select a Vendor

After possible suppliers have been identified, they are carefully evaluated. Often, several vendors offer acceptable products, but the vendors may vary on other factors important to the buyer. A decision will have to be made to determine what combination of vendor characteristics best meets the buyer's needs. A procedure called vendor analysis may be used to help with the decision. **Vendor analysis** is an objective rating system used by buyers to compare potential suppliers on important purchasing criteria. An example of a vendor analysis for the purchase of vehicles for a business is shown in Figure 12-3.

Negotiate a Purchase

The purchasing team will determine which of the products and suppliers best meet the business's needs, and the purchasing department will begin negotiations with them. This is another difference from the process used by final consumers. Usually, retail businesses specify the conditions of the sale, and the consumer decides whether to accept those conditions. In business-to-business marketing, the buyer often specifies the requirements the seller needs to meet. The buyer and seller may discuss those criteria and make changes.

Negotiations are completed in several ways. If the company is buying a standard product or one that has been purchased in the past, the negotiations are simple. The buyer and seller will discuss price, quantity, and delivery and will agree on the terms of the sale. If the buyer has not developed a complete set of criteria or selected a specific product to purchase, the company may develop a request for proposal. A **request for proposal (RFP)** contains a specific description of the type of product or service needed and the criteria that are important to the buyer. Suppliers then develop proposals that contain detailed descriptions of the product or service they can supply and the way they can meet the buyer's criteria.

For the company that has completely determined its needs, product specifications are provided to the suppliers who then demonstrate how they can meet those specifications. Finally, the most restrictive type of negotiations is known as bidding. In **bidding**, several suppliers develop specific prices at which they will meet detailed purchase specifications and other criteria prepared by the buyer. The supplier that is able to respond to the buyer's requirements at the lowest price is usually selected. A bidding process is a common practice in selling to government agencies.

FIGURE 12-3

If a company is planning to buy several new vehicles, it will usually analyze potential suppliers on important criteria in order to select the best vendor.

Vendor Analysis					
Vendor	**Purchasing Criteria**				
	Specifications	**Warranty**	**Service**	**Price**	**Availability**
Dodge	10	8	5	6	4
Ford	9	9	6	4	5
GMC	7	7	9	8	7
Toyota	8	4	7	5	6
Scoring: 10 = high; 1 = low					

Make a Decision

After analyzing the information available, the buying team selects a supplier. Because several people are involved in the decision, it may involve conflict and politics. Each person has different needs to satisfy—both business needs (what is best for the department) and personal needs (what is best for the person's career). Businesses try to specify criteria and develop purchasing procedures that should be followed to avoid those types of problems.

When a decision is made, the purchasing department prepares a detailed purchase order or contract to send to the supplier to ensure that products are supplied in the form and quantity needed at the correct time and price.

Evaluate the Purchase

After a purchase is made, the buyer determines if the product meets the needs as well as possible. If businesses develop detailed specifications, they use those specifications in evaluating purchases. They also consider their customers' needs. Sometimes, businesses complete the evaluation process before the products are used. When the product is received, it may be inspected to ensure that it meets requirements. For products purchased in large quantities, such as raw materials or component parts, it may not be feasible to inspect every product. The purchaser may inspect small quantities and evaluate the samples.

When purchases meet the buyer's needs, the buyer will usually continue to purchase from the same supplier unless

COURTESY OF GRUNER & JAHR USA PUBLISHING

Inc is reaching out to business customers by inviting them to participate in an online business panel. In doing so, businesses gain access to information that could assist them in future decision making.

needs change or unless the supplier is no longer able to meet the buyer's purchasing requirements. If purchasing needs remain the same, the procedure becomes a repeat purchase, and reordering is managed by the purchasing department or the user department. The purchasing procedure may even be automated so reorders can be placed by a computer that monitors inventory levels.

Checkpoint ▶▶

What are the steps in the business purchasing process?

Marketing, Sales & Service

"My dad's wife is very excited about her new job. She is working on supplier relationships at a newly built automotive factory. The majority of the suppliers have located distribution sites close to the plant to facilitate just-in-time (JIT) delivery of parts to the plant. She also has oversight of the manufacturing specifications of the parts. She helps the suppliers understand what they need to do to ensure their products meet her company's specifications and also how they can apply the same quality controls to their vendors."

How do companies ensure that their vendors understand their needs? Whether it is raw materials for manufacturing or finished goods for retailing, companies need to have a coordinated strategy for communicating and managing their needs—both within their own organizations and with their suppliers.

Employment Outlook

- An average rate of employment growth is expected.

Job Titles

- Demand Forecasting Specialist
- Logistics Supervisor
- Materials Manager
- Supply Chain Integration Manager
- Regional Logistics Director

Needed Skills

- A bachelor's degree is often required. A master's degree can be helpful for more advanced positions.
- Strong analytical, interpersonal, and negotiation skills are needed.

- Professional certification or training in production and inventory management or lean manufacturing is an asset.

What's it like to work in... *Supply Chain Management*

Ingrid, a distribution analyst for a large plastics manufacturer, is attending her group's monthly forecasting meeting. Demand for Ingrid's product line, the plastics used to produce laundry detergent containers, is being reviewed. Representatives from Sales, Marketing, and the Forecasting Analysis groups are in the meeting.

Her company utilizes forecasting software that uses historical sales to project future demand. Information from sales representatives regarding the anticipated loss or growth of business can be manually entered into the forecasting system.

After the forecasts are electronically updated, Ingrid reviews their impact on the production schedule. When planning production, Ingrid needs to balance existing customer orders, forecasted customer orders, and current inventory levels against future manufacturing schedules. Her job is to make sure that each type of product is available when customers need it without excess inventory.

Rumors about raw material shortages cause Ingrid to call her counterpart at the manufacturing plant to see if there is need for concern. If shortages are anticipated, she will contact the sales manager so that he can have his sales force talk to its customers about immediate needs. Order prioritization can occur after all needs are assessed.

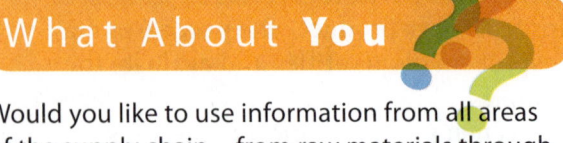

What About **You**

Would you like to use information from all areas of the supply chain—from raw materials through finished product demand—to help a company optimize its production and operations?

PHOTO: ©GETTY IMAGES/PHOTODISC

Judgment Call

What If Buyers Become Too Close to Suppliers?

The trend toward more cooperative relationships between purchasing professionals and suppliers has increased the chance for ethical problems. Most people recognize that bribes and kickbacks are wrong. The line between proper and improper behavior is clear. The real danger lies in gray areas where friendships mix with business.

Businesses that emphasize the development of strategic relationships with suppliers often have less objective procedures in place for awarding contracts. In such cases, it is easier for buyers to allow subjective personal feelings to interfere in the decision-making processes. Also, strategic relationships often involve sharing confidential internal information.

About two-thirds of businesses have written ethics policies for purchasing personnel. Some purchasing professionals believe those policies are flawed because they are too lenient, not too strict.

Think Critically

1. How do clearly defined policies help purchasers and suppliers avoid ethical problems?

2. What kinds of policies might a company adopt to prevent purchasing employees from feeling like they owe suppliers a favor for gifts?

Improving Purchasing Procedures

Companies know that effective purchasing does a great deal to improve the success of the business while poor purchasing causes serious problems. One company that manufactures instant breakfast drinks spent several million dollars on a new piece of equipment to seal the plastic liners that held the product inside an outer package. After using the machine for several months, the company found that the time needed to seal the packages slowed the pace of production by 20 percent. The manufacturer's salespeople were unable to make commitments to customers about quantity and delivery schedules. Because production was reduced, inventories of raw materials increased. The hours of work for many of the company's employees had to be reduced. So, one purchase had a very big negative effect on the business.

Improved Performance

An example of how purchasing improves business performance comes from a large retailer. The retailer found that some manufacturers gave significant price discounts for the purchase of very large quantities of certain products. The retailer usually purchased the higher quantities believing that the low prices could be passed on to its customers, resulting in increased sales. After several years of taking advantage of

Fast FACTS

Businesses are getting much better at managing inventory. In 1992, inventories averaged $1.56 for every $1 of sales. By 2006, inventory levels had dropped to $1.26, about a 20% cost savings.

the price discounts, an evaluation of the purchases was completed. The retailer learned that the large-quantity purchases resulted in two problems. First, both transportation and inventory costs increased. Second, the retailer had difficulty selling all of the products in a timely fashion. Some of the inventory had to be sold at very low prices just to get rid of it. And some of the products were never sold before their "sell-by" dates expired. Therefore, the total cost of the unsold products was wasted.

After that analysis, the retailer put together a new purchasing plan. Purchase quantities were more closely matched with customer demand. Even though the cost of merchandise purchased was higher, the savings in inventory, transportation, and fewer unsold products allowed the retailer to keep customer prices nearly as low as before while profits increased by almost 15 percent.

The examples show that there is more to effective purchasing than just the cost of the product. Identifying and monitoring the total costs of the business that are affected by a purchase are important business activities.

Supply Chain Management

Distribution is a part of a larger process known as supply chain management. A **supply chain** is the flow of products, resources, and information through all of the organizations involved in producing and marketing a company's products. A supply chain is complex and usually involves several businesses. Those businesses must cooperate rather than compete to ensure that customer needs are satisfied and all businesses make a profit.

One way to improve a supply chain is with just-in-time supply. **Just-in-time (JIT)** means that the inventory level is kept low

Why should a business closely monitor its inventory needs?

and resupplied by supply chain members just as it is needed. Another tool used in supply chains is total quality management. **Total quality management (TQM)** establishes specific quality standards for all procedures. TQM teams made up of employees in each organization in the supply chain study procedures and make recommendations for quality improvements.

Members of a supply chain benefit from close cooperation and sharing of information. Effective supply chains have developed secure procedures to coordinate the electronic exchange of information through their marketing information systems. They cooperate in marketing research and cost controls to collectively achieve customer satisfaction.

Checkpoint ▶▶

Why do purchasing decisions need to take into consideration more than just the direct cost of products and services?

Processing Purchases

From the time decisions are made to order products until the products are ready for use or resale in a business, a number of procedures must be completed. A variety of records, including inventory and purchasing records, must be maintained to make sure the purchasing procedures are completed correctly.

Inventory Records

Inventory is the assortment of products maintained by a business. Inventory includes the products and materials needed to produce other products and services to operate the business or to be sold to customers. Inventory management is needed so that managers are aware of the supply of products on hand at any time. That information helps to control costs and to ensure that operations can continue without interruption.

Inventory records are maintained to provide information about the products on hand in the business. That information can include the type of products, their source, age, condition, and value. It should also indicate how rapidly the inventory is used, when it should be reordered, and the sources of supply.

Two types of inventory systems are typically used by businesses: physical inventory and perpetual inventory. A **physical inventory system** determines the amount of product on hand by visually inspecting and counting the items. A physical inventory count is conducted on a regular basis, often every few months or each half-year.

A **perpetual inventory system** determines the amount of a product on hand by maintaining records on purchases and sales. Daily inventory levels determined through the perpetual system are maintained on computers. When a sale is made, information from the product label is entered into a computer system (usually via sales terminals), and the inventory level is automatically adjusted. Most businesses combine the use of physical and perpetual inventory systems. There will be differences between the inventory levels of each system. The discrepancies can result from products that have been stolen or lost or from poorly maintained records. An important task in inventory management is to reduce losses and inventory records errors.

Purchasing Records

A **purchase order**, a form listing the variety, quantity, and prices of products ordered, is completed by the buyer and sent

©DIGITAL VISION

What are the advantages and disadvantages of a physical inventory system?

to the seller to begin the purchasing process. The seller fills the order and sends it to the buyer with a **packing list**, an itemized listing of all of the products included in the shipment. At the same time, the seller sends an invoice to the buyer. The **invoice** is an itemized billing statement with terms of payment for the order.

When the merchandise is received by the purchaser, it will be unpacked and inspected for damage. A **receiving record** is completed listing all of the merchandise received in the shipment and its condition. The receiving record is compared to the packing list, and any discrepancies are noted. Both are forwarded to the accounting department to be compared to the purchase order and invoice before payment is made. Finally, the products that have been received are entered into the inventory records of the company and are distributed to the departments where they will be used or sold.

Checkpoint ▶▶▶

Why are accurate inventory and purchasing records so important to a business?

12-3 Assessment

Xtra! Study Tools
school.cengage.com/marketing/marketing

Key Concepts

Determine the best answer.

1. True or False: Business purchasing procedures are totally different from the way final consumers make purchase decisions.

2. Which of the following is true about business purchasing?
   a. Demand for business products is derived from the needs of customers.
   b. Only the needs of the department that will use the product or service should be considered.
   c. After a vendor has been identified, the business should develop product specifications.
   d. All are true.

3. True or False: The businesses that make up a supply chain should view each other as competitors.

4. A _____ inventory system determines the amount of a product on hand by maintaining records on purchases and sales.

5. An itemized listing of all of the products included in a shipment is a(n)
   a. invoice
   b. packing list
   c. purchase order
   d. inventory record

Make Academic Connections

6. **Math** Using the Fast FACTS information from this lesson, if a company had average monthly sales of $565,500 in 1992 and $823,750 in 2006, what would be the value of its inventory in each of those years? Prepare a bar graph to show your results.

7. **Technology** Use the Internet to research how technology is being used to increase the coordination of activities and information within supply chains to improve their effectiveness. Prepare a one-page report on your findings. Prepare a bibliography of the resources used for your report.

Connect to **DECA** *An Association of Marketing Students*

8. Your marketing team has been asked to prepare complete purchasing procedures to be followed by all departments in a large manufacturing business when ordering new equipment. Prepare a flow chart that illustrates the procedure you recommend including a description of each step, who is involved, and how the effectiveness of each step will be determined. Present your flowchart to your teacher (judge) for evaluation.

Retail Purchasing

GOALS

- Describe how retailers identify customer needs and how to satisfy them.
- Identify the ways retailers locate the products they need to satisfy their customers.

KEY TERMS

merchandise plan, *p. 352*

basic stock list, *p. 353*

model stock list, *p. 353*

marketing matters

Retailers buy products from selected manufacturers and wholesalers for resale to final consumers in their target markets. Because retailers make a relatively small profit on each item sold, they spend a lot of time and effort studying their customers to make sure they stock what customers want to buy. Retailers develop detailed merchandise plans to organize the hundreds and thousands of items they carry.

Retail buyers locate the products they want to offer for sale through manufacturers' and wholesalers' sales representatives, trade shows, catalogs, and increasingly through web sites maintained by the sellers. Once they decide what to buy, they follow carefully developed procedures to get the products on their shelves as quickly and efficiently as possible. For many retailers, customer needs change rapidly, new products are added frequently, and old products are removed from their merchandise plans.

Make a list of eight things that you have purchased recently. For each item, list three retailers you think carry that item or a similar alternative.

Planning to Satisfy Customer Needs

Retail businesses purchase products for resale. Market conditions for products change rapidly. A buyer for a large supermarket chain may review more than 200 new products each week for possible purchase. Also, many products sold in retail stores are seasonal, meaning the products sell well during a particular time of the year but not at other times. Retailers make very little profit on the sale of any one item. Therefore, if a product remains unsold, the business quickly loses money.

Retailing is very competitive, so retailers study customer needs carefully when making purchase decisions. If Company A offers a product that customers want, and its competitors do not have that product,

Company A has a real advantage. If a company is able to sell a similar product at a lower price than its competitors, it will usually sell a larger quantity. Retailers constantly evaluate their direct competitors to determine what products are being sold at what prices.

Determining Customer Needs

Retailers use a great deal of marketing information and research to anticipate customer needs. Most retailers collect customer and product information each time a sale is made. Many have consumer panels and focus groups that meet regularly to evaluate new products. Most businesses encourage customers to identify

Get the Message

Using Social Media

One of the advantages of the Internet over other forms of media is that it allows anyone with a computer to create and share information, opinions, and other content. This aspect makes the Internet a "social medium."

Studies show that social media usage is still small, but growing rapidly. Between April 2006 and April 2007, social media usage increased almost sevenfold, especially among young people. Nearly 70% of people between the ages of 12 and 21 now use some sort of social networking web site.

Web sites such as MySpace, YouTube, Wikipedia, Flickr, and Amazon all use this concept in different ways, fostering communities and relying on them to create content. Marketers try to tap into these communities to spread their messages. Using pre-existing social networks to spread marketing messages is sometimes called "viral marketing," and it can be incredibly effective and efficient if done properly.

Think Critically

1. How do the web sites mentioned above foster social networking? What content do they depend on their communities to create?

2. What advantage does viral marketing have over traditional media approaches? What disadvantages?

---

products they want that are not available in the store.

Retail buyers and merchandise managers study market information including the economy, competition, and new product developments. They attend meetings and trade shows and talk with the salespeople of their suppliers. They carefully track the offerings, prices, and services of competitors in order to be aware of any changes or apparent advantages of those businesses.

Tracking Product Sales

Retailers carefully track the sales of each product in inventory to immediately determine sales trends. Computer technology aids in that process. Scanners at checkout counters are connected to computers that store inventory information. When a purchase is made, the scanner reads the bar code on each product. The bar code provides information such as product name, product type, price, manufacturer, and the date of purchase by the business. That information is immediately analyzed by the computer. Managers can determine if special displays, sales, or advertising programs affect the sales volume of specific products.

Most retail store computer systems are connected to other computers in regional or national offices. This allows purchasing decisions as well as marketing plans to be adjusted quickly to ensure that products are sold rapidly, products that do not sell are not reordered, and new purchases respond to customers' needs.

Developing a Purchasing Plan

Retail stores must offer an adequate assortment of products to meet customers' needs. Larger department stores and discount retailers offer hundreds of different products in many merchandise categories. Specialty stores offer less variety but a complete assortment of products in specialized categories.

Businesses prepare merchandise plans to guide decision making. A **merchandise plan** identifies the types, assortments, prices, and quantities of products that will be stocked by the business for a specific period of time. The merchandise plan is like a budget in that it provides the basis for ordering merchandise and maintaining the store's inventory. The merchandise plan is used to determine the products to order, delivery schedules, the space allocations required, initial pricing strategies, and promotional plans.

The merchandise plan may be developed for a short time period, such as one month for a specific season in which unique merchandise will be sold, or for a longer time period. Few stores have plans that last longer than six months. Customer needs and interests and competitive conditions can change dramatically in that time, so the inventory would be out of date.

The merchandise plan is developed from a basic stock list or a model stock list. A **basic stock list** identifies the products a store must have available to meet the most important needs of its customers. The products on the basic stock list will be reordered time and time again until there are major changes in the market or economy. The basic stock list will not change a great deal over time. It includes the products customers expect to find anytime they visit the store.

A **model stock list** identifies the complete assortment of products a store would like to offer to customers. The model stock list is more extensive than the basic stock list. It is also subject to change more frequently based on economic conditions, the financial resources of the business, and the changing needs of customers. A large national retailer may have a model stock list that identifies all possible product choices for local stores to offer. Each store manager then tailors the individual location's inventory to the specific needs and conditions in that area from the model stock list.

Checkpoint ▶▶

Why do retailers need a merchandise plan?

Obtaining the Needed Products

Retail buyers make purchases from both manufacturers and wholesalers. They have several ways of learning about vendors and their products.

Selling to Retail Businesses

Most vendors use salespeople to sell to retail buyers. They will meet with the store owner or manager for smaller businesses. For large regional or national retail chains, the salespeople visit buying offices where buyers make decisions for many stores. Often in buying offices, buyers specialize in one type of product, so a salesperson may have to visit with several buyers during one trip to the office. Some cities have trading centers for specific industries. For example, many furniture manufacturers open showrooms in High Point, North Carolina, where furniture retailers from

NETBookmark

Trade shows offer manufacturers a chance to show their merchandise to large numbers of wholesalers and retailers at one time. The American International Toy Fair, sponsored by the Toy Industry Association, is the largest toy trade show in the Western Hemisphere. Access school.cengage.com/marketing/marketing and click on the link for Chapter 12. According to the show's web site, how many manufacturers and other businesses display their merchandise at the toy fair? From how many countries? How many buyers typically attend the fair? Identify at least three companies that might send buyers to the American International Toy Fair.

school.cengage.com/marketing/marketing

all over the world travel to see the latest product lines.

Trade shows also offer an opportunity for many manufacturers to display their merchandise. There is a large electronics trade show each year in Las Vegas. Companies spend thousands of dollars on exhibits, demonstrations, and advertising because they know retailers will be looking for new products.

A final method of purchasing is through vendor catalogs and web sites. This buying method is particularly useful for small retailers who cannot afford to travel to trade centers or trade shows and who do not purchase large enough quantities to warrant frequent visits from salespeople. Catalogs and web sites are also used to sell standardized and frequently purchased items that are sold primarily on the basis of price and availability. Most manufacturers and wholesalers are moving many of their sales and customer support functions onto web sites. Many automate the online ordering process for regular customers so that routine purchases can be made and orders can be filled automatically via the Web.

Completing the Purchase Process

Retail buyers continually identify and study vendors for the many purchases they will make. Vendors must meet specific criteria in order to be considered. Each retailer will have its own criteria and will communicate them to vendors. Those criteria may vary for different products in the store's merchandise assortment. Some products may be unique and can only be obtained from one source. Others may be rather common and can be obtained from a variety of vendors.

A product may be fast-selling or perishable, requiring the retailer to quickly replace items in inventory. The retailer will want to purchase from a supplier who can guarantee

rapid and reliable delivery. Other items may be very competitive products that can be purchased in many stores. The retailer's customers will shop for the lowest price, so a supplier must be located that will sell at competitive prices.

For new products, fashions, or seasonal items, the retailer may not be certain of the total amount of inventory that can be sold. The buyer may want to work with a vendor who will initially ship a small amount of inventory but who will be able to rapidly provide additional quantities if sales are higher than expected.

Most businesses have a standard procedure for ordering merchandise. The order must be placed far enough in advance to be sure it is delivered before the current stock is completely sold or in time for the selling season for the product. The timing of orders is often a difficult problem for retailers. If the order is placed too soon, the merchandise arrives before it is needed,

Why is product delivery an important factor when selecting a vendor?

taking up space and adding to storage and handling costs. If the order is late, the merchandise is not in stock when customers want it, and sales are lost.

For retailers with many stores, the seller ships the merchandise to the buyer's distribution center or store. The distribution center is used to assemble product orders for local stores and then to quickly reship them. For small stores, sellers will ship orders directly to the business.

When orders are received at the store, they are unpacked and prepared for sale. Again, each business has specific and careful procedures to be followed in receiving, unpacking, inspecting, and preparing products for sale. Those procedures may require assembly, cleaning, pricing, or other types of processing, depending on the type of products. Some stores have large storage areas where merchandise

is maintained until needed on the selling floor. Others move most of the stock immediately onto shelves or into displays for sale. Preparing merchandise for sale and moving it into inventory must be done carefully and efficiently with as little disruption to customers as possible.

Merchandise can be lost, stolen, or damaged during the receiving process. Because most retail businesses have very low margins of profit, any significant loss at this time can affect the business's ability to make a profit.

Checkpoint ▶▶▶

What methods do vendors use to make products available to prospective retail buyers?

12-4 Assessment

Key Concepts

Determine the best answer.

1. True or False: Retailers typically carry the same items for a long period of time since customer needs seldom change.

2. Retailers track sales and inventory using scanners that read the _____ on each product that is sold.

3. A _____ stock list identifies the important products a store must have available to meet the most important needs of its target market.
   a. basic
   b. model
   c. complete
   d. perpetual

4. For large regional or national retail chains, vendors' salespeople visit _____ where buyers make decisions for many stores.

5. True or False: Most retailers purchase products from only one vendor in order to be assured of responsive service.

Make Academic Connections

6. **Career Success** Go to the employment section of a national retailer's web site and gather information on retail buying jobs. If no information is provided, send a professional e-mail to the company requesting information. Based on your research, write a one-page report on the company, the career, and your interest in it.

7. **Economics** Review local newspapers and other information sources to identify economic information that could affect retail sales in your community in the next six months. Prepare a two-minute oral report discussing the information and how retailers should respond to it.

Connect to ◆ DECA
An Association of Marketing Students

8. You are the fresh organic foods buyer for a regional supermarket chain. Prepare a vendor analysis form that identifies five important criteria you expect vendors to meet in order to sell fresh organic foods to your stores. Present the form to your teacher (judge) and describe the reasons for your choices.

Check Your Understanding

Now that you have completed the chapter, check your understanding of the lessons with these questions. Record the score that best represents your understanding of each marketing concept.

1 = not at all; 3 = somewhat; 5 = very well

If your score is 42–50, you are ready for the assessment activities that follow. If you score 33–41, you should review the lessons for the items you scored 1–3. If you score 32 or less, you will want to carefully reread the lessons and work with a study partner on the areas you do not understand.

Can you—

___ list five categories of business customers?

___ identify ways in which the business market is different from the final consumer market?

___ describe how procedures will be different for new, modified, and repeat purchases?

___ offer reasons why several people representing different parts of a business should be involved in major purchase decisions?

___ suggest several factors that should be considered when purchasing from international suppliers?

___ identify the general process business customers follow when making purchase decisions?

___ define the meaning and importance of supply chain management?

___ describe the purpose of each of the records that are a part of the purchasing process?

___ describe several ways that retailers can identify customer needs?

___ give examples of methods vendors use to provide product information to retail buyers?

Review Marketing Terms

Match the terms listed with the definitions. Some terms may not be used.

1. Contains a specific description of the type of product or service needed and the criteria that are important to the buyer
2. Determines the amount of product on hand by visually inspecting and counting the items
3. An itemized billing statement with terms of payment for the order
4. Inventory level is kept low and resupplied just as it is needed
5. Companies that offer products for sale to other businesses
6. The assortment of products maintained by a business
7. Identifies the types, assortments, prices, and quantities of products that will be stocked by the business for a specific period of time
8. The exchange of products and services between businesses
9. Detailed requirements for construction or performance of a product
10. A form listing the variety, quantity, and prices of products ordered

a. basic stock list
b. bidding
c. business-to-business marketing
d. inventory
e. invoice
f. just-in-time (JIT)
g. merchandise plan
h. model stock list
i. packing list
j. perpetual inventory system
k. physical inventory system
l. purchase order
m. purchase specifications
n. purchasing
o. receiving record
p. reciprocal trading
q. reorder point
r. request for proposal (RFP)
s. supply chain
t. vendors

Review Marketing Concepts

11. True or False: The majority of exchanges involving products or services are between businesses and final consumers.

12. True or False: Businesses that purchase products for resale to final consumers typically do not change the form of those products.

13. True or False: An example of a poor purchasing decision is selecting a supplier that is not able to deliver the product when promised.

14. True or False: The most difficult purchasing situation for a business is when it buys a product for the first time.

15. True or False: The only types of companies classified as business consumers are producers.

16. True or False: Because there are fewer business customers than final consumers, the total amount of possible sales revenue will be smaller for those selling business products.

17. True or False: The majority of products purchased by businesses are for final consumption.

18. True or False: Direct distribution from the producer to the customer is common in business-to-business marketing.

Marketing Research and Planning

19. Use the Internet to find the web site of a company engaged in each of the types of businesses listed below. Develop a table to provide the following information: company name, its URL address, major products or services it sells, and how it markets those products or services to other businesses.
    a. automobile manufacturer
    b. insurance company
    c. office supplies
    d. industrial chemicals
    e. financial services
    f. work uniforms
    g. freight transportation
    h. temporary personnel

20. Identify a major purchase decision you might make within the next five years (college, new automobile, apartment, etc.). Then, specifically outline the steps you could follow to make the purchase in the objective way followed by businesses. After you have outlined the steps, prepare a vendor analysis form. List the factors that you will consider when making the purchase. Develop numerical values for each factor that reflect its relative importance to you. Create the form so that it can be completed as you evaluate several companies that provide the product or service.

21. Form a team with two or three other students. As a team, select one of the following topics related to business-to-business marketing. Research the topic by reading marketing books, current business magazines, and other business resources. You might be able to identify a business person or other resource person in your community who is an expert on the topic to interview. Prepare a three- to five-minute oral report on the topic and include three visuals.
    a. Census data on business customers
    b. Working with international vendors
    c. Using benchmarking to develop product specifications
    d. Developing an effective supply chain
    e. What occurs at manufacturers' markets and trade shows
    f. New technology for retail inventory management

Marketing Management and Decision Making

22. A vendor wanted to determine what factors were most important to its customers when making purchase decisions. It conducted a survey of purchasing agents and asked them to assign a value from 0 to 5 for six factors they consider when purchasing products. The values ranged from 0 (not considered when making a purchase decision) to 5 (most important factor in the purchase decision). The first table on the next page shows results from 140 respondents.

Factors	Value					
	5	4	3	2	1	0
Price	0	40	55	32	13	0
Delivery Schedule	45	38	36	20	1	0
Vendor Reputation	0	24	38	52	18	8
Past Experience with Vendor	7	10	68	55	0	0
Vendor Service after Sale	0	5	12	22	36	65
Product Quality	110	24	6	0	0	0

Factors	Product		
	Vendor	Competitor B	Competitor C
Price	6	8	10
Delivery Schedule	8	5	7
Vendor Reputation	7	7	5
Past Experience with Vendor	3	9	6
Vendor Service after Sale	8	4	6
Product Quality	10	7	8

a. The vendor wanted to use the data to develop an average value for each of the factors. Calculate the mean value for each factor by multiplying the value by the number of respondents selecting that value, totaling the result for all six value scores for the factor, and then dividing the result by 140 (the total number of respondents).

b. The vendor asked a focus group to compare one of the vendor's products to similar products sold by two other competitors using the six factors from the research study. The focus group assigned each product a score ranging from 1 to 10 for each of the six factors, with 1 being the lowest rating and 10 being the highest rating. The results of the focus group ratings are shown in the second table.

The vendor then used the information from the original marketing research study to develop a product score for each company. The mean score for each factor (calculated from the research study results in Part a) was multiplied by the rating assigned to that factor by the focus group (from the second table). Then the results for each of the six factors were totaled, giving each company a final score. That procedure would predict that the company whose product received the highest score would be the one that best met the purchaser's needs. Calculate the total product score for each company using the procedure described. Then be prepared to discuss the meaning of the results in terms of customer perceptions of the three companies' products.

23. May Randall is the purchasing manager for Protective Insurance Company. The company is installing a wireless network and is providing a new desktop computer or laptop for office personnel. The company maintains all company records in a large mainframe computer. It is important that the computers purchased are compatible with the wireless network and current mainframe hardware and software. Working with managers from each of the major divisions of the company, May has developed purchase specifications for new computers and has identified four potential vendors. One of the vendors is the supplier of the current mainframe, but each of the other vendors has assured May that their machines meet the specifications.

May is now faced with important decisions. First, should Protective Insurance buy all of the computers from one vendor or allow divisions to order from more than one? Each division has different computing needs and preferences among the vendors. By choosing only one vendor, everything is standardized, there may be a lower price, and service is handled by one company. But if the vendor is not reliable, it will affect the entire company. Using more than one supplier allows each division to choose its preferred computer, but it can create service and support problems as well as less room for price negotiations with each vendor. May wonders if preference should be given to the vendor of Protective's current equipment. The company and its equipment have been very reliable, and service has been efficient and effective. However, the company has less experience with wireless systems. How would you recommend that May resolve these issues?

Retail Merchandising Individual Series Event

The owner of Luxury Furniture wants to increase sales. He has asked you to develop both customer and sales associate incentive plans to increase sales.

The customer incentive plan must include special discounts and sales promotions when customers' annual furniture purchases reach different levels throughout the year. The incentive plan for sales associates must reward employees for reaching different sales goals throughout the year.

You have also been asked to describe a database for customer information that will be used to communicate with customers. The owner wants to know what information will be included in the database. He is interested in how the database can be used for bulk mailings that will be sent to loyal customers of Luxury Furniture.

Your plan for increasing sales must include training and development for sales associates to improve customer satisfaction. You must describe follow-up communication that sales associates will send to customers after their purchase of furniture. You must also describe a special sales event that will create excitement and increase customer traffic in the store.

You will meet with the owner of Luxury Furniture in his office to explain your plan for increasing the company's furniture sales. You are allowed ten minutes to describe your plan for increasing sales and maintaining a loyal

customer base. During or after the presentation, the judge can ask questions.

Performance Indicators Evaluated

- Identify information monitored for marketing decision making. (Marketing-Information Management)

- Explain the types of promotion. (Promotion)

- Explain the selling process. (Selling)

- Explain the role of customer service as a component of selling relationships. (Selling)

- Plan follow-up strategies for use in selling. (Selling)

Go to the DECA web site for more detailed information.

Think Critically

1. Why is follow-up communication so important for customer satisfaction?

2. What type of promotion would require the customer to come to the furniture store?

3. What types of credit incentives might be offered to increase furniture sales?

4. Why is a customer database a good marketing tool?

www.deca.org

Getting Products to Customers

©RUBBERBALL/JUPITER IMAGES

Newsline

Image or Value—Can't We Have Both?

For a long time, the idea of shopping in discount stores was not appealing to many consumers. Those who did shop at Wal-Mart and Kmart were attracted by the significant cost savings they could realize. However, for other shoppers, image meant everything. They were willing to sacrifice price in the belief that discount stores did not offer the brand names or the quality they demanded. But over time, discount stores began to change. New, upscale discounters such as Target and Kohl's demonstrated that quality, image, and value pricing attracted customers who had not shopped at traditional discount stores or were not satisfied with the choices of those stores. They have been followed by wholesale membership stores including BJs Wholesale Club and Costco, which feature broad assortments, well-known brand names, and discount prices. Outlet malls have transitioned from offering dated, imperfect, and clearance merchandise to featuring the latest offerings from nationally known manufacturers and even designer labels. Even Wal-Mart and Kmart are paying more attention to brand name and style while still trying to maintain their low-price leadership.

Today's customers are very aware of the many store and product choices. They now realize that if they shop and compare before making a purchase, they can save money on their purchases and still get the brands, quality, and image they want. As a result, many traditional department stores have struggled. Some have failed, others have been acquired by stronger businesses, and a few, such as JCPenney, Bloomingdale's, and Dillard's, have responded with a more targeted product assortment, higher levels of customer service, and stronger branding and promotion. The future of retailing suggests that the concept of "image is everything" will still appeal to a select few, but "high quality and high value" will have the greatest appeal.

Think Critically

1. Should retail stores attempt to attract both image-conscious and value-conscious customers? Why or why not?

2. How has the high-quality and high-value approach affected other types of retail businesses such as grocery, electronics, and home improvement stores?

Prepare for Performance

This chapter develops the following Performance Indicators from the DECA Competitive Events program.

Core Performance Indicators

- Acquire foundational knowledge of channel management to understand its role in marketing
- Manage channel activities to minimize costs and to determine distribution strategies
- Develop channel-management strategies to minimize costs
- Assess channel-management strategies to improve their effectiveness

Supporting Performance Indicators

- Explain the nature of channels of distribution
- Describe ethical considerations in channel management
- Evaluate channel members
- Select channels of distribution
- Develop channel-management strategies

Go to **school.cengage.com/marketing/marketing** and click on Connect to DECA.

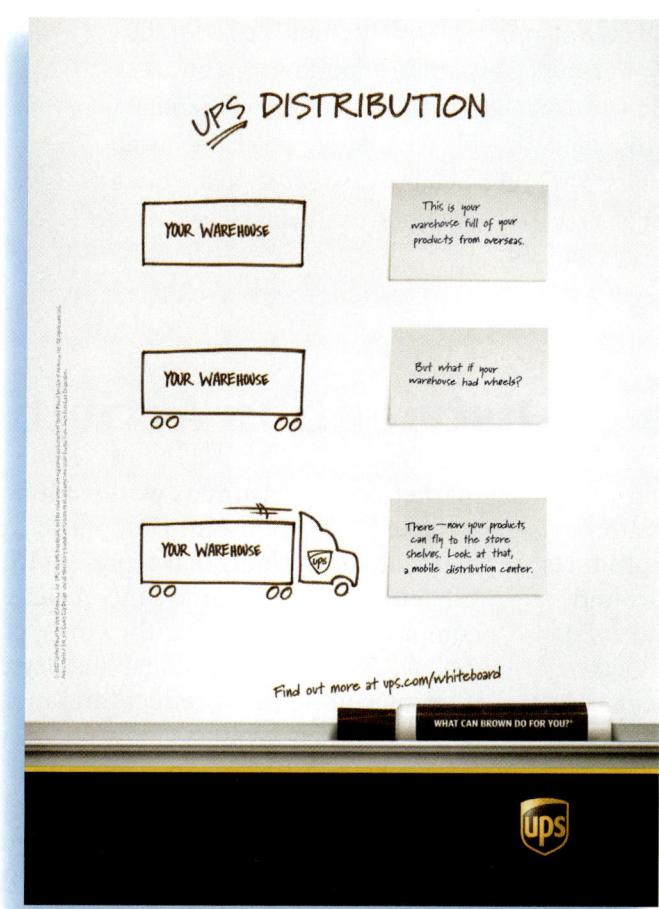

©UPS

Visual Focus

For hundreds of years the major marketing challenge facing businesses was distribution. Getting products from the producer to the locations where customers could purchase and use them was difficult, expensive, and time-consuming. Today, while businesses focus on many more marketing activities, effective distribution still is an important factor in customer satisfaction and profitable sales. Companies such as UPS specialize in the variety of activities that are part of a complex channel of distribution.

Focus Questions:

What is the unique product or service that UPS is offering to prospective customers in the ad? Do you believe the simplicity of the advertisement is effective? Why or why not?

Use the same basic visual concept to create your own advertisement that illustrates a different way that UPS can improve product distribution for a manufacturer or retail business. If necessary, visit the UPS web site for ideas. Show your advertisement to other students and compare it to their ads.

Marketing through Distribution

GOALS

- Explain why the distribution function is so important to effective marketing.
- Illustrate how a well-planned distribution system supports the marketing plan.

KEY TERMS

distribution function, *p. 363*

marketing matters

Distribution is the most complex and challenging of marketing functions. Often the largest percentage of the marketing costs for products and services is spent on distribution-related activities. Distribution is crucial to the matching of production with consumption, which is one of the essential requirements for an effectively functioning free enterprise economy. Distribution also plays a key role in improving the four economic utilities—form, time, place, and possession.

Distribution usually involves several businesses in what is known as a distribution or supply channel. The distribution system can only work as planned if all the members of the channel agree on and follow a plan. Because each member of a distribution channel has its own marketing strategy, it is especially important for a business to choose its distribution partners wisely and manage its distribution system carefully.

Choose a product that you or your family bought recently for which the distribution channel involved several businesses from the point of production to the place where it was purchased. Make a list of all of the distribution steps you believe had to be completed for the product to reach you.

The Importance of Distribution Activities

Welcome to the world marketplace! U.S. consumers have access to hundreds of thousands of products. Products come from companies around the world. Any time of the day and every day of the week, most people can locate a store to purchase the products they need or a business that performs a desired service. If a store is not convenient, other choices are available. Customers can purchase by telephone, by mail, or over the Internet and be assured of delivery within days or, for local purchases, even hours or minutes.

In the same way, U.S. businesses now can send their products throughout the world reaching almost any international marketplace. Consumers worldwide are attracted to fashions, movies, music, and many other products that represent the U.S. culture. At the same time, American companies recognize that they must compete with other international businesses offering competitive products and must be able to get their products to international customers quickly and inexpensively.

The most complex and challenging part of marketing is distribution. Many companies, activities, and people are involved in the distribution of products and services from the producer to the consumer. Large percentages of marketing budgets are spent on the activities involved in distribution.

For most products and services, distribution activities account for over 50 percent of the total marketing costs.

The Distribution Function

Distribution is the oldest and most basic part of marketing. In fact, before the term *marketing* was even a part of business language, *distribution* was used to describe the activities that directed the flow of goods and services between producers and consumers. Today, because marketing activities have expanded, distribution is just one of the important marketing functions. The **distribution function** involves determining the best methods and procedures to use so that prospective customers can locate, obtain, and use a business's products and services.

When distribution works well, consumers are not really aware of its importance. Products and services are available where and when people want them and in a usable condition. However, when distribution does not work, it is very evident. Products are out of stock, backordered, available only in the wrong styles or sizes, out of date, or damaged. Prices are incorrectly marked or missing. Salespeople do not have adequate product information, or products advertised in the newspaper are not available in the store. Much of the dissatisfaction consumers have with businesses results from poor distribution.

Distribution as an Economic Concept

Distribution is an important activity for the effective operation of any economic system, and it is essential in a free enterprise economy. Free enterprise is based on the matching of production and consumption decisions. When business people decide to produce a product, the product will not be successful unless consumers can obtain it. When consumers have a demand for a particular type of product or service, that demand will not be satisfied until they can locate the desired product. Distribution aids in matching supply and demand.

©DIGITAL VISION

Why does distribution play an important role in customer satisfaction?

Distribution has a major impact on economic utility. Economic utility is the amount of satisfaction a consumer receives from the consumption of a particular product or service. Businesses can increase customer satisfaction by improving the form of a product or service, making it available at a more convenient time or place, or making it more affordable. As you consider the four types of economic utility, you can see that distribution has the most direct effect on time and place utility. However, it can also affect the form of a product by making sure that products are fresh and undamaged when they are distributed. Efficient distribution also affects the final product cost, so it is a factor in possession utility.

Distribution as a Marketing Mix Element

Another way of seeing the importance of distribution is to examine the marketing mix. Distribution as a part of the marketing mix involves the locations and methods used to make the product available to customers. When a marketer develops a marketing strategy and prepares a marketing plan, the distribution decisions made can determine whether the customer is able to easily locate and purchase the products and services needed.

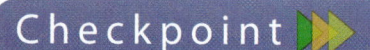

Checkpoint ▶▶

Why is distribution so important to effective marketing?

Development of a Distribution System

Edu-Games was a new company that produced high-quality board games for children. The company carefully researched the market and identified a target market of parents aged 25 to 45 with from one to three children under the age of 10. At least one parent had a college education, and total family income was over $55,000. The families in the target market spent an average of $3,000 a year on education-related purchases, including toys and games.

The Marketing Plan

Based on the target market information, Edu-Games prepared a marketing plan for its board games. The games were constructed of finished wooden pieces and packaged in sturdy boxes. Package designs illustrated the games in use, and descriptions of the educational value were clearly printed on the outside of each box. Prices were set high ($56 per game) to match the quality image, and prices were printed on the package so that customers could be certain they would pay the same price no matter where they purchased the game.

Because Edu-Games was not large enough to have its own sales force, it used distributors of games and toys to sell the product to retailers. To help the distributors, the company identified the types of retail stores where the product should sell best. Those stores were primarily bookstores with special children's collections and stores that specialize in children's apparel. The company did not want the games sold through large toy stores or discount stores because those stores did not fit the high-quality, high-priced product image. Besides, the target market did not purchase most of its educational products in those types of stores. Edu-Games produced an easy-to-assemble display that provided space for 300 games. It contained information describing the games, and their educational value.

Disappointing Results

Six months after beginning distribution, sales were much lower than expected. An evaluation of marketing activities revealed that most of the games had been distributed to large toy stores because they were the traditional customers of the distributors, and the distributors believed higher sales would result from those stores. The toy stores used a mass marketing strategy and cut the suggested price by 10 percent or more. Even with the discounts, the price was much higher than the average board game sold by the stores. Because of space limitations, many of the stores did not use the displays. Instead, the games were stacked on shelves, which did not allow customers to see the unique packaging.

Working in **Teams**

Identify personal experiences team members have had with businesses that illustrate effective and ineffective distribution. Discuss how the experiences shaped your views about the companies. As a team, develop several recommendations about how companies can improve customer satisfaction through effective distribution.

The experience of Edu-Games shows that the success of a product or a business is usually influenced by many other businesses. Even businesses that apply the marketing concept and try to respond to the needs of a target market can have problems if the businesses they use to distribute products do not follow the marketing plan.

Decision Time

Any time a product or service is marketed to a customer, several distribution decisions must be made for a satisfactory exchange to occur. Those decisions include:

- Where and when will the product be produced, sold, and used?
- What characteristics of the product or service will affect distribution?

- What services or activities must be provided in order for the product to be successfully sold?
- Is special physical handling needed?
- Who will be responsible for each of the needed distribution activities?
- When will each activity occur?
- Who is responsible for planning and managing the distribution process?

Checkpoint ▶▶

Why is merely designing an effective distribution system not enough to ensure that products will be where customers want them when they want them?

13-1 Assessment

Xtra!
Study Tools
school.cengage.com/marketing/marketing

Key Concepts

Determine the best answer.

1. True or False: For most products and services, distribution activities account for over 50 percent of the total marketing costs.

2. Distribution has the greatest effect on which of the following economic utilities?
   a. time
   b. place
   c. possession
   d. both a and b

3. When a marketer develops a marketing strategy, the distribution decisions made can determine whether the customer is able to
   a. obtain a product at the lowest cost
   b. choose from an assortment of products
   c. easily locate and purchase the products and services needed
   d. obtain the highest-quality product

4. True or False: Once a business decides on a distribution strategy, all other businesses in the channel of distribution are required to follow that plan.

Make Academic Connections

5. **Statistics** Ask 20 people to identify a recent problem they had when shopping for a product or service at a local business. Classify each response according to the marketing mix element that seemed to be the reason for the problem—product, price, distribution, or promotion. Total the numbers for each mix element and develop a graph that illustrates the results of your research.

6. **Economics** Review newspapers, business magazines, and the Internet to locate information on a situation where there is an imbalance of supply and demand resulting from a distribution problem. Write a short report on the situation, identifying who is affected, the problems that have resulted, why the situation occurred, and what is being done to resolve the economic imbalance.

Connect to

7. Develop a two-minute presentation on the importance of distribution in implementing the marketing concept. Provide examples of effective distribution to illustrate your points. Give your presentation to your teacher (judge).

Assembling Distribution Channels

GOALS

- Identify the differences between producers and consumers that are addressed by distribution channels.
- Describe the differences between direct and indirect channels of distribution.

KEY TERMS

direct channel, *p. 369*

indirect channel, *p. 369*

channel captain, *p. 371*

marketing matters

Channels of distribution are developed by businesses to perform the many marketing functions that have to be accomplished any time an exchange takes place with a final consumer. Products are sometimes distributed directly from the producer or manufacturer to the final customer. More often, there are other specialized businesses that complete the activities needed to move products from producers to final consumers. When there are businesses involved other than the producer, it is referred to as indirect distribution. The involvement of other businesses makes the distribution channel indirect rather than direct. Businesses often use both direct and indirect distribution, depending on the target market selected. The number and type of businesses in the channel are selected to help adjust differences in quantity, assortment, location, and timing that would otherwise prevent a satisfying exchange between the producer and the consumer.

Name a product that you have bought recently directly from its producer or manufacturer. Describe how you and the producer were brought together in order for the exchange to take place and what activities each of you performed to complete the exchange.

The Need for Distribution Channels

When products and services are exchanged, they move through a channel of distribution. A *channel of distribution* is made up of the organizations and individuals who participate in the movement and exchange of products and services from the producer to the final consumer. The channel can be very simple, involving only the producer and the final consumer, or it can be very complex, involving many businesses.

If you buy a local newspaper, it is often edited, printed, and distributed by one company. If you buy a copy of *USA Today*, it is written and edited by one company in Mclean, VA, printed by one of several other companies located in various parts of the country, and then distributed and sold by other companies. There are several reasons that channels of distribution are needed in marketing.

Adjusting Differences between Producers and Consumers

There are many differences in what producers develop and what consumers need. Channels of distribution allow for adjustments to be made in those differences so that the available products match the customers' needs. Consumers want to be able to buy a variety of products from many different companies (see Figure 13-1).

Adjustments are usually needed in the quantity and assortment of products, the location of the products, and the timing of production and consumption.

Differences in Quantity

Businesses sell their products to large numbers of customers. They produce thousands and even millions of those products in order to meet the total market demand. Individual consumers usually buy only a very small quantity of a product at any time. So, a channel of distribution must be able to adjust the large quantity produced by the business to match the small quantity needed by a consumer.

Differences in Assortment

A producer or a manufacturer often specializes in production. A company typically produces only a limited variety of products in one or a few product classifications. Yet consumers have needs for a great variety of products. Another adjustment made through a channel of distribution is in the assortment of products. The channel will accumulate products from a number of manufacturers and make them available in one location to give consumers adequate choice and variety to meet their needs.

Differences in Location

Customers are usually not conveniently located next to the places where products are produced. They live throughout the country and the world. It would be nearly impossible for each manufacturer and consumer to meet to complete an exchange. A channel of distribution moves the product from the place where it is produced to the variety of places where it will be consumed.

Differences in Timing of Production and Consumption

For efficiency, most manufacturers operate year-round to produce an adequate

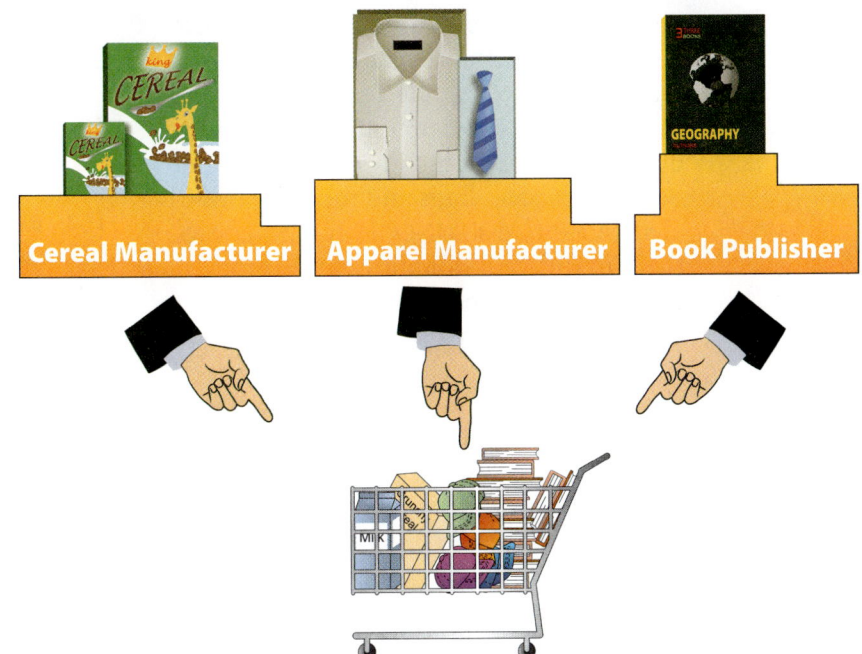

Adjusting Differences between Producers and Consumers

FIGURE 13-1

Channels of distribution help to match what businesses produce with what consumers want to buy.

supply of products. Consumers do not use many of those products year-round. Snow blowers, swimwear, gardening equipment, and children's toys are all examples of products that are purchased in much higher quantities during certain times of the year.

Producers of agricultural products may only be able to produce some products in specific growing seasons. Consumers want products such as fresh fruits and vegetables throughout the year. This presents a challenge to distributors to match seasonal agricultural production with year-round consumer demand. Making adjustments between the time of production and consumption is another responsibility of the channel of distribution.

Walk through a supermarket and study the adjustments made for the products sold there. Food has been accumulated from throughout the world. Some is fresh and some is processed. The wheat used in the bread and cereal may have been produced many months ago, processed into the products you see on the shelf, and distributed to many stores. The fruits and vegetables may have been rushed by airplane and refrigerated truck from fields in the United States or South America and delivered to the store only a few days after being harvested. Eggs and meat are evaluated and sorted so that you can purchase them in different quantities and grades. Soft drinks have been accumulated from several local and regional bottlers so that you can have a variety of choices. If the channels of distribution have worked well, the supermarket will be well stocked with all of the products you want to buy.

Providing Marketing Functions

In any exchange between producer and consumer, all of the marketing functions must be performed. If no other organizations or individuals are involved in the exchange, the functions will need to be performed by either the producer or consumer. Often neither of those participants is willing or able to perform some of the functions. Other organizations or individuals then have the opportunity to become part of the channel of distribution and perform the needed functions.

Consider marketing activities such as transportation, financing, or promotion. Some businesses do not have the special equipment or the personnel to complete those functions, but they must be completed if the product is going to be sold to the consumer. Trucking companies, railroads, and airlines can provide transportation. Banks and finance companies provide credit to businesses and consumers. Wholesalers and retailers purchase products from manufacturers, hoping to resell them at a profit. Advertising agencies, television and radio stations, magazines,

newspapers, Internet web sites, and search engines provide promotional assistance.

Increasing Marketing Efficiency

If all exchanges of products and services occurred directly between producers and consumers, a great deal of time would be required for marketing activities. Consider the number of products that you and your family purchase during one week. What if you had to locate and contact each producer and manufacturer, agree on a price, and find a way to get the product from the business to your home? You would spend most of your time on those marketing activities, and it would be an expensive process.

Figure 13-2 illustrates the efficiency of exchange that can result from a carefully planned channel of distribution. When other businesses enter the channel of distribution, they take over many of the marketing responsibilities, saving you

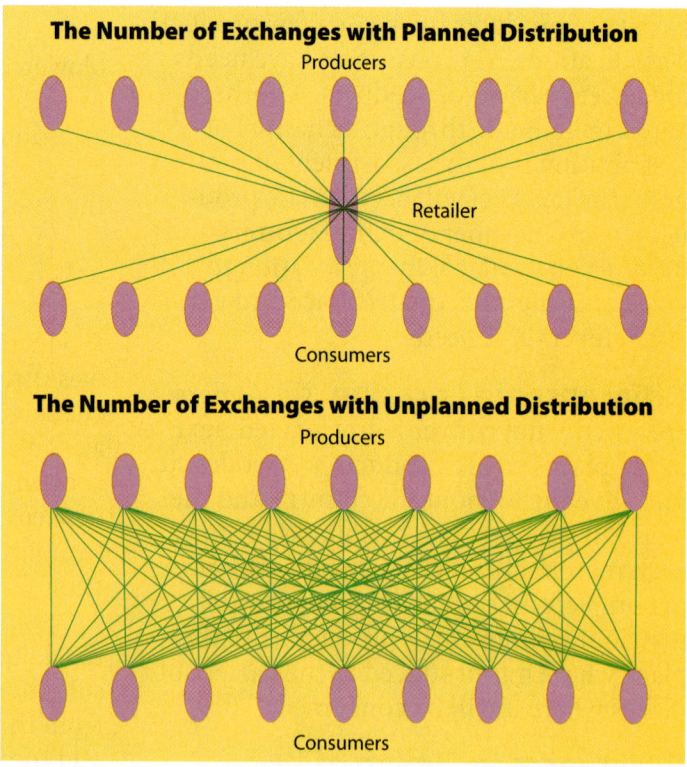

The Number of Exchanges with Planned Distribution
Producers

Retailer

Consumers

The Number of Exchanges with Unplanned Distribution
Producers

Consumers

FIGURE 13-2
A planned channel of distribution makes the exchange process much easier and more efficient than an unplanned channel.

both time and money. The retailer determines your needs and the needs of many customers like you. It then contacts the manufacturers of the needed products and has all of the products shipped to its location. You can then make one shopping trip to the business and purchase the needed products. In addition to saving time for you and the manufacturers, the other businesses are very effective at locating and purchasing the needed products and finding the most efficient ways to ship them to their locations. Therefore, the cost of the marketing functions should be reduced compared to what it would be if you had to complete those functions yourself.

Checkpoint ▶▶

What are the four differences between producers and consumers that are adjusted by distribution channels?

Planning and Managing Channels of Distribution

In order to have an effective distribution system, the channels of distribution must be carefully planned. Participants should be identified, and methods for developing and managing the channel should be considered. The channel of distribution will be most effective if all participants believe in the marketing concept, cooperate with each other, and direct their efforts at satisfying customer needs.

Channel Participants

Channel members include all of the businesses in the distribution channel. There are both direct and indirect channels of distribution. In a **direct channel**, the producer sells the product to final consumers. In a direct channel, either the producer or consumer is responsible for completing each

©GETTY IMAGES/PHOTODISC

Do you think a snowboard producer should use a direct or indirect channel of distribution?

marketing function. An **indirect channel** includes other businesses between the producer and the consumer. They buy the product from the producer or other channel members and sell to consumers or other businesses. Each channel member provides one or more of the marketing functions in an indirect channel.

A business chooses between a direct channel and an indirect channel based on several factors. Indirect channels are used most often in the sale of consumer products while direct channels are more typical in business-to-business marketing. But

Fast **FACTS**

In many international cities, McDonald's is now delivering fast-food orders to customers using drivers on motor bikes. Deliveries account for up to 80% of revenues in some Egyptian stores and are more profitable than walk-up sales. Delivery fees run 50 cents to $1 per order, but customers say it is much more convenient than standing in line.

there are many exceptions to that pattern. Some manufacturers use direct marketing methods such as catalogs, telephone sales, and factory outlets to directly reach final consumers. Increasingly, the Internet allows more direct marketing for consumer products, although many businesses still use indirect channels and include sales, distribution, and customer service specialists as a part of their Internet marketing efforts. Also, manufacturers that sell to businesses across large geographic areas and in other countries often rely on other businesses to help them with selling, distribution, financing, and other marketing functions.

Direct channels of distribution are most often selected when

- there are a small number of customers

- customers are located in a limited geographic area

- the product is complex, is developed to meet specific customer needs, or requires a great deal of service

- the business wants to maintain close control over the marketing mix

If the opposite market characteristics exist, an indirect channel of distribution will usually be developed.

Many manufacturers use multiple channels of distribution for the same product. This decision is consistent with the marketing orientation because several target markets can exist for the same product. The needs and purchasing behavior of each target market can be quite different.

Think of all of the different customers and needs that must be met by a carpet manufacturer. The same basic product may be sold directly to a contractor who is building several large office buildings. To reach a variety of target markets, the carpet might be sold through department stores, home improvement centers, and specialty carpet and flooring businesses. Some of those businesses will be contacted by the carpet manufacturer's salespeople while some very small retail businesses might buy from a wholesaler or another business that sells carpets for several manufacturers. The possible channels of distribution for a carpet manufacturer are illustrated in Figure 13-3.

Developing and Managing a Channel System

The Edu-Games example in the previous lesson showed that developing an effective channel of distribution is important if a marketing strategy is going to be

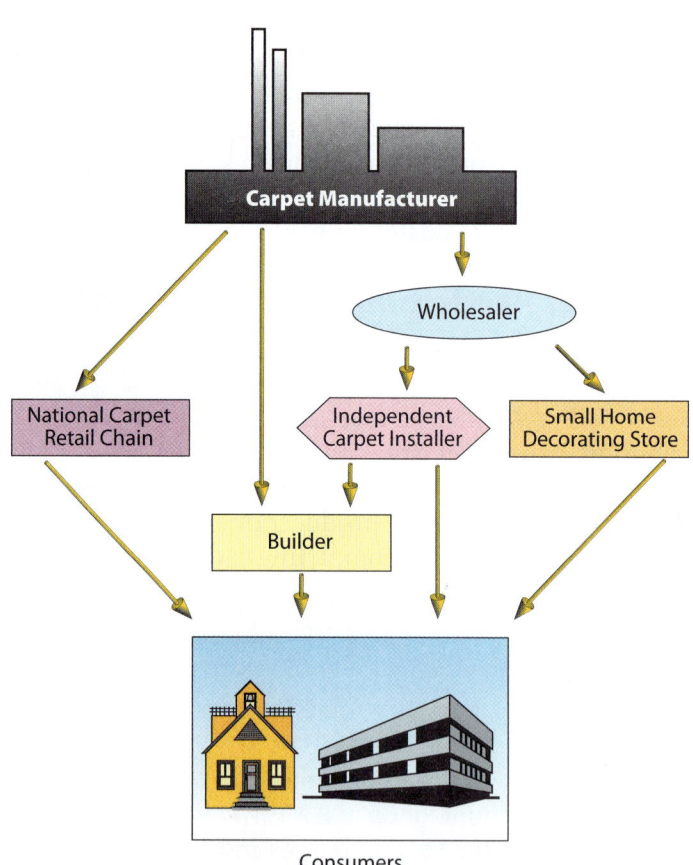

Multiple Channels of Distribution for Carpets

FIGURE 13-3
The same product may move through several channels of distribution before reaching the final consumer.

successful. Few products can be distributed using a direct channel. Therefore, channels must be developed carefully so that the product reaches the customers in the form they want, at the appropriate time and location, and at a price they can afford. Channel development and management is an important task for marketers.

Any business or individual can take responsibility for developing a channel of distribution. A manufacturer that develops a new product wants to find the best way to get the product to the target market. A retailer who discovers an important customer need will try to find a source of products that will satisfy that need. Even consumers can create channels of distribution by locating a supplier for a product they want that is not currently available in the market.

Cooperation or Conflict?
Channels of distribution are usually made up of independent businesses that treat each other as suppliers and customers as products move between them. They each have their own goals and customers and cooperate only when it is to their benefit. This often leads to problems and conflict. If a manufacturer has a very large inventory of one product and a limited supply of another, it is more likely to try to sell the first to retailers without being too concerned about what the retailer will do with the product. If a retailer is competing with another business that is cutting prices, it will try to force manufacturers and wholesalers to cut the prices the retailer has to pay. The retailer will usually not worry whether those companies are able to make a profit. Because businesses are used to competing with each other and working independently, it is sometimes difficult for a business that

©COURTESY OF ROCKWELL AUTOMATION

Automation and technology speed distribution and help channel members share information.

is a member of a channel of distribution but does not work directly with the final consumer to be concerned about satisfying the final consumer's needs.

Channel Management Responsibilities
A channel of distribution must be well managed to effectively coordinate all of the activities needed to achieve a satisfying exchange. Managing a channel of distribution is the responsibility of the channel captain. The **channel captain** takes responsibility to identify channel members, assign distribution activities, help members agree

Figure This

Downstream Activity Offers Clue to Future Sales

In order to gauge how well their products are doing in the marketplace, businesses that use intermediaries such as independent wholesalers and distributors need to distinguish between two measures of product movement. One is the businesses' own sales and orders from their distributors. The other is the sales or deliveries that their distributors make to retailers. The latter measure of product movement is often referred to as "depletion" because it is a measure of the rate at which distributors are depleting their product inventories.

The relationship between sales and depletions can be a valuable indicator of future sales trends. If sales are lower than depletions, then inventories are decreasing. In that case, distributors will have to buy more products to maintain inventory levels. On the other hand, if sales are exceeding depletions,

it means inventories are building. That might be a bad sign, indicating that sales will have to slow to keep inventories from becoming overstocked. On the other hand, it could be a favorable signal if distributors and retailers are building inventories because they anticipate a pickup in sales.

Think Critically

1. If company sales for the just-completed quarter fell by 2,000 cases, and distributor depletions increased by 10,000 cases, what is the implied change in inventory levels at the company's distributors?

2. If a car manufacturer finds that its shipments to dealers for the past month increased by 25,000 cars while dealers' depletions increased by 15,000 cars, what is the implied change in dealers' inventory levels?

---

on performance standards, and facilitate communication among channel members. The channel captain is often the biggest company in the channel of distribution but will not be effective if it uses its size to "bully" the other companies. Instead, the captain must work to satisfy the needs of each business and allow each to make a reasonable profit.

When a company works independently to achieve its goals, effective channel management is difficult. However, when several organizations work cooperatively, they often find new opportunities and methods to successfully meet customer needs better than the competitors that do not cooperate.

Channel Management Tools Technology is available to help manage a channel of distribution. *Supply-chain management (SCM) software* is used to collect

and manage the information needed by each channel member. The needed information includes raw materials and finished product inventories, production and sales records, storage and shipping data, and costs of each distribution activity. Customer information is tracked using *customer-relationship management (CRM) software*. The software analyzes target market and individual customer sales records, product requests, returns, and new market opportunities.

The efficient exchange of information between departments in a company and among the businesses in a supply chain has been improved with the introduction of *electronic data interchange (EDI)*. EDI allows direct computer-to-computer exchanges of information such as invoices, sales and inventory records, and product location and transportation records.

©GETTY IMAGES/PHOTODISC

How does EDI improve the distribution function?

Because information is converted to a standard EDI format, the information can be easily shared and analyzed in order to speed decisions and distribution activities. Also, because the information is exchanged from computer to computer, there is no need to enter information more than once, which will help cut costs and reduce the chance of human error.

Checkpoint ▶▶

What is the difference between a direct and an indirect channel of distribution?

13-2 Assessment

Xtra! Study Tools
school.cengage.com/marketing/marketing

Key Concepts

Determine the best answer.

1. When products and services are exchanged, they move through a channel of _____.

2. Which of the following is *not* one of the major differences that need to be adjusted between producers and consumers?
   a. quantity and assortment
   b. location
   c. timing
   d. each is an adjustment that needs to be made

3. Only the producer and consumer are involved in a _____ channel.
   a. direct
   b. indirect
   c. retail
   d. business-to-business

4. Under which of the following conditions would a manufacturer most likely involve other businesses in a channel of distribution?
   a. there are a small number of customers
   b. customers are located close to each other
   c. the product is simple and will require little service
   d. all are correct

5. True or False: Effective channel management is easier when each business works independently to achieve its goals.

Make Academic Connections

6. **Math** A tomato farmer has used direct distribution to sell her products to local consumers through an area farmers' market. Last year, she sold 400 bushels of tomatoes at $2.49 a pound. (There are 53 pounds in a bushel of tomatoes.) This year she is considering using an indirect channel by selling to two area supermarkets. She estimates that she can sell 650 bushels at $1.63 a pound. What will be the difference in revenue if she makes the change? What other factors should the farmer consider before changing to indirect distribution?

7. **English** Prepare a one-page written analysis of the following statement: "If there are conflicts among channel members, the channel captain should make decisions that are in the best interest of his or her business."

Connect to ◀ **DECA**
An Association of Marketing Students

8. Your team works for a small manufacturer of sunglasses with a unique film coating that offers greater UV eye protection than existing products. Identify one method of direct distribution and two possible indirect channels. Analyze the advantages and disadvantages of each and choose the one your team believes is best for consumers and the business. Make a three-minute team presentation of your analysis and recommendation to your teacher (judge). Prepare two visuals to support your presentation.

Wholesaling Manages the Middle

GOALS

- Describe the benefits that wholesalers provide to other members of a channel of distribution and to final consumers.

- Explain how the role of wholesalers is changing in an economy where many of their traditional retail customers prefer to deal directly with manufacturers.

KEY TERMS

wholesalers, *p. 375*

wholesale member clubs, *p. 376*

marketing matters

While wholesale businesses are not evident to many consumers, they play an important part of many distribution channels. They perform several specialized distribution activities as products and services move from producers to their final points of use. Wholesalers are used when they can provide marketing services more effectively and at a lower cost. They can be more effective at a lower cost because they are able to specialize and achieve economies of scale.

As industries are consolidating and large producers and national retailers are dealing directly with one another, wholesalers have been concentrating on small- to medium-sized customers who need their services to remain competitive. Wholesalers can provide less-risky access to new markets and to new research and communications technologies. They also play important roles in the expansion of international product distribution.

Identify two local retailers who obtain at least some of their products directly from producers. Why is it possible and appropriate for each company to deal directly with a producer? Discuss with other students why it is difficult for many retailers, especially small businesses, to deal directly with producers and manufacturers.

Who Needs Wholesaling?

Many marketing functions must occur in the exchange between a producer and consumer. They can be shifted and shared, but they cannot be eliminated. In many cases, producers or consumers are unwilling or unable to perform some of the functions. In other cases, they can and will perform the functions, but other organizations can complete those activities more effectively, in less time, or at a lower cost. In those cases, an organization is likely to become part of the channel of distribution.

A traditional indirect channel of distribution for consumer products would involve a producer, a retailer, and the final consumers. However, the producer may find that there are so many retailers needed to reach all of the consumers in its target markets that it cannot serve all of the retailers effectively. To obtain all of the products it wants to sell, a retailer may see the need to work with such a large number of producers that it is almost impossible to work well with each one. In those cases, the traditional channel expands to add a wholesaler.

Benefits of Wholesaling

Wholesalers are companies that assist with distribution activities between businesses. They do not work with final consumers in any significant way. Their role is to provide needed marketing functions as products and services move through the channel of distribution between producers and other businesses.

Wholesalers provide important marketing services for the channels in which they participate. Some businesses are unable to complete the marketing tasks required because of the cost or specialized resources or skills needed. Others choose not to do some tasks because they want to focus on their production or selling activities.

Wholesalers may provide one or more of the needed marketing activities better or at a lower cost. For example, a small retailer is not able to purchase most products in large quantities. Some manufacturers do not want to sell their products in small quantities. A wholesaler combines the orders of several small retailers and purchases in efficient quantities. Shipments for businesses in the same location can be combined, allowing less costly transportation methods to be utilized.

In the same way, a manufacturer usually tries to produce products throughout the year, but consumer demand for the products may be seasonal. The manufacturer may not have adequate facilities to store the products until they can be sold to retailers. The manufacturer may use wholesalers who specialize in storage and inventory management, allowing it to focus on production rather than storage.

Wholesaling Activities

The typical wholesaling activities include buying, selling, transporting, storing, and financing. Specifically, wholesalers accumulate the products of many manufacturers, develop appropriate assortments for their customers, and distribute the products to them. Wholesale businesses may finance the inventories of manufacturers until they can be sold and may extend credit to retailers to enable them to make purchases.

Wholesalers also assist manufacturers in determining needs of retailers and final consumers and provide market and product information to retailers. They help collect and analyze information on sales, costs, changes in demand, and inventory levels. Some wholesalers support the promotional efforts of manufacturers and retailers.

Most wholesalers purchase products from producers and manufacturers and then resell them to their customers. In that way, they are assuming risk by investing their money. If the products are damaged or cannot be sold at the desired price, the wholesaler loses money.

Types of Wholesalers

Wholesalers fall into three major categories—*full-service wholesalers, limited-service wholesalers,* and *agents and brokers.*

Full-service (or merchant) wholesalers take title to the products they sell and provide a full range of distribution activities. In addition to providing or arranging transportation services, they usually offer credit,

What marketing activities do wholesalers perform?

Get the Message

Truck-Side Ads

Selling advertising space on the side of semi-trailers might become a lucrative source of revenue for trucking companies. Until now, their fleets mostly have promoted only themselves. The problem with selling truck sides as roving billboards has been the inability to gauge how many people are seeing the ads. Now there is a way to do that.

Fleet Advertising, which operates a fleet of truck-side billboards, and 3M Graphics funded the development of a system that uses a global positioning satellite to track the whereabouts of trucks. It combines that information with traffic data to produce estimates of how many people are exposed to a roving truck ad.

With the high cost of billboards and with restrictions on billboards in many localities, mobile truck-side ads could find a ready market. There are numerous companies that already specialize in this medium.

Think Critically

1. How do you think traffic data are used to estimate the number of people who see a mobile ad?

2. What are the advantages of truck-side ads compared to stationary billboard ads?

---

promotional assistance, product research and information, and even product installation and repair. Full-service wholesalers may offer a broad assortment of products, such as general merchandise for supermarkets, or they may specialize in a narrow product category, such as hardware.

Limited-service (or specialized) wholesalers may not provide services such as research, credit, or promotional support. They concentrate on one or two important functions such as warehousing and storage, product delivery, or accumulating products for sale in a convenient location such as a produce or fresh fish market for supermarkets.

Agents and brokers are independent businesses that provide specialized exchange functions such as locating suppliers, selling, financing, or arranging shipments. They do not take title to products. They essentially work as an extension of the workforce of the manufacturer or retailer.

Other Wholesaling Businesses

Wholesale franchises and cooperatives are groups of small businesses that affiliate because of the benefits gained from cooperation in completing marketing and distribution activities. In a wholesale franchise, small retailers follow the guidance of a large wholesaler in operating their businesses. In return, they receive purchasing advantages and support from the wholesaler. They normally operate under the same business name, such as IGA (Independent Grocers Alliance) and NAPA (National Automotive Parts Association).

Wholesale cooperatives are wholesale organizations owned jointly by member businesses. The wholesale businesses are owned by producers or retailers to provide distribution services to members. Farmers form wholesale cooperatives to jointly brand and market their products, such as Sunkist and Land-O-Lakes. Examples of wholesale cooperatives organized by small retailers include Ace Hardware and FTD (Florists' Transworld Delivery, Inc.).

There has been a recent increase in the popularity of a unique wholesaling business. **Wholesale member clubs** are businesses that offer a variety of consumer products to members through a warehouse outlet. Many of the clubs are open to both final consumers and businesses, although the membership requirements and prices may vary for each group. Well-known wholesale clubs include Sam's Club and Costco. Products are displayed in large warehouses. Product assortments may be limited but are available in large quantities. Customers are responsible for transporting their purchased products.

The wholesale clubs initially targeted small businesses. Most now offer memberships to employees of large businesses and organizations and also to individuals.

Because individuals as well as businesses buy products from wholesale clubs, these companies cross the line between retailing and wholesaling.

Checkpoint ▶▶▶

What types of benefits does a wholesaler provide to other members of a distribution channel?

The Changing Role of Wholesalers

As many manufacturers and retailers get bigger and as distribution and communication methods improve, it would seem that the need for wholesalers would decrease. In fact, some large retailers refuse to deal with most wholesalers. They believe that they can get better service and prices if they work directly with manufacturers. As marketing has changed, wholesalers have adjusted their business practices to continue to participate in channels of distribution.

There are still many more small- and medium-sized retailers and manufacturers than there are large businesses. Those smaller businesses need effective purchasing and distribution methods to compete with the large businesses. Wholesalers perform those functions because they evaluate the products of many manufacturers, buy and ship in large quantities, and assist with financing and many other marketing activities.

Access to Markets

Wholesalers provide access to new markets with less risk than if the retailer developed that market alone. Wholesalers help retailers become aware of new products and new manufacturers. They make products available from businesses located long distances away. For manufacturers who want to expand into new markets or sell to different types of businesses, wholesalers may already have experience in those markets.

They can develop new business opportunities more effectively than if the manufacturer attempts it alone.

Export and import organizations are very important in building international business. They are informed of the conditions and customer needs as well as business procedures and legal requirements for operating in the international market. Without the help of wholesalers, many companies would not be successful in international markets.

Of the recent changes in wholesaling, among the most important are better communications and information, improved technology, and broader customer service. Effective wholesalers believe in the marketing concept. They work to identify their customers and understand their needs. They learn of the problems the customers are having with products and marketing activities and help them to solve those problems.

Fast FACTS

According to the 2002 U.S. Economic Census report, 435,521 U.S. wholesalers generated sales of more than $4.6 trillion dollars. At the same time, 1.1 million retail businesses reported total U.S. sales of just under $3.1 trillion. Wholesalers generated one-fifth of their total sales in foreign markets.

Specialized Services

Many wholesalers are adding marketing research and marketing information services. They help their customers gather information and provide them with data that will help the businesses improve their operations and decisions. Computer technology can process orders more rapidly and keep track of the quantity and location of products. New methods of storing and handling products reduce product damage, the cost of distribution, and the time needed to get products from the manufacturer to the customer. Wholesalers are providing additional services to their customers such as marketing and promotional planning, 24-hour ordering and emergency deliveries, specialized storage facilities, and individualized branding and packaging services.

Checkpoint ▸▸▸

How are wholesalers adapting to consolidation in the marketplace?

13-3 Assessment

school.cengage.com/marketing/marketing

Key Concepts

Determine the best answer.

1. True or False: The costs of distribution activities are usually higher when a wholesaler is used to complete them.

2. True or False: When a producer or manufacturer uses a wholesaler to sell consumer products, the need for retailing is eliminated.

3. Independent wholesale businesses that provide specialized exchange functions but do not take title to goods are known as
   a. limited service wholesalers
   b. merchant wholesalers
   c. agents and brokers
   d. wholesale franchises and cooperatives

4. Wholesale member _____ are businesses that offer a variety of common consumer products for sale to selected members through a warehouse outlet.

5. Which of the following is *not* one of the ways wholesalers are responding to changing market conditions?
   a. developing and providing access to new markets
   b. offering export and import services for foreign markets
   c. gathering and providing information and data to customers to improve operations
   d. reducing the number of marketing services offered to cut costs

Make Academic Connections

6. **Research** The Fast FACTS feature in this lesson identifies the number of wholesale businesses in the United States and their total revenues in 2002. Use the Internet to locate the U.S. Economic Census for 1992. Determine the number of wholesale businesses and their total revenues reported in that census. Construct a table and a graph that compares the changes in the wholesale industry during the ten-year period.

7. **History** Identify and conduct research on one wholesale franchise or cooperative. Prepare a report that identifies when and how it was started, the reasons it was formed, how it has expanded and changed over the years, and future plans for the organization. Include a picture of the company's logo in your report.

Connect to ◀DECA

8. As a sales representative for a full-service merchant wholesaler, you are contacting a new restaurant owner who does not currently use a wholesaler. The owner purchases fresh foods from local growers and buys most other products and supplies from a local wholesale member club or through online purchases from other businesses. Prepare and deliver a three-minute sales presentation to your teacher (judge) on the benefits to the owner of using your wholesale business for all purchases rather than the current practice.

Retailing Reaches Consumers

GOALS

- Define retailing and describe ways to distinguish various types of retailers.
- Describe ways that retailing is changing in response to changes in consumer preferences and the business environment.

KEY TERMS

retailer, *p. 379*

inventory shrinkage, *p. 380*

specialty or limited-line retailers, *p. 380*

mixed merchandise retailers, *p. 380*

service retailers, *p. 381*

non-store retailing, *p. 382*

franchising, *p. 383*

atmospherics, *p. 384*

marketing matters

Consumers purchase most of their products and services from retailers. While retailers do not develop the product, they are responsible for the marketing mix that consumers see. Retailers choose the product assortment and select the locations where consumers can make purchases, set prices, and control much of the promotion. They often provide information and customer service during and after the sale. They are usually responsible if customers have questions or problems with a purchase. Because retailers are the consumer contact for all members in a channel of distribution, their role is critical. As consumer preferences and the business environment change, retailing quickly changes in response. The growth of Internet sales and the adoption of new store designs and sales technology are among the important challenges facing retailers.

Make a list of the ten retailers that you have visited most recently. Classify each as a local independent business, franchise, or regional or national chain. What products or product categories does each retailer carry? What factors led you to buy or not buy from each retailer during your visit.

The Role of Retailing

The final business organization in an indirect channel of distribution for consumer products is a **retailer**. While some large discount retailers sell products to other businesses, their primary customers are individual consumers purchasing to meet their own needs. Retailers accumulate the products their customers need by buying from manufacturers or wholesalers. They display the products and provide product information so that customers can evaluate them. Most retail businesses help customers purchase products by accepting credit cards or providing other credit or financing choices. Additional services such as product assembly, installation, alterations, repairs, layaway, gift-wrapping, and delivery are provided by many retail stores.

In addition to offering products and services for consumers, retailers support the marketing activities of wholesalers and manufacturers. They often finance the inventory by paying the manufacturer or wholesaler before the products are sold to consumers. In addition to purchasing products for resale, retailers store large amounts of inventory so that customers have a variety of product choices and ready availability if they decide to make a purchase. Because of that, the retailers are reducing the storage costs of the other businesses and assuming much of the risk involved in maintaining an inventory of products. Products can be lost, damaged, stolen, or go out of style before they are sold. A major cost to retailers results from inventory shrinkage. **Inventory shrinkage** is a loss of products due to theft, fraud, negligence, or error.

Promotion is an important marketing activity of retailers. Increasingly, retailers are involved in marketing research and marketing-information management. Some retailers even take responsibility for transporting products from the manufacturer to their distribution centers and on to individual stores.

Types of Retailers

It is difficult to describe retailing with precision because of the variety of businesses that sell to final consumers. Because there are so many consumers and their needs and purchasing behaviors are so different, retail businesses develop to respond to those differences.

Some consumers carefully plan their purchases, gather information in advance of shopping for products, and want to complete their shopping as quickly as possible. Other consumers use very little planning, gather information about products while they are in a store or mall, and enjoy spending a great deal of time shopping.

You probably know people who make frequent trips to stores and make a large number of both small and large purchases. There are other consumers who shop infrequently but spend large amounts of money when they make a purchase decision. Some people prefer to do their

Why is it important for retailers to understand the purchasing behavior of customers?

purchasing through catalogs or over the Internet rather than travel to the stores. Retail businesses are available that match each of these types of shopping behaviors. There are several ways to examine the various types of retailing.

Product Mix of Retailers One way of categorizing stores is by the types of products offered in the businesses. Some retailers specialize in one or a few product categories while others offer customers a wide range of products.

Specialty or limited-line retailers offer products from one category of merchandise or closely related items. Examples include food, automotive, apparel, lawn and garden, music, or travel. Some stores in this category offer a wide variety of types of products while others may be very specialized. For example, within the category of food, it is possible to find businesses that sell only coffee, cookies, or fresh fruits and cheeses while other businesses offer many varieties of food in hundreds of product categories.

Mixed merchandise retailers offer products from several different categories. Common examples of mixed merchandise retailers are supermarkets in which you can buy many products other than food, department stores that may offer 20 or more distinct departments of products, and large drug stores that sell pet food, automotive products, electronic equipment, and health-related products in addition to medications.

A recent successful example of mixed merchandise retailing is the "dollar" store. Dollar stores typically are smaller, convenience-type stores that offer a limited assortment of household and packaged food items at deep discounts. The stores are often targeted at families and singles seeking bargain prices for routine household purchases.

A newer concept in retailing is the superstore. *Superstores* are very large stores that offer consumers wide choices of products at lower prices. Many of today's superstores began as discount stores such as Wal-Mart and Kmart. They have now developed much larger stores that combine groceries, home products, electronics, garden centers, and even food courts. Most superstores combine a variety of product categories so that consumers can use the store for one-stop shopping. Limited-line superstores sell products in a narrower product category but offer consumers many choices of products, brands, and features within that category. Two of the most popular types of limited-line superstores today are computer stores and consumer electronics stores.

A final category is **service retailers**, which have services as their primary offering with a limited number of products for sale that complement the services. Examples include barber shops, movie theaters, and auto service centers.

Location of Retailers An important characteristic of retailing is the location of the store. The location can be studied in relation to the customer or to other businesses. *Convenience stores* are located very close to their customers, offering a limited line of products that consumers use regularly. Most convenience stores sell gasoline, food, and household products. Other convenience stores are becoming popular, including businesses that provide packing and mailing, photocopy and printing services, and movie and computer game rentals.

Judgment Call

When Is Cooperative Pricing Ethical?

In some industries, controlling prices is difficult. That is especially true in an oligopoly where a few large businesses offer very similar or identical products. If a customer wants to purchase a car and several dealers sell the same models, the customer will shop to find the lowest price. Dealers know they must be competitive.

When business people see that they are competing in an oligopoly, they might be tempted to agree with other businesses to keep prices high. To protect consumers, the federal government makes it illegal for businesses to "fix" prices. Recently, there have been high-profile investigations of alleged price fixing in both the oil industry for gas prices and the dairy industry for the price of milk. Both of these industries sell commodities that do not vary from company to company.

It is difficult for the government to regulate pricing when a few large firms compete. For example, it is not unusual for an airline to announce a price change to take place in several weeks. Then competing airlines can determine if they are going to match the price change. While this pricing practice is not illegal, it has much the same effect as illegal price fixing.

Think Critically

1. Do you think the legal pricing practice described for the airline industry is ethical?

2. How is pricing affected when large competing companies merge?

Shopping centers are a set of stores located together and planned as a unit to meet a range of customer needs. There are several types of shopping centers, based on size and types of businesses. *Shopping strips* contain about 5 to 15 stores grouped together along a street. They offer a limited number of emergency and convenience products such as fast food, gasoline, laundry services, and drug stores. *Neighborhood centers* have between 20 and 30 stores that offer a broader range of products meeting the regular and frequent shopping needs of consumers located within a few miles of the stores. *Regional shopping centers* contain 100 or more businesses. These large shopping centers attempt to meet most or all of consumers' shopping needs. The centers are developed around several large department or discount stores. They often attract customers from ten or more miles away.

The world's largest mall is the South China Mall in Dongguan, China. It includes 1,500 stores and covers 9.6 million square feet. In comparison, the 4.2-million-square-foot Mall of America in Minneapolis, Minnesota, offers customers the opportunity to visit over 520 businesses, 50 restaurants, an indoor amusement theme park, aquarium, and entertainment district. It is an international travel destination as well as a retail shopping extravaganza.

Stand-alone stores are large businesses located in an area where there are no other competing businesses nearby. They offer either a large variety of products or unique products. Stand-alone businesses must have products that customers cannot easily find in more convenient locations or products so important or unique that consumers will make a special trip to the business. Examples of stand-alone businesses are some auto dealerships, superstores, and lawn-and-garden centers.

Non-Store Retailing A unique category of retail businesses is non-store

NET Bookmark

As your textbook explains, the world's largest mall is the South China Mall in Dongguan, China. However, business at the mall has not met owners' expectations. Access school.cengage.com/marketing/marketing and click on the link for Chapter 13. Read the article from the *International Herald Tribune*. Then give some reasons why you think the mall has not yet been successful.

school.cengage.com/marketing/marketing

retailing. **Non-store retailing** involves selling directly to the consumer at home rather than requiring the consumer to travel to a store. Two of the oldest and most common forms of non-store retailing are door-to-door selling and catalog sales. Many years ago, traveling salespeople sold many consumer products. The salespeople traveled to the customers' homes because consumers took infrequent shopping trips. This method is used less frequently today because of cost and changing shopping behavior, but organizations such as Avon Products and the Girl Scouts still use door-to-door selling. Some home sales are done through organized home parties where friends gather for food and activities as well as to see the latest products in categories from jewelry to art and even specialty food products.

The sale of general merchandise through mail order catalogs once was popular, but it declined as shopping centers became more convenient and travel became easier for more and more people. However, in the past decade, catalog sales have regained much of their past popularity as a result of express delivery services and strong guarantees and warranty programs by businesses. Rather than offering general merchandise, the most popular catalogs today offer specialty merchandise products.

Other types of non-store retailing include vending machines, telephone sales, televised shopping clubs, and direct mail selling. The newest and potentially the most lucrative form is Internet retailing such as Amazon.com. In addition, numerous supermarkets, restaurants, and other retail businesses now allow local customers to place orders from a home computer, pay by credit card, and have the order delivered in a matter of minutes, if needed.

Checkpoint ▶▶

What are three common ways to distinguish or classify various types of retailers?

How Is Retailing Changing?

Retailing has always been known for variety as well as rapid change. There is nothing to suggest that change will not continue. Retailing is likely to be very different in the next ten years than it is now. Also, because of the large number of retailers and the choices available to consumers, it will be increasingly difficult to compete in many types of retail businesses. Consumers expect variety, quality, service, and low price. Retailers will have to be very effective at purchasing, selling, and business operations. To be profitable, they will have to find the most efficient ways to operate in order to keep costs low.

Changing Types of Retailers

It is likely that there will continue to be a need for both specialty and mixed merchandise stores. Some people predicted that specialty stores would disappear as people did more one-stop shopping. Yet there are a large number of consumers who are willing to invest more time in shopping and are looking for a wider choice as well as unique or unusual items that are not widely available. The number of small specialty retail businesses has begun to increase again after going through a period of decline. The very large specialty businesses also continue to grow.

The Expanding Internet

The growth of the Internet and an increased level of consumer comfort in making online purchases is expanding Internet retailing opportunities. Very small businesses and even individuals have found that they can compete effectively when selling merchandise online. Easy to use web design and shopping-basket software and the availability of businesses that will manage online stores, financial transactions, shipping, and even customer service make Internet retailing possible for almost anyone who has a product for sale. While the first Internet retailers were usually click-only businesses, meaning they sold products online only, most of the major retailers today offer products for sale online as well as through their brick-and-mortar stores. Customers are able to search for merchandise online before going to a store, make the purchase through the Internet and pick it up at the store, make merchandise returns to the store, or arrange customer service for in-store purchases online. The lines between Internet and in-store retailing are becoming increasingly blurred.

The Growth of Franchising

Franchising is a very popular type of retail ownership. **Franchising** is a business

Working in **Teams**

Select a retail business that has made a change in the way it does business. For example, perhaps the business has incorporated technology, made changes to its shopping environment, or moved into international markets. As a team, discuss why you believe the change was made and whether it has been effective. Explain your answer.

relationship in which the developer of a business idea sells others the rights to the business idea and the use of the business name. In a franchise business, the owner (the *franchiser*) develops a basic business plan and operating procedures. Other people (*franchisees*) purchase the rights to open and operate the businesses according to the standard plans and operating procedures. Franchise fees are paid to the franchiser for the business idea and assistance.

Franchises allow people with limited experience to enter a business. They are guided by the franchise plan and training, which can reduce the risk of failure. Popular franchises increase customer awareness of a business because many businesses operate in different locations using the same franchise name and promotions. Examples of successful retail franchises include restaurants, financial services, hotels, oil change services, and copying businesses.

Increased Use of Technology

Technology is having a big impact on retailers. Not only are most business operations managed with computers, but also new types of equipment are being used in businesses to store, distribute, and display products. For example, customers can shop for products by using a computer screen on a kiosk rather than by walking around a store. When a product is selected from the description and picture on the screen, the consumer inserts a credit card into the computer. The product is packaged and available for pickup at the front of the store when the customer is finished shopping.

Technology has particularly enhanced the merchandising function of retailing. Starting with electronic inventory systems using bar codes or electronic tags on all merchandise, products can be tracked from the point of manufacture until they are sold. Retailers use optical scanning sales terminals to instantly record sales and merchandise returns. A detailed record of each product is maintained and instantly updated so that the store can track sales, prices, merchandise shortages,

©GETTY IMAGES/PHOTODISC

How has the use of bar codes changed the way retailers do business?

damage, returns, and even detailed customer data matched to sales. That information can be shared with channel members to replenish inventory of fast-moving merchandise, cancel orders of products customers do not want, and improve pricing and promotional strategies.

The Shopping Experience

While some shoppers want to spend very little time in a store and expect an efficient shopping experience, others are attracted to shopping as an exciting social experience. Retailers are increasingly concerned about atmospherics. **Atmospherics** are the elements of the shopping environment that are appealing to customers, attract them to a store, and encourage them to buy. The major elements of atmospherics are the store location, exterior and interior appearance, store layout and display, and the shopping environment.

Many stores have reduced product display space and widened aisles, changed interior colors and lighting, and used more visual features and appealing product presentations. Some stores have organized merchandise so that shoppers can see products displayed in the types of settings where they would be used and can participate in product demonstrations. They have product experts available to answer questions and help with purchase decisions.

The Global Marketplace

Global retailing holds a great deal of promise for the future. While many manufacturers and wholesalers have been involved in international marketing for a number of years, retailers are often reluctant to expand into other countries. Several types of retail businesses have successfully moved into Eastern and Western Europe, Central and South America, and Asia. As countries of the former Soviet Union and Africa develop their economies, retail opportunities will expand there as well. Many of the U.S. fast-food businesses have been quite successful in international marketing as have businesses in the travel industry, including hotels and automobile rental agencies. U.S. fashions have wide acceptance, so specialty apparel stores are looking at other countries as likely places to expand their businesses.

Checkpoint ▶▶

In what ways is retailing changing in response to shifting consumer preferences and changes in the business environment?

13-4 Assessment

Key Concepts

Determine the best answer.

1. In an indirect channel of distribution for consumer products, the final business organization is a
   a. manufacturer
   b. wholesaler
   c. retailer
   d. customer

2. _____ offer products from one category of merchandise or closely related items.
   a. Specialty or limited-line retailers
   b. Mixed merchandise retailers
   c. Superstores
   d. Non-store retailers

3. True or False: The person who purchases the rights to open and operate a franchise is known as the franchisee.

4. The elements of the shopping environment that are appealing to customers, attract them to a store, and encourage them to buy are
   a. pricing strategies
   b. store location
   c. employee training
   d. atmospherics

Make Academic Connections

5. **Research** Use the Internet or business publications to identify the five largest U.S. retailers in the following categories:
   a. specialty or limited-line stores
   b. department stores
   c. discount stores
   d. retail franchises
   e. Internet retailers
   Prepare a table to present your findings.

6. **History** A concept that describes how retail businesses change over time is known as the "wheel of retailing." Use the Internet or business textbooks to gather information on this concept. Prepare a visual that illustrates the concept and a two-minute speech that describes the concept and its effect on retail businesses.

Connect to

7. Your marketing team has been asked to plan a neighborhood shopping center for the community near your school. Select a location, create a drawing of the layout of the center and select 20 stores that you believe would be effective tenants based on characteristics of local shoppers. Present and describe your plan to your teacher (judge).

Physical Distribution

GOALS

- Describe the various means by which products are transported within a channel of distribution.
- Explain the common options for storing and handling products while they are moving through the distribution channel.
- Examine the importance of order processing and inventory control to the overall effectiveness of a physical distribution plan.

KEY TERMS

physical distribution (logistics), *p. 386*

warehouse, *p. 389*

distribution centers, *p. 390*

marketing matters

It is important to have the right combination of businesses in a channel of distribution. Merely selecting businesses does not ensure that products will move effectively from the producer to the consumer. An important part of channel planning is physical distribution, the handling and movement of products through the channel. Businesses that specialize in specific physical distribution activities are often included in a channel of distribution. All parts of the physical distribution process must be carefully planned, coordinated, and controlled in order for products to reach customers on time and in good condition. The primary physical distribution activities are transportation, storage and product handling, and information processing.

Identify a small, fragile product and a large, heavy product. Identify several ways each of the products could be transported from the manufacturer to the customer.

Choosing Transportation Methods

When most people think of physical distribution, they probably think of shipping or transportation. It is much more complicated than that. **Physical distribution** (also known as *logistics*) is the process of efficiently and effectively moving products and materials through the distribution channel. The main physical distribution activities are transportation, storage, and product handling. Physical distribution also requires information processing to make sure accurate records are maintained throughout the process.

The Physical Distribution Process

Products are usually handled many times as they move from manufacturing through several forms of transportation and many locations to the place where they will be consumed or sold. Products may be grouped into large units for transportation and then divided into smaller units for display, sale, storage, or use, all requiring further handling and packaging.

Usually products do not move continuously through the channel of distribution.

They are stored as each business processes paperwork, sells to the next channel member, and determines the location of distribution. Storage facilities must be arranged to hold and protect the product. Inventory control procedures must be developed so that the product does not become lost.

Moving the Product

The first step in physical distribution planning is deciding how products will be moved from the producer to the customers. There are several transportation methods used to move most common products—railroad, truck, airplane, ship or boat, and pipeline. As you consider those alternatives, some are automatically eliminated because they are not available in certain locations or are not equipped to handle the type of product to be shipped. You clearly would not send small packages by rail or by ship, and you would not ship iron ore and coal by airplane. Other factors such as the speed of delivery needed, any special handling required, and cost enter into the choice of transportation methods.

Railroads Railroads are useful for carrying large quantities of heavy and bulky items. Raw materials, industrial equipment, and large shipments of consumer products from the factory to retailers often are moved by rail. The cost of this method is relatively low if a large quantity of a product is moved, but the total cost to ship one or more carloads of a product is high. Products move quite slowly on trains compared to other methods of transportation.

Problems exist in using railroads for shipping products. Equipment is not always available where it is needed, and it takes time to move empty cars to new locations. Many areas of the country are not served by rail, so other forms of transportation will be needed to and from the closest rail site. The time needed to load and unload freight from rail cars is long.

Safety is a major factor in choosing the transportation method to move many industrial products such as chemicals.

Railroads are responding to the need for improved service to customers. Railroad tracks and equipment are being upgraded, and routes are being rescheduled to improve customer service. Newer methods of product handling have been developed, including packing products into large containers or truck trailers which are then hauled on flatbed rail cars. To speed rail shipments to customers, it is now possible for a business to send several carloads of products from the production point and redirect them to customers en route as sales are made.

Trucks Trucks are the most flexible of the major transportation methods. They can handle small or large shipments, goods that are very durable or require special handling, and products that are going across town or across the country. Trucks can reach almost any location and can provide relatively rapid service. Trucking costs are relatively low for short distances and easy-to-handle products but increase for longer-distance or more difficult shipments.

Many companies own their own trucks. Small companies can often afford to own and maintain a delivery vehicle. Large manufacturers, wholesalers, and retailers often own fleets of trucks to be able to move products where and when needed. Trucking firms are important channel members. They provide the specialized service of transporting products to other channel members. They often have special product handling equipment, storage facilities, and well-trained drivers to insure that products are moved rapidly and safely.

Ships and Boats A large number of products sold internationally are transported by water. While airlines move small shipments rapidly, ships can handle large quantities and large products very well at a much lower cost than air shipments. The major problem with this form of transportation is speed. Ships are relatively slow, and it may take several weeks after a product is loaded on the ship before it is delivered to the customer. Also, there is a risk of large losses if a ship is damaged by weather or other conditions. Ships usually must be used in combination with trucks or railroads, as they are limited to travel between major ocean ports with terminals that have the appropriate product-handling capabilities.

Boats on inland waterways such as lakes and large rivers are another type of water transportation used for shipping. Barges and other cargo-handling boats are used to ship products such as coal, grain, cement, and other bulky and nonperishable items. Like ships, they are rather slow, but they can handle large quantities at relatively low prices.

Airplanes If you want products delivered rapidly and can afford a higher cost, air transportation will often be the choice. Small parcels can be carried on commercial flights while large products

Virtual Marketing

Tracking Shipments Online

Transportation companies use the Internet to let their customers and clients know precisely where shipments are, when they are due to arrive at their destinations, and even what is inside various packages. Providing detailed shipping information is part of a larger trend toward integrating information among senders, transportation companies, and recipients. Properly executed, it can let retailers automatically manage inventory, anticipate and fulfill supply needs, and reduce the valuable time lost when shipments unnecessarily sit in warehouses. It can also give retailers more information to relay to customers who might be waiting for an item to arrive.

An early hurdle that prevented many companies from fully embracing consolidated online shipping and inventory information was data security. However, as encryption technology has improved and the security threat has become minimal, companies have been more willing to adopt these online services.

Think Critically

1. How can better information reduce the amount of time a valuable part sits in a shipper's warehouse before it is put to a productive use?

2. Search the Internet for a web site of an package delivery company. What kinds of information about a shipment can customers obtain from the web site?

or large quantities of a product can be moved using cargo planes.

Because of the high transportation costs, many companies do not consider air as a transportation choice. When other factors are considered, air transportation may not be as expensive as it seems. For example, the speed of air delivery reduces the need for product storage. Products may need to be handled less, and the speed of distribution reduces spoilage, damage, and theft. Companies that do not regularly use air transportation may choose that method for special or emergency deliveries.

Pipelines While not used for many products, pipelines are an important transportation method. Gas, oil, and water are moved in large volumes over long distances through pipelines. Even some products you would not think of move by pipe. Small coal and wood particles can be mixed with water into a slurry and sent through a pipeline between locations. Pipelines are expensive to construct and can be difficult to maintain. Once built, though, they can be a very inexpensive method to use because a large amount of product can move through the pipeline. It may also be the only choice to deliver products from some locations, such as crude oil from remote oil fields.

Combining Methods Products often move through long distribution channels among several businesses. It is likely that many will be transported using combinations of transportation methods. A

Why are trucks a popular mode of transporting products?

shipment of appliances may be moved from a factory to a rail site by truck, moved across the country by rail, and then loaded onto other trucks to be delivered to retailers.

Companies like FedEx, UPS, and the U.S. Postal Service employ their own fleets of cargo planes and delivery trucks to move small shipments between cities throughout the world overnight. Gasoline and other petroleum products are moved from a refinery to locations across the country by pipeline. Then trucks are used to transport the products to wholesalers, retailers, and business customers.

Checkpoint ▶▶

What are the common transportation methods used in channels of distribution?

Storage and Product Handling

Since production and consumption seldom occur at the same time, products must be held until they can be used. This means that methods and facilities for storage must be developed as a part of marketing. Effective storage allows channel members to balance supply and demand, but it adds to the costs of products and adds the risk that products may be damaged or stolen or become outdated while being stored.

Warehouses

Storage of most products is usually done in warehouses. A **warehouse** is a building designed to store large amounts of raw materials or finished products until they can be used or sold. Warehouses can be privately owned by any of the companies in the channel of distribution. Private ownership allows the company to develop the specific type of facility needed for the products being handled at the locations where they are most needed. For companies that need limited storage space or need it less frequently, public warehouses are available. Public warehouses are often used for overflow storage or for products that are seasonal.

If you live in a medium- to large-sized city, you may have an area of town that was a warehouse district. Large, old, multistory buildings were used in the past by many wholesalers and manufacturers. They were often located near the center of town to be close to the retail businesses. Today, you will find storage facilities located at the edge of town near interstate highways or airports. The buildings are still large, but they are usually only one story tall. If you enter the building, you will likely see long conveyor belts or chains that move products through the building. There may even be computer-controlled trucks and carts (robots) that move products from area to area. Special storage shelves and equipment can move products in and out without the need for handling by people. Bar codes on the shelves, containers, and packages allow computers to keep track of the location of products and the length of time they are in storage.

Distribution Centers

The newest kind of storage facility is known as a distribution center. A **distribution center** is a facility used to accumulate products from several sources and then regroup, repackage, and send them as quickly as possible to the locations where they will be used. A large retailer may have a number of distribution centers located throughout the country and the world. Thousands of products are ordered from many manufacturers and shipped in huge quantities from the manufacturers to the distribution centers. The products are needed in various assortments and quantities in the hundreds of stores owned by the retailer. The costs of storage and transportation are high, so the distribution centers must be good at receiving the products, combining the different products into shipments for each store, and routing those shipments quickly. The goal of the distribution center is to reduce the costs of physical distribution while increasing the availability of products to customers. That can be done by using efficient product-handling methods and reducing the time products remain in the distribution center.

Packaging

Another important part of product handling is packaging. Packaging is a part of product development in that it aids in the effective transportation, storage, and use of the product. For many products, packaging also serves as a promotional tool. But the primary purpose of packaging is to protect the product from the time it is produced until it can be consumed. If the product is damaged or destroyed as it moves between companies, a great deal of money that has been invested in the product by manufacturers and other channel members will be lost.

Packaging materials need to be selected and packaging methods developed that protect the product and allow it to be shipped in appropriate quantities. A product being handled with a forklift and shipped in large containers by trucks and rail cars needs to be packaged differently from a product being shipped in small quantities to the consumer using a parcel service. Products sent across town require different packaging and packing than those shipped around the world.

Checkpoint ▶▶

What are the common options for storing and handling products while they are moving through the distribution channel?

Understand Personal Financial Statements

Just as corporations use financial statements to track and analyze their financial status, individuals should use personal financial statements to measure their personal financial health. An important measure of your long-term financial strength is an increasing net worth. Your net worth is determined from a personal balance sheet using the basic formula: Net Worth = Total Assets − Total Liabilities.

Total assets are made up of current and long-term assets. Current assets include checking and savings accounts, money owed to you that will be paid in the near future, and cash on hand or in the bank. Long-term assets might include long-term savings and investments, such as certificates of deposit, stocks, bonds, and things you own such as a car. Later on, long-term assets might include the cash value of life insurance, real estate, retirement plans, and other long-term investments.

Current liabilities include current bills owed, money you may have borrowed, and payments on purchases. If you have a job, income taxes you will owe at the end of the year are current liabilities. Later, your rent will be a current liability. Long-term liabilities are amounts you owe that will be paid over a period longer than a year, such as a car loan. In future years, long-term liabilities may include a home mortgage or payments on loans to finance your education.

Determining your net worth by preparing a balance sheet can help you assess whether you have sufficient assets to pay for your immediate and long-term debts.

A personal cash flow statement is another tool for evaluating your financia health. The cash flow statement shows where immediate income (cash) is coming from and how it will be used during a defined short time period, such as a month. Your monthly personal cash flow can be defined as: Monthly Cash Flow = Monthly Income Received − Monthly Expenses Paid.

Cash income could be money from your job, any sporadic income (from baby-sitting or snow shoveling jobs or birthday gifts), or your allowance. Interest on savings is considered income when it is paid. Later, if you have income from investments, rental property, or loans, it would appear in your cash flow statement in the month it is received.

Cash expenses are the payments you make for clothing, entertainment, and other living expenses. If you borrowed money, the payments you make are expenses. In the future, cash expenses may include mortgage payments, utilities, insurance, and taxes.

You should calculate cash flow to make sure you have enough cash on hand to meet all required payments. If not, you will have to use savings or borrow money, which hurts your overall financial position. Your goal should be to have a positive cash flow most months and a growing net worth over time. If your net worth is negative, but your current cash flow is positive, you can construct a plan to improve your net worth.

Develop Your Skill

To analyze your current financial health, use the Internet to locate forms for a personal balance sheet and cash flow statement and complete them as accurately as possible.

Share your financial statements with your parents or another trusted adult and ask for feedback on your financial health. Discuss your future plans and financial goals and how they can be accomplished with financial planning.

Construct financial statements you believe might reflect the financial condition you would like to have in ten years. What will you have to do to achieve that goal?

PHOTO: ©GETTY IMAGES/PHOTODISC

Information Processing

Physical distribution systems must match the supply of products with the demand for those products. First, products must be available in adequate assortments and quantities. Then, the inventory of products can be matched with the needs of consumers and channel members. An effective information system must be able to predict consumer demand to be sure that an adequate supply is available. The system must assure that the supply matches demand so there is not too much or too little of a product. Products must be routed to where they are needed as quickly as possible. The two important parts of the physical distribution information system are order processing and inventory control.

Order Processing

Order processing begins when a customer places an order. Typically the order is placed with a salesperson, but the order may be placed by telephone or fax, by computer using a direct connection, or on the Internet.

When the supplier receives the order, a system must be in place so that the order can be sent to the department in the business where it can be filled. At the same time, the order is also being processed by the accounting department to determine the terms of the sale, method of payment, and cost of the products. Other business people are determining the method, cost, and timing of transportation.

When the order is filled, it must be packaged and prepared for shipment. The order is checked to make sure it is complete, and information is forwarded to the accounting department so that an invoice can be prepared. The shipper is notified so that transportation is available. The customer is informed that the order has been processed and shipped. This procedure is repeated at each stage of the channel of distribution until the product is delivered to the final consumer. Order processing is not complete until payment has been received and recorded, the product has been delivered and accepted by the customer, all shipping and delivery records have been completed, and product inventory records have been updated.

Inventory Control

The level of inventory affects the cost of marketing and the level of customer satisfaction. If too much inventory is maintained, storage costs will be too high. There is also a risk that customer needs will change or the product will spoil or become outdated and will not be sold. If not enough inventory is available, customers will not be able to buy what they need, and sales and goodwill will be lost.

An inventory control system must maintain several types of information. It is important to know what products are in inventory, what quantity of each product is available, and how long each has been in inventory. Effective inventory control methods maintain information in a computer, so it is not necessary to look at the inventory each time there is a question.

A second important feature of an inventory system is a method to determine what products to order and what quantities to order. An inventory control system should identify how much of each product is being sold and how rapidly. The people responsible for maintaining adequate inventory levels should know how long it takes to replenish the supply for each

Working in Teams

As a team, identify a large industrial product and a small consumer product. Create two flowcharts that show the activities and businesses that the team believes will be required to complete the physical distribution process. Discuss the differences between the two flowcharts.

product so that an adequate inventory can be maintained to meet anticipated customer demand. They should also be aware of products that are selling more rapidly or more slowly than planned. When sales are higher than expected, the company may want to order more to be able to meet customer needs. When sales are slow, reasons for the reduced level of sales should be determined and a decision made as to whether or not to reorder.

Today's computerized inventory systems allow information to be exchanged instantly between channel members. For many Internet sites, and increasingly for retail stores and industrial salespeople, a possible order can be instantly checked to determine if an adequate supply is on hand and, if not, when it will be available. Salespeople and customers can identify the number of days it will take for the product to be delivered as well as the shipping costs for alternative transportation methods.

Checkpoint ▶▶▶

What types of information should be available in a physical distribution information system?

13-5 Assessment

Xtra!
Study Tools
school.cengage.com/marketing/marketing

Key Concepts

Determine the best answer.

1. Another name for physical distribution is
   a. storage
   b. transportation
   c. logistics
   d. inventory control

2. The most flexible of the major transportation methods is
   a. railroads
   b. airlines
   c. trucks
   d. pipelines

3. A(n) _____ is a facility used to accumulate products from several sources and then regroup, repackage, and send them as quickly as possible to locations where they will be used.

4. The two important parts of the physical distribution information system are
   a. ordering and shipping
   b. invoicing and transportation
   c. order processing and inventory control
   d. data processing and data management

Make Academic Connections

5. **Communication** You are the transportation specialist for an auto manufacturer in South Carolina. You have been asked by the logistics manager to compare shipping new cars to dealers in the northeastern states using auto transport trucks or rail cars. Prepare a one-page memo analyzing the alternatives and making a recommendation.

6. **Technology** Use the Internet to gather information on a technology that is being used by shipping companies to improve the physical distribution of products in terms of speed, security, information, or other factors. Prepare a report on the technology and include examples of how companies are benefiting from its use.

Connect to ◀ DECA
An Association of Marketing Students

7. A company is producing a recordable CD shaped like a business card, which business people can present to clients. They can print standard business card information on the CD label and record information and visuals about their business on the CD that would provide details about the company and its products. Design a package that can be used to sell sets of the blank business card CDs in office supply stores that both protects and promotes the product. Present your design and discuss it with your teacher (judge).

Chapter 13 Assessment

Check Your Understanding

Now that you have completed the chapter, check your understanding of the lessons with these questions. Record the score that best represents your understanding of each marketing concept.

1 = not at all; 3 = somewhat; 5 = very well

If your score is 42–50, you are ready for the assessment activities that follow. If you score 33–41, you should review the lessons for the items you scored 1–3. If you score 32 or less, you will want to carefully reread the lessons and work with a study partner on the areas you do not understand.

Can you—

___ offer several reasons why distribution is so important to successful marketing?

___ list the distribution decisions that must be made in order for a satisfactory exchange to occur?

___ identify several adjustments that must be made between producers and consumers through the channel of distribution?

___ describe the difference between a direct and indirect channel of distribution and when each should be used?

___ discuss how wholesalers can add value in many distribution channels?

___ describe changing roles of wholesalers?

___ identify common types of retailers based on their product mix and their location?

___ discuss how today's retailing is changing?

___ compare the major transportation methods used in physical distribution?

___ provide examples of how effective order processing and inventory control improve marketing?

Review Marketing Terms

Match the terms listed with the definitions. Some terms may not be used.

1. Selling directly to the consumer at home rather than requiring the consumer to travel to a store

2. A loss of products due to theft, fraud, negligence, or error

3. A business that offers products from one category of merchandise or closely related items

4. A building designed to store large amounts of raw materials or products until they can be used or sold

5. The producer sells the product to final consumers

6. Businesses that offer a variety of common consumer products for sale to selected members through a warehouse outlet

7. A business that offers products from several different categories of merchandise

8. The process of efficiently and effectively moving products and materials through the distribution channel

9. Businesses that have services as their primary offering with a limited number of products for sale that complement the services

10. Companies that assist with distribution activities between businesses

a. atmospherics
b. channel captain
c. direct channel
d. distribution centers
e. distribution function
f. franchising
g. indirect channel
h. inventory shrinkage
i. mixed merchandise retailers
j. non-store retailing
k. physical distribution (logistics)
l. retailer
m. service retailers
n. specialty or limited-line retailers
o. warehouse
p. wholesale member clubs
q. wholesalers

Review Marketing Concepts

11. Most producers make only a small number of goods, yet consumers need a wide variety of products and want to buy many of them at the same time and place. This disparity represents which kind of difference?
    a. quantity
    b. assortment
    c. location
    d. timing

12. True or False: The business that produces a product always has the primary responsibility for developing the channel of distribution that will get it to final consumers.

13. True or False: For a channel of distribution to work effectively, all of the channel members must adopt the same marketing strategy.

14. Which of the following factors supports the choice of a direct channel of distribution?
    a. a large number of customers
    b. customers who are spread out over a wide geographical area
    c. a complex product developed to meet specific customer needs
    d. the producer is not concerned with having control of the marketing mix

15. An Internet service that sells custom-made CDs to individual consumers is an example of which of the following?

a. non-store retailer
b. indirect distribution channel
c. mixed merchandise store
d. wholesale member club

16. True or False: Retailers are responsible for the marketing mix that consumers see because they are the last business in an indirect channel of distribution.

17. Which type of shopping center typically has between 20 and 30 stores and offers a range of products meeting the regular and frequent shopping needs of consumers?
    a. shopping strip
    b. neighborhood center
    c. regional shopping center
    d. none of the above

18. True or False: Pipelines are only used to transport oil, gas, and water.

19. True or False: Transportation on inland waterways such as rivers and lakes is seldom used in the United States because bulk materials can be moved faster and less expensively by truck.

20. The most costly of the major transportation methods is
    a. railroad
    b. truck
    c. ship
    d. airplane

Marketing Research and Planning

21. When products are exchanged between producers and consumers, all of the marketing functions must be performed. In a direct channel of distribution, either the producer or the final consumer is responsible for marketing functions. In an indirect channel, other channel members will perform some of the functions. Two examples of common exchanges are listed in the next column. For each of the examples, identify the channel of distribution as either direct or indirect. Then identify which of the channel members will be responsible for each of the nine marketing functions. Prepare a brief written justification for each of your decisions. (It is likely that more than one channel member can perform some of the functions.)

a. A consumer travels to a strawberry farm to pick and buy fresh fruit.
b. A homebuilder orders a truckload of plywood from a building supply wholesaler to be delivered to the job site by the supplier. The supplier fills the order from a shipment of plywood delivered last month by rail car from the plywood manufacturer.

22. The number of franchises is growing rapidly, with opportunities available in manufacturing, service, wholesaling, and retailing. Identify a franchise that interests you. Gather information about the franchise through Internet or library research, by writing to the franchiser, or by interviewing the owner of a local franchise. Gather the following information:

a. Is the franchise a manufacturing, wholesale, retail, or service business?
b. What are the primary products and services offered?
c. Who are the customers?
d. What other businesses does the franchise work with?
e. Where is the franchise located in the channel of distribution?
f. What marketing functions does the franchise perform?
g. What types of physical distribution activities are completed by the business?

Gather additional information you believe will help you understand the franchise business. Prepare a written or oral report on your findings.

23. The location of a retail business is very important to its success. Unless the product is extremely important to customers and they do not have a choice of where to buy, they will not spend a long time looking for a place to purchase it. For each of the products listed, consider who the typical consumer would be, and then determine whether the business should be located in a shopping strip, a neighborhood shopping center, a regional shopping center, or a stand-alone store. Develop a written justification for each decision.
a. homeowners' and renters' insurance
b. personal computers for home and business use
c. new automobiles
d. movie rentals
e. building materials and home improvement products

24. Many e-commerce businesses have struggled to find effective ways to distribute products to customers and to accept product returns. Parcel delivery service companies such as FedEx and UPS have grown as a result of agreements with e-commerce businesses to manage their distribution activities. Visit the web sites of two parcel delivery services and gather information on the physical distribution services each offers to e-commerce businesses. Prepare a table that lists at least ten distribution activities. Develop two columns that compare the services offered by each company for the activities identified.

Marketing Management and Decision Making

25. Edu-Games, the company discussed in the first lesson of this chapter, was trying to develop an effective channel of distribution for its unique product. The company was having difficulty because the distributors and retailers were not implementing the marketing mix as planned. If a manufacturer is unable to get the necessary cooperation from other channel members, it is difficult to successfully market the products. To solve the problem, Edu-Games is considering three alternatives:
a. selling the games directly to customers by mail or the Internet
b. developing its own sales force to replace the distributors
c. finding ways to work more closely with its current distributors to implement the marketing plan that was already developed

Prepare a written analysis of each of the three alternatives, identifying advantages and disadvantages of each. Then select the alternative you believe is best and develop a rationale for your choice based on principles of effective marketing and distribution.

26. Using a computer spreadsheet program, compile a list of 15 to 20 household products that you and your family purchase regularly. Find the per-unit prices that these or comparable products sell for at a superstore or wholesale member club, a mixed merchandise store such as a supermarket or department store, a limited-line specialty store, and an Internet store. Use a spreadsheet program to record the prices. Select the products that are carried by each of the businesses and compute the total cost of purchasing all of those products from each type of retailer. Calculate the percentage difference in the cost of all products between each type of retailer.

Quick Serve Restaurant Management Individual Series Event

The Quick Serve Restaurant Management Individual Series Event consists of a 100-question, multiple-choice comprehensive exam and role-plays. The role-play portion of the event requires participants to accomplish a task by translating what they have learned into effective, efficient, and spontaneous action. The five performance indicators specify the distinct tasks the participant must accomplish during the role-play. Students have ten minutes to prepare their strategy and ten minutes to explain it to the judge. The judge can ask questions during or after the presentation.

Obesity is a serious issue in the United States. Many children and adults have unhealthy weight issues. Society has blamed much of the obesity problem in the United States on fast-food restaurants that serve food with high levels of calories and fat. Many of the fast-food restaurants are also blamed for their super-sized portions. Much of the food offered at quick serve restaurants is fried and not very healthy.

Burger Barn has been in operation since 1960. Large juicy burgers, french fries, onion rings, malts, and sweet desserts have made Burger Barn a popular restaurant. Your marketing team has been asked to create healthy food alternatives for Burger Barn's customers. The healthy items you offer should not increase the price of the meals.

You must also develop an advertising campaign that shows how Burger Barn is helping to fight obesity by giving customers more healthy choices. The advertising campaign must give young people incentives for making healthy diet choices. Also, Burger Barn must become active in the community to promote physical fitness. You must determine an event for Burger Barn to sponsor that confirms its commitment to a healthier population.

Performance Indicators Evaluated

- Lead the way for change. (Emotional Intelligence)
- Identify product opportunities. (Product/Service Management)
- Generate product ideas. (Product/Service Management)
- Explain nutritional standards. (Product/Service Management)
- Explain the components of advertisements. (Promotion)

Go to the DECA web site for more detailed information.

Think Critically

1. Who is the target market for a healthy diet campaign?

2. Why must quick serve restaurants be accountable for a personal problem like obesity?

3. What kinds of commercials are used by Subway to emphasize a healthy lifestyle?

4. What kinds of commercials should Burger Barn use to help distance itself from the obesity epidemic?

www.deca.org

Determining the Best Price

©PHOTOGRAPHERS' CHOICE/GETTY IMAGES

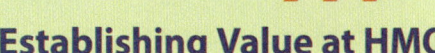

Newsline

Establishing Value at HMOs

The rising cost of health care is one of the most serious problems facing the United States, where costs now top $1 trillion a year. Stressing preventive health care can help control costs. If people see doctors regularly, problems can be identified and treated before they become more expensive.

Preventive health care is a key characteristic of health maintenance organizations (HMOs). HMOs offer medical services to subscribers for a flat fee rather than requiring patients to pay based on the services they receive. In the past, people visited physicians infrequently, seeking attention only when they were sick or injured. Now people go to HMOs to prevent illness.

A problem is that some subscribers go to HMOs without good cause, raising costs unnecessarily. Costs that had been brought under control by HMOs are now increasing again. Studies of subscribers' attitudes identify two reasons for the increasing costs. First, they view the services as "free." Second, they strongly believe in preventive care, and they visit HMOs regularly to ensure that they remain healthy.

HMO managers needed a way to increase the perceived value of their services without diminishing the importance of prevention. So they introduced small service fees for each visit. Ideally, the fee is low enough that it does not discourage people who need to see a doctor, yet high enough to discourage unneeded visits. Subscribers typically will not visit unless their problem is worth at least the amount of the service fee.

Attitudes and perceptions are an important part of marketing. Marketing personnel for HMOs need to be concerned about their customers' views of price and value if they are going to continue to control the rising cost of health care.

Think Critically

1. What do you think is a good amount to charge for an HMO service fee to accomplish the two goals stated above? Why?

2. How do HMO subscribers benefit from service fees?

school.cengage.com/marketing/marketing

Prepare for Performance

This chapter develops the following Performance Indicators from the DECA Competitive Events program.

Core Performance Indicators

- Understand concepts and strategies utilized in determining and adjusting prices to maximize return and meet customers' perceptions of value
- Employ pricing strategies to set prices for marketing services
- Assess pricing strategies to identify needed changes and to improve profitability
- Evaluate the effectiveness of the marketing-communications mix to make product-mix decisions

Supporting Performance Indicators

- Explain the nature and scope of the pricing function
- Describe the role of business ethics in pricing
- Explain factors affecting pricing decisions
- Evaluate pricing decisions
- Assess changes in price structure
- Select approach for setting a base price

Go to **school.cengage.com/marketing/marketing** and click on Connect to DECA.

©LEXUS

Visual Focus

Of the four marketing mix elements, price ultimately can have the biggest impact on consumers. Price is an important factor in the consumer's perceived value of a product or service. Price alone can determine whether or not a customer can afford to make a purchase. Price is just as important to businesses. It determines how much profit can be made. Because pricing plays an important role in the economy, the government will step in when necessary to help regulate prices. Businesses must carefully determine their selling prices by using demand analysis, studying the market conditions, and setting pricing strategies.

Focus Questions:

What is the focus of the advertisement for *The Week?* What pricing strategy do you think is being used by offering an online publication free of charge? How does this add value for the customer? Locate another advertisement that focuses on price. Share your example in class and determine the price objective of the advertiser.

The Economics of Price Decisions

GOALS

- Explain the reasons why price is an important marketing tool.
- Demonstrate how the economic concept of elasticity of demand relates to pricing decisions.
- Describe the three primary ways in which government influences prices.

KEY TERMS

elasticity of demand, *p. 403*

inelastic demand, *p. 403*

elastic demand, *p. 403*

marketing matters

Price is an important part of marketing because the prices people pay largely determine how they value an exchange and how satisfied they are with purchase decisions. Expectations of value are closely tied to the price of a product or service. Sellers and buyers devote a lot of attention to prices because prices are easy to change, unlike other elements of the marketing mix.

Price is also central to the economic concepts of supply and demand. Marketers who understand whether the demand for a product is elastic or inelastic are better able to set the optimum price for it.

Government in a free enterprise economy plays a limited role in the pricing of products and services. The main ways it influences prices are by regulating competition, controlling unfair pricing practices, and taxing.

Make a list of all the things you've bought in the last week. For which ones did the price significantly affect your purchase decision?

Price as a Marketing Tool

"That was a great value!" "You didn't get your money's worth." "It can't be very good at that price."

People make many decisions about what to buy based on the prices they pay. Their satisfaction with purchases is often based on their view of the prices. The lowest price is not always viewed as the best price. Many years ago, the Yugo automobile was imported into the United States as the lowest cost automobile on the market. However, it didn't have the style, size, power, or quality to attract customers. Kmart established an image as a low-cost retailer but had difficulty competing with Wal-Mart's low pricing or attracting customers

who shop at stores with a higher-quality image. You can probably think of many products you buy that could be purchased at a lower price. Why do you decide to pay a higher price?

The prices charged for products and services are important to the businesses selling them as well as to consumers. The price determines how much money a business will make to cover the costs of designing, producing, and marketing its products or services. If the price is not high enough to pay those costs and generate a profit, the business will not offer that product or service for long.

The Importance of Price

We know that effective marketing results in satisfaction for both the consumer and the business. A satisfactory price means that the consumer views the purchase as a value. It also means that the business makes a profit on the sale.

Price is the money a customer must pay for a product or service. But price is much more complicated than that. Think of the various words used to identify the price of something. They include admission, membership fee, service charge, donation, retainer, tuition, and monthly payment. In some cases, money is not used at all. In bartering, people must agree on the value of the items being exchanged rather than setting a monetary price.

Price is such an important part of marketing that it is one of the four elements of the marketing mix. *Price* is the actual cost and the methods of increasing the value of the product to the customers. As one of the nine functions of marketing, *pricing* is defined as establishing and communicating the value of products and services to prospective customers. When planning any marketing activity, business people must consider the impact of the cost to the business, the price customers must pay, and the value that is added to the product or service as a result of the activity.

Price Adjustability

Price is an important tool because it can be changed much more quickly than other marketing decisions. Once a product is designed and produced, it is very difficult to change its form or features. A channel of distribution takes a great deal of time to develop. After the wholesalers and retailers are selected and the product is distributed, it is not easy to change the locations where customers can purchase the product. Even promotion is not easy to adjust. Advertisements must be written and produced, time or space in media must be purchased well in advance, and salespeople have to be hired and trained.

Digital Digest

Outsourcing the Drive-Thru

When you place your order at the drive-thru at a fast-food restaurant, you expect that you're talking to someone inside the restaurant. But thanks to technology, this may no longer be the case. Many major fast-food chains, including McDonald's, Wendy's, and Hardee's, have experimented with or implemented remote call centers to take your order from the drive-thru. The person you're talking to may be in a different state, or even some day in a different country. They take your order, enter it into a computer, and the order is sent back to the restaurant to be fulfilled.

For the restaurant, this allows employees to be more specialized. The same person doesn't have to take the order *and* fulfill it—employees focus on either taking the order *or* fulfilling it. Early studies show that this increases efficiency of the drive-thru and helps get more customers through, increasing profitability. And because employees have less to focus on, they make fewer mistakes, which makes the customer happier.

Think Critically

1. What problems might arise when the person who takes the order is not in the same building as those who fulfill the order?

2. What would the pros and cons be of chain restaurants outsourcing their drive-thru order-taking to call centers overseas?

By contrast, changing a price is often as simple as adding a new price sticker or marking out an old price. Even manufacturers can change the price charged by a retailer by offering a coupon or a rebate. Because prices can be changed more easily than other marketing tools, marketers must be careful not to make pricing mistakes.

Checkpoint ▶▶

Name three reasons why price is an important marketing tool.

Price as an Economic Concept

Price is also an important economic concept. People have unlimited wants and needs that they try to satisfy with the limited resources that are available to society. Price allocates available resources among people. If there is a small quantity of a product or service but a very large demand, the price will usually be quite high. On the other hand, if there is a very large supply of a product or if demand is low, the price will be low. Figure 14-1 illustrates how supply and demand affect price.

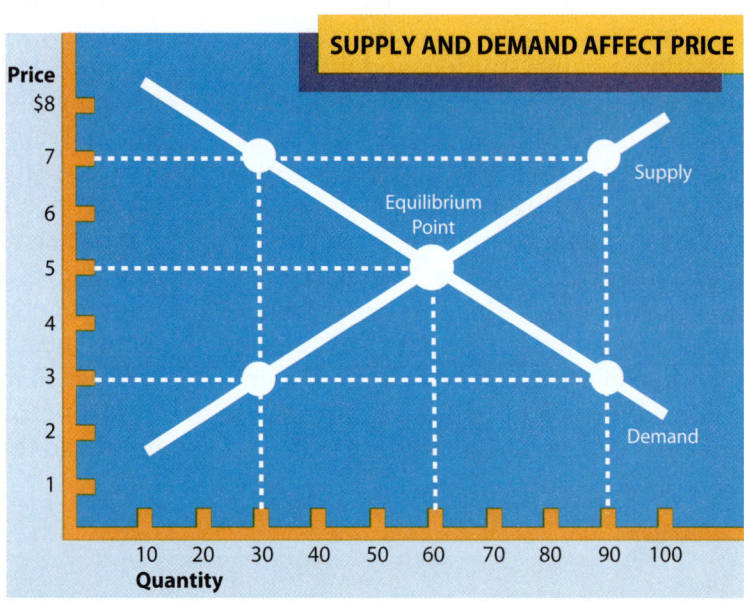

SUPPLY AND DEMAND AFFECT PRICE

FIGURE 14-1

At a price of $3, demand (90) is greater than supply (30). At a price of $7, supply (90) is greater than demand (30). At a price of $5, supply equals demand (60), and the market is in equilibrium.

Economic Utility

The value customers receive from a purchase results from more than just the product or service itself. The concept of economic utility demonstrates that value is added through changes in form, time, place, or possession. Therefore, customers believe a product is a greater value and will often pay a higher price if the product is available with preferred features at a better time or place than other choices, if it is more accessible, or if it can be purchased on credit.

Elasticity of Demand

It may seem that an easy way to get consumers to buy your product is to decrease the price. It seems logical that if the price decreases, more products will be sold. Many people believe that if sales increase, profits will increase as well. That is not always the result.

The table in Figure 14-2 shows several prices charged by a supermarket for one dozen eggs. The table also shows the quantity sold and the total revenue the store received from the sales. As you can see, the decrease in price does not result in enough additional sales to increase the total amount of money received.

A different result is shown in Figure 14-3. When the supermarket decreases the price of ice cream, the additional quantity sold increases total revenue.

The difference between these examples illustrates a key economic concept. **Elasticity of demand** describes the relationship between changes in a product's price and the demand for that product. Elasticity is based on the number of good substitutes for a product and the willingness of consumers to go without a product if the price gets too high. In Figure 14-2,

Inelastic Demand

Price of a Dozen Eggs	Quantity Sold	Total Revenue
$0.65	305	$198.25
$0.68	300	$204.00
$0.71	292	$207.32
$0.74	285	$210.90
$0.77	277	$213.29
$0.80	264	$211.20

FIGURE 14-2
When the price is decreased for one dozen eggs, a larger quantity will be sold. The increase in quantity sold is not enough to increase the total revenue from the sales.

Elastic Demand

Price of a Gallon of Ice Cream	Quantity Sold	Total Revenue
$3.65	180	$657.00
$3.70	165	$610.50
$3.75	158	$592.50
$3.80	147	$558.60
$3.85	136	$523.60
$3.90	122	$475.80

FIGURE 14-3
When the price of one gallon of ice cream decreases, the quantity sold increases a great deal. The increase in quantity sold results in higher total revenue.

the result occurs because there are few substitutes for consumers who purchase eggs. When consumers need to purchase eggs, they will do so even if the price is increased. If the price decreases, they will not buy many more eggs than they would have at the higher price. This is an example of inelastic demand. With **inelastic demand**, a price decrease will decrease total revenue.

Figure 14-3 illustrates elastic demand. With **elastic demand**, a price decrease will increase total revenue. Demand is elastic when customers have several good substitutes for a product. Consumers view ice cream as one choice among many desserts. If the price of ice cream increases, some customers will not buy ice cream or will buy other desserts that are now a better value. If the price of ice cream decreases, people who were buying other products may switch now that ice cream seems more affordable.

If price changes are too great, the type of demand elasticity may change. If eggs become extremely expensive, people will stop buying them. There is a limit to the amount of ice cream people will buy, no matter how inexpensive it is. Therefore, marketers can use price elasticity only for price changes that consumers believe are reasonable.

Working in **Teams**

As a team, make a list of items that you frequently purchase. Next to each item, record the average price paid for it. Then discuss whether you would continue to purchase the item if the price increased. Would you purchase more of the item if the price dropped? Determine the elasticity of demand for each item on your list.

Checkpoint ▶▶

How are prices related to elasticity of demand for a product or service?

Planning a Career in... *Global Sourcing*

"My uncle just got back from India. His company just established a customer service department in India to accept orders for printer ink cartridges. My uncle trained employees how to handle U.S. orders. Given the lower labor costs in India, his company expects to achieve an improved profit margin."

Did you ever wonder why so many companies are locating their customer service departments offshore? Have you ever considered why so many popular consumer items are manufactured in foreign countries?

Global Sourcing is a field that considers the most cost-effective way to manage product development while maintaining high-quality marketing and customer service procedures. With evolving technologies that streamline communications, the barriers to sending work offshore have diminished.

Employment Outlook

- Slower than average growth is anticipated. Improved software has contributed to increased efficiency among currently employed sourcing specialists.
- The Internet facilitates relationships among companies and worldwide locations.
- Improved supply chain management has streamlined the global sourcing process.

Job Titles

- Global Customer Service Specialist
- Global Logistics Specialist
- Supply Manager
- Global Sourcing Associate
- Strategic Sourcing Manager

Needed Skills

- A bachelor's degree is usually required. A master's degree will improve chances of promotion.

- A strong knowledge of international finance, operations, and logistics is important.
- Understanding foreign cultures and proficiency in a foreign language is helpful.

What's it like to work in...
Global Sourcing

Perry, a global sourcing specialist for a large toy manufacturer, is compiling manufacturing specifications for a new toy. The toy's packaging will be used for storage of the toy pieces. Via e-mail, Perry will distribute the specifications to his preferred vendors. Each vendor is required to place its bid for the toy and the packaging according to the manufacturing specifications.

Perry then set up a meeting for next week with a member of his finance department. Because many of the bidding vendors are from foreign countries, Perry and the financial analyst will formulate a 12-month estimate of the anticipated value of the dollar relative to each of the respective foreign currencies. Fluctuations of the dollar relative to the foreign currencies will affect the cost-effectiveness of the bids.

Later that day, Perry participated in an International Product Safety Standards meeting. As product safety is one of the key attributes parents consider prior to buying a toy, the meeting focused on how to insure safety standards are translated accurately for offshore vendors.

What About **You**

Would you like to participate in worldwide efforts to develop the most economical and effective supply chain to produce and market quality products and services for your company?

Government's Effect on Prices

In private enterprise economies, businesses and consumers interact to determine prices and what is bought and sold. Governments play a role only when laws or regulations are needed to prevent unfair competition or to encourage activities that benefit society. When governments are involved in the economy, they often affect prices. The most important methods governments use to influence prices involve regulation of competition, controlling unfair pricing, and taxation.

Regulating Competition

A foundation of private enterprise is that competition benefits both businesses and consumers. Whenever one business is large enough to control a market or when a few businesses cooperate to take advantage of smaller businesses or consumers, the government may regulate those businesses. Years ago, the federal government believed that AT&T had too much control of the telephone service industry. A court ruling required AT&T to divide itself into several smaller independent companies. This allowed other businesses, such as MCI and Sprint, a better chance to compete.

The government also wants to encourage the development of new products and services so consumers have additional choices. One way to help businesses is to protect new products from competition until they can become profitable. Patents are granted to inventors of unique products for a period of 20 years. During that time, no other business can market exactly the same thing unless the inventor grants permission or the patent is sold. In the same way, people who develop artistic works such as books, films, recordings, or artwork can be protected by copyrights. If a company has a patent or copyright, it has greater control over the price it charges, since there will be no other product just like it for a period of time.

Regulating Prices

The federal government has specific legislation to regulate the pricing practices of businesses. Some of the most important areas regulated by laws include:

- Price-fixing: Competing companies at the same level in a channel of distribution (manufacturers, wholesalers, retailers) cannot cooperate in establishing prices.

- Price discrimination: Businesses cannot discriminate in the prices they charge to other businesses in their channel of distribution. A manufacturer must offer equivalent prices, discounts, and quantities to all wholesalers or retailers.

- Price advertising: Businesses cannot mislead consumers through the advertising of prices. Examples of misleading advertising include using phony list prices (prices at which the products are never sold), incorrect comparisons with competitors' prices, or continuous promotion of a sale price. Companies must also clearly communicate the terms of credit offered to customers.

- Bait-and-switch: Companies cannot lure customers with offers of low prices and then tell them the low-priced product is unavailable or inferior.

- Unit pricing: Many products sold in varying quantities or package sizes must list the price for a basic unit of measurement, such as a liter, ounce, or pound, so consumers can make price comparisons.

Taxation

Taxes are another way that governments affect the products and services marketed, the prices paid, and the level of competition. An increase in the tax on a product makes it less attractive to consumers and often reduces the level of sales. Taxes on products such as tobacco and liquor not only collect revenues for the government but also reduce the consumption of products that are believed to be harmful. In the same way, import taxes increase the cost of foreign products, making domestic products a better value for consumers. For products that are considered luxuries such as expensive automobiles and jewelry, a tax may not reduce the quantity of the products purchased, but it increases the amount of taxes collected from people who are viewed as most able to pay.

Occasionally, the government wants to encourage a particular type of business or the development of certain products or services. Legislators use a tax reduction for that purpose. When businesses disappear from the central part of cities, city and state governments may reduce or eliminate some taxes for several years to encourage businesses to relocate in those areas. To promote the use of alternative fuels, some states reduced the tax on ethanol-based gasoline.

Checkpoint ▶▶

What are the three main ways that government influences prices in a private enterprise economy?

14-1 Assessment

Xtra! Study Tools
school.cengage.com/marketing/marketing

Key Concepts

Determine the best answer.

1. True or False: Product manufacturers prefer elastic demand over inelastic demand.

2. Marketers need to be concerned about pricing mistakes for all of the following reasons *except*
   a. prices are difficult to change
   b. prices that are set too high allow competitors easy entry into the market
   c. prices that are set too low result in lost revenue
   d. if prices are raised, consumers may resist

3. How does government encourage new product development?
   a. by regulating competition
   b. by granting tax breaks for research and development
   c. by granting patents
   d. all of the above

4. The _____ determines how much money a business will make to cover the costs of designing, producing, and marketing its products or services.

Make Academic Connections

5. **Government** Competition among businesses helps keep prices lower. Research a recent merger or sale between two large corporations in which the government became involved to ensure there would be no adverse effect on competition. Prepare a one-page report.

6. **Economics** Select two products or services that consumers can purchase. Record three prices for each product or service—a low, average, and high price. Survey 20 people and ask them (1) if they would buy the items at the various price levels and (2) how many of the items they would buy at one time at the various price levels. Create a table as shown in Figures 14-2 or 14-3 to determine the elasticity of demand for each item based on your survey results.

Connect to ◀DECA

7. Today, many restaurants use price as a marketing tool to promote their value menus, which include menu items for $1 or less. You work for a movie theater. Determine how the theater could use a similar pricing strategy to help increase its business. Present your pricing strategy to your teacher (judge).

Developing Pricing Procedures

GOALS

- Describe three common pricing objectives for businesses.
- Explain how businesses establish a price range for a product.
- Identify the three components that must be considered when determining the selling price.

KEY TERMS

breakeven point, *p. 409*   operating expenses, *p. 411*

selling price, *p. 410*   net profit, *p. 411*

product cost, *p. 410*   markup, *p. 411*

gross margin, *p. 410*   markdown, *p. 412*

marketing matters

In order to achieve optimal results, businesses need to carefully plan the prices they charge for their products and services. Price planning begins with establishing price objectives. Three common objectives are maximizing profits, increasing sales, and supporting an image.

To narrow down their choices, businesses analyze demand to determine the maximum price that customers will pay. Breakeven analysis helps to determine the minimum price at which a business can cover its fixed and variable costs. In the end, the selling price must cover product costs and operating expenses and leave room for a profit. Some businesses, especially retailers, set prices by applying markups, such as a fixed percentage of product cost, to the merchandise.

Make a list of three things you or family members owned that were subsequently sold. Describe how the selling prices were determined and the actual prices buyers paid.

Setting Price Objectives

It is not easy to determine the best prices to charge for products. Companies want prices that cover their costs and contribute a reasonable profit. Consumers are not particularly concerned about the company's costs or whether the company makes a profit on the sale. Consumers want to get the best value and expect comparably priced products. Because it is not easy to determine the actual costs for marketing a product or what customers are willing to pay, many companies do not take enough care in setting prices. They may set their prices based on what competitors are charging. Or they may set their prices high, believing that they can reduce them if customers are unwilling to pay the original prices. Such practices are risky and may result in unsold products or loss of profits. Prices should be planned as carefully as the other mix elements.

To begin price planning, marketers need to determine what objectives they want to accomplish with the price. Examples of possible pricing objectives are to maximize profits, increase sales, or maintain a particular company image.

Maximize Profits

Companies that seek to maximize profits carefully study consumer demand and determine what the target market is willing to pay for their products. The prices are set as high as possible while still satisfying customers. In this way, there is more money to cover the costs of production and marketing and return a profit. Companies that want to maximize profits usually select smaller target markets where unique products can be developed. Their products are quite different from competitors' and meet important customer needs in those markets.

Increase Sales

Sales-based pricing objectives result in prices that achieve the highest possible sales volume. Companies that want a greater share of the market or have high levels of inventory may choose this objective. Prices will usually be quite low to encourage customers to buy. Companies using a sales-based objective need to set the price high enough to cover costs. Also, they must have an adequate supply of the products to meet customer demand. They will usually sell their products in markets with a large number of available customers.

Maintain an Image

Companies can use the prices of products to help create a specific image for the product or the company. Many consumers believe that price and quality are related, that higher prices mean better quality while lower prices suggest poorer quality. Therefore, companies that are building a quality image use higher prices than competitors do.

Have you shopped at a business where no prices were posted for the products? Have you eaten at a restaurant where the menu did not contain prices? These businesses are creating an image that price is unimportant in the purchase decision. They are using non-price competition to sell their products and services.

Some companies, such as Wal-Mart, are trying to build a low-price image. These companies try to appeal to cost-conscious customers by offering better value for less money. They need to keep their prices as low as or lower than competitors' prices. Some companies advertise that they will "meet or beat" their competitors' prices. The intention of that strategy is to convince customers that the company will always have the lowest prices.

Checkpoint ▶▶

What three objectives do businesses commonly choose from when setting prices?

Determining a Price Range

After a company determines the basic objective that will guide pricing, the next step is to determine the possible prices for products and services. Study almost any product and you will see that it is sold at various prices depending on the brand, store, time of year, and other factors. To set an effective price, maximum and minimum prices for the product must be determined. Those prices determine the *price range*.

Maximum Price

The highest possible price that can be charged is determined by the target market. It is based on demand analysis. Marketing research is used to identify the customers in the target market and determine their needs. Then alternative products and services that the target market will consider in satisfying its needs are identified. Finally, the customers in the target market are asked to identify what they would be willing to pay for each of the alternatives. The highest price that results from this analysis of demand is the maximum price. Customers will not be willing to pay more than that amount as long as needs and alternatives do not change.

Minimum Price

The lowest price in the price range is determined by the costs of the seller. A company can sell a product at a loss only for a short time and then only for a very few products. Most prices must be set so that when all products are sold, the company has covered its costs. The minimum price should also contribute profit to the company.

To determine the minimum price, calculate all production, marketing, and administrative costs for the product. That is difficult because some costs cannot be directly related to specific products. Also, costs are often highest for new products but then decrease as more products are sold.

Breakeven Analysis

One way that companies determine the minimum price is through breakeven analysis. The **breakeven point** is the quantity of a product that must be sold for total revenues to match total

costs at a specific price. The breakeven point is calculated using the following information.

- Fixed costs: The costs to the business that do not change no matter what quantity of the product is produced or sold
- Variable costs: Those costs that are directly related to the quantity of the product produced or sold
- Total costs: Fixed costs plus variable costs for a specific quantity of the product
- Product price: Price at which the business plans to sell the product
- Total revenue: The anticipated quantity that will be sold multiplied by the product price

The formula for finding the breakeven point is:

$$\text{Breakeven point} = \frac{\text{Total fixed costs}}{\text{Price} - \text{Variable costs per unit}}$$

Figure 14-4 illustrates a breakeven analysis table for an Ascroe Garden Weeder. Using the information in Figure 14-4, you can calculate the breakeven point if the weeder sells for $14. The total fixed costs for the product are $85,000. The variable costs for each tool are $2.80. Ascroe wants to determine how many weeders

Breakeven Analysis for Ascroe Garden Weeder

Units Sold	Variable Costs Per Unit	Total Variable Costs	+	Fixed Costs	=	Total Costs	Price	Total Revenue
5,522	$2.80	$15,462	+	$85,000	=	$100,462	$14	$77,308
6,054	$2.80	$16,951	+	$85,000	=	$101,951	$14	$84,756
6,998	$2.80	$19,594	+	$85,000	=	$104,594	$14	$97,972
7,589	$2.80	$21,249	+	$85,000	=	$106,249	$14	$106,246
8,225	$2.80	$23,030	+	$85,000	=	$108,030	$14	$115,150
9,110	$2.80	$25,508	+	$85,000	=	$110,508	$14	$127,540

FIGURE 14-4

The breakeven point is the quantity where total costs equal total revenue. Based on the figures in this table, that quantity would be about 7,589 units for a price of $14.

Price Range for a Pair of Shoes

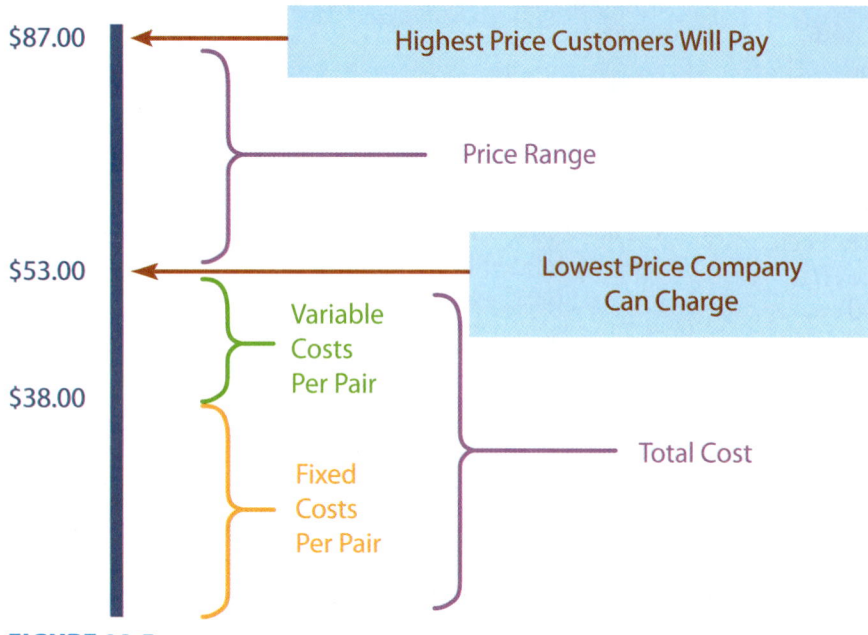

FIGURE 14-5

A company can price its product anywhere between its total cost per unit (minimum price) and the amount customers are willing to pay (maximum price). All of the possible prices are known as the price range.

Price Range

Figure 14-5 shows a price range that was calculated for a pair of shoes. Using demand analysis, it was determined that customers in the target market would pay as much as $87 for the shoes when they are compared to all of the other choices. The company must charge at least $53 to cover fixed and variable costs. The shoes can be sold at any price between the maximum and minimum. The company will select a price that meets its pricing objective and gives it the flexibility to increase or decrease the price as market conditions change.

If the goal is to sell the greatest quantity of shoes possible, the company will set the price near $53. If the goal is to establish a high-quality image and provide a higher level of customer service, the price will be closer to $87. A goal of being competitive with the price may result in a price that is close to the prices of competing brands.

must be sold to break even if the price is set at $14. Use the following formula:

$$\text{Breakeven point} = \frac{85,000}{14.00 - 2.80} = \frac{85,000}{11.20} = 7,589 \text{ units}$$

Ascroe must determine if it will be able to sell at least this number of units. If so, it will not lose money at a price of $14. Additional calculations can be made at other possible prices to determine the relationships between prices, costs, and demand.

Checkpoint ▶▶

What are the endpoints that define a price range for a product, and how are they determined?

Calculating a Selling Price

The price charged for a product or service is known as the **selling price**. For a successful product, the selling price has three components. The largest part of the selling price for most products is the **product cost**, the cost of producing (or buying) the product. The product cost includes the cost of parts and raw materials (or the price paid to a supplier for finished

products), labor, transportation, insurance, and an amount for damaged, lost, or stolen products. The difference between the cost of the product and the selling price is known as the **gross margin**. The gross margin is the amount that is available to cover the business's expenses and provide a profit on the sale of the product.

The next component of the selling price is operating expenses. All costs associated with actual business operations are **operating expenses**. The costs of buildings, equipment, utilities, salaries, taxes, and other business expenses need to be calculated and added to the product cost. Marketing costs are incorporated into the operating expenses or included as a separate amount.

The final component of the selling price is profit. **Net profit** is the difference between the selling price and all costs and operating expenses associated with the product sold. Profit is not guaranteed to businesses when they sell products. Often costs and expenses are higher than anticipated, or the selling price had to be reduced to make the sale. In those cases, the business may not be able to make a profit or might even lose money on the sale. Businesses try to set selling prices high enough that reasonable profits are possible even when some costs are higher than expected or selling prices are reduced.

Markups and Markdowns

Some businesses, especially retailers, use markups to set prices. A **markup** is an

amount added to the cost of a product to determine the selling price. Markups are usually stated as a percentage rather than a dollar amount. Businesses determine the percentage needed to cover operating expenses and provide a profit and use that percentage to calculate the selling price.

Markup can be calculated as a percentage of the product cost, or alternatively as a percentage of the selling price. A box of 500 envelopes is sold at an office supply store for $3.50. The cost to the store is $2.80. The markup as a percentage of cost is 25 percent ($0.70 ÷ $2.80). The markup as a percentage of the selling price is 20 percent ($0.70 ÷ $3.50).

A few businesses use a standard markup for most products. For example, all products could be marked up the same percentage, such as 45 percent, to determine

Virtual Marketing

Internet Advertising Services

The advent of Internet shopping has rattled many businesses, because it is now so much easier for buyers to comparison shop. With so much pricing information in consumers' hands, many businesses are forced to focus on other elements of the marketing mix to attract customers. Fortunately, the Internet has also made that easier.

Advertising services are available that can send ads directly to potential buyers while they are shopping on a competitor's web site. The ads are sent via the shopper's web browser when they sign up for the service. They enable businesses to, in effect,

steal customers away from their competitors with better offers right at the time those very customers are most likely to be making buying decisions.

Think Critically

1. How do you think businesses like the idea that a competitor can reach their prospective customers while they are viewing the businesses' web sites?

2. Most Internet businesses that offer these services have very strict privacy policies. Why do you think those policies are necessary?

the selling price. Other businesses determine the differences in operating and marketing costs or differences in the type of competition for various product categories. Then they develop a separate markup percentage for each product category.

When products are not selling well, a markdown will be used. A **markdown** is a reduction from the original selling price. Markdowns can be expressed as specific dollar amounts or as a percentage of the original selling price. Markdowns are usually viewed as business mistakes since the product did not sell at the planned price. The mistakes may be a result of poor product quality or overestimating customer demand. Markdowns can also result from changes made by competitors or poor marketing mix decisions involving location and promotion.

Effect on Profit

Businesses must consider the effect of markups and markdowns on profits. High markups do not always mean that the business will make a larger profit on the product. Usually a high markup reduces the quantity sold or results in slower sales and higher costs to the business. On the other hand, business people must be careful in using very low markups. While the lower price may result in higher sales, the markup may not cover all expenses. On the other hand, markdowns will usually result in lower profits, but they can help reduce inventory expenses. Marketers must carefully study the effects of different markup and markdown percentages before determining the one to be used.

Checkpoint ▶▶

What are the three components that should be considered when determining the selling price?

14-2 Assessment

Key Concepts

Determine the best answer.

1. True or False: Businesses determine the maximum price that customers will pay for a product through demand analysis.

2. What three variables do businesses commonly analyze using breakeven analyses?
   a. variable costs, price, and fixed costs
   b. variable costs, fixed costs, and breakeven point
   c. variable costs, price, and demand (units sold)
   d. none of the above

3. True or False: A company should always select the price that is at the lowest point of the price range for a product.

4. The difference between the cost of the product and the selling price is the _____.

Make Academic Connections

5. **Math** A company manufactures and sells photo key chains for $3.50 each. Its fixed costs for the product are $40,000. The variable costs are $0.95 per unit. How many key chains will the company need to sell to break even?

6. **Ethics** Do you think it is ethical for a business to use a high markup on its products? Explain why or why not. How can consumers influence the markup used by a business?

Connect to DECA

7. You and a partner are opening a clothing boutique that sells designer clothing and accessories. You are locating your shop in an upscale neighborhood. Write a price objective for your products. Select one product you will sell and determine the price range for it. Then, calculate the selling price. Describe your price objective and explain how you determined the selling price to your teacher (judge).

Pricing Based on Market Conditions

GOALS

- Identify two marketing tools that illuminate competitive conditions and help marketers set prices.
- Describe the various criteria businesses use in establishing the final price a customer pays.
- Explain why extending and managing credit is an important part of marketing.

KEY TERMS

skimming price, *p. 414*

penetration price, *p. 414*

non-price competition, *p. 415*

one-price policy, *p. 415*

flexible pricing policy, *p. 415*

price lines, *p. 416*

FOB pricing, *p. 416*

zone pricing, *p. 416*

discounts and allowances, *p. 416*

consumer (retail) credit, *p. 418*

trade credit, *p. 418*

marketing matters

Determining the best price is as much a function of the target market as it is a matter of marketing objectives. Much also depends on conditions in the market. In addition, product life cycles and consumer purchase classifications help marketers tailor prices to the competitive environment. Depending on the type of market being targeted and the expectations of customers, various criteria can be used to adjust the final price for each transaction.

Credit is a component of the price element that businesses use to facilitate transactions and to enable customers to make purchases that they otherwise might not be in a position to complete. Businesses need to manage credit effectively, or it can be costly.

Make a list of ten items purchased by you, a friend, or a family member. For how many of those ten items was the final price the same as other people paid who purchased the same item at about the same time? What caused prices paid by various customers to differ?

Competitive Environment

When planning the prices of products and services, marketers need to be aware of the competition in the market. If customers see many good alternatives, the prices of those products will remain very similar. If customers view a product as having few substitutes, the price of that product can be set at a higher level than competing products.

There are certain types of market conditions where customers view products as very similar. Consider the difference between pure competition and monopoly. In pure competition, customers see all product choices as identical. Therefore, it is almost impossible for a business to charge more for its products than other companies charge. On the other hand, a business operating in a monopoly has the advantage that customers have no good substitutes. Therefore, the company has more control over the price. That is why government often regulates monopoly markets.

In-Theater Advertising

If you go to see a movie in a theater, you'll probably see several ads before the movie starts. In the past, those ads were limited to previews of other movies, but in the last decade or so, ads for other products have become part of the movie-going experience. You might see as many as five commercials before the previews begin.

Statistics show that in-theater commercials are more likely to be remembered than those on television. This may be because moviegoers are a "captive audience," meaning that they aren't likely to get up and leave and can't change the channel. In this regard, they are very attractive to marketers. But many movie fans are resentful of in-theater commercials. They've already paid $10 for a movie ticket and feel they shouldn't be subjected to watching commercials. Some complain that the movie is delayed because of the ads, and others feel the theater is taking advantage of them.

When it comes to in-theater advertising, marketers must weigh these potentially negative feelings against the advantages of better brand recall.

Think Critically

1. If a company is going to run in-theater commercials, how might it alter them so that the audience will be more accepting of their message?

2. Do you think younger audience members are more accepting of in-theater commercials than older moviegoers? Can you think of a compromise that satisfies both marketers and moviegoers?

Product life cycle analysis and consumer purchase classifications are two marketing tools that are helpful in making pricing decisions. Some businesses also use non-price competition as a marketing strategy.

Product Life Cycle

Throughout the stages of a product life cycle, the type of competition changes. Those changes affect the prices that companies can charge. In the introductory stage, only one brand of a new product is available, allowing the business to control the price charged. Some companies enter the market with a skimming price. A **skimming price** is a very high price designed to emphasize the quality or uniqueness of the product. The target market must be closely studied to ensure customers would be willing to pay a high price for a new product. A skimming strategy usually results in higher profits for the company, but those higher profits encourage other companies to enter the market.

Other companies use a penetration price in the introductory stage of the product life cycle. A **penetration price** is a very low price designed to increase the quantity sold of a product by emphasizing the value. A penetration price may result in higher total revenues, but the initial level of profit is much lower. Companies use a penetration price to attract a large share of the market early and discourage competition.

In later stages of the life cycle, competition increases, and there is an emphasis on price competition. In the maturity stage, customers see many choices that look very similar. Therefore, a small price change might encourage them to switch from one brand to another.

Consumer Purchase Classifications

Consumer purchase classifications also provide an example of different levels of price competition. Staple convenience goods and price-based shopping goods illustrate intensive price competition. In each case, customers see few product differences and, thus, are drawn to lower prices. For products such as emergency or specialty goods, price is not as important to customers as other factors, so they are willing to pay higher prices.

Companies selling products with many similar competitors (common household products, basic clothing items, business supplies) have to be very careful of the prices they charge. They must pay close attention to the prices of competitors. On the other hand, companies with unique products (special jewelry or fashion designs, expensive automobiles, personal services) can be less concerned about the prices of competing products or services.

Non-Price Competition

When businesses emphasize price as a reason for customers to buy a product or service, two problems can result. First, the emphasis on price may encourage customers to view price as the most important reason for buying. That view causes them to see the other parts of the marketing mix (product, distribution, and promotion) as less important. Second, the emphasis on price means that businesses must keep prices as low as possible. With low prices, less profit will be made on each product sold. With lower profits, the company has

less money to spend on marketing activities or new product development.

To avoid those problems, some companies use non-price competition. **Non-price competition** de-emphasizes price by developing a unique offering that meets an important customer need. Few people ask the price to be charged when they go to a physician. Price is not an important factor when purchasing a one-of-a-kind painting, applying for admission to an exclusive college, or planning a wedding or other special celebration.

Companies using non-price competition need to carefully study the needs of a target market. The products and services that people in the target market view as possible alternatives must be examined. Market research can identify the things customers find dissatisfying about the competition. The company uses that information to develop a better marketing mix that is much more satisfying to those customers. If the company is successful in developing a unique marketing mix that meets important customer needs, price will not be an important factor in the purchase decision.

Checkpoint ▶▶

What are two tools that help marketers identify the competitive environment and make better pricing decisions?

Pricing Strategies

Few people expect to pay the price that is listed on the window sticker of a new automobile. Yet, when you go bowling or play miniature golf, you pay the price set by the business. Companies develop pricing strategies based on various criteria to help them establish the final prices.

Price Flexibility

Customers may not have a choice about the price they pay for a product. They

either pay the price set by the business, or they do not buy. A **one-price policy** means that all customers pay the same price. In other cases, such as the purchase of a new car, the price paid by customers is based on how effectively they negotiate with the salesperson. A **flexible pricing policy** allows customers to negotiate the price within a price range.

It may seem unfair to offer different prices for the same product. In some cases it is actually illegal to use flexible pricing. But consider a farmer selling fresh vegetables at a market. On days when there are a number of other farmers with the same products at the market, the farmer may need to lower the price in order to sell all of the products. On the other hand, when there are fewer products available, the demand will be higher, resulting in higher prices.

Automobile dealers traditionally have used flexible pricing to obtain the highest price possible from each customer. They often reduce the price if a customer is unwilling to pay the sticker price. Recently many auto dealers have begun using a one-price policy, in part because so many customers have been obtaining dealer cost information on the Internet. With this policy, a lower initial price is set, and all customers are expected to pay that price for the automobile. The dealers believe that they can reduce selling costs and customers will feel they are being treated more fairly under the one-price policy.

Price Lines

Many companies offer several choices of the same product to appeal to different customer groups. Appliance stores sell refrigerators, stoves, and dishwashers with several choices of options ranging from basic to full-featured. To make it easier to analyze the choices, the products are grouped into two or three price lines. **Price lines** are distinct categories of prices based on differences in product quality and features. Companies must decide whether or not to offer price lines, the number of lines to offer, and the difference in prices among those lines. For example, an appliance store may sell stoves with price lines of $300, $500, and $800. Price lines make customers aware of the differences among products or services.

Geographic Pricing

Increasingly, companies sell products in different parts of the country and throughout the world. Costs of distribution and selling are quite different at various locations. Customer expectations of price and the level of competition are often different. Companies must determine how prices will be set in each geographic area.

Some companies keep the product price the same but charge a different amount to cover transportation costs. A method for setting transportation costs based on geographic location is known as FOB (free on board) pricing. **FOB pricing** identifies the location from which the buyer pays the transportation costs and takes title to the products purchased. For example, "FOB factory" means the customer pays all transportation costs from the point where the product is manufactured. A seller can negotiate with the customer and agree to pay some or all of the transportation costs by identifying a selected city between the buyer's and seller's locations for the FOB designation. Another type of geographic pricing is zone pricing. With **zone pricing**, different product or transportation costs are set for specific areas (or zones) of the seller's market.

Discounts and Allowances

Sellers may choose to offer discounts and allowances to buyers of their products. **Discounts and allowances** are reductions in a price given to the customer in exchange for performing certain marketing activities or accepting something other than what would normally be expected in the exchange. Some common discounts and allowances include the following:

- Quantity discount: Offered to customers who buy large quantities

- Seasonal discount: Offered to customers who buy during times of the year when sales are normally low
- Cash discount: Offered to customers who pay cash rather than using credit or who pay their credit accounts quickly
- Trade discount: Reduction in price offered to businesses at various levels in a channel of distribution (wholesalers and retailers)
- Trade-in allowance: Reduction in price in exchange for the customer's old product when a new one is purchased
- Advertising allowance: Price reduction or specific amount of money given to channel members who participate in advertising the product
- Coupon: Price reduction offered by a channel member through a printed promotional certificate
- Rebate: Specific amount of money returned to the customer after a purchase is made

Added Value

The customer's perception of value can be changed by making additions to the purchase. This is typically done through services provided during and after the sale. Another way of adding value is to provide complementary products or a larger quantity for a reduced unit price, such as "buy two and get a third item free." Some businesses offer prizes and premiums for purchases or use incentives for regular purchasing. Examples of such incentives are the frequent flyer programs used by

*E*Trade Financial is using two pricing strategies—a rebate and added value by offering a free portfolio review.*

airlines. Customers are given free tickets after they have traveled a certain number of miles on one airline.

Checkpoint ▶▶

Name three strategies businesses use to determine the final price a customer pays.

Offering Credit

Companies that market very expensive products or services may have a difficult time selling them even if customers believe the price is fair. Few companies have the cash to pay for a $30 million building. Few individuals are able to pay the full amount for a new car. Credit makes it possible for expensive purchases to be made. A company must determine if credit is necessary as a part of the price mix element.

Types of Credit

Consumer credit (retail credit) is credit extended by a retail business to the final consumer. The credit may be provided by the seller or may be offered by another business that is participating in the marketing process, such as a bank, finance company, or a credit card company like Visa.

Most sales between businesses are made on credit. **Trade credit** is offered by one business to another business. It is often used when there is a time lag between when a sale is negotiated and when the products are actually delivered. Credit sales are a traditional business practice in many channels of distribution. Businesses rely on waiting 30 days or longer before making payment.

Developing Credit Procedures

Credit provides a method for obtaining additional customers and sales. If credit is poorly managed, though, costs may be very high, and the money may never be collected from some customers. Business people responsible for credit sales must plan procedures carefully to be sure that credit is a successful part of a marketing strategy. The procedures include developing credit policies, approving credit customers, and developing effective collection procedures.

Credit Policies

The first decisions for a business regarding credit are whether to offer it and whether to offer it on all products and to every customer. Next, the credit plan is developed. The business decides whether it will offer its own credit plan or rely on other companies to offer credit. Finally, the credit terms are developed. The terms include the amount of credit that will be extended, the rate of interest to be charged, and the length of time given to customers before payment is required.

Credit Approval

Not all customers are good credit customers. If a customer is unable to pay for purchases, the seller loses all of the money invested in producing and marketing the product as well as incurs the cost of extending credit. Even if the product is recovered from the customer,

World View

The American-Japanese Car Company

Sometimes a barrier for a company entering a foreign marketplace is simply the fact that the company is foreign. It may offer a superior product at a lower price, and it may be a well-known brand, but in some markets, and in some industries, customers have a sense of patriotism involved with buying locally manufactured products.

The U.S. auto industry is one such market. In the post-9/11 environment, there has been a resurgence of American patriotism, and many U.S. automakers have capitalized on that sentiment and encouraged consumers to "buy American." Chevy, in particular, with its slogan "An American Revolution," has positioned itself as *the* American pickup truck.

To combat this, Toyota launched a campaign focusing on the number of manufacturing plants it has in the United States, how many Americans it employs, and how much it helps the American economy. Toyota's goal is to simply inform people that even though it is a Japanese-owned car company, many of its cars are made in the USA.

Think Critically

1. Why do you think people are more likely to buy cars built in their own country?

2. How might an American car company position itself to combat Toyota's marketing strategy?

it is not likely that it can be resold for an amount that will cover the costs.

A business that plans to offer credit must determine the characteristics and qualifications of the customers that will be extended credit. Those factors typically include customers' credit history, the resources they have that demonstrate their financial health, and the availability of the money with which they can make payments. Most businesses have a procedure through which customers apply for credit and provide financial references. These references include banks and other businesses from which they have obtained credit in the past. Commercial credit services such as Experion for final consumers and Dun & Bradstreet for business customers are used to provide information on credit histories.

Collections Effective collection procedures are an important part of a credit plan. The procedures are needed so that customers are billed and payments are made at the appropriate time. Procedures for collecting overdue accounts are an important part of a credit system. Most businesses that offer credit have a small percentage of their accounts that are never collected. Even a small percentage of uncollected funds can make a credit plan unsuccessful. This results in losses and the need to increase prices for other customers.

Checkpoint ▶▶▶

Why should businesses extend credit, since it exposes them to a risk of not being paid for their products or services?

14-3 Assessment

Key Concepts

Determine the best answer.

1. When high-tech companies bring out new products and initially charge very high prices, what kind of price are they setting?
   a. penetration price
   b. skimming price
   c. zone price
   d. value-added price

2. True or False: Non-price competition is more prevalent among luxury products and services targeted to very affluent consumers.

3. A flexible pricing policy is more likely to be used in all of the following businesses *except*
   a. antique shop
   b. automobile dealer
   c. real estate
   d. grocery store

4. Effective _____ procedures are an important part of a credit plan because they ensure that customers are billed and payments are made on time.

Make Academic Connections

5. **Geography** Research the price of a ticket for a Major League Baseball game in several states. Why do you think the price of a baseball game ticket varies depending on the geographic location where the game is held?

6. **Consumer Economics** Select a product or service that has two to three price lines. Create a table with one column for the name of the product or service and one column for each price line. In each price line column, list the features that correspond to the price. Based on the information you gather, which price line is most appealing to you? Explain why.

Connect to ◀ DECA
An Association of Marketing Students

7. You work in the marketing department for a computer manufacturer that sells to businesses and consumers. To increase sales, you have been asked to develop a discounts and allowances program for both markets. Describe the discounts and allowances programs you would recommend for each target market to your teacher (judge). Explain why the programs will be effective and profitable.

Chapter 14 Assessment

Check Your Understanding

Now that you have completed the chapter, check your understanding of the lessons with these questions. Record the score that best represents your understanding of each marketing concept.

1 = not at all; 3 = somewhat; 5 = very well

If your score is 42–50, you are ready for the assessment activities that follow. If you score 33–41, you should review the lessons for the items you scored 1–3. If you score 32 or less, you will want to carefully reread the lessons and work with a study partner on the areas you do not understand.

Can you—

___ explain why price is such an important part of marketing?

___ describe the relationship between price and consumer demand for a product?

___ identify the government's role in influencing prices?

___ describe price objectives commonly set by businesses?

___ explain how to determine the price range of a product or service?

___ perform a breakeven analysis to determine the minimum price to charge?

___ identify the three components that must be considered when calculating the selling price?

___ discuss how the competitive environment affects prices?

___ describe pricing strategies that are used to determine the final price?

___ explain how credit plays a role in the price mix element?

Review Marketing Terms

Match the terms listed with the definitions. Some terms may not be used.

1. A reduction from the original selling price
2. The relationship between changes in a product's price and the demand for that product
3. The difference between the selling price and all costs and operating expenses associated with the product sold
4. Increases total revenue when prices decrease
5. All customers pay the same price
6. A very high price designed to emphasize the quality or uniqueness of the product
7. A very low price designed to increase the quantity sold of a product by emphasizing the value
8. De-emphasizes price by developing a unique offering that meets an important customer need
9. The quantity of a product that must be sold for total revenues to match total costs at a specific price
10. Costs associated with business operations
11. Allows customers to negotiate price within a price range
12. An amount added to the cost of a product to determine the selling price

13. Distinct categories of prices based on differences in product quality and features

a. breakeven point
b. consumer credit
c. discounts and allowances
d. elastic demand
e. elasticity of demand
f. flexible pricing policy
g. FOB pricing
h. gross margin
i. inelastic demand
j. markdown
k. markup
l. net profit
m. non-price competition
n. one-price policy
o. operating expenses
p. penetration price
q. price lines
r. product cost
s. skimming price

Review Marketing Concepts

14. A(n) _____ is offered to customers who buy large numbers or a large amount of a product.

15. A(n) _____ is a specific price reduction offered by a channel member through a printed promotional certificate.

16. A(n) _____ is a specific percentage reduction in price offered to businesses at various levels in a channel of distribution.

17. A(n) _____ is a specific amount of money returned to the customer after a purchase is made.

18. A(n) _____ is offered to customers who pay without using credit or who pay their credit accounts quickly.

19. A(n) _____ is offered to customers who buy during times of the year when sales are normally low.

20. A(n) _____ is a price reduction or cash payment given to channel members who participate in advertising a product.

21. A(n) _____ is a reduction in price in exchange for the customer's old product when a new one is purchased.

Marketing Research and Planning

22. There are many terms used to present the price of products and services. Also, the price or value of a product or service can be represented in a variety of ways with numbers, graphics, and pictures. Look through newspapers, magazines, direct mail advertisements, and other print materials from businesses and organizations and find examples of the many ways prices are communicated to consumers. Cut out examples and create a collage of price and value.

23. Identify at least ten consumers who will participate in a price study. Ask each person to respond to the following three items and record his or her answers.
    a. Identify five products or services that you purchase regularly for which price is one of the most important factors in the decision.
    b. Identify five products or services that you purchase regularly for which price is not one of the most important factors in your decision.
    c. Compare the products from the two lists and identify up to three reasons why price is more important for the first list than for the second.

    After you have collected the information, analyze the responses and develop several conclusions about the importance of price in consumer purchase decisions.

24. Using the following price and cost information for four products, determine the breakeven quantity. Then construct a graph for each product that illustrates total fixed costs, total variable costs, total revenue, and total costs. Identify the breakeven point on each graph.

Product	Price	Total Fixed Costs	Variable Costs Per Unit
A	$ 42.00	$ 20,000.00	$ 18.00
B	550.00	980,500.00	86.00
C	1.20	1,500.00	0.90
D	150.50	75,250.00	102.00

25. Identify one form of consumer credit to study. It can be a credit card from a retailer or a manufacturer, a bank credit card such as MasterCard or Visa, installment credit, a loan from a bank or finance company, or other types of credit plans. Collect information by interviewing a credit manager or other person from the company who understands the credit system. Collect a copy of the credit application and other print information that explains the terms of credit. If possible, interview one or more people who use that particular form of credit. When you have finished your study, prepare a written report on the credit policies and procedures. Include the following information: who is offered credit, the application and approval procedure, the type of credit plan, the major credit terms, how billing is done, and the collection procedures for past due accounts.

Marketing Management and Decision Making

26. Jerry Englebrecht has operated a successful dog grooming service for ten years. Each year his number of customers has grown. His expenses have always been quite low since he is the only employee and operates the business from his home. For many years, the number of dog owners has increased in his town, but that growth has now almost stopped.

   In the past two years, three other competing grooming services have opened. One is being offered by a veterinarian to serve her customers primarily. Another is part of a large chain of pet grooming stores located in a larger city 15 miles away. The newest competitor is a small partnership consisting of two people who offer grooming on a part-time basis. They are open only two nights a week and on Saturdays.

   Until recently, Jerry had not been too concerned about the competition. He believed he had loyal customers and had been getting inquiries from new pet owners. Recently he has noticed that fewer new people are asking about grooming services, and some of his regular customers have not returned. In talking to some of his customers, he learns that the chain store and the partnership are both offering grooming services at a much lower price than he is.

   Jerry does not want to lower his price because that will decrease his profits. His goal has always been to use the profits to buy a building and expand his business.
   a. How can Jerry decide whether he should lower his price?
   b. If Jerry wants to emphasize non-price competition, what are some recommendations you would make to him in the areas of product, distribution, and promotion to increase customer satisfaction?

27. A small company has just created a new type of greeting card. It looks the same as the typical greeting card you can buy in most retail stores. The unique feature is a microchip in the card on which the sender can record a 30-second personalized message. Initially, the cards are being produced in two categories—Valentine cards and New Year's cards—for times when people may want to send more unique and personalized messages. If these cards are successful, the company may choose to expand its line of cards for other holidays, seasons, and special events.

   Because of the computer technology and special envelopes needed to protect the card, the company's cost before distribution is higher than other cards—$3.40 each. The business has decided that the cards will be sold to a select set of specialty retailers throughout the world. A few wholesalers may be used for distribution if they follow a carefully developed marketing plan. The cards will also be sold directly to consumers who purchase in quantities of at least 50 cards. Those cards will be distributed by a parcel delivery service.

   Your task is to develop a proposed set of pricing strategies for the company. Develop a specific strategy for each of the following items: price objective, price range, price flexibility, price lines, geographic pricing, discounts and allowances, and added value. The pricing strategies must be consistent with the product, its image, the type of competition that will exist, and the marketing strategies described.

28. Using the information in the following table, calculate the missing amounts.

Product Cost	Gross Margin	Operating Expenses	Selling Price	Net Profit	Markup (Selling Price)	Markup (Cost)
$120.00	$____	$40.00	$____	$15.00	____%	____%
____	36.00	16.00	58.00	____	____	____
0.75	0.30	0.12	____	____	____	____
865.00	____	____	995.00	27.50	____	____
____	____	12.75	38.50	5.25	____	____
10.00	____	____	____	2.00	____	50
____	25.00	25.00	80.00	____	____	____
____	____	27.00	____	64.00	70	____

Hospitality and Recreation Marketing Research Event

The Hospitality and Recreation Marketing Research Event provides an opportunity for participants to demonstrate skills needed by management personnel. Hospitality and recreation marketing includes marketing and management functions in a business primarily engaged in satisfying customers' desire to make productive or enjoyable use of leisure time.

A customer service gap is the difference between customers' expectations of a service and the actual service they receive. The Hospitality and Recreation Marketing Research Event requires participants to select a hotel or restaurant and analyze the customers' perceptions of service they receive from the business. Participants will survey current customers and prospective customers to determine their expectations of the hospitality business. Participants will then develop a customer service/promotion campaign to expand the customer base using the most cost-effective media available.

This project can be completed by one to three members. You will have ten minutes to present your project and five minutes to answer the judge's questions. The written project consists of the following parts:

Executive Summary Write a one-page description of the project.

Introduction Include a description of the business and the community where it is located.

Research Methods Used in the Advertising Media Analysis Describe the design of and methods used to conduct the advertising media analysis.

Findings and Conclusions Analyze the available advertising media, define their cost, describe their potential effectiveness, and identify the most cost-effective media.

Proposed Institutional Promotion Campaign Include goals, objectives, and rationale of the institutional promotion campaign; include activities, timelines, and budget for the campaign.

Bibliography and **Appendix** Include additional sections as needed.

Performance Indicators Evaluated

- Design an advertising media analysis. (Promotion)
- Conduct an advertising media analysis. (Information Management)
- Prepare an institutional promotion campaign to improve public perception of a business. (Promotion)
- Analyze results from the research and identify the most cost-effective advertising media available. (Financial Analysis)
- Present the research findings and institutional promotion campaign to the company. (Communication Skills)

Go to the DECA web site for more detailed information.

Think Critically

1. Why are more hotels and restaurants emphasizing customer service in their advertisements?

2. Why should businesses be aware of the customer service gap?

3. What is the best way to survey customers about their hotel or restaurant experience?

4. What is the meaning of hospitality?

www.deca.org

Chapter 15

Effective Promotion Means Effective Communication

©PHOTOS.COM/JUPITER IMAGES

Newsline

Why Do You Buy What You Buy?

Walk into the grocery store and look at all the products on the shelves around you. There's an entire section of bar soaps. There are a dozen brands of toilet paper and an entire aisle of cereals.

You may not have tried all of these products, but you probably recognize many of them. You know how some products smell and how others will make you smell. You know the names of the characters on the cereal boxes. Maybe you know a jingle for some of the cereals. In the soup aisle, you may be able to name sports stars who are associated with certain brands.

The grocery store is full of choices. With all the different brands of bar soap available, why do you choose one over the other? Do you like the fragrance better? Is it on sale? Does the package make you

think it will clean better? What color is the soap? Is the brand a name you recognize? Did you see a television commercial for the soap that made you laugh?

Some of these questions may seem silly. Why would you buy a bar of soap just because you thought a television commercial was funny? Does it matter if the soap is featured in a colorful display? If the soap is on sale, you are more likely to buy it, right? But what if there's another soap that is not on sale but is still cheaper?

What we buy is not always based on a completely rational decision. And it is not always planned. Some estimates suggest that 80 percent of the things people buy at the supermarket are unplanned. That is, they didn't decide to buy the product until they saw it. Then,

for some reason, they wanted or thought they needed that product, so they picked it off the shelf and put it in their cart.

Companies spend millions of dollars trying to influence the split-second decisions you make in the aisles of the grocery store. Much of this money goes into what is known as promotion.

Think Critically

1. When you are buying something at the grocery store, on what factors do you base your decision?

2. Inside the grocery store, does the placement of a product on the shelf affect your decision? On which shelves do you believe grocery stores stock the most popular brands?

school.cengage.com/marketing/marketing

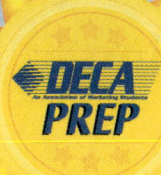

Prepare for Performance

This chapter develops the following Performance Indicators from the DECA Competitive Events program.

Core Performance Indicators

- Explain the nature of effective communications
- Acquire a foundational knowledge of promotion to understand its nature and scope
- Understand the relationship between marketing and marketing communications

Supporting Performance Indicators

- Explain the role of promotion as a marketing function
- Explain the types of promotion
- Identify the elements of the promotional mix
- Describe the use of technology in the promotion function

Go to **school.cengage.com/marketing/marketing** and click on Connect to DECA.

©CREATED BY JWT ATLANTA FOR THE UNITED STATES MARINE CORPS

Visual Focus

Sometimes a brand may have barriers that it must overcome in order to become successful. Companies use promotion to inform, persuade, and remind people about their product or service. This chapter will introduce you to the various forms of promotion, their strengths and weaknesses, and how companies decide what forms of promotion to use.

Focus Questions:

What kind of person comes to mind when you think of the Marine Corps? Picture that person in your mind. Now look at the advertisement to the left. How does this ad compare with your preconceptions? Sometimes a company must overcome well-established perceptions to persuade people to try its product. What barriers do you think the Marines are challenging with this ad?

Locate another ad that you believe is attempting to overcome preconceived notions about a product or service. Share the ad with the class and discuss whether it has changed your opinion about the product or service.

Promotion as a Form of Communication

GOALS

- Identify the function of promotion as part of the marketing mix.
- Describe the communication process and identify its eight elements.
- Explain the three roles of promotion in marketing.
- Define the two types of communication that are important to marketers.

KEY TERMS

promotion, *p. 426*

communication process, *p. 427*

sender, *p. 427*

message, *p. 428*

encoding, *p. 428*

message channel, *p. 428*

receiver, *p. 428*

decoding, *p. 428*

noise, *p. 428*

feedback, *p. 429*

interpersonal communication, *p. 431*

mass communication, *p. 432*

marketing matters

This year, the average person will see or hear approximately one million marketing messages—almost 3,000 messages a day. Most of those will be promotional messages about various products and services. They will be on television and radio, on the Internet, on billboards, in stores, from telemarketers and salespeople, and through text messages on cell phones. Most of those messages will be lost in the clutter. For marketers to effectively reach the people they are trying to reach, they need to choose the right target, develop a persuasive message, and devise the right mix of advertising, public relations, sales promotion, and personal selling. With the right balance of promotions, they can deliver a consistent message that will help lead to a purchase decision by the consumer.

Identify a marketing message you have seen or heard recently. Describe how you received the marketing message. What action or result occurred or will occur because of that message?

Promotion as Part of the Marketing Mix

When you want to buy a car, you have many choices. You choose from hundreds of makes, models, and dealerships. The same is true of cheeseburgers, guitars, and toothpaste. Because you are free to choose where to spend your dollars, companies must compete for your business. They want you to believe that they offer a product or service that is superior to their competitors, and they ultimately want you to choose their product or service.

One of the most important tools for a company trying to attract customers is promotion, one of the four elements of the marketing mix. **Promotion** is any form of communication that a company uses to inform, persuade, or remind consumers about its products or services.

As part of the marketing mix, promotion should complement the other three elements as illustrated in Figure 15-1. A product may be exactly what consumers want, may sell for the right price, and may be available to them because of good distribution. However, if they don't know about the product, don't know where to get it, or don't think that it will fill a need or desire in their life, the product will not sell. That is why good promotion is critical. Promotion is how a company communicates with consumers.

FIGURE 15-1
Promotion is a key element of the marketing mix. It relies on and complements the other elements.

Checkpoint ▶▶

What is promotion?

Promotion Is a Form of Communication

Promotion is a **communication process**, or the transfer of a message from a sender to a receiver. In marketing, the process usually involves a company or organization sending a sales message to a potential customer. To understand how this process works, a marketer must first understand the basics of the communication process, as illustrated in Figure 15-2 on the next page.

The Sender

The communication process originates with a sender. The **sender** is the source of the message being sent, the *who* in the communication process. This can be a person, a company, or an organization. In marketing, the sender is typically a company trying to send a message to consumers. When you see an advertisement, the sender is the company that planned the ad. For example,

the U.S. Marine Corps was the sender of the ad that opened this chapter.

What components of the communication process are represented by this simple "sale" sign?

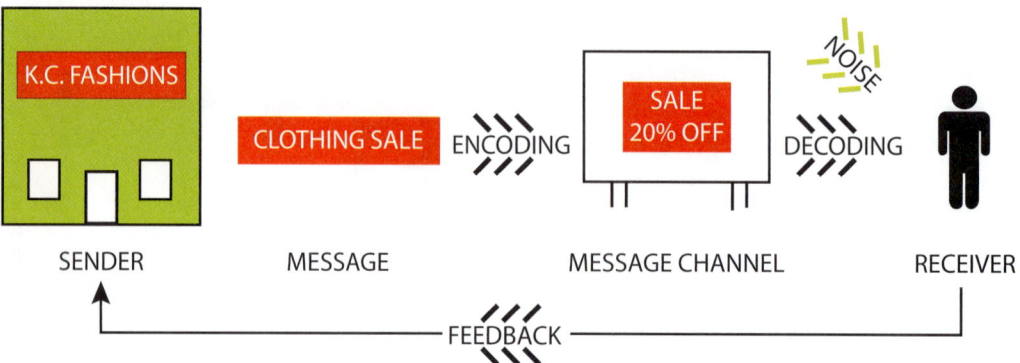

FIGURE 15-2
Promotion is a form of the communication process by which a company sends its message via a message channel to potential customers.

The Message

The **message** is *what* is being communicated. In the promotion process, there can be several messages conveyed at once, on several different levels. A simple message might be that a store is having a sale. But there may be other less explicit messages conveyed in the process. For instance, if the materials used to promote the sale look very elegant, they may send the message that the store is elegant and classy.

Encoding by the Sender

When the sender converts an idea into a message that the receiver can understand, this is called **encoding**. Encoding relies on basic units of meaning such as language, words, and symbols, but it can also include more subtle cues: colors, design, music, and imagery. When the store having the sale creates its promotions, decides what words and pictures to include, and how each type of promotion will work, this is all a part of the encoding process.

The Message Channel

The vehicle by which the message travels is the medium, or **message channel**. The message channel is *how* the message will be distributed. In marketing, the message channel can be television, radio, magazines, a salesperson, text message, the Internet, or anything else that carries a promotional message.

The Receiver

The message travels to the receiver. The **receiver** is the person or persons *to whom* the message is directed or any person who understands the message that is sent. In marketing, receivers are the target audience or potential customers.

Decoding by the Receiver

Before the message can be said to be fully received, it must be decoded by the receiver. **Decoding** is the process by which the receiver interprets the transmitted language and symbols to comprehend the message. People may see a sign, but if the sign uses words or images they do not understand, they will not receive the intended message.

Noise

Any distracting information in the transmission, the message channel, or the receiver's environment that may inhibit or distract from the message is called **noise**. Noise includes TV or radio static or interference, competing messages, unfamiliar words, or even a crying baby—anything that makes it harder to receive the message. Marketers also refer to some types of noise as "clutter."

Chuck E. Cheese's Goes Bilingual to Target Hispanics

Chuck E. Cheese's is a children's pizza chain that operates more than 500 restaurants across the country. In recent years, Chuck E. Cheese's began to expand its market and focus on the Hispanic youth market. The Hispanic market is growing rapidly in the United States, and experts predict that by 2010 the purchasing power of the Hispanic-American market could reach $1 trillion. This presents a great opportunity for many marketers, and Chuck E. Cheese's, a Texas-based company, is trying to capitalize.

For several years, the chain has been creating bilingual commercials in English and Spanish in the hope of reaching Hispanic children. It sponsors the popular Spanish-language animated series Maya & Miguel and has partnered with Hispanic children's networks such as Sorpresa! Chuck E. Cheese's has also worked more Spanish-language elements into its promotions, web site, and operations over the years.

As the Hispanic-American population continues to grow, more companies like Chuck E. Cheese's will target it with Spanish-language marketing campaigns.

Think Critically

1. Do you think non-Spanish-speaking kids would be confused or turned off by bilingual ads?

2. Why is it important for Chuck E. Cheese's to promote its restaurants to Hispanic children and families?

Feedback

Sometimes there is a feedback step in the communication process. **Feedback** is the receiver's response to the message. It can be direct feedback, such as a letter sent from the receiver to the sender or a survey taken by the sender. It can also be indirect feedback, such as the redemption of a promotional coupon or the purchase of a company's product.

Feedback is very important because it helps marketers determine if their promotions are working effectively and how to improve them.

Checkpoint ▶▶

What are the eight elements of the communication process?

The Role of Communication in Marketing

Before marketers begin a promotion program, they should outline the goals of the program. What results do they want to achieve with it? Promotion fulfills three main roles for marketers: it can inform, persuade, or remind an audience, or it can involve some combination of the three.

Inform

A company will often use promotion to inform people about a product. This is particularly true when a company introduces a new product or a new product feature. If a store is opening or moving to a different location, they will want to let customers know.

Sometimes a company wants to inform people of a feature that has always existed but that people just did not know about. At other times, a certain aspect of a product will become more appealing, and the company will want to publicize that aspect. For instance, when gas prices rise, car companies will often advertise the gas mileage of their more fuel-efficient cars because that feature, though it has not changed, has become more relevant to consumers.

More complex products and services are more likely to use promotions that inform customers about their products. When a buying decision is complicated—when people are looking to buy a boat, life insurance, or a computer, for example—consumers will want to collect as much information as possible and compare their options. The price of a product can also impact the amount of information a consumer seeks. People want more information before they purchase a car than they do before they purchase a pack of gum.

By providing people with information they need to make informed decisions, marketers hope that consumers will decide to buy the product. In this way, the role of informing can sometimes overlap with or be combined with the role of persuading customers.

Persuade

Sometimes a company will need to make a case for why a customer should buy its product. The company will create a promotional program with the goal of persuading customers. The company may say why its product is better than the competitor's product, or it may explain how the product will fulfill a need or desire of the consumer. "These shoes will make you look

Ella está feliz porque
sus vacaciones
son en un Marriott.

El está feliz
porque son gratis.

Y esto es posible con nuestro premiado programa de viajero frecuente Marriott Rewards. Cuando viaje por negocios en América Latina, usted puede acumular puntos o millas. Al cabo de un tiempo, los podrá canjear por vuelos u hospedaje gratis con su familia en los Hoteles Marriott alrededor del mundo. Marriott cuenta con 393 hoteles en 56 países, donde encontrará el servicio y la atención que usted merece. Ningún otro sistema de membresía le ofrece tantas recompensas.

pensamos en usted

Marriott.
HOTELS · RESORTS · SUITES

©MARRIOTT CORPORATION

This Marriott ad targets the Hispanic market. If you cannot read Spanish, the decoding step in the communication process would be ineffective.

cool." "Fly our airline because it costs less." "This car is better for the environment." These are all persuasive arguments.

Sometimes, a promotion will both inform and persuade. For instance, if Pepsi says that people preferred Pepsi to Coke in a taste test, that information is intended to persuade you that Pepsi is better and that you should buy it instead of Coke. The persuasive message is supported by the information that people tried both products and preferred Pepsi.

Persuasive promotions can be used throughout the life cycle of a product, but they are typically used more after consumers are familiar with the product. It is also common for a company to change its persuasive tactics over time. Chevy may advertise the pulling power of its pickup trucks in one campaign, their longevity in another, and the fact that they are American-made in another. These can all be important features, and all are reasons a person might buy a Chevy truck. Chevy changes its promotional approach because different people find different aspects of Chevy trucks more persuasive as they consider what to buy.

Remind

The final role of promotional activities is to remind customers about existing products. These products are typically mature in their life cycle and familiar to consumers. Marketers want to remind people that a successful product exists and why people like it. When you see a sign in a football stadium with just a Snickers logo, it is a reminder promotion. Marketers are depending on the fact that you know what Snickers is and how it tastes. They hope that by just seeing the sign, it will remind you to purchase one from the concession stand.

Checkpoint ▶▶

What are the three roles that promotion plays in marketing?

Types of Communication

Marketers study the communication process to determine the types of communication necessary for their products or services. The type of communication used depends on the product or service and the intended target market characteristics. There are two main types of communication used by marketers: interpersonal and mass communication.

Fast FACTS

It has been reported that managers spend over half of their time involved in interpersonal communications—30% is spent on speaking and 25% is spent on listening.

Interpersonal Communication

Interpersonal communication is any person-to-person exchange. In marketing, this may be a telemarketing call, an in-person sales call, a customer service desk, an online chat with a company representative, or a salesperson in a store. The greatest benefit of interpersonal communication is that it is a two-way conversation. Customers can ask questions, and the salespeople can give an immediate response and tailor the message accordingly. They can tell if a customer is interested, bored, irritated, or needs more information.

Interpersonal communication is very specifically targeted, so for certain types of products, such as complex and high-end products, it can be very advantageous. A salesperson can explain the differences between one product and another and help the customer make a knowledgeable purchase decision. An experienced salesperson can also earn a customer's trust in ways that other types of communication cannot.

Interpersonal communication is frequently used in business-to-business marketing. Because business-to-business marketing can involve large sums of money, many companies have a professional sales staff. This sales staff can form relationships with its clients and be more responsive to their needs.

One of the main weaknesses of interpersonal communication is that it is often costly in terms of its efficiency. One salesperson can only deal with one or two people at a time. Also, while a knowledgeable sales force can be a great asset, it can be expensive to train them and pay sales-related expenses.

Mass Communication

Mass communication is the opposite of interpersonal communication, which gives customers the one-on-one attention of a salesperson. **Mass communication** attempts to reach a wide audience, sometimes millions of people, through mass media such as radio, television, magazines, and newspapers.

Mass communication is a one-way flow of information. It does not provide the opportunity for instantaneous feedback since the receiver cannot directly respond to the sender. This limits how much the message can be tailored for the recipient. While marketers do their best to target their messages, with mass communication they cannot be sure who will see the promotion. It may not reach all of the intended audience, and it may reach some people for whom it was not intended.

The strength of mass communication is that it can be much more cost-efficient than personal selling. One advertisement, for instance, can be used over and over to reach many more people in a shorter amount of time than a salesperson ever could. And although direct feedback is limited with mass communication, marketers have developed methods of gauging the effectiveness of a promotion. For example, they might issue coupons and track their use or use market research to gather consumers' reactions to an advertisement.

Checkpoint ▶▶▶

What are the two types of communication that are commonly used by marketers?

15-1 Assessment

Key Concepts

Determine the best answer.

1. Promotion is how a company communicates with a potential _____.

2. Which of the following is not an element of the communication process?
   a. sender
   b. message channel
   c. interceptor
   d. feedback

3. One advantage of mass communication is
   a. instant feedback from the receiver
   b. it can reach a large audience
   c. it has a personal touch
   d. all of the above

4. Interference in the message transmission that may inhibit or distract from the message is called
   a. information
   b. barrier
   c. noise
   d. static

Make Academic Connections

5. **Visual Art** Select an ad or other promotion you have seen or heard recently. Draw or use technology to create a picture, graphic, or other visual representation of the communication process as it pertains to that promotion.

6. **Research** Use the Internet or library to research how a major brand has changed its promotions over time. Describe the changes and explain why you think they were made and whether or not the changes have been effective.

Connect to

7. You and your team members work for an advertising firm that has been hired by a home electronics store. The owner of the store wants your team to create a television commercial for a new stereo. Determine the target market for the stereo and the communication goal. Write a script for the commercial. Your team should act out the commercial for your teacher (judge). Be sure to provide props to help make the commercial realistic.

Types of Promotion

GOALS

- Explain the advantages and disadvantages of advertising as a type of promotion.
- Describe the ways that public relations can be used to generate publicity.
- Identify the benefits and drawbacks of using personal selling to promote a product or service.
- Explain the advantages and disadvantages of using short-term incentives as sales promotions.

KEY TERMS

advertising, *p. 433*

broadcast media, *p. 433*

publicity, *p. 435*

public relations, *p. 435*

personal selling, *p. 437*

sales promotion, *p. 438*

marketing matters

There are many different types of promotion marketers can use to communicate with customers. Some types of promotion are more appropriate than others, and marketers must know what factors to consider when deciding which types of promotion to use. The four common types of promotion are advertising, public relations, personal selling, and sales promotion.

Marketers strive to find the right mix of these four ingredients. In a good promotional mix, all the elements work together, complementing each other so that consumers get a consistent message about the product or service. In order to create the best promotional mix, marketers must understand the characteristics, strengths, and weaknesses of each form of promotion.

Think of a product that you like. Describe the types of promotions used for that product. Do the promotions all communicate the same thing about the product? Which form of promotional activity do you find most effective? Why?

Advertising

The most popular and familiar form of promotion is advertising. **Advertising** is any form of paid, nonpersonal communication that uses mass media to deliver a marketer's message to an audience. As shown in Figure 15-3 on the next page, the major types of media used for advertising are television, radio, print, direct mail, outdoor, ambient, and the Internet.

Television and radio are known as **broadcast media**, meaning that a signal is sent from a central transmitter to receivers in a geographic area. Ads on TV and radio take the form of commercials, or "spots."

Print advertising is any paid message run in a magazine or newspaper. Print advertisements can be several pages long, but they are more commonly one page or a part of a page.

Direct mail is any marketing message sent to an audience through the mail. It is sometimes referred to as "junk mail," but it can be a very effective way to efficiently target messages.

Outdoor advertising, also called "out-of-home" advertising, includes billboards, signs on buses or taxis, messages on the sides of buildings, posters, ads on bus shelters or benches, signage at sporting events, or any other space designed specifically for ads outside the home.

Because marketers are always looking for ways to make their message stand out and get noticed, there has been a rise in recent years of *ambient advertising*. This type of advertising includes any nontraditional medium in the environment of the audience. Stickers on bananas, messages chalked onto sidewalks, hot-air balloons, stunts or "guerilla" advertising, and messages on bathroom stall doors all fall into the category of ambient advertising.

Internet advertising is the fastest-growing and most dynamic type of advertising. Marketers are developing new ways to use the Internet beyond the simple banner ad. The greatest benefit of Internet advertising is that it can be targeted by interest and location, and unlike most other forms of advertising, it provides marketers with instant feedback. Many experts believe the Internet is the future of advertising.

FIGURE 15-3

Marketers use various forms of advertising to send messages to consumers.

has great potential to move people emotionally because of the film style, music, and other production factors. When it comes to building strong brands, creating an emotional tie between a consumer and a product can be invaluable.

Advantages of Advertising

Because advertising has the ability to reach a wide audience, it is an efficient medium in terms of cost-per-viewer. Advertising is also a very controllable, repeatable form of promotion, delivering the exact same message again and again if necessary. Marketers know that an ad run at one time in Seattle and at another time in Atlanta will be exactly the same. The ad can be run multiple times in those places to reinforce the message.

This example also points out another advantage: many forms of advertising are not limited by geography. Ads can reach people anywhere in the country and most places in the world.

The final advantage of advertising, particularly television advertising, is that it

Disadvantages of Advertising

For all the advantages of advertising, there are also some disadvantages. First, even though advertising is very efficient in cost-per-viewer, the overall cost can be prohibitively expensive, especially for smaller companies. The average professionally produced television spot costs nearly $400,000 not including the cost of running it on television. To run a 30-second commercial just once on a show like *American Idol* can cost more than $700,000. A company with a national advertising plan will need to budget millions of dollars for it to be effective.

The second disadvantage is the impersonal nature of advertising. In most cases, there is no instant feedback, no ability to modify the message for the viewer, and no

Virtual Marketing

Big Advertisers Find Better Role for Internet

When the Internet was developed, it was obvious that it would present great opportunities for marketers. But early on, many companies simply used the Internet as they would use a billboard or magazine. They placed banner ads and put information on their web sites. But forward-thinking companies realized that the Internet differs greatly from other media. While television or print media allow only one-way communication (the company can send its message to the audience), the Internet allows a two-way flow of information.

Companies developed web pages that gave their customers helpful information but also invited them to engage in a dialogue with the company and with each other. Customers could ask questions about products, give the company feedback, and share tips and product uses with each other.

Companies also realized they could tap into the social potential of the Internet and create a community around a product or issue.

For example, Unilever launched a campaign for Dove that encouraged people to re-examine their concepts of beauty as defined by the media. The company used television and outdoor billboards, but much of the dialogue took place online where people could share their views with each other about an important topic.

Think Critically

1. What are the implications of this trend for Internet sites that rely on revenues from selling banner advertising? Will banner ads still have a place?

2. Think of a popular social networking web site like MySpace.com. How could this kind of site be used as a model by a company to promote a product?

---

way to make the personal connection that face-to-face communication allows.

Finally, with so much advertising clutter and other noise and with new technologies such as digital video recorders, it has never been easier for audiences to tune out or skip past ads. This is a major problem for marketers—one they are constantly trying to solve.

Checkpoint ▶▶

Name some advantages and disadvantages of advertising as a type of promotion.

Public Relations

Marketers often try to get their message to consumers by generating publicity through existing mass media, often news outlets. **Publicity** is any nonpaid communication about a product, service, company, or cause. The effort to reach consumers by generating positive publicity is known as **public relations**, or PR.

Working in **Teams**

As a team, select a school event or program that needs funding or supplies. For example, perhaps the school band needs to raise money for new uniforms. Discuss how publicity might benefit the cause. Develop a public relations campaign to create community awareness.

Judgment Call

Cause-Related Marketing Requires PR Savvy

Cause-related marketing refers to a company promoting itself by supporting a social cause or charity. It used to be that these partnerships were short-term. A company might fund a charity event in exchange for being mentioned during the event. The company and charity would then part ways. Recently, however, the trend has been for more long-term partnerships between companies and charities. Because a corporate sponsor can typically provide much more financial assistance to a charity than private donors can, it has become commonplace for charities to court corporate sponsors.

For their part, companies spend a lot of time analyzing which causes to attach themselves to. The hope is that people will have a more favorable view of that company. Companies must ensure that the cause they are supporting matches their overall mission. For instance, the Clorox Company, which manufactures products that clean and disinfect, partners with the Red Cross. This partnership makes sense because both Clorox and the Red Cross share the mission of keeping people healthy.

Think Critically

1. If a company has engaged in unpopular practices in the past and now wants to improve its image to help repair the damage, would a cause-related marketing initiative be a good idea? Why or why not?

2. Is cause-related marketing good for society or just a way for a company to take advantage of a situation while appearing to exhibit corporate citizenship?

Although the actual media coverage of the product or service is nonpaid, companies often have a PR department or hire a PR firm to identify media opportunities. They will often write press releases to send to the news media about their product or service or contact talk shows, magazines, and other media outlets to try to get their product mentioned.

Sometimes PR is a response to negative publicity. If a product is faulty or unsafe or if there is a recall, a company may use public relations to control the amount of damage done to its image. The company will contact media outlets in the hope that any coverage of the issue will include the company's point of view and what it is doing to resolve the problem.

Advantages of Public Relations

Publicity generated through public relations is very valuable because a third-party source such as a news program is perceived as being more objective than a commercial. When a product gets a favorable mention on a news program or a favorable review by a talk show host or celebrity, people are more likely to listen and try the product than if they had just seen a television commercial. When Oprah Winfrey, for example, mentions a product on her show or selects a book for her book club, those products fly off the shelves because so many people trust and respect Oprah. For that reason, many companies work to get their products on her show.

The second advantage of public relations is that it can be relatively inexpensive. If the release of a new product from a company becomes a big news story, it can be worth millions of dollars in free publicity. Apple, maker of the popular iPod music player, masterfully uses the news media to create buzz anytime a new iPod is released, and it has helped Apple lead the industry.

Disadvantages of Public Relations

The biggest disadvantage of public relations is that it is hard to control. Because it relies on third-party media outlets, exactly what is said about a product is up to the media, not the marketer. While coverage of a product by one media outlet may lead to more coverage and create a big story, it is nearly impossible to predict or control what kind of coverage, if any, a product gets. If the news media covers a product but reviews it negatively, it can be disastrous for a company.

Checkpoint ▶▶

What are some of the advantages and disadvantages of public relations?

NETBookmark

Businesses often sponsor individuals or teams in a number of sports, such as cycling, tennis, and automobile racing. Access school.cengage.com/marketing/marketing and click on the link for Chapter 15. The auto racing organization NASCAR maintains a list of corporate sponsors on its web site. View the list of sponsors and identify three that seem surprising or unlikely in some way. Explain your reaction. Why might a company that does not have a direct relationship to auto racing sponsor a NASCAR driver? Can you think of any risks involved in corporate sports sponsorship?

school.cengage.com/marketing/marketing

Personal Selling

As the name suggests, **personal selling** is person-to-person communication with a potential customer in an effort to inform, persuade, or remind the customer to purchase an organization's products or services. It usually involves interaction with a salesperson.

Personal selling is most commonly used in business-to-business promotion, where salespeople from one company meet with the people in charge of making the purchasing decisions for another company. Business-to-business deals can sometimes involve large sums of money. These meetings can involve elaborate presentations and follow-up meetings before a sale is completed.

Other forms of personal selling include salespeople at a retail store, telemarketers, car dealers, real estate or insurance agents, or even customer service representatives available online or over the phone. Effective salespeople are trained and knowledgeable so that they can help inform customers about products, answer questions, and eventually lead them to a purchase decision.

The types of products for which personal selling is appropriate are usually complicated and relatively expensive products with many features. Cars, auto insurance, homes, stereos, and business equipment are all good examples.

Advantages of Personal Selling

An advantage of personal selling is the personal contact. It can be much more informative and persuasive than advertising because of the person-to-person interaction.

Also, with person-to-person contact, feedback from the customer is immediate, and the sales presentation is flexible. A salesperson in a computer store can ask and answer questions, demonstrate features, and make a good product recommendation based on a customer's needs.

Disadvantages of Personal Selling

The major disadvantage of personal selling is the per-person cost. Though the cost of advertising is high, advertising reaches millions of people. Personal selling reaches one customer at a time and makes one sale at a time, so the cost per customer can be quite high. Sometimes, especially in business-to-business marketing, the selling process can go on for months and ultimately may not result in a sale.

Checkpoint ▶▶▶

Name an advantage and a disadvantage of personal selling as a type of promotion.

Sales Promotion

Sometimes marketers will want to boost sales through the use of short-term incentives with the hope that consumers will repeat the purchase later without the incentive. Any activity or material that gives consumers a direct incentive to buy is called **sales promotion**. The use of sales promotions is a common tactic when a company introduces a new product and wants to entice consumers to try it or when a company needs to increase the short-term sales of a product. An ice cream brand may want consumers to try a new flavor or a car dealership may want to sell last year's model before the newer model arrives.

Common types of sales promotions include price promotions through sales, coupons, or rebates; product incentives such as limited-time models or free product features and options; or giveaways like sweepstakes, contests, free product samples, or free toys with purchase. Special in-store or point-of-purchase displays provided by a manufacturer to encourage sales are also types of sales promotion.

Companies will often use price promotions and contests to boost short-term sales of a product.

Advantages of Sales Promotion

The greatest advantage of sales promotion is that it can generate short-term sales. A company can use a sales promotion for a boost that can also create loyal customers.

Another advantage is that sales promotion results are usually measurable. Stores know how effective a coupon program is because they can count how many coupons were redeemed, or the traffic during a contest can be compared with normal store traffic. This information can be used to improve future sales promotions.

Disadvantages of Sales Promotion

The biggest advantage of sales promotion can also be one of its drawbacks. Most successful businesses strive to create and maintain loyal customers. Sales promotion, on the other hand, focuses on the short-term. It builds customer relationships motivated by incentives rather than a true preference for the brand. Once the promotion has ended, the business hopes that the customers will return, but often they do not.

Other disadvantages of sales promotion can be the cost of providing the incentives, the loss in profit by cutting the price of products, and the cost of advertising the promotion. A promotional program that nobody knows about does not work, so companies must run ads promoting the promotion.

Checkpoint ▶▶

List common types of sales promotion.

15-2 Assessment

Key Concepts

Determine the best answer.

1. Which form of advertising has the best chance of emotionally moving a viewer?
   a. print
   b. direct mail
   c. television
   d. radio

2. Which is the biggest disadvantage of public relations?
   a. cost
   b. speed
   c. limited impact
   d. difficult to predict and control

3. What product would be the best candidate for personal selling?
   a. bar soap
   b. a piano
   c. chocolates
   d. movie tickets

4. The short-term nature of a sales promotion can be
   a. an advantage
   b. a disadvantage
   c. both an advantage and a disadvantage
   d. neither an advantage nor a disadvantage

Make Academic Connections

5. **Language Arts** Create a fictional person and write a one-page account of his or her day. Describe how the person comes into contact with each of the four types of promotion during the normal activities of a day and how he or she reacts to them. The promotions can be for the same product or for different products.

6. **Math** A grocery store usually makes a 10 percent profit on a box of detergent that sells for $5.00. In an average week, it sells 30 boxes of detergent. The store runs a coupon promotion for 25 cents off each box of detergent. How many boxes does it need to sell per week to break even on the reduced product price during the promotion?

Connect to DECA

7. You own a high-end clothing store in the mall. Determine how each type of promotion might be used to attract customers to your store and produce sales once they are there. Create a chart outlining your promotional choices and how each would be used. Present the chart to your teacher (judge) and discuss your decisions.

Mixing the Promotional Plan

GOALS

- Explain the five major factors that affect the promotional mix.
- Describe the seven steps in the promotional planning process.

KEY TERMS

promotional mix, *p. 440*

promotional plan, *p. 443*

marketing matters

Each of the four types of promotion has its strengths and weaknesses. Marketers typically use several or all of the types of promotion. They fill different roles and reach consumers in different ways, but they deliver essentially the same message. The specific way in which the promotional elements are used depends on several factors: the product itself, the target market, the product price and distribution, the availability of resources, and the company's overall philosophy.

Select a product you own. What types of promotion would you use for the product if you were planning the promotional mix? How would you decide what types of promotion would be most effective?

The Promotional Mix

As Figure 15-4 illustrates, the **promotional mix** is the combination of advertising, public relations, personal selling, and sales promotion that marketers use to reach a target market. It is critical that the elements of the promotional mix complement each other. If they deliver conflicting messages, the consumer might become confused. A carefully planned promotional mix can capitalize on the strength of each type of promotion and reach customers from several different angles to deliver on the promotional objective. How marketers determine which promotional tools to use depends on several factors as shown in Figure 15-5 on the next page.

Promotional Objective

You will recall that promotional communication can serve three purposes for a marketer: to inform, persuade, and

FIGURE 15-4

Each element of the promotional mix impacts the other elements, so they must work together to be effective.

remind. Different types of promotions are better suited for certain objectives. For instance, personal selling is an excellent tool for persuading customers with detailed, personalized information. However, it wouldn't make sense to hire salespeople to stand at the dairy case and remind people to buy milk at the supermarket.

Target Market

It is critical to consider the target market in formulating a promotional mix. Who are the people the company is trying to reach, and what do they find compelling? If your target market is upper-income, health-conscious women, offering coupons for 25 cents off a nutritional supplement may not be as effective as advertising the product's health benefits. You also need to consider where the target market lives. A target market that is dispersed across the country might make telemarketing a better approach than a billboard.

Marketing Mix

The type of product, the price, and its distribution affect the promotional mix as well. Certain products are better served by certain types of promotions. Bar soap, for instance, is not a good candidate for personal selling. However, a low-priced product such as soap would probably benefit from a coupon. On the other hand, consumers want more information before buying expensive items like a new house, which is why personal selling is a good fit. Distribution also plays a role. Internet advertising works particularly well for products sold online because of its ability to easily link to web sites selling the item.

Company Philosophy

Some companies believe in certain values that impact the promotional mix. For example, a hiking boot company may feel that outdoor billboards clutter the landscape and, therefore, will not use billboards. In 2006, Volkswagen ran a promotion in which it gave away an electric guitar with its cars because the promotion fit the company philosophy of freedom in self-expression.

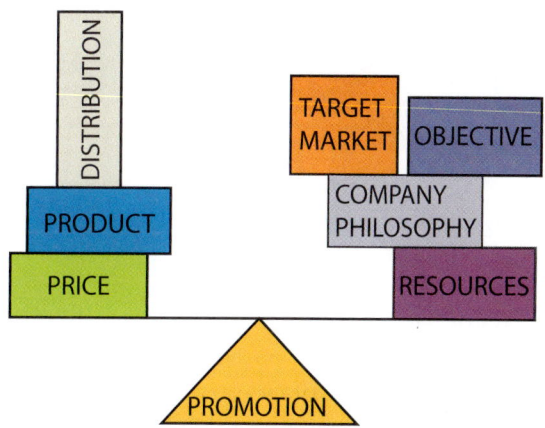

FIGURE 15-5

Many factors impact promotional plans, which makes developing the right promotional mix a balancing act.

Resources

The final factor to consider is the company's financial situation. Promotion can be expensive, and the marketer must determine which elements will have the greatest chance at achieving the company's objectives for the least amount of money. Small companies may not have the budget to use all the promotional tools available.

Checkpoint ▶▶▶

What five major factors affect marketers' choices when developing the promotional mix?

What promotional mix would you recommend for a new cell phone that has many unique features?

Design a Promotional Display

Have you ever been to a large, organized event, like a fundraising run for a charity, and noticed all of the booths set up near the finish line? Which booths catch your eye and draw you in? Why do you go to one booth instead of another?

Promotional displays are utilized by businesses and organizations in a variety of settings. Common settings for promotional displays include malls and stores, community events, and trade shows.

Displays have a variety of objectives. The display should inform prospective customers about the product. It should be enticing enough to pique their curiosity and pull them in to look at it. The display should be attractive to view and stimulate an appropriate response or action. The display reflects not only the product being promoted but also the image of the sponsor.

Here are some guidelines for a retail display.

- Make sure displays are well-balanced and proportional. They should fit within their allocated space and blend with the overall environment of the store.

- Decide what feeling the display is trying to evoke and choose colors accordingly. Warm colors, like red, are stimulating. Cool colors, like blue, are relaxing.

- Be sure the design will attract the target audience of the display. For example, a golf product display might incorporate a background image of a golf course.

- Consider whether the display will be located at the end of an aisle, in the middle of a walkway, in a window, or on a tabletop. There is an optimal design for each of these areas related to how customers view and use the space.

- Think about the location of the display relative to the products being sold. Items should be displayed with related merchandise. For

example, displaying tennis racquets with tennis apparel makes sense, while locating them next to camping equipment could distract or confuse consumers.

The reason merchandise is featured will impact the design of the display. Value might be the focus of a display that features sale merchandise.

Each item in the display should support the overall theme of the display. For example, including a large blanket, a cooler, disposable dishes, hand sanitizer, a portable volleyball net, and a Frisbee together in a picnic display makes sense because each of these items could be of interest to customers planning a picnic.

Develop Your Skill

Plan a display geared toward increasing attendance for an upcoming event at your school or in your community.

Using posterboard, draft two different designs for a display promoting the event. Ask several students, teachers, and target audience members for feedback to determine which display is the most appealing.

Refine the display that received the strongest feedback. On posterboard, develop a layout of all the elements you would include in the display. On a chart, outline why each element was included and how it supports the overall goals of the display.

Attend a school or community event that might have been an appropriate venue for your display. Try to determine why some displays draw more visitors than others. What are the characteristics of the displays that appear to be the most effective?

Promotional Planning

It is important to remember that each type of promotion serves a different purpose in the promotion mix and should be used to complement the other methods of promotion. Advertisements, for example, reach larger audiences and create awareness. Without them, the personal sales effort would be much more difficult, time-consuming, and expensive. Publicity resulting from public relations adds credibility to the message, but it is more difficult to control. Personal selling, on the other hand, offers personalized contact, can provide specific information a customer needs, and can close a sale. Without personal selling, the initial interest generated by advertising might be wasted. Sales promotion supplements the other methods and fills in the gaps by stimulating short-term sales efforts.

The promotional mix must be carefully planned around a common theme so that all the elements work together and, when viewed as a whole, deliver the message to the consumer. The blueprint for how the elements of the promotional mix will work together is called the **promotional plan**.

Creating an effective promotional plan is something that takes time. Most large companies plan well in advance to ensure that their promotions budget is used as efficiently as possible. Companies of all sizes follow a basic process for developing their promotional mix. They carefully analyze the current situation and identify opportunities. Then they formulate a promotional plan to take advantage of those opportunities. After the plan is implemented, marketers study the results and use what they learn to guide future efforts. The seven steps in the promotional planning process are shown in Figure 15-6 and are discussed below.

Research and Analyze the Market

Marketers can conduct market research as needed or use existing research to gain an

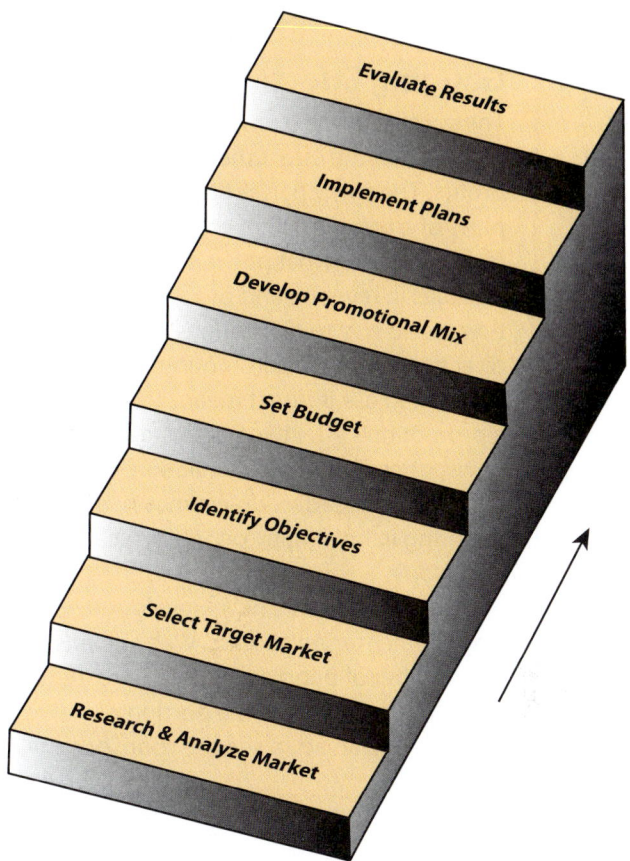

Promotional Planning Steps

FIGURE 15-6
Marketers follow a step-by-step process to develop a promotional plan that is focused, efficient, and based on achievable goals.

understanding of the market. They then analyze the research and identify the strengths and weaknesses of their product, opportunities in the market, and competitive threats.

Select the Target Market

Based on the opportunities identified in the research, the marketer can select a specific target market for the promotional plan. In this stage, the marketer should identify key characteristics of the target market and fully understand what might motivate the target market to buy the product. This allows the marketer to create a focused promotional strategy.

Figure This

Gauging Effectiveness

The success of most promotions ultimately depends on the effect they have on business profits. The tricky part is figuring out which parts of a complex promotional mix are responsible for what portion of subsequent changes in revenue and profits. In most cases, there is no way to tie changes in revenue directly to a specific promotion, so marketers have to use indirect means to estimate a promotion's effectiveness. Magazines and newspapers track paid circulation, total circulation, and readership estimates, the latter factoring in how many people typically read each copy.

Electronic media have developed new ways of measuring success. Web site hits are the number of people who log on to a site. Clickthrough rates are the portion of viewers who click on an ad to see the sponsor's site, where the amount of time each spends at the site is also tracked. Conversion rates are the portion of viewers who follow through by buying something or registering for whatever is being promoted.

Think Critically

1. If the weekly Rabbit Hash Business Journal has a paid circulation of 5,000, gives out 800 free copies, and estimates that 5.5 people read each copy, how many people read the paper each week?

2. If a popular web site averages 10 million hits a day, and an advertising agency estimates that a banner ad for a contest promotion on the site will yield a clickthrough rate of 3% and a conversion rate of 22%, how many people per day can it expect to register for the promotion?

Identify Promotional Objectives

With an understanding of the market, the marketer can then define the objective of the promotion. What does the company want to achieve with its promotional plan? The objective should be realistic and measurable.

Set the Promotional Budget

At this point, the marketer determines what it will cost to accomplish the objectives. While in reality budgets are sometimes dictated by the funds available, the ideal promotional budget is set to fit the plan, not the other way around. Previous annual budgets or predicted sales are often used to help determine a reasonable promotional budget.

Develop the Promotional Mix

With the available budget set, the marketer can then decide the appropriate mix of advertising, public relations, personal selling, and sales promotion, balancing all the factors that affect the mix.

©DIGITAL VISION

Why is it important to follow each step in the promotional planning process?

Implement the Promotional Plan

Once the promotional mix is developed, money from the total promotional budget is allocated to each effort. An activity schedule is developed, and decisions are made determining when the various promotional efforts take place. Sometimes promotions run simultaneously and sometimes they are staggered, depending on the stated objectives. Then the promotional materials are created, and the plan goes into effect.

Evaluate the Results

Marketers evaluate their promotional plan during and after the promotions, comparing the results with the objectives. They may change the promotional mix or

certain elements of it based on what they learn. The results can also be used to help plan future promotional efforts.

Working in **Teams**

Working with a team, identify a product or service that is commonly promoted. Discuss the various forms of promotion used and the message conveyed in each promotion. Based on this information, determine the target market that the company is trying to reach. Then identify the promotional objectives you think the company is trying to achieve.

Checkpoint ▶▶

What are the seven steps in the promotional planning process?

15-3 Assessment

school.cengage.com/marketing/marketing

Key Concepts

Determine the best answer.

1. True or False: A promotional plan will not be effective if all four elements of the promotional mix are not used.

2. Which is *not* a factor in developing a promotional mix?
   a. budget
   b. company philosophy
   c. length of television commercial
   d. available financial resources

3. A company that skips a step in developing a promotional plan runs the risk of
   a. misunderstanding the target market
   b. setting unrealistic objectives
   c. wasting money
   d. all of the above

4. What is the main purpose of research in the promotional planning process?
   a. understand the target market
   b. determine available funds
   c. select a marketing mix
   d. create an implementation schedule

Make Academic Connections

5. **Technology** Some people say that the Internet should be counted as a fifth element in the promotional mix. Why do you think this is? How many elements of the promotional mix can be fulfilled via the Internet?

6. **Management** You are the marketing manager for a designer shoe manufacturer. You have spent weeks developing a promotional mix that involves all four elements. Today you found out that your budget has been cut in half and you must cut two of the elements. Which two elements would you cut? Why?

Connect to **DECA**
An Association of Marketing Students

7. Your team has been hired by Ben & Jerry's Homemade Ice Cream to create a promotional mix for its company. Research Ben & Jerry's and consider what elements of the promotional mix would be the best fit for the company. Present a promotional objective and a proposed promotional mix, with specific media recommendations to your teacher (judge).

Check Your Understanding

Now that you have completed the chapter, check your understanding of the lessons with these questions. Record the score that best represents your understanding of each marketing concept.

1 = not at all; 3 = somewhat; 5 = very well

If your score is 42–50, you are ready for the assessment activities that follow. If you score 33–41, you should review the lessons for the items you scored 1–3. If you score 32 or less, you will want to carefully reread the lessons and work with a study partner on the areas you do not understand.

Can you—

— identify the function of promotion as part of the marketing mix?

— define and describe the communication process?

— identify the eight major elements of the communication process?

— name the three roles that promotion plays in marketing?

— describe two types of communication used by marketers?

— compare and contrast the two types of communication?

— list the four major types of promotion?

— describe the advantages and disadvantages for each type of promotion?

— name the five factors affecting the promotional mix?

— describe the seven steps in developing a promotional plan?

Review Marketing Terms

Match the terms listed with the definitions. Some terms may not be used.

1. The transfer of a message from a sender to a receiver

2. The combination of advertising, personal selling, public relations, and sales promotion that marketers use to reach a target market

3. The medium by which the message travels

4. Paid form of nonpersonal communication sent through mass media to deliver a marketing message to an audience

5. Interpreting language or symbols to comprehend the message

6. The person or persons to whom the message is directed

7. The blueprint for how the elements of the promotional mix will work together to deliver a consistent message

8. Any form of communication used to inform, persuade, or remind consumers about a company's products or services

9. An activity or material that offers consumers a direct incentive to buy a product or service

10. An attempt to reach a wide audience through mass media such as radio, television, magazines, and newspapers

11. The effort to reach consumers by generating positive publicity

a. advertising
b. broadcast media
c. communication process
d. decoding
e. encoding
f. feedback
g. interpersonal communication
h. mass communication
i. message
j. message channel
k. noise
l. personal selling
m. promotion
n. promotional mix
o. promotional plan
p. public relations
q. publicity
r. receiver
s. sales promotion
t. sender

Review Marketing Concepts

There are four types of promotional activities within marketing: advertising, personal selling, public relations, and sales promotion. Read the following activities and identify which type of promotional activity is involved.

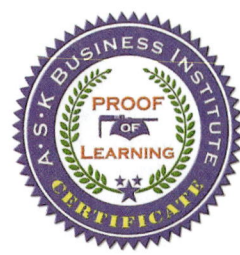

12. A press conference announcing a new automobile safety feature.

    _____

13. A coupon for 50 cents off the purchase price of toothpaste.

    _____

14. A shoe salesperson suggesting the purchase of shoelaces to a customer.

    _____

15. An athlete wears a certain brand of basketball shoes.

    _____

16. A full-page ad in a newspaper devoted to the sale of seafood products.

    _____

17. A chance to instantly win a car with the purchase of a soda.

    _____

18. An end-of-aisle display offering a free cooler with the purchase of a case of bottled water.

    _____

19. A sports drink sponsoring a marathon to raise money for cancer research.

    _____

20. A telemarketer encouraging you to buy a magazine subscription.

    _____

21. A realtor holding an open house.

22. A school sending its drama troupe to entertain in a retirement home.

    _____

23. The logo of a candy bar on a sign in the outfield of a baseball stadium.

    _____

Marketing Research and Planning

24. Choose a national brand and research how it uses advertising, public relations, personal selling, and sales promotion to effectively grow its business. Prepare a report on the specific promotional efforts of the brand and why they have worked for that company.

25. Find and record each of the following:
    a. five different types of advertisements
    b. five examples of personal selling that you have witnessed
    c. five promotions in a local store
    d. five public relation activities related to companies, products, or services

26. Select an advertisement from a magazine or newspaper. Show the ad to eight people and ask them the following questions:
    a. What is the central message of this ad?
    b. What does it tell you about the company that is running it?
    c. Does it make you want to buy this product or use this service?
    d. What other promotions are you aware of from this company?

    When you have completed the interview, write a summary of your findings using a word processing program. Do the people agree in their interpretation of the ad's meaning? If there are any differences in opinion, speculate as to what might cause those differences.

27. Companies benefit greatly from promotional elements that work together and complement each other. Give specific examples that illustrate how the following promotional elements can work together.
    a. advertising and public relations
    b. sales promotion and personal selling
    c. advertising and personal selling

28. Search the Internet for web sites that have promotions related to the products listed below. Write a half-page summary for each product site, indicating the address (URL) of the web site, the sponsor of the site, and the kinds of promotions offered. Select the promotion that you think is the most effective and explain why.
    a. boat
    b. organic food
    c. pet care products
    d. lawn and garden supplies
    e. computer
    f. home decor products

29. Select a product or service with which you are familiar. Walk through the promotional planning process using the product or service you have selected, and answer the questions that you think the company had to answer to create its promotional plan. Use the Internet to research anything you do not know, such as budget and results. Outline your findings in a written report.

30. Four magazines that direct their messages at a similar target audience are *Vogue*, *Harper's Bazaar*, *Elle*, and *Redbook*. The following chart

THE IMPACT OF ADVERTISING			
Magazine	Year 1 Ad Pages	Year 2 Ad Pages	Year 3 Ad Pages
Vogue	885.12	906.26	832.43
Harper's Bazaar	376.90	301.14	499.19
Elle	553.58	490.06	367.96
Redbook	323.12	264.83	268.27

shows the number of ad pages sold between January and June for each of these publications over a three-year period.
    a. Calculate the total number of pages sold every year.
    b. Calculate the percentage share each magazine has for each time period.
    c. Create a bar graph comparing Year 1, Year 2, and Year 3 for the four publications, based on total pages sold.

31. Search the Internet for recent industry data on business spending for promotional activities. Write a one-page report summarizing the information you find.

Marketing Management and Decision Making

32. Marketing managers are responsible for meeting the promotional objectives they set for their products or services. They also understand that thoughtful, well-written objectives can help focus and direct a promotional effort.

    The following list contains several products and services. It is your task to develop two promotional objectives that are appropriate for each of these products or services. Make certain the objectives are achievable through promotion. You may want to focus on a specific role of promotion: to inform, persuade, or remind.
    a. Six Flags theme park
    b. a local used car dealer
    c. fat-free frozen yogurt
    d. a national rental car company

33. A marketing manager oversees the development of the promotional mix based on the objectives set forth. For each of the objectives you developed in the previous activity, create a promotional mix that includes a description of how at least one element from each type of promotion might be used to help achieve the objectives.

34. It is very important for marketing managers to evaluate the results of their promotional plans and analyze what worked and what could be improved. This analysis helps them prepare future objectives and create promotional plans in upcoming years.

    Select one of the promotional mixes you developed in the previous activity. Assume that your promotional plan was a success and that your company wants to be even more aggressive next year. If your plan calls for it, the company is willing to double the money allocated for your promotional efforts. Write a new promotional objective and develop a new promotional mix that will aggressively grow your business. Be prepared to defend and support your decisions.

Community Service Project

The Community Service Project provides an opportunity for DECA members to develop a better understanding of the role civic activities have in society, to make a contribution to a community service or charity, and to learn and apply the principles of marketing management.

One to three members can participate in the Community Service Project. Participants are required to develop a manual on the procedures for planning, organizing, implementing, coordinating, and evaluating the project.

The project consists of the written document and oral presentation. The written entry will consist of the following parts:

Executive Summary Write a one-page description of the project.

Introduction Provide a historic background of the selected community service or charity; include a description of the local DECA chapter, school, and community.

Contributions to a Needed Community Service or Charity Include the description and purpose of the project, rationale for selecting the project, and description of the benefits of the project to the chapter members' understanding of leadership development, social intelligence, and community service.

Organization and Implementation Include an organizational chart, member involvement, and job descriptions; include the description of the project, documentation, and impact goal for the beneficiary.

Evaluation and Recommendations Include an evaluation of the project, the impact of the community service or charitable project, and recommendations for future projects.

Bibliography and **Appendix** Include additional sections as needed.

Performance Indicators Evaluated

- Demonstrate an understanding of the role of community service within the community. (Emotional Intelligence)
- Plan and conduct a project to benefit a community service or charity. (Operations)
- Evaluate the community service project's effectiveness in meeting the stated goals. (Strategic Management)
- Determine priorities and manage time commitments and deadlines. (Operations)

Go to the DECA web site for more detailed information.

Think Critically

1. What are some of the personal benefits from participating in community service?
2. What kind of publicity does an organization receive from participating in community service?
3. What strategy can be used to rally members of an organization to participate in a community service project?
4. Why are committees important for completing community service projects?

www.deca.org

Be Creative with Advertising

©DIGITAL VISION/GETTY IMAGES

Newsline

Selling an Image

Conventional wisdom, and some might say common sense, tells us that a person buys a computer because of what is inside it—the technology, circuit board, hard drive, and processor. A computer is a tool, and it doesn't matter what it looks like. It is not a pair of jeans. It certainly does not make someone "cool" to own one kind of computer instead of another. At least, that was conventional wisdom until the late 1990s when Apple Computer launched its "Think Different" campaign.

By saluting revolutionary thinkers like Albert Einstein, Miles Davis, Jim Henson, and John Lennon, Apple positioned itself as the computer for people who think outside the box, the non-traditionalists. Ridiculed at

first, the campaign launched Apple into a new era of rapid growth. Customers responded, and Apple's sales soared, bringing the company back from nearly going out of business.

And then Apple began to redesign its computers to look sleeker and more modern, almost like pieces of artwork. Experts again questioned the move. Why would people buy a computer because of how it looked? And again, customers proved the experts wrong. People did want a computer that looked cool. People wanted a computer that made them *feel* cool and rebellious.

That is the power of a brand. The purchase decisions people make are seldom completely rational. Often, they are buying into the idea of a

brand as much as they are purchasing a product. Companies dedicate much time and money to understanding these human motivations and then capitalizing on them by creating advertising that appeals to both the logical and emotional sides of consumers. They want people not just to *think* but also to *feel* that their brand is the right one to buy.

Think Critically

1. People have immediate associations with certain brands. Where do these associations come from?

2. Do you think every product can be sold with the type of emotional appeal that Apple made? Why or why not?

school.cengage.com/marketing/marketing

Prepare for Performance

This chapter develops the following Performance Indicators from the DECA Competitive Events program.

Core Performance Indicators

- Explain the use of advertising agencies
- Evaluate advertising copy strategies that can be used to create interest in advertising messages
- Understand design principles to be able to communicate needs to designers
- Assess advertisements to ensure achievement of marketing communications goals

Supporting Performance Indicators

- Select advertising agencies
- Evaluate advertising agencies
- Describe effective advertising layouts
- Determine advertising strategies for campaigns
- Identify effective advertising headlines

Go to **school.cengage.com/marketing/marketing** and click on Connect to DECA.

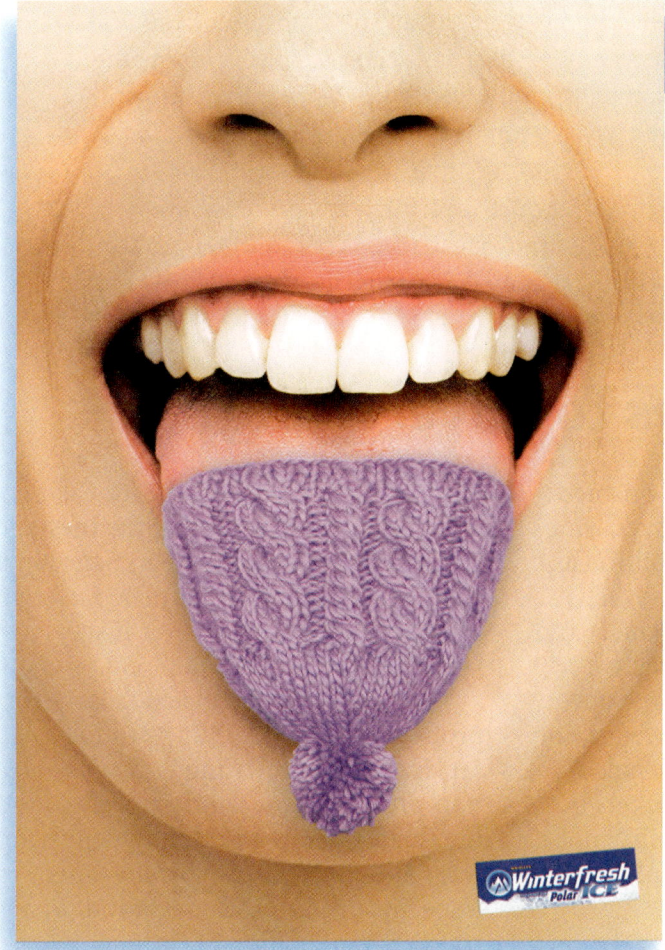

©WINTERFRESH POLAR ICE

Visual Focus

Advertising is one of the main ways that brands communicate with their customers. Through paid media, companies carefully control the messaging in their advertising to inform, persuade, or remind people about their brand. Many businesses hire advertising agencies to help them create an advertising campaign. Because advertising has influential powers, it is important that it be regulated to protect consumers.

Focus Questions:

Advertising is capable of communicating messages in many different ways, sometimes several messages at once. In this Winterfresh ad, the main message is communicated visually. What is the main message? How does it make you feel? Does it make you want to try Winterfresh gum?

Locate another ad that makes you want to buy the product or service. Share the ad with the class and explain why it moves you to take action.

What Is Advertising?

GOALS

- Define product advertising and brand advertising and distinguish between the two types.
- Describe the major roles at an advertising agency.

KEY TERMS

product advertising, *p. 453*

brand advertising, *p. 453*

corporate advertising, *p. 453*

advertising agency, *p. 454*

account executive, *p. 454*

account planner, *p. 454*

media plan, *p. 454*

media planner, *p. 455*

art director, *p. 455*

copywriter, *p. 455*

creative director, *p. 455*

producer, *p. 455*

marketing matters

You will recall that advertising is any paid, one-way communication delivered through a mass medium. Companies advertise in order to inform, persuade, or remind their customers. In addition, companies use a mix of product advertising and brand advertising to deliver specific product messages to their audience and to help build their brands so that their audience has positive associations with them.

A company will often hire an advertising agency to help develop the communication strategy and marketing message and then to create and execute advertisements that communicate that message. Sometimes the advertising agency will create just one advertisement for a product, but it is also common for an agency to develop a campaign of ads with a similar theme that work together across several media.

Working in a small group, list several product advertisements that you have recently seen or heard. What medium was used for each product's ad? Have you seen or heard the same product advertised in other media? Discuss the results of your list.

Two Approaches to Advertising

Advertising is a very complex business. In the United States, total advertising expenditures are over $250 billion a year. Companies rely heavily on advertising to drive demand for their products and services. Developing targeted, effective ads is a lengthy and expensive process. Successful advertising requires knowledge not only of marketing but also of psychology, an understanding not only of markets but also of cultural trends, and an ability not only to communicate clearly but also to do it artfully and persuasively.

Marketers spend a lot of time determining what the most persuasive advertising message will be for their business and ensuring that the message is delivered to their target audience in a clear and convincing manner. Advertising targets everyday people. It speaks their language and touches their emotions.

We think of advertisers as large for-profit corporations selling products or services, but advertising is also used by non-profit groups, politicians, and other organizations. In addition to delivering a message, advertising typically aims to sell a specific product, build a brand or, most often, a combination of the two.

Product Advertising

Product advertising gives the benefits of a specific product or service and relies on rational arguments why a customer should buy it. It may include product information, prices, or comparisons with competitors.

Product advertising gives at least one product attribute as a reason for purchasing a product. For example, "Phillips energy-saving light bulbs save money on your power bill."

Brand Advertising

A *brand* is the accumulation of all the tangible and intangible qualities of a company, product, or product line. It includes elements such as the name, logo, slogan, and designs associated with the brand. It also includes associations such as attitude and personality. These rational and emotional elements comprise the *brand character*.

Think of a well-known brand such as Coca-Cola. If you were to describe Coca-Cola, you might offer a product attribute such as the taste, or you might give a brand attribute such as the colors red and white. You might also mention a less tangible attribute, such as "young" or "fun." These are all part of the brand.

Part of what makes brands important is that in Western culture, our purchase decisions help define who we are. When we purchase a car or even a soda, those choices say something about us. Certain brands are "cool" or "rebellious." Others are "classic" or "dependable." Part of the character of that brand is transferred to us. If this seems surprising, consider that in a 2007 survey

of Toyota Prius owners, 57 percent said they bought their Prius hybrid car because "it makes a statement about me." It wasn't because the Prius got good gas mileage or looked nice. They bought it for what the brand represented.

Brand advertising is advertising that aims to build an image. It uses common elements to define what a product or company stands for and to give it a personality in the minds of consumers. Brand advertising may be done for a company brand, such as Nike. Advertising for a company is called **corporate advertising**. Brand advertising may also be done for a branded line of products, such as Swanson frozen dinners.

Brand advertising can even be used for vacation destinations, such as the Cayman Islands, to help build an image.

Even product advertising will include some elements of branding. An advertisement for Snickers, for instance, will sometimes deliver a message about the candy bar—that it satisfies hunger—but it will also make you feel something about the brand. Perhaps the ad makes you laugh or makes you think that Snickers is for young, energetic people. Those associations are brand associations. Almost all advertising is a mix of product and brand advertising.

Checkpoint

Explain the difference between product advertising and brand advertising.

The Advertising Agency

A business will often hire another company to handle the advertising for some or all of its brands. An **advertising agency** is a company that specializes in creating advertising. Many people within an advertising agency work together to create an ad from start to finish. These people all bring different expertise to the process.

An **account executive** is the key liaison between the client and the agency. Account executives help clients plan the advertising and relay information from the clients to other people in the agency.

To learn about the target market, the agency looks to its **account planner**. Account planners spend a lot of time talking to the target markets. Sometimes they conduct research in focus groups, where a moderator leads a discussion about the advertising with a small group of people. At other times, they travel to the homes of the target markets to see how they live, work, and think.

Some ad agencies will also develop a media plan for the business. A **media plan** is a detailed listing of where and when ads will run. It is designed to give the business

Digital Digest

DVRs Make Ad Avoidance Even Easier

Digital video recorders (DVRs) that can record and skip through TV programming give viewers a power that advertisers have long feared—the power to skip commercials. Advertising time is only valuable if the audience watches the commercials.

With the introduction of the remote control and then again with the VCR, advertisers feared that viewers could easily avoid commercials. Now, with 50 million DVRs predicted to be in the market by 2009, advertisers are scrambling for answers.

One possible solution is to embed special billboards containing a logo and a quick message that pops up on the screen if someone skips through the commercial. Networks have also experimented with inserting contests or bonus show content into the commercial breaks. Some advertisers argue that the simplest way to get viewers to watch commercials is to make them more entertaining so viewers will *want* to watch.

Think Critically

1. Based on the fact that the remote control and VCR did not spell disaster for advertisers, do you think DVRs will cause problems?

2. What is the likely outcome if advertisers conclude that TV ads are no longer reaching the desired audiences?

the best coverage of its target market for the least amount of money. The person who develops the media plan is the **media planner**.

The team that actually creates the advertising is typically made up of an art director and a copywriter. Generally speaking, the **art director** has a background in design or fine art and is responsible for how the ad will look. The **copywriter** has a writing background and writes the words in the ad. However, good creative teams work together, and their roles are not so rigid.

Sometimes, a creative director oversees the creative team. The **creative director** helps guide the creative process and ensures that the creative team's work conveys the right message and is in line with the client's needs.

An advertising agency may also have a production department. The job of the **producer** is to facilitate everything that happens after the client agrees to develop an ad or campaign. This includes hiring a director and editor to make a television commercial or a photographer for a print ad. The producer is also responsible for ensuring that an ad does not exceed the client's budget.

Checkpoint ▶▶

Name the major roles at an advertising agency.

16-1 Assessment

Key Concepts

Determine the best answer.

1. Which of the following is an element of a brand?
   a. color
   b. personality
   c. design
   d. all of the above

2. What is the primary aim of brand advertising?
   a. to illustrate a product feature
   b. to provide a rational reason to make a purchase
   c. to help create a brand image
   d. to make comparisons with competitors

3. Who is the key liaison between the client and the ad agency?
   a. creative director
   b. copywriter
   c. account executive
   d. producer

4. True or False: Product advertising gives at least one product attribute as a reason for purchasing a product.

Make Academic Connections

5. **Visual Art** Pick a brand that you like. Create a collage or "mood board" with pictures, words, colors, symbols, or other elements that you associate with the brand you selected.

6. **Writing** Carry a notebook with you throughout your day. Write down the brands that you come in contact with. Make a note of how they make you feel and any associations you might have with them. Write a one-page summary of your findings.

Connect to ◀DECA

An Association of Marketing Students

7. Your advertising agency has been given a new assignment: to create brand advertising for a new soda called Silver Cola. Develop a two-minute presentation for your client on the elements you would use to create a brand for Silver Cola. What colors, designs, and music would you use? What kinds of people would you use in your commercials? How would you want your target audience to think of your cola? What would be its "personality"? Give your presentation to your teacher (judge).

Advertising Planning

GOALS

- Describe the process of setting objectives, determining the budget, and developing the creative strategy.
- Describe the different types of media and the factors that must be considered when selecting which media to use.

KEY TERMS

advertising plan, *p. 456*

advertising campaign, *p. 456*

creative strategy, *p. 458*

strategic brief, *p. 458*

reach, *p. 460*

frequency, *p. 461*

lead time, *p. 461*

marketing matters

When a company decides to include advertising as part of its promotional mix, the first step is to develop an advertising plan. An advertising plan describes the activities and resources needed to create and execute an advertising campaign that will reach the target market with a focused, compelling message.

The first steps in developing an advertising plan are to set the advertising objectives and work out a budget. A creative strategy that will guide the creative message of the advertising is then written. As the project moves into the hands of the writers, art directors, and others who will execute it, the media planner begins to select the media types, such as television or magazines, and vehicles, such as *Survivor* or *Newsweek*.

Select an ad you have seen recently that seemed to be out of place, either appearing in the wrong medium or at the wrong time. What medium and time would have been more appropriate? Explain why.

The Planning Process

An **advertising plan** is a document that outlines the activities to be completed and resources needed to create advertising. It specifies objectives and a budget and includes the basis for creating and evaluating the advertising strategy and creative strategy. An advertising plan may be for a single advertisement, but it is most often written for an advertising campaign.

An **advertising campaign** is a series of related advertisements with a similar look, feel, and theme that centers on a specific product, service, or brand. Since advertising involves huge sums of money, advertisers follow a specific process to create the advertising plan and develop the most effective, cost-efficient campaign.

1. Set objectives
2. Determine the budget
3. Develop the creative strategy
4. Select and schedule the media
5. Develop the creative concept
6. Produce the advertising
7. Evaluate the plan's effectiveness

Set Objectives

The first step in the development of an advertising plan is to determine the advertising objectives. *Objectives* are the desired results to be accomplished within a certain time period. Objectives may be to increase sales, to increase awareness, or to communicate an idea to an audience. It is important for objectives to be specific and measurable. As part of the objectives, advertisers specify the main communication of the advertising, the target audience, and the time frame.

Objectives for a specific advertising plan will vary from organization to organization and from product to service. For example, an advertising plan for a municipal library might have as its objective to attract 1,000 new library cardholders between the ages of 5 and 10 during the next month. An advertising plan for the Nissan Xterra might have as its objective visits to Nissan dealerships by 9,000 Hispanic residents of West Texas, Arizona, and New Mexico during the months of June, July, and August. Figure 16-1 presents an objective for the advertising plan of Seaside Resorts.

Determine the Budget

Once the advertising objectives are defined, the budget can be developed. Managers identify a total advertising budget early in the planning process. A more detailed budget is prepared as planning is completed. There are four common methods of determining budgets for advertising.

What You Can Afford In the what-you-can-afford method of determining the ad budget, organizations account for all of their other expenses, and whatever is left over is budgeted for advertising. This is not the ideal method, but sometimes, especially with smaller companies, it is the reality.

Percentage of Sales The percentage-of-sales approach budgets a percentage of past, current, or projected future sales for advertising. For example, a firm that sold $50 million in tractors last year might allocate five percent of sales to advertising, for an ad budget of $2.5 million.

One drawback of this method is that advertising varies directly with sales. If sales drop, more advertising, not less, may be what the company needs to bring sales back up. In addition, past sales are not always the best predictor of future sales. Markets are volatile, and changes like increased competition, evolving customer tastes, or new technology can impact sales drastically. Companies are better off considering the current situation and future trends, and then using a percentage of predicted future sales when calculating the budget.

Competition Matching The competition-matching approach suggests that an organization should have an ad budget similar to its competitors. Although it is smart to be aware of what the competition is doing in terms of advertising, competitors may have different advertising objectives and different resources. Also, it is difficult to determine competitors' budgets until after the fact. Therefore, this approach can be problematic.

Objective and Task The best method of determining an advertising budget is to base it on the objectives to be achieved. The advertising team determines the desired goals of the advertising effort,

FIGURE 16-1
Objectives are the results to be attained by the advertising plan.

Advertising Objective for Seaside Resorts	
Sales Objective	Increase reserved summer rentals by 10% by February 15
Communication	Make reservations by February 15 and save $100 off the weekly rental rate
Target Market	Families living in California who spend one week or more at the beach every year

Why is an advertising budget determined early in the planning process?

outlines the activities needed to accomplish those goals, and then calculates the cost of completing each necessary task in order to determine the advertising budget.

Develop the Creative Strategy

Effective advertising campaigns are targeted to deliver a clear message to a defined target audience. The process of deciding what to say and how to say it starts with the creative strategy. The **creative strategy** is how a company positions its brand or product in its advertising. At this phase of the process, an advertising agency's account executive works with the client to define certain parameters for the advertising. To whom is the advertising targeted, and what

should the advertising communicate to that target market?

Members of the account team then write a **strategic brief**, also known as a creative brief, which is a short document that defines the target market and articulates the main message of the advertising. The strategic brief is very important because it guides the rest of the advertising process.

Checkpoint ▶▶

What are the four common methods of determining an advertising budget, and which one is usually the most effective?

Select the Media

As an agency's creative department begins work on developing the advertising, media planners simultaneously work on where and when to place it. The media plan answers questions regarding what types of media, which vehicles, in what units, and at what time.

The media type refers to the format, such as TV, radio, or print. The vehicle is

Fast FACTS

Between 2005 and 2006, advertising spending in all traditional media types increased, with the exception of newspaper advertising, which declined 2.4%.

the programming or publication in which the advertising appears, such as *Lost, Sports Illustrated,* or *USA TODAY.* The unit refers to the length or size of the advertisement, such as a 30-second commercial or quarter-page print ad. The timing of an ad campaign might be *continuous,* which means that it runs continually over a period of time. Or it might be *pulsing,* which means that the campaign runs more often during specific times, such as holidays.

Each type of media has its strengths and weaknesses (see Figure 16-2). The job of the media planner is to create a plan that takes advantage of the strengths of the media vehicles and reaches the target market with just the right frequency. The goal is to reach the most people in the target market for the least amount of money.

FIGURE 16-2
The media planner must determine the right balance of media to use for the advertising.

Advantages and Disadvantages of Major Advertising Media

Media	Advantages	Disadvantages
Television	Reaches large audiences Low cost per viewer Has emotional impact Highly segmented markets	High total cost Long lead time Strong potential for interference from other sources
Radio	Highly mobile Relatively low cost Short lead time Highly segmented markets	Message limited to audio Strong potential for interference from other sources
Outdoor	Low cost High visibility Short lead time	Increasingly regulated Message length is limited Strong potential for interference from other sources
Direct Mail	Highly segmented Easy to measure effectiveness Stimulates action Hidden from competition	Often considered junk mail Expensive
Magazines	Long life span Can carry response vehicles (coupons, response cards) High pass-along rate Highly segmented	High cost Long lead time
Newspapers	Short lead time Large circulation Can carry response vehicles (coupons) Inexpensive	Lower print quality Short life Limited segmentation High clutter (competing ads)
Internet	Highly targeted Instantly measurable Built-in response vehicles Interactive	Limited audience High clutter (competing ads) Security and privacy concerns

Media planning is a balancing act of many factors, and advertisers are constantly looking for new ways to break through the clutter of traditional media. However, traditional media remains an enormous industry, with television as king. Advertisers in the United States spent $65 billion on TV in 2006. Following this, in order of spending, were magazines, newspapers, and radio. Internet advertising, the newest form, has grown rapidly since its inception, to nearly $10 billion a year, jumping 17 percent from 2005 to 2006.

Each type of media has characteristics that should be analyzed before a choice is made (see Figure 16-3). The cost, reach, frequency, lead time, and fit of each format must be considered to determine the best choice.

Cost

Media costs depend on the type of media, the specific vehicle, and the unit. The media planner tries to balance these factors to reach the most people at the least expense. The planner must figure out whether the total cost of a specific medium is affordable for the budget and whether it is cost efficient. Efficiency is measured by the per-reader or per-viewer cost. The total cost of an ad in a national magazine might be $50,000. The per-reader cost of magazines is expressed as the cost per thousand readers, or CPM. The CPM for an ad that costs $50,000 and reaches 500,000 people is $100 ($50,000 ÷ 500 thousand = $100).

Reach

The **reach** is the total number of people who see an ad. In TV advertising, it is based on the number of people watching the programming. In outdoor advertising, traffic statistics help estimate the number of viewers.

For a magazine or newspaper, the number of copies distributed is called

FIGURE 16-3

There are several factors to consider when determining which medium to use.

Questions to Consider When Selecting Media	
Cost	What is the total cost of the medium? What is the cost per viewer? Does the cost fit into the advertising budget? Is it the most effective use of advertising dollars?
Reach	What is the overall circulation or viewership? Will it reach the target audience? Is there a strong pass-along rate?
Frequency	How often will the target audience see the advertising message? How many viewings does it take for the message to "stick"? After how many viewings does "wear-out" occur?
Lead Time	How long before running the advertising does the medium outlet require the ad materials? How flexible is this medium? Can the ad materials be ready by the medium's deadline?
Creative, Brand, and Corporate Fit	Does the medium fit the message? Is the medium a good fit for the brand? Does the medium fit the company philosophy?

the *circulation*. But with those media, there is also the *pass-along rate*, which is how many people read a single printed copy. One copy of *Newsweek*, for example, is read on average by about six people. Therefore, its reach is higher than its actual circulation.

Frequency

The number of times a member of the target audience is exposed to the advertising message is the **frequency**. Radio, television, and newspapers can be used quite frequently. In fact, advertisers can run the same message daily or, in the case of radio and television, even hourly. But a message also loses effectiveness after a certain number of exposures. This is called "wear-out." For example, if you see a commercial once or twice, you will get much more out of it than when you see the commercial the tenth time. By then, its effect on you has worn off.

Advertising executive Donald Gunn believes that all television ads fall into one of twelve basic categories or "master formats." Access school.cengage.com/marketing/marketing and click on the link for Chapter 16. Read the brief *Slate* article, play the slide show, and watch the video examples of the twelve categories. Then brainstorm a list of current television commercials or take note of them as you watch television one evening, and place each commercial into one of Gunn's twelve categories. Explain your selections. Can you think of any other categories beyond Gunn's original twelve?

school.cengage.com/marketing/marketing

Lead Time

The amount of time required to place an ad is the **lead time**, which varies tremendously among media types. The lead time

World View

Ethnic-Focused Media

Since the encoding and decoding of messages are essential parts of the communications process, using ethnic-focused media would seem to be a natural way to reach minority consumers such as African-Americans, Hispanics, and Asian-Americans. They make up approximately one-third of the U.S. population and are growing at a much faster rate than the general population. Yet ethnic-focused media garner only a tiny fraction of U.S. ad expenditures.

Ethnic-media executives say their media deserve a bigger share of ad expenditures but don't get it because there are few minorities among media buyers, advertisers think of ethnic media only as an afterthought,

advertisers do not understand minorities' buying habits, and targeting narrow market segments is more expensive than a one-size-fits-all approach.

An example of a company targeting ethnic groups is American Airlines. It developed a special Spanish-language portal on its web site to allow Spanish-speaking users to more easily book travel and receive e-mail newsletters with fares to their preferred countries.

Think Critically

1. Why are ads in ethnic-focused media effective with the targeted groups?

2. Why is targeting ads to narrow segments more expensive than a one-size-fits-all approach?

for a newspaper ad might only be a day compared to several months for a magazine ad. The timeline for the production of the ads should factor in the lead time to ensure the ads will be finished by the media deadline.

Creative, Brand, and Corporate Fit

There are also issues of whether or not the medium is appropriate for the advertising, the brand, or even the company running the ads. For example, if the creative message is long and complex, an outdoor board on a highway would not be a good fit. It is hard to read a long message when you are driving past at 65 miles per hour.

Likewise, a brand or company may not wish to associate itself with certain media vehicles or types of programming. Family companies such as Disney are very sensitive to the types of media vehicles in which they advertise. Even if its target audience is watching a show, Disney may not want to appear during the show if it contains material considered objectionable by the company or is in opposition to the brand's values.

Checkpoint

What are the five primary considerations in selecting the types of media in which to run an advertisement?

16-2 Assessment

Xtra! Study Tools
school.cengage.com/marketing/marketing

Key Concepts

Determine the best answer.

1. Which of the following is *not* included in advertising objectives?
   a. the overall goal of the campaign
   b. the main message to be communicated
   c. the media vehicles to be used
   d. the timeframe for achieving goals

2. The best way to determine a budget is by
   a. matching what the competition is spending
   b. determining how much is required to meet the advertising objectives
   c. setting it at 15% of predicted annual sales
   d. allocating the amount remaining after research and development

3. Which medium would be best suited for a complex message that requires a viewer response?
   a. outdoor
   b. radio
   c. Internet
   d. television

4. True or False: The *media type* refers to the programming or publication in which the advertising will run.

Make Academic Connections

5. **Communication** Create a chart that shows an example of each type of media. You can use photos, cut out advertisements, or draw examples that you find, but each type of media should be represented in some way.

6. **Research** Pick an advertising campaign that you particularly like. On the Internet, conduct research to learn what company and ad agency are responsible for the campaign. Find as much information as you can and write a one-page report about the campaign. Identify the brand or company being advertised and the type of media and vehicles used in the campaign. Also, include an explanation of why you like the advertising.

Connect to DECA
An Association of Marketing Students

7. Select a product that you would find in a grocery store. Put together a media plan for that product that uses at least one media vehicle in each media type. Present your media plan to your teacher (judge) with any necessary visual aids. Be prepared to explain why you chose those vehicles based on the advertising objectives and the overall effectiveness of the media plan.

Advertising Execution and Evaluation

GOALS

- Name common creative advertising formats.
- Explain what happens during the production phase of the advertising process.
- Differentiate between quantitative and qualitative research.
- Name the four types of advertising regulation.

KEY TERMS

quantitative research, p. 468

qualitative research, p. 468

cease-and-desist order, p. 469

corrective ads, p. 469

fine, p. 469

marketing matters

After the advertising plan is created, the budget set, and the creative strategy developed, the strategic brief is given to the creative team to develop the creative concept. There are several common formats of creative advertising, all with the goal of standing out among the clutter and delivering the message in a memorable way. After the creative concept is approved by the client, the advertising is produced. Once the advertising has run, its effectiveness is gauged using several research techniques.

Various review boards and other individuals work together to oversee advertising and to help ensure that it is fair, honest, and not deceptive or harmful to the public.

Find and make copies of four print ads. List all the things you like and dislike about each ad.

Creative Development

After the media decisions are made, the creative work begins. This is the step during which the advertising is actually created. The advertising must reach the target audience, be consistent with the objectives set, and fit within the budget.

Creative Formats

Because advertising aims to stand out, the creative team tries to develop a concept that is completely original. However, there are some common creative formats they might use, alone or in combination with other formats.

Musical Some commercials revolve around a song: a jingle, characters or famous musicians singing, or simply background music. Over the years, Pepsi has used many different musicians from Ray Charles to Beyonce. And jingles like "I wish I were an Oscar Mayer wiener" can stay in your mind for life, creating strong brand awareness.

Dramatization Sometimes commercials present a realistic scene played by actors, often with the product solving a problem of some sort. Dramatizations are supposed to give us the feeling that we are watching or hearing a real event.

Advertising as a Game of Chance

To see how difficult it can be to accurately predict the effectiveness of an advertising plan, look at the number of variables and calculations involved. Most plans rely on getting a message out to many people hoping that a few will buy the product. But a few small changes can seriously affect the plan.

Consider a company that buys a TV spot during the World Series, expecting to reach 30 million baseball fans with an ad for a credit card. Based on prior experience, the plan estimates that one in every 200 people (0.5%) will apply for a card. That number of people yields 150,000 applications, of which 120,000 (80%) can be expected to qualify, which satisfies the objective of 100,000 new cards.

But what happens if the game is a blowout by the end of the second inning, and the ad runs in the fifth inning when only 60% of the viewers are still watching? And what if 25% of them drift out of the room during the break? The audience has now shrunk to 13.5 million. Now suppose that because of overexposure to prior promotions, the response rate is weak, and only 1 in 500 (0.2%) apply. And suppose those still watching have below-average credit, so only 67% qualify. All of these factors leave the company with only 18,000 new credit cards. How could it have been so far off? It is the result of cumulative changes in a long series of variables.

Think Critically

1. A banner ad is seen by 20 million Internet users, and 0.4% of them click through to the sponsor's site, at which point 2% buy the product being promoted. How many product sales result?

2. By what percentage do product sales decrease if the click-through rate is reduced to 0.2%?

Testimonial Celebrities, knowledgeable professionals, or everyday people sometimes endorse a product by giving a testimonial. Whether it is Sean "Diddy" Combs selling skin care products, a doctor recommending a medicine, or an everyday person talking about the Saturn Ion, the idea is that an audience is more likely to trust a message from a third party than one directly from a company.

Comedy One way of giving a brand personality is to make the audience feel an emotion, and humor is a popular emotion in advertising. Even if they don't want to buy your product, viewers who laugh at a commercial will have positive associations with that brand.

Image Advertising Image ads evoke some sort of mood or attitude for a brand or product. The iPod and nearly all fashion advertising is pure image.

Product Demonstration This creative format shows the product in action. It may be a simple demonstration of a cleaning product removing dirt or something

Working in Teams

As a team, make a list of commercials you have seen recently and decide which type of creative format each exemplifies. They may be a combination of two or more formats. Discuss which of these commercials you like and which ones you don't like. Is there a format common to the commercials you like?

exaggerated like a Chevy truck pulling a spaceship.

Competitive Competitive advertising makes a claim of superiority over the competition. It may show competing products side by side, or it may just refer to some aspect of the competition.

The Creative Concept

Once the creative team has developed the creative concepts and the creative director has approved them, they are drawn up in rough form and presented to the client. At the client presentation, the agency may act out ideas for TV commercials, read scripts, or show rough versions of print ads to help bring the creative ideas to life.

Because advertising is very expensive, clients will sometimes conduct research on a concept to make sure it will be effective. They may present the concept to focus groups for quick feedback, or they may use more extensive testing techniques that require them to produce a rough version of the ad and then ask an audience questions about it. Research helps gauge if an

©DIGITAL VISION/GETTY IMAGES

What is the purpose of the client presentation meeting?

audience will like an ad and understand its main message. If the advertising concept passes these tests, the client will be more likely to approve it for production.

Checkpoint ▶▶▶

Why is it important for creative concepts to be unique and original?

Get the Message

Ad Clutter

Clutter is the industry term for anything other than programming that is broadcast on television. For decades, the amount of clutter per hour of programming on television slowly crept upward, reaching about 15 minutes of clutter per hour in 2005. Since then, the amount of clutter has remained relatively stable. Daytime television has the most clutter, with some networks carrying as much as 20 minutes of clutter per hour. Cable television tends to have slightly more clutter than the broadcast networks.

Advertisers hate clutter even more than viewers do, because it tends to obscure the messages they are trying to get across (never

mind that commercials make up the greatest bulk of clutter). The more clutter there is in an hour, the greater the chance that a viewer will tune out and miss a company's message. Advertisers must do everything they can to make sure their advertising is attention-grabbing, so it stands out from the clutter.

Think Critically

1. Why is there a natural tendency for clutter to grow even though viewers and advertisers hate it?

2. What effect do you think the abundance of cable channels and new networks has on the amount of clutter carried per hour?

Planning a Career in... *Virtual Creative Services*

"My brother has landed an internship as an assistant Web marketing writer for a car manufacturer. The company is developing a hybrid vehicle targeted toward environmentally conscious adults in their early 20s. My brother will review print and online marketing materials and suggest ways the content can be more engaging. He will also evaluate the company's web site from the perspective of a typical end user and make suggestions on how to improve site navigability."

How do companies decide on the best advertising content to inform and excite consumers about their products? How are messages customized for various audiences?

Creative services is a field that focuses on the thematic content, graphics, and presentation of advertising. Selecting the mass media distribution channel, from billboards, radio, TV, or the Internet, is also within the realm of creative services.

Employment Outlook

- A growing but increasingly competitive field.
- Faster-than-average growth is anticipated based on the growth of Internet marketing and advertising.
- Opportunities may be industry-dependent. Demand is expected to be strong in technology, professional, and service industries but may decrease in more traditional industries.

Job Titles

- Web Content Manager
- Content Strategy Director
- Lead Web Content Editor
- Director of Content
- E-Communications Editor

Information Technology

Needed Skills

- A bachelor's degree including liberal arts, writing, and business courses with an emphasis on marketing is recommended.
- Excellent writing, communication, and computer skills are needed.
- Experience with Web content management and Web publishing tools is important.

What's it like to work in...
Virtual Creative Services

Bashira, a Web content editor for an online mortgage company, just finished a presentation to the product management team about an addition to the company's web site. During the development process, Bashira held group meetings with representatives from product management and marketing to ensure that the content was aligned with brand objectives. She also received input from a focus group of prospective customers who matched the target market.

Now that the copy has been approved, Bashira is meeting with her company's web site designer. Bashira wants to be sure that the web site design provides an easy way for customers to navigate the web site and review the new mortgage materials in order to make the best product choice.

At the end of the day, Bashira prepares for tomorrow's meeting with the media communications manager. The meeting objective is to review the editorial style guides for both print and electronic media to ensure a consistent look, feel, and voice for all published materials.

What About **You**

Would you like to be a part of the creative process, helping a company develop customer-focused product information for new electronic media?

PHOTO: ©PHOTODISC/GETTY IMAGES

Production

Once the client feels comfortable with the creative concepts, the agency will start the production phase. For a print ad, this may involve hiring a photographer, selecting models for the ad, and finalizing the design and layout.

A television commercial is a more involved process. The producer and creative team hire a director, cast the actors, select locations, and work with a crew of as many as 100 people to shoot the commercial. This can be a time-consuming process.

After the commercial is filmed, the creative team works with a variety of people—an editor, a sound engineer, and possibly special effects artists—to finish the project, sometimes adding music, sound effects, and an announcer. The goal is to create a commercial that grabs the audience's attention while communicating the message effectively.

The agency then presents the advertising to the client and continues to work on the commercial until the client is confident that it will be effective. The final step is to transmit the ads to the TV stations, magazines, or newspapers that will run them. Figure 16-4 shows the steps in the creative development and production processes.

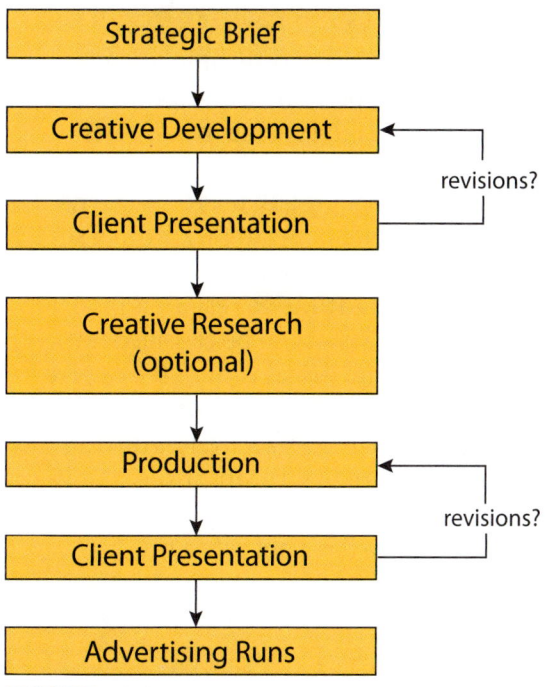

Creative Development and Production Process

Strategic Brief

Creative Development

Client Presentation

revisions?

Creative Research (optional)

Production

revisions?

Client Presentation

Advertising Runs

FIGURE 16-4
Creating and producing the advertising begins with the strategic brief.

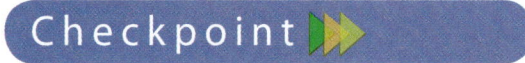

Checkpoint ▶▶

At what stage of the process of creating an ad does a producer get involved?

Gauging Advertising Effectiveness

Advertisers must evaluate ad campaigns to measure how well they meet the objectives of the advertising plan. Sometimes the impact of advertising is difficult to measure because there are many other variables that can affect sales, but it is an important step that helps the advertiser collect data to improve future efforts.

If the advertising has a built-in evaluator, like a redeemable coupon or a rebate offer, then the advertisement's effectiveness can be determined from the number of coupons or rebates redeemed for these promotional items. However, many advertisements do not have built-in measures and need to be evaluated using other techniques.

Advertising is sometimes evaluated before it is run. This is common especially with television concepts because television is expensive and the advertiser wants to make sure it is using its money wisely. After the advertising has run, it is also evaluated to see how effective it was. There are various methods to evaluate advertising.

Advertisers choose which type of research and specifically what method they will use based on their budget and what they hope to learn.

Quantitative Research

Sometimes advertisers want to ask a large number of people simple questions. Surveys about the advertising, recall tests that see if people remember the ads, and other types of testing that ask questions and allow respondents to pick from a set of answers are all types of quantitative evaluation. **Quantitative research** involves collecting data that can be classified into meaningful numerical values. It can give advertisers valuable information such as the increase in brand awareness during an ad campaign or a comparison of how respondents who have seen a commercial and those who have not rate a product.

Qualitative Research

On the other hand, research that interprets the *why* and *how* of people's opinions is called **qualitative research**. Qualitative research presents customers with open-ended questions rather than specific choices. This method includes such techniques as focus groups, one-on-one interviews, or other types of face-to-face discussions. Although qualitative research typically has a much smaller number of respondents than quantitative research, the great advantage is that it allows the researcher to deeply probe the issues and ask follow-up questions. "Tell me why you like the commercial." "How could we make it better?"

Checkpoint ▶▶

Describe the difference between quantitative and qualitative research.

Regulating Advertising

Although it ultimately is best for marketers to be forthright in their advertising, there are a number of systems in place to protect consumers and ensure that advertisers are honest and ethical.

Government Regulation

The Federal Trade Commission (FTC) and the Federal Communications Commission (FCC) oversee all commerce and commercial communications in the United States. They uphold laws, decide cases, and enforce standards to ensure that misleading and deceptive advertising does not occur. In cases where advertising is judged to be deceptive, these government bodies have the power to require corrective measures.

Network Regulation

Because networks (and publications) are ultimately responsible for everything they air, all networks have standards and guidelines regarding advertising claims and content. Advertisers must follow these regulations, or the networks can reject their advertising.

Regulatory Boards

There are a number of advertising regulatory boards that regulate truthfulness in advertising. These boards are usually organized by consumer groups, business associations, or the advertising industry itself. The National Advertising Review Council, National Advertising Review Board, and

©PHOTODISC/GETTY IMAGES

Why do you think it's important to regulate advertising in the media?

Children's Advertising Review Unit all oversee various aspects of advertising to protect consumers.

Competitive Regulation

A large part of regulation actually comes from competing companies. Companies watch each other closely to ensure that competitors are not gaining an unfair advantage by making untruthful claims. They may file complaints or lawsuits if a competitor makes a claim that it cannot adequately substantiate.

Corrective Actions

Regulatory forces work together to make sure that advertisers can support any product claim and that they disclose all information necessary for a customer to make an informed decision. When advertisers fail to meet these requirements, there are a number of corrective measures that can be imposed by the FTC. Advertisers may receive a **cease-and-desist order**, which is a legal order to discontinue the deceptive advertising. The company may be forced to run **corrective ads** that correct any false impressions left by the deceptive ads. There may also be a monetary penalty, or **fine**, imposed on the offending company. Depending on the violation, those fines can be large amounts.

All of these reviews, regulations, and corrective measures are intended to keep advertising honest, keep competition fair, and protect the public. Upholding these standards is in everyone's best interest.

Checkpoint ▶▶

What are the four systems working to regulate advertising?

16-3 Assessment

Key Concepts

Determine the best answer.

1. Which creative format uses a person to talk about the benefits of a certain product?
   a. image advertising
   b. product demonstration
   c. testimonial
   d. competitive

2. Who is *not* a part of the production process?
   a. creative team
   b. producer
   c. strategic planner
   d. director

3. Which of the following does *not* help to regulate advertising?
   a. competition
   b. government
   c. pricing strategies
   d. review boards

4. True or False: Surveys and recall tests are two types of qualitative research methods.

Make Academic Connections

5. **Writing** Write a radio commercial for a hair salon that also offers spa services. Determine the main message you want to communicate about the salon. Be creative. Your radio commercial should be 60 seconds long.

6. **Research** Use the Internet to learn more about focus groups. Locate a company that is using a focus group to conduct research related to advertising. Prepare a one-page report on the company and the purpose of the focus group.

Connect to **DECA** An Association of Marketing Students

7. Select a product or service and create an advertising campaign for it. Write a strategic brief that outlines your target market and main message. Then, create ads for at least three different media. Video and audio tape television and radio ads, and draw or create on a computer all print and outdoor ads. Present your campaign to your teacher (judge).

Check Your Understanding

Now that you have completed the chapter, check your understanding of the lessons with these questions. Record the score that best represents your understanding of each marketing concept.

1 = not at all; 3 = somewhat; 5 = very well

If your score is 42–50, you are ready for the assessment activities that follow. If you score 33–41, you should review the lessons for the items you scored 1–3. If you score 32 or less, you will want to carefully reread the lessons and work with a study partner on the areas you do not understand.

Can you—

___ describe the difference between product and brand advertising and how they work together?

___ identify the major roles at an ad agency?

___ list the seven steps in the advertising planning process?

___ describe the four methods of determining an ad budget and indicate the best one?

___ describe the different types of media?

___ list the five considerations when selecting media?

___ name some common advertising creative formats?

___ describe the production phase of the advertising process?

___ explain the difference between quantitative and qualitative research?

___ name four ways of regulating advertising?

Review Marketing Terms

Match the terms listed with the definitions. Some terms may not be used.

1. Builds an image for a brand or company
2. Series of related advertisements with a similar look, feel, and theme
3. Document that defines the target market and articulates the main message of the advertising
4. How a company positions its brand and product in its advertising
5. Outlines the activities and resources needed to create advertising
6. A company that specializes in creative advertising
7. Collecting data that can be classified into meaningful numerical values
8. The person responsible for how the ad will look
9. Legal order to discontinue deceptive advertising
10. The person that facilitates everything that happens after the client agrees to develop an ad or campaign
11. Gives the benefits of a specific product or service and relies on rational arguments why a customer should buy it
12. A detailed listing of where and when ads will run
13. The person who writes the words in the ad

a. account executive
b. account planner
c. advertising agency
d. advertising campaign
e. advertising plan
f. art director
g. brand advertising
h. cease-and-desist order
i. copywriter
j. corporate advertising
k. corrective ads
l. creative director
m. creative strategy
n. fine
o. frequency
p. lead time
q. media plan
r. media planner
s. producer
t. product advertising
u. qualitative research
v. quantitative research
w. reach
x. strategic brief

Review Marketing Concepts

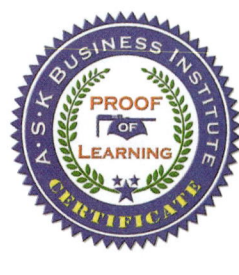

14. _____ gives the benefits of the product or service and relies on rational arguments for why a customer should buy it.

15. With the what-you-can-afford approach to budgeting, organizations account for all of their other expenses, and then whatever is _____ is budgeted for advertising.

16. The _____ approach budgets a percentage of past, current, or projected future sales for advertising.

17. The competition-matching approach to budgeting suggests that an organization should spend a similar amount of money on advertising as its _____.

18. The objective-and-task approach to budgeting involves determining the objectives to be achieved, identifying the activities required to accomplish the objectives, and then calculating the total _____ of each task.

19. Reach refers to the number of people who see a(n) _____ .

20. _____ refers to the number of times a member of the target audience is exposed to the advertising message.

21. _____ is the amount of time required to place an advertisement prior to the time it runs.

22. An ad showing a glass cleaner removing handprints and smudges from a patio door is an example of the _____ creative format.

23. _____ advertising is a format that evokes a mood or attitude for a brand or product.

24. A(n) _____ uses either celebrities or everyday people to endorse a product.

25. The _____ is the person on the agency staff responsible for facilitating the production process.

26. A focus group is an example of _____ research.

27. _____ occurs when an advertisement loses effectiveness after a certain number of exposures.

28. The FCC and FTC are government organizations that help _____ advertising.

29. A(n) _____ ad corrects any false impressions left by deceptive ones.

30. A(n) _____ is a monetary penalty imposed on a company that uses false or deceptive advertising.

Marketing Research and Planning

31. Annual advertising costs in the United States exceed $250 billion. Clearly, marketers spend a great deal of money on advertising. Your task in this activity is to become acquainted with advertising costs in a local market. Select an advertising medium used by marketers in your community, such as a radio station, a newspaper, a shopper's guide, an outdoor advertising agency, or a television station.

    Contact the organization or use reference materials to obtain information regarding its advertising rates. Be prepared to report to your class regarding the cost of advertising per minute, per inch, per week, per day, or whatever measurement is used.

32. One of the major concerns of organizations that advertise is the effective use of their advertising dollars. A recent survey of 259 successful companies asked what type of evaluation they use. The responses are summarized in the following table. (Respondents could select more than one evaluation method.)

Evaluation Method	Number of Respondents
Coupon redemption	179
Toll-free customer line	114
Focus groups	114
Customer survey	44
Rebate redemption	41
Recognition tests	26

a. Calculate the percentage of each of the response types and create a bar graph to illustrate the results.

b. Based on these results, how have the companies decided to allocate evaluation dollars? Do you think this is the best approach for all companies? Explain your answer.

33. You are the owner of the only hardware store in a city of 100,000 people. You have been able to reduce your promotional efforts because of the lack of competition.

Recently, however, a large hardware store chain has purchased land on which to build a new store. Describe your marketing response in terms of price, product, distribution, and promotion. Provide details about the type of advertising you would do.

34. New companies, or companies with new products, often use very different advertising strategies than do experienced and trusted companies with established products. For each example below, explain how the advertising for a new product or company might differ from an established one.
a. Family restaurant
b. SUV
c. Energy drink

35. Many businesses experience seasonal fluctuations in sales. Listed below are three products or services that often experience high and low sales periods. Suggest two advertising strategies for each product/service that could help reduce these sales fluctuations.
a. Lawn maintenance
b. Ski resort
c. Toy manufacturer

Marketing Management and Decision Making

36. You are the chief executive officer of a company that manufactures golf equipment. Your marketing research determines that there is a large market for an oversized driver golf club. Your company invests heavily in designing and manufacturing this new driver.

The advertising agency you have hired is developing an advertising plan for the new golf club. As CEO, list five factors you will be looking for in the advertising. List five questions you will want to ask the agency to ensure its ideas will help your sales.

37. Not all advertising is done by companies selling products and services. Find an example of advertising for a charity, cause, or political campaign and prepare a 200-word report describing the advertising, the strategy, and how it differs from product advertising. Be prepared to present your findings to the class.

38. Research one of the laws or agencies that deal with illegal advertising and prepare a 200-word report. Be prepared to present your findings to the class.

39. Log on to the web site of one of the organizations listed below and prepare a one-page report of the services it offers to its members and the kinds of information available on its site. Be prepared to give a presentation to the class.
a. Advertising Research Foundation
b. American Advertising Federation
c. Association of National Advertisers
d. Audit Bureau of Circulations
e. Direct Marketing Association
f. Internet Advertising Bureau
g. Outdoor Advertising Association of America
h. Radio Advertising Bureau
i. Television Bureau of Advertising

40. Search the Internet for a web site that carries a lot of online advertising. Browse the site for 15 minutes and count the number of different ads that you see. Write a one-page report on the ad content of the site, including the types of advertisers you see, the formats of the ads they display on the site, and any notable ads that stood out in the clutter. Explain why the ads captured your attention.

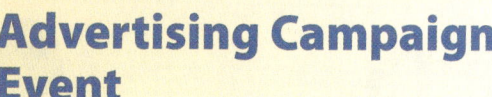

Advertising Campaign Event

The purpose of the Advertising Campaign Event is to prepare an advertising campaign of any length for a real product, service, company, or business for a prospective client/advertiser. Students must also present an appropriate budget for their proposed advertising campaign. This event can be completed by one to three students.

You will prepare up to ten fact sheets in outline form for your presentation. All members of the team must participate during the 15-minute presentation to the client/advertiser. Five minutes are allotted for the judge to ask questions about the presentation. Each participant must respond to at least one question posed by the judge.

The ten outline fact sheets must include:

Executive Summary Write a one-page description of the campaign.

Descriptions Identify the product, service, and company or business selected as well as the client/advertiser.

Objectives of the Campaign Provide major reasons for the advertising campaign.

Identification of the Target Market Describe the primary and secondary markets.

List of Advertising Media Selection Necessary for the Campaign Describe the types of media and their reach.

Budget Provide detailed projections of actual costs.

Schedules of All Advertising Planned Include outlines of the frequency and timing of ads.

Schedules of All Sales Promotion Activity(ies) Planned Describe sales promotions that will complement advertising.

Statement of Benefits to the Client/ Advertiser Describe anticipated outcomes of the ad campaign.

Bibliography List all sources used.

You will assume the role of advertising personnel with the goal of selling your idea to the judge (client/advertiser).

Performance Indicators Evaluated

- Exchange information and ideas with others through writing and speaking. (Communication Skills)
- Explain the components of advertisements. (Promotion)
- Analyze product information to identify product features and benefits. (Selling)
- Set priorities and demonstrate effective time management. (Emotional Intelligence)
- Demonstrate critical thinking/problem-solving skills. (Emotional Intelligence)

Go to the DECA web site for more detailed information.

Think Critically

1. Why is the budget a very important part of the advertising campaign?

2. Why must the advertising campaign consider buying behavior of primary and secondary markets?

3. How can the scheduled events for an advertising campaign stimulate sales?

4. What is the bottom line for a client considering an advertising campaign?

www.deca.org

Selling Satisfies Customers

©DIGITAL VISION/GETTY IMAGES

Newsline

Technology Is Integral to the Sale

Several hundred thousand dollars are at stake as the salesperson for a truck manufacturer sits in an office with clients from a mining company. The customer will place an order for three trucks, but only if the manufacturer meets some very specific requirements. Using Bluetooth technology the salesperson links her laptop computer to a miniature projector that displays images on a wall screen for everyone to see. She selects a design menu, and an outline of a truck appears. As she asks questions of the purchasing team, she adds features to the truck design that meet the company's requirements. The price of the truck is displayed, and each time a feature is added, the price is adjusted. The customer sees the cost of each change.

When the design is completed, the salesperson uses a secure wireless connection using a satellite relay in order to contact the factory to check production schedules. The customer makes an offer that is 5 percent below the listed price for the trucks. The salesperson uses instant messaging software to involve her manager with the price negotiations. The manager agrees on the price if three trucks are ordered on the production schedule the factory has available and the customer can make full payment within 90 days of delivery. The finance representative on the purchasing team quickly sends a text message to his manager using his wireless PDA and receives approval on the payment plan. With all details in order, the salesperson prepares a personalized contract, which is electronically signed by the customer and the manufacturer.

In her hotel that evening, the salesperson prepares for the next day by using the Internet to access records from her office computer for the two companies she plans to visit. She also confirms her flight schedule with her online travel agent. After a final check of her online calendar, e-mail, and text messages, she heads for a relaxing meal.

Salespeople rely on information and communications. Small and powerful laptop computers, sophisticated but easy-to-use software, and a variety of wireless and other electronic technologies reduce the time needed for each of those activities and make information instantly available to salespeople.

Think Critically

1. Describe how the sales transaction would occur without the electronic technologies.

2. How does technology change the selling process? Is it easier or more difficult as a result?

school.cengage.com/marketing/marketing

Prepare for Performance

This chapter develops the following Performance Indicators from the DECA Competitive Events program.

Core Performance Indicators

- Understand sales activities to show command of their nature and scope
- Acquire information about the sales industry to aid in making career choices
- Acquire product knowledge to communicate product benefits and to ensure appropriateness of product for the customer

Supporting Performance Indicators

- Explain the impact of sales cycles
- Describe the use of target marketing in selling
- Explain the nature of professional selling
- Discuss the economic and social effects of professional selling

Go to **school.cengage.com/marketing/marketing** and click on Connect to DECA.

©AVAYA COMMUNICATIONS

Visual Focus

To many customers, the salesperson is the face of the company. The way salespeople present themselves, interact with clients, listen to customer concerns and questions, and provide appropriate solutions with their company's products and services often determines the success of a marketing mix. As a wise businessperson once said, "Nothing happens in business until somebody sells something." This chapter offers a detailed description of the selling function, including the careful preparation salespeople make and the follow-up and support activities they perform after the sale has been made.

Focus Questions

What message does this ad convey? How do instant electronic communication technologies improve the customer/salesperson relationship? What negative effects can those technologies have if they are not used carefully and professionally?

Communication skills are especially important in business-to-business selling. Discuss with other students examples from your own experience of effective and ineffective communications demonstrated by retail salespeople.

The Value of Selling

marketing matters

Professional, personalized communications, which are at the core of selling, are an effective promotional tool for many businesses. Personal selling allows a company to respond to the unique needs of customers with specific messages designed to help customers make purchasing decisions.

Selling is not the best promotional method for every situation. There are distinct advantages and disadvantages to be weighed to determine where and when personal selling fits a business's needs, either alone or in conjunction with other promotional methods. Salespeople find management skills are important to success. Salespeople need to develop skills in self-management, customer management, and information management.

Write a description of the procedure followed the last time you or a family member sold something. If you had it to do over again, how would you improve the process to get a better result?

The Process of Personal Selling

When the selling function is a part of a company's marketing mix, salespeople provide the link between the customer and the business. The key link in the marketing process is when the salesperson sells the products of the business to the target market.

The ultimate goal of any business is to sell its products and services profitably. The resources of a business are wasted and the efforts of the employees are of no value if the products remain unsold. Those resources and efforts often rest on the shoulders of one group of people—the salespeople. The selling process involves people who work for or represent the company. These people communicate directly with customers in order to persuade them to purchase the company's products and services.

Successful sales occur when customers are able to locate and purchase the products and services they need and are satisfied with the result. The business is then able to make a profit on the money invested in developing and marketing those products and services. For businesses that understand the marketing concept, all business efforts are coordinated, and marketing activities are directed toward the profitable sale of products and customer satisfaction.

Selling is a part of the promotion element of the marketing mix. *Promotion* includes the methods and information communicated to customers to encourage purchases and increase their satisfaction. There are a variety of promotional methods that businesses use, and each has a specific purpose. **Selling** is direct, personal communications with prospective customers in order to assess needs and satisfy those needs with appropriate products and services.

Direct and Personal

All promotional methods involve communication with customers. Most are directed at large groups of customers. Those methods must be more generalized to appeal to the common needs of the audience. The larger and more diverse the audience, the less specific and individualized the promotional messages can be. Personal selling, however, is used to communicate with one or a few customers. Salespeople work directly with customers. If they devote time and effort to getting to know the customer, they can tailor the information to meet individual needs.

Direct communication means that the salesperson can meet and talk with the customer. Usually the meeting is face to face but may be completed via telephone or newer technologies such as video conferencing or web conferencing. Based on the discussions, the salesperson provides additional, specific information as needed. If a customer has concerns or asks questions, the salesperson is able to respond. By listening to the tone of voice or observing body language, the salesperson may determine that the customer is still uncertain about a decision. Based on that feedback, the salesperson personalizes the communication to address the customer's doubts and resolve concerns.

Assess and Satisfy

Effective marketing matches the most appropriate products and services to customer needs. Salespeople can tailor the choices of a business's products to individual customer needs and preferences. They can also determine where each customer is in the decision-making process. Some people may be ready to buy while others

need more information. Some may not yet have fully clarified their needs, so they are not ready to choose a specific product.

Sometimes salespeople try to substitute a product they want to sell for the one that is best for the customer. It is appropriate to offer a product that the customer did not originally intend to buy, but only if it is the best match with customer needs. It is not appropriate to sell a product just because customers are uninformed or because the salesperson needs to make a sale. The salesperson should discuss the purchase decision with each customer to make sure that specific needs and concerns are addressed. The salesperson should then offer each customer the best possible solution the company can provide to meet those needs.

Concerns about any part of the marketing mix should be addressed to the satisfaction of the customer. If a company's products will not meet a customer's needs,

©DIGITAL VISION/GETTY IMAGES

How might this jewelry salesman assess his customer's needs?

Selling Yourself with Internet Job Services

The development of the World Wide Web and the proliferation of Internet-based employment and personnel services has been a boon for freelancers (self-employed professionals). Instead of wasting nonbillable hours and dollars searching classified listings and networking for contacts of questionable value, they can now post their qualifications and requirements on the Internet and clients will come to them.

Even better, their search is no longer as limited by geography as it used to be. With a few keystrokes, they can send their resume to millions of potential clients around the world. Meanwhile, they can also conduct highly targeted searches of Internet databases for assignments to pursue. The same technology that allows freelancers to find work easily will also permit them to perform many tasks in the comfort of their home rather than at a client's office hundreds of miles away.

Almost all Internet services geared to freelancers are available without charge to job seekers. A key to success is writing a profile or resume that includes the right buzzwords, or keywords. Companies conduct their own searches to find qualified freelancers, and you will draw their attention only if your information matches their search criteria. Another key is to include realistic expectations so that you are not wasting time with offers that don't meet your requirements. When you are selling yourself, qualifying customers is most important.

Think Critically

1. What keywords might you include in a personal profile if you wanted to find freelance marketing work?

2. Does the advent of Internet job services mean that face-to-face networking is no longer necessary?

---

there is no benefit in selling something. The customer will quickly realize that the purchase was not appropriate and will likely return the product to the company, resulting in a lost sale and higher costs. Even if the product is not returned, the customer will be unhappy with the company and salesperson and will be reluctant to make another purchase in the future.

Checkpoint ▶▶

How does selling differ from other promotional methods?

When to Use Personal Selling

There are advantages and disadvantages to personal selling. Those advantages and disadvantages are summarized in Figure 17-1 on the next page. Business people need to understand when personal selling is appropriate and when it may not be the most effective promotional tool.

Advantages

Personal selling offers many advantages that other forms of promotion do not. It allows a business to meet customer needs on an individual basis.

Information When a business provides information through an advertisement, there is a limited amount of information

FIGURE 17-1

Organizations need to consider the advantages and disadvantages of personal selling when deciding whether to use it.

Evaluating Personal Selling

Advantages of Personal Selling	Disadvantages of Personal Selling
More information	Cost per customer
More time	Time required
Flexible	Less control
Uses feedback	Skills required
Persuasive	
Follow-up	

that can be included. An outdoor billboard or electronic display is usually restricted to fewer than ten words because viewers pass by very quickly. Television and radio commercials last no more than a minute, with most fitting into even shorter time slots. While newspaper and magazine advertisements can be longer, few people will spend more than a minute or two reading a print advertisement. More product information can be disbursed through personal selling.

Time Salespeople spend a considerable amount of time with customers. Even in the very shortest sales presentation to a customer, the conversation may last for several minutes. Effective salespeople often meet with customers several times. Each meeting may last from ten minutes to one hour. With that amount of time, a great deal of information can be exchanged.

Flexibility Personal selling is very flexible. The sales presentation is typically scheduled at a time and place that is convenient for the customer. During the meeting, if it is clear that a customer understands certain information or if that information is not important to the customer, the salesperson can move on to another topic.

Feedback Because personal selling is two-way communication, the customer provides feedback. An effective salesperson asks questions, listens to customers' concerns, and determines if additional information is needed. That feedback is used to make the information even more specific to the individual needs of the customer. In addition to obtaining feedback from the customer, the salesperson provides feedback to the company. If the customer is dissatisfied with any part of the marketing mix or if competing products appear to meet customer needs better, the salesperson can inform the company so that changes and improvements can be made.

Persuasion Selling is typically used near the end of the consumer decision-making process. At that time the customer is deciding whether or not to make the purchase. The customer may be comparing one or two very similar products before making a final decision. A salesperson is able to be persuasive at that time. By knowing the important needs of the customer and understanding the product and those of main competitors very well, customer needs can be matched with the features of the company's product and compared to those of competitors. The salesperson needs to be sure that the product will satisfy the customer. If it does, the salesperson is in a position to help the customer make the decision to purchase.

The salesperson also may be able to offer adjustments in the marketing mix such as offering credit, delivery service, or even a modification in the product, if needed. By knowing what changes are possible and matching them with specific customer needs, the salesperson can be very effective in making a sale.

Figure This

Pay-for-Performance Incentives

Salespeople are paid to sell, and many have compensation packages that provide incentives based on their sales. Some receive base salaries plus incentives. Others are compensated solely on what they sell. These incentive packages are designed to motivate the salespeople and keep them hungry for more sales.

Common forms of incentives include quotas, commissions, bonuses, long-term incentives, contests, or a combination of these methods. For example, car salespeople are commonly paid a flat fee for each car they sell plus a commission based on a percentage of the gross profit from each sale. If they reach a certain level—say, 20 cars in a month—their percentage of the profit is increased.

Given that kind of pay structure, it is no wonder that car salespeople are notorious for high-pressure tactics. Many businesses have found that such compensation systems hurt customer relationships. They try to balance compensation packages with long-term incentives and management systems that rein in overly aggressive salespeople.

Think Critically

1. A salesperson is paid $100 for every car she sells plus 10% of the gross profit from each sale. She also receives a bonus of $100 for each car in excess of 20 in a given month plus an additional 1% of her total gross profits for each car she sells in excess of 25 cars in a month. How much will she be paid if she sells 28 cars for a total gross profit of $65,000?

2. A salesperson is paid $2,000 per month plus a 5% commission on sales in excess of $40,000 in a month. If he already has booked sales of $31,000 by the last day of the month, how much is it worth to him if he can close on a $10,000 order by the end of the day? If he is confident of getting a $50,000 order from another customer the following month, what might he be tempted to do with the $10,000 order?

Follow-up A sale is not completed at the time the customer makes a purchase. The customer must use the product and decide if it meets the customer's needs. If the customer is dissatisfied with the product, it will probably be returned. The customer may not want to buy other products from the company.

An important responsibility of a salesperson is to follow up with the customer after the sale. The follow-up provides an opportunity to ensure that the customer is able to use the product correctly, has everything needed, and is satisfied. Often a customer just needs additional product information or reassurance to be fully satisfied with the purchase. If, however, the product does not work as expected or does not fully meet the customer's needs, a salesperson who is willing to make adjustments or accept a product return and replacement can usually turn a negative situation into a positive one.

Disadvantages

While there are many advantages of personal selling, there are also some disadvantages. One of the most important disadvantages is cost. You often hear of the high cost of advertising. A magazine ad can cost tens of thousands of dollars, and a nationwide television advertisement on a popular show can cost hundreds of thousands. It does not seem possible that personal sales could be more expensive, but businesses are concerned about the cost per customer as well as other issues.

Cost Per Customer If an advertisement reaches thousands of potential customers, the cost per person might be as low as one dollar or often even less. A salesperson's expenses can include the cost of salary, travel, time spent with a customer, and equipment and materials needed for sales presentations. A salesperson may talk to only a few customers each day. Therefore, the cost per customer can be very expensive. For sales of products to businesses, the cost of selling to each customer can easily be several hundred dollars. For very high-value products requiring months of negotiations and often involving several people as a part of a sales team, the cost of personal selling can be tens of thousands of dollars. However, if the process results in a multimillion-dollar sale, that cost is well worth it.

Time Because a salesperson meets with either one or a very few customers at a time, it takes a great deal of time for a large number of customers to be contacted. Compare that to an advertisement that reaches millions of people at the same time. The length of time needed to reach a large number of customers is a disadvantage of personal selling. A company can solve that problem by employing a large number of salespeople, but that adds to the costs of selling. Usually personal selling is used when the number of customers in the target market is small.

Control The salesperson is responsible for deciding what information to provide as well as how and when activities are completed. Therefore, the company's managers have limited control over the sales process. Salespeople often work alone or in small selling teams. During the time they are with a customer, they provide the information they believe is needed to help the customers decide to buy. When salespeople are not meeting with customers, they can plan additional sales calls, follow up on previous sales,

and complete a variety of record-keeping tasks. Individual time management, personal responsibility, and self-discipline are important attributes for an effective sales professional.

Skill The last disadvantage involves the knowledge and skill required to be an effective salesperson and the difficulty of the selling job. Salespeople need to understand selling procedures, communications, psychology, accounting, and management. They also need a great deal of knowledge about their products and services and those of their competitors. The selling process requires people who are outgoing and creative, able to adjust to different people and situations, and good at solving problems. The job often requires long work hours and travel. It is not easy for companies to find skilled salespeople.

Choosing Personal Selling

Personal selling should be used when it improves the marketing efforts. It can be the only method of promotion used by a company. Usually it is combined with other methods as a part of a promotional plan. Characteristics of products and markets that indicate the need for personal selling include the following:

- Complex or expensive products
- Markets made up of a few large customers
- New or very unique products with which customers are unfamiliar
- Customers located in a limited geographic area
- Complicated or long decision-making process
- Customers who expect personal attention and help with decision making

Checkpoint ▶▶

How can time be both an advantage and a disadvantage of personal selling?

Make a Persuasive Presentation

There are many times when the most efficient way to move an issue forward is by making a persuasive presentation. An effective presentation requires a great deal of preparation. First, you should define specifically what you want to accomplish with your presentation. What actions are you trying to motivate your audience to take? Do you want them to become active supporters of a cause? Do you want them to purchase the product or service you are selling?

The presentation should be tailored specifically to your audience members. If you do a presentation on the same topic to different audiences, you should adjust the presentation to effectively influence each audience.

It is important for the audience to believe that you are a credible source on the information being presented. You need to "sell" yourself and your knowledge base. Working in comments and information that show you have thoroughly researched your topic is one way to do this. You should also put your presentation in the context of any related issues important to the audience. This way your audience members will know that you studied not only the topic you are presenting, but also other factors that could impact them.

Dress in a manner that is appropriate for your audience. If you are making a pitch for a new sports product, you could dress in neat, crisp casual apparel. If you are presenting a business proposal for which you are seeking funding, then dressing in professional business attire would be appropriate.

Presentation content should be carefully considered. The product, service, or issue should be clearly defined. It should be well supported with simple, understandable facts and reasons.

The audience should obtain a clear understanding of how they will benefit from what you propose. You should define how your idea or proposal is superior to other choices. That superiority might arise from providing an improvement on existing technology or it could stem from an entirely new innovation in the field.

Any visual tools used in the presentation should be attention getting, easy to understand, and memorable. Determine the most effective way to present your ideas visually and make sure you are comfortable with the technology.

Engage the audience in the presentation. Meaningful examples and experiences as well as language that evokes an emotional response are ways to accomplish this. Compelling endorsements from others that the audience identifies with are an effective way to sway an audience. Since you are passionate about the topic, let that passion show through in your tone, mannerisms, and presentation style.

Construct your closing to move your idea forward. Whether you are asking for a sale or asking for support, your goal is to persuade the audience. Address any questions or concerns.

Finally, define the next steps and make it easy for people to take action. End with enthusiasm, conviction, and a positive tone.

Develop Your Skill

Define an issue you are passionate about. Decide what action you would like people to take in support of the issue.

Using the methods noted above, prepare a persuasive presentation. Practice the presentation several times to become comfortable. Then deliver it to a close friend, family member, or adult mentor to get feedback before presenting it to your target audience.

Personal Sales Management

Personal selling is a demanding career. Most salespeople are responsible for their own time, with limited direction from their managers. Often they are paid on commission. This means they are not paid unless they sell something.

A sales career can also be very rewarding. Professional salespeople who do their jobs well are paid more than many other business people. Because salespeople are responsible for the sales presentation, there is a great deal of satisfaction when a sale is made and the customer is satisfied. Even though they may not manage other people, successful professional salespeople have the qualities of good managers. The important areas of personal sales management are self-management, customer management, and information management.

Self-Management

Selling requires motivation and an effective use of time. It is difficult to call on yet another customer at the end of a long day. It is demanding to complete the necessary research needed to plan a personalized sales presentation. Much of a salesperson's time is spent on non-selling activities— paperwork, research, studying customer needs, and solving customer problems. A salesperson must be able to determine what needs to be done, set an efficient work schedule, and devote the necessary time until the work is completed. At times, it may require more than an 8-hour day or a 40-hour week.

Salespeople need to be emotionally and physically healthy. Salespeople may feel stressed because success depends on customers deciding what to purchase and when they will purchase. They may be expected to achieve specific levels of sales for the company in a given time. Long hours of work may seem to leave little time for exercise and relaxation.

Finally, an important part of self-management is personal development. Salespeople must be well educated and informed. They need to continue to learn about new selling procedures, the applications of technology, and information about products, customers, and competitors. It may seem that time is better spent with customers, but time has to be scheduled for personal and professional development as well.

©PHOTODISC/GETTY IMAGES

Customer Management

Selecting and scheduling customers is a difficult challenge for salespeople. Some customers offer a greater potential for sales because they purchase more frequently or in larger quantities. Certain customers require a greater amount of time from salespeople because they are at an earlier stage in decision making. Some customers require more time because their needs are not well identified or they ask for a great deal of information. Salespeople must be able to decide how much time to spend with each customer to maximize their sales.

When salespeople travel to meet customers, they have to carefully schedule their time. They need to limit the amount of time they are traveling in order to spend more time selling. Also, they need to keep their travel costs as low as possible to increase profits.

Information Management

The Newsline at the beginning of the chapter illustrates the importance of information to salespeople and their customers. Consider what would happen if a salesperson has almost no information about specific customers yet attempts to develop a sales presentation. That presentation will be very general and based on the salesperson's assumptions. In the same way, if the salesperson does not have immediate access to updated product information, price changes, distribution schedules, service records, and the like, it will be difficult to respond to customer needs and answer customer questions in a timely manner.

Salespeople must be able to identify needed information, develop effective record-keeping systems, and use the company's information system. In addition, salespeople must complete orders and other sales records carefully and completely. If a salesperson makes an error in the price or quantity of an order or other required information, it can result in problems for the company, such as added expenses or lost profits, and possibly even greater problems, such as legal liabilities.

Checkpoint ▶▶▶

Identify three important elements of personal sales management.

17-1 Assessment

Key Concepts

Determine the best answer.

1. Which of the following is *not* true about the process of personal selling?
   a. The selling process involves people who work for or represent the company.
   b. Salespeople communicate directly with customers to persuade them to purchase a company's products and services.
   c. Selling is a part of the distribution element of the marketing mix.
   d. All are true.

2. True or False: The larger and more diverse the audience, the less specific and individualized the promotional messages can be.

3. True or False: An advantage of personal selling over advertising is that it can provide more information than the typical advertisement.

4. Which of the following is true about the use of personal selling in the marketing mix?
   a. It should be used when it reduces the cost of marketing.
   b. It should not be combined with other promotional methods.
   c. It should be used when there is a large number of customers located in many different areas.
   d. It should be used when customers have a long or complicated decision-making process.

Make Academic Connections

5. **Math** A top business magazine has a total readership of 971,435, and 57 percent of readers report seeing a company's advertisement in one issue. The cost of the ad was $104,300. The company's salespeople have a prospective client list of 8,327 business people and are able to arrange a meeting with 93 percent of them. The total sales budget for those calls was $37,280. Calculate the cost per customer of each method.

6. **Career Success** Use Internet career boards or the employment section of a large-circulation newspaper to identify four different personal selling job opportunities in business-to-business and retail sales. Study each job and prepare a table that compares the jobs, identifying things that are similar and different. Based on the analysis, write a one-paragraph statement identifying which of the jobs you would prefer and why.

Connect to ◀ DECA
An Association of Marketing Students

7. You are the sales manager of a neighborhood office of a major cellular telephone service provider. Your goal is to make sure the company's service plans are well matched to the needs of each customer. Prepare a list of five questions you want each salesperson to ask new customers to gather information about their needs. Present your list of questions to your teacher (judge) and discuss the reasons for each question.

Preparing for Effective Selling

GOALS

- Describe the way effective salespeople qualify prospective customers and use their decision-making processes to plan their sales presentations.
- Explain why salespeople need to know their product thoroughly and how product features will benefit their customers.
- Demonstrate why it is important to understand the competition's products and marketing plans.

KEY TERMS

cold calling, *p. 485*

qualifying, *p. 486*

feature, *p. 489*

benefit, *p. 489*

marketing matters

The success of a salesperson is typically measured by the sales that are made and the satisfaction of the customers. That success is often determined well before the salesperson ever meets with the customer. Many salespeople spend more time preparing for sales than they do in actual contact with customers. In addition to developing effective selling skills, three areas are important—understanding the customer, understanding the product, and understanding the competition.

Imagine that you are preparing to interview for a well-paying job that you want very much. You need to sell yourself to the employer, who in this situation is the customer to whom you want to sell your services. You are the product, and other job applicants are the competition. Make a list of two points each about the customer, the product, and the competition that will determine your chances for success.

Understanding Customers

Marketing is responsible for creating satisfying exchanges between a business and its customers. Because salespeople negotiate the sale of products and services with the customer, they need to ensure that the customer is satisfied with the purchase. Understanding each customer helps a salesperson organize the presentation to meet that customer's needs. Effective selling requires a great deal of preparation.

Identifying Customers

Just as a business identifies its target market, salespeople need to identify appropriate customers. Not everyone is a potential customer for the products a salesperson represents. Even when high-potential customers are identified, additional information is needed to tailor the best possible match of products and services for each one. A great deal of time is wasted if the salesperson is talking to people who are uninterested or unable to buy the company's products.

Some salespeople use a process called cold calling. With **cold calling**, a salesperson contacts a large number of people who are conveniently located without knowing a great deal about each person contacted. Examples of cold calls include a salesperson for business products who plans to call on every business listed in a city business directory with annual sales over $1 million.

A telemarketer selling family health insurance plans uses a computer dialing system programmed to randomly call all nonrestricted residential telephone numbers. A salesperson for a carpet cleaning business knocks on the door of every home on a block to locate prospective customers.

You can imagine that using cold calling is both difficult and discouraging for a salesperson. A large number of customers will have to be contacted before finding someone who is interested in the salesperson's products. Also, the salesperson has a difficult time beginning the selling process if almost nothing is known about the prospective customer, whom the salesperson has just met. Most important, people contacted by the salesperson may be quite upset about the intrusion if they are not interested in the products being sold. They will have a belief that the salesperson and the company are bothering them for no good reason. The salesperson is not just wasting the time of people who have no current needs related to those products. Also wasted are the resources of the company that could be better spent on interested consumers.

A marketing-oriented business does not use cold calling as a part of personal selling. Salespeople gather information on possible customers and determine if they fit the characteristics of the company's target market. Often, through the company's marketing information system or marketing research, information on prospective customers is already available to assist the salesperson. Also, other promotional or marketing efforts such as coupons and product registration cards are frequently used to identify customers and gather other information before the salesperson makes the first face-to-face contact. The selling process will be a much more positive experience for both the customer and the salesperson. It is also more productive when the salesperson knows who prospective

©STOCKBYTE/GETTY IMAGES

How can a salesperson identify prospective customers?

customers are, where they are located, what their important needs are, and when and how each customer prefers to be contacted.

Qualifying Prospective Customers

Not all people in a target market are prepared or able to purchase a product at a particular time. A salesperson will complete a procedure known as qualifying a customer. **Qualifying** involves gathering information to determine which people are most likely to buy.

Three identifying characteristics qualify a person as a prospective customer. Without all three characteristics present, the person will not purchase the product. The characteristics include:

- A need for the product

- The resources to purchase the product

- The authority to make a decision to purchase

While everyone in a target market has a general need for the product being marketed, that need may not be as important as other needs. The customer may have already purchased another product to meet the need. Salespeople identify customers who have the strongest need and who are ready to make a purchasing decision. Most people have many more needs than they can satisfy at a given time.

A common limitation on purchasing is a lack of resources to buy the product. It is possible that a customer does not have the money or adequate financing through the use of credit. No matter how hard the salesperson works or how effective the sales presentation is, a sale is not possible if the customer is unable to afford the product. Part of the information-gathering process of salespeople is determining if the customer has adequate resources or if financing will make resources available.

Many times people want to buy a product but do not have the authority to make the decision. A child may have to ask a parent, a manager may need to get approval from the purchasing department, or a partner in a business may need to have the agreement of the other partners. Salespeople often need to work with several people before a purchase decision is made. It is important to determine which person or people will make the final decision and to make sure they are included in the selling process at the appropriate time.

Understanding Customer Decisions

Consumers go through a series of steps when they make a decision. Those steps include identifying a problem or need, gathering information, evaluating alternatives, making a decision, and evaluating the decision. Consumers need specific and different types of information as they move through each step. If the consumer is gathering information on possible products to satisfy a need, information on financing alternatives will not be helpful. On the other hand, if the customer has already narrowed the choice to two products and is comparing them, it will not help to provide general information on the needs a product satisfies. Salespeople often translate the consumer decision-making steps into a series of mental stages that lead to a

sale. Those mental stages are summarized with the letters AIDCA. The meaning of each letter is shown in Figure 17-2.

A salesperson knows that the customer must first focus *attention* on the salesperson and the sales presentation. It is important to get the customer's *interest* in the product early in the presentation. A customer moves from interest to *desire* when it is clear that the product meets important needs. The desire turns to *conviction* when the customer determines that the product is a good value and the best choice. That leads to *action*, or the purchase of the product.

A salesperson who understands consumer decision making and is able to determine which of the AIDCA stages each customer is in will be able to provide

Mental Stages of Consumer Decision Making

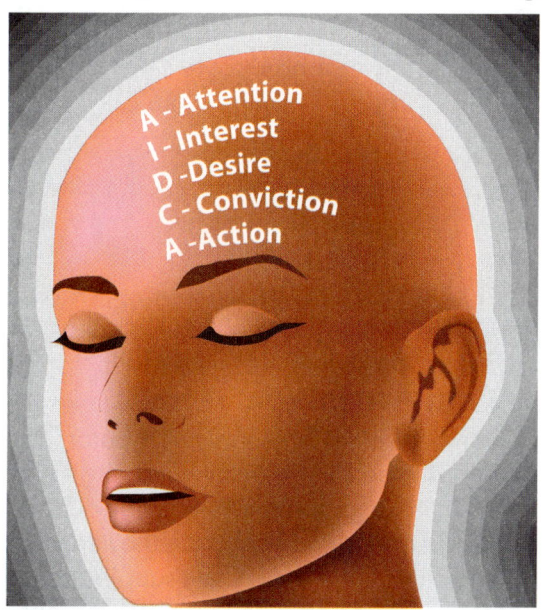

FIGURE 17-2
Salespeople need to understand the mental stages consumers complete in making a decision and use that information to plan each sales presentation.

Working in **Teams**

Have team members identify a purchase they have recently made and describe how they completed each mental stage leading to a decision. Discuss the similarities and differences in how each person moved through the stages.

the specific information that each customer needs at a particular time to assist with an appropriate decision. An important advantage of personal selling is the capability of providing specific information to each customer when it is needed.

Checkpoint

Why is it important to qualify prospective customers before involving them in a sales presentation?

Understanding the Product

As the representative of the company to the customer, the salesperson is responsible for providing the information needed for the customer to make a good decision. There are two parts to that responsibility. The salesperson must have adequate product knowledge and must also be able to communicate the information effectively to the customer.

Product Knowledge

Choosing the best product to satisfy a customer's needs is often not an easy task.

Customers may not be able to determine by examining a product, or even by reviewing the information that accompanies a product, whether it is the one they should buy. Salespeople need to know a great deal about the products they represent. They must also be able to quickly access additional information when needed to answer customers' unique questions.

An effective salesperson is familiar with all parts of the marketing mix. Customers are concerned not only about the product but also about the price and

Get the Message

Web Sites for Distributor Communication

For many industrial supply distributors, the World Wide Web is evolving into the key medium for getting their message out to prospective customers. Since they are dealing with standard parts and supplies that can usually be obtained through a number of distribution channels, successful selling frequently hinges on price, availability, and reliability. Getting up-to-date information out to customers is vital to staying competitive in what many believe has become an "information transfer" business.

Even for small distributors, the Web opens the door to a potential worldwide market for products, particularly those for which shipping is not a big expense. Its big advantages are cost-effectiveness and timeliness. Distributors can publish a

web-based catalog that is available to anyone with a web browser, 24 hours a day, seven days a week. Unlike print catalogs, it can be updated continuously, so product listings and prices are always current.

From a buyer's perspective, online catalogs allow a business to query dozens of suppliers by e-mail at the touch of a few keystrokes. Distributors have learned to reply promptly or risk losing an order to a competitor.

Think Critically

1. What role does personal selling have in an "information transfer" business that relies heavily on a web site to generate sales?

2. What are the advantages and disadvantages of web-based catalogs versus printed catalogs?

availability. They may have seen other company promotions and have questions about that information. While an individual customer is not interested in all of the marketing mix information, the salesperson must be able to tailor a sales presentation to the needs of each customer.

One customer may want to know about the construction and durability of a product. Another may be concerned about the warranty and repair services. Still another may need to know about financing. A salesperson who does not know that information or who is unable to obtain it quickly will not be able to satisfy potential customers and will lose their confidence and respect. Sales will be lost to other salespeople who can provide the needed information.

Information Sources

A variety of sources of product information is available to salespeople. Companies prepare information sheets and product manuals. Advertisements and other types of promotions often contain valuable information including price changes and special incentives. The product's marketing plan and marketing research reports are sources of useful information, as are other salespeople and company personnel including engineers, production personnel, and other marketers.

Many companies offer frequent training for salespeople that emphasizes important and up-to-date product information. They also prepare sales aids and other materials for salespeople to use as a part of their sales presentations. Effective salespeople regularly read business publications, attend conferences and trade shows, and study other information sources to keep up to date on the products and services they sell. Knowing that they are well prepared with a great deal of product knowledge makes salespeople confident that they can answer customer questions and provide the marketing mix each customer needs.

Communicating Product Information

A **feature** is a description of a product characteristic. A **benefit** is the advantage provided to a customer as a result of the feature. Figure 17-3 illustrates this difference. To further illustrate, decide which of the following statements is more effective as a part of a sales presentation?

"The standard engine in this vehicle is a 3.5 liter V6."

"Our standard engine offers the best combination of efficiency and power. You will average 29 miles per gallon, but it will also give you immediate acceleration, so you won't have trouble merging into faster traffic when entering the freeway."

The statements provide examples of features and benefits. The first statement describes a feature—the standard 3.5 liter V6 engine. The second statement describes how the customer will benefit from the engine—fuel efficiency and adequate acceleration when needed. Salespeople communicate most effectively when they

Feature-Benefit Comparison

FIGURE 17-3

Salespeople need to communicate the benefits of important product features based on each customer's needs. In this case, the feature is an airbag, and the benefit is driver safety.

can describe the benefits of a product for a customer in terms of important needs.

Frequently a product's features are similar to those of competitors. Other features are different, and a few may be unique. Customers want to know how various products and brands are similar and how they are different. They also want to know how the features will meet their needs. The salesperson needs to understand the features, compare them to competitors, translate them into customer benefits, and communicate the important benefits in an understandable way to each customer.

Checkpoint ▶▶

Why is merely describing a product's features not enough for an effective sales presentation?

Understanding the Competition

A customer will seldom make a purchase without considering several choices. The consumer wants to buy the most appropriate product and the best value. It is not always easy for customers to make the final decision. With products that are very similar, quite complex, or for which little information is available, consumers may have a difficult time determining which is best. It is not unusual for a customer to buy one product only to realize later that another choice would have been better.

Salespeople want to sell the products and services they represent, but they will be more successful in the long run if the customer is satisfied with the purchase. The salesperson who is familiar with competitors' products can help the customer understand differences among the choices. Understanding competitors' products and incorporating that information into a sales presentation is not easy. Some salespeople believe all they need to do is provide general and obvious information about competing brands or to make only negative comments about competitors. However, customers will not find that information helpful. They are deciding between two or three alternatives and will not feel positive if the salesperson inappropriately

How can salespeople help customers make informed purchasing decisions?

©PHOTODISC/GETTY IMAGES

downgrades one of their final choices. Customers will have a different view of a salesperson who demonstrates an understanding of the competition and carefully helps customers compare advantages and disadvantages so that they can make the most informed choice.

It is not unusual for customers to study several brands or similar products before making a decision. A knowledgeable salesperson can explain important differences to customers to assist them with the comparison. The customer may not make a final decision immediately but may spend additional time comparing competing products. The customer will be able to use the information provided by the salesperson when examining a competitor's product and see the advantages of the first brand. Just as with their company's products, it is important that salespeople study all of the important parts of the marketing mix for competitors' products and call attention to benefits of each of the mix elements when appropriate.

Checkpoint ▶▶▶

Why is it necessary for a salesperson to understand competitors' products?

17-2 Assessment

Xtra! Study Tools
school.cengage.com/marketing/marketing

Key Concepts

Determine the best answer.

1. True or False: Salespeople who work for a company that believes in the marketing concept will not need to gather customer information because detailed target market information is already available.

2. With _____ , a salesperson contacts a large number of people who are conveniently located without knowing a great deal about each person contacted.

3. The characteristics of a qualified prospective customer include all of the following *except*
   a. a need for the product
   b. the resources to make a purchase
   c. the authority to make a purchase decision
   d. all are qualifying characteristics

4. The letters that summarize the correct order of the mental stages of a customer decision are
   a. FIFO
   b. AIDCA
   c. EFFORT
   d. none are correct

5. A _____ is a description of a product characteristic, and a _____ is the resulting advantage provided to the customer.

Make Academic Connections

6. **Research** You are a salesperson for an athletic uniform company. Your assigned market is all public and private schools within 200 miles of your community. Locate two resources you can use to identify all of your potential customers. Describe the information in each resource that will help you qualify the customer. List other information you will need to fully qualify each school that is not available in the resources.

7. **Ethics** As an automobile salesperson, you know that you can often sell customers expensive cars by offering lower monthly payments requiring six years of payments. It increases your current commissions, but it means that customers will struggle to make monthly payments for many years. Write a three-paragraph analysis of your responsibility to the customer, to your business, and to yourself.

Connect to ◆ **DECA**
An Association of Marketing Students

8. Select a popular brand of luggage and gather information on a wheeled suitcase that can be carried on an airplane. Develop a chart that identifies five important product features and a specific customer benefit statement for each feature. Use your own words for the benefit statements rather than those of the manufacturer. Present the chart to your teacher (judge).

The Selling Process and Sales Support

GOALS

- Detail the seven steps of the selling process.
- Explain why salespeople need support from other areas of the business.

KEY TERMS

approach, *p. 493*

preapproach, *p. 494*

demonstration, *p. 495*

close, *p. 496*

trial close, *p. 496*

suggestion selling, *p. 497*

follow-up, *p. 497*

marketing matters

A salesperson carefully assesses the needs of customers and uses the company's resources to design an effective marketing mix. The salesperson then presents that mix and describes how it meets the customer's needs. The salesperson asks questions to determine if the mix is satisfactory or if adjustments must be made and helps the customer make the best decision. The best salespeople do not feel they are finished once the sale is made. They will follow up with customers to make sure they are satisfied and to provide any additional support needed.

Describe the last time you worked with a salesperson to buy something. What did the salesperson do to convince you to buy? What could he or she have done differently to be more effective?

Steps in the Selling Process

The selling process that is based on the marketing concept may not fit your perception of selling. Remember that not all companies and salespeople understand or believe in the marketing concept. It is not unusual to find salespeople who believe their responsibility is to convince the customer to buy their company's products no matter what. They look at the selling process as a type of contest between the customer and the salesperson. Each tries to negotiate the best deal possible. These salespeople use information and the resources of the business as well as their personality and persuasion skills to convince the customer to buy.

The marketing concept suggests another approach to selling. The salesperson represents the company to the customer but also is responsible for satisfying customer needs. The selling process is a cooperative process rather than a competition. The salesperson's responsibility is to help the customer through the steps of the decision-making process so that the final decision is the best choice. A salesperson does need to be persuasive, but it is easier to persuade people to buy if they believe you understand their needs and have their best interests in mind.

Effective selling is a very demanding profession. People who are skilled at selling are in high demand in business because their customers are very loyal and return again and again to buy. They are well compensated for their abilities because they help a company sell products profitably.

The procedures of effective salespeople can be summarized in the seven steps of the selling process. Those steps are listed in Figure 17-4.

Approach

The **approach** is the first contact with the customer when the salesperson gets the customer's attention and creates interest in the product. The approach may be initiated by the customer or by the salesperson. In either case, the salesperson is responsible for the result.

Retail Selling Consider the situation in which a customer enters a retail store. The salesperson must decide whether to approach the customer or to allow the customer to look around the store. Some customers have a particular product in mind. Others are making initial judgments about whether the store offers products that interest them. Still others are simply spending time in the store without any real interest in making a purchase. A salesperson who approaches the customer in a pleasant way can quickly determine if the customer wants assistance and where the person is in the mental stages of decision making.

For the customer who is just beginning to search for a product, the salesperson provides information on the basic characteristics of products that might meet the customer's needs and may direct the customer to the appropriate location in the store. The salesperson allows the customer to examine several choices but will step in if the customer appears to need help or has a question. With information gathered by observing and talking to the customer, the salesperson can offer information on

FIGURE 17-4

Effective salespeople follow a specific procedure to match customer needs with the company's products and services.

Steps in the Selling Process	
Step	**Purpose**
Approach	Contact customers, gain their attention and interest, and create a favorable first impression
Determine Needs	Gather information to determine customers' needs and how they can be met
Demonstrate	Present the product in a way that emphasizes cutomer benefits
Answer Questions	Overcome objections and ensure the marketing mix meets customers' needs
Close	Obtain a decision to purchase
Suggestion Selling	Suggest other products customers may see as valuable
Follow-up	Continue contact to ensure satisfaction, determine other needs, and build relationships

the few products that appear to meet the customer's needs.

As the customer is nearing a decision, the salesperson might review advantages of certain product features, payment options, or any final important factors that will help the customer decide to buy. Even if the customer does not buy, the salesperson should be courteous and remind the customer of important features and benefits to keep in mind. That will usually impress the customer and encourage a return visit.

Business-to-Business Selling

Salespeople who call on business customers have different factors to consider when planning an approach. Since several people may be involved in making a purchasing decision, the salesperson must decide whom to contact. Business people receive frequent visits from many salespeople. They do not have time to meet with all of them, so they select only those who they believe can be of help. Telephone calls, letters of introduction, or special promotional materials sent to the prospective customer can be used to make the customer aware of the salesperson, the company, and its products.

When an appointment is set with a business customer, the salesperson needs to be on time and well prepared with all materials required to discuss products and services with the customer. The salesperson needs to clarify who will participate in the initial meeting and whether others are involved in the final purchase decision. The initial call may be used to acquaint the customer with the business and its products and to gather information in order to facilitate follow-up meetings. On the other hand, many business-to-business sales are completed in one sales call, so the salesperson needs to be well prepared with customer information and the capability to negotiate an order. It is beneficial if both the salesperson and the customer are in agreement on the purpose and goals of the first meeting.

Determine Needs

Determining needs is central to the marketing concept and the selling process. This step can be performed both before and after the initial customer contact. Whenever possible, salespeople should gather information about customers and their needs before the first meeting. Based on that information, they can outline and practice their sales presentation.

Efforts to prepare for a sales presentation in advance of the first customer contact are called a preapproach. The **preapproach** includes gathering preliminary information and preparing a preliminary sales presentation for a customer. Salespeople study target market information available on the specific customer. They also review information about their own company, its products, and the marketing mix. The intention is not to memorize a sales presentation. Rather, preparation and practice make the salesperson

Digital Digest

Effective Technology Boosts Sales

Increasing the productivity of a sales force takes more than just handing out hand-held digital organizers to manage appointments and contacts. If information technology merely streamlines administrative tasks to give salespeople more time to make unproductive sales calls, it is not worth the investment in money or time. Technology consultants stress that truly productive systems provide salespeople with the very latest information on products, customers, competitors, orders, and market conditions. And they include training to help salespeople get the most out of the technology.

The best-regarded information systems not only give salespeople the latest information available but also enable them to integrate any new information that they come across. This two-way movement of information ensures that everyone in an organization, including independent dealers, can access the latest information when and where they need it. It also ensures that everyone is working with the same information at all times.

As a result, salespeople can target their sales presentations more precisely and, if appropriate, make adjustments to the marketing mix to fit the situation. That results in a reduction in unproductive activities and an increase in effective selling.

Think Critically

1. What kinds of information about a business customer would you want to have before making an important sales call?

2. Why is sales force information technology most beneficial for large organizations?

more comfortable and allow the salesperson to concentrate on the customer during the meeting.

Once customers are contacted, they become the primary sources of information. Salespeople confirm and fine-tune the information they have and then zero in on determining the customer's specific needs by direct questioning. The goal is to find the best way to satisfy those needs and lead the customer effectively to a decision through a sales presentation. Preapproach work with a customer may be done through surveys and questionnaires, e-mail and telephone contacts, or even a meeting with the stated goal of gathering information.

Demonstrate

The major part of the sales presentation is the demonstration. The **demonstration** is a personalized presentation of the features of the product in a way that emphasizes the benefits and value to the customer. The salesperson tailors the product information directly to the customer and emphasizes the parts of the marketing mix that best meet the customer's needs. The demonstration is designed to turn the customer's interest into desire.

As the salesperson moves from the approach to the demonstration, the main needs of the customer should be identified. The salesperson confirms those needs and determines the information that will help the customer make a decision by asking questions and listening carefully to the customer.

The most effective demonstrations are based on a feature-benefit presentation. The salesperson must identify the features

©DIGITAL VISION/GETTY IMAGES

How could a vacuum cleaner demonstration help persuade a customer?

of the marketing mix that are most important to the customer and describe how the customer will benefit from each of the features.

Characteristics of an effective demonstration include the following:

- Use active, descriptive language that is understandable and meaningful.

- Direct the customer's attention to a specific feature and explain the benefit.

- Observe reactions and listen to comments to keep the demonstration focused on the customer's needs.

- Demonstrate the feature rather than just describing it when possible.

- Involve the customer. Let the customer handle and test the product.

- Make the presentation dramatic so that the customer remains interested and remembers important features.

- Use sales aids such as pictures, charts, and computer demonstrations to enhance understanding.

- Review the benefits that seem to be most meaningful to the customer.

Answer Questions

A salesperson uses a customer's questions to resolve concerns and provide additional

Fast FACTS

A study by Dartnell Corp. found that salespeople spend less than half of their work time selling. More than half of their time is spent traveling, waiting to see customers, and completing paperwork and other administrative tasks.

information. As a salesperson successfully responds to each question, the customer is mentally moving from desire to conviction.

This step in the selling process is often referred to as *overcoming objections*. In the traditional view of selling, it was believed that customers raised objections to avoid making a purchase decision. Salespeople had to overcome that resistance by handling the objection. Again, that approach set up the selling process as a competition between the customer and the salesperson.

When the salesperson has the interests of the consumer in mind and is presenting a product or service that meets customer needs, there is less reason for resistance. Customers want to be certain that they are making the correct decision. They ask questions to gather information and to clarify their understanding.

A salesperson should welcome and encourage questions. Questions will often help the salesperson identify the most important needs of the customer. They indicate the parts of the marketing mix that the customer does not yet understand. By answering each question well, the salesperson demonstrates an interest in the customer's needs and the customer's understanding of the product. An effective procedure for answering questions is shown in Figure 17-5.

Close the Sale

The **close** is the step in the sales process when the customer makes a decision to purchase. A well-planned sales presentation helps the customer move from attention to interest to desire and then to conviction. A customer must be confident that a product or service will meet important needs and that it offers the best value. At that point, the final step in the decision-making process can be completed—action.

It is not easy for the customer to make a decision to buy. This is especially true for an expensive product or one that the customer has not purchased before. A salesperson needs to be skillful in closing the sale. A customer who feels pressured will resist buying the product. On the other hand, some customers need encouragement. If the salesperson does not ask for the order, the customer may postpone the decision and buy something later. The salesperson must provide opportunities for the customer to purchase the product and be willing to continue the sales presentation if the customer is not ready to buy.

Providing the customer with the opportunity to buy during the sales presentation is known as a **trial close**. A customer who repeatedly handles the product, appears satisfied with answers to questions, or responds favorably to a feature-benefit description or demonstration may be ready to buy. The salesperson should take that opportunity to ask for the order.

There are several ways a salesperson can close a sale. The goal is to make the decision easy for the customer. Methods of closing a sale include:

Close on an important benefit. "You obviously are concerned about safety. This automobile not only has front and side air bags but also has built-in child safety seats in the rear. You can't find a safer family automobile."

Offer the customer a choice. "We have both the green and blue in stock. Which would you prefer?"

Provide an extra value. "This month we are offering a 3 percent discount if you decide to order 500 or more units."

Answering a Customer's Questions

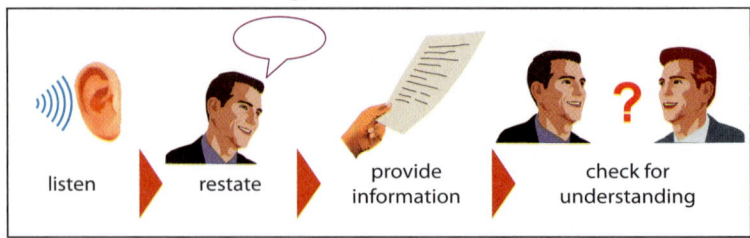

listen → restate → provide information → check for understanding

FIGURE 17-5
Answering questions requires effective communication skills.

Ask about the method of payment. "Will you pay cash, or would you like to use the 6-month financing plan we discussed?"

Emphasize availability. "If you place the order today, we can have it delivered and installed by Friday."

Guarantee satisfaction. "You can try it for two weeks. If you are not satisfied for any reason, we will gladly replace it or offer a full refund."

As soon as the customer decides to buy, the salesperson should reinforce that decision. Customers want to believe they made the right choice, but they often have concerns after the decision is made. The salesperson should re-emphasize the value and briefly summarize the benefits the customer will receive from the purchase.

Suggestion Selling

One of the responsibilities of the salesperson at the completion of a sale is to be certain the customer's needs are as fully satisfied as possible. Frequently, a product can be used more effectively if the customer purchases related merchandise. A bicycle rider needs a bicycle helmet. A coffee table may be useful for someone who just purchased a living room suite. If customers go home without all of the things needed to use the product, they will probably be dissatisfied. Offering additional products and services after an initial sale in order to increase customer satisfaction is known as **suggestion selling**. Products offered after a sale should be clearly related to the product purchased and beneficial to the customer. A customer who believes that the salesperson is just trying to add to the sale or is pushing products that the business is currently promoting will no longer have a positive view of the salesperson.

Follow-Up

Customers who purchase products and services from a company and are satisfied with their purchases are likely to buy from that company again. Making contact with the customer after the sale to ensure

NETBookmark

The *close* is the step in the sale when the customer makes a decision to purchase. This can be the most difficult part of a transaction for a salesperson to handle. Access school.cengage.com/marketing/marketing and click on the link for Chapter 17. Read the online article about closing techniques. According to the article, how do retail sales closes get customers to buy? Why does the author believe that retail close techniques do *not* work well in business-to-business selling? Do you agree?

school.cengage.com/marketing/marketing

satisfaction is known as **follow-up**. Follow-up also provides another opportunity to reinforce the customer's decision and determine if the customer has additional needs that the business can meet. Following up each sale is an important part of relationship building that can lead to repeat sales and referrals to additional customers.

Part of the follow-up responsibility may include activities such as checking on

©PHOTODISC/GETTY IMAGES

How can salespeople follow up with their customers?

delivery schedules, making sure warranty or product registration information is accurate, scheduling product installation and maintenance, or making sure financing paperwork is complete and accurate. If the customer has any problems, the salesperson should arrange to resolve them quickly. When the customer sees the salesperson completing follow-up activities, it will be evident that the customer is important.

Checkpoint ▶▶

Identify and describe each of the seven steps in the selling process.

Providing Sales Support

For selling to be effective, the salesperson must receive support from many parts of the business, including other marketing personnel. To meet customer needs, the salesperson must have products and services that are well designed, readily available, and priced competitively. People in production, finance, and management need to coordinate their work with the salespeople to match the supply of products with sales. Order processing, customer service, and many other business activities are required.

Each of the following descriptions of important marketing activities demonstrates how they support the work of salespeople.

- *Marketing-Information Management:* Salespeople need access to a wide variety of information throughout the selling process. In the preapproach, the salesperson needs information on customers and their needs. During the sales presentation, the salesperson may need to gather additional information about products, competitors, or the customer that should be maintained in the company's MkIS.

- *Financing:* Many customers need to finance their purchases. Salespeople must have access to credit services to offer their customers. They may also

There are many technology businesses, such as SAS, that offer systems to help improve the effectiveness of salespeople.

need assistance in explaining financing and completing the paperwork.

- *Pricing:* Many prices are not firm and can be negotiated by the customer. Offering discounts, accepting trade-ins, and other methods can be used to adjust the price. A salesperson must have the authority to negotiate the price or must be able to get pricing information quickly.

- *Promotion:* Usually customers obtain information from sources other than the salesperson to aid in making a buying decision. Other types of promotion, including advertising and publicity, can create interest, inform customers of product choices, or reinforce a purchase decision.

- *Product/Service Management:* Salespeople can provide information on customer needs and customer reactions to the current products and services offered by the business. That information should be used to improve existing products and develop new products.

- *Distribution:* Products and services often need to be delivered to customers. Salespeople rely on transportation services to get the products delivered at the time the customers want them. Salespeople need to have information on transportation schedules and costs when they work with their customers.

Checkpoint ▶▶

Why do salespeople need support from other areas of the business including other marketing personnel?

17-3 Assessment

Xtra! Study Tools
school.cengage.com/marketing/marketing

Key Concepts

Determine the best answer.

1. True or False: The selling process needs to be viewed as a contest between the customer and the salesperson to see who can negotiate the best deal.

2. The first contact with a customer when the salesperson gets the customer's attention and creates interest in the product is the
   a. preapproach
   b. approach
   c. contact
   d. cold call

3. Which of the following is *not* a characteristic of an effective product demonstration?
   a. use technical language to impress the customer
   b. keep the customer from asking questions until the demonstration is complete
   c. don't let the customer handle the product to prevent confusion and damage
   d. none are effective procedures

4. Offering additional products and services after an initial sale in order to increase customer satisfaction is known as _____ .

5. True or False: For selling to be effective, the salesperson must receive support from many parts of the business, including other marketing personnel.

Make Academic Connections

6. **Communication** Choose a partner and as a team, select a product that each of you is familiar with and would be comfortable selling. For each of the methods of closing a sale, write a short script that a salesperson could use to sell the product. Use the script to role-play each closing method for the class.

7. **Science** When customers make expensive purchases, they often use a scientific decision-making process. Develop a chart that outlines the steps in the decision-making process (see Chapter 6). Next to each of those steps, list the step or steps in the selling process that help a customer with that part of the decision-making process. Write a one paragraph statement discussing how salespeople can help customers make the best decision possible.

Connect to  An Association of Marketing Students

8. You are a salesperson meeting with a prospective customer to sell a new laptop computer. Select the brand and model of computer you want to sell, gather product information, and prepare a five-minute sales presentation that includes the appropriate approach, demonstration, response to questions, trial close, close, and suggestion selling. Meet with your teacher (judge) to complete your sales presentation.

Chapter 17 Assessment

Xtra!
Quiz Prep
school.cengage.com/marketing/marketing

Check Your Understanding

Now that you have completed the chapter, check your understanding of the lessons with these questions. Record the score that best represents your understanding of each marketing concept.

1 = not at all; 3 = somewhat; 5 = very well

If your score is 42–50, you are ready for the assessment activities that follow. If you score 33–41, you should review the lessons for the items you scored 1–3. If you score 32 or less, you will want to carefully reread the lessons and work with a study partner on the areas you do not understand.

Can you—

— define selling and describe the characteristics of effective personal selling?

— describe when businesses should use personal selling based on its advantages and disadvantages?

— describe the three important areas of personal sales management?

— explain why cold calling is not an effective method of identifying prospective customers and what makes a qualified customer?

— identify each of the mental stages in consumer decision making?

— provide examples that demonstrate the difference between features and benefits?

— explain why salespeople need to understand competitors' products as well as their own?

— identify each of the steps of an effective selling process in the correct order?

— describe the importance of follow-up with customers after the sale is completed?

— suggest several important marketing activities that support the work of salespeople?

Review Marketing Terms

Match the terms listed with the definitions. Some terms may not be used.

1. Direct, personal communications with prospective customers in order to assess needs and satisfy those needs with appropriate products and services

2. The step in the sales process when the customer makes a decision to purchase

3. A description of a product characteristic

4. Providing the customer with the opportunity to buy during the sales presentation

5. Gathering information to determine which people are most likely to buy

6. Gathering preliminary information and preparing a preliminary sales presentation for a customer

7. A salesperson contacts a large number of people who are conveniently located without knowing a great deal about each person contacted

8. Making contact with the customer after the sale to ensure satisfaction

9. The advantage provided to a customer as a result of the feature

10. A personalized presentation of the features of the product in a way that emphasizes the benefits and value to the customer

a. approach
b. benefit
c. close
d. cold calling
e. demonstration
f. feature
g. follow-up
h. preapproach
i. qualifying
j. selling
k. suggestion selling
l. trial close

Review Marketing Concepts

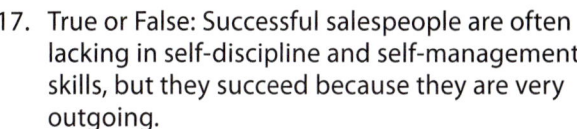

11. True or False: Cold calling is usually a cost- and time-effective method of finding sales leads.

12. Personal selling is _____ in that a salesperson can provide additional information or move on to another topic depending on a customer's reaction to the sales presentation.

13. True or False: Personal selling generally has a higher cost per customer than other methods of promoting a product or service.

14. The mental stages of consumer decision making are represented by the acronym _____.

15. The step of the selling process referred to as answering questions is also known as _____.

16. When a customer indicates that he or she has decided to place an order, the salesperson should take the first opportunity to _____ the decision to assure the customer that he or she has made the right move.

17. True or False: Successful salespeople are often lacking in self-discipline and self-management skills, but they succeed because they are very outgoing.

18. Successful sales occur when customers are able to buy what they need and the business is able to _____.

Marketing Research and Planning

19. The following is a list of important personal selling concepts. Match each concept with the correct example or description.
    a. assess and satisfy needs
    b. customer decision-making process
    c. feedback
    d. flexibility
    e. follow-up
    f. product knowledge
    g. qualifying
    h. time
    ____ During a sales presentation, the salesperson can respond to the customer's questions or determine if specific information is needed.
    ____ Salespeople listen and ask questions to respond to the needs of each customer.
    ____ Customers get more detailed product information than they can with other methods of promotion.
    ____ Lin Chung estimates that she spends about one-third of her time with customers to help them with products they have purchased.
    ____ Rosa Garcia likes to make sure her customers get the best products possible to solve their problems.
    ____ Salespeople use marketing research information to determine the customers who are interested in and able to buy the company's products or services.
    ____ Fred March listens carefully to his customers so he can understand when they are ready to make purchase decisions.
    ____ Sales publications, manuals, promotional pieces, conferences, trade shows, and trade publications are studied and used by effective salespeople.

20. Salespeople are often paid bonuses or commissions on their total sales. Each of the following salespeople earns $60,000 per year and, in addition, earns 2 percent commission on all sales over $250,000 per year.
    a. What is each salesperson's total income for the year?
    b. What is the average amount of each salesperson's sale?
    c. What percentage of calls resulted in a sale for each salesperson?

Salesperson	Total Sales	Number of Sales Calls Per Year	Number of Sales Per Year
Chin Miller	$2,345,200	250	107
Jane Brown	3,395,200	350	120
Marcus Gonzalez	2,930,400	400	99

21. Before making a sales call, the salesperson should be armed with information about the customer, the product, and the competition. Assume you are a salesperson of vehicle tires to be sold to automobile manufacturers. List three pieces of information that would be helpful to know about your customer, your product, and the competition. List three methods or sources you can use to find the necessary information.

22. Effective salespeople help to solve customer problems by explaining how a product or service will benefit the consumer. It is helpful to prepare a feature-benefit chart for each product a salesperson represents. Assume you are a salesperson selling a video camera. For each of the following features, describe a customer benefit using descriptive, meaningful language.
    a. automatic focus
    b. date and event imprinter
    c. case with carrying strap and ID tag
    d. removable flash memory storage
    e. six-hour battery
    f. low-light lens
    g. detachable microphone
    h. image stabilization system

Marketing Management and Decision Making

23. As the CEO of a company that offers web site design and web hosting services to other businesses, you understand how important it is to provide support to your salespeople as they plan sales presentations and work with prospective and current customers. For each of the marketing activities listed below, specify one way that the people working in these areas can provide the necessary support for the salespeople.
    a. Distribution
    b. Financing
    c. Marketing-Information Management
    d. Pricing
    e. Product/Service Management
    f. Promotion

24. Search the Internet for six full-time job openings in sales. Prepare a table that compares the industry and product/service to be sold, job duties, qualifications (education and experience) and type of compensation (wage, salary, commission). Add notes from the job announcement that identify whether or not you believe the company expects the salesperson to understand and follow the principles of the marketing concept.

25. Pick one of the following products listed below, and go comparison shopping for a particular brand and model of that product at three different retailers. Obtain data on the list or sticker price, the prices of features or options you prefer, and the final price offered by the salesperson. Input the data into a computer spreadsheet program and calculate the average list price, the average price of each option, and the average final price. Calculate the difference between each list and offered price. Using a word processing program, write a one-page report of the actions taken by salespeople you encountered to determine your needs and help you make a good purchase decision.
    a. motor scooter
    b. a set of golf clubs
    c. large screen plasma or LCD television
    d. the newest full-featured cellular telephone
    e. work desk and chair for your room
    f. a musical instrument

26. Form a three-person sales team with two classmates. Your team represents a local vending company that wants to enter into an exclusive contract with your school to supply vending machines that will offer only healthy beverages and snack foods. You hope to be the only vendor, place ten machines in the school, and offer the school 20 percent of all revenues from the machines. Your company is willing to negotiate on the types of items in the machines, the number of machines, and the percentage of revenue shared, if necessary. As a team, identify the person in the school who will be your initial contact, the other school personnel you expect to be involved in the final decision, and how you will make your initial contact. Prepare a team sales presentation following the steps in the selling process. Prepare printed or computer-displayed materials and visuals to support your sales presentation. Practice the presentation as a team, and then make the presentation to a group of your classmates who will role-play the school's decision makers.

Technical Sales Event

The purpose of the Technical Sales Event is to provide an opportunity for students to demonstrate knowledge of a technical product. Participants will organize and deliver a sales presentation for their selected technical product to meet the needs of customers. The target customers are parents of students in elementary, middle, and high school. (New product and/or service target market customers will be identified annually by DECA.)

Society is becoming increasingly concerned with the number of young people being abducted each day. You have been asked to do an analysis of the Student Tracker—an electronic device that allows parents to know the location of their children at all times. First Alert sells a broad line of security products, ranging from home security systems to GPS tracking devices frequently used by business travelers to find their way around major cities.

You must convince the CEO from First Alert that the Student Tracker is an important product with great potential for profitability. You must analyze Student Tracker features and benefits. The Student Tracker must be inconspicuous, convenient to wear, and dependable with a long battery life. You must explain a strategy to convince students to wear the Student Tracker. Your presentation must explain how easy it is to monitor people wearing the Student Tracker.

You must organize appropriate information and present/defend a sales presentation. The 20-minute oral presentation will consist of 15 minutes for the sales presentation and 5 minutes for the judge's questions. Your presentation will be evaluated for effectiveness of public speaking and presentation skills and how well you respond to the judge's questions.

Acceptable visual aids include three standard-sized posters not to exceed 22" × 30" each and one standard-sized presentation display board not to exceed 36" × 48" to be placed on chairs or free-standing easels. Electronic presentations with no sound effects may also be used in the Technical Sales Event.

Performance Indicators Evaluated

- Communicate reasons for buying a new technical product. (Communication Skills)
- Take a concept from an idea to an actual product. (Product/Service Management)
- Analyze product information to identify product features and benefits. (Selling)
- Set priorities and demonstrate effective time management. (Emotional Intelligence)
- Demonstrate critical-thinking/problem-solving skills. (Emotional Intelligence)

Go to the DECA web site for more detailed information.

Think Critically

1. How has the media been a driving force behind the need for the Student Tracker product?
2. Why must the Student Tracker device be small and inconspicuous?
3. Where are the best opportunities for First Alert to present the Student Tracker to its target markets?
4. Why might students resist the Student Tracker device?

www.deca.org

Marketing in a Global Economy

18-1 The Expanding World Economy

18-2 How Businesses Get Involved

18-3 Understanding International Markets

©DIGITAL VISION/GETTY IMAGES

Newsline

Responding to the World Economy

Are NAFTA, WTO, and EU the names of rock groups or characters from a science fiction movie? No, but they have become as important in our lives as music or movies. The acronyms stand for the North American Free Trade Agreement, the World Trade Organization, and the European Union. They represent a few of the growing number of agreements among nations.

NAFTA is an example of a regional trade pact. It was implemented between the United States, Canada, and Mexico in 1994. The purpose was to eliminate trade barriers, facilitate cross-border movement of goods and services, and increase business investment opportunities. It has been opposed by people in the United States who fear the loss of manufacturing jobs to Mexico and the erosion of environmental and safety safeguards.

The World Trade Organization deals with the rules of trade among nations. Founded in 1995, it now includes almost 150 member countries. It builds international trade agreements and resolves trade disputes. The WTO works to support free trade and to change laws and regulations that businesses view as restrictions to international trade. Critics fear that the WTO shifts power from citizens and national governments to a global group of unelected officials.

A unique regional agreement is the European Union because it extends beyond improving trade among countries. The EU started in 1957 with six western European countries and continues to expand. In 2007, it included 27 member countries. The EU promotes economic growth and social equality across country borders with an EU parliament and a common currency, the euro.

There is concern that international agreements may damage the economies of some countries, resulting in lost jobs and limited protection for a country's companies and products. Competition between groups of countries may be fiercer than it is between individual countries, and governments may become more committed to regional and worldwide economic development than to the economic well-being of its own citizens.

Think Critically

1. Why would individual governments be willing to change some laws and regulations to gain regional economic cooperation?

2. What are possible advantages and disadvantages to citizens of individual countries from the increasing unified planning and economic cooperation of the EU?

school.cengage.com/marketing/marketing

Prepare for Performance

This chapter develops the following Performance Indicators from the DECA Competitive Events program.

Core Performance Indicators

- Understand global trade's impact to aid business decision making
- Employ marketing information to develop a marketing plan
- Determine global trade's impact on business decision making
- Explain labor issues associated with global trade

Supporting Performance Indicators

- Identify the effects of global trade on retailing
- Explain current retail trends driven by global trade
- Access global trends and opportunities
- Explain the nature of global trade
- Discuss the impact of cultural and social environments on global trade

Go to **school.cengage.com/marketing/marketing** and click on Connect to DECA.

INSURANCE | REINSURANCE | FINANCIAL

The XL Capital group is rated A+ by AM Best (15 August 2006)
Visit www.xlcapital.com

XL
FUNDAMENTAL STRENGTH – CAPITAL AND PEOPLE

The strength to cover the world's leading businesses and financial centers.

©XL

Visual Focus

A business's greatest competition traditionally came from companies in its own back yard. Now the competition can come from across the country and even around the world. Businesses are becoming globally focused, not only to respond to competition but also to identify new and potentially profitable market opportunities. When competing internationally, the marketing concept still applies, but target markets and marketing mixes may be very different. Businesses moving into the global market may look for help from other businesses that have more international experience.

Focus Questions:

Based on the ad, what types of products and services does XL Capital offer and who are its customers? How would a business involved in international trade benefit by working with XL?

Locate another ad of a company that provides products or services to international customers. Share your ad in a class discussion on how marketing may be similar or different in international markets.

The Expanding World Economy

marketing matters

Businesses often try to sell their products or services in international markets when they run out of new customers in their home markets. Another reason for reaching out to customers in other countries is to try to match the competition from foreign firms that have entered their home markets. They hope to be able to satisfy a growing demand from foreign consumers for a greater variety of products.

Make a list of ten assorted products that are regularly used in your home, such as food, electronics, medicine, clothing, and furniture. Identify the country or region of the world where you believe each product was produced. What percentage of the products did you identify as being produced or manufactured in a foreign country? Do you believe that percentage reflects in general how consumer dollars in the United States are spent on goods produced in foreign countries versus the United States? Compare your answers with those of other students in a class discussion.

The United States and International Trade

In 2006, the total value of all goods and services produced in the world was nearly $66 trillion. That amount has more than doubled in just five years. The United States has the world's largest economy. In 2006, it produced products and services valued at more than $13 trillion, which is about one-fifth of the total production of all countries in the world. The United States is a very productive country with only China and the combined production of countries in the European Union approaching the output of the U.S. economy. The top world economies are shown in Figure 18-1.

Worldwide Interdependence

Most of the products and services produced in the world are still consumed by people in the countries where they are produced. Yet about one-third of all world production is sold outside of the country in which it is produced. The sale of products and services to people in other countries is known as *international trade*. Some countries are more involved in international trade than others, but almost all countries are expanding their involvement.

It is easy to find examples of international trade. Spend a short time looking at all the products and services you consume during just one day to determine where they were produced. You will quickly see that many are not produced in the United States but come from countries around the world. Products or services purchased from another country are known as **imports**.

You may start your morning with fruit and cereal grown in El Salvador and transported here in ships from Panama. The clothes you wear may have been manufactured in Taiwan, and you may ride to school on a bus that was assembled in Canada. Your textbooks may have been published by a company that is part of a British corporation. After school, you may call your friends on a telephone that was produced in Japan and use a computer made in Korea for homework. That evening you watch a movie that was filmed in Kenya on a DVD player assembled in Poland. Certainly, you will likely see that many of the products and services you use were produced in the United States, but you and the people in your community are indeed international consumers.

International business is also important to other countries. Just as you use products produced in foreign countries, consumers in those countries are important customers for U.S. businesses. Products and services that are sold to another country are known as **exports**. Important consumer products exported from the United States to other countries include music, movies, automobiles, and food products. U.S. manufacturers of airplanes, computers, and communications equipment also have a large number of international customers.

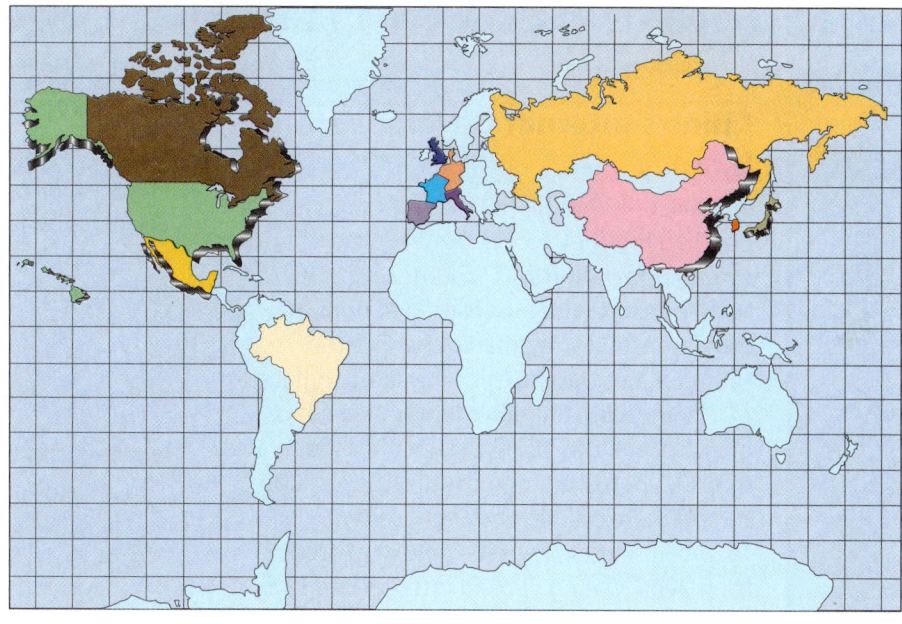

The World's Largest Economies (2006)*

*CIA World Factbook, 2007

World	$ 65.950	trillion
United States	$ 13.130	trillion
European Union	$ 13.060	trillion
China	$ 10.170	trillion
Japan	$ 4.218	trillion
Germany	$ 2.630	trillion
United Kingdom	$ 1.930	trillion
France	$ 1.891	trillion

Italy	$ 1.756	trillion
Russia	$ 1.746	trillion
Brazil	$ 1.655	trillion
South Korea	$ 1.196	trillion
Canada	$ 1.178	trillion
Mexico	$ 1.149	trillion
Spain	$ 1.109	trillion

FIGURE 18-1

The United States is the world's largest producer of goods and services, but other countries are increasing their production rapidly.

Working in **Teams**

As a team, identify three products for which you believe U.S. companies are the largest producers based on worldwide sales. Now identify three products for which you believe foreign-owned companies are the worldwide sales leaders. Use the Internet to determine whether or not you are correct.

Virtual Marketing

China's Internet Develops from Infancy

In 2000, only 2 percent of China's population had Internet access. But because China's overall population was so large, even this small percentage of users made China the fifth largest Internet market behind the United States, Japan, Germany, and England.

Since 2000, China's Internet usage has grown rapidly. In 2007, it was estimated that 12.3 percent of the country's 1.3 billion people were online. That represents 162 million Internet users, up 620 percent from 2000. Over half of all Internet users in the country are under 25 years old.

China has invested heavily in its Internet infrastructure, but because China has many rural areas, a good portion of the population still does not have Internet access. Many people go online at their workplace, colleges, or in Internet cafes. U.S. companies recognize the potential for growth. Companies such as Google have moved into the Chinese market, but because the Chinese government censors information that its people can access, Google limits the information on its site to adhere to Chinese law.

Think Critically

1. Even with the rapid growth of China's online population, why might businesses decide to avoid that market?

2. What does the age of Chinese Internet users say about its potential as a business market?

The Changing Nature of International Trade

The type of products and services exchanged between countries is changing. Years ago, a great deal of international trade was devoted to obtaining raw materials. Some countries had an abundance of raw materials (timber, iron ore, petroleum) but had not developed their manufacturing capabilities. Other countries were heavily involved in manufacturing but did not have adequate supplies of needed resources to operate their factories. Therefore, they purchased the raw materials from other countries. At that time, raw materials made up almost all of the products traded between countries. Today, raw materials are less than one-third of the world's exports. Most exports now consist of manufactured goods and services.

Currently, international trade in services is growing faster than trade in products. Common types of services exchanged between countries include communications, travel, education, financial services, and information. One interesting example of the exchange of services is in the area of data management. Banks and other financial institutions in the United States are using companies in India, Ireland, and South Africa to complete a large amount of the data processing for their businesses. At the end of the business day in the United States, data is transferred to another country via telephone lines, fiber optic cable, or satellite transmission. The data processors in the other countries complete work on the information, update the customers' accounts, and transfer the data back to the U.S. location in time for use the next business day.

Checkpoint ▶▶

What is the difference between imports and exports?

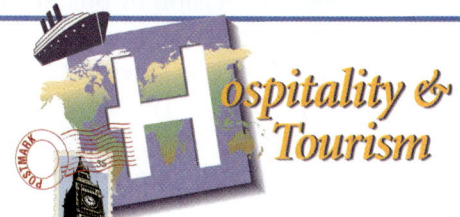

ospitality & Tourism

"My grandpa is finally going to travel to Japan to study a culture that has always intrigued him. Since he has some health issues, he wanted to be sure that his tour includes interpreters who are well versed in medical terminology in addition to the usual tourist information. His travel agent has assured him that competent interpreters will be available on his tour, so he should just relax and start packing!"

How do corporations conduct business in foreign countries? How do tourists manage daily life needs in foreign countries?

International hospitality coordinators work to ensure successful, stress-free trips for international travelers. Because a variety of languages and cultures may be represented, both interpreters and translators need to be available in the host countries. Interpreters focus on verbal language translations. Converting one written language into another is the role of translators.

Employment Outlook

- Consolidations in some parts of the industry may reduce management opportunities, but growth is expected in international business services.
- Excellent job prospects exist in countries with developing economies and where business and tourism is expanding.

Job Titles

- International Travel Coordinator
- Hotel Concierge
- Translator and Interpreter
- Cruise Line Guest Services Director
- International Convention Planner

Needed Skills

- Interpreters and translators must be fluent in multiple languages.
- A bachelor's degree in Hospitality Management is beneficial.

- An understanding of and experience with varied cultures is an advantage.
- High school students may participate in a two-year program developed by The Hotel and Lodging Association. Program completion results in a professional certification in hospitality.

What's it like to work in... *International Hospitality*

Arden, an international sales agent for a hotel chain, is preparing a sales proposal. Tomorrow she will be calling on the conference coordinator for an international professional society. The society has booked the local convention center for its annual conference. Although the conference will not occur for two years, the organizers want to ensure that the hotel they use responds to the needs of international visitors.

Arden has arranged the services of several international language specialists for the entire conference. Given the variety of countries represented by conference attendees, Arden needed to secure a broad spectrum of interpreters and translators.

Arden's sales plan incorporates recommendations from the hotel staff that focus on accommodating the cultural needs of guests from various countries. The entire hotel's staff receives extensive training about cultural differences.

Proactively catering to the needs of international travelers should give Arden's hotel a competitive edge.

What About You

Would you like to work with international travelers to help make their visit to your country more enjoyable?

Why Businesses Are Going Global

The decision by businesses to become involved in international trade is not always as carefully planned as you might think. There are a number of reasons why businesses typically get involved in international trade.

Changing Markets and Competition

Some businesses first decide to market products in other countries out of necessity. They find that competition is becoming very intense in their current markets and their sales and profits are declining. To gain sales and increase profits, companies begin to look at other countries for potential markets.

When the birth rate declined in the United States, companies that manufactured products for babies (formula, baby food, diapers) looked for markets in other countries. And when attendance at U.S. movie theaters declined for several years, film distributors increased their efforts to market films abroad.

Other companies consider international markets when they see companies from other countries entering their own markets. Rather than just competing with the foreign companies in their own country, they decide to enter international markets to keep the competition more balanced. In the 1970s, automobile manufacturers from Japan and Germany moved into the U.S. market to take advantage of the need for smaller, more fuel-efficient cars. One of the responses of U.S. firms was to increase efforts to sell their brands in other countries.

A third reason for global marketing is the increasing worldwide demand for products. Consumers in many countries look to the United States for product and service ideas. As economies expand throughout the world and standards of living increase, consumers in those countries are willing to spend money for a variety of products. Businesses that recognize the increasing demand offer their products for sale wherever customers are willing to buy, including internationally. Manufacturers of products ranging from blue jeans to music and hamburgers are finding success in world markets.

To some businesses, the idea of selling products or services internationally seems complicated or difficult, so they may decide not to become involved in international trade. But with improvements in transportation, communication, banking and finance, and other business processes, it is often as easy to serve markets in other countries as it is to sell in markets that are several states away.

Assistance with International Marketing

Every country benefits from international business because of the availability of a greater variety of products and services and the profits available from exporting the country's products. Most governments are developing support for companies that want to increase their business conducted in other countries.

There are several examples of government support for U.S. businesses. The

Germany's Volkswagen Beetle has been a popular U.S. import for many years.

Department of State maintains embassies in most countries that can help with passports, documents, and laws. The U.S. Department of Commerce maintains the Trade Information Center and Export Assistance Centers to provide support for U.S. businesses involved in international trade. Even the Small Business Administration has an office to provide assistance for small U.S. businesses wanting to expand into foreign markets. Many states have trade promotion offices to help businesses develop markets in other countries.

In addition to government support, an increasing number of other sources, such as banks and other financial services companies, insurance businesses, accounting firms, transportation companies, and communications services firms, may provide assistance to their customers.

Checkpoint ▶▶

What are three reasons that businesses try to sell their products or services in international markets?

18-1 Assessment

Xtra! Study Tools
school.cengage.com/marketing/marketing

Key Concepts

Determine the best answer.

1. True or False: As of 2006, the United States had the world's largest economy.

2. Products or services purchased from another country are known as
   a. exports
   b. imports
   c. quotas
   d. joint ventures

3. Today, raw materials make up about _____ of the world's exports.
   a. one-tenth
   b. one-third
   c. one-half
   d. three-fourths

4. Which of the following is *not* one of the reasons for U.S. businesses to enter international markets?
   a. Competition is becoming very intense in their home markets.
   b. Foreign companies are entering U.S. markets to compete.
   c. There is an increasing worldwide demand for consumer products.
   d. U.S. markets are getting smaller and are no longer profitable.

Make Academic Connections

5. **Math** Use the information in Figure 18-1 to calculate: (a) the total value of goods and services produced by all of the countries listed (do not include the EU) and (b) the percentage of the world's total production represented by each country, by the EU, and by the combined total of all countries excluding the EU.

6. **Government** Use the Internet to identify one federal agency or office and one agency or office from your state that provides information and support for businesses seeking to become involved in international marketing. Based on your research, prepare a two- to three-paragraph description of each agency or office identifying the types of businesses they support, the services they provide, and contact information.

Connect to ◀ DECA
An Association of Marketing Students

7. Your employer manufactures electric-powered scooters that have been very popular among U.S. teenagers and young adults as well as commuters. The company is deciding whether to begin selling the scooters internationally. Prepare a two-minute presentation with at least one chart or handout describing the advantages and disadvantages of international marketing for the company. Give your presentation to your teacher (judge).

How Businesses Get Involved

GOALS

- Define indirect and direct exporting and balance of trade.
- Explain how foreign production, foreign investment, and foreign joint ventures operate.
- Describe the way in which multinational companies compete by thinking globally.

KEY TERMS

indirect exporting, p. 512

direct exporting, p. 512

balance of trade, p. 513

foreign production, p. 513

foreign investment, p. 514

joint venture, p. 514

multinational companies, p. 515

marketing matters

International trade is important to the U.S. economy. Nearly 250,000 businesses are involved in exporting, accounting for more than 11 percent of all products and services produced in the United States. Over 95 percent of exporting firms are small- to medium-sized businesses. Manufacturers accounted for the largest portion of the value of U.S. exports at nearly $500 billon. Wholesalers made up the next largest portion at just under $100 billion.

Make a list of five manufacturing companies in your area. Identify the products they produce. Do you believe these products are exported? What countries would be good markets for the products manufactured by the companies you identified?

The Importance of Marketing in International Trade

There are many forms of international trade. Most businesses first get involved through exporting or selling their existing products in other countries. When businesses have been successful selling products in their own country, they may begin to look for additional markets that they believe would want to buy their products. Or customers from other countries may become aware of the company's products and seek to purchase them. **Indirect exporting** is the process in which marketing businesses with exporting experience represent the exporting company and arrange for the sale of products in other countries. The producer or manufacturer will not be directly involved in exporting activities but will rely on the exporting business to serve the international markets. With more experience, a company may try **direct exporting**, which involves taking complete responsibility for marketing its products in other countries.

In 2006, the United States was the world's second largest exporter selling $1.024 trillion of products and services to other countries. That accounted for about 7 percent of the entire world exports. Germany led the world in exports with $1.133 trillion. The United States was the largest world importer, with $1.9 trillion or nearly 16 percent of the world total in that year. Germany was second with $916 billion in imports.

Those figures suggest one of the problems countries face concerning international trade. The difference between the amount of a country's imports and exports is known as its **balance of trade**. As you can see from the figures above, in 2006 the United States had an $876 billion negative balance of trade while Germany had a $217 billion positive balance of trade. In the short run, the balance of trade may not have an effect on a country. But many economists believe that continual negative balances can create problems. A negative balance of trade shows that a country is sending more of its financial resources to other countries through the purchase of products than it is receiving from the sale of products abroad. It also demonstrates

that businesses from other countries are satisfying the needs of consumers better than the country's own businesses.

Checkpoint ▶▶

How is a country's balance of trade determined?

Foreign Production, Investment, and Joint Ventures

Some other examples of ways that businesses participate in international trade are through foreign production, foreign investment, and joint ventures.

Foreign Production

With **foreign production**, a company owns and operates production facilities in another country. As companies expand into international markets, it becomes difficult to maintain manufacturing in only one country and meet all of the new market demands. With foreign production, manufacturing occurs where needed. Raw materials and resources can often be acquired inexpensively close to the markets where the products will be sold.

In the past, all of the production activities for a product would be completed in a country in the region where the product would be sold. Today, it is not unusual for the production process to occur in more than one location. Computers, automobiles, and medical equipment are manufactured using parts produced in one country and then shipped to another country for final assembly. Multicountry production requires very effective planning and distribution systems.

There is a concern that too much foreign production can have a negative effect on a country. One of the major issues is the loss of jobs in the country from which the production is being moved. A U.S. company may decide to open a manufacturing facility in a country with much lower wage rates. If it closes a U.S. factory to open a foreign facility, U.S. jobs are lost and overall consumer purchasing power is reduced.

People defending foreign production argue that companies from other countries with U.S. markets are investing in production facilities in this country. As more U.S. consumers purchase Toyotas, BMWs, and other foreign brands of automobiles, those companies have opened automobile plants in the United States. Those companies hire employees from the area and attract other

Global Travel: Representing Your Country

It used to be that international business was left to the large corporations. However, because of the Internet, adding an international element to even the smallest business is now possible. Today, there are approximately 40,000 multinational companies compared to just 7,000 in 1975.

As global business and travel grows, it is increasingly important for American business people to be sensitive to the diverse cultures around the world. An American traveling on business in the Middle East, for example, is a representative not only of his or her company but also of the United States. How people in other countries perceive the United States is often based on their encounters with Americans.

A new industry has popped up that educates business travelers on courteous foreign travel. Special schools of global management offer business travelers classes on global corporate diplomacy. The nonprofit group Business for Diplomatic Action works through business travelers to maintain a positive image of America around the globe. Good, courteous diplomacy while traveling is not just good for business; it is good for America.

Think Critically

1. In Europe, it is common for people to speak more than one language. How does this compare to people in the United States, and what impression might it give of Americans?

2. What kinds of cultural differences must business travelers be sensitive to as they travel to different parts of the globe?

businesses that produce component parts used in the production of the vehicles.

Foreign Investment

Some companies have identified businesses in other countries that have already developed production or marketing capabilities. Rather than entering the country and starting a new business, the company purchases the existing business. Owning all or part of an existing business in another country is known as **foreign investment**. Through foreign investment, businesses can move more quickly into another country. They can also use the past financial performance of the purchased business to determine whether it is a good investment. The new owners may decide to change the business or continue to operate it in the same way as the previous owners. That decision will be based on the past success of the business and the needs of the company making the foreign investment.

U.S. companies have been active in foreign investments for many years, but recently other countries have increased their foreign investments. Today, the United States has about one-third of the world total with about $14 billion invested in other countries. In addition, the United States is an attractive country in which foreign businesses like to invest. Currently, it is the leading host country for foreign investments with over $16 billion of foreign assets invested in the United States.

Joint Ventures

When two or more companies in different countries determine that they have common interests, they may form a joint venture. In a **joint venture**, independent companies develop a relationship to cooperate in common business activities. The agreement may be in the form of a contract where the companies agree to a specific set of activities for a predetermined period of time. In another form of joint venture, each company actually agrees to purchase a portion of the other company to create joint ownership. They then have a continuing relationship based on that ownership.

One of the largest joint ventures involves ten international airlines that have signed agreements to cooperate in coordinating flight schedules, marketing activities, travel reward programs, and airport resources. Called **one**world®, the companies believe the cooperative activities make them more competitive for the international traveler. It offers ways to reduce costs and increase customer service. It is not always an easy alliance since each of the cooperating airlines is still an independent company serving its own markets and customers.

> ## Checkpoint ▶▶
>
> **If a U.S. company wants to expand its manufacturing operations in other countries, what options does it have?**

Multinational Companies

Some companies have been involved in international business for a long time. They may use several of the strategies described above and sell services and products in a large number of countries throughout the world. They probably are purchasing products and services from companies in many countries to use in production and operations. Businesses that are heavily involved in international business usually develop factories and offices in several countries in order to keep operations closer to the customers. Businesses that have operations throughout the world and that conduct planning for worldwide markets are **multinational companies**. Multinational businesses no longer think of themselves as being located in one country selling to customers in other countries. They think globally.

There are many businesses that you may think of as U.S. companies that are really multinational. They operate throughout the world and derive a large part of their sales and profits from countries other than the United States. McDonald's is an example of a multinational company. It operates over 32,000 stores in more than 100 countries. U.S. stores account for only 35 percent of the company's annual sales. Other examples of well-known multinational companies that started in the United States are Coca-Cola, Hilton Hotels, John Deere, 3M Corp., Nike, and IBM. There are also many multinational firms that started in other countries. Some familiar examples include Nestle S.A., Panasonic, Seiko, Hyundai, L'Oreal, and Ciba-Geigy.

Figure 18-2 shows there are many employment opportunities in multinational

FIGURE 18-2

Multinational companies offer many employment opportunities throughout the world.

The World's Largest Employers		
Company	**Home Country**	**No. of Employees**
Wal-Mart Stores (retailing)	United States	1,900,000
China National Petroleum (petroleum)	China	1,086,966
U.S. Postal Service (mail services)	United States	796,199
Sinopec (petroleum)	China	681,900
Siemens (electronics)	Germany	475,000
McDonald's (food service)	United States	465,000
Deutsche Post (mail services)	Germany	463,350
Carrefour (retailing)	France	456,295
Agricultural Bank of China (financial)	China	452,464

companies. Multinational companies hire employees, including managers, from many countries. They expect their employees to be able and willing to work with people from all over the world. Employees often travel, and some even relocate and live in other countries while they work for the multinational company.

Competitors for multinational businesses also come from many different locations. A business may compete with one set of companies in Australia and another in Africa or South America. There are an increasing number of large multinationals that compete for customers in all parts of the world. Thinking globally opens up many opportunities for businesses, but it also makes business and marketing decisions even more complex.

Checkpoint ▶▶

Why do multinational companies operate in so many different markets and hire employees and managers from so many countries?

18-2 Assessment

Key Concepts

Determine the best answer.

1. True or False: In 2006, the United States was the world's largest exporter of products and services.

2. The difference between the amount of a country's imports and exports is known as its
   a. trade deficit
   b. amount of foreign investment
   c. balance of trade
   d. export balance

3. When independent companies develop a relationship to cooperate in common business activities, they are involved in
   a. foreign investment
   b. foreign production
   c. a joint venture
   d. forming a multinational company

4. True or False: While U.S. businesses are active in foreign investments, our laws prevent foreign companies from investing in the United States.

5. Businesses that have operations throughout the world and that conduct planning for worldwide markets are _____ companies.

Make Academic Connections

6. **Economics** Use the library or Internet to gather historical information about the amount of foreign trade for the United States during the most recent ten years for which information is available. Prepare a line graph that illustrates the values of exports and imports for each year. Write one paragraph summarizing what the graph illustrates.

7. **Geography** Select a large retail business that operates in countries around the world (McDonald's, Wal-Mart, Starbucks, Holiday Inn, and others). Visit the company's web site and determine the countries in which the business operates and the number of locations it has in each country. Locate and print a map of the world. Identify the countries and number of locations for the business on the map.

Connect to ◆DECA

8. You have been asked by a local citizens' group to speak to the organization on how the local community benefits from international trade. Prepare a two-minute informational speech. Deliver the speech to your teacher (judge).

Understanding International Markets

GOALS

- Explain how economic conditions affect the ability to market within a country.
- Describe the factors that determine the best marketing mix for particular countries.
- Examine how conditions in international marketing affect the completion of marketing functions.

KEY TERMS

preindustrial economy, *p. 518*

industrial economy, *p. 518*

postindustrial economy, *p. 519*

gross domestic product (GDP), *p. 520*

gross national product (GNP), *p. 520*

standard of living, *p. 520*

productivity , *p. 520*

purchasing power, *p. 520*

consumer price index, *p. 520*

inflation, *p. 520*

recession, *p. 520*

business cycles, *p. 521*

quotas, *p. 522*

tariffs, *p. 522*

subsidy, *p. 522*

marketing matters

The marketing concept applies in other countries' markets like it does in the United States. While the same marketing functions are needed in international business, there are differences in how specific marketing activities are completed from one country to another. Business people involved in international business often work with marketing experts from the foreign country in which they are operating to be sure they use the most effective procedures that are understood and accepted by the country's consumers.

Try to identify three consumer products that are popular in other countries but which are not in high demand in the United States. Why are these products popular elsewhere but not in the United States? Now identify three products that originated in another country but are popular in the United States? What makes them attractive to U.S. consumers?

The International Economic Environment

The concept of a market in other countries is the same as a market in this country. A market refers to the prospective customers a business wants to serve and their location. Business people should not assume that all countries have the same kinds of markets as are found in the United States or that all people in a country have the same characteristics, needs, and interests (see Figure 18-3). Just as it would be a mistake in the United States to market to all consumers as if they were the same, businesses need to recognize important differences among prospective customers in other countries.

There are many similarities but also some differences between marketing internationally and marketing within one country. The idea of identifying target markets and developing a marketing mix

FIGURE 18-3

Businesses must gather a great deal of information in order to determine if they can successfully market their products and services in another country.

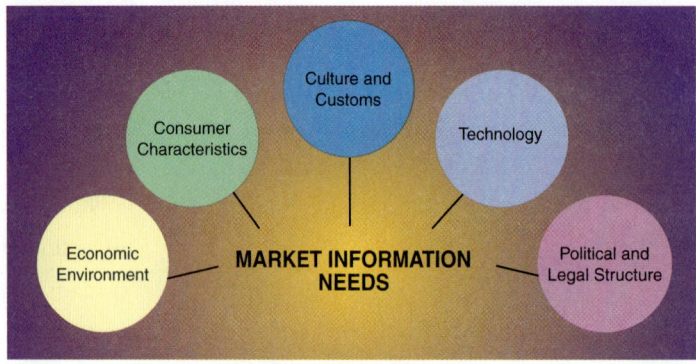

remains the same. So does the need to complete each of the major marketing functions. The characteristics of markets, the information needed and how it is obtained, and the procedures used to develop each of the marketing mix elements will change as companies concentrate on target markets in other countries.

The level of economic development of a country and the current condition of the economy must be understood for effective marketing. A country that has a high standard of living will already have well-established businesses that manufacture and sell a variety of both consumer and business products. That country will offer very different marketing opportunities than a country that is struggling to meet basic social and economic needs for its citizens. Economies of the world's countries can be grouped into three broad categories: preindustrial, industrial, and postindustrial.

Preindustrial Economies

The **preindustrial economy** is based on agriculture and raw material development through activities such as mining, oil production, and harvesting timber. In this type of economy, many of the country's citizens provide for all of their own needs and have a very low standard of living. Manufacturing, distribution, and retail systems are just beginning to develop. This makes it difficult for businesses to produce,

distribute, or sell products until the economy is further developed.

Leaders in a country at the preindustrial economy stage recognize the importance of moving to the next stage. They see their natural resources being consumed and few job choices for their citizens. Those countries are unable to participate in the international economy except through the sale of raw materials. The leaders of the countries are looking for help in developing their economies.

Countries with preindustrial economies were once viewed as offering few opportunities for foreign businesses. Some companies purchased raw materials from the countries. Others actually developed mining, lumbering, or oil drilling activities. Often, those companies were accused of exploiting the countries. Some companies took natural resources and returned very little to the economies. Today, many preindustrial countries provide opportunities for companies that want to sell manufacturing equipment, cooperate in the development of manufacturing businesses, or improve production processes.

Many countries also seek assistance in developing distribution systems. There must be effective methods of getting products to customers and places for the products to be sold. Roads, railroads, river systems, and airports are needed to distribute products as manufacturing develops. Developing distribution systems and organizing wholesale and retail businesses will make it possible to sell products.

Industrial Economies

Today, most countries have industrial economies. In an **industrial economy**, the primary business activity is the manufacturing of products. Much of the manufacturing in the early stages of an industrial economy is devoted to the production of equipment and materials for businesses and the development of marketing systems. Later, as people work in the factories and other businesses, wages increase and the standard of living improves. There is greater demand for a variety of consumer products, and businesses develop to meet those needs.

There are many opportunities for international businesses in industrial economies. There is demand for both business and consumer products. Often, products and services that are successful in countries with more developed economies can be sold in the industrial economies as those countries develop. Businesses in industrial economies may be willing to participate in joint ventures with businesses from other countries in order to obtain needed expertise and experience.

Postindustrial Economies

The largest and most-developed economies in the world have moved into the postindustrial stage. A **postindustrial economy** is based on a mix of business and consumer products and services produced and marketed in the global marketplace. Countries with postindustrial economies have very high standards of living with many international business opportunities. Companies use up-to-date technologies and business procedures. Countries with postindustrial economies work with other countries to develop effective laws and procedures that encourage and support international trade.

People living in postindustrial economies are very aware of products and services available from other countries. They expect the businesses in their country to produce similar products of equal or higher quality at a reasonable price, or they will buy from companies in other countries.

Condition of the Economy

A country's stage of economic development shows the long-term picture of its economy. The short-term condition is important as well. If a country's economy is strong and growing, citizens will have more job opportunities and money to spend. Businesses will have a better environment for sales and profits. The government will

Judgment Call

Bribery Common but Not Legal

Offering bribes or demanding kickbacks to facilitate international business is widespread even though it is outlawed in virtually every country. Because it is so common and so difficult to fight, it is one of the toughest barriers to international trade faced by U.S. businesses.

Unlike some countries, U.S. law makes it illegal for a U.S. company to bribe a foreign official. So Americans generally have no good choices when they encounter foreign officials who demand payment before they will award them a contract or issue necessary permits. They can either break the law to get the contract, or they can decline to pay and lose the business.

Some U.S. businesses opt to transact foreign business through foreign partners or subsidiaries. Then foreign employees handle the distasteful transactions while the parent company avoids violating U.S. laws.

Think Critically

1. If a business person encounters a foreign citizen who expects an illicit payment to facilitate a business deal, what options does he or she have?

2. Why are attempts to combat bribery in international trade so difficult?

Working in Teams

Use the library or Internet to identify three countries, each representing one of the economic categories. A good source of information is the *CIA World Factbook*. As a team, prepare a chart that compares the three economies to illustrate the reasons for your classification.

have more resources for roads, schools, education, and other services.

There are several important measures of a country's economy. One of the most used measures is gross domestic product. **Gross domestic product (GDP)** is the total value of goods and services produced within a country during the year. It is sometimes referred to as *gross domestic income (GDI)*. A related measure is gross national product. **Gross national product (GNP)** is the total value of all goods and services produced by a country during the year, including foreign investments. GNP is a broader measure and includes the production of multinational companies that occurs outside a country's borders. A growing GDP and GNP is a sign of a strong economy.

A country's **standard of living** is a measure of the quality of life for its citizens. It is based on factors such as housing, food, education, clothing, transportation, and employment opportunities. A country's standard of living is calculated by dividing the total income of the country (GDP) by its population. This figure is also referred to as *GDP per capita*. A country with a high standard of living produces and sells larger quantities of goods and services, meaning more jobs, higher wage rates, and better markets for businesses.

A fourth economic measure is productivity. **Productivity** is the average output by workers for a specific period of time. For example, if a business has 20 employees working 40 hours a week and produces 80,000 units of a product during the week, the productivity is 100 units (80,000 units ÷ 800 work hours per week). If the same

employees produce a larger number of units working the same number of hours, businesses have increased their productivity. Productivity shows the efficiency of a country's work force and technology used in production. Productivity can increase as a result of a more educated and skilled workforce, more efficient operations, and increased use of technology to support work procedures.

A final measure of the condition of an economy is purchasing power. **Purchasing power** is the amount of goods and services that can be purchased with a specific amount of money. A specific measure of purchasing power is the consumer price index. The **consumer price index (CPI)** is the change in the cost of a specified set of goods and services over time. If a country's CPI declines, the number of purchases consumers can make with the same amount of money will be fewer. Purchasing power declines with **inflation**, where prices increase faster than the value of goods and services, and during a **recession**, a period of time in which the economy slows resulting in

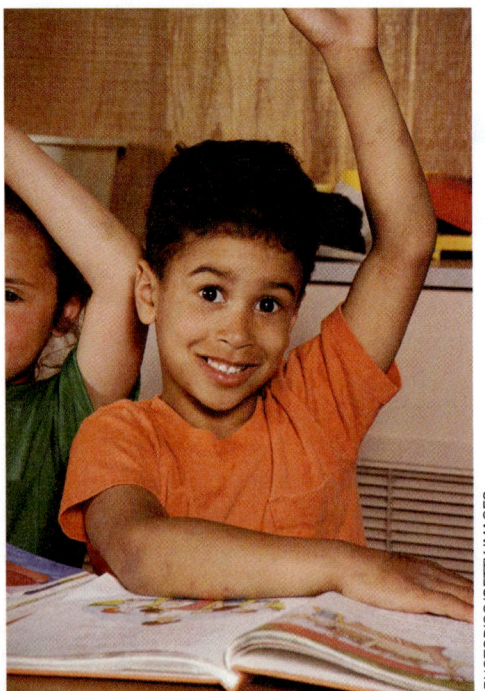

Why is education a factor in a country's standard of living?

lower production, employment, and income. Even while economies grow, they go through periods of expansion and decline. Those recurring changes in an economy are called **business cycles**.

Checkpoint ▶▶▶

What are the three stages of economic development that can affect a country's receptiveness to international trade?

Finding the Right Mix for Foreign Markets

Each international market can be very different and may require changes in the marketing mix. A company that believes in the marketing orientation will carefully study the consumers in each country to determine if appropriate markets exist. If so, the company will study the markets to identify unique characteristics. It will then begin to design an appropriate product or service, determine how the product will be distributed, establish pricing policies, and develop promotion strategies that are appropriate for the country and the specific market. This strategy is likely to result in differences from the way the products are marketed in the original country but will provide the best opportunity for the company to be successful.

Consumer Characteristics

Information needs to be gathered about the people in a country. Businesses need to determine if there are enough prospective customers. They need to know demographic characteristics such as age, income, employment, and education. Businesses must determine where prospective customers are located in the country, where and how they typically buy products, what methods of transportation will work best, and which communications media are available.

Culture and Customs

The culture and customs of a country may determine whether certain products or marketing methods will be appropriate or acceptable. *Culture* is the common beliefs and behaviors of a group of people who have a similar heritage and experience. *Customs* are accepted or habitual practices. Family structures, religion, beliefs and values, language, personal habits, and daily activities may be quite different from what the marketers are used to in their own culture. Failure to recognize differences may result in misunderstanding and mistrust. Businesses moving into countries with different cultures for the first time should seek advice and assistance from people who are knowledgeable about the country's cultures and customs. Many multinational companies employ people from the countries they are entering to provide the needed expertise.

Technology

The technology of business and marketing is changing rapidly. Businesses are adopting new methods of manufacturing, transportation, product handling, and communication. Consumers have access to computers, new types of appliances, and changing technology.

Once these new technical products are developed in one country, they are usually distributed and accepted in many other countries. Businesses cannot assume, though, that the same technology used in their home country is available or used in other countries. Even if the technology is used, there might be important differences. An excellent example is the metric system. Several years ago, there was an attempt to convert most of the measurement systems in the United States to the metric system, which is widely used throughout the rest of the world. That attempt was not successful,

NETBookmark

International marketing activities can be quite different when serving customers in another country. Access school.cengage.com/marketing/marketing and click on the link for Chapter 18. A wealth of information about doing business in other countries can be found on the Executive Planet web site. Look through the site, and then briefly describe the tone that should be taken in promotional material aimed at the German market. Also, find a country that would not appreciate an advertising campaign that pokes fun at older folks. Explain your answer.

school.cengage.com/marketing/marketing

although metric measures are used more widely than before.

Other interesting examples of possible conflicting technologies in international business include different cell phone communication frequencies used in most other countries compared to the United States and the voltage requirements and power supplies for a country's electrical systems.

Political and Legal Structure

One of the most important factors that can affect the success of international marketing is a country's political and legal systems. The types of political systems range from democratic, in which the citizens of the country control the decisions of the government, to autocratic, where power is in the hands of a very small group of people. In the recent past, one of the major political structures, communism, was rejected in many Central European countries and in the former Soviet Union. Those countries reorganized their political systems to adopt more democratic principles. Even the largest communist country, China, is adopting many of the free enterprise principles for operating businesses.

The stability of the political system is important for businesses. If a country is politically unstable, it is possible that business ownership and operating procedures may be threatened. There have been many examples of countries in which the government was overthrown and the businesses owned by people from other countries were destroyed or taken over by the new government.

Countries develop laws to regulate business. Many of those laws affect international business operations. Some countries have laws that provide strong support for their businesses in the sale of products in other countries or protect the country's businesses from foreign competition.

Because the leaders of industrial economies want the businesses in their countries to be successful, they may try to restrict the amount of imports through the use of quotas or tariffs. **Quotas** are limits on the numbers of specific types of products that foreign companies can sell in the country. **Tariffs** are taxes placed on imported products to increase the price for which they are sold. Countries may also support their businesses through subsidies. A **subsidy** is money provided to a business to assist in the development and sale of its products. International free trade efforts have attempted to reduce these types of restrictions and protections.

©PHOTODISC/GETTY IMAGES

Why would U.S. businesses be concerned about the political structure of another country?

Checkpoint ▶▶

Name four factors that can affect the success of a marketing plan in an international market.

Digital Digest

Video Conferencing: The Global Conference Room

Ask any salesperson, and they will probably tell you that the best way to interface with clients is in person, face-to-face. Likewise, meetings that take place between marketers, advertisers, and other businesspeople are typically more efficient when everyone is in the same room. However, with some companies having offices and clients in multiple countries on multiple continents, it is often not possible or cost-effective to fly people around the globe for meetings. That's where video conferencing comes in.

A video conference is a meeting of two or more people in different locations via a digital transmission that allows the parties to see and hear each other. Currently, it is the closest thing to meeting in person available.

Although video conferencing was first invented in the late 1960s, it wasn't until the technology boom in the 1990s that it became feasible for businesses. Even then, it was expensive because it required special equipment and used a large amount of bandwidth. More recent technology, however, has made video conferencing much easier and more affordable with a much higher quality. Many personal computers even have cameras, microphones, and software built in that allow people to video conference from their own desks or workstations. These advances have made video conferencing an important tool in global business.

Think Critically

1. Why do you think it is so important to meet "face-to-face" with clients and co-workers?

2. Can you think of any negative aspects of a company relying heavily on video conferencing?

International Marketing Activities

Before a business can begin to plan the marketing mix that will be used for an international market, it needs reliable information about that market. The procedures for gathering and analyzing market information are quite similar for international markets to those used in a business's home country. The business needs to develop a marketing information system to collect and analyze information. It also may need to complete marketing research or work with local or international research companies to answer specific questions about customers and competitors.

Gathering Market Information

The characteristics of specific countries require special attention to both marketing-information management and marketing research. The sources of information, the types of technology and research capabilities, the ways that people respond to research procedures, and the laws relating to information collection will likely be quite different. For example, in the United States, much of today's consumer research is completed using Internet or telephone surveys, or data is collected using technology at the time of sale. In some countries, technology is not as well developed, eliminating those options. And in some cultures, asking many types of personal questions is considered discourteous.

Companies often work with businesses and business people from the country in which they hope to market products to gather needed information. This helps to ensure that those doing the research better understand the unique characteristics of the country and that the research will be completed in a way that does not harm the image of the business. People in international business need to listen carefully to people from the countries they want to serve in order to avoid biases and stereotypes.

Adjusting the Marketing Mix and Marketing Functions

After business people have gathered the necessary information to understand the new market, they can develop the marketing mix. With this information, the mix can be specifically designed to meet the needs of each international market. The types of marketing activities often will be the same or similar to those previously used by the company. However, there are some important differences in the marketing functions as shown with the following examples.

Product/Service Management
Products and services must be developed to meet the needs of customers and market conditions. Important activities for international markets include packaging for protection and for easy use by customers. In addition, brand names must be carefully selected to fit the language of the country. Finally, any product information must be written to meet the laws of the country and to clearly communicate with the customers.

Distribution
Effective distribution of products to and within other countries is often one of the most challenging marketing functions. Decisions need to be made on the appropriate shipping method from country to country and within the new markets. How effective, reliable, and safe are the various methods of transportation and how are products normally stored and distributed?

Selection of the types of businesses in which the product will be sold is part of distribution. It is important to know the amount of time it will take from processing an order until the product is available to customers. Also, laws regulating distribution, including taxes, tariffs, and quotas, must be observed. Most countries require inspection of imported products, which must be arranged either before the product is shipped or when it reaches the country.

Selling
A country's customs play an important role in successful selling. Salespeople must be aware of the need to be formal or informal, who initiates conversations, how a business card is presented, and whether it is appropriate to conduct business during a meal. In some cultures, salespeople are expected to present a gift to a prospective customer while in other countries the gift would be seen as a bribe and would be illegal or offensive.

Financing
In most cases, the company will need to extend credit to the businesses that will distribute its products in the other country. It will also need to consider the accepted credit practices for consumers and ensure the procedures used to assist customers in purchasing conform to the country's laws and customs. The types of contracts and forms used, as well as the monetary system, may be different. While some credit cards are used internationally, they may not be the form of payment used by consumers in each country. The business also will need to develop relationships with banks and other financial organizations in the new country.

Pricing
It is not likely that customers from another country will have the same perception of value as those in the business's home country. Even if that perception is similar, a different money system is

used, and the costs of marketing are often higher, so prices may have to be changed. The customs of the country may require a new approach to deciding how prices are set, changed, and communicated to the customer.

Promotion Promotion is the marketing function where a country's customs and culture are particularly important. Promotion relies on effective communication. Language and pictures communicate a business's message to customers. There are many examples of promotional mistakes where words were not translated correctly or had very different meanings.

Promotional planning for international markets includes careful selection of the media to be used. Mass media may not be as available in some countries or may not be used for promotion. In many countries, television is not used extensively for advertising. Use of the Internet is growing rapidly in many countries, but it may not be used in the same ways for communication between businesses and customers.

Checkpoint ▶▶

What must be done before developing a marketing mix for a targeted international market?

18-3 Assessment

Key Concepts

Determine the best answer.

1. True or False: The concept of a market in other countries is the same as a market in this country.

2. The economy that is based on agriculture and raw material development through activities such as mining, oil production, and cutting timber is
   a. preindustrial
   b. industrial
   c. postindustrial
   d. self-sustaining

3. Which of the following should be completed first by a company entering an international market?
   a. establish product prices
   b. make sure companies are available to distribute the products
   c. adjust promotion to avoid stereotypes and biases
   d. gather reliable information about the market

4. True or False: The Internet is now an effective method for communicating between businesses and consumers in most international markets.

Make Academic Connections

5. **Math** A method to calculate a country's standard of living is to divide its GDP by its population. Use the Internet to determine the amount of the GDP for the top ten countries in the world and the population for each country. Use the information to calculate the standard of living for each country. Prepare a table that compares the GDP and standard of living rankings of the ten countries.

6. **Research** Choose a foreign country in which you might be interested in working if you have a career in international marketing. Use the library or Internet to gather information about the country's population, economy, culture, political and legal system, and business environment. Prepare a two-page report discussing what you learned.

Connect to DECA

7. A Chinese bicycle manufacturer wants to begin selling its most popular model in the United States and has asked your marketing team for advice on effective marketing. Prepare one important recommendation on selecting a target market and on each marketing mix element that will help the manufacturer understand the U.S. market for bicycles. Make a team presentation of your recommendations to your teacher (judge).

Chapter 18 Assessment

Check Your Understanding

Now that you have completed the chapter, check your understanding of the lessons with these questions. Record the score that best represents your understanding of each marketing concept.

1 = not at all; 3 = somewhat; 5 = very well

If your score is 42–50, you are ready for the assessment activities that follow. If you score 33–41, you should review the lessons for the items you scored 1–3. If you score 32 or less, you will want to carefully reread the lessons and work with a study partner on the areas you do not understand.

Can you—

___ describe several reasons for the growing importance of international trade?

___ differentiate between imports and exports?

___ identify why businesses decide to become involved in international trade?

___ provide examples of direct and indirect exporting?

___ demonstrate how to calculate a country's balance of trade?

___ discuss the differences between foreign production, foreign investment, and joint ventures?

___ identify why multinational businesses no longer think of themselves as located in one country?

___ describe the three broad categories of economies and how each affects international marketing?

___ list several factors about a country and its people that businesses need to consider when developing a marketing strategy?

___ provide examples of how marketing functions might need to change in international markets?

Review Marketing Terms

Match the terms listed with the definitions. Some terms may not be used.

1. A measure of the quality of life for its citizens
2. The difference between the amount of a country's imports and exports
3. The average output by workers for a specific period of time
4. The primary business activity is the manufacturing of products
5. Owning all or part of an existing business in another country
6. The change in the cost of a specified set of goods and services over time
7. Products or services purchased from another country
8. A company takes complete responsibility for marketing its products in other countries
9. Taxes placed on imported products to increase the price for which they are sold
10. Based on a mix of business and consumer products and services produced and marketed in the global marketplace
11. Products and services sold to people in other countries

a. balance of trade
b. business cycles
c. consumer price index
d. direct exporting
e. exports
f. foreign investment
g. foreign production
h. gross domestic product (GDP)
i. gross national product (GNP)
j. imports
k. indirect exporting
l. industrial economy
m. inflation
n. joint venture
o. multinational companies
p. postindustrial economy
q. preindustrial economy
r. productivity
s. purchasing power
t. quotas
u. recession
v. standard of living
w. subsidy
x. tariffs

Review Marketing Concepts

12. True or False: The total value of goods and services produced in the world is growing rapidly, having doubled in the five years before 2006.

13. True or False: Preindustrial economies offer good opportunities for foreign businesses, but these opportunities are limited due to the economies' needs and resources.

14. True or False: Most of the countries in the world have industrial economies.

15. True or False: The decisions of businesses to become involved in international business are always very carefully planned.

16. True or False: Because of cultural and language barriers, there is very little international trade in services.

17. True or False: There is almost no foreign investment in the United States by companies from other countries.

18. True or False: A multinational company usually competes with the same countries no matter in what part of the world it operates.

19. True or False: There is almost no similarity in the way a company markets internationally and the way it markets within its home country.

20. True or False: A country's gross national product (GNP) is usually larger than its gross domestic product (GDP) because the GNP includes foreign investments.

21. True or False: International free trade efforts include increasing the use of subsidies, quotas, and tariffs.

Marketing Research and Planning

22. In order to be successful, businesses that sell their products in other countries must be able to offer a product that has advantages compared to the competing products in the country.

    Look at several products you own or use regularly and identify five that were manufactured outside the United States. For each product, identify the part of the marketing mix (product, price, distribution, or promotion) that was the most important reason you decided to purchase the product. Then make a recommendation for U.S. manufacturers on how they can improve their marketing mix to be more competitive.

    Next, identify five products you own or use that were manufactured by U.S. companies. For each product, identify the part of the marketing mix that was the primary reason you selected that product rather than one manufactured in another country. Make a recommendation to foreign manufacturers on how they could offer a more competitive marketing mix.

23. Choose one of the following:
    a. Large piece of equipment used for road construction
    b. Vitamins and mineral supplements for use by consumers
    c. Movies

    d. Fresh flowers
    e. Auto repair service

    Assume you are deciding how to market the product or service to another country. For each of the nine marketing functions, describe a specific marketing activity that must be completed in order to market that product internationally.

24. Search the Internet for a site that contains economic and demographic statistics for various countries. Pick a continent or region with at least ten different countries. Using a computer database or spreadsheet program, compile a database of statistics for each country, including population, GDP, and GDP per capita. Sort and rank the countries by each of the statistics.

25. Use the Internet to search the U.S. Department of Commerce web site or another source for statistics on U.S. exports for the latest full year that has been reported. List the top ten countries for U.S. exports and the main types of goods and services they purchase. Now, complete the same activity for U.S. imports. Identify the top ten countries that sell goods and services to the United States and the main types of goods and services the United States imports from each country. Prepare two tables to illustrate your results.

Marketing Management and Decision Making

26. Businesses must make decisions that are ethical and socially responsible. When marketing products internationally, the cultures and values of countries may conflict. Business people may be criticized for decisions that seem to be positive and acceptable in another country but are not viewed as appropriate in their home country.

   The following scenarios describe ethical decisions faced by U.S. businesses when marketing in other countries. Read each scenario carefully and consider the effects of the decisions on the company, its customers, and the country in which it plans to market the products. Also, consider the business's social responsibility in the United States and internationally. For each scenario, write two paragraphs that describe how you would respond to the ethical situation facing the company and provide reasons for your decision.

   a. A prescription drug manufacturer has spent over five years of research to develop a new medication to help young children with asthma. The company is certain the medication is safe although there have been minor side effects in some who used it during testing. The company has spent over $40 million developing the medication and wants to begin selling it as quickly as possible to begin to recover those costs and return a profit. The U.S. Food and Drug Administration (FDA) requires an additional three years of testing before the medication can be approved for sale in the United States. A large international wholesaler is willing to purchase the drug and sell it over the Internet from its distribution facilities in another country that does not require the lengthy testing period. The procedure would allow people from any country, including the United States, to order the medication online as long as they could fax a letter from their physician certifying that the patient was under treatment for asthma.

   b. A U.S. airline recognized that the number of business people and vacationers traveling to the United States from a Southeast Asian country was growing faster each year than from any other country in that region. It wanted to enter the market and capture a large percentage of that growing business. However, it had to compete with a successful smaller airline based in the Asian country that already had many flights into the United States, making it difficult to get new customers. The U.S. company's advertising agency suggested it could find former employees of the smaller airline who would say that they were concerned about the safety and quality of the airline's service. The statements would all be true, but they clearly did not represent the beliefs of most of the company's employees. The goal would be to raise questions in the media about the airline, causing travelers to question whether they would fly with that airline. At the same time, the U.S. airline would begin an ad campaign promoting its expanded service to the United States as well as its quality and safety record.

   c. A hotel chain was considering a joint venture with a company in another country. The plan was to build five new hotels in resort areas that were growing rapidly. The businesses already located in the resorts were experiencing a great deal of success, and it was clear that other hotels would be built in the resorts as soon as companies could purchase the land and obtain financing. The advantage of the joint venture for the hotel chain was that the company it was working with already owned land in several of the resort areas and had available cash to begin hotel construction while additional financing was being arranged. As the hotel company management was preparing the paperwork to finalize the joint venture, it received a letter from a civil rights group providing evidence that the company with which it was planning to cooperate had an unwritten but clear policy to discriminate in its hiring practices. A check of the company's employment records showed that the employees were 96 percent white in a country that had a 35 percent nonwhite population. Also, no women had ever been promoted beyond the level of supervisor in the company. The management knew that if the joint venture was not successful, it was unlikely that they would find a similar company with which to work.

Food Marketing Individual Series Event

The Food Marketing Individual Series Event consists of a 100-question multiple-choice comprehensive exam and role-plays. The role-play portion of the event requires participants to accomplish a task by translating what they have learned into effective, efficient, and spontaneous action. Students have ten minutes to prepare their strategy for the role-play and an additional ten minutes to explain their strategy to the judge. The judge can ask questions during or after the presentation.

The highly competitive supermarket industry has tried new strategies to market and distribute products to consumers. Many of the smaller grocery stores have closed due to the competition from larger supermarkets. Larger supermarkets offer customers a wide array of goods and services. While grocery store customers are usually price-conscious, their loyalty can be fickle.

Fresh Produce is an independent neighborhood grocery store that is known for its fresh meats, vegetables, and fruits. Customer service is a top priority. Fresh Produce employees carefully bag groceries and carry them to the customers' vehicles. Fresh Produce also excels at fulfilling and delivering telephone orders. This service is greatly appreciated by senior citizens in the community. Employees at Fresh Produce know customers by name.

Some major supermarkets have unsuccessfully tried to sell groceries online. Fresh Produce believes that a web site showcasing its unique qualities could be a successful promotional tool.

You are a web designer who must design an attractive web site for Fresh Produce. You must explain how the web site will emphasize the grocery store's uniqueness and contribute to this image by offering features such as an online newsletter and recipes for healthy living. You must present a plan for collecting the e-mail addresses of Fresh Produce's loyal customers. The web site should provide clear instructions on how to order online and how to access coupons for items offered at Fresh Produce.

Performance Indicators Evaluated

- Identify ways that technology impacts business. (Information Management)
- Describe current business trends. (Information Management)
- Identify issues and trends in retailing. (Information Management)
- Explain ways that technology impacts food marketing. (Information Management)
- Explain issues and trends in the food marketing industry. (Information Management)

Go to the DECA web site for more detailed information.

Think Critically

1. How will senior citizens react to using Fresh Produce's web site? How can you overcome their objections?
2. How can the web site make Fresh Produce more efficient?
3. What type of contest could the web site offer customers?
4. Why must the web site be user-friendly?

www.deca.org

Managing Risks

©RUBBERBALL/GETTY IMAGES

Newsline

Successful New Products Are No Easy Task

American businesses are apparently finding it harder than ever to develop new products. Managers from America's top retail and manufacturing businesses were asked about the success rate of their new products. While the typical success rate had been reported at between 10 and 20 percent in the past, the managers responding to the survey indicated that only 8 percent of their new product ideas ever reach the market. Of those that are introduced to consumers, fewer than 20 percent succeed. Simple analysis of those results shows that nearly 99 percent of product ideas developed by businesses fail.

Why does it appear that new product results are moving in the wrong direction? The managers

participating in the survey believe it is because the costs of new product development are too high and it takes too long to see a profit. Therefore, companies are not willing to spend the time and money needed to develop new products. Another problem reported is the tendency for company managers to change new products to fit their own ideas rather than relying on research gathered from the target markets for the new products. When managers think they know more than customers about what will work and what will not work, the result may be a product that customers will not buy.

Managers report that their new product development process is much faster than it was in the

past. New products can be developed and moved to the market quickly. However, managers believe that is one of the biggest weaknesses of the process. When a company needs to move fast, it is more likely to make mistakes.

Think Critically

1. Why do you think business managers would change new products to fit their own ideas rather than follow their market research?

2. If companies can develop new products quickly and get them to the market faster than ever before, why aren't more new products successful?

school.cengage.com/marketing/marketing

Core Performance Indicators

- Understand economic systems to be able to recognize the environments in which businesses function
- Identify potential business threats and opportunities to protect a business's financial well-being

Supporting Performance Indicators

- Identify speculative business risks
- Explain the nature of risk management
- Identify factors affecting a business's profit
- Determine factors affecting business risk

Go to **school.cengage.com/marketing/marketing** and click on Connect to DECA.

Visual Focus

Businesses have to make decisions every day that involve some kind of risk. While risks can result in opportunities for business success, they can also lead to financial loss or business failure. Marketers need to understand the types of risks they face and ways for dealing with them. Risk management involves providing security and safety for the business and its customers and reducing risk. Marketers must consider the risks associated with each element of the marketing mix and address them as they are developing the marketing plan.

Focus Questions:

What service is being offered by Zurich in this advertisement? How do insurance providers help businesses manage risk? As this ad indicates, Zurich can help businesses identify hidden risks. Why are insurance companies better at finding hidden risks?

Locate another ad that focuses on risk. Share your example in class and explain the type of risk identified in the ad.

Assessing Business Risks

GOALS

- Explain why businesses take risks and how they are classified.
- Describe the four ways available for businesses to deal with risks.

KEY TERMS

risk, *p. 532*

opportunity, *p. 533*

natural risk, *p. 533*

human risk, *p. 533*

economic risk, *p. 533*

pure risk, *p. 533*

speculative risk, *p. 533*

controllable risk, *p. 534*

uncontrollable risk, *p. 534*

insurable risk, *p. 534*

uninsurable risk, *p. 534*

marketing matters

Risks can be classified in four ways—based on the source of the risk, result of the risk, control of the risk, and insurability of the risk. Business people deal with risks in one of four ways or in a combination of ways. They can avoid a risk by choosing an alternative that does not entail that risk. They can transfer a risk to someone else, usually at a cost. They can insure the potential loss from a risk. Or they can assume the risk and accept the consequences.

Describe a risky course of action that you chose to undertake in the recent past and the potential losses and gains that you faced. What was the outcome? Would you repeat your action if you faced the same risk again?

The Nature of Business Risk

Every year thousands of people decide to open their own businesses. Most entrepreneurs will use all of the money they have saved. They will borrow thousands of additional dollars. They may quit their current jobs to devote all their time to the new business. Each believes he or she has an idea that will attract customers, earn a living, and maybe even make a lot of money.

At the same time that thousands of entrepreneurs are opening new businesses, many others are closing their doors. Their dreams did not come true. They are disappointed and discouraged. Most lost the money they invested in the business. Many will never attempt a new business again.

When a person decides to open a business or a company decides to develop

What are some risks new business owners face?

©PHOTODISC/GETTY IMAGES

a new product, there is a chance for success and a chance for failure. The possibility that a loss can occur as the result of a decision or activity is known as **risk**.

Seeking Opportunities

Why do people invest a great deal of time and money in new businesses or products when there is a risk of loss? While there is a chance of loss, there is also an opportunity. An **opportunity** is the possibility for success.

Success takes many forms. For both individuals and businesses, it can mean recognition, being viewed as a leader, or providing personal satisfaction and satisfaction for others. An important measure of success in business is profit. The private enterprise economy is organized to encourage risk-taking. People invest money and take risks in business to make a profit.

Each of us takes risks every day. You might decide whether to speak to a new person you meet. The risk is that the person might not respond in a positive way. The opportunity is that you will establish a new friendship. You may have spent a great deal of time and effort in the past few years selecting difficult courses, completing homework, and preparing yourself for college. Nevertheless, there is a risk that your effort will not pay off. Your grades might not be high enough, or you may not have the money needed to attend the college you have chosen. But you have chosen to assume these risks for the opportunities provided by a college education.

Classification of Risk

Marketers need to understand the risks they may face in order to deal with them. There are four classifications of risk. The classifications are based on the source of the risk, the result of the risk, the control of the risk, and the insurability of the risk.

Source of the Risk Business risks generally arise from one of three things. A **natural risk** is caused by the

You can't forsee all injuries. But you can **plan for them.**

Insurance companies such as Liberty Mutual can help businesses plan for unexpected risks.

unpredictability of nature, such as the weather or an earthquake. **Human risk** arises because of the potential actions of individuals, groups, or organizations. The uncertainty associated with market forces, economic trends, and politics creates **economic risk**.

Result of the Risk A risk that presents the chance of loss but no opportunity for gain is known as a **pure risk**. When you are driving, you are at risk of being in an accident. If you have an accident you will likely suffer a loss. You could be injured, you could injure others, or there could be damage to the vehicles. You do not gain anything if you simply avoid an accident.

The result is different for other risks. If you have the chance to gain as well as lose from the risk, it is known as a **speculative risk**. If you invest money in the stock market, it is possible you could lose a great deal of money if the value of the stock goes down. On the other hand, there is an opportunity for making money if the stock price increases.

Control of the Risk A risk that can be reduced or even avoided by actions you take is a **controllable risk**. If you are concerned about losing jewelry or cash, you might decide to put it in a safe or a safety deposit box in a bank. If the roads are slippery, you can avoid driving or drive very carefully to reduce the chance of an accident.

If your actions do not affect the result of a risk, it is an **uncontrollable risk**. The weather cannot be controlled although the type of weather has a big impact on businesses such as farms. If the weather is favorable, farmers have the opportunity to grow and harvest crops. With poor weather, crops will not develop.

Insurability of the Risk If a risk is faced by a large number of people, if the risk is pure rather than speculative, and if the amount of the loss can be predicted, it is an **insurable risk**. For example, many people who own homes or buildings face the risk that their property could be destroyed by flooding. Insurance companies look at the amount of losses from flooding in past years and sell insurance that would pay for the buildings that could be damaged.

For an **uninsurable risk**, it is not possible to predict if a loss will occur or the amount of the loss. Speculative risks are usually not insurable. A business is not able to buy insurance that will pay for losses suffered because customers did not buy a new product. The person who invests in the stock market must accept any losses or gains because it is not possible to accurately predict the result of the investment.

Checkpoint ▶▶

Why do businesses take risks even when failure and financial losses may result?

Dealing with Risk

Clearly, people prefer success rather than failure. Marketing activities are subject to many risks. Every activity performed has the chance of success or failure. Each target market may provide a profit or loss for the company. Marketers need to be familiar with ways to deal with risks.

People responsible for risk management go through a careful process to decide the best way to deal with each risk faced by the business. Four methods can be considered (see Figure 19-1).

Avoid the Risk

It is possible to avoid some risks. For example, some shipping methods are more likely to result in lost or damaged products. To avoid that risk, the marketer would choose another shipping method. If there is evidence that it will be very difficult to enter a market to compete with several larger businesses, that market can

Dealing with Risk	
Management Strategy	**Result**
Avoid the Risk	Business chooses a different strategy that doesn't involve that risk
Transfer the Risk	Business lets another business complete the risky activity
Insure the Risk	Business pays insurer to reimburse the amount of losses from the risk
Assume the Risk	Business proceeds with the decisions made and takes full responsibility for the results

FIGURE 19-1
When facing a risk, managers have several choices of how to respond.

Judgment Call

Chinese Protest Starbucks at Cultural Landmark

The global economy is in full swing. Some of the largest American companies now have customers in almost every country on every populated continent. But there is always room for growth, and restaurant chains are always looking for new, high-traffic places to open profitable stores. What happens, though, when a company wants to open a store somewhere, but the citizens do not want that store in that place?

This is exactly what happened when Starbucks opened a store in China's historic Forbidden City in 2000. The former imperial palace is China's top tourist attraction. Chinese critics claimed that the presence of an American coffee shop in such a symbolic location was inappropriate and denigrated Chinese culture.

After years of controversy, and after considering many options, Starbucks decided to close the store in 2007. Starbucks continues to operate more than 250 stores in other parts of China.

Think Critically

1. What factors do you think went into Starbucks' decision to close its store?

2. What are the positive and negative results of the store closing for Starbucks?

3. Are there any places in the United States where companies should not open stores?

---

be avoided. Market research can be a good way for a business to anticipate such risks in advance.

Transfer the Risk

A common method of dealing with risk in marketing is to transfer the risk to others. A business that believes it will have difficulty collecting money from credit customers does not offer its own credit. Instead, it accepts several national credit cards. The credit card companies accept the risk for the opportunity to make a profit.

Fast FACTS

When businesses transfer the risk of credit to credit card companies, there is a cost. Every time a retail business accepts a national credit card like Visa or Discover for payment, it is charged a transaction fee of anywhere from one to five percent of the price of each sale.

Insure the Risk

If a financial loss is possible from the risk and that loss can be predicted, the risk can be insured. The company facing the risk pays a small amount of the potential loss to an insurer. If the loss occurs, the insurer guarantees payment to the company. The company accepts a small, certain loss (the cost of insurance) for protection from a larger, uncertain loss. Remember that many risks are not insurable because they are speculative.

Assume the Risk

A company that assumes a risk faces the risk and deals with the result. This strategy is sometimes referred to as *risk retention*. Some risks are unlikely to occur. Other risks have relatively small losses compared to the opportunities. And some risks are simply a normal part of doing business. In each case, it may be best to assume the risk because it will not have a serious negative effect on the business.

Sometimes a business *must* adopt a risk retention strategy because a risk

What outcomes does a business face if a product does not sell well?

cannot be avoided, transferred, or insured. For example, once a product is in the market, many things can happen that may result in much lower sales than expected. The business accepts that possibility and attempts to make the product as successful as possible. Economic conditions sometimes change rapidly, and the business faces a risk that was not anticipated. There is not enough time to make changes, so the business must assume the risk.

Checkpoint ▶▶▶

What are the four ways people deal with the risks that are inherent in operating a business?

19-1 Assessment

Key Concepts

Determine the best answer.

1. True or False: Speculative risks are generally uninsurable.

2. A(n) _____ is the possibility of success.

3. If your actions do not affect the outcome of a risk, it is a(n)
   a. pure risk
   b. uncontrollable risk
   c. human risk
   d. insurable risk

4. If a business decides to hire a third party to dispose of hazardous material rather than disposing of the material itself, the business is
   a. transferring the risk
   b. assuming the risk
   c. insuring the risk
   d. avoiding the risk

5. Which of the following conditions is necessary in order for a risk to be insurable?
   a. the amount of the potential loss must be unpredictable
   b. it must be a speculative risk
   c. it must be faced by a large number of people
   d. all of the above

Make Academic Connections

6. **Visual Art** Work as a group to draw or use technology to create a picture, graphic, or other visual representation of the different types of risks. Present your visual to the class and explain how each image represents a category of risk.

7. **Communication** How might the formation of a joint venture between two companies be a way of dealing with risk? What method of dealing with risk does it represent? Explain your answer in a one- to two-page report.

Connect to **◀DECA**
An Association of Marketing Students

8. Because many employees have trouble finding adequate day care for their children, your company is considering opening an on-site day care facility for employees' children. You have been asked to develop a report for management that outlines the potential risks involved with such a venture. You must also describe the four management strategies the company could use to handle the risk, weighing the pros and cons of each. Present your report to your teacher (judge) and recommend a strategy, explaining your choice.

Identifying Marketing Risks

GOALS

- Explain how changes in the economic and competitive environment create marketing risks.

- Describe marketing risks associated with each of the marketing mix elements.

KEY TERMS

risk management, *p. 537*

liability, *p. 539*

marketing matters

Marketing poses many different kinds of risks. Many factors combine to determine whether or not a business is successful. These factors include the type of competition, the economy, laws and regulations, technology, and customer needs. As factors change in unpredictable ways and market conditions shift, each poses risks and also offers opportunities. Marketers try to take advantage of the opportunities before conditions change at the risk of making a decision that ends up being inappropriate by the time it is implemented.

When a company has choices of marketing mixes, the company often selects the one that emphasizes its strengths and can be completed successfully. Yet each of the marketing mix elements—product, distribution, price, and promotion—is subject to certain risks. Marketers consider those risks when planning and implementing marketing decisions.

Make a list of five factors in the current economy and legal environment that pose serious risks to area businesses. Explain why each should be considered a risk.

The Risk of Change

Business people, including marketers, face a variety of risks. Risk management is an important marketing function. **Risk management** in marketing includes providing security and safety for products, personnel, and customers and reducing the risk associated with marketing decisions and activities. It is possible to analyze the marketing environment and marketing mix to identify the areas where risks are likely to occur.

Many factors combine to determine whether or not a business is successful. These factors include the type of competition, the economy, laws and regulations, technology, and customer needs. Each factor poses risks and also offers opportunities. Marketers are always looking for profitable new opportunities. They are willing to take a risk if there is a real possibility of success.

©PHOTODISC/GETTY IMAGES

How can a business provide security for its personnel and customers?

Economy

Businesses regularly face the risk of a change in the economy. Sales may be high and customers may value the product until faced with a recession. Suddenly, the business is unable to maintain sales, and profits fall. High unemployment or an increase in taxes could have similar effects on a business.

Laws and Regulations

Failure to follow laws and regulations can put a company at risk. For example, if a restaurant does not follow the proper health regulations, it could be shut down. Implementation of new laws or a court ruling can require a major change in operations. Even inadvertently breaking the law could have disastrous consequences for a business.

Competition

A company can lose market share by failing to consider the actions of its competitors. New technology and products can enter the market at any time. Those changes can have an immediate effect on a business. Consider how quickly a new video game or a new version of computer software can cause existing products to become outdated. When a few supermarkets and retail stores converted to self-service scanner technology to speed customer checkouts, other stores had to decide if they should install the equipment or risk losing customers.

How can technology, such as bar code scanners, be a risk factor for businesses?

©DIGITAL VISION/GETTY IMAGES

Customer Needs

Customer needs can change with little notice. Marketing responds to customers' needs, so such a change will cause a loss of business if the needs go unmet. Product life cycles illustrate how demand changes for products. Some life-cycle stages last only a very short time and require the business to make changes to maintain sales and profits.

Checkpoint ▶▶▶

How do changes in the economic environment affect marketing risks?

Risks to Elements of the Marketing Mix

When selecting from among several target markets, a company reduces its risk if it works with markets that can be clearly identified and located. The company should choose a market for which adequate information is available. A group of customers that has purchased a company's products before and has been very satisfied presents a better opportunity for introducing a new product than a group that has no previous experience with the company. When a company has choices of marketing mixes, the company will often select the one that emphasizes its strengths and that can be completed successfully.

Each marketing mix element is subject to some risks. Marketers should consider those risks when planning and implementing marketing decisions.

Product

The product itself faces several risks. Probably the most obvious is the risk of damage before the product is sold or used. The product needs to be designed so it is sturdy and durable. Packaging needs to protect the product while it is transported and stored. You have probably purchased products that were damaged or broken when you opened them. Perhaps they did not perform the way you expected when you used them. It is likely that you returned the product for a refund. You may have lost confidence in that product and others with the same brand name. A company risks a great deal with a poorly designed product.

Businesses must study how the consumer will use the product. They must be sure it is designed to meet consumer expectations for use. The product also must not spoil or deteriorate before it is used if it will not be consumed immediately. Many food products are dated to tell consumers when they were processed or when they should be used. Restaurants that prepare foods in advance must discard food if it sits too long before being ordered.

The product design must be up to date. If competing products have improvements or incorporate new technology, customers will quickly see the differences and switch to those brands. There are many examples of businesses that failed because their products did not change with the times. Even the most loyal customers will not

continue to buy the same product when they see that a superior design is available.

The product risk that concerns businesses most is liability. **Liability** is a legal responsibility for loss or damage. You frequently hear or read of a company that has to pay millions of dollars to a person who was injured while using the company's products. Companies are responsible for the design and use of their products. When injury, death, or financial loss occurs that involves a company's product in any way, the company may be held legally liable. Even services are subject to that risk. One of the highest expenses for physicians is the cost of malpractice insurance. The insurance is needed for protection from the cost of lawsuits brought by patients who believe they were mistreated or injured while under the doctor's care.

Distribution

When planning for the distribution of products, businesses need to be concerned about safety, security, and performance of distribution activities. Safety risks include the safety of products, buildings, and equipment. They also include the safety of people involved in distribution activities and customer safety. Whenever products

NETBookmark

Businesses supply information with all products informing customers about their safe handling and use. However, product warnings sometimes appear to be a bit excessive or unnecessary. Access school.cengage.com/marketing/marketing and click on the link for Chapter 19. Watch the video from ABC News reporter John Stossel about product warning labels. Do the warnings seem excessive to you? Why or why not? What kinds of risks do you think the companies using these labels are trying to prevent?

school.cengage.com/marketing/marketing

Working in Teams

As a team, brainstorm a list of consumer products that have become obsolete because of advances in technology. Next to each item, record the new consumer product that replaced it. For example, the typewriter was replaced by the computer. Then, discuss some actions that the manufacturers of the obsolete items might have taken to reduce or eliminate the risk posed by the new technology.

Coca-Cola Angolan Gamble Pays Off

In 2000, during a long-running civil war where even major roads were too risky for transporting goods because of guerrilla attacks, Coca-Cola opened a $36 million plant in Bon Jesus, Angola. Coca-Cola was already making a lot of money in Africa, but it saw room for growth and determined that the risk of opening a new plant in the unstable environment was worth the risk.

The risk paid off. With the help and protection of the Angolan government, which had a 45 percent stake in the Coca-Cola venture, production at the Bon Jesus plant reached 14 million cases in the first year, and Coca-Cola opened a second plant in Lubango in southern Angola. The government also helped put a damper on black-market suppliers of canned Coke who undercut prices by evading import duties.

Today, Coca-Cola is the largest consumer goods provider in Africa. Its sales on the continent continue to grow, and its production and distribution centers employ over 55,000 Africans and help strengthen the growing African markets.

Think Critically

1. How did the formation of a joint venture with the Angolan government help to reduce Coke's risks?

2. What political and economic risks did Coke take by investing in a country amid a civil war?

---

are moved from one location to another, there is a possibility for damage or injury. Procedures for product handling, storage, and transportation are planned carefully to reduce that possibility. People are trained in proper handling procedures. Safety standards are used in the design of facilities and equipment.

As products move through a channel of distribution, there are many opportunities for theft. Products can be stolen by burglars, by customers who shoplift, and by employees. Surveillance equipment, security procedures, and personnel are used to protect against theft.

You can see the importance that is placed on security when you visit most retail stores. Well-designed merchandise displays, security tags, video monitors, security personnel, and electronic sensors at all exits are used to reduce shoplifting and employee theft. Even with the thousands of dollars invested in security, shoplifting loss in many businesses is as much as 10 percent of sales. That loss adds tremendously to the price of products. It also requires special product handling procedures that are an inconvenience to customers and an extra expense to the business.

The final area of business risk related to distribution is the performance of the distribution system. Products need to be available to the customer at the place and time they are needed. If the product is not there, a sale is missed. Products must move through the distribution system efficiently. Ordering and order processing, inventory control, materials handling, and transportation must all work effectively. If an order is misplaced, a shipment is sent to the wrong location, or inventory levels are not maintained correctly, customers cannot obtain the products they want. Product damage is another concern in the distribution system. Procedures and equipment are used that protect the products while they move through the channel of distribution.

It is even possible for factors outside the control of a business to interfere with distribution. Poor weather conditions can slow transportation or damage or destroy buildings, equipment, and inventory.

SOS Skills for Occupational Success

Evaluate Information Sources

In modern society, we are bombarded by information. Electronic information is available through text messaging, blogs, spam, pop-ups, forums, and listservs. Traditional information outlets—such as radio, TV, newspapers, magazines, and billboards—also remain prevalent.

The Internet has dramatically changed the way information is gathered and distributed. By providing an inexpensive and instantaneous distribution channel for information, the Internet has enabled everyone, from individuals to special interest groups to large corporations, to distribute their message quickly and expansively. But the quality of that information can sometimes be questionable.

Traditional information outlets typically employ people to check the accuracy of data before it is published. In contrast, bloggers and other online information providers often work independently with no one monitoring the accuracy of their facts. Inaccurate information is frequently published online, and the speed of distribution simply compounds the problem.

Informed readers can use a variety of strategies to evaluate the accuracy of information. These strategies are appropriate for both electronic and traditional media.

1. **Consider the source of the information.**
   - Where did it come from?
   - Who published it?
   - What qualifications does this person or organization have to discuss this topic?
   - Is the person or organization widely recognized as a source of reliable information?
   - What other information can you find about the author or organization responsible for this information?

2. **Determine the objectivity of the information.**
   - Does the author have an obvious bias concerning the topic?
   - Are all sides of the issue presented, or only one point of view?
   - Is the language calm and reasoned or emotional and inflammatory?
   - Are the statements factual? Can they be proved?

3. **Identify the purpose for the information.**
   - To whom is the information directed?
   - Is someone trying to sell you something or change your mind?
   - Are opinions stated as facts?
   - Does the presenter express a preference for a person, group, or idea?

4. **Is the information current?**
   - Is this a topic on which it is important to have up-to-date information?
   - Is there copyright or footnote information that will help you determine when the content was created?

Develop Your Skill

Pick a topic that you know is controversial. Research a claim within that topic. Look for information that will support both sides of the claim. Gather information from both electronic sources and traditional sources.

After you have located a number of sources, compare and evaluate their accuracy, timeliness, and reliability using the above strategies. Prepare a table listing the sources and assign each one a "credibility rating" of 0–5. Explain how you arrived at that rating.

PHOTO: ©PHOTODISC/GETTY IMAGES

Price

Customers must see the product price as a value. They must also be able to afford the product. Companies face two risks when pricing products and services. The price can be set too high, reducing demand and causing products to remain unsold. On the other extreme, if products are priced too low, the company is unable to make a profit.

Setting a product price is very difficult. A number of factors enter into the price, including the costs of production, marketing, and operations. Any services offered, discounts, markdowns, and the cost of credit must be figured into the price for a profit to be earned. Every business in a channel of distribution must be able to make a profit after paying its costs. Finally, customers will usually compare the price of a product with those of competitors.

Promotion

The goal of promotion is to communicate with consumers to influence them to purchase the company's products. Anything that interferes with that goal is a business risk. The media need to perform as planned. If a radio or television commercial is not aired as planned, or if a newspaper or magazine is not distributed on schedule, the promotional plan is less effective. If a salesperson cannot meet with a customer or does not communicate effectively, sales are lost.

Just as companies are subject to product liability, there are legal responsibilities related to promotion. Information must be honest and accurate, or the company may be liable for the harm caused by inappropriate or illegal promotion.

Another area of risk is the damage that can result from other businesses'

To reduce the risks associated with introducing new products, French's used a coupon and a contest to encourage customers to try its new mustard flavors.

promotions or from information communicated by people or other organizations. Sometimes other companies' promotions contain misleading or incorrect information about a competitor's products. While it may be possible to get the company to stop using those promotions, damage may already be done. It is difficult to correct misinformation. Customers who have had a negative experience with a product will often tell many other people about their experiences. That word-of-mouth publicity can be very damaging.

Checkpoint ▶▶

For most businesses, what is the product risk that most concerns them?

What problems might occur if a newspaper ad contains inaccurate information?

19-2 Assessment

Xtra! **Study Tools**
school.cengage.com/marketing/marketing

Key Concepts

Determine the best answer.

1. Risk _____ in marketing includes providing security and safety for products, personnel, and customers as well as reducing the risk associated with marketing decisions and activities.

2. True or False: Product life cycles illustrate how demand changes for products.

3. The legal responsibility for loss or damage is called
   a. liability
   b. exposure
   c. indemnity
   d. insolvency

4. Which of the following is a risk associated with the product element of the marketing mix?
   a. a product is priced higher than a competitor's product
   b. a restaurant undercooks the food it prepares
   c. a television commercial is not aired as planned
   d. inventory is too low to meet customer demand

Make Academic Connections

5. **Ethics** To minimize competition risk, employees from a local restaurant regularly "keep tabs" on competitors by posing as potential customers. Do you think this is ethical? Explain why or why not. What are some ways a business can legitimately research the competition?

6. **Economics** The economy can be a contributing factor to the success or failure of a business. Examine the current state of the U.S. economy. Identify three potential risks a business faces today based on current economic conditions. Summarize these risks in a one-page report.

Connect to DECA

7. Your team members manage an auto parts company that provides parts and supplies to a wide variety of local auto repair businesses. As a team, talk about the types of distribution risks your business faces. Discuss some procedures your business can take to minimize performance errors in the distribution system. Develop a plan to implement those procedures. Make a three-minute team presentation of your plan to your teacher (judge).

Managing Marketing Risks

GOALS

- Explain how the various sections of the marketing plan should be used to avoid risks and limit the business's exposure to risks.
- Describe other ways to eliminate or control marketing-related risks.

KEY TERMS

surety bond, *p. 547*

product liability insurance, *p. 547*

professional liability insurance, *p. 548*

marketing matters

Businesses need to find ways to prevent risks from interfering with marketing plans, either by eliminating risks or minimizing the effects of risks that cannot be eliminated. The marketing plan provides an excellent tool for developing risk management strategies. Each of the three sections of the marketing plan includes elements related to risk management. The action plan needs to identify activities and responsibilities for controlling and reducing risks.

In addition to managing risks through the marketing planning process, businesses can effectively manage risks by training marketing personnel in safety and security policies and by purchasing various types of insurance to cover damages that arise from risks.

Make a list of the safety and security policies your school has that are designed to eliminate risks or reduce the damage potential of risks that cannot be eliminated entirely.

Handling Risks with Marketing Planning

With the large number of risks in marketing, businesses must find ways that prevent those risks from interfering with the marketing plans. The first goal should be to prevent risks. If it is not possible to prevent a risk, plans should be made to reduce the negative effects of a risk on the business and its customers. Remember that there are four ways to deal with risks. They are to avoid the risk, transfer the risk, insure the risk, or assume the risk. No matter which method is used, careful planning is needed. Risk management is so important to the success of a business that it should be incorporated into the company's marketing plan.

Developing a marketing plan provides an ideal opportunity for a business to

©DIGITAL VISION/GETTY IMAGES

Why is planning an important component of risk management?

identify potential risks and make plans to avoid or reduce those risks. Each of the three sections of a marketing plan provides opportunities to identify and develop plans for managing risks (see Figure 19-2).

Analysis

When completing a market analysis, information is gathered on current marketing strategies, competitors, the marketing environment, and strengths and weaknesses of the company. Each of these areas can be studied to determine risks and opportunities. Changes in the economy, new technology, and competitors' actions that can affect a business should be identified as part of the market analysis.

Strategy

The second section of the marketing plan is used to develop the marketing strategy. Target markets are identified and the marketing mix needed for each market is described. When identifying market segments within the target markets, the risks that exist in each market should also be examined. The study of marketing mix alternatives should also include a review of the possible risks. Likely, the business will have choices of mix alternatives. Some will be more risky than others.

For example, small retail businesses must decide whether to accept credit and debit cards and personal checks. The alternative is to accept only cash. Credit and debit cards add an additional expense for the business, and accepting checks is an added risk. Then again, the payment options may help attract customers who otherwise would not shop at the store. The business must decide if the lower risk and cost of accepting only cash is worth the potential lost business of credit customers. It will analyze the risks and compare them to the opportunities presented with each choice.

Action

The final section of the marketing plan is the action plan. In this section, the

Reducing Risk Using the Marketing Plan

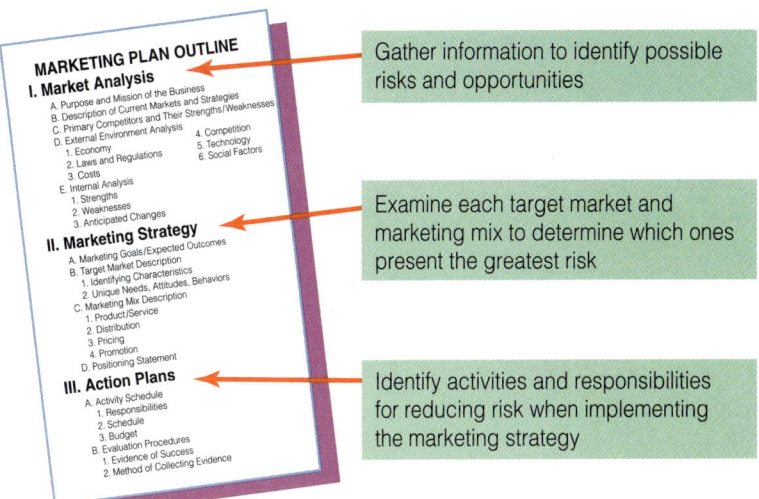

FIGURE 19-2

The marketing plan is a tool that can be used to reduce and manage risk. Risk management should be a part of each section of the marketing plan.

activities and responsibilities for the marketing strategy are identified. Some of the activities and responsibilities will relate to risk reduction. For example, people are given responsibility for quality control, scheduling and coordinating distribution activities, checking promotional plans to make sure they meet all

How can a business reduce risk by assigning responsibilities to its employees?

legal requirements, and the many other activities that deal with the risks in marketing. A responsibility of the marketing manager is to carefully review each part of the action plan to determine if risks are adequately addressed.

Checkpoint ▶▶▶

What are the three sections of the marketing plan that can be used to identify and develop plans to manage marketing risks?

Other Ways of Dealing with Marketing Risk

In addition to planning, most businesses implement specific security and safety plans, purchase insurance to protect against financial loss, and regularly review marketing activities and operations to identify and reduce risks.

Security and Safety

Because of its importance, security and safety planning is often a responsibility of people specifically trained in that area. In many businesses, security and safety management is part of the operations area. It must be coordinated throughout the business, including marketing activities. Marketers will work with security and

Fast **FACTS**

Every minute, an average of 640 acts of shoplifting occur in U.S. retail businesses. That adds up to more than 300 million occurrences per year. It is estimated that shoplifting costs retailers nearly $10 billion in losses annually.

safety experts to identify areas needing attention and procedures to use that will reduce those problems.

All marketing personnel should receive special training in safety and security procedures. They should:

How can retailers prevent shoplifting and theft?

©PHOTODISC/GETTY IMAGES

Figure This

Risks, Rewards, Expected Value

With almost any business or investment activity, the results are uncertain but not wholly unpredictable. In most cases, there is a known range of possible outcomes. For example, investing in a company's stock will result in a complete loss if the company goes bankrupt. On the other hand, if it does very well, the value of the stock might double or triple over a period of time.

Through detailed analysis, reasonably accurate estimates can be made of the likelihood of the various outcomes. Those estimates, expressed as probabilities, can be used to derive what is known as the "expected value" of a course of action. Expected value is calculated by multiplying each possible outcome by the probability of its occurrence and then adding all of the subtotals. That final sum is the expected value, although "expected value" is something of a misnomer since for any single action the outcome is not likely to be the expected value. Still, the expected

value can be used to determine whether a course of action is a worthwhile risk. For a large number of actions, the average outcome should approximate the average expected value.

Business people need to keep in mind that an expected value is only as good as the probability estimates from which it is derived. If a highly favorable outcome is given an unreasonably optimistic (high) probability, a risk might seem well worth taking when it actually is not.

Think Critically

1. In a game of chance played by flipping a coin, when a coin comes up heads the player wins $5, and if it comes up tails the player pays $5. If there is a 50% chance of getting heads or tails, what is the expected value of each flip?

2. What would the expected value be if the player had to pay $6 when the coin came up tails?

- know how to recognize problems
- know how to prevent accidents and injuries
- be aware of company policies regarding surveillance, shoplifting, and theft prevention

Salespeople and customer service personnel need to discuss risks and safety concerns related to product use with customers. Products and packaging should be analyzed to ensure that they meet all safety and health requirements. Information should be supplied with all products informing customers about safe handling and use of the products.

Insurance

One method of transferring risk is to purchase insurance. The payment of insurance premiums transfers some or all of

the financial loss for the insured risk to the insurance company. There are some common areas of marketing in which businesses purchase insurance.

Insurance on marketing personnel includes health and life insurance as well as surety bonds. A **surety bond** provides insurance for the failure of a person to perform his or her duties or for losses resulting from employee theft or dishonesty.

Property insurance protects the buildings, equipment, and in some cases, the inventory of the business. Liability insurance pays for damage caused to other people or their property. Theft insurance also provides property protection. There are several types of insurance available to protect against damaged and lost merchandise while it is being transported. Another important type of insurance is **product liability insurance**, which provides protection from consumer

Why do personal service businesses and professional organizations need insurance?

claims arising from the use of the company's products. Similar insurance is available for service businesses. **Professional liability insurance** protects against claims of negligent or harmful actions by business professionals. Examples of professional liability insurance include malpractice insurance for physicians and errors and omissions insurance for financial advisors, attorneys, and accountants.

Risk Reduction

Marketers are constantly searching for opportunities. Those opportunities include new target markets and improved marketing mixes. With every opportunity comes a certain amount of risk. Risks can never be eliminated entirely. However, careful planning and effective marketing management can help companies avoid some risks and limit damages.

The most important way to reduce risks is with careful planning. The marketing

Digital Digest

The Newest Business Risk

After the terrorist attacks on the United States in September 2001, security threats took on a much different meaning to U.S. businesses. They began paying increased attention to possible attacks on buildings, distribution systems, and sources of energy and raw materials. But computer security also became a greater priority.

Many security specialists believe that the greatest damage could be done to the United States by attacking its information and communication systems. A cyber attack could shut down air transportation, emergency services, major media, energy distributors, major financial centers like Wall Street, and many other forms of commerce.

In the past, the greatest threat to companies' computer systems had been hackers attempting to demonstrate their prowess in breaking through a corporate firewall or by utilizing a glitch in technology. But with the new awareness of terrorism, companies reassessed their vulnerability to a cyber attack from terrorists.

U.S. businesses now spend an average of 12 percent of their information technology budgets on security for their computer systems. Security experts warn that amount may not be enough, but the added attention to computer security certainly helps reduce the chances of a cyber attack.

Think Critically

1. What type of damage might result from a cyber attack on a large business?

2. How would your personal life be affected if there was a cyber attack on businesses supplying energy or communications?

plan provides a useful structure to identify risks and develop ways to deal with them. Another important method of reducing risk is with the careful selection and training of marketing personnel. Employees should be selected based on their concern about customers and their needs. Employees should want to perform their jobs effectively. Then they should be trained to follow safety and security procedures. Finally, all marketing employees should be constantly alert to possible risks that can cause problems for the business or harm to customers or other people. When problems are identified, changes should be made to reduce the risk and avoid damage or loss.

Checkpoint ▶▶

Which marketing personnel should receive special training in dealing with surveillance techniques and with safety and security risks?

19-3 Assessment

Xtra! Study Tools
school.cengage.com/marketing/marketing

Key Concepts

Determine the best answer.

1. Which of the following is the *first* step to take to reduce risk by using the marketing plan?
   a. gather information to identify possible risks and opportunities
   b. examine each target market and marketing mix to determine which ones present the greatest risk
   c. incorporate a risk retention strategy into the marketing plan
   d. identify activities and responsibilities for reducing risk when implementing the marketing strategy

2. True or False: Salespeople and customer service personnel do not need special training involving safety and security risks.

3. A _____ bond provides insurance for the failure of a person to perform his or her duties or for losses resulting from employee theft or dishonesty.

4. Malpractice insurance is an example of what type of marketing-related insurance?
   a. property insurance
   b. professional liability insurance
   c. theft insurance
   d. life insurance

5. True or False: The marketing manager is responsible for determining if marketing risks are adequately addressed.

Make Academic Connections

6. **Government** The Occupational Safety and Health Administration (OSHA) aims to ensure employee safety and health in the United States by working with employers and employees to create better working environments. Prepare a two-page report about OSHA focusing on its mission, history, and impact on workplace safety. Also, explain how compliance with OSHA regulations can help a business reduce workplace risks.

7. **Social Studies** Doctors' groups, patients, and insurance companies have criticized medical malpractice litigation as expensive, unpredictable, and inefficient. These critics claim that the cost of malpractice insurance has forced many doctors to go out of business. Others claim that the "malpractice crisis" is a myth. Research the issues surrounding medical malpractice litigation, including potential solutions to the problems. Present your findings in a three-page paper.

Connect to ◀ **DECA** An Association of Marketing Students

8. You manage a clothing store. The owner has asked you to prepare a presentation about the types of insurance your company should purchase to reduce risks. Develop a three-minute presentation using visual aids for your teacher (judge) in which you describe the types of insurance your company should have and explain why the company needs this type of insurance.

Chapter 19 Assessment

Xtra!
Quiz Prep
school.cengage.com/marketing/marketing

Check Your Understanding

Now that you have completed the chapter, check your understanding of the lessons with these questions. Record the score that best represents your understanding of each marketing concept.

1 = not at all; 3 = somewhat; 5 = very well

If your score is 42–50, you are ready for the assessment activities that follow. If you score 33–41, you should review the lessons for the items you scored 1–3. If you score 32 or less, you will want to carefully reread the lessons and work with a study partner on the areas you do not understand.

Can you—

__ distinguish between a risk and an opportunity?

__ explain why businesses take risks?

__ identify the various ways risks are classified?

__ describe the four ways available for businesses to deal with risks?

__ define the term *risk management?*

__ explain how changes in the economic and competitive environment create marketing risks?

__ describe marketing risks associated with each of the marketing mix elements?

__ explain how the various sections of the marketing plan can be used to avoid risks?

__ discuss the role of insurance in risk management?

__ describe other ways to eliminate or control marketing-related risks?

Review Marketing Terms

Match the terms listed with the definitions. Some terms may not be used.

1. A risk that presents the chance to gain as well as the chance to lose

2. A risk that is caused by the unpredictability of nature, such as the weather

3. A risk that can be reduced or even avoided by actions you take

4. Provides protection from claims arising from the use of the company's products

5. A risk that is present when a person's actions do not affect the result

6. A risk that is faced by a large number of people, is pure rather than speculative, and the amount of the loss can be predicted

7. The possibility for success

8. A risk that is caused by the uncertainty of market forces, economic trends, and politics

9. A risk that presents the chance of loss but no opportunity for gain

10. In marketing, it includes providing security and safety for products, personnel, and customers as well as reducing the risk associated with marketing decisions and activities

11. A risk for which it is not possible to predict if a loss will occur or the amount of the loss

12. The possibility that a loss can occur as the result of a decision or activity

13. A risk that arises because of the potential actions of individuals, groups, or organizations

14. A legal responsibility for loss or damage

15. Provides insurance for the failure of a person to perform his or her duties or for losses resulting from employee theft or dishonesty

a. controllable risk
b. economic risk
c. human risk
d. insurable risk
e. liability
f. natural risk
g. opportunity
h. product liability insurance
i. professional liability insurance
j. pure risk
k. risk
l. risk management
m. speculative risk
n. surety bond
o. uncontrollable risk
p. uninsurable risk

Review Marketing Concepts

16. If a business chooses an alternative strategy because the strategy does not pose a particular risk, what kind of risk management strategy is it practicing?
    a. avoiding risk
    b. transferring risk
    c. insuring risk
    d. assuming risk

17. When a business hires another company to perform a risky activity that it does not want to undertake itself, it is practicing which type of risk management strategy?
    a. avoiding risk
    b. transferring risk
    c. insuring risk
    d. assuming risk

18. When a business forms a joint venture with other companies that are better prepared to handle certain risks, it is practicing which type of risk management strategy?
    a. avoiding risk
    b. transferring risk
    c. assuming risk
    d. all of the above

19. If a risk cannot be avoided, transferred, or insured, a business must adopt a risk _____ strategy.

20. True or False: A surety bond is a financial investment that pays a guaranteed rate of return and cannot decrease in value over the stated term.

21. A(n) _____ risk presents the chance for loss but no opportunity for gain.

22. Business people assume the risk of failure in order to gain the _____ for success.

23. Incorrect or inadequate product information is a risk associated with the _____ element of the marketing mix.

24. Late delivery of a product is a risk associated with the _____ element of the marketing mix.

25. When businesses buy insurance to cover their risk of financial loss, they exchange the certain cost of the _____ for the uncertain cost of the covered damages.

26. The three sections of a marketing plan are marketing _____, marketing _____, and _____.

27. Employees should be trained to
    a. be aware of company safety policies
    b. recognize problems
    c. prevent injuries
    d. all of the above

28. True or False: The marketing plan is not an effective tool for businesses to use to help avoid risks.

29. A toy company that manufactures a motorized scooter would most likely have _____ insurance to protect against claims of injuries due to use of the scooter.

Marketing Research and Planning

30. The management of a local drug store has just received the monthly figures for gross sales and losses due to shoplifting for the past year (see the table).
    a. Calculate the percentage of gross sales lost to shoplifting each month.
    b. Calculate the total gross sales and the total dollars and percentage of sales lost to shoplifting for the year.
    c. Develop a bar graph by month showing the dollar amount lost to shoplifting.

31. Interview a local businessperson concerning the types of risk faced by his or her business. Use the following questions as a guide for your discussion, but do not limit yourself to these questions.

Month	Gross Sales	Dollar Losses Due to Shoplifting
January	$200,356	$2,003.56
February	237,595	4,039.11
March	377,920	7,558.40
April	394,395	9,859.75
May	420,400	4,204.00
June	310,497	7,762.42
July	292,304	2,923.04
August	230,422	5,760.55
September	379,295	11,378.85
October	599,395	29,969.75
November	735,284	40,440.62
December	923,502	55,410.12

- What industry is your business in?
- What types of risk does your business face?
- How can you prevent, reduce, or avoid these risks?

After you have completed your interview, bring your results to class and share them with your classmates. Tabulate the class results and answer the following questions.

a. What types of risks did each business name?
b. Are there similarities and/or differences in the types of risks faced by various businesses?
c. What types of solutions or remedies did the businesses employ to prevent, reduce, or avoid their risks?

32. The best method of reducing risk is to be an informed marketer. The information needed by a marketer is usually gained by maintaining a marketing information system and doing specific market research. Marketers cannot make good decisions without knowing as much as possible about all internal and external influences on their products or services. Using your knowledge of marketing information, describe a marketing risk associated with each of the following areas. Explain how a marketing information system can reduce the risk.

a. New tax laws
b. Increased cost of raw materials needed to manufacture your product
c. Possible strike of transportation workers
d. Price-cutting tactic of a major competitor

33. You are a marketing student and a part-time employee of an ice cream store. You decide that you need to explain to your manager the value of competitive positioning in reducing the risks associated with operating the business. Recently, a chain of ice cream stores has opened in your town. They have taken many of your customers away. Your manager is unsure of how to respond to these problems. In your discussion, remember to explain problems versus opportunities, competitive positioning, and customer satisfaction.

Marketing Management and Decision Making

34. Digital televisions that can also access the Internet are gaining in popularity although design standards are still unsettled and most people have had little or no experience with them. It is predicted that in the near future, these systems will replace most standard televisions. Millions of dollars have been invested in the research and development of these systems. Using your knowledge of new product development and risk management, answer the following questions:

a. What type of risk is involved in the development of this revolutionary product?
b. How can a company attempt to minimize the risks? Can it avoid these risks completely?
c. Explain how the steps in the new product development process help minimize risk.

35. Using correct pricing strategies is an effective way of managing risk. Explain how the following pricing strategies are used in effective risk management:

a. Penetration pricing
b. Price skimming
c. Non-price competition
d. Discounts
e. Price lining

36. Search the Internet for the web site of an insurance company that specializes in insuring business risks. Write a one-page report on the types of services it offers, the types of business risks it insures, and how it uses its web site to market its insurance coverage to businesses.

37. Search the Internet for a news article describing a corporate bankruptcy filing or financial reorganization. Describe the circumstances that led to the company's financial problems and explain how it failed to successfully manage the risks it faced. What could it have done differently to avoid those risks or minimize the damage it suffered?

Business Services Marketing Individual Series Event

The Business Services Individual Series Event consists of a 100-question, multiple-choice, comprehensive exam and role-plays. The role-play portion of the event requires participants to translate what they have learned into effective, efficient, and spontaneous action. The five performance indicators specify the distinct tasks participants must accomplish. Students have ten minutes to prepare their strategy for the role-play and ten additional minutes to explain their strategy to the judge. The judge can ask questions during or after the presentation.

Some of the nation's largest banks are offering online banking through the use of cell phones. Banks send customers a text message when their account balance falls below a certain level or unusual activity occurs in their account.

Currently consumers' interest in cell phone banking is limited. Young consumers who are comfortable using their cell phones to browse the Internet are the most likely users of the newest bank services. Banks do not charge for cell phone services, but this does not mean that the service is free. The cell phone banking services can increase the customer's cell phone bill because of charges incurred for text messages received. Many cell phone customers have plans that do not include online minutes. They will incur extra charges for time spent online monitoring their account balance.

Banks that offer cell phone banking have security measures to protect customers. Banks require customers to use a six-digit access code to use the banking service. Customers will not be liable for losses caused by fraud, but it can be a difficult process to get the money back. Customers who choose to use cell phone banking should make sure the bank requires the use of a password or PIN (personal identification number) to access cell phone accounts and should contact the bank immediately if the cell phone is lost or stolen.

You must prepare a presentation to persuade customers to use cell phone banking and present it to the bank's CEO (judge).

Performance Indicators Evaluated

- Describe the use of technology in the product/service management function. (Product/Service Management)
- Identify consumer protection provisions of appropriate agencies. (Product/Service Management)
- Explain the concept of product in business services. (Product/Service Management)
- Describe the concept of promotion in business services. (Promotion)
- Analyze product information to identify product features and benefits. (Selling)

Go to the DECA web site for more detailed information.

Think Critically

1. Which age groups should be targeted first for cell phone banking?

2. Why might customers hesitate to use cell phone banking?

3. What joint venture opportunities exist for the banks and cell phone providers?

4. Will the growth of cell phone banking be gradual or rapid?

www.deca.org

Marketing Requires Money

©BLEND IMAGES/JUPITER IMAGES

Newsline

Improving Quality While Cutting Costs

Xerox was focused on cutting costs and increasing profits when it decided to reduce the number of administrative service centers from 36 to 3 in 1999. At the same time, it reorganized its sales organization to broaden the responsibilities of the salespeople to include customer service and administrative tasks. The results were disastrous. Billing errors resulted in customers receiving invoices for products they never ordered or prices to which they never agreed. Months were spent resolving customer complaints. Customers left, revenues decreased, employee morale dropped, and turnover increased.

With the help of General Electric Capital, Xerox discovered a way to change its operations using a tool called Lean Six Sigma. It evaluates all work from the simplest to the most complex throughout the company, removing unnecessary steps and improving those that remain. It brings together people from each department involved in a process to evaluate it and make changes.

The Lean Six Sigma process focused the attention and energy of Xerox on two important issues—how to get people working together and how to maintain both quality and efficiency in every procedure. Its impact soon became evident. The time taken to design and build a complex machine was reduced by a full year. Reviewing a document management process resulted in a savings of nearly $200,000. Xerox's sales and profits have since rebounded, and both employee and customer satisfaction have been restored. Cost cutting alone did not make the difference. It required a company-wide commitment to improving the work process.

Think Critically

1. Why did the efforts of Xerox to cut costs have such a negative result?

2. Why does involving people from several departments increase the chances of improving quality?

school.cengage.com/marketing/marketing

Prepare for Performance

This chapter develops the following Performance Indicators from the DECA Competitive Events program.

Core Performance Indicators

- Analyze cost/profit relationships to guide business decision making
- Manage financial resources to ensure solvency
- Understand tools, strategies, and systems used to maintain, monitor, control, and plan the use of financial resources

Supporting Performance Indicators

- Determine relationships among total revenue, marginal revenue, output, and profit
- Describe the concept of economies of scale
- Understand promotional and marketing budgets
- Plan sales activities to meet sales quotas

Go to **school.cengage.com/marketing/marketing** and click on Connect to DECA.

Some think relaxing moments.

We think hard-working money.

Investment Banking • Private Banking • Asset Management

We look at things from a different perspective – for the benefit of our clients. By building on our experience and expertise globally, we help our clients realize new opportunities. This has been our ambition since 1856. www.credit-suisse.com

Thinking New Perspectives.

CREDIT SUISSE

©CREDIT SUISSE

Visual Focus

Although marketing is vital to the success of a business, it can be a big expense for the business. Expenses are incurred for each element of the marketing mix—product, distribution, price, and promotion. The costs of marketing activities must be carefully planned and monitored. If marketing costs are not controlled, profits will suffer. Marketers must be skilled at financial management. Financial forecasts, budgets, and financial statements can help marketers anticipate expenses and revenues related to marketing activities. This information can be used to develop marketing plans that will meet the needs of both customers and the business.

Focus Questions:

What is the focus of the advertisement for Credit Suisse? Why do both consumers and businesses need to manage their finances? What are the benefits to both? Discuss with other students the importance of financial planning for a business. How could poor financial planning affect a business?

Marketing Affects Business Finances

GOALS

- Explain how marketing affects a business's financial planning.
- Define short- and long-term marketing expenses and the various types of financing for marketing activities.

KEY TERMS

revenue, *p. 556*

capital expenses, *p. 559*

operating expenses, *p. 560*

marketing matters

Marketing can be very expensive. There are several important categories of marketing costs including capital expenses, inventory costs, and operating costs. Sources of financing need to be developed for each category of costs. Those sources include financial institutions, credit offered by sellers, cash available in the business, and money obtained from the sale of products and services.

Marketing activities also affect the revenue of a company. Target markets and marketing mixes should be studied to identify ways to increase revenue and control costs. The result should be increased profits for the company.

Choose a local business or nonprofit organization in your area. Identify what you believe are the primary types and sources of revenue and expenses. Discuss why the business or organization must carefully plan and monitor both its revenues and expenses.

Marketing Costs Affect Business Success

Marketing costs money. On average, 50 percent or more of the retail price of products and services is needed to pay the cost of marketing activities. Therefore, managing marketing costs is important to the profitability of a business. If marketing costs are carefully controlled, there is more money available to use for important activities such as marketing research, product improvement, and customer services. The result should be greater customer satisfaction. On the other hand, if marketing costs are not well managed, the company does not have the money to improve the marketing mix. Production costs may need to be reduced, marketing activities cut back, or prices increased to customers. The result is a product or service that is less satisfying to customers and not as competitive with other brands.

In the end, there will be reduced profits for the company. This makes financial management an important marketing skill.

The Importance of Finances

One of the results of effective marketing is **revenue**—the money received from the sale of products and services. In order to sell products, money must be spent to pay for the products and services to be sold. The cost of operating and managing the business must be covered. The expenses of the marketing activities needed to facilitate the exchanges between the business and its customers must be paid. When all of those costs are subtracted from the revenue, the result is a profit or loss for the business. This basic financial equation is:

Revenue − Costs = Profit or Loss

Even in nonprofit businesses or other organizations, finances are important. If the expenses of those organizations are higher than the available funds, they cannot operate at the level they would prefer. If expenses exceed revenue, they cannot offer the products and services their clients need or expect.

For example, a day care center might operate as a nonprofit organization, but it is still involved in marketing. The center must offer the appropriate services in a safe and comfortable facility. It must be open when clients need child care services, and it must offer affordable prices. The organization needs to communicate with current and prospective clients about the center's services. If the revenue collected from the clients is not adequate to support the marketing mix, the center will not be able to continue to operate. Therefore, the manager of the day care center must carefully plan and control finances in order to keep the center open and available to families in the community.

The Role of Marketing in Financial Planning

Most large organizations have departments that deal specifically with financial planning and management. Experts in finance and accounting are responsible for maintaining the best financial position for their company. These experts assist other managers with planning. They maintain financial resources and records and provide information on revenue and expenses.

Even small businesses and other organizations usually have assistance to help managers with financial planning and record keeping. A business may employ an accountant full- or part-time, use an accounting service, or consult a financial planner. Several easy-to-use computer software programs can help even the newest and smallest organizations with financial decisions.

While marketers may employ people and other resources to help with financial planning, they are still responsible for the

©PHOTODISC/GETTY IMAGES

Why is it important for all types of businesses to increase revenues and control marketing costs?

revenue and expenses related to marketing activities. Marketers need to identify ways to increase revenues while controlling the costs of marketing. They must decide which markets present the most profitable opportunities and which choices in a marketing mix are the most cost-effective.

Target Markets A variety of decisions that marketers make affects the financial performance of a company. One example is the choice of target markets. Suppose a company has a choice between two markets. One market has a smaller number of potential customers, but those customers spend a higher percentage of their income on the product. There are also fewer competitors. Would this be a good fit for the company? Also, what about international markets? On one hand, it may be difficult and expensive for the business to enter a distant market with which it has no experience. If the business is not successful in the market, a great deal of money will be lost. On the other hand, successful entry could mean substantial profits for many years to come and opportunities to enter adjoining markets in other countries. In each of these examples, decisions about the target markets determine the amount of sales and revenue that can be obtained.

Marketing Mix In the same way, decisions about the marketing mix have an important impact on the company's financial resources. As the product element of the marketing mix is developed, marketers may decide that additional customer services or improved packaging to prevent product damage is needed. Each of those choices increases the cost of the product. The changes may also result in increased sales or customers who are willing to pay more because of the improvements.

Distribution decisions can also increase expenses. Examples include using several channels for distribution or operating regional warehouses to reduce the time needed to get products to customers. Expenses involved with the pricing element include offering credit, coupons, or rebates. Expenses associated with the promotion mix element include more frequent advertising, direct marketing efforts such as telemarketing, or additional training for salespeople. Each time marketers consider changes in the marketing mix, they need to study the costs of those changes and predict the effect of the changes on sales.

Checkpoint ▶▶

Why are marketing and its effectiveness so important to an organization's financial planning process?

Managing Marketing Costs

To determine the amount of money needed for marketing, marketing expenses need to be classified as either long term or short term. Long-term expenses are for items that the company can use for several years. Short-term expenses are for current activities or items used within a short time, typically less than one year. Long-term expenses are usually paid over an extended period of time. They are often financed by borrowing money from a bank or other financial institution. Normally, short-term expenses must be paid when they are purchased. Sometimes they are financed with credit from the seller and must be paid within one or a few months.

Long-Term Expenses

Most long-term business costs apply to production or operations rather than marketing. The costs of land, buildings, and equipment are the typical expenses in this category. Some marketing plans identify land and building needs. A company that distributes products may need buildings, vehicles, and equipment for product storage and handling. Manufacturers using

©DIGITAL VISION /GETTY IMAGES

How would you classify the construction costs for a new retail site?

direct sales to customers through factory outlet stores need to build or rent facilities and equipment for retail operations. The increased use of technology in other parts of marketing requires investments in special equipment. For example, computers are essential for effective marketing research and marketing information management. Companies that use telemarketing or provide customer information and service often invest in high-speed Internet access, telephone systems, computers, and other office equipment. Advertising and other types of promotion require sophisticated audio, video, and print production equipment and facilities. While most companies hire advertising agencies and production companies to develop their advertising and promotional materials, some larger companies maintain their own facilities, equipment, and personnel for those tasks.

Short-Term Expenses

Most marketing expenses result from performing specific marketing activities that are completed in a short period of time. These types of expenses depend on the marketing mix, but most businesses commonly incur short-term expenses in areas such as salaries and wages, administrative costs, operating expenses, order processing, customer services, advertising and promotion, and transportation costs.

Financing Marketing Activities

An important part of financial planning is identifying the sources of money needed to pay for marketing activities and expenses. Marketers work with a company's executives and financial managers to identify financial needs. They must also identify the methods that will be used to obtain the needed money. The three main types of financial needs are capital expenses, inventory expenses, and operating expenses.

Capital Expenses
Long-term investments in land, buildings, and equipment are **capital expenses**. They are usually financed with money borrowed from a financial institution such as a bank or insurance company. Some manufacturers provide long-term loans to their customers to help finance a major equipment purchase. It is also possible to lease equipment and buildings instead of buying them. The financial personnel of an organization are usually responsible for arranging the financing of capital purchases.

Creative ad campaigns, such as the Chick-fil-A ads, can be a big marketing expense but are designed to increase sales and revenues.

Inventory Expenses
The assortment and quantities of products that a company maintains for sale to customers is inventory. Inventories for manufacturers are produced with the anticipation that they will be sold to customers. For other channel members, inventories are purchased and then resold to their customers. The cost of the inventory is not recovered until the products are sold and the customer pays for the purchase.

Financing of inventory is usually done in one of two ways. Short-term loans may be obtained from financial institutions. Most banks will not loan the full value of the inventory since it may not sell as expected. The other common method of financing inventory is through credit extended by the seller. Since most sellers will finance the sale for only a short period, often 30 to 60 days, the purchasing

Get the Message

Billboards Enter the Computer Age

Billboards are perhaps the oldest form of advertising, going back to when merchants in small towns put signs out to attract customers to their shops. Today, they line many of the nation's highways and interstates, advertising hotels, restaurants, theme parks, radio stations, and much more. Although the media dollars spent on outdoor advertising is only about 15 percent as much as television, billboards remain effective, especially for local businesses.

Some advertisers see billboards as an out-of-date medium when compared to the flash of television and Internet. But technology is changing that. While a traditional billboard message remains static for a month or more, new electronic billboards allow for bright, animated messages. High-traffic places like Times Square in New York

is a veritable carnival of lighted, animated, spectacular billboards. These types of billboards are expensive, but they can be very captivating, and they allow advertisers to deliver dynamic messages to their audience. The message can even change from moment to moment during the day.

Although electronic billboards are generally limited to extremely high-profile areas, they have been popping up more and more on highways across the country. While they may never completely replace traditional static billboards, we will probably be seeing much more of them in the future.

Think Critically

1. What about billboards makes them especially appropriate for local businesses?

2. What types of businesses might change the message on their billboard depending on what time of day it is?

---

company must be able to sell the inventory quickly to pay for the order on time. In both cases, the purchaser pays interest on the money borrowed and factors the cost of financing into the price of the products.

Operating Expenses The final category of marketing expenses is operating expenses. **Operating expenses** are the costs of day-to-day marketing activities. They include salaries and wages, materials and supplies, advertising and special promotions, and customer services.

Working in Teams

As a team, make a list of expenses typically incurred by all businesses. Next to each expense, record whether it is a capital expense, inventory expense, or operating expense. Then discuss potential ways to finance each of the expenses your team has listed.

Operating expenses include the variety of other marketing activities completed regularly to sell products and services and to meet customer needs. Operating costs are normally paid as they are incurred or shortly thereafter. The money for payment of operating expenses comes from the cash on hand in the business and the income from sales. Monthly and weekly budgets and financial reports monitor operating expenses and income to ensure that money is available to pay the expenses. Marketing managers pay careful attention to operating budgets and make changes rapidly if it appears that operating expenses are too high or revenues are too low.

Checkpoint ▶▶

What is the difference between capital expenses and operating expenses in terms of how they typically are financed?

Why is it important for marketing managers to monitor operating expenses?

20-1 Assessment

Key Concepts

Determine the best answer.

1. True or False: If costs consistently exceed revenues, a business cannot offer the products and services its clients need or expect.

2. Most marketing expenses result from
   a. specific marketing activities that are completed in a short period of time
   b. long-term costs such as building and equipment
   c. unexpected costs arising from changes in the marketplace
   d. paying off long-term loans used to finance marketing activities

3. _____ expenses are usually financed with money borrowed from a financial institution such as a bank or insurance company.

4. Which of the following is *not* considered an operating expense?
   a. salaries and wages
   b. advertising
   c. major equipment purchase
   d. customer services

Make Academic Connections

5. **Economics** Read through the business section of your local newspaper or an online edition of a newspaper from another community and find at least one story related to a company's capital expenses. Find a second story related to another company's operating expenses. Summarize each article and explain why you classified each as relating to capital or operating expenses.

6. **Math** Suppose your company takes a $25,000 loan for one year at 8 percent interest with equal monthly payments. Calculate the monthly payment on this loan so the principal and interest will be paid at the end of the year.

Connect to DECA

7. You work as a classroom aide at a nonprofit day care center. Today, the director of the center remarked to you that she had been told by a board member not to worry about watching expenses and revenues because the day care center is a nonprofit organization. She asked you to prepare a brief but tactful report explaining to the board member why this perception is incorrect. Present your report to your teacher (judge).

Tools For Financial Planning

GOALS

- Describe the principal planning and operating tools used by business.
- Detail how marketers develop forecasts, budgets, and financial statements.
- Explain the kinds of financial analyses marketers perform to increase profits.

KEY TERMS

financial forecast, *p. 562*

budget, *p. 563*

financial statement, *p. 564*

income statement, *p. 564*

balance sheet, *p. 565*

assets, *p. 565*

liabilities, *p. 565*

capital, *p. 565*

marketing matters

Three factors contribute to the financial performance of a business—revenue, costs, and results (profit or loss). Managers are responsible for operating the business so that customers are satisfied and the business makes a profit. Several financial tools help managers meet that responsibility. Those tools can be classified as planning tools and operating tools.

The primary planning tools are forecasts and budgets. Forecasts predict long-term financial performance, generally for periods of a year or longer. Budgets are shorter-term tools used to develop detailed plans for specific activities. The primary operating tools are income statements and balance sheets. Managers use these summaries of financial performance to determine the effectiveness of business operations. Marketers must be able to interpret financial statements to develop marketing plans and improve decision making.

Obtain a copy of an annual report for a publicly owned corporation from the library or Internet. Make copies of the income statement and balance sheet in the annual report. How many months or years of financial information does each statement cover? What items are reported on the financial statements? Discuss with other students why understanding the financial information is important to managers and investors.

Planning and Operating Tools

Businesses have a number of tools they can use for planning and operating the company. These tools include forecasts, budgets, the income statement, and the balance sheet.

Planning Tools

Businesses operate from plans. Plans identify the goals of the business and determine the best ways to achieve those goals. Business plans guide the activities of employees. Plans are used to evaluate the progress of the business in meeting its goals. Two important types of financial plans are forecasts and budgets.

Forecasts Plans are based on estimates of future events. Managers want those estimates to be as accurate as possible. They prepare forecasts to aid in planning. A **financial forecast** is a numerical prediction of future performance related to revenue and expenses. Forecasts are usually made for a period of at least one year or more into the future.

Digital Digest

Screen Out Costly Customers

The layout of a typical income statement indicates why sales or revenues are commonly referred to as the "top line" and profits are called the "bottom line." In between top-line sales revenues and bottom-line profits are all the costs. A key to business success is making sure that as much of the top line as possible makes it to the bottom line rather than being eaten up by expenses.

Modern information management systems make it possible to analyze in detail which parts of a business are the most efficient in terms of the percentage of revenues that are delivered to the bottom line. In many cases, data can be analyzed customer by customer.

Marketing experts recommend two steps to increase that percentage—screen out undesirable customers and increase sales to desirable existing customers. By getting rid of hard-to-please customers who cost more than they are worth, businesses have more time to spend on cultivating satisfied customers who are likely to buy more. Unfortunately, too many businesses spend 80 percent of their time and energy trying to appease chronic complainers who account for 20 percent of their sales.

They would be better off turning that ratio on its head by identifying their best existing customers and spending 80 percent of their time and energy on them. Good, reliable customers are the least expensive sources of increased sales revenue. Tracking marketing costs by customer allows businesses to see which are supporting the bottom line and which are eating it up.

Think Critically

1. How do information management systems make it easier to screen out undesirable customers?

2. Why are existing customers usually a business's best prospects for increased sales?

Some companies develop forecasts for as long as five years, although they are usually not as accurate as shorter forecasts. Conditions can change that cause long-range forecasts to become inaccurate.

The most important financial forecasts for marketing are sales, market share, and marketing expenses. Sales forecasts predict the quantity of sales or the dollar volume of sales for a product or a specific market. For example, a sales forecast may predict the sales of a product to increase by 6 percent for each of the next two years and then by 4 percent for the third year. Forecasts of market share anticipate the percentage of sales in a market that will be made by each of the major competitors. An appliance store that currently has 14 percent of the market in a city will need to determine how to respond to a forecast that projects its share dropping to 10 percent in two years. Expense forecasts project changes in the amount a company will need to spend for specific operations or activities. For example, a forecast for an office supplies company that uses trucks to make deliveries to customers might project that transportation costs will increase by 24 percent over the next five years due to an anticipated gasoline shortage.

Budgets When planning for a shorter time period, managers use budgets. A **budget** is a detailed projection of financial performance for a specific time period, usually one year or less. When managers identify the activities that must be completed to accomplish the goals of the business, they develop budgets to anticipate the costs of those activities and the revenue that can be expected to be generated by them. Two common examples of budgets used in marketing are sales and advertising budgets. Separate budgets are usually developed for each product, market, and major marketing activity.

analyze the performance of all of the stores operating in a specific country or region of a country. Additionally, each store will have its own income statement. Managers may also want to determine the profitability of specific parts of the business

Operating Tools

Managers use several tools, known as financial statements, to determine the effectiveness of operations. A **financial statement** is a detailed summary of the specific financial performance for a business or a part of the business. The important financial statements for marketers are income statements and balance sheets.

Income Statement

An **income statement** reports on the amount and source of revenue and the amount and type of expenses for a specific period of time. The purpose of an income statement is to determine if the business earned a profit or loss on its operations. A sample income statement is shown in Figure 20-1.

An income statement can be developed to analyze the profitability of the entire company or just one operating unit of the company. For example, Starbucks operates stores in many different countries. It can develop an income statement for the entire corporation, which includes the income and expenses of all stores in every country. It can also

FIGURE 20-1

An income statement shows the relationship between sales and expenses in order to determine if operations are profitable.

Dendum Products, Inc.
Income Statement
For the Six-Month Period Ending June 30, 20—

Revenues:
  Gross Sales:
    NE region $123,528
    NW region 195,426
    SE region 232,965
    SW region 148,258
        Total Gross Sales $700,177
  Less Sales Returns:
    NE region .... $ 6,123
    NW region 5,896
    SE region 8,344
    SW region 7,421
        Total Sales Returns........................... 27,784
  Net Sales $672,393
Cost of Products Sold:
  Inventory, Jan. 1, 20— .... $ 86,593
  Purchases $583,226
    Less: Purchase Returns........ −6,048
        Purchase Discounts........ −3,582
  Net Purchases 573,596
Total Cost of Products for Sale $660,189
  Inventory, June 30, 20— .... −78,190
  Net Cost of Products Sold........................... 581,999
Gross Margin .... $ 90,394
Operating Expenses:
  Rent Expense.................................... $ 8,225
  Bad Debts Expense 695
  Credit Card Fee Expense 1,200
  Transportation Expense 10,150
  Equipment Purchases 860
  Equipment Depreciation 620
  Insurance Expense 1,050
  Salaries and Wages 12,845
  Payroll Taxes..................................... 1,926
  Supplies Expense.............................. 734
  Advertising Expense 18,040
    Total Operating Expenses .... $ 56,345
Net Income before Taxes .... $ 34,049

operations. An income statement can be developed for a specific market, a category of customers, or a product or product category. The income statement in Figure 20-1 analyzes the financial performance of a company for a six-month period, with sales figures for four different regions of the country.

Marketers use income statements to determine if marketing activities are achieving an adequate sales volume. Income statements are also used to identify the costs of the activities needed to attain that sales volume.

Balance Sheet A **balance sheet** describes the type and amount of assets, liabilities, and capital in a business on a specific date. **Assets** include the things the business owns. **Liabilities** are the amounts the business owes. The difference between the amount of assets and the amount of liabilities is the actual value of the business, or **capital**. Managers must be able to identify changes in those amounts to determine if the financial condition of the business is improving or declining. Figure 20-2 shows an example of a balance sheet.

Important information that marketers obtain from balance sheets includes the value of assets used for marketing activities, the levels of inventory of products for sale, and the amount owed by customers who have been offered credit. A balance sheet also identifies whether the company has money available

to spend on such things as new product development, buildings, equipment, and other resources needed to improve marketing activities.

Checkpoint ▶▶

What kinds of financial information do income statements and balance sheets contain?

FIGURE 20-2

A balance sheet shows the relationship between the assets, liabilities, and capital of a business.

Froerich Fundamentals
Balance Sheet
December 31, 20—

Assets

Current Assets:

Cash	$ 95,436	
Accounts Receivable	42,827	
Product Inventory	135,673	
Supplies	21,128	
Prepaid Insurance	2,442	
Total Current Assets		$ 297,506

Capital Assets:

Buildings	$647,545	
Vehicles	97,221	
Equipment	228,322	
Capital Assets	$973,088	
Less: Depreciation of Capital Assets	13,286	
Total Capital Assets		959,802
Total Assets		$1,257,308

Liabilities

Current Liabilities:

Accounts Payable	$ 92,286	
Mortgage Payable	296,243	
Notes Payable	63,552	
Payroll Taxes Payable	71,074	
Insurance Payable	6,995	
Total Liabilities		$ 530,150

Capital

Retained Earnings	$286,680	
Owners' Equity	440,478	
Total Capital		727,158
Total Liabilities and Capital		$1,257,308

Using Financial Tools

Marketers work with finance and accounting experts to develop and use financial tools. Some of the information used to prepare forecasts, budgets, and financial statements comes from the marketing department and its operations. Marketers help to collect and report the necessary information. When the reports are prepared in accounting and finance, they are distributed to marketing personnel for use in decision making. Marketers must be able to understand and interpret financial statements. Marketers use the information to develop marketing plans and to improve marketing operations.

What methods could a new window washing business use to prepare financial forecasts and budgets?

Developing Forecasts and Budgets

Financial plans are not helpful unless they are reasonably accurate. Planners use several methods to develop accurate forecasts and budgets.

Past Performance
The most common planning method to use is past performance. By comparing the forecasts and budgets from previous years with the actual results, planners can see which ones were accurate and which were not. Using that past experience makes planning more accurate.

Industry Performance
A second method is to use information from comparable businesses and markets to develop plans. New businesses frequently rely on this method to develop forecasts and budgets since they have limited past performance on which to base projections. Often, trade associations or information services collect and report on the financial performance of businesses in a particular industry. Some government agencies, including the U.S. Department of Commerce, also gather and report financial information on businesses.

Marketing-Related Data
Additionally, planners can look for related figures that help to predict performance. For example, the number of tires that an auto service business might sell can be based on the number of cars in a market and the age of those cars. The original tires on a car will normally need to be replaced between two and three years after the car is sold.

Identifying the number of those cars in the shopping area of the business will help in developing a forecast for tire sales.

Marketing Plan The most effective way to develop a budget for marketing expenses is to calculate the costs of performing the necessary marketing tasks. Here again, the marketing plan is an effective tool. A marketing plan describes the marketing activities necessary to implement the marketing mix. The marketing manager analyzes each of the planned activities to determine what personnel and resources will be needed. Then the wages, costs of resources, and the amounts of all other expenses are matched with each activity. When all of those items are totaled, the marketing manager has a specific estimate of the amount that needs to be budgeted for that activity. An example of that type of budget development is shown in Figure 20-3.

Gathering Information for Financial Statements

The information needed to prepare income statements and balance sheets is the actual financial performance of the business. Therefore, the marketing department is responsible for maintaining accurate records on sales, expenses, inventory levels, customer accounts, and equipment.

Traditionally, employees were asked to record information while completing a marketing activity. For example, when a sale was made, information about the customer, product, and terms of the sale would be recorded on a purchase order, invoice, or sales receipt. In retail businesses, the information may have been recorded

FIGURE 20-3

This budget helps the manager analyze the costs and benefits of operating a customer service department.

Developing a Budget for a Marketing Activity

Planned Monthly Customer Service Department Expenses

Management Salary	$ 4,028
Personnel Wages	18,840
Facility Expense (space and utilities)	3,526
Office Equipment	305
Telephone Expense	498
Computer Expense	295
Postage	86
Supplies	175
Travel Expense	830
Product Returns and Replacements	644
Total Budgeted Expenses	$29,227

using a cash register or a point-of-purchase computer.

Today, much of this information is captured by electronic scanners that read bar codes on products and then automatically enter data into computer databases. As products move through a manufacturing and distribution process, the bar codes are scanned automatically or by employees using scanning equipment. Additional information can be entered along with the bar code data using a keyboard, a touchscreen, or an electronic pen.

FedEx, UPS, and other delivery companies track each item they handle using this kind of technology. From the time packages are received to the time they are delivered, information on each item at each step along the way is maintained in computers. Reports on numbers of items delivered, speed of delivery, costs, and location can be obtained at any time.

Fast FACTS

According to recent financial statements, Wal-Mart is the largest corporation in the United States, with annual revenues of more than $351 billion and total assets of over $151 billion.

Checkpoint ▶▶

Where does the information come from that businesses use to develop financial statements, forecasts, and budgets?

Planning a Career in... *Credit Marketing Management*

"Since starting a new job, my brother has been getting multiple credit card offers from his company's credit union. After reviewing a brochure, he realized that he would be able to not only save on his annual usage fee but also receive one percent of his monthly charges back. Now that he has received the new credit card, he likes to use it frequently. In effect, it provides him with a one-percent discount on all purchases."

How do credit card companies obtain new card holders? How do they approach existing card holders whose cards have expired from prolonged non-use? Credit marketing managers work to increase the use of credit cards among consumers. Enticing potential customers to obtain credit cards through various promotional efforts and determining the appropriate target groups for direct mail marketing campaigns are among the strategies they employ.

Employment Outlook

- Average growth is anticipated.
- Increased demand for credit managers resulting from economic growth will be offset somewhat by industry consolidations.
- Fierce competition for customer retention and for new customers will drive the demand for marketing specialists working in credit services.

Job Titles

- Online Promotions Manager
- Co-Branding Credit Card Marketer
- Direct Mail Credit Manager
- Credit Card Portfolio Manager
- Credit Sales Manager

Needed Skills

- A bachelor's degree with a major in a quantitative business discipline (like accounting or finance) is usually required.

- A thorough knowledge of laws, regulations, and tax implications specific to the credit card industry is necessary.
- Continuing education, either through a university or professional society, is needed to remain current with changes affecting the industry.

What's it like to work in...
Credit Marketing Management

As a credit marketing manager at a large department store, Miguel is responsible for expanding the use of credit cards within each division of his corporation. This morning he is analyzing the effectiveness of a direct mailing campaign to prospective customers that he had initiated. By comparing the forecasted growth of credit cards to the actual growth of credit cards for each division, Miguel can gauge the campaign's effectiveness. Miguel needs to follow up with representatives from each of the two divisions that did not meet their forecast. He wants to understand why the forecasts were not met so that a new, more effective campaign can be developed.

Tomorrow Miguel is teaching a course for recently hired credit marketing representatives. Miguel wants to ensure that each representative is well versed in the incentives offered to credit card holders. For example, many consumers were eager to sign up for a store credit card when they learned that periodically they would receive an additional 10 percent off all store purchases made with the store credit card.

What About **You**

Would you like to help a corporation increase its credit card revenue from its customers?

PHOTO:©DIGITAL VISION/GETTY IMAGES

Analyzing Financial Information

Information available from financial tools can be very valuable in improving marketing decisions. Forecasts and budgets are evaluated to determine their accuracy. The projections are compared with actual performance. When differences are found, they are studied to determine why the differences occurred. It is possible that the projections proved to be inaccurate, indicating that methods used to develop the forecasts and budgets need to be modified. Or it could be a sign that marketing activities were less effective than anticipated and need to be improved.

Using Financial Information

Financial statements are evaluated to determine the changes that occur from one period of operations to the next. A marketing manager studies various markets to determine if sales are increasing or decreasing. Inventory levels can be compared from year to year as can the amounts owed by customers. If the information shows that the financial performance is improving, the marketing manager will want to continue with the same activities. If sales are decreasing or inventories and customer accounts are increasing too quickly, marketing activities may need to be changed.

Another method of analysis is to compare one type of financial performance to another. For example, sales volume can be compared to advertising expenses. If expenses are going up at a faster rate than sales, a problem may be developing. Other important comparisons in marketing are the level of inventory to sales, costs of transportation compared to costs of product handling and storage, and product costs compared to marketing expenses.

Information is essential for effective marketing. Marketing research provides information to aid in understanding customers. Financial information is needed to determine what marketing activities the organization can afford to complete and the impact of those activities on profits. Financial planning is a critical marketing skill.

Marketers use financial information to identify how to increase revenue and reduce costs. As shown in Figure 20-4, if a greater volume of sales can be achieved while controlling expenses, profits will increase. In the same way, if sales can be maintained while reducing the costs of marketing, the company will also be able to increase profits.

Increasing Revenues

Increased revenue results from selling more products and services. Financial information is analyzed to determine the products that sell the best and the customer groups that buy the most products. Efforts are directed at the best products and markets. Poorly performing products and markets are either improved or dropped. Each time a new marketing plan is developed, the most important products and markets are identified.

FIGURE 20-4

When the goal of a business is increased profits, marketers have two basic ways of getting there: (1) They can increase sales while holding costs steady. (2) If sales are not increasing, they can reduce the cost of achieving those sales.

Marketing Strategies to Increase Profits

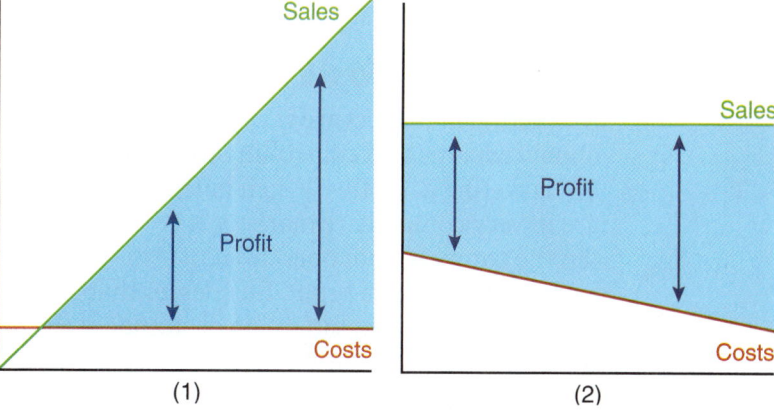

How could providing laptops to its salespeople help a business control costs?

Marketers are also concerned that an effective price for a product is maintained. It is possible that more products can be sold to customers if discounts are offered or the price is reduced. Some salespeople who have control over price are quick to reduce the price, believing that is the only way the customer will buy. Yet the lower price may reduce revenue to the point where a profit cannot be made. Salespeople who understand customer needs make an effective presentation of the entire marketing mix in response to those needs. They know that customers look for the best value, not the lowest price.

Controlling Costs

Marketing managers are very concerned about reducing and controlling the costs of marketing activities. When businesses are in very competitive markets, it is often the company that operates most efficiently that makes a profit. Businesses that are concerned about satisfying customer needs must be very careful in cutting costs. Marketing activities that are important to

customers cannot be eliminated without considering the impact on customer satisfaction. It is often possible to find ways to perform marketing activities in a less costly way while keeping the same level of customer service. For example, an insurance company provided its salespeople with laptop computers to reduce the time it took to complete the required forms and to exchange information between the salespeople and the company. The company found that the use of laptops not only reduced expenses by over 15 percent but also cut the number of errors on insurance applications by nearly 5 percent.

Another example of reducing marketing expenses comes from a large supermarket in the Southeast. It operates a very large fleet of trucks to deliver products from its warehouses to its stores. The trucks would deliver the products and return to the warehouse empty. The transportation manager started to identify suppliers of products that were located in the towns where the supermarket had stores. When a truck was delivering a load from the warehouse to a store, the manager would determine if a nearby supplier had an order to be sent to the warehouse. If so, the supermarket's truck would pick up the order rather than driving back empty. This procedure saved the company several thousands of dollars each month in transportation costs.

Marketing employees as well as managers need to be aware of the costs of marketing activities and identify ways to reduce expenses. It is often possible to identify ways that marketing activities can be performed more efficiently, the amount of supplies or materials can be reduced, or waste can be eliminated. Many companies provide incentives for employees who identify cost savings.

Checkpoint ▶▶▶

What are the two basic ways that businesses can increase profits?

20-2 Assessment

Xtra! Study Tools
school.cengage.com/marketing/marketing

Key Concepts

Determine the best answer.

1. True or False: A financial forecast is a detailed summary of the specific financial performance for a business or part of the business.

2. A budget differs from a financial forecast in that it
   a. predicts the long-term financial performance of a business
   b. is usually not as accurate as a financial forecast
   c. does not take capital expenses into account
   d. typically covers short-term rather than long-term financial performance

3. The difference between the amount of a business's assets and the amount of its liabilities is the actual value of the business, or _____.

4. The most effective way to develop a budget for marketing expenses is to
   a. calculate the costs of performing the necessary marketing tasks
   b. use data from comparable businesses and markets
   c. look at last year's figures and increase them based on the current rate of inflation
   d. ask all marketing personnel to submit a sample budget, and then average the figures to arrive at the final budget

Make Academic Connections

5. **Finance** Use the library or Internet to locate the financial statements of a business you admire and find (a) the company's net income before taxes last year and (b) the dollar amount of the company's value (capital). Record these figures and explain which financial statement you used to find the information.

6. **Ethics** Suppose a radio manufacturer decides to cut costs by reducing the terms of its product warranties from two years to one year. Do you think this decision is ethical? Why or why not? What if data show that about 8 percent of the company's best-selling model becomes defective after about 18 months of use?

Connect to ◀DECA
An Association of Marketing Students

7. You and a friend have decided to start a small computer repair shop. Since you are new entrepreneurs, your business has no past performance on which to base a budget. Using the library or Internet, compile a list of resources you can use to help you prepare the first budget for your business. Estimate revenues and expenses and create a startup budget for your new business. Present it to your teacher (judge) and explain how you arrived at the amounts in your budget.

Budgeting for Marketing Activities

GOALS

• Explain the various ways that businesses raise revenue through marketing activities.

• Describe the kinds of marketing expenses that arise in conjunction with each element of the marketing mix.

KEY TERMS

accounts receivable, *p. 576*

marketing matters

Every activity in a business costs money. Decisions need to be made on the most effective use of that money. Marketing managers then decide on the best way to use the marketing budget. They do that by analyzing the expenses involved in marketing.

Marketing activities generate revenue. Most of the revenue comes from the sale of primary products and services. Secondary and after-sale products and services can also contribute substantially to revenues and profits. Offering credit can generate interest revenues.

Completing marketing activities also incurs costs. There are expenses associated with each of the four marketing mix elements.

Make a list of five activities that you or your family performed in the past month that resulted in revenue. Also list five expenses associated with those activities.

Effects of Marketing on Revenue

A marketing strategy provides the basis for developing the marketing budget. The marketing strategy identifies the target markets that the business intends to serve and the marketing mixes to be used for each market. A written marketing plan is prepared to show how the business will implement the marketing strategy. The plan describes the activities to be completed and the resources needed.

The people who develop a marketing plan often find that they do not have adequate resources to develop the most effective marketing mix. For example, research might show that customers prefer a product with several options that is sold through a large number of outlets. Yet the company cannot afford to spend money on both product improvements and more extensive

distribution. A decision needs to be made whether to put more money into the product or into distribution. That decision is often based on which of the mix elements is most important to the customer, the type of mix offered by the competition, and the actual costs of each choice to the company.

The marketing mix and budget are also affected by the way the company has spent money in the past. If the company was responsible for the transportation of its products, it may have invested in trucks or other equipment needed to move products from the business to customers. Warehouses or distribution centers may have been built to handle the inventory. If the company has already made those investments, it will typically try to use marketing mixes that take advantage of those resources. If a

Virtual Marketing

Consumer-Generated Advertising

The term Web 2.0 refers to the perceived shift in the way people began to use the Internet in the early 2000s. Although the technology did not fundamentally change, in this second generation of the Internet, social networking sites, blogs, discussion boards, and wikis allowed for much more user-generated content. Companies slowly began to embrace this approach, recognizing that while traditional media like television and print were a one-way stream of communication, the strength of the Internet was that it allowed for users to also contribute meaningful content. Rather than companies talking at consumers, they could now engage in a dialogue with them.

In 2007, the approach of letting consumers generate content spilled over into traditional media. Both Frito-Lay and the NFL held contests in which consumers submitted ideas for television commercials. The winning commercials were broadcast during the Superbowl.

As judges of the contests, Frito-Lay and the NFL could control what was said in the commercials. But one of the negatives of consumer-generated content is that companies do not have as much control over the messaging. When Chevy provided consumers with footage of its Tahoe and invited them to make their own commercials and post them online, they got over 30,000 entries in four weeks. Some touted the benefits of the Tahoe, but a small percentage were criticisms of the Tahoe's low gas mileage and negative impact on the environment. Surprisingly, Chevy did not remove the negative entries from the web site. To them, keeping an honest dialogue was more important than ensuring that all the messages were positive.

Think Critically

1. From the company's standpoint, what are some positives of consumer-generated advertising? What are some negatives?

2. Do you think consumers care whether a commercial message was created by another consumer instead of the company doing the advertising? Why or why not?

---

company has relied on other businesses to store and transport products in the past, it may be very expensive for the company to change and instead provide those marketing activities itself.

Marketing activities are completed in order to generate revenue. Most of the revenue for a business results from the sale of products and services. The marketing plan identifies the markets that the company plans to serve. Marketing activities are developed to meet the needs of customers in the market so that they will purchase the products or services offered by the company. There are several parts of the marketing mix that can affect the amount of revenue. Sources of revenue affected by mix elements include sales, after-sale products and services, and interest earned on credit services.

Sales of Products and Services

The primary objective of a marketing strategy is for the business to obtain the most profitable level of sales possible while satisfying a target market. The marketing mix is developed to increase customer satisfaction by offering a product or service that is different from and better than those offered by competitors. It is possible for a company to improve a product by offering additional features and options, better packaging, or customer services. The product can be made available in a more convenient or more appropriate location. Credit can be offered to make the product more affordable.

What kinds of products and services might a garden center offer to generate after-sale revenue?

Promotion and other types of communication can clearly show the customer the value of the product and how it can be used most effectively. Marketers need to study the impact of each mix choice on sales and profits and then select the mix that achieves the best combination for the company. The most important source of revenue for an organization is the sale of its primary products and services.

Several factors can reduce the level of sales. Customers may not be satisfied with a product because it is damaged, is not what the seller promised, or does not meet the customers' needs. In those cases, customers will return the product to the seller and expect a replacement or a refund. Returned and replacement products reduce the level of sales and add to the seller's costs.

The seller may offer the customer a discount on the price charged if the customer is not satisfied or receives less than promised. Again, the amount of discounts reduces the sales volume. If the company offers a rebate to customers, the amount of the rebates must be subtracted from the total sales.

After-Sale Revenue

It has been said that a current customer is more profitable than a prospective customer. There are ways to increase sales to existing customers while satisfying their needs. Automobile dealers and movie theaters provide two examples of this marketing strategy. Selling automobiles today is a very competitive business. Customers carefully shop for the best price, so dealerships often have to cut prices so low that they make little profit on the sale of the automobiles. Profit for the business comes from activities that occur after the sale. A very important source of revenue and profit for automobile dealers comes from servicing and repairing automobiles they have sold. They work very hard to encourage customers to return to the dealership for service.

In the same way, many movie theaters rely on the sale of other products to operate profitably. Most movies are shown several times a day for many weeks. The first few times a new movie is shown, the theater may be full of customers, and the sale of tickets by itself will make a profit. Later on, however, fewer customers will come to see the movie. The sale of concession items (popcorn, soft drinks, candy) provides the opportunity for the theater to make a profit when ticket sales alone do not. Think of the number of businesses that have a variety of products they sell that complement the original purchase.

Sometimes businesses identify other ways of generating revenues in addition to the sale of the primary products and services. Restaurants may sell baseball caps, coffee mugs, or packaged popular food items such as pasta sauce or baked goods. Those sales are both effective promotional tools as well as another source of revenue. In the northern states, landscaping and grass-cutting businesses often see their profits reduced during winter months because of poor weather. People simply do not need to have much yard work done in the late fall and winter. However, some of these companies may contract with cities, large businesses, and even homeowners to clean the snow from streets, parking lots, and driveways. This provides some revenue during a time when they otherwise would not be able to operate.

Credit and Interest

Many purchases are made with cash, and the seller receives payment as soon as the sale is made. If credit is offered to

Figure This

Unit Sales Provide Another Perspective

While higher sales are generally a good sign for a business, the way those higher sales are achieved can be even more important. One way marketers analyze sales is to distinguish between the dollar volume of sales and unit volume. Dollar volume is measured by the revenue derived from sales. Unit volume is the number of products or services that are sold. Regardless of the dollar volume on an income statement for a given period, the number of units sold can be a good indication of where the business is headed.

Marketers can quickly derive unit sales from dollar volume by dividing sales revenue by the price per unit or by the average price per unit. Conversely, the average price per unit sold can be calculated by dividing dollar volume by the number of units sold. Either figure can be a valuable tool for analyzing sales trends.

If unit sales are flat or declining, it is usually a sign of trouble. Perhaps one of the target markets for a product or service is maturing, and new markets need to be developed to resuscitate growth. Or maybe competitors have grabbed a larger share of the market.

If a decline in unit sales is accompanied by increasing revenues, it might indicate that the company has raised its prices too high. Often, price increases will boost dollar volume initially. Customers may continue to buy the product because that is what they are accustomed to doing, or because other aspects of their business have been developed to work best with that product. As time goes by, however, they begin to search for and find cheaper alternatives that are equally effective. Also, competitors might be drawn to the market by high margins and a chance for easy profits. So after an initial increase in revenue following a price hike, a business might see future revenues start falling. Declining unit sales are an advance warning of future revenues.

Think Critically

1. If the dollar volume of sales for a product increases 4.5 percent, and the number of units sold increases 10 percent, what happens to the average price per unit?

2. An income statement indicates that total revenue for a product line was $10 million. The basic model costs $250, and a new advanced model costs $400. The unit volume of basic models was 30,000. How many advanced models were sold?

customers, the sale is not complete. Financial statements often include an item called accounts receivable. **Accounts receivable** are sales for which the company has not yet been paid. Credit is often offered to increase sales beyond the amount that is possible if customers had to pay cash.

Credit Cards Many businesses use credit services offered by other companies rather than developing and managing a credit department. For example, a retail store may accept credit cards such as Master-Card, Visa, or Discover. The credit card company pays the retailer who accepted the customer's credit card for the amount of the purchase. It is then the credit card company's responsibility to collect the account from the customer who made the credit purchase. In return for using the credit card company, the retail business is charged a fee that usually amounts to 2 percent or more of the total amount of its credit sales.

Some companies have their own credit systems, or even their own credit cards, that can be used only for the purchase of products from their business. There are several costs for companies that choose to manage their own credit services. The company needs to design the credit system and determine the terms that will be offered to customers. Then personnel must be hired and trained to manage the credit system. Computers and

Do the benefits of extending credit to customers outweigh the risks? Why or why not?

©PHOTODISC/GETTY IMAGES

other equipment are needed to maintain the credit records, billing, payments, and other information. Since credit customers do not pay for their purchases for a month or more after the sale is made, additional money is needed to finance the expenses of the company until payment is received.

Businesses offering credit frequently charge interest to their customers to pay for the credit services. If most accounts are paid in full, it is possible that the interest charges will even provide a profit for the company.

Unpaid Credit Even with the most careful and effective credit system, some customers do not pay their accounts when billed. Even a small amount that is unpaid can eliminate any profit the company makes on credit sales and reduces the total dollar amount of sales. Companies offering credit to customers work to develop effective credit procedures to

Fast **FACTS**

As of 2007, there were more than 1.55 billion Visa cards in circulation around the world—more than any other credit card on Earth. MasterCard has about 750 million cards in circulation. Together, Visa and MasterCard control 75 percent of the $1.3 trillion credit card market in the United States.

reduce the amount of unpaid accounts. They carefully track the age of the unpaid accounts. If an account remains unpaid for several months beyond its due date, it will likely never be paid.

No matter how carefully credit accounts are managed by a company, it is normal to have at least a small percentage of credit sales that are uncollectible. Those uncollected accounts and the cost of collection activities are an important business expense. While credit may appear to be an important service to offer customers, businesses must carefully study whether the increases in sales resulting from credit actually add to or reduce their profits.

Regulation Companies that offer credit need to be aware of laws that regulate credit activity. Among the important federal laws is the Equal Credit Opportunity Act, which prevents companies from discriminating among the people to whom they offer credit. The Truth-in-Lending Act specifies the type of information businesses must provide to credit customers. The Fair Credit Reporting Act regulates the use of the credit information that businesses gather about individual customers. Also, the methods companies use to collect money owed by customers are controlled under the Fair Debt Collection Practices Act.

Checkpoint ▶▶

What activity has the biggest impact on the amount of revenue a business generates?

Expenses Associated with the Marketing Mix

Just as the sale of products and services by marketers results in income for a business, the completion of marketing activities adds to the business's expenses. Expenses are associated with each of the marketing mix elements.

Product Expenses

The majority of expenses related to product development for manufacturers is a part of the production budget. Those expenses include the cost of materials, equipment, and personnel needed to produce the product. Also, the cost of packaging is considered a production cost. For wholesale and retail businesses, products must be purchased from other companies, so their costs are determined by the prices paid for the merchandise.

There are other expenses related to the product mix element. The expenses associated with offering a guarantee or warranty, as well as the costs of repairing items that are damaged or fail, must be included. In addition, many businesses offer customer services, some of which can be very expensive.

Some services, such as delivery and setup or training, are offered as part of the actual sale. Other services are provided for a long time after the sale while the customer is using the product. For example, many companies that manufacture and sell home theater components have technicians who will work with customers if they are having problems with a product. KitchenAid has a toll-free telephone number that customers can call to get information about the use of any product the company manufactures, ranging from small appliances to large industrial equipment. Several automobile manufacturers offer 24-hour-a-day roadside repair service for their customers.

Distribution Expenses

Distribution costs are a major area of marketing expenses. Companies must pay to

How could a business decrease promotion-related costs, such as travel expenses for salespeople?

transport, store, and display their products. These costs include long-term expenses, such as buildings and equipment, and short-term expenses, such as wages and supplies. Even service businesses have expenses associated with delivering the services to customers or operating the location where customers come to purchase the services. In addition to the obvious costs of distribution, other expenses for most businesses include the costs of developing and managing the channels of distribution, inventory control costs, materials handling expenses, and the costs of order processing.

Price Expenses

The major expense related to the price mix element is the cost of offering credit. Another price expense item is the cost of communicating prices to customers. This may seem like an unimportant item, but consider the thousands of items that a business stocks and sells during one year. If each item needs a price tag, the cost of printing the stickers or tags and the expense of placing them on the products can be high. This cost increases if a price change needs to be made. Many retail businesses have found that the time and

expense of pricing products is so great that they have introduced other methods. The products no longer carry price stickers. Instead, the price is posted on the display shelf. The price is stored in the company's computer and is identified through a bar code on the product package. A price change is made by simply changing the amount in the computer and updating the price on the product display shelf.

Promotion Expenses

Many costs are associated with promotion. Few inexpensive ways are available for companies to communicate with customers. Each type of promotion has its own set of expenses.

Advertising is the most common type of promotion. The major cost of advertising is the expense of purchasing space in newspapers or magazines or buying time on television or radio. It is also expensive to create and produce the advertisements. These expenses include the salaries of a variety of creative people as well as the equipment and materials they need for their work.

Selling is also an expensive promotional method. The biggest cost of selling is the salaries of salespeople. Additional costs include training and management as well as the equipment, materials, and product samples salespeople use. Salespeople for manufacturers often travel regularly to meet with customers. Their sales territories can cover several states or countries. The costs of operating an automobile, air travel, hotel rooms, meals, and other related expenses can be hundreds of dollars each day. Salespeople need to be very effective in order to make enough sales just to cover their expenses.

It is said that the most inexpensive form of promotion is word of mouth. But companies that want customers to help sell their products often spend money to ensure that it is done well. When a customer buys a product, the company may make a follow-up phone call to make sure the customer is satisfied. Letters and gifts may be sent to show that the company appreciates the customer's business. Some companies offer satisfied customers money or other incentives if they identify a prospective customer who then buys a product.

Checkpoint ▶▶▶

Which elements of the marketing mix give rise to related marketing expenses?

20-3 Assessment

Key Concepts

Determine the best answer.

1. True or False: When a company offers its customers credit, profits always rise due to increased sales.

2. The major expense related to the price mix element is the
   a. cost of packaging
   b. profit margin
   c. cost of offering credit
   d. production cost of the product

3. Sales for which the company has not yet been paid are called accounts _____.

4. The most common type of promotion is
   a. word of mouth
   b. advertising
   c. press releases
   d. personal selling

5. All of the following are expenses related to the distribution mix element *except*
   a. inventory control
   b. materials handling
   c. storage
   d. warranty costs

6. True or False: Many businesses rely on after-sale revenue to operate profitably.

Make Academic Connections

7. **Research** There are many costs associated with promotion. The costs of each type of promotion vary. Research the costs of at least five different advertising media (radio, television, newspaper, outdoor advertising, etc.) by contacting various media companies to obtain pricing information. Some companies may be able to send you a media kit containing advertising prices. Prepare a table listing each type of media and its costs.

8. **Government** Use the library or Internet to find information about the Fair Debt Collection Practices Act. When was the Act passed? What are its major provisions, and what effect has it had on the debt collection industry? Report your findings in a two- to three-page paper.

Connect to

9. You work in the marketing department for a local chain of coffee shops. To increase revenue in your stores, you have been asked to develop some ideas involving the sale of products other than the primary product your stores offer—hot coffee. Describe the target markets and the types of products you would recommend to your teacher (judge). Explain why your ideas would be effective and profitable.

Chapter 20 Assessment

Check Your Understanding

Now that you have completed the chapter, check your understanding of the lessons with these questions. Record the score that best represents your understanding of each marketing concept.

1 = not at all; 3 = somewhat; 5 = very well

If your score is 42–50, you are ready for the assessment activities that follow. If you score 33–41, you should review the lessons for the items you scored 1–3. If you score 32 or less, you will want to carefully reread the lessons and work with a study partner on the areas you do not understand.

Can you—

___ explain how marketing affects a business's financial planning?

___ define short- and long-term marketing expenses and the various types of financing for marketing activities?

___ list and describe the three main types of financial needs a business typically has?

___ describe the principal planning and operating tools used by business?

___ detail how marketers develop forecasts, budgets, and financial statements?

___ explain the kinds of financial analyses marketers perform to increase profits?

___ distinguish between an income statement and a balance sheet?

___ explain the various ways that businesses raise revenue through marketing activities?

___ describe the ways credit can increase or decrease a business's revenues?

___ describe the kinds of marketing expenses that arise in conjunction with each element of the marketing mix?

Review Marketing Terms

Match the terms listed with the definitions.

1. The money received from the sale of products and services
2. Long-term investments in land, buildings, or equipment
3. The costs of day-to-day marketing activities
4. A numerical prediction of future performance related to revenue and expenses
5. A detailed summary of the financial performance for a business or a part of a business
6. A description of the type and amount of assets, liabilities, and capital in a business on a specified date
7. A detailed projection of financial performance for a specific time period, usually one year or less
8. Things a business owns
9. Sales for which the company has not yet been paid
10. A report on the amount and source of revenue and the amount and type of expenses for a specific period of time

11. The amounts a business owes
12. The difference between the amount of assets and liabilities, or the actual value of a business

a. accounts receivable
b. assets
c. balance sheet
d. budget
e. capital
f. capital expenses
g. financial forecast
h. financial statement
i. income statement
j. liabilities
k. operating expenses
l. revenue

Review Marketing Concepts

13. The basic financial equation is _____ − _____ = _____.

14. True or False: Decisions about distribution rarely impact expenses.

15. Which of the following would *not* be considered a short-term expense?
    a. supplies
    b. a new fleet of delivery trucks
    c. the monthly utility bill
    d. salaries and wages

16. Which of the following is a typical way to finance inventory?
    a. through a short-term loan
    b. through credit extended by the seller
    c. both a and b
    d. neither a nor b

17. True or False: An income statement can be used only to analyze the profitability of an entire company, not just one operating unit of the company.

18. True or False: The most common method of developing financial forecasts or budgets is to use information from comparable businesses.

19. The marketing department is responsible for maintaining accurate records on
    a. inventory levels
    b. customer accounts
    c. sales
    d. all of the above

20. True or False: Generally, current customers are more profitable to a business than prospective customers.

21. If a greater volume of sales can be achieved and expenses can be controlled, profits will _____.

Marketing Research and Planning

22. Two important methods of planning and analyzing financial information are (1) comparable information from similar businesses and (2) the costs of performing specific marketing tasks and activities.

    A number of reference books published by the federal government, trade and professional associations, and private businesses contain this information. Using the library, a business information encyclopedia, business reference books, the Internet, or the resources of a businessperson you know, identify at least two sources of financial information available to marketers. Review one of the sources and prepare a written summary of the information contained in the reference. Provide examples of the specific information.

23. You are the marketing manager for EnviroSaf, a company that has developed a new type of lawn care product that controls weeds and insects without chemicals. The product is currently sold through garden centers in eight states in the northwestern United States. You are responsible for all distribution and promotional activities and for completing marketing research. You work with other managers to set product prices, to develop and provide customer services, and

to complete new product planning. You believe that you can make the most effective decisions if you have financial information available related to the marketing activities you control.

Write a one-page memo to Frances Payton, chief financial officer of EnviroSaf. Identify the types of financial information you need, list the financial tools that will help you with planning and operations, and explain why it is important for the marketing manager to be involved in financial planning. Use information from the chapter to help you prepare the memo.

24. One of the methods of forecasting sales for products and services is to identify relationships between two products or services. In the chapter, it was suggested that the volume of automobile sales can be used to predict the sale of automobile tires. If business people can identify similar relationships among products and services, they can increase the effectiveness of their forecasts. List at least ten other product/service relationships where you believe the sale of one affects the sale of the other. Two more examples are given to help you.

The sale of	*Is related to the sale of*
computers	computer software
winter coats	gloves and hats

Marketing Management and Decision Making

25. The school club to which you belong needs to raise funds to pay for a trip to a state conference. The members want to plan a fundraiser that will be fun, provide a community service, and result in a reasonable profit for the club. The idea being considered is an ethnic food celebration. Your club would be responsible for contacting community groups to staff a booth in which a specific type of ethnic food would be sold. The group would also develop a display representing each ethnic culture or provide a short presentation (dance, historical story, and so on) about each culture. The event would be held on a Saturday afternoon for three hours in the school's gymnasium. People would come to sample the food and to enjoy the presentations.

    For financial planning, some of the anticipated costs are:

    Gymnasium rental $300
    Table rental for booths . . . . $3 per table
      (minimum of 50 tables)
    Security . . . . $45 per hour
    Insurance $80
    Cost of possible promotional materials:
    Flyers . . . . $0.08 each
    Posters . . . . $0.45 each
    Envelopes and postage . . . . $0.32 each
    30-second radio ad . . . . $58 each
      (10 for $500) + $80 production costs
      (fixed)
    Salesperson commission . . . . . . $8/booth sold
    Labor costs (Set up, tear down,
      cleaning) . . . . $6 per hour

    The plan is to sell booths for the celebration. There is space for up to 40 booths in the gymnasium if three tables are used per booth. The groups would be able to sell their foods and keep all revenues from the sale after paying the booth fee. Also, an admission could be charged, and other products, such as t-shirts and souvenir cups, could be sold.

    Develop a plan of activities to be followed by your class in planning and managing the celebration. Include all aspects of a marketing mix (product development, distribution, pricing, promotion). Based on the plan of activities, prepare a budget for the celebration using the income statement format illustrated in the chapter. Include projections of all types of revenues and reasonable expenses. Estimate those expenses for which no costs are given. Develop at least three projections of revenues using alternative prices charged for the booths, varying admission prices, or different attendance levels. Calculate the impact on profit or loss.

26. A hardware store has decided to add free delivery as a service for customers who purchase over $250 of merchandise in one order. Delivery will also be available to other customers, but a delivery fee will be charged. The store can purchase a delivery van for $18,000. Three methods of financing the van are being considered.
    a. The store's bank will provide a one-year capital improvement loan at 9 percent interest. To qualify for the loan, the company must maintain 150 percent of the value of the vehicle in checking or savings accounts with the bank.
    b. A finance company will purchase all of the company's accounts receivable for 86 percent of their value. The store's accounts receivable currently are valued at $26,000.
    c. The store can use cash on hand to make the purchase. The current balance sheet for the store shows the cash balance is $31,800. The cash budget for the coming 12 months shows that the highest projected cash total during that time is $38,000 and the lowest projected cash total is $12,200.

    Analyze the three sources of financing to determine the direct cost of each to the business and the possible advantages and disadvantages of each method. Prepare a written recommendation of the method you believe the store should use to finance the delivery van.

27. Search the Internet for a public corporation's annual report and find the section that discloses its revenues, expenses, and income for three or more years. Using a spreadsheet program, calculate the percentage increase or decrease in sales revenue for each year. Also, calculate the annual ratio of sales revenue to earnings or net income. Print the results of your calculations.

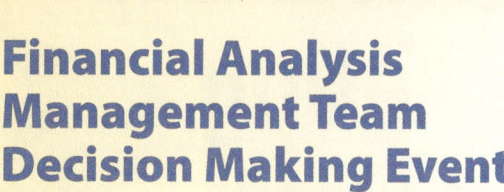

Financial Analysis Management Team Decision Making Event

Student Lawn Services has been a successful lawn service operation for the past two years. It is located in a growing suburb of a large city that has a mild climate year round.

The owner of Student Lawn Services started the business by maintaining the yards for five customers. He gives satisfied customers poinsettias in December as an expression of customer appreciation. The business has grown rapidly through word-of-mouth promotion from satisfied customers. It has expanded to 50 customers who require weekly lawn services. Profits from the business operation allowed him to upgrade his lawn equipment.

The owner has become overwhelmed with the growth of the business. Much of the demand is due to an expanding community and numerous new housing developments. Competitors have entered the market in hopes of intercepting some of his business. However, customers still prefer the personal touch provided by Student Lawn Services, and the prices are reasonable compared to the competition.

The owner of Student Lawn Services has called upon your financial management team to suggest strategies for maximizing sales without negatively impacting the personalized services offered. The owner began the business as a sole proprietorship. He is considering partnering with some of the competing lawn service businesses in the community.

Your team must outline a strategy for Student Lawn Services to successfully grow the business. Your team must explain the advantages and disadvantages of partnering with another business. Your team must also explain pricing strategies for lawn services.

You have 30 minutes to prepare your presentation, 10 minutes to present your plan to the owner of Student Lawn Services (judge), and 5 minutes to answer the judge's questions about your plan.

Performance Indicators Evaluated

- Explain the concept of productivity. (Economics)
- Explain the concept of economic resources. (Economics)
- Describe the concepts of economic scarcity and economic activities. (Economics)
- Explain the principles of supply and demand. (Economics)
- Determine factors affecting business risk. (Economics)
- Explain the nature of positive customer/client relations. (Emotional Intelligence)
- Identify factors affecting a business's profit. (Economics)

Go to the DECA web site for more detailed information.

Think Critically

1. Why is financial management important for a growing business?

2. How does this case involve supply and demand?

3. What is the advantage of partnering with a competitor?

4. What public relations campaign can Student Lawn Services use to maintain positive relationships with customers?

www.deca.org

Entrepreneurship and Marketing

©CORBIS

Newsline)))

Avoiding the Glass Ceiling

Many people have been known to hit the "glass ceiling" in business. What is the glass ceiling? Over the years in some companies, it was very difficult for women and racial or ethnic minorities to move onto and up the management ladder in their career. Older white males held the top management spots. When they retired or moved to other positions, other white males usually replaced them. It may not have even been an apparent attempt by the older managers to discriminate. They just felt more comfortable with and had greater confidence in the people with whom they worked. While most businesses have attempted to make changes, there is a belief that the glass ceiling is still in place in some organizations.

Entrepreneurship has been a way for women and other minority business people to get to the top

of a company. When you start your own business, no one can place a glass ceiling over your head. Statistics bear out the growing diversity of small business ownership. According to the most recent data from the Small Business Administration (SBA), nearly 10.4 million firms are owned by women. They employ more than 12.8 million people and generate $1.9 trillion in sales. For the past two decades, women-owned companies have continued to grow at around two times the rate of all businesses.

The number of companies owned by other minorities has more than doubled in that same time to now represent 18 percent of all businesses. Those companies sell more than $600 billion of products and services each year. Of all U.S. businesses, 6.6 percent are owned by Hispanic-Americans, 5.0 percent by African-Americans, 4.6 percent by

Asian-Americans, and 0.9 percent by Native-Americans.

Think Critically

1. Do you believe the glass ceiling has been a major reason for the growth in new business ownership by the groups identified? If the glass ceiling disappears in large businesses, do you believe the growth in minority-owned small businesses will slow? Why or why not?

2. While the number of women-owned and minority-owned businesses is increasing, the percentage is much smaller than the percentage of the total U.S. population that each group represents. Why do you believe that percentage remains low?

Prepare for Performance

This chapter develops the following Performance Indicators from the DECA Competitive Events program.

Core Performance Indicators

- Understand the concepts, processes, and skills associated with identifying new ideas, opportunities, and methods and with creating or starting a new project or venture
- Employ entrepreneurial discovery strategies to generate feasible ideas for business ventures

Supporting Performance Indicators

- Develop a concept for a new business venture to evaluate its success potential
- Determine needed resources for a new business venture to contribute to its startup viability

Go to **school.cengage.com/marketing/marketing** and click on Connect to DECA.

Potential Energy of Wind/sec
P = ½ (ρAV) V² = ½ ρ A V³

Air Density [ρ, kg/m³]
Wind Velocity [V, m/sec]

Air Temp
59°F

Air Density
1.225 kg/m³

Wind Direction
NW // 315°

Wind Velocity
10 m/sec

Wind Turbine

It can shape mountains.
It can move oceans.
Now the wind can even
heat up your toaster.

Together, all the GE Energy wind turbines in the world could produce enough power for 2.4 million US homes. Something maybe to chat about over your next round of toast. It's yet another example of our blueprint for a better world.

imagination at work

ecomagination.com

©GENERAL ELECTRIC

Visual Focus

Every large business that is an industry leader once started as a small business. Often it was the creation of an entrepreneur who was willing to risk financial resources, time, and effort to develop a product or service idea. A goal of most entrepreneurs is to make a profit, but they are also driven by the need for personal achievement. This chapter introduces you to entrepreneurship and how entrepreneurs start and develop effective businesses. You will determine if you have the characteristics of an entrepreneur and if it would be a career choice that interests you.

Focus Questions:

General Electric was formed from the business ideas of inventor and entrepreneur Thomas Edison. Today the multibillion-dollar company is still viewed as one of the most innovative in the world. Why do you believe GE focuses on innovation and new product ideas in many of its advertisements? What image do you have of the company after viewing and reading the ad shown here? Discuss with your classmates whether you believe large companies can be as creative and innovative as new companies led by entrepreneurs.

Understanding Entrepreneurship

GOALS

- Provide examples of successful entrepreneurs and the businesses they started.
- Describe the importance of entrepreneurship to the U.S. economy.

KEY TERMS

entrepreneur, *p. 587*

entrepreneurship, *p. 587*

marketing matters

Entrepreneurs are unique people. They are willing to take risks to start businesses. Successful entrepreneurs often start several companies during their business careers. They are usually not content to start the business and then continue to operate it for years and years as the manager. In fact, once the business is well established, many entrepreneurs do not succeed when they are required to switch to the role of manager.

Consider the following questions. Why is it important in a free enterprise economy to have people who are willing to take risks to start new businesses? How do the personal characteristics and skills needed to start a business differ from those needed to manage a business? Do you believe you would rather be an entrepreneur responsible for creating a new company or a manager responsible for the continuing success of an existing company? Share your ideas with other students.

Starting a Business

You may have heard the story of Henry Ford, who created Ford Motor Company. Today, Ford Motor Company is a giant international corporation. But it had its beginnings in 1896 when Henry Ford produced his first automobile in a Michigan garage.

Bill Gates provides another example of a person who started with an idea and developed a successful large business, in his case, Microsoft. The idea for the company began when, as college students, Bill and his friend Paul Allen developed a computer program to operate the first personal computers.

Many other people have put their personal stamps on the U.S. economy with business ideas and the commitment to bring the ideas to life in new companies.

Why do you think starting a business is the American Dream of many people?

©PHOTODISC/GETTY IMAGES

Examples include Madam C. J. Walker, who started a business in the early 1900s to produce and distribute hair-care products and cosmetics for African-Americans who were not being served by other businesses. Levi Strauss invented a process in 1873 to use rivets in the manufacturing of denim work pants to add strength to the seams, creating a clothing company that still manufactures blue jeans today. Ben Cohen and Jerry Greenfield began mixing unique flavors of ice cream in a renovated Vermont garage in 1978. Ben and Jerry's Ice Cream is known worldwide for its high-quality products and its unique company environment. Margaret Rudkin developed the Pepperidge Farm company that she later sold for several million dollars. The business idea grew as she baked and then sold bread and cookies from her home in the 1930s.

Ben & Jerry's unique ice cream flavors as well as its unique view of ownership responsibilities help it stand out from its competitors.

The American Dream

Starting your own business has been called the American Dream. People go into business to make a profit, but they also start their own businesses to have the freedom to do work that they enjoy and to take responsibility for the success or failure of the business. There is little that is more rewarding than seeing your ideas and efforts grow into a profitable business, offering jobs to others, and providing products and services that satisfy customers. On the other hand, being a business owner presents a continuing challenge to meet a payroll, pay the bills, and find ways to compete successfully.

An **entrepreneur** is someone who takes the risk to start a new business. That risk involves investing his or her money in the business. **Entrepreneurship** is the process of planning, creating, and managing a new business.

An entrepreneur is different from a business manager. A manager is responsible for a business created and owned by others. The manager is an employee and so takes direction from the owners of the business. The owners must approve any major change in the business. On the other hand, the manager does not take on the financial risks faced by owners. If the business fails, the manager will lose a job but will not have lost any money invested in the business.

While entrepreneurship is an important part of U.S. business, there are

Working in **Teams**

Individually, team members should think about the work of entrepreneurs and of business managers and prepare two lists: (1) things that are different and (2) things that are the same. As a team, compare the items in the two lists and discuss whether entrepreneurs and managers are more alike or more different.

Get the Message

Making Convincing Presentations

A new business will not be successful if the entrepreneur cannot obtain funding from investors, loans from banks, or financing from other companies to be able to purchase or lease buildings, equipment, and materials needed to operate the business.

The entrepreneur prepares a business plan to provide the information needed by others in deciding whether to invest or provide financing. Most people will not read the full plan, though, until they are interested in the business idea.

So an entrepreneur must be able to make a short oral presentation when meeting with potential investors and business people that will cause them to be interested in the new company. If the presentation does not get their attention in the first minute and present two or three meaningful points and supporting information in the first few minutes, it will probably not be successful.

Think Critically

1. Why do prospective investors and other business people want to hear a short presentation from the entrepreneur?

2. If you were an entrepreneur, what would be your first statement to generate interest in your new company?

3. Create a presentation outlining the major topics you would cover in three to five minutes to interest investors in a new business.

---

entrepreneurs starting businesses around the world. In developing economies, entrepreneurs are often the first to start businesses to produce and sell products and services. Some of the most renowned global businesses, such as Sony, Mercedes-Benz, and IMAX theaters, were originally the ideas of international entrepreneurs.

Entrepreneurship Opportunities in Marketing

Entrepreneurs start all types of businesses. Manufacturing businesses tend to be the most recognized, but marketing opportunities also exist for entrepreneurs. Some of the best-known entrepreneurs had marketing ideas.

Sam Walton developed an efficient method to distribute products from manufacturers to his discount retail stores. He grew his small Arkansas business into today's Wal-Marts and Sam's Clubs. Frederick Smith wrote a paper as an undergraduate student at Yale on how packages and other deliveries could be moved rapidly by airfreight through a system of hub cities. From that idea, he created FedEx, which today is the world's largest express transportation company. Mrs. P.F.E. Albee took the products of the California Perfume Co. and pioneered the now famous door-to-door selling and distribution methods of Avon Products.

Those are just a few examples of people who had ideas for how to distribute, sell, promote, and service the thousands of products consumers demand. Retail and wholesale businesses, finance and credit companies, transportation businesses, advertising agencies, and many other organizations are involved in the distribution and exchange of products and services between producers and consumers. All provide opportunities for entrepreneurs.

Checkpoint ▶▶▶

What is the difference between an entrepreneur and a manager?

Writing a Press Release

A press release is a communications tool used by organizations and companies to inform the media about exciting new developments. The purpose of a press release is to "sell" the media outlet on the newsworthiness of whatever the press release is seeking to promote so that it provides media coverage to inform the public.

A variety of media outlets are available for press release distribution. These outlets include newspapers, magazines, radio, and web sites. Press releases are distributed using fax, e-mail, or "snail mail" to the decision makers in media organizations. These organizations are bombarded by competing press releases, so a concise, well-written, professional press release is crucial. A press release should be written with a particular media outlet in mind.

To catch the reader's attention, each press release should lead with a thought-provoking, attention-grabbing heading. Effective press releases have a tantalizing tone that motivates the reader to finish reading the entire release.

Always consider the target audience of the development or event that is the focus of the press release. For example, if your school drama club is trying to raise money by performing as clowns at children's birthday parties, you might want to send a press release to a local publication that focuses on children's activities.

A press release should use language and content that evokes an emotional response. Quotes can be used effectively. Sometimes a quote from an expert expressing enthusiasm adds credibility. A quote from a typical "person on the street" can make the product or event seem relevant to a general audience.

Just as answering the "who, what, when, where, and why" questions are mandatory for journalism articles, it is necessary to include the same information in a press release. Other types of information are essential as well. If you are promoting an event, include a description of the sponsoring organization and the cost of

attending the event. For people who might have questions, provide as much contact information as possible. Phone numbers, web sites, and e-mail addresses are all good. Decide who in your organization will be responsible for answering inquiries.

A variety of press release templates are available online and in popular word processing programs.

Carefully think about when to distribute the press release. Consider the time each media outlet will take to make a decision, prepare, and run the news feature to provide adequate lead time before the event.

Follow up on the press release by calling the decision maker who received the release. Prepare a brief outline of pertinent points prior to the call. When you have the decision maker on the phone, engage him or her in a brief conversation to "sell" the importance of your press release.

Develop Your Skill

Volunteer to write a press release for an upcoming school event. Work with an advisor to clarify the target audience of the release and the key information to include. Develop the content of the release using the guidelines described.

After distributing the press release to the appropriate media outlet, follow up with the decision maker and review the results with your advisor.

Save copies of your press release and any media reports that resulted. They provide a good addition to your educational and career portfolio.

The Importance of Entrepreneurship

It is sometimes easy to confuse small business with entrepreneurship. Not all small businesses are owned and operated by entrepreneurs. Many people buy an existing small business or operate a franchise and may not be considered entrepreneurs. Nevertheless, almost all businesses developed by entrepreneurs start out as small businesses.

Economic Role

Entrepreneurs develop small businesses, and small businesses are important to the U.S. economy. Over 600,000 new small businesses are started each year. Over 10 percent of the working population in the United States is self-employed. Some additional important small business statistics provided by the Small Business Administration are shown in Figure 21-1.

Small businesses are more likely to hire younger and older workers and workers who need part-time jobs. Small businesses have historically been the source of the initial job training for many people. A first part-time or full-time job working for a small business teaches important lessons such as time management, human relations, and good work habits as

©PHOTODISC/GETTY IMAGES

Why are small businesses more likely to employ younger and older workers?

well as the knowledge and skills to perform the job.

Personal Benefits

Entrepreneurs work long hours to make their businesses successful. They sacrifice to invest their savings and often have little or no income for the first few years of operations. They are responsible for the success of the business, so they have to handle complaints and solve problems. With all of those difficulties, why would anyone want to be an entrepreneur?

Owning a small business offers many personal benefits. Many people are able to add to their income by operating a part-time business in addition to their full-time job. Most entrepreneurs start their first business while they are still working for another company. They often start the business at home on a part-time basis and expand it to a full-time business if it is successful.

FIGURE 21-1

The role of small businesses (20 or fewer employees) in the U.S. economy.

Small businesses...
• Make up over 97% of all businesses
• Employ 52% of all non-government workers and 38% of workers in high-tech occupations
• Provide about 75% of all new jobs
• Are responsible for over half of all goods and services produced
• Make up over 95% of all companies involved in exporting

Entrepreneurs receive a great deal of personal satisfaction from developing an idea into a business and completing work that is interesting and uses their skills. Watching a business grow, opening new businesses, providing jobs for people in the community, and being able to control the profits from the company are all identified by entrepreneurs as reasons they prefer business ownership.

©PHOTODISC/GETTY IMAGES

Checkpoint ▶▶

Why are small businesses an important part of the U.S. economy?

How can small businesses help their communities grow?

21-1 Assessment

Key Concepts

Determine the best answer.

1. The American Dream is
   a. starting a new business
   b. getting rich
   c. retiring early
   d. becoming a manager in a large business

2. True or False: There are very few opportunities to start new marketing businesses in today's economy.

3. True or False: Not all small businesses are owned and operated by entrepreneurs.

4. Which of the following is *not* true of the role of small businesses in the American economy?
   a. make up over 97% of all businesses
   b. employ over 50% of all non-government workers
   c. provide about 75% of all new jobs
   d. all of the above are true

5. True or False: Most entrepreneurs start their first business while they are still working for another company.

Make Academic Connections

6. **History** Identify a large, well-known corporation that is a successful business today. Use the Internet to conduct research on the original owner(s) and how the business was started. Prepare a short report on that history and whether or not it is an example of entrepreneurship.

7. **Technology** Use information from the lesson on the role of small businesses in the U.S. economy or gather additional or more recent information. Use a computer and graphing software to prepare three bar or pie charts that illustrate that role. Make sure to prepare specific and meaningful titles and labels for each chart.

Connect to

8. Your team has been asked to prepare a presentation for a local community television channel to promote the importance of entrepreneurship. Develop a five-minute presentation that uses an informational poster as a visual aid. Videotape your team presentation so that it can be viewed by your teacher (judge).

Characteristics of Entrepreneurs

marketing matters

Some characteristics that make a successful marketer also make a successful entrepreneur. Creativity, determination, risk-taking, and willingness to take responsibility and make decisions are all important both in marketing and in starting a new business.

You are often involved in activities in school, in clubs and other organizations, and in part-time jobs that demonstrate the qualities needed for success as an entrepreneur and as a marketer. List the characteristics identified above. Now make a list of the school activities, clubs, organizations, and jobs in which you have participated. Compare the lists and identify specific assignments, activities, and leadership roles that gave you an opportunity to develop and demonstrate each of the characteristics. After you have finished, consider which of the characteristics are currently personal strengths and which are not yet as well developed.

What Does It Take?

Why is it that some people have started several successful businesses, often when they are still quite young, while other people have never considered starting one? What makes one person suited to be a business owner and other people suited to be managers or employees? Researchers have studied successful entrepreneurs and have identified qualities that make them different from other people.

Characteristics of Entrepreneurs

It is important to recognize that almost anyone can be an entrepreneur if he or she has a strong desire and will. Women and men of all races, ages, and educational backgrounds have become successful

Why do you think some entrepreneurs succeed while others fail?

©PHOTODISC/GETTY IMAGES

entrepreneurs. People are not born with entrepreneurship skills. The skills can be developed if you want to start your own business.

Studies of successful entrepreneurs show that they usually have the following characteristics.

- *Entrepreneurs are focused and goal-oriented.* Many successful entrepreneurs thought about and planned their business for many years. They may have faced a number of obstacles before they were able to succeed, but they did not give up on their plan.

- *Entrepreneurs are risk-takers.* **Risk-taking** is a willingness to risk the chance of failure in order to be successful. Entrepreneurs invest time and money in ideas that others may not have tried. Yet entrepreneurs are not gamblers. They carefully consider the risk. They work hard to reduce the risk and increase the chances of success.

- *Entrepreneurs want to achieve.* They set high personal goals, and then do everything they can to meet those goals. They may stubbornly keep working at the goal even when it does not seem likely they will succeed.

- *Entrepreneurs are independent.* They are often not involved in team activities and may not do well when asked to cooperate with others. They are more comfortable when they are in charge and responsible for results.

- *Entrepreneurs have a high level of self-confidence.* When people are **self-confident**, they believe in themselves and their abilities and expect to be successful. If they do not succeed at an activity, they will either decide it was not important, put the responsibility for failure on others, or work hard to improve to succeed the next time.

- *Entrepreneurs are creative.* **Creativity** is the ability to use imaginative skills to find unique ways to solve problems. Creative people often approach problem

©DIGITAL VISION/GETTY IMAGES

Why is it important for entrepreneurs to be goal-oriented?

solving differently and are likely to develop original ideas and solutions. That creativity is often the reason that entrepreneurs develop products and services others have not considered.

You can see by looking at the list of characteristics that not everyone is suited to be an entrepreneur. Also it is apparent why an entrepreneur may not make a good business manager or team player and may prefer to work independently rather than working for someone else.

Often, the business started by an entrepreneur fails when it begins to grow and the owner has to spend time managing the growing business. The entrepreneur may not have the patience or the interpersonal skills needed to successfully manage the business. It is not unusual for an entrepreneur to sell the business after several years and then begin the process of starting a new business all over again.

Do You Want to Be an Entrepreneur?

Most people know whether they want to be an entrepreneur. Remember, you can be a small business owner without being an entrepreneur. You can buy and operate a business that was successfully started by another person. You can become a franchisee and operate a business using the standards and procedures developed by the franchiser.

If you have thought about starting your own business, you should assess your potential. Determining whether you have what it takes to be a successful entrepreneur is an important step. If your desire to start a business is strong, you can develop the characteristics and skills that are necessary.

Use the checklist in Figure 21-2 to determine if you have the qualities needed to successfully start your own business. For the items for which you cannot place a checkmark, plan ways to develop the quality so that you can improve your chances for success as an entrepreneur.

FIGURE 21-2
Check your entrepreneurship characteristics.

— I usually set realistic and achievable goals for myself.
— I like to take responsibility for my own actions.
— I like to solve problems and identify new ways to do things.
— I'm willing to take risks when I know there is a chance to be successful.
— I am able to manage my time well and usually complete the tasks I start.
— When I am doing something I enjoy, I will commit many hours to the work.
— I like challenges and don't mind the pressure.
— Things do not have to be simple; I can manage several things at the same time.
— I usually have confidence in the things I choose to do.
— I often put personal priorities ahead of socializing.
— I would rather do things where I can control the results rather than relying on others.
— When I don't have the answer to something, I will go out and find it.
— I understand my strengths and weaknesses.
— When I have accomplished an important goal, I often want to move on to something else.

Checkpoint ▶▶

Why do some businesses started by entrepreneurs fail when they begin to grow?

Preparing for Entrepreneurship

You may know others your age who have already started successful businesses on a part-time basis, or you may have done so yourself. If you have not, but you have the desire, you should begin planning now if you want to become an entrepreneur. When you begin planning, you may well find that you have already done several things that will improve your chances for successfully starting a new business.

In the early part of the 20th century and before, many entrepreneurs did not have a great deal of education. It was not unusual for an entrepreneur to drop out of school, work in business for many years, and then start a business. However, that was a time when business was not as complex as it is today and fewer people were educated. It was possible to run a business based on what the person had learned through experience.

Today, consumers and business people are more educated, and business procedures and technology are more complex. While there are certainly successful young entrepreneurs and older entrepreneurs with a high school education or less, most people who start successful businesses today have completed high school and often have one or more college degrees.

An Inventor and an Entrepreneur

Combine the curiosity of an inventor and the business skills of an entrepreneur and you have multimillion-dollar international business success.

Erno Rubik was a Hungarian designer who was intrigued by mathematical problems. He developed a cube comprised of 26 smaller six-colored cubes that were connected but could be rotated independently. Mr. Rubik wanted to determine how to solve the problem of aligning all of the same-colored sides of the small cubes on the same side of the larger cube. He invented and applied for a patent for the cube.

When Hungarian businessman Tibor Laczi saw the cube, he believed there was potential for both a children's toy and an adult puzzle. Working with Erno Rubik, Mr. Laczi signed agreements with companies in several countries to produce and market the Rubik's Cube.

It has become the most popular puzzle in history and has made both men multimillionaires. More than one-eighth of the entire world's population has played with a Rubik's Cube.

Think Critically

1. What personal characteristics do you believe are similar and different between an inventor and an entrepreneur?

2. Why do you believe the Rubik's Cube was such a successful international product?

Education is an important part of preparing to become an entrepreneur. The classes you select should develop academic abilities, technology skills, and an understanding of business.

Academic Preparation

To plan and start a business, you will need to work with many people, develop and communicate your business plans, seek financing, prepare and review financial documents, make decisions, and solve problems. A strong academic preparation will provide the knowledge and skills needed for these tasks.

Communications Skills
Writing and speaking are essential entrepreneurial skills. You will write business letters, memos, and reports. You will prepare written materials such as employment advertisements, job descriptions, and product information. Use classes in English and composition to develop your ability to write clearly and efficiently using the form and style expected by the reader.

Oral communications are especially important to entrepreneurs. You will make presentations to investors, bankers, lawyers, other business people who will provide products and services for your business, and prospective customers. You must communicate effectively with employees to conduct meetings, give directions, and explain procedures.

Public speaking, speech, and other oral communications courses are important to you if you are planning to be an entrepreneur. In addition, find leadership roles in class projects, become an officer in

Fast FACTS

A survey by QuickBooks of 1,300 of its small business customers revealed that 43% of the entrepreneurs said they were loners as kids, 25% considered themselves nerds, 10% identified themselves as jocks, and 1% said they had been bullies.

clubs and other organizations, and participate in activities in which you are responsible for formal and informal presentations.

Math Skills As an entrepreneur, you are responsible for the profitability of your new business. If the business is not profitable in a short time, it will fail. If there is no profit, you will not be able to pay yourself, so you will need to work at another job to receive a paycheck.

Basic math skills are used to develop financial plans for the business as well as in day-to-day business operations. You will need to make calculations quickly and accurately involving the mathematical functions of addition, subtraction, multiplication, and division. You will frequently calculate percentages and use fractions and decimals. The ability to estimate the accuracy of a calculation will allow you to quickly check a budget, an invoice, or a sales estimate.

Advanced math skills, including statistics and accounting, will be useful in conducting research and in preparing and analyzing financial reports. You will be able to select the best investment opportunities, negotiate favorable loan terms, and compare the performance of your business with similar businesses.

To develop the needed skills, you should take a number of mathematics classes, including algebra, and business classes that include mathematics, such as accounting, finance, business statistics, and marketing research.

Scientific Skills You may believe that science classes cannot contribute a great deal to helping you become an entrepreneur unless the business is a scientific business. Yet science classes are an important way to learn to solve problems, conduct research, and make decisions

What kinds of math skills would be valuable for entrepreneurs? Why?

based on careful and objective analytical procedures.

Scientific skills include identifying problems, reviewing information, considering alternative solutions, and basing decisions on objective information. Science classes also teach careful observation skills, note taking, and the preparation of written reports.

Using Technology

Many tools are available to help entrepreneurs plan and manage their businesses. You are probably familiar with many of the tools since they are commonly used by students in schools and are available in many homes.

The most common and important business tool is a computer. Business planning can be completed much more easily and accurately using a computer and available software. Business records, including payroll, taxes, budgets, accounts payable and receivable, and others can be developed, maintained, and analyzed using a computer.

In addition to being computer literate, entrepreneurs need to be able to use a variety of business software including word processing, spreadsheet, database, graphics and presentation design, web design, accounting, and statistics programs. Other technology used by business people includes printers, fax machines, cell phones, and personal digital assistants (PDAs). In addition to being able to use these types of technology, entrepreneurs need to be able to select the technology that will perform the needed tasks.

The Internet is becoming an essential personal and business communication medium and information resource. Entrepreneurs need to be able to use the Internet to quickly gather information, analyze competition, and communicate with other business people, investors, bankers, customers, and employees. Understanding search engines, web site design, and communication resources is an important technology skill. Effective use of the Internet also involves understanding and following security procedures and following netiquette principles for professional communication. **Netiquette**, or Internet etiquette, is the informal code of conduct regarding acceptable online behavior.

It is possible to learn how to use business technology in a number of ways. Many classes in your school will help you develop computer skills. Business classes will introduce you to common business software. Part-time jobs and internships also provide opportunities to use technology. Many of your interests, hobbies, clubs, and activities will allow you to develop technology skills.

Business Skills

In the past, many entrepreneurs developed business skills

through experience. They often worked in another business for many years and advanced to become managers before deciding to start their own business. Others learned from the mistakes they made when starting a business. If they were lucky, they were able to correct the mistakes, but many entrepreneurs had to suffer one or more business failures before succeeding.

Today, there are many opportunities to learn about business and develop the knowledge you will need as an entrepreneur. High schools and colleges offer

©PHOTODISC/GETTY IMAGES

Why do today's entrepreneurs need to complete higher levels of education compared to entrepreneurs in years past?

many business classes. Often, you can take courses in entrepreneurship that actually help you develop your business idea and business plan.

Important business classes for entrepreneurs are accounting, business communications, business law, finance, business management, and marketing as well as computer classes. Because many new businesses are using the Internet, e-commerce is an increasingly important business class. You should also participate in cooperative education or internship programs and become a member of a student business organization such as DECA. These activities will give you practical experience, allow you to identify and work with business mentors, and develop important leadership, interpersonal, and teamwork skills.

Checkpoint ▶▶▶

What are the academic skills that are important for entrepreneurs?

21-2 Assessment

Xtra! Study Tools
school.cengage.com/marketing/marketing

Key Concepts

Determine the best answer.

1. Which of the following is a characteristic of most entrepreneurs?
   a. enjoy participating in team activities
   b. are willing to gamble
   c. are goal-oriented
   d. all of the above

2. True or False: In the early part of the 20th century, many entrepreneurs did not have a great deal of education.

3. Which of the following is *not* an academic area that is useful in preparing to be an entrepreneur?
   a. communications
   b. math
   c. science
   d. all are important

4. _____ is the informal code of conduct regarding acceptable online behavior.

5. True or False: Since entrepreneurs do not work well in teams, there is little benefit in participating in a student business organization as a way to prepare to be an entrepreneur.

Make Academic Connections

6. **Visual Art** Work with a team to create a bulletin board in your classroom titled "Characteristics of Successful Entrepreneurs." Use both text and pictures to illustrate each of the characteristics discussed in the lesson.

7. **Reading** Use the library and Internet to collect and read newspaper and magazine articles that have been written about a well-known entrepreneur. Based on your reading, how do the personal characteristics of the entrepreneur compare to those discussed in the lesson? Make a list of the characteristics you were able to identify.

Connect to ◀DECA
An Association of Marketing Students

8. You are a mentor for a middle-school student who will enroll in your high school next fall and wants to start a business after graduation. Prepare a written educational plan in which you recommend the courses from your school's curriculum for each year, student organizations and activities to consider, and other experiences that would help the student prepare for the career choice. Present the plan to your teacher (judge) and discuss the reasons for your recommendations.

Business Ownership Opportunities

GOALS

- Identify business opportunities related to marketing functions.
- Describe how marketing can help you identify business ownership opportunities.

KEY TERMS

viral marketing, *p. 599*

microcredit, *p. 600*

marketing matters

Entrepreneurs start all types of businesses. Many entrepreneurs open businesses that use special skills they have developed. For example, a person who has developed web design skills may start a business developing web sites for other businesses. Others start a business that is related to the type of business experience they have. For example, a person who manages the accounting department of a large company may decide to open her own accounting business. A third area for business ideas is a person's hobby or interests. If someone likes to cook, a catering business could be a possibility. A person who enjoys traveling may start a business organizing and leading tours.

Think carefully about specific skills, work experience, and interests and hobbies you have. List them on a sheet of paper. Then under each category, list several businesses you could start related to the category. Share your ideas in a discussion with other students and brainstorm other ideas to add to each student's list.

Business Opportunities in Marketing

There are unlimited opportunities for starting your own business. Entrepreneurs own manufacturing, retail, wholesale, and service businesses. Specialized areas such as farming, clothing design, home remodeling, fitness training, and computer programming provide entrepreneurship opportunities.

We have learned that marketing businesses are an important part of our economy. Both retailing and wholesaling companies are marketing businesses that provide a number of marketing activities in completing the exchange process.

Even if you decide not to start a retail or wholesale business, there are many other marketing opportunities available for entrepreneurs. Each of the marketing functions needs to be performed as products

and services are exchanged between producers and consumers. Businesses can be developed to provide these functions.

Promotion

Several types of businesses offer promotional services. Advertising agencies, public relations firms, graphic design, copywriting, and printing companies are examples of businesses involved in promotion. Other companies build displays for stores or design billboards and electronic signs to promote businesses and products. The new area of viral marketing offers the opportunity to offer unique promotional services. **Viral marketing** is a promotional approach that encourages people to pass along marketing messages through word of mouth, creating a rapid dissemination

Figure This

Return on Investment

To finance a new business, an entrepreneur was able to invest $75,000 of her own money. She obtained $490,000 of additional funds from a group of people who owned a venture capital company. Venture capital companies look for attractive new business ideas where they can get a good return on the money they invest. The table below shows the amount of money invested and the profit received at the end of three years of operation.

	Entrepreneur	Investors
Amount of Investment	$75,000	$490,000
3-Year Profit	$9,500	$112,000

Think Critically

1. What was the 3-year return on investment of the entrepreneur and of the investors (profit ÷ investment × 100)?

2. What was the total amount invested in the business and the total amount of profit?

3. Why would an entrepreneur be willing to accept a smaller return on investment than the venture capital group is willing to accept?

of information. The use of viral marketing on the Internet has allowed marketers to have an almost instantaneous impact on large numbers of people.

Selling

Sales agencies are hired to sell the products and services of companies. This is often done when it is not profitable for a company to employ its own sales force. Another type of business opportunity related to selling is offering sales training or developing resources that are used by salespeople, such as computer programs, sales materials, or product models.

Distribution

Many types of companies are involved in storing and distributing products from producer to consumer. Trucking companies, express delivery businesses, and couriers handle thousands of products each day. Warehouses and storage centers ensure that products are held safely until they are needed.

Pricing

It is difficult to identify businesses related to the pricing function. Yet a number of

companies help determine the value of products and negotiate agreements between the buyer and seller. An example of that type of business is an auction house, where products are presented and sold to the highest bidder. eBay is an example of an Internet business that helps buyers and sellers negotiate a fair price for products. Other companies provide pricing information to prospective buyers so that they know how much they should pay for products.

Financing

Banks and credit card companies are marketing businesses that provide financial services to businesses and consumers. Financial advisors help in obtaining credit and making investments. Newer entrepreneurial companies are providing very small amounts of financing for people who are considering starting new part-time businesses. **Microcredit** provides small value loans to people who cannot qualify for traditional bank loans. Microcredit has become a way of increasing the number of small businesses in rural and high poverty areas that can benefit from economic development and in preindustrial countries that are just starting to develop their business economies.

Risk Management

Businesses constantly face risks that challenge business operations. Entrepreneurship opportunities exist for people who have expertise in security, safety, and the application of technology to help businesses anticipate, manage, and reduce their risks. Today, many businesses face security issues resulting from terrorism threats as well as maintaining the privacy and security of business and customer information. They often look to experts to help them respond to those new issues.

Marketing-Information Management

Gathering and analyzing information and conducting marketing research are important marketing activities. Many types of businesses perform this marketing function. Some companies pay consumers to test products, conduct surveys in malls, or send shoppers into businesses to determine the effectiveness of customer service. Businesses gather information and prepare reports for other companies.

Product and Service Management

You can find a company that will provide assistance to other businesses in new product research and design. Other companies will provide testing to ensure the quality of a product or to compare the strengths and weaknesses of competing products.

Market Planning

Many companies need assistance in identifying new markets and determining the feasibility of entering those markets. Entrepreneurs with expertise in underserved markets (ethnic consumers, international markets) can offer specialized services to other businesses. Many exporting and importing businesses have been formed by entrepreneurs.

Checkpoint ▶▶▶

Why do each of the marketing functions provide entrepreneurship opportunities?

Identifying Business Ownership Opportunities

Understanding marketing gives you an important set of skills to help you identify possible business opportunities. Many entrepreneurs select a business idea based solely on their interests, skills, and experience. It is important to choose a business that you like and for which you are skilled to operate successfully. But that is not enough.

Successful marketing uses a two-step process. The first step is to identify customers and their needs. The second step is to develop a marketing mix to meet the needs of the customers. A successful business should follow the same procedure. Rather than starting with an idea for products and services, an entrepreneur should begin by studying the market.

Identify a Target Market

Before you decide to start a business, you should determine if a target market exists for the business. Who are the possible customers and where are they located? What are their specific needs? Are those needs generally satisfied by existing products and services or are they unsatisfied with current choices?

Study the Competition

A new business will have difficulty competing with an existing business unless the existing business has a weakness. Identify companies offering similar products. Determine the prices they charge and the services they offer. Find out what customers in your target market like and dislike about each competitor.

Develop a Unique Offering

Based on a study of the customers and competitors, determine if you can provide a competitive product. Unless you can identify something your business will offer that is better than the competition in some important way, it is not likely that your new business will be successful. Using your understanding of marketing planning will help you identify successful business opportunities.

Checkpoint ▷▷

What is the two-step marketing process that can be used to identify business opportunities?

21-3 Assessment

Key Concepts

Determine the best answer.

1. True or False: Starting a retail or wholesale business is an example of entrepreneurship opportunities in marketing.

2. _____ provides small value loans to people who cannot qualify for traditional bank loans.

3. True or False: The first step an entrepreneur should take in starting a new business is to identify an idea for a product or service that he or she wants to offer.

4. After an entrepreneur identifies a target market and studies the competition, the next step in planning is to
   a. find an effective location
   b. obtain needed financing
   c. create a unique offering
   d. develop a memorable business name

5. A company that assists businesses in identifying global markets performs which of the following functions?
   a. promotion
   b. financing
   c. pricing
   d. market planning

Make Academic Connections

6. **Math** There are 5,789 fitness center customers in a community. Research shows that 18 percent are very dissatisfied with their current fitness center. If a new business can enroll 25 percent of the dissatisfied customers, how many members will it have? What percentage of the total market will the fitness center enroll?

7. **Finance** Use the Internet to gather information on an organization that offers microcredit to support new entrepreneurs in a country with a developing economy. Prepare a written report on the organization and the results of the program.

Connect to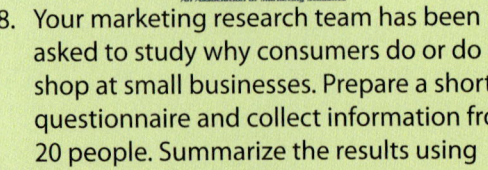

8. Your marketing research team has been asked to study why consumers do or do not shop at small businesses. Prepare a short questionnaire and collect information from 20 people. Summarize the results using tables and charts. Make an oral presentation to your teacher (judge).

Legal Needs of Entrepreneurs

GOALS

- Describe the legal forms of ownership for a business.
- Discuss legal steps to follow in starting a new business.

KEY TERMS

proprietorship, *p. 603*

proprietor, *p. 603*

partnership, *p. 605*

partnership agreement, *p. 605*

corporation, *p. 605*

charter, *p. 605*

marketing matters

Entrepreneurs are quite independent and want to be totally responsible for business decisions. This makes it difficult to share ownership of a new business with other people. However, having multiple owners in a business often increases the chances that the business will be successful. Form small groups with other students and discuss the advantages and disadvantages of each of these three scenarios:

1. An entrepreneur starts a new business with his or her own money and is the sole owner and decision maker.
2. An entrepreneur identifies another person to be a partner in a new business. The partners contribute an equal amount of money and share in the ownership and decision making.
3. An entrepreneur sells stock to four other people to finance a new business. The entrepreneur owns half of the stock, and the other four own equal amounts of the remaining stock. The entrepreneur manages the business, and the other owners serve as the board of directors to approve major plans for the business.

The Ownership Decision

One of the first decisions made by an entrepreneur is the legal form of ownership for the new business. While it would seem that an entrepreneur would be the sole owner, there are three common ownership choices. They are proprietorship, partnership, or corporation. Each form of ownership offers advantages and disadvantages.

Proprietorship

A business owned and managed by one person is a **proprietorship**. A **proprietor** is a person who has sole ownership of a business. Proprietorship is the most common form of business ownership, with

©DIGITAL VISION/GETTY IMAGES

Why is a proprietorship a popular form of ownership for entrepreneurs?

Judgment Call

Whose Idea Is It?

Sometimes entrepreneurs will have an idea for a new product while they are working for another company. If the company they are working for decides to develop and market the product, the person who developed it may not share in the profits if the product is successful.

Some entrepreneurs take their idea and start their own business rather than sharing it with their employer. In this case, the idea was developed while they were employed, but the former employer does not share in the profits of the new product.

Some companies now ask employees to sign legal agreements that they will not start a business from an idea developed on the job. The agreements usually give the employee rights to some of the profits the company makes from ideas developed by the employee.

Think Critically

1. Do you believe employees should be able to take ideas they developed while employees and start their own businesses?

2. Should a company be obligated to share profits from a new product with the employee who had the idea?

3. Do you agree with the idea of the legal agreement described? Why or why not?

---

nearly three-quarters of all businesses organized in this way. Under the proprietorship form of organization, the owner is responsible for the money needed to start and operate the business as well as all business planning and management.

Advantages of Proprietorships

The sole owner of the business is the boss and can make all decisions. That feature suits many entrepreneurs, who are generally quite independent.

The proprietor receives all profits of the business. Because of the profit motive, entrepreneurs work very hard to make their businesses successful. The proprietor also has full claim to all of the business's assets if there are no debts.

The owner can make decisions without consulting others, so he or she can act quickly when needed. As a result, proprietorships are very flexible and can adjust rapidly to changing conditions.

Forming a proprietorship is relatively easy. There are few legal requirements to start the business or to end it. As a result, people who are trying to form their first business are drawn to this form of business ownership.

Disadvantages of Proprietorships

Running a business successfully requires many skills. A proprietor is totally responsible for the business and may not have all of the skills needed. There is a greater chance that the business will fail due to lack of planning and management skills or other areas where the proprietor is not well prepared.

While a few businesses can be started without a lot of money, most new businesses are quite expensive to form. One person may not have the needed money and may not be able to borrow adequate funds. Many business ideas are never developed due to a lack of funds.

In a proprietorship, the owner assumes a great deal of risk. While the owner receives all the profits of the business, that person also suffers all the losses if the business is not profitable. Creditors can make claims on everything the entrepreneur owns, not just the assets of the business if it fails.

The business will not be able to continue to operate for long if the owner becomes ill or dies. The business will either have to be sold or must close. Sometimes an entrepreneur loses interest in the business or does not have adequate time to devote to developing and managing it. With no other owners, the business is likely to fail.

Partnership

A **partnership** is a business that is owned and operated by two or more people who share in the decision making and profitability of the company. A partnership is formed using a **partnership agreement**, a legal document that specifies the responsibilities and financial relationships of the partners.

Advantages of Partnerships
Partnerships pool the knowledge and skills of all the owners. There are more people available to manage the business.

Because more than one person owns the business, there is usually more money available. Also, banks are more likely to loan money to companies when more than one person is responsible for repaying the loan.

If one person decides to leave the business or dies, the business does not have to close. Partnership agreements specify how a partner can be replaced. The remaining partners can continue to operate the business until a new partner is located.

Disadvantages of Partnerships
Disagreements on important decisions can occur among partners. It may take time for partners to discuss issues and agree on the best solution. Many partnerships fail due to disagreements that cannot be resolved among the partners. In a partnership, all partners are generally responsible for any actions and decisions made by another partner. If money is owed, each partner is liable for the entire debt.

Corporation

A **corporation** is a business owned by people who purchase stock in the company. Corporations are granted a charter by the state in which they are formed. A **charter**

What are the advantages of the partnership form of business?

is a legal document allowing the corporation to operate as if it were a person. That means the business can borrow money, enter into contracts, and is liable for its decisions and actions.

Advantages of Corporations

A corporation is most often formed by an entrepreneur to raise money and to limit the liability faced by the owners. Because an owner invests in stock, the losses suffered by the business in case of failure are limited to the amount of the investment.

The life of a corporation does not depend on any one owner. If an owner decides to sell his or her stock, another person can buy it, and the business continues to operate.

As a corporation grows, it is easier for the owner to turn day-to-day management responsibilities over to managers. Policies and direction of a corporation are controlled by a board of directors who hire well-prepared executives to manage the business.

Disadvantages of Corporations

Because corporations operate based on a charter, they face more rules and regulations than other forms of businesses. They are watched carefully by the states in which they operate and must file regular reports.

The people who own the company's stock usually do not have as much interest in the business as the entrepreneur. They may be more concerned about the profits earned by the company than they are about the day-to-day operations. No one individual has to take responsibility for business operations and decisions.

Corporations usually are taxed at a higher rate than the other forms of business. Also, individual investors must pay taxes on any profits distributed to them.

Checkpoint ▶▶

How is ownership different in each of the three legal forms of business ownership?

Starting Your Business

Once you have decided to start a business, several legal steps need to be completed before you can open for business.

- Select the form of ownership. Decide if your business will be a proprietorship, partnership, or corporation. If it is a partnership, prepare and sign the partnership agreement. If it is a corporation, prepare and file a charter and complete the other forms required by the state.

- Decide on a business name and register it with the state and local government.

- Determine the licenses and permits that are needed to operate your business. Complete the procedures to obtain each one.

- If you are creating a new product, determine if a patent, copyright, or trademark can be obtained. If so, file an application.

- Purchase or lease buildings and equipment. Obtain necessary financing for the purchases and for business operations. Complete mortgage, lease, and loan applications and financial documents.

Fast FACTS

A leading business consultant lists the top reasons for new business failure as: starting the business for the wrong reason, poor management, lack of money, wrong location, lack of planning, expanding too quickly, and no business web site.

- Create necessary business records.

- Identify insurance needs and purchase the necessary policies.

- Prepare personnel policies and procedures if employees will be hired. Identify and comply with all employment and tax laws.

- Develop procedures and prepare forms you will use to sell products to customers and make sure they meet all legal requirements. Be prepared to collect and report all local, state, and federal taxes.

You can see that starting a business involves many steps and requires a great deal of legal information. An entrepreneur should work with a lawyer skilled in business startups and should seek assistance from experienced business people, business associations, and government offices to make sure all procedures are followed and all legal requirements are met.

Checkpoint ▶▶

Why is it important to get legal assistance from a lawyer and others when starting a new business?

21-4 Assessment

Xtra!
Study Tools
school.cengage.com/marketing/marketing

Key Concepts

Determine the best answer.

1. A business owned and managed by one person is a
   a. small business
   b. proprietorship
   c. charter
   d. new venture

2. A disadvantage of a partnership compared to a corporation is
   a. there can only be two owners in a partnership
   b. each partner must assume all of the financial risks
   c. the government controls partnerships more carefully than corporations
   d. a partner cannot be involved in the day-to-day management of the business

3. A _____ is a legal document allowing the corporation to operate as if it were a person.

4. True or False: Because starting a new business is quite simple, an entrepreneur generally does not have to obtain advice and assistance from lawyers, accountants, or other business professionals.

Make Academic Connections

5. **Government** Use the Internet to identify the procedures that must be followed to form a corporation in your state. Prepare a written list of the procedures including the name of the state department or office that administers the process.

6. **Visual Art** Use the flowcharting function on a computer graphics program to prepare a flowchart of the legal steps described in the lesson that an entrepreneur should take to start a new business. Compare your flowchart with those prepared by other students and discuss similarities and differences.

Connect to ◀ DECA
An Association of Marketing Students

7. A family friend has worked for a large advertising agency and now wants to start a new business to provide promotion and public relations services to other small businesses. He plans to form the business as a proprietorship since it is very simple to start. You want to convince him that the business will be more successful if organized as a partnership or corporation. Participate in a role-play with your teacher (judge) to present the reasons for your beliefs and to answer questions.

Developing a Business Plan

GOALS

- Discuss the importance of a business plan for a new business.
- Identify and describe the parts of a business plan.

KEY TERMS

business plan, *p. 609*

executive summary, *p. 611*

marketing matters

The characteristics of entrepreneurs make them more interested in starting and operating the business than in taking the time to carefully plan for a business. Yet studies have identified that one of the most important tools to the success of a new business is a carefully developed, well-written business plan.

Before you study this lesson, consider all of the information needed and all of the decisions that must be made before a business can open. Think about the activities that must be completed to successfully operate a business.

Make a list of all the things you would include if you were preparing a written plan for a new business. For each item listed, write a short statement describing why you believe it would help an entrepreneur to carefully plan for that business element. Share your list with other students to identify the similarities and differences. As you complete this lesson, compare your list to the information in the lesson.

The Importance of Planning

An entrepreneur will make many decisions before the business ever opens. Many more decisions must be made after the business begins operations. If the correct decisions are made, the business will be successful, but if enough of the owner's decisions are incorrect, the business will join the thousands that fail each year.

An experienced business owner may know enough about the business to make many of the important decisions quickly with the information available at the time. A new entrepreneur does not have that experience or the information to easily make good decisions. It will be valuable if the entrepreneur has help readily available when problems are encountered and decisions must be made.

©STOCKBYTE/GETTY IMAGES

How can inexperienced business owners improve their chances of success?

The Business Plan

A **business plan** is a written document prepared to guide the development and operation of a new business. It contains the information used and the initial decisions made to manage each of the major areas of the business.

Each new business will have a slightly different plan. The business plan should be prepared by the business owner and should reflect the owner's knowledge, ideas, and experience. But all business plans must communicate several things.

Why would a lending institution want to see a business plan?

- The purpose of the business and the types of products and services it plans to offer

- Descriptions of the business's customers and their important needs

- Major business activities that will be completed

- Resources needed, including materials, equipment, and people

- Sources of financing and the amount of money needed to start and operate the business

- The type of competition to be faced and major competitors

- Financial requirements and profit projections

Using the Business Plan

A business plan would be important even if only the entrepreneur used it. By gathering and studying information and using that information to make decisions about the business, the owner will usually be more careful and more objective in determining how the business will operate.

The business plan becomes an important guide for starting and operating the business. Because of the detailed planning, the entrepreneur can use it to determine if the business is developing according to the plan and if changes need to be made.

In addition to the value of the plan to the business owner, however, other people who are involved in starting the business benefit from a well-prepared business plan.

Prospective Partners and Stockholders

If the entrepreneur wants to organize the business as a partnership or a corporation, potential owners will want information about the business to determine if they want to participate.

Bankers and Investors

Most new businesses will need to borrow money to finance buildings, equipment, product purchases, and several months of operations. Bankers and other people who might consider making loans will need detailed information to make sure the business is a solid investment. Most investors and financial institutions insist that entrepreneurs provide a well-developed business plan.

Employees of the Business

The owner of a new business works many hours each week and is very busy making sure the business is successful. Employees are an important part of the operations. The business plan provides information to employees so the owner will not have to orally communicate the information to employees when they need it or when the owner is not available.

Other Business People Other businesses will be a part of the success of the new business. If the new business manufactures products, it will need cooperation from retailers to sell products. It will need to purchase raw materials, supplies, and equipment and usually will want credit from suppliers. The new business may need the help of lawyers, accountants, advertising agencies, and others. A business plan assures the cooperating businesses that the owner is well prepared to work with them.

Checkpoint ▶▶

Why is it important for a new entrepreneur to have a written business plan?

Developing a Business Plan

A business plan is used to make important decisions about business operations, to communicate those decisions to others, and to serve as a guide for business operations. The parts of a business plan are shown in Figure 21-3.

The sections of the business plan present the specific decisions that have been made and describe how the business will be organized and managed. The written plan identifies the resources that will be needed to operate the business successfully. Financial plans describe the money that will be needed to operate the business and how the money will be used. Detailed financial projections are made to show income, expenses, profit, and the return on investment that investors, including the entrepreneur, can expect from the financing they provide.

FIGURE 21-3
Each section of a business plan provides detailed information on decisions made for that part of the new business.

Outline of a Business Plan for a New Business

I. Introduction to the Business
    A. Description of products and services
    B. Owners and form of ownership
    C. Business organization
    D. Long- and short-term objectives
    E. Strengths and weaknesses

II. Description of the Industry
    A. Economic conditions
    B. Types of competition
    C. Strengths and weaknesses of competitors
    D. Anticipated changes in the industry

III. Market Analysis
    A. Description of target markets
    B. Analysis of needs and purchase behavior
    C. Sales forecasts for major markets

IV. Operations
    A. Organization of operations and departments
    B. Descriptions of major activities
    C. Identification of equipment, materials, and other operating resources needed
    D. Staffing requirements and management plans

V. Marketing
    A. Description of marketing mix
    B. Procedures for implementing marketing activities
    C. Resources needed for marketing

VI. Financial Plans
    A. Startup costs
    B. Semiannual income and expense projections
    C. Monthly cash flow budgets
    D. Annual balance sheet projections
    E. Analysis of financial plan
    F. Sources of financial and funding requests

Working in **Teams**

As a team, review the sections of a business plan listed in Figure 21-3. Using a local telephone or business directory, identify an organization or individual that could serve as an advisor or resource to help develop each section of the plan. Consider business professionals, experienced business owners, government agencies, college and university personnel, and others.

After the business plan is complete, the owner should prepare a one- or two-page summary of the plan. The **executive summary** provides an overview of the business concept and the important points in the business plan. It highlights the major planning decisions made by the business owner. The executive summary is useful when the owner needs to present the plan to others in order to build understanding and support for the new business. It should capture the attention of readers and make them want to learn more about the entire business plan.

Checkpoint ▶▶▶

What are the major sections of a business plan?

21-5 Assessment

Key Concepts

Determine the best answer.

1. True or False: A business plan is not needed unless the entrepreneur needs to obtain financing from a bank or other investors.

2. True or False: Each new business will have a slightly different business plan.

3. A business plan should be prepared by
   a. the business owner
   b. a communications specialist
   c. an experienced entrepreneur
   d. all would be appropriate

4. A business plan should be shared with each of the following groups *except*
   a. prospective partners and stockholders
   b. bankers and investors
   c. employees of the business
   d. competitors

5. True or False: An entrepreneur only needs to prepare a one- or two-page summary of a business plan rather than a long, detailed written plan.

Make Academic Connections

6. **Communication** Plan and practice a persuasive speech to persuade new business owners that they can benefit from preparing a detailed written business plan. The speech should include at least four specific benefits of the written business plan. Present your speech to other students.

7. **Reading** Use the library or Internet to locate a sample business plan for a new business. Read the plan as if you were a prospective investor to determine if it provides the information you need to understand the business and make a financing decision. Write a three-paragraph analysis of the strengths, weaknesses, and effectiveness of the plan.

Connect to DECA

8. Identify a target market and choose a small business idea to serve that market. Use the outline of a business plan shown in Figure 21-3 to prepare a one- or two-page executive summary of the planning decisions for your small business. Use the executive summary to present your business idea and plans to your teacher (judge).

Chapter 21 Assessment

Check Your Understanding

Now that you have completed the chapter, check your understanding of the lessons with these questions. Record the score that best represents your understanding of each marketing concept.

1 = not at all; 3 = somewhat; 5 = very well

If your score is 42–50, you are ready for the assessment activities that follow. If you score 33–41, you should review the lessons for the items you scored 1–3. If you score 32 or less, you will want to carefully reread the lessons and work with a study partner on the areas you do not understand.

Can you—

___ define entrepreneur and entrepreneurship?

___ discuss ways in which entrepreneurs and entrepreneurship benefit the U.S. economy?

___ list several characteristics that are common to most entrepreneurs?

___ describe the academic, technology, and business skills needed to prepare for entrepreneurship?

___ identify new business opportunities that are related to each of the marketing functions?

___ compare the steps in the marketing strategy to a procedure entrepreneurs should follow in identifying new business opportunities?

___ explain the advantages and disadvantages of each of the three legal forms of business ownership?

___ identify several important legal steps that should be followed when starting a new business?

___ justify the value of a written business plan for a new business?

___ outline the major sections of a business plan?

Review Marketing Terms

Match the terms listed with the definitions. Some terms may not be used.

1. A person who has sole ownership of a business
2. A legal document allowing the corporation to operate as if it were a person
3. The informal code of conduct regarding acceptable online behavior
4. A business that is owned and operated by two or more people who share in the decision making and profitability of the company
5. A willingness to risk the chance of failure in order to be successful
6. A written document prepared to guide the development and operation of a new business
7. The process of planning, creating, and managing a new business
8. Provides small value loans to people who cannot qualify for traditional bank loans
9. A business owned by people who purchase stock in the company
10. Someone who takes the risk to start a new business
11. The ability to use imaginative skills to find unique ways to solve problems

12. A legal document that specifies the responsibilities and financial relationships of the partners

a. business plan
b. charter
c. corporation
d. creativity
e. entrepreneur
f. entrepreneurship
g. executive summary
h. microcredit
i. netiquette
j. partnership
k. partnership agreement
l. proprietor
m. proprietorship
n. risk-taking
o. self-confident
p. viral marketing

Review Marketing Concepts

13. True or False: Few new small businesses today succeed due to the competition from large international businesses.

14. True or False: One of the reasons people start businesses is to have the freedom to do work they enjoy.

15. True or False: All small businesses are owned by entrepreneurs.

16. True or False: Small businesses represent about half of all of the businesses operating in the United States.

17. True or False: Often, a business started by an entrepreneur fails when it begins to grow.

18. True or False: Successful small businesses are seldom owned by people from minority groups.

19. Which of the following is *not* a characteristic of entrepreneurs?
    a. Entrepreneurs want to achieve.
    b. Entrepreneurs are independent.
    c. Entrepreneurs are wealthy.
    d. Entrepreneurs are risk-takers.

20. When selecting an idea for a business to start, an entrepreneur should choose one that
    a. has never been tried before
    b. meets his/her interests and skills
    c. requires only a small investment
    d. is recommended by friends and family

21. True or False: Unless an owner can identify something a business will offer that is better than the competition in some important way, it is not likely that the business will be successful.

22. The form of business ownership in which the owners assume the least amount of risk is
    a. entrepreneurship
    b. partnership
    c. proprietorship
    d. corporation

23. True or False: A disadvantage of a partnership is that if money is owed, each partner is responsible for the entire debt.

24. True or False: The business plan should be shared with prospective customers so that they are more confident in the business's success.

25. The financial section of a business plan includes
    a. an analysis of customer needs
    b. a description of the marketing mix
    c. identification of startup costs
    d. staffing requirements

26. True or False: The complete written business plan should be no more than one or two pages long.

Marketing Research and Planning

27. Identify a small business you would be interested in starting as an entrepreneur. Use the Internet to locate the following information about that type of business:
    - Two existing businesses that offer the same type of product or service
    - Two businesses that could supply products or services needed by the business for its operations
    - Two sources of small business assistance available to a new entrepreneur
    - Two financial institutions in your area that may provide startup financial support for the new business

28. Use a word processing program to develop a questionnaire using the items in Figure 21-2. Add three additional items asking respondents to identify their age, gender, and number of years of education.

    Give a copy of the questionnaire to five people and ask them to complete it. When you have all of the completed questionnaires, enter the items into a spreadsheet. Calculate the totals for each item. Prepare a report of your findings.

    Working with other students in your class, enter the information from all questionnaires into one spreadsheet and calculate the class totals for each item. Discuss the results. Identify any differences in responses that seem to relate to age, gender, and education.

29. The number of businesses formed as proprietorships, partnerships, and corporations is identified and reported by state and federal governments each year. Use the Internet to obtain the most recent information on the number and type of businesses for the entire United States and for your state.

    Develop a spreadsheet to report the information you obtained. Use the spreadsheet to calculate the total number of businesses in the country and in your state. Calculate the percentage of U.S. businesses in each category, the percentage of the total number of businesses in your state in each category, and the percentage of the U.S. totals represented by the businesses in your state. Prepare national and state pie charts to illustrate the results. Make sure to label the charts and all data presented.

Marketing Management and Decision Making

30. Becoming a successful entrepreneur requires a person who has the necessary personal characteristics, education, and experience, as well as the financial resources to be able to provide some of the initial financing of a new business.

    Prepare a personal analysis of your current status as a possible entrepreneur and a plan to improve your preparation. Use a word processing program and prepare a two-column table titled "My Entrepreneurship Preparation." The heading of the left column is "What I Have." The heading of the right column is "What I Need."

    Using information from the chapter, complete the table to describe what you have already done to prepare to be an entrepreneur and what you need to do to continue your preparation. Use the following headings for the rows in your tables:

    Entrepreneurship Characteristics
    Academic Preparation
       Communication Skills
       Math Skills
       Scientific Skills
    Technology Skills
    Business Skills
    Work Experience

31. Entrepreneurship opportunities often result from the design of new products or the development of improvements in existing products. Select one of the following products or identify another product category approved by your teacher:
    a. portable television and video player
    b. miniaturized computer keyboard
    c. student backpack
    d. cellular telephone
    e. beverage cooler for the beach

    Use a computer graphics program or craft materials to create a new design for the product that you believe improves on the current design (added features, easier to use, more portable or efficient, etc.). When you and your classmates have finished your designs, display the new products around the classroom. Have a "gallery walk" where small groups walk from product to product and the designer describes the product, its features, and its benefits.

32. Working in small groups and with the help of your teacher, identify a small business owner from your community who is a graduate of your high school. Contact the person and arrange an interview. If possible, obtain a video camera and videotape the interview. If it is not possible to meet the business owner in person, it may be appropriate with the permission of your teacher to complete the interview using the telephone or e-mail. Make sure to take careful notes during the interview.

    Ask the business owner the following questions:

    1. Why did you decide to start your own business?
    2. What did you do to prepare for business ownership?
    3. What steps did you take to start your business?
    4. Who is your target market?
    5. Who are your main competitors?
    6. What are the characteristics of your marketing mix: product, price, distribution, and promotion?
    7. What do you believe are the most important factors in being a successful small business owner?

    When your interview is completed, summarize the information your team obtained and prepare an oral report on the entrepreneur to present to your class.

Entrepreneurship Participating Event

The purpose of the Entrepreneurship Participating Event (Creating an Independent or Franchising Business) is to provide an opportunity for the participant to develop and present a proposal to form a business. The event provides an opportunity for participants to develop and demonstrate mastery of essential skills as they apply to the analysis of a business opportunity, the development of a marketing/promotion plan, and the development of a financial plan.

After conducting research, participants must choose an independent or franchise business for a selected location. The written plan will consist of the following sections:

Executive Summary Write a one-page description of the project.

Description and Analysis of the Business Situation Include rationale and marketing research, introduction, self-analysis, analysis of business opportunity, and proposed organization for the business.

Proposed Marketing/Promotion Plan Describe the proposed product or service, proposed pricing policy, personal promotion, nonpersonal promotion, and place (distribution).

Proposed Financing Plan Include projected income/cash flow statement, projected three-year plan, capital, and repayment plan.

Bibliography List all resources used.

Participants will have 15 minutes to present and defend their business prospectus to the judge. The judge has an additional five minutes to ask the participant questions about their business plan. Your presentation must convince the judge to invest in your idea. The business plan should convince financial institutions and/or venture capitalists to invest money in your idea.

Performance Indicators Evaluated

- Analyze the opportunity for starting a business. (Communication Skills)
- Interpret financial statements. (Financial Analysis)
- Take a concept from an idea to a business proposal. (Information Management)
- Set priorities and demonstrate effective time management. (Emotional Intelligence)
- Demonstrate critical thinking/problem-solving skills. (Emotional Intelligence)

Go to the DECA web site for more detailed information.

Think Critically

1. Why is the executive summary for the business plan so important?

2. Why would financial institutions and venture capitalists want to see projected financial statements for a three-year period for a proposed business?

3. Why is it important to analyze the existing competition when proposing a new business?

4. What is the major advantage of proposing a franchise business rather than an independent business?

PHOTOS: ©DECA INC.

www.deca.org

Take Control with Management

© PHOTODISC/GETTY IMAGES

Newsline

Quality Is a Top Management Responsibility

One of the most important responsibilities of a retail manager is maintaining quality. And it is more than the quality of the products offered in the store. The look of the store, the atmosphere, employees, and the entire shopping experience must meet customers' expectations. Even the lowest prices will not attract customers to a store if they are not comfortable and satisfied with their experience in the store. So what is required to maintain the quality of the retail shopping experience?

A survey asked nearly 1,000 shoppers to rate 21 specific factors that influenced their attitudes about a store. The most important quality feature to consumers is time. Time was rated twice as important as any other category. Time includes how long it takes to check out, total time to complete shopping, and how quickly the store processes credit and debit cards or other forms of payment. Second in importance was how the customer is treated. Consumers want to feel that the store is concerned about their needs and that each employee is helpful, friendly, and courteous.

Efficiency, including the number of open checkout lanes or registers and the ease of locating and choosing merchandise, was rated third. Price and the physical environment were tied for fourth place. Customers are concerned that prices are clearly marked and accurate and advertised specials are easy to locate. They want to shop in a pleasant, roomy, uncluttered atmosphere. Finally, consumers are concerned about technology. They want stores to use modern technology. They also want employees to know how to use the cash registers quickly and accurately.

Improving the quality of the shopping experience is one of the best ways to ensure customer satisfaction. If managers are unwilling to spend the time and money to improve the factors customers see as important, they will pay through lost sales and lost customers.

Think Critically

1. Why do you think time was so important to the survey respondents?

2. What retail stores in your community provide the highest-quality shopping experiences? What makes each effective in your view?

school.cengage.com/marketing/marketing

Prepare for Performance

This chapter develops the following Performance Indicators from the DECA Competitive Events program.

Core Performance Indicators

- Understand the tools, techniques, and systems that businesses use to plan, staff, lead, and organize their human resources
- Utilize planning tools to guide an organization's/department's activities
- Manage internal business relationships to foster positive interactions

Supporting Performance Indicators

- Provide input into strategic planning
- Manage staff growth and development to increase productivity and employee satisfaction
- Involve staff in company activities
- Determine and respond appropriately to personality types

Go to **school.cengage.com/marketing/marketing** and click on Connect to DECA.

©BMCSOFTWARE

Visual Focus

Management involves making sure that the right things happen in the right way. Even small businesses with only a few employees require management to plan, coordinate people and activities, and make sure the expected results are being achieved. Think of the challenges that face the managers of a huge multinational company. Ultimately the effectiveness of management determines the success of a company. Marketing managers must plan, organize, staff, lead, and control the many marketing activities and employees needed to satisfy customers and ensure a profit for the business.

Focus Questions:

What are the main responsibilities of each of the types of managers listed in the ad—CFO, COO, CMO, CEO, and CIO? Why is it important for them to be able to easily communicate and share information with each other? If you were a manager in a large company, would this ad interest you? Why or why not?

Locate another advertisement or visual example of a product or service designed to help managers complete their work. Share your example in a class discussion.

The Functions of Management

GOALS

- Explain the importance of management in business and the role of managers in effective marketing.
- Define the five functions of management.

KEY TERMS

managing, *p. 619*

marketing management, *p. 619*

planning, *p. 621*

long-range planning, *p. 621*

short-term (operational) planning, *p. 621*

organizing, *p. 623*

staffing, *p. 623*

leading, *p. 623*

controlling, *p. 623*

marketing matters

The people in a business complete thousands of activities intended to achieve certain goals. If the goals are going to be reached, those activities and the people who perform them have to be coordinated. Each business activity must occur at the proper time and place, using procedures that accomplish the tasks in the correct way. All of the resources needed to complete the tasks must be available as well. Making sure that business activities are well planned and occur as planned is ultimately the responsibility of management.

All parts of a business including marketing require management to be successful. Market managers plan and implement an efficient marketing strategy and coordinate the people, activities, and resources needed to accomplish the company's marketing goals. Business management entails five basic functions—planning, organizing, staffing, leading, and controlling. These five functions apply to all organizations, large and small, and to every manager from the chief executive officer to the newest supervisor.

Make a list of ten activities that must be coordinated in order for this marketing class to be effective and successful. Compare the items on your list with those of other classmates.

Coordinating People and Resources

The work of an organization consists of thousands and thousands of activities. Those activities often seem unrelated to each other. Many employees in a business and most customers are unaware of the variety of activities that go on every day in many different locations. However, all of that work is necessary for products and services to be produced and distributed and for customer orders to be received and processed. Each activity needs to be completed on time and accurately. Each activity must be coordinated with other related activities.

Key to Success

What makes a company successful? A quality product? Satisfied customers? Well-trained and motivated employees? Efficient operations? Profit? Each of these is important, but successful organizations have another key factor—effective management.

Effective managers are able to organize the resources and work of a company in ways that result in success. Companies with effective managers usually have good products, employees, and operations resulting in satisfied customers.

Management is one of the most important functions of a business. Very simply, **managing** is getting the work of an organization done through its people and resources.

Are managers important to a business? Consider the following scenarios. If the resources available are not the ones needed for a task, that task cannot be performed. If employees are dissatisfied with their jobs or are not well trained, motivation will be low and work quality will decline. If customer service is not performed well, customers will not get what they expect and are likely to complain. If someone in order processing is not careful in calculating prices on an invoice, someone in accounting will face the problem of explaining an overcharge or the need for an additional payment to a customer.

Each of these problems will require management attention and will need to be resolved. If they can be anticipated and prevented, the business will have a much better chance of success.

Marketing Management

You are aware of the many resources and people involved in planning and implementing a marketing strategy. Customer and market information needs to be gathered and studied. Products and services need to be planned, priced, distributed, and promoted. Each of the marketing mix elements must be coordinated with the others. If a product is not distributed in the time or the way that is expected by salespeople or advertisers, customers may be promised a product that cannot be

delivered. If product development costs much more than budgeted, pricing decisions will need to be changed.

Marketing management is the process of coordinating resources to plan and implement an efficient marketing strategy.

The work of more than one company usually needs to be coordinated as products move through a channel of distribution. The channel may include a manufacturer, transportation company, finance company, wholesaler, retailer, advertising agency, and others. You can see how the work of marketing managers can be very complex.

Now that you understand what a marketing strategy is, you are able to describe the work of marketing managers. Marketing managers are responsible for the success of the company's marketing efforts. Those marketing efforts are all of the activities involved in planning and implementing a marketing strategy. They manage the people and resources needed to identify markets and plan marketing mixes.

You also know how to determine if marketing managers are doing a good job.

According to the marketing concept, effective marketing results in satisfying exchanges. Marketing managers are successful when customers in the target markets are satisfied and the company is profitable.

©DIGITAL VISION/GETTY IMAGES

Why is marketing information important to marketing managers?

Working in **Teams**

As a team, create a diagram of the marketing mix with each mix element identified. Draw a line from one element to another and discuss how a problem in one element can have a negative effect on the other elements. Connect each element with another until all of the relationships have been discussed.

Checkpoint ▶▶▶

What is the role of marketing managers in making sure that a company's marketing efforts are successful?

Joshua Mannes was nearing his 67th birthday, which put him at the mandatory retirement age for his company. Even though he was the CEO, he would have to step down, yet he did not feel ready to retire. In 45 years of work, he had moved from an entry-level sales position through four levels of management, spending the past 12 years as the top executive. Mr. Mannes wanted to pass his expertise on to others, and he decided that the best way to do that was to become a business coach.

A business coach is an expert in many aspects of business who provides individualized information, advice, support, evaluation, and feedback to people who are trying to improve their job performance and career success. Business coaches are different from mentors in that they work on specific tasks for defined periods of time and are paid for their efforts. Business coaches may be hired by a company to provide support for one or more of its employees or by individuals looking for professional support. Business coaches work with top executives, beginning managers, employees in key positions in a company, or individuals who want to move up professionally.

Employment Outlook

- The career field is relatively new so current employment opportunities are limited but with expected future growth.

- Success is dependent on each business coach's ability and results.

Job Titles

- Business Coach
- Career Coach
- Life Coach
- Executive Coach

Needed Skills

- A broad knowledge of business derived from a variety of successful business leadership positions

- Expertise in problem solving, performance evaluation, and planning

- Ability to build rapport, listen, provide positive feedback and encouragement, and motivate improved performance.

What's it like to work in...
Business Coaching

Joshua Mannes is now in the third month of his new business and loves his work as a business coach. Today he has meetings with three clients. The first is a CEO who is having difficulty communicating with her board of directors. Joshua is working with her on ways to keep the board members updated with short written reports and follow-up telephone calls. The second client is a sales manager who has accepted his first international assignment. Joshua is drawing on his eight years as a sales manager in South America to provide advice on working with different cultures. At the end of the day, he will meet for the first time with a young entrepreneur who wants to be sure he has the management skills needed to effectively lead his rapidly growing business. Joshua is especially interested in working with this new client because he wants to see the young person realize his dream.

What About **You**

As you increase your knowledge and experience in business, would you like to pass what you know on to others to help them flourish in their careers?

Management Functions and Activities

The definition of managing presented earlier in the lesson is a general view of the role of managers. It is hard to determine specifically what managers do from that definition. A better understanding of the work of managers comes from examining the five functions of management—planning, organizing, controlling, staffing, and leading.

Planning

Planning involves analyzing information, setting goals, and determining how to achieve them. The president of a company is responsible for determining the direction of the business and making sure that plans are in place to move forward. Supervisors determine what their work groups need to accomplish each day and assign duties to each person they supervise. Even though the two managers work at very different levels in the organization with quite different responsibilities, both have planning as a part of their jobs. There are two types of planning that managers complete—long-range planning and short-term planning.

Long-Range Planning In
long-range planning, information is analyzed that can affect the business over a long period of time. Long-range plans are typically developed to cover a year or more and may include long-term goals and direction for five to ten years. Long-range planning includes setting broad goals and direction. Examples of long-range planning in a business are the strategic plan and business plan. In marketing, the marketing plan is often considered a long-range plan because it sets direction and goals for all marketing functions and personnel. However, it must be coordinated with the company's overall strategic plan and business plan.

Why is planning an important function of management?

Long-range planning is difficult because it relies on information from a variety of sources. The information available to managers cannot accurately predict the future. Managers need to use the information to help them anticipate what might occur over the time that the plan will be in place. They rely on their experience, a variety of data, and the help of planning experts and tools to make decisions. Using management skills, they will make decisions that will guide the business in the future.

Short-Term Planning
Short-term planning (often known as *operational planning*) identifies specific objectives and activities for each part of the business for a time period of a year or less. Often managers prepare a plan for a three-month period and then review or extend the plan on a month-to-month basis. In that way, they are always looking three months in advance.

Short-term planning is based on the long-range plan, so that all of the areas of the business are working to achieve the same goals. The objectives and activities of each part of the organization that are described in short-term plans must be coordinated with each other to avoid conflicts and inefficiency.

Spam: It Isn't Just a Meat Product

Anyone with an e-mail address is probably familiar with spam. Spamming is the use of any electronic messaging system to deliver unsolicited bulk messages. The most recognized type of spam is e-mail, but it can also take the form of instant messages, newsgroup posts, blog posts, or faxes.

Spamming is basically electronic junk mail. But unlike junk mail, technology allows spammers to operate at very little cost. The collection of e-mail addresses, the mailing of messages, and even response mechanisms for anyone who replies to the spam can all be automated. Spam has a very low response rate, but with such a low operating cost, spamming can still be profitable.

In general, spamming is viewed as annoying and unethical. It is often a vehicle through which fraud, identity theft, and numerous other scams are perpetrated. In addition, people collectively waste thousands of hours a year deleting spam messages from their work and personal e-mail inboxes. For these reasons, respectable companies avoid spamming, and the U.S. government regularly debates ways to curb spamming without infringing on the right to free speech.

Think Critically

1. Should spam be treated differently than traditional "junk mail"? Why or why not?

2. How would your perception of a company change if it began sending you spam messages?

Marketing planning in a large organization provides a good example of long-range and short-term planning. The marketing plan serves as the long-range plan for the company's marketing efforts. It identifies the target markets that the business plans to serve and describes the marketing mix that must be developed to meet the needs of each market. It also sets goals that the company will use to evaluate whether the plan is successful.

The managers of each specific area of marketing, such as marketing information, distribution, sales, and customer service, use the information from the marketing plan to guide short-term planning. They must determine the objectives and activities for each of their areas. They will need to communicate with each other and share information about their plans and activities. In this way, each of the specific short-term plans will coordinate with each other to meet the long-range goals outlined in the company's marketing plan.

Marketing information managers determine the information needed to make good decisions about each part of the marketing mix. They make sure the needed information is available to all other managers when needed for their planning. The distribution managers determine what products need to be moved to specific locations at what times and in what quantities. They determine how products will be packaged, stored, and transported at the lowest cost with the least damage.

Sales managers provide training and product information to salespeople. They help identify detailed information about customers and prepare the salespeople to use the information. They make sure customers understand the entire marketing mix and how it meets customer needs.

Customer service managers ensure that personnel and resources are available to respond to customer needs after a product purchase. They may develop delivery, installation, and repair services. They make sure that problems are solved and that customers are satisfied with their purchases.

Organizing

Organizing resources is important so that work can be accomplished effectively and efficiently. **Organizing** as a management function means arranging people, activities, and resources in the best way to accomplish the goals of an organization. Many businesses develop organizational charts to illustrate how the company is divided into divisions or departments and to show the relationships among those work units.

There are many ways to divide the work in a business. Managers organize by assigning responsibility and authority to others to get work done. They identify the types of resources that will be needed by employees including buildings, equipment, and supplies. Managers develop effective working relationships within the work group and with other work groups to make sure the organization works effectively.

Staffing

The activities needed to match individuals with the work to be done are known as **staffing**. Managers prepare job descriptions, recruit and select employees, determine how personnel will be compensated, and provide the necessary training so that employees can complete their work well.

Staffing is often considered the most difficult of the management functions. There are a number of activities involved in staffing, and the manager must be able to work well with a variety of people. It may be difficult to find people with the skills that match the jobs in a company. Effective training requires time and money. Some companies are not willing to invest in good training programs, making the manager's job more difficult. Managers are

Why is staffing one of the most difficult management functions?

©DIGITAL VISION/GETTY IMAGES

also responsible for evaluating the performance of each employee. They can reward those who are doing well, but they may need to dismiss employees who cannot meet the requirements of their jobs.

Leading

Is there a difference between being a manager and being a leader? Who do you identify as leaders—in your class, school, community, or country? What are the characteristics of an effective leader? Today in business, leadership is identified as one of the most important qualities of effective management. **Leading** is the ability to communicate the direction of the business and to influence others to successfully carry out the needed work. Effective leadership includes having commitment and motivation, using effective communication, establishing good working relationships, and recognizing and rewarding effective performance.

Controlling

When **controlling**, managers measure performance, compare it with goals and objectives, and make adjustments when necessary. If a company establishes a goal that 95 percent of all customer orders will

What activities are involved in the controlling function of management?

be delivered within 24 hours, the manager must regularly review information on order processing and delivery to be certain the goal is met. When the manager sees that fewer than 95 percent of the orders are being delivered on time, quick action must be taken. The manager must determine why orders are late and take steps to improve performance.

Specific controlling activities include setting standards, collecting and analyzing information, considering methods of improving performance, changing plans when necessary, solving problems, and resolving conflicts. Several common tools are used by managers to control operations, including plans, budgets, financial reports, and management information systems.

Checkpoint ▶▶

What are the five functions of management?

22-1 Assessment

Key Concepts

Determine the best answer.

1. Which of the following is an important factor in the success of a company?
   a. well trained and motivated employees
   b. efficient operations
   c. effective management
   d. all of the above

2. Managing is getting the work of an organization done through its _____ and _____ .

3. Which of the following is *not* one of the functions of management?
   a. planning
   b. organizing
   c. marketing
   d. controlling

4. True or False: Short-term planning identifies specific objectives and activities for a specific part of the business for a time period of a year or less.

Make Academic Connections

5. **Technology** Make a list of the five functions of management. Using the Internet or other resources, identify one technology product that could be used by a manager when completing each of the functions. Write a two-sentence description of the technology and how it supports the specific management function.

6. **Math** A marketing vice-president estimates her time at work in an average week is divided among the management functions in this way: planning, 16 hours; organizing, 8 hours; staffing, 4 hours; leading, 20 hours; and controlling, 18 hours. Prepare a pie chart to illustrate the hours and percentage of time devoted to each function.

Connect to DECA

7. Develop a three-minute presentation on why each of the management functions contributes to an effective marketing strategy in a business. Prepare visual aids to support your ideas. Give your presentation to your teacher (judge).

Managing Effectively with a Marketing Plan

GOALS

- Describe how a marketing plan serves as a guide for effective marketing management.
- Explain how marketing managers determine effectiveness by gauging customer and business satisfaction.

KEY TERMS

performance standard, *p. 628*

marketing effectiveness, *p. 629*

self-directed work team, *p. 632*

marketing matters

Marketing plans, which are detailed, written documents, help marketing managers perform each of the management functions effectively. Marketing managers are engaged in planning when they develop the marketing plan. Details in the marketing plan provide direction and support for each of the other management functions—organizing, staffing, leading, and controlling. So the act of developing a marketing plan establishes direction for marketing management.

A marketing plan also provides a means for evaluating the effectiveness of the company's marketing efforts. Overall marketing effectiveness is determined by how well customers and the organization itself are satisfied. Customer satisfaction is based on how well important needs are met. Organizational satisfaction is gauged by meeting its goals.

Work with a group and identify two goals. The first should deal with how to increase the overall academic performance of students in your school. The second should relate to improving the school environment. Identify the activities, people, and resources needed to accomplish each goal. Describe how you will determine how well the goals are met.

Improve Management with a Marketing Plan

Studies have been done that compare successful companies with unsuccessful companies. One of the most important differences typically seen is that successful companies develop and follow written marketing plans while unsuccessful ones do not. Figure 22-1 on the next page shows the outline of a typical marketing plan.

Information for Planning

It is easy to see how the marketing plan is related to the planning function. It is a long-range plan that sets goals and direction for the company for the length of time that the plan is in effect. The first part of the plan, Market Analysis, describes and reviews internal and external information that affects marketing. By studying this part of the plan, managers learn about the competition, the economy, and other important factors that can affect the success of their plans. They are made aware of strengths and weaknesses of the business so that weaknesses can be improved and strengths can be emphasized.

The second section of the marketing plan is the Marketing Strategy. In this section, target markets are identified and the marketing mix is described. Most important, the goals and outcomes that will be used to measure the success of the marketing plan are described. Every manager who has marketing responsibilities needs to be very familiar with this section of the plan. Every planning activity in the company is directed at implementing that strategy and achieving those goals and objectives. The managers responsible for each marketing function must determine how their function supports the overall marketing strategy. The goals and objectives they develop for their part of the business must contribute to the goals identified in the marketing plan.

In the final section, the Action Plan, specific activities and responsibilities are identified to guide short-term operations. All of the managers of marketing activities contribute to the development of this section. It identifies the work needed in their part of the business and guides them in planning day-to-day activities, including creating schedules and budgets.

Direction for Organizing

Much of the organizing work in a company is done before a marketing plan is developed. A company decides which marketing functions and activities it will perform and which will be provided by other companies. It develops a structure that organizes marketing personnel and activities into departments. It identifies the responsibilities of managers for the various departments and activities. Those decisions usually will not change a great deal even though many marketing plans will be written. If a company is successful with its target markets and makes only minor adjustments in the marketing mixes, it will not want to change its basic organizational

FIGURE 22-1
Each section of a marketing plan is important to a marketing manager in completing the five functions of management.

Marketing Plan Outline

I. Market Analysis
   A. Purpose and Mission of the Business
   B. Description of Current Markets and Strategies
   C. Primary Competitors and Their Strengths/Weaknesses
   D. External Environment Analysis
      1. Economy
      2. Laws and Regulations
      3. Costs
      4. Competition
      5. Technology
      6. Social Factors
   E. Internal Analysis
      1. Strengths
      2. Weaknesses
      3. Anticipated Changes
II. Marketing Strategy
   A. Marketing Goals/Expected Outcomes
   B. Target Market Description
      1. Identifying Characteristics
      2. Unique Needs, Attitudes, Behaviors
   C. Marketing Mix Description
      1. Product/Service
      2. Distribution
      3. Pricing
      4. Promotion
   D. Positioning Statement
III. Action Plan
   A. Activity Schedule
      1. Responsibilities
      2. Schedule
      3. Budget
   B. Evaluation Procedures
      1. Evidence of Success
      2. Method of Collecting Evidence

structure unless it sees ways to improve performance or save money with the change.

Support for Staffing Decisions

Effective marketing requires people with the skills necessary to perform the required marketing activities. Again, the marketing plan provides a useful tool for managers to determine staffing needs. The Action Plan is important because it describes activities and responsibilities that need to be accomplished by marketing personnel.

Managers match those activities with the current marketing employees. If the employees do not have the necessary skills to perform the activities, managers will need to develop training programs. If there are not adequate numbers of employees to perform the necessary work, new employees must be hired, or other businesses can be brought into the marketing channel to perform those activities. In some instances, current employees may not be needed for the activities required in a new marketing plan. Managers will have to make difficult decisions about the future for those employees and may need to help them find other jobs in the company or elsewhere.

Using the marketing plan to evaluate staffing needs is an important way for managers to determine where problems are likely to occur. You are probably familiar with businesses that had problems because they did not have adequate numbers of employees or the employees did not have the needed skills or were not motivated to serve customers well. Managers who pay careful attention to staffing needs, training, and employee motivation often have a decided advantage over their competitors.

Managers as Leaders

Many marketing efforts fail because the people responsible for the activities do not perform them well. Poor performance does not always occur because people do not have the skills to do the work. It may be due to a lack of leadership. Even though a manager has developed an effective plan and has the people and resources needed to carry out the plan, another ingredient is necessary—leadership.

Employees need to be a part of the business for it to be successful. They want to be involved and understand why the work they do is important. A marketing manager who is a leader involves employees in developing the plan and discusses the

Why should managers involve employees in marketing planning?

plan with employees when it is completed. In that way, the employees see why the plan is important. They understand how it can lead to success for the business and the people who work for the business.

The marketing manager also determines the working relationships that are necessary to implement the plan. Those relationships may be among people in the same department, in different departments in the company, and even with people in other businesses. A good leader develops effective working relationships and finds ways to recognize and reward the people who do their work well. When activities are completed that are an important part of the marketing plan, the people who are responsible need to know that they are doing the right things and that their manager and coworkers appreciate the good work.

Fast FACTS

Hewlett-Packard requires every business that is a part of its business-to-business sales channel to participate in customer satisfaction surveys. HP uses customer satisfaction as a competitive weapon in the marketplace and expects high customer satisfaction numbers from its business partners.

Gaining Control of Marketing

An old proverb says, "If you don't know where you're going, you will never know when you get there." A marketing plan states clearly whom the business wants to serve, what marketing activities are required, and the goals the business expects to achieve. Each of those decisions is used to measure the effectiveness of marketing. Evaluating effectiveness is a part of the controlling function of management.

Evaluating Effectiveness Marketing managers study how well they are reaching and serving each target market. They determine the market potential, the company's market share, and the share held by each competitor. Most businesses evaluate customer satisfaction with products and services as well as with other parts of the marketing mix. They want to see high satisfaction levels. A business becomes concerned if satisfaction begins to decline or if customers rate competitors higher.

The marketing mix is developed as a part of the overall marketing strategy in the marketing plan, and then the activities and resources needed to implement each mix element are identified. Schedules, budgets, and other planning tools are prepared to guide implementation. Finally performance standards are developed for marketing activities. A **performance standard** specifies the minimum level of expected performance for an activity. Marketing managers evaluate each one to see if the performance standards are being met. Whenever managers receive information that shows activities are not being performed as expected, they must take immediate action to correct problems.

Environmental Change There is another valuable way that the marketing plan helps managers with the controlling process. The first part of the marketing plan carefully describes the internal and external environment on which the plan is based. A change in any part of

©DIGITAL VISION/GETTY IMAGES

How can managers learn about changes in the external environment that may affect their marketing plans?

that environment could affect the success of the marketing plan. Managers read research reports, magazines, and newspapers. They attend conferences, talk to colleagues, and review other information so that they will be up to date and prepared to respond to changes.

The types of environmental factors that often change are the economy, technology, competition, and laws and regulations. For example, during 2000 and early 2001, many economic signs indicated that businesses were changing their spending patterns, particularly for technology and related products and services. Manufacturers immediately began to adjust their own inventory levels and production capacities so that they would not be caught carrying too much inventory or have to write down the value of outdated products. In 2005 and 2006, mixed economic signals were seen in the worldwide economy. Since consumer spending remained strong, most businesses continued with their plans but kept an eye on both U.S. and worldwide economic forecasts.

Checkpoint ▶▶

Why is a marketing plan a key to effective marketing management?

Ethical Decisions = Profits

Some business people argue that ethics and profits are not always compatible. But in 2001, the Co-operative Bank of Manchester, England, enacted an ethics policy stating that the bank would not work with companies with poor human rights and environmental records.

Some people predicted that the bank would fail due to this new ethics policy. In fact, it did turn down over $12 million in business early on. However, the company has seen a significant increase in investors attracted by the ethical stance. Thirty percent of its 2003 profits could be directly attributed to those customers, an increase of 6 percent in just one year. The bank carefully targets prospective customers who share its ethical and social values, leading to consistent growth in profits and clientele.

In recent years, other businesses in various industries, from clothing labels and auto manufacturers to diamond companies, have adapted ethics policies reflecting their stance on workers' rights, fair trade, and the environment. Many of these ethics policies attract new, like-minded customers.

Think Critically

1. Why would people believe that acting ethically might reduce profits?

2. Why would a business want to select a bank with the ethical and social policies described?

Determining Marketing Effectiveness

Managers are responsible for getting the work of the business done through other people and resources. If the work is not done well, the managers have not been successful. An important management responsibility is determining the effectiveness of marketing.

How can managers decide if marketing is effective? Is it based on the highest sales, largest market share, or most profit? Is the company with the best products or the products that have been on the market longest the most effective?

Managers may not always agree on what effective marketing is. The definition of marketing presented at the beginning of the book states that effective marketing results in satisfying exchanges. Accordingly, **marketing effectiveness** means that both customers and the business are satisfied. Based on that definition, to determine if marketing is effective, marketing managers need to be able to determine when the customers and business are satisfied.

If you were the marketing manager of a company, how would you know whether or not marketing is effective?

Measuring Customer Satisfaction

Customers are satisfied when they select a company's product or service to meet a need, use it, and choose it again when they have the same need. Therefore, an increasing level of sales is usually a good indication of customer satisfaction. However, companies should be careful to gather information on repeat purchases and use. They should be able to identify the level of sales for specific target markets and, if sales are growing, how much is from new customers and how much is from repeat purchases by satisfied customers.

Many companies spend a great deal of time and money studying customer satisfaction. They telephone customers or ask them to complete surveys. They may ask customers who have just made a purchase to provide feedback on their shopping experience and satisfaction.

Many retailers and other businesses have customer service centers in each store to make it easy for customers to return products, make exchanges, or get help with problems. Internet businesses also try to make customer service easy by providing options for customers to contact the business through telephone, e-mail, or instant messaging. Easy procedures to make product returns or to obtain service and repairs are also important to companies that sell products via the Internet, telephone, or catalog.

It is important to keep records of customer questions, problems, and complaints as well as positive responses. Customer service employees should complete a report of each contact, the reason for service, and the results so that common problems can be identified and eliminated. Any customer contact, its purpose, and the actions taken should be documented.

Figure This

Rule of 72 Makes Quick Work of Projections

Calculating market share is not always as simple as it looks, even when companies have information about the current size and spending habits of a market segment they want to target. That is because market segments are always shifting, and businesses want to target those that are growing or that can be expected to grow if the right strategies are applied. What is really important is not how big the segment is today, but how big it will be in the future. In other words, by how much and how quickly can it grow?

The Rule of 72 is a simple tool that can be used to quickly estimate how fast a market share can be doubled, assuming a constant rate of annual growth. Here is the formula: Years = 72 ÷ Rate where Rate is the annual rate of growth and Years is the number of years needed to double a beginning value. It can also tell you how fast a market needs to grow if a business wants it to double in a given number of years. In that case the formula is: Rate = 72 ÷ Years.

The Rule of 72 works well for rates of growth up to about 20 percent per year. For rates ranging from 20 percent to 36 percent, substitute 78 for the 72 in the formulas.

Think Critically

1. If Samco Inc. wants to double its Midwest sales in five years to justify a new warehouse, how fast must sales grow each year?

2. If Samco wants to double its Midwest sales in three years, what rate of growth is required?

3. If Samco's marketing manager estimates that segment sales will grow 12 percent annually indefinitely, how long will it take to double sales? How long will it take to quadruple sales?

Companies should not ignore the satisfaction of other businesses in the channel of distribution. Retailers and wholesalers are customers of manufacturers. If they are not satisfied with the manufacturer's products and services or their working relationships, they may decide to work with a competitor. Retailers and wholesalers need to inform manufacturers of any problems customers have with their products so that the problems can be resolved. Many businesses now involve other channel members in planning customer service and evaluation procedures. They regularly check with those businesses to make sure they are receiving the support needed to be effective and to provide customer feedback that relates to the cooperating business.

Measuring Business Satisfaction

Every business operates for a purpose. For many businesses, the purpose is to make a profit. For some businesses, however, profit is not the most important purpose. Some people start and operate a business because they enjoy the work. Some organizations are developed because of the contribution they make to the community. The success of schools, churches, city missions, public health centers, and other similar organizations is usually not measured by the level of profit. These organizations determine their success by looking for improvements in the community or society that result from their work.

Analyzing Goals The success of a business is determined by its goals. If the goal of a business is to increase sales or market share, it will not be successful if sales or market share decline. If a business sets a goal to achieve a profit of 4 percent of all sales or an 11 percent return on the owners' investment, it will be successful when it achieves that goal. Even if the goal of an organization is to change the attitudes or behaviors of people (stop smoking, stay in school), it will be successful only if people in its target market change those attitudes or behaviors.

Most goals of businesses and organizations are quite specific and can be measured. Businesses gather information on sales, costs, market share, and profits to determine their success. Nonprofit organizations gather information on increases in attendance, use of services, changes in behavior, or differences in attitudes and beliefs.

Financial Analysis When people think of marketing, they often fail to recognize the importance of budgets and financial performance. Marketing managers must understand and use financial information to determine the success of marketing activities. Sales of products in various markets can be compared from one year to the next. Costs associated with specific activities can be analyzed. Profits from one target market can be compared with those from another. The profitability of a specific marketing strategy can be analyzed.

Employee Satisfaction Managers also need to be concerned about the satisfaction of the people who work for the business. There is a great deal of evidence that employees who enjoy their work are more productive.

Marketing managers need to determine the level of employee satisfaction. Some companies ask their employees to complete surveys. Others hold regular meetings where employees can discuss problems and make suggestions.

Today, many companies form self-directed work teams. A group of employees who work together toward a common purpose or goal without the usual managerial supervision is a **self-directed work team**. While the work team is not a part of management, it is given many of the management responsibilities for planning, organizing, and evaluating its work. The teams have a great deal of responsibility for setting goals. They may determine the ways that work should be completed or how to solve customer problems. They may even be responsible for hiring other members of the team and determining how bonus money is distributed. Involving employees in decisions usually increases their satisfaction. A company that uses self-directed work teams will want to evaluate the effectiveness of that strategy and prepare the team members to be able to evaluate the results of their work.

Checkpoint ▶▶▶

When marketing managers use the marketing concept, what gauge do they use in determining marketing effectiveness?

22-2 Assessment

Xtra! Study Tools
school.cengage.com/marketing/marketing

Key Concepts

Determine the best answer.

1. _____ companies develop and follow written marketing plans while _____ ones don't.

2. The first major section of a marketing plan is the
   a. market analysis
   b. marketing strategy
   c. management plan
   d. action plan

3. True or False: Marketing effectiveness means that either customers or the business must be satisfied.

4. Which of the following would be the *best* specific measure of customer satisfaction?
   a. increasing sales
   b. increasing percentage of repeat customers
   c. increasing profits
   d. increasing number of new products for sale

5. A group of employees who work together toward a common purpose or goal without the usual managerial supervision is a(n)
   a. unsupervised group
   b. experienced employee team
   c. self-directed work team
   d. executive committee

Make Academic Connections

6. **Management** Identify three activities you complete on a regular basis at home, school, and in your after-school activities or hobbies. For each activity, prepare a specific performance standard that specifies the minimum level of expected performance for the activity in order for it to be completed successfully. For example, "A student can have no more than two unexcused absences in a semester."

7. **Research** Use the library and Internet to locate information on factors that contribute to employee satisfaction. Prepare a two-page report of your findings. Make sure to reference the information sources you used to prepare your report.

Connect to DECA
An Association of Marketing Students

8. Your team has been asked to develop a survey that can be given to customers of a local movie theater to determine their level of satisfaction with important aspects of the entertainment experience. Prepare an easy-to-complete survey of no more than ten items. Present the survey to your teacher (judge) and discuss the importance of each item as a measure of customer satisfaction.

The Work of Marketing Managers

marketing matters

The activities managers perform while carrying out the five management functions vary. The activities will depend largely on the specific position and the type of organization. Senior executives tend to do long-range planning and develop strategies. Lower-level managers often spend time implementing the decisions made by senior executives. Marketing managers, of course, work on marketing activities while managers in other parts of the business concentrate on the business functions for which they are responsible.

Choose a retail business and a manufacturing business. For the businesses chosen, identify several activities the top executive of the business would spend most of his or her time doing. Now identify several activities a supervisor of marketing employees would spend most of his or her time doing. Which of the five management functions do the activities of each manager represent? Discuss with other students how management is similar or different for the two positions.

Planning and Organizing

Oyang Chen is the executive vice president of marketing for an international automobile manufacturer. James Swathmore is a field sales manager for a food products wholesaler. He supervises five salespeople in a large northeastern U.S. state. The partial organization charts in Figure 22-2 on the next page illustrate the differences between Chen's and Swathmore's positions.

Planning

Ms. Chen spends most of her time planning with four other top executives and the CEO to set direction for the company. She is involved in long-range strategic planning, which identifies how the company must change over the next five to ten years. Ms. Chen studies consumer purchasing and economic trends throughout the world. She is very concerned about international trade agreements, increases and decreases of quotas, and changes in tariffs among several countries that have a major impact on the international automobile industry. Energy sources and prices, inflation, and the values of world currencies are also concerns for Ms. Chen.

The major responsibility of Ms. Chen's office is to prepare the company's marketing plan. The plan is developed for a five-year period, with specific plans for each of the five years. Each year the plan is revised and extended for another year so that the company is always planning five years in advance. The marketing plan is used by seven regional managers to prepare more specific plans for their regions of the global market.

Mr. Swathmore is also involved in planning, but he concentrates on short-term plans. He develops quarterly plans, but he implements monthly and weekly plans. While Mr. Swathmore must be familiar with the entire company's marketing plan, he is most concerned with the promotional mix element and the selling responsibilities. However, he must be very familiar with the product mix element, distribution, and pricing strategies because each of those has a major impact on the work of his salespeople.

Mr. Swathmore spends most of his planning time identifying customers, assigning them to salespeople, developing schedules and budgets for each person, and helping salespeople to develop specific sales strategies for major customers.

Organizing

Mr. Swathmore and Ms. Chen have very different organizing responsibilities. The overall marketing structure of each company is already set. The automobile

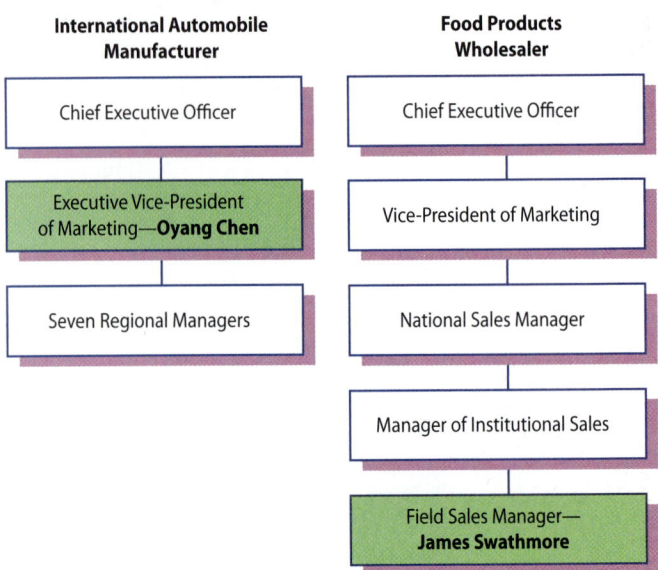

FIGURE 22-2

Oyang Chen and James Swathmore hold very different positions within their companies. Both must be effective at planning, organizing, staffing, leading, and controlling.

manufacturer is organized into seven worldwide regions. The food wholesaler is organized by customer type and geographically by state. Several common ways that companies organize their marketing operations are shown in Figure 22-3.

Ms. Chen's organizing activities focus on developing marketing policies and procedures for the entire company. **Policies** are rules or guidelines to be used in a company to make consistent decisions. **Procedures**

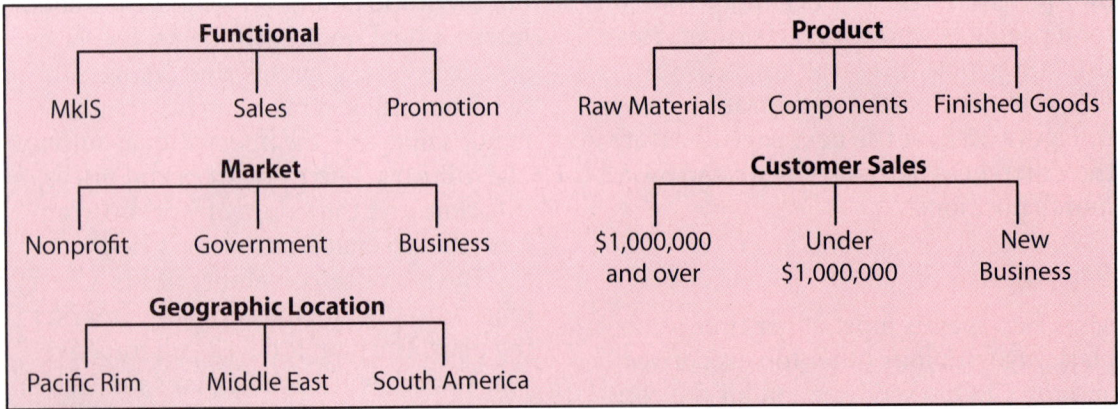

FIGURE 22-3

Marketing activities can be organized in several different ways depending on the type of business and its markets.

are the steps to be followed for consistent performance of important activities. Those policies and procedures will help determine the organizational structure for marketing, the functions that are performed, and the types of companies that will participate in marketing the automobiles.

Mr. Swathmore must work within the policies and procedures established by his manager. He is responsible for determining the activities that need to be performed and assigning those duties to the salespeople. He delegates authority and responsibility to each salesperson to complete the necessary selling tasks.

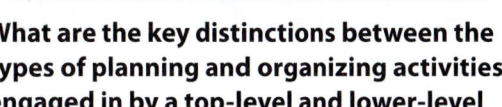

What are the key distinctions between the types of planning and organizing activities engaged in by a top-level and lower-level marketing executive in a business?

Managing the Work of Marketers

Both of the managers are responsible for getting the work of the organization done through other people. Therefore, they need to identify the need for personnel and fill those positions with the most qualified people.

Staffing

Ms. Chen will hire a few people to be her assistants. Her main responsibilities for staffing are to work with the company's human resources personnel to develop employment policies and procedures. She makes decisions about the percentage of the marketing budget that will be allocated to employee salaries, benefits, and expenses.

Mr. Swathmore is directly responsible for the salespeople who work in the territory he manages. He may not have total responsibility for hiring each person, but he identifies when an opening exists and describes the requirements for any open position. He helps with recruiting, interviewing, and selecting the person to fill the position. Most sales managers are very active in training new salespeople and helping to improve the selling skills of experienced employees.

Leading

Leading is an important responsibility for each of the managers. Some people would expect that Ms. Chen has more leadership responsibilities because she is the top marketing executive in the company. Yet Mr. Swathmore must be an effective leader if the selling team is to be successful in its territory. All managers must be able to involve people in planning, communicate expectations, and build effective teams to accomplish the work. They need to be able to recognize performance that contributes to the goals of their company and provide rewards that encourage people to continue to perform well.

Controlling

Controlling is another area of marketing where both managers have similar responsibilities. Each prepares objectives and specific plans to guide their work. They have developed standards for performance of the various marketing activities for which they are responsible. The major controlling activity is to gather and review information to determine if the objectives, plans, and

Working in **Teams**

A student club will operate a school concession stand at the varsity athletic events this fall, and your team will manage the project. List each of the five management functions on a separate sheet of paper. For each function, make a list of the activities your team will need to complete to successfully operate the concession stand.

Judgment Call

Technology Raises Privacy Issues

The development and spread of digital information technologies in the workplace has greatly increased the ability of employers to monitor employees' work habits. While the technology has raced ahead, the ethical issues raised by those advances have multiplied. In many cases, the issues have arisen much faster than businesses and managers have been able to confront and resolve them.

Typically, the legality of employers' actions is not in question because the actions they are monitoring (or capable of monitoring if they choose to do so) are conducted on company time using company equipment or property. Telephone records, e-mail and Internet traffic records, and computer files are all kept and stored as standard business practices by many if not most businesses. The information has many possible business uses aside from the monitoring of employee activities.

The ethics of using those resources to evaluate employees, however, is far from clear. On one hand, employers have openly used timekeeping and surveillance systems for decades to monitor workplace activities. Moreover, the availability of phone and computer records should be no secret to employees in today's working environment. Still, there are lines that most employers would not think of crossing. As technology advances, the question is where those lines should be drawn.

Think Critically

1. What guidelines would you set for businesses in establishing privacy policies for management and employees?

2. What responsibilities do managers and employees have in preserving ethical behavior and respect for privacy in the workplace?

---

standards are being met. Ms. Chen will be concerned about the entire marketing plan and performance in all of the marketing departments. Mr. Swathmore will concentrate on the activities and results of his specific department and salespeople.

An effective marketing information system is important to both managers. Without an efficient MkIS, neither manager will be able to analyze and understand the many activities under their control. The marketing information system gathers and analyzes information. It identifies when problems are occurring. Both Mr. Swathmore and Ms. Chen spend a great deal of time studying reports. They must identify the parts of their plans that are working well and the areas where problems may be developing. Ms. Chen concentrates on products or regions that have high and low performance. Mr. Swathmore is concerned about individual customers and salespeople.

When a specific problem is identified, the managers work quickly to correct it. They review budgets, schedules, and activities from their plans to see if some are not being performed in the way that was expected. They may have to revise the plans if it is clear that the original plans will not work.

Checkpoint ▶▶

For which management functions do top-level and lower-level marketing managers tend to have similar responsibilities?

How can a manager determine if objectives are being met?

22-3 Assessment

Key Concepts

Determine the best answer.

1. True or False: An important planning responsibility of most top marketing executives is to prepare the company's marketing plan.

2. Which of the following is true about the planning done by lower-level marketing executives?
   a. They do not do any specific planning but follow the plans developed by top executives.
   b. They concentrate more on short-term planning than on long-range planning.
   c. Their plans do not need to be in writing.
   d. They do not need to be familiar with the entire company's marketing plan.

3. The steps to be followed for consistent performance of important activities are known as
   a. plans
   b. policies
   c. procedures
   d. none of the above

4. True or False: Top marketing executives have more leadership responsibilities than lower-level managers.

Make Academic Connections

5. **Visual Art** Work with a team to create a poster that illustrates the types of activities marketing managers complete for each of the management functions. Other than the names of the functions, use only pictures and other graphics on the poster. Show the finished poster to other students and see if they can identify the activities represented.

6. **Career Success** Based on the descriptions of the two marketing management jobs discussed in the lesson, decide whether you would prefer to hold an executive management position or a specialized management position as a career choice. Prepare a three-paragraph report on the reasons for your choice.

Connect to

7. Work with another student to prepare two role-play scenarios of a retail store department manager meeting with a salesperson to discuss the importance of customer service. One role-play should demonstrate effective leadership, and the other should demonstrate ineffective leadership. Present both role-plays to your teacher (judge) and be prepared to answer questions about your demonstrations.

Check Your Understanding

Now that you have completed the chapter, check your understanding of the lessons with these questions. Record the score that best represents your understanding of each marketing concept.

1 = not at all; 3 = somewhat; 5 = very well

If your score is 42–50, you are ready for the assessment activities that follow. If you score 33–41, you should review the lessons for the items you scored 1–3. If you score 32 or less, you will want to carefully reread the lessons and work with a study partner on the areas you do not understand.

Can you—

___ offer definitions of management and marketing management?

___ list and describe the five management functions?

___ explain how the work of top executives and lower-level managers is similar and different?

___ identify the three major sections of a marketing plan and the important planning information included in each section?

___ explain the need for performance standards for marketing activities?

___ describe the two parts of marketing effectiveness?

___ discuss why self-directed work teams need to understand the functions of management?

___ identify the types of planning activities that are completed by top marketing executives?

___ describe the difference between a policy and a procedure?

___ provide examples of how a marketing information system helps marketing managers with the controlling function?

Review Marketing Terms

Match the terms listed with the definitions. Some terms may not be used.

1. Both customers and the business are satisfied

2. The process of coordinating resources to plan and implement an efficient marketing strategy

3. The activities needed to match individuals with the work to be done

4. A group of employees who work together toward a common purpose without the usual managerial supervision

5. Identifies specific objectives and activities for each part of the business

6. Measuring performance, comparing it with goals and objectives, and making adjustments when necessary

7. Arranging people, activities, and resources in the best way to accomplish the goals of an organization.

8. Rules or guidelines to be used in a company to make consistent decisions

9. The ability to communicate the direction of the business and to influence others to successfully carry out the needed work

10. Specifies the minimum level of expected performance for an activity

a. controlling
b. leading
c. long-range planning
d. managing
e. marketing effectiveness
f. marketing management
g. organizing
h. performance standard
i. planning
j. policies
k. procedures
l. self-directed work team
m. short-term (operational) planning
n. staffing

Review Marketing Concepts

Read each of the following statements and determine if it describes a planning, organizing, leading, controlling, or staffing function.

11. The home office of a drugstore chain sends directions on how merchandise should be displayed on the shelves.

12. The owner of XPert Hardware surveys her customers regarding the hours the store should be open and decides to open one hour earlier.

13. Aries Stavros holds a staff meeting every week to make sure that staff members understand their job assignments and to hear any complaints and questions they may have.

14. The owners of a dog grooming service decide to offer training classes to their employees in customer service.

15. Su Lee Han finds it necessary to review the budget allocations for her department once a week.

16. Jack Erbinsky attends a training session to learn about a new line of refrigeration products his company will carry.

17. Julio Chavez reduces the number of employees by three employees when his boss reassigns two product lines to another supervisor.

18. A multinational corporation restructures its marketing operations by product lines rather than by countries or regions.

19. The sales manager at Brevardo's Auto Sales holds a weekly meeting with his sales staff to keep them focused on sales goals.

20. Marketing executive Carol Hoerst skims through five online newspapers every morning for news that might affect the competitive environment for her company's products.

21. Melvin B. Goode hires an executive assistant in order to free up more of his own time for strategic planning.

22. The CEO of an international conglomerate anticipates retiring in two years and brings together an executive team to begin discussing the company's future.

23. The general manager of a restaurant reviews menu prices every three months to determine if changes are needed to keep prices in line with fluctuating food costs.

Marketing Research and Planning

24. Look at the classified ads in your local newspaper. Cut out at least five ads for managers. Paste each ad on a piece of paper and list the qualifications for each job. Is there one qualification that is predominant in all of the ads? If so, which one?

25. Identify a specific business and the product or service it markets. In a memo to your teacher, explain how each section of a marketing plan can be used as a guide for each of the management functions within that organization. Describe the function and the marketing management activities that would be completed to market the product or service.

26. There are many management tools such as total quality management, six sigma, benchmarking, balanced scorecard, continuous process improvement, and others to help managers improve the effectiveness of their organizations. Search the Internet for articles on a management tool of your choice. Write a 400-word paper explaining the tool, how it is used, and whether or not it is considered effective. Cite at least three research sources. Be prepared to present your paper to the class.

27. Mark Peters is the owner/manager of a wholesale electrical supply house. He has 40 employees and until recently has managed the entire operation himself. Lately his business is growing. He has decided he needs to reorganize the business and have a layer of management that reports to him.

    Eighteen people work in the warehouse. They are responsible for shipping, receiving, and inventory. The supply house has five employees who work the counter, maintain inventory records, and handle some of the more routine paperwork. There are ten truck drivers who deliver and pick up merchandise. And finally, seven people work in the office handling budgets, accounts receivable, and orders.

Develop a complete organizational chart for the business, adding the new layer of management. Indicate management and employee levels and areas of responsibility.

28. Managers realize that a good product or service will go unsold unless the employees do the best job possible in dealing with customers. Managers spend a great deal of time motivating and encouraging employees to do their very best. From your personal experience or using research, identify and describe five ways that managers can support their employees through positive motivation. State which ones in your view are the most effective and why.

29. A business will usually be successful if satisfactory exchanges are made. Both the company and the customer must be satisfied that they have received the most value for their money. List five specific things that indicate a customer is satisfied and five that indicate business satisfaction. Describe how each of the types of customer and business satisfaction can be measured. Be specific.

Marketing Management and Decision Making

30. A home improvement store recently decided to survey its final and business consumers to determine if they were satisfied with the type of service they were receiving. The results shown in the following table were obtained.
   a. The company surveyed 1,100 final consumers and 550 business consumers. Develop a table that identifies the number of yes and no responses to each of the questions for final consumers and business consumers.
   b. Develop a bar graph comparing the responses of business and final consumers for each of the survey items.
   c. Identify three problems that company managers can address and recommend an action that can be taken to correct the problems.
   d. For each of the actions you identified develop a specific performance standard that can be used to measure its effectiveness.

31. Form a team as directed by your teacher for this project. Using the Internet or the school library, access the Statistical Abstract of the United States published by the U.S. Census Bureau. On the Internet, use a search engine to locate the publication. Find the section titled *Income, Expenditures, and Wealth* and go to the table that lists the most recent year's gross domestic product (GDP) for each state.

   Use a computer to create a spreadsheet. Enter each state name and the state-by-state GDP figures into two columns of the spreadsheet.

   Use a map of the United States to organize the states into ten contiguous sales regions. Include Alaska and Hawaii in a region with west coast states. Cut and paste the information in your spreadsheet to organize it into ten groups representing the sales regions your team developed. Use the spreadsheet functions to calculate the total GDP in dollars for each sales region. Also calculate the percentage GDP (based on total U.S. GDP) for each region. Prepare a report that identifies the ten sales regions with their constituent states, showing the GDP in dollars and the percentage GDP for each region. Use the spreadsheet to prepare one or more pie charts for your report that illustrate the sales region information.

	Final Consumers		Business Consumers	
	Yes	No	Yes	No
Are sales items usually available?	45%	55%	75%	25%
Do you wait more than two minutes to be helped?	15%	85%	37%	63%
Is sales staff knowledgeable?	95%	5%	83%	17%
Are prices competitive?	50%	50%	94%	6%
Is sales staff courteous?	82%	18%	85%	15%

Public Relations Project

Successful business leaders understand the importance of developing good community relations. Students participating in the Public Relations Project will demonstrate the skills needed in planning, organizing, implementing, and evaluating a single public relations campaign conducted by the group. The campaign may focus on any topic or subject of interest to the group and should involve the majority of the chapter members.

The Public Relations Project can be completed by one to three students. The project consists of two major parts: the written document and an oral presentation by chapter representatives. The body of the written entry must be limited to 30 numbered pages, including the appendix (if an appendix is attached) but excluding the title page and the table of contents. The oral presentation will consist of ten minutes for students to present their public relations project and five minutes for the judge to ask questions about the project.

The body of the written entry consists of the following parts:

Executive Summary Write a one-page description of the project.

Campaign Theme or Focus Describe the issue to be addressed, rationale for selecting the issue, and the target population.

Local Media and Other Promotional Possibilities Describe the local print and broadcast media available, other possible promotional activities, media mix, and rationale for media and other promotional activities.

Campaign Organization and Implementation Include organizational chart, member involvement and job descriptions, description and documentation of the campaign, and estimated impact on the target population.

Evaluation and Recommendations Include evaluation and recommendations for future campaigns.

Bibliography List all resources used.

Appendix Inclusion is optional.

The Public Relations Project gives students an opportunity to promote their organization, a project, school, DECA chapter, or marketing department in a favorable manner to the community.

Performance Indicators Evaluated

- Develop and/or identify a theme for a public relations campaign. (Operations)
- Plan and organize a public relations campaign for the local community. (Operations)
- Work as a team to successfully complete a public relations project. (Emotional Intelligence)
- Implement a public relations campaign. (Operations)
- Evaluate the planning and implementation process. (Strategic Management)

Go to the DECA web site for more detailed information.

Think Critically

1. Why do businesses have public relations departments?
2. What types of personalities are best suited for successful public relations departments?
3. Why is it important for organizations such as DECA to establish positive relationships with the local media?
4. When should publicity be used as part of a public relations campaign?

www.deca.org

Planning Your Future in Marketing

©STOCKBYTE/GETTY IMAGES

Newsline

What Do Employees Want?

It's a startling statistic. In a recent survey, only 3 percent of employees said they were satisfied with their current job. Half of the respondents said they would consider changing their careers to entirely different types of work. Almost one-fourth are planning to make changes in the next year. Less than one in five employees said they would never consider a career change.

What are people looking for? Nearly 30 percent want to be able to make more money and don't believe their current job offers that opportunity. Coming in second was the desire to increase their personal happiness. Nearly 25 percent of the people wanting a career change believed they would be happier in another job. The third and fourth reasons for changing careers were greater job satisfaction (7 percent) and better working hours (4 percent).

Do people who change careers obtain the things they are looking for? Almost three-fourths of voluntary job changers do make more money. In order to get those increases in pay though, most had to complete additional education or training.

The results related to the other reasons for change are less encouraging. Respondents were nearly evenly divided about whether they were happier with their new jobs. Most reported the new job was more challenging and satisfying but believed they spent too many hours working and had only limited control over the hours they worked. One of the greatest values is that the individuals who changed jobs believed they were in a better position to withstand changes in the job market and to take advantage of other job opportunities that might become available.

Think Critically

1. Does the percentage of people who are dissatisfied with their jobs surprise you? Why or why not?

2. What does the information about job satisfaction say about the way that people choose their careers? Why do you believe people choose careers that they later find dissatisfying?

3. Why do you think "to make more money" is cited so frequently as the most important reason for wanting to change jobs?

4. If people report being dissatisfied with their jobs, why do only 7 percent want to change jobs to increase job satisfaction?

5. If you were an employer reading this report, what would you do about it?

school.cengage.com/maketing/marketing

Prepare for Performance

This chapter develops the following Performance Indicators from the DECA Competitive Events program.

Core Performance Indicators

- Understand concepts, tools, and strategies used to explore, obtain, and develop a business career
- Acquire self-development skills to enhance relationships and improve efficiency in the work environment
- Participate in career planning to enhance job success potential

Supporting Performance Indicators

- Assess personal interests and skills needed for success in business
- Explain possible advancement patterns for jobs
- Identify skills needed to enhance career progression
- Develop personal traits to foster career advancement

Go to **school.cengage.com/marketing/marketing** and click on Connect to DECA.

Visual Focus

The world is opening to you. As you continue your education and gain work experience, more and better career opportunities will be available. You may have decided that marketing jobs match your interests and abilities. If so, the choices are almost limitless. Even if you choose another career interest, your knowledge of marketing will be useful. This chapter explores the many career opportunities in marketing and helps you plan for an exciting career no matter what choices you make.

Focus Questions:

What products do you think of when you see the name IBM? In the past, IBM was a world leader in computer hardware and software. Today it emphasizes how its employees can help other businesses. Based on this ad, how does IBM want to help its customers? What does it want customers to think about when it asks, "What makes you special?"

Locate an ad that emphasizes the importance of a company's employees and their skills. Discuss why employees are such a valuable resource to businesses.

Benefits of a Marketing Career

GOALS

- Identify the impact of marketing careers on the economy.
- Describe the benefits of choosing a marketing career.

KEY TERMS

marketing job, *p. 644*

job, *p. 647*

career, *p. 647*

career planning, *p. 648*

marketing matters

Marketing jobs exist in every community and almost every business. Many people get their first job while they are still in high school or even earlier. That first job is often a marketing job. It may be delivering newspapers, taking tickets at a movie theater, or serving customers in a fast-food restaurant.

While those first jobs do not require a great deal of education and experience, they are important in developing an understanding of business operations as well as important career skills that are used even by people who hold the highest jobs in a company.

Make a list of any part-time or full-time jobs you have held. For each job, identify two or three things you learned that will be helpful in advancing into higher positions in a business. Compare your answers with the answers of other students to see what the jobs have in common in preparing people for careers in business.

The Importance of Marketing Careers

Marketing is one of the most important functions of business today. It provides employment for millions of people. Many of the fastest-growing and highest-paying jobs in our economy are marketing jobs. Whether you are still in high school, have a two- or four-year college degree, or have a graduate degree such as an MBA or PhD, there are employment opportunities in marketing that match your interests and skills.

Between one-fourth and one-third of all jobs in the United States are marketing jobs. In a **marketing job**, the completion of marketing activities is the most important or only job responsibility. The people who are employed in marketing are responsible for research and product planning, advertising and selling, distribution

of products from manufacturers to consumers, customer service, assistance with financing and credit procedures, and many other activities. Because of people who effectively perform their marketing jobs every day, customers are able to obtain the products and services they need at a fair price, and businesses are able to sell their products and services at a profit.

Marketing and Business Opportunities

Marketing jobs are found in all types of businesses. The primary purpose of some businesses, such as advertising agencies and retail stores, is to complete marketing activities. They are responsible for one or more of the marketing mix elements or

Have one team member name a type of business that exists in your community. Then, have other team members, in turn, identify a marketing job that they believe is needed by that business. Continue until no more jobs can be identified. Then, have the next team member name another type of business and continue the process.

marketing functions. Most of the jobs in those businesses are marketing jobs.

Other businesses have a non-marketing activity as their primary purpose. Those businesses include manufacturers and service providers as well as government agencies, schools, public utilities, and many other types of organizations. Even in those businesses, however, many people are employed to complete marketing activities that are an important part of the business's regular operations.

Even people who are not directly employed in marketing jobs often need to understand marketing and use marketing skills as a part of their work. Physicians and dentists often operate practices by themselves or in partnership with other professionals. Owners of small businesses—from daycare centers to catering or landscaping businesses—need to be able to plan, promote, price, and distribute their products and services in order for the enterprises to be successful. Marketing is an important part of almost every business and many jobs. You will find an understanding of marketing useful to you as you choose and prepare for a career.

Marketing is a part of every industry. Therefore, you can combine your interest in that industry with your marketing background for a choice of jobs. Important marketing jobs are found in the airline industry, the military, entertainment, healthcare, agriculture, and construction. Marketers are an essential part of the newest industries, including e-commerce and biotechnology. If you want to work in science, research, publishing, or education, you can find numerous opportunities to combine those interests with your marketing skills.

Marketing Jobs Improve the Economy

Consider what our lives would be like without people employed in marketing jobs. Without marketing researchers, our views would not be heard in business as new products are planned. Fresh fruits and vegetables would not be available year-round in the local supermarket without people in distribution to ship those products from other states and countries. We could not use newspapers, magazines, television, or the Internet to gather information about the products we want to buy if people did not work in advertising and promotion.

Marketers who work with us when we make hotel or rental car reservations or reschedule a flight on an airline help to ensure that we enjoy business travel or vacations. Customer service personnel solve problems with a product that we have just purchased, realtors help us rent an apartment or purchase a home, buyers for retail stores get the latest fashions for us, and automobile salespeople locate and arrange financing for the car we have always wanted to own.

What kinds of marketing jobs are found in the education industry?

New Media Redefines Advertising Roles

Traditional advertising media—television, print, outdoor, and radio—are saturated. There are so many advertising messages bombarding consumers every day that advertisers must look for new ways to reach customers. This drive to find new and innovative ways to reach consumers has changed the way marketers and advertisers must work. Where once copywriters and art directors at an ad agency might spend their entire careers specializing in print and television, they now must be able to think of online and guerilla tactics.

Crispin Porter + Bogusky, the advertising agency for Burger King, has done a very good job of reaching consumers in new and innovative ways. They have changed the way an advertising agency works, requiring their creative department to think outside the box of traditional advertising. In addition to creating print and television ads, they have created web sites, competitions, events, stunts, and even video games. At ad agencies like Crispin Porter + Bogusky, traditional roles are becoming less defined, and everyone is being asked to think creatively to help the clients.

Think Critically

1. Why is it important for advertisers to be able to think beyond traditional media?

2. If you were in charge of staffing at an advertising agency, what characteristics would you look for in a new hire?

Marketing personnel are involved in many of our daily activities as we purchase products, enjoy restaurants and entertainment, and use the services of businesses and other organizations. We notice, and often are not very happy, when marketing activities are not performed well. Marketing activities performed effectively by business people who are concerned about customer satisfaction save us time and money and make our lives more enjoyable.

There are thousands of marketing jobs that most of us know little about because we do not come into contact with the people performing that work. Those jobs are in business-to-business marketing. Many businesses provide products and services to other businesses rather than to consumers. Farmers sell the products they grow to food processors. Steel and plastic producers develop materials used by the auto industry, appliance manufacturers, construction firms, and many other types of businesses. Transportation companies move the products of one company to other companies to be used in their businesses or resold to consumers.

Each of those companies is involved in marketing and employs many people to complete the marketing activities needed to satisfy its business customers. The same types of jobs described earlier that are performed to meet consumers' needs are also completed in business-to-business marketing.

While you may not be aware of those jobs, if they are not performed well, you would not be able to purchase your morning cereal or lunchtime sandwich. Automobiles, microwave ovens, and shopping malls would not be built. And the computers and paper needed to print your favorite book or magazine would not get to the publisher.

We are more familiar with the marketing jobs in our own town or city and even in our own country. But marketing occurs worldwide to meet the needs of people in every country and to support international trade. Locate the names of the countries in which the products you use daily are produced and you will realize the importance of marketing worldwide. Those products would not be available to you and U.S. companies would not be able to sell their products in other countries without the daily work of millions of people in marketing. International marketing is providing more and more career opportunities.

Checkpoint ▶▶▶

Why are marketing jobs important to businesses that have non-marketing activities as their primary purpose?

Why Choose a Marketing Career?

This may be your first experience studying marketing. You may not have understood marketing very well before beginning this class and may not have been aware of the variety of marketing career opportunities. It is not unusual for people to end up in marketing careers without careful planning or without being aware of the benefits of those careers. Understanding marketing will allow you to select a career that is exciting, challenging, and rewarding. You can also plan the education you will need and the types of work experiences that will help you prepare for the career of your choice.

Benefits of Working in Marketing

You have choices of many different jobs and careers. A **job** is any full- or part-time work in a specific position of employment. Most people hold many jobs during their working lives. Many jobs, especially the first ones, are often taken with little thought of the future. Instead they are selected to meet the immediate needs of the worker. On the other hand, a **career** is a chosen area of work, usually made up of a progression of jobs, that provides personal and professional satisfaction. While you may have more than one career in your lifetime, the choice of careers is usually made more carefully based on individual interests, abilities, and preparation. People who move from job to job without a great deal of thought, considering only their immediate needs, often are not particularly happy or satisfied with their work.

©PHOTODISC/GETTY IMAGES

What is the difference between a job and a career?

With careful planning and preparation, including continuing your education, you will find many career choices open to you. Those choices will likely be more in line with your interests and abilities, and you will be more informed of the advantages and disadvantages of each career area. Marketing offers many diverse jobs and career choices that fit a variety of individual needs, interests, and lifestyles. While you may ultimately choose to work in a career area other than marketing, you should still be aware of the many benefits of working in marketing as you make job and career choices.

Many Choices Marketing jobs exist in every industry and within most companies. Marketing jobs are found at the lowest and highest levels of a company and are available for people with varied amounts of education and experience. No matter what your interests, job opportunities in marketing are available that match those interests.

Interesting Work Marketing is usually not boring. Marketers work with customers and people from other businesses as well as with people in their own company. Most marketing jobs involve creativity and decision making. Marketers are involved in planning, communicating, evaluating, and problem solving. As companies develop new products and services or identify new market opportunities, marketers will be involved from the beginning.

Financially Rewarding Some beginning marketing jobs will pay no more than minimum wage. Yet employees in those jobs who prove to their employer that they understand business operations and have a customer-service attitude are promoted quickly to higher-paying jobs with more responsibility. Marketing jobs are among the highest-paid positions in most companies. Because effective marketing results in higher profits for a company, effective marketers are often compensated with commissions, bonuses, or profit sharing to increase the salaries they earn.

Stable Employment As the economy changes, people may find that job opportunities change as well. People worry that they will lose their jobs when the economy is poor. Because marketing activities are so important to most businesses, marketing employees are often the last to be dismissed and the first to be rehired. Marketing skills are useful in many types of businesses and industries. If one

industry is not doing well economically, marketing jobs are likely available in industries that are experiencing better economic conditions.

Entry-Level to CEO

Most people will change jobs many times during their lifetime. Marketing skills are useful in a number of jobs. Entry-level jobs in marketing usually lead to advanced jobs with greater responsibility and higher salaries. A clerk in a store can become a department manager, store manager, and regional manager. Survey specialists working in marketing research can become product and brand managers. A sales associate can progress to salesperson, sales manager, and vice-president of sales and marketing. A recent study of the largest businesses in the United States found that people who started in marketing are often chosen to lead the entire company as the chief executive officer, or CEO.

No matter if you choose marketing or some other career, careful career planning is important. **Career planning** is an ongoing process involving self assessment, career exploration, and decision making leading to a satisfying career decision. You

Why do marketing skills lead to more stable employment?

will need to identify the knowledge and skills required for the career you select, the educational preparation needed, and the jobs you will likely hold as you progress through your career. Lack of appropriate preparation is often cited as the reason why a person is not considered when a position is filled in an organization.

There are a number of important resources available to help you plan a career in marketing. Libraries and the Internet provide many career planning resources and references. Business organizations and many individual businesses provide materials that describe career opportunities and the preparation necessary for each career. People with experience in the careers that interest you are often willing to discuss their work, provide career advice, and even serve as mentors to those who are beginning their careers. Career centers and counselors are also valuable resources for planning.

You are now familiar with marketing and the many career opportunities available in marketing. You can decide if you want to consider a career in marketing and then identify the career planning activities you will need to complete to prepare for the career of your choice.

Checkpoint ▶▶▶

What are the main benefits of working in marketing?

23-1 Assessment

Xtra!
Study Tools
school.cengage.com/marketing/marketing

Key Concepts

Determine the best answer.

1. Between _____ and _____ of all jobs in the United States are marketing jobs.

2. Which of the following is an example of a non-marketing business?
   a. a retailer
   b. a farmer or rancher
   c. an advertising agency
   d. a wholesaler

3. A transportation company moving the products of one company to other companies for use in their businesses is an example of
   a. business-to-consumer marketing
   b. direct marketing
   c. manufacturing
   d. business-to-business marketing

4. True or False: A chosen area of work, usually made up of a progression of jobs, that provides personal and professional satisfaction is a marketing job.

Make Academic Connections

5. **Visual Art** Work with other students to create a bulletin board or other display for your classroom that illustrates the range of marketing jobs that exist in your community. Illustrate jobs that are located in marketing and non-marketing businesses and in business-to-business marketing.

6. **Writing** Write a 300-word essay on "The Importance of Career Planning." The essay should define career planning and explain the career planning process, the benefits of planning, and what may happen to people who do not develop and follow a career plan.

Connect to ◀DECA
An Association of Marketing Students

7. You have been asked to speak to an eighth-grade careers class about marketing careers. Prepare a five-minute speech that describes the variety of marketing careers and the reasons that students might be interested in marketing jobs. Give your speech to your teacher (judge).

Employment Levels in Marketing

marketing matters

Do you like working as a team or are you more comfortable taking individual responsibility for your work? Do you believe you would like to lead and manage a work group? Do you have a vision of yourself in the future being the top executive of a large company or an entrepreneur who has started a successful business from scratch?

In the past, a measure of business success was starting at the bottom of a company and moving as high as possible into management. Today, career progression is more likely to mean changing jobs from one company to another, from one career area to another, and attempting to balance personal, family, and professional goals at the same time.

Make a list of five factors that you believe will be important to you as you plan your future. Identify how you believe the jobs you hold will relate to the factors you have identified.

Progressing through Marketing Jobs

Many people have an idea of their ideal job. However, the job in which you will spend the most time in your career will not be your first or second job. Each of us will hold many jobs before we find the job we really want. Some people will never achieve the job of their dreams because they do not develop and follow a career plan.

Completing Career Planning

Planning for a marketing career involves a number of choices. A way to increase your chances for a successful career is to complete career planning. Planning for a career in business is made up of several components. First you identify a career area. A **career area** is the type of business or the business function in which you plan to work. Examples include marketing,

finance, information management, and production.

How can career planning help you climb the "career ladder"?

©DIGITAL VISION/GETTY IMAGES

The next step is to consider a career path in the career area. A **career path** is a series of related jobs with increasing knowledge and skill requirements and greater amounts of responsibility. The third step is to compare your current academic preparation and experience with the jobs in the career path and then to prepare a career plan. A **career plan** identifies the progression of jobs in your career path, your plans for education, training, and experience to meet the requirements for those jobs, and a time schedule for accomplishing the plan.

It may seem like an almost impossible task to develop a realistic career plan when the business world is changing so much. There will likely be jobs available ten years from now that do not exist today. The knowledge and skills needed to be successful in a job will likely be quite different in a few years.

A career plan cannot be totally accurate and will probably change several times in the future. However, without a plan you will likely not pay attention to important changes and will seldom be prepared to pursue promotions, advancements, and job changes. People who complete career planning are more likely to have jobs they like and are better prepared to perform them than those who do not have a career plan.

Employment Levels in Marketing

Employment opportunities in marketing are available to people with a range of education levels, work experience, and interests. To help with career planning, those opportunities are organized within five levels. The levels of marketing employment are entry (*prerequisite*), career, specialist, supervisor/manager, and executive/owner. Those five levels are illustrated in Figure 23-1.

Entry-Level Marketing
People employed in entry-level marketing jobs perform routine activities with limited authority and responsibility. Entry-level jobs require limited education and

FIGURE 23-1
The five levels of marketing employment.

experience. They are often held by individuals who are still enrolled in high school or who have only a high school diploma. You can often obtain an entry-level marketing job with no previous experience. Entry-level jobs usually pay an hourly wage, often beginning at the minimum wage. Examples of entry-level jobs in marketing are clerk, cashier, stock person, and delivery person.

Quite often, people who hold entry-level positions do not view the job as the first step in a career path. They just want part- or full-time employment to earn money. They may move from job to job with no specific plans for the future. Career planning helps people select entry-level jobs that will be interesting, use existing knowledge and skills, and help prepare them for career advancement. Entry-level jobs are referred to as *prerequisite jobs* because most employers expect people to have developed prerequisite work skills in these beginning jobs before considering them for career employment.

Career-Level Marketing
Career-level positions are more complex than entry-level jobs. People in career-level positions have more control over their work, have a variety of tasks to complete that require specific knowledge and skill to perform well, and usually are involved

knowledge of a particular area of business operations. They will generally have special training and considerable experience in one particular area of marketing or a type of marketing activity required by the business in which they work. They will usually have a four-year college degree or even a graduate degree or advanced training in their area of work.

Marketing specialists are often considered the most skilled and expert people in their part of the business. Examples of marketing specialists include brand and product managers, advertising account executives, lead sales representatives, marketing research specialists, and buyers.

Marketing specialists will usually continue to work in the specific area of marketing and be promoted to advanced positions. They may be hired by other companies because of their specialized marketing expertise.

Supervisor/Manager-Level Marketing
People who work for some time in a business and have held career-level or specialist positions may want to move into management. They will usually begin as a supervisor or assistant manager with responsibility for a few people in a specific area of the business. Supervisors usually devote only a portion of their work time to management responsibilities. They spend additional time completing the work of their department. If they like the responsibility of managing others and do it well, they will likely be moved to higher levels of management and will be responsible for a broader set of management activities that consume most, if not all, of their work time.

Supervisors and managers need to have an understanding of and usually some experience working in the area for which they have management responsibilities. They must also have effective communications, human relations, and leadership skills. People promoted to the position of supervisor or manager usually have several years of experience in the company. However, some people are hired as supervisors

in problem solving and decision making. As people develop experience and are successful in career-level marketing positions, they may be given some limited supervisory responsibilities over a few entry-level employees or may be selected for leadership positions in work teams.

To qualify for career-level jobs, a person will need a year or two of successful experience in the company or a similar business. In lieu of or in addition to that experience, a person may need to complete education beyond high school and obtain a two-year or four-year degree.

People in career-level positions usually view the work as more than a job to earn money. They work in an area of general interest and in a job they believe will lead to career advancement. Businesses hire people for career-level positions in marketing who demonstrate understanding of marketing principles and business operations and who have an enthusiasm for developing skills in the area of work that will contribute to the business's success.

Specialist-Level Marketing
Marketing specialists perform very specific work in a business that requires advanced

or managers with less experience but with specific education or training in management. Companies often have management training programs to help employees learn to be effective managers.

Supervisors and managers are needed in all areas of marketing. Examples include sales manager, inventory manager, customer service manager, marketing information systems manager, and many others.

Executive/Owner-Level

Marketing The people with the greatest amount of authority and responsibility for marketing are executives and business owners. Executives hold the top marketing positions in a company, such as vice-president of marketing or president of international marketing operations. Business owners are responsible for the entire operation of their companies, including marketing.

Marketing executives and business owners need to have a thorough understanding of business principles and procedures, management, and all areas of marketing. They are responsible for all of the major marketing plans and decisions made and the implementation of the plans. They spend most of their time gathering and reviewing information, planning, and evaluating marketing effectiveness to make sure it is contributing to the profitability of the business.

Executives will have spent many years in the business, often working in many different marketing jobs. They often will have a graduate degree in business. Business owners do not always have as much experience or education. They do have a strong desire to start their own business. Today, many owners without academic preparation in business and marketing and several years of business experience will find it difficult to develop a business that continues to grow and make a profit.

Checkpoint ▶▶▶

What are the five levels of employment in marketing?

Skills for Marketing Success

Marketing today is becoming very complex. It involves many specialized but related activities. The people asked to complete marketing activities in companies must be more knowledgeable than ever before. In the past, people could learn to perform marketing on the job, but that is seldom possible today.

To prepare for a marketing career, you need to understand the skills that will be required for the job that you want. Marketing jobs demand two types of fundamental knowledge. First, you will need foundational skills that are useful in all business careers. Second, you will need to develop an understanding of the basic functions of marketing. You will then be prepared to develop skills in the specialized area of marketing in which you want to work.

Foundational Skills

Marketing is necessary for business success. But marketing skills alone are not enough for a successful business career. Marketing personnel need to develop foundational skills including

Fast **FACTS**

The U.S. Department of Labor, Bureau of Labor Statistics predicts employment of marketing professionals is expected to increase 18 to 26 percent through 2014. An even higher rate of growth is projected for marketing jobs in the scientific and professional services.

Digital Digest

Work Outside the Office

Telecommuting is a work arrangement in which an employee works outside the office, sometimes with flexible hours. Telecommuting, or "working from home" became more popular in the late 1990s when advances in Internet and mobile technology gave employees access to clients, coworkers, and information regardless of their location.

Some sales and marketing jobs allow employees to work outside the office as long as they continue to handle their responsibilities and meet their job's requirements. This arrangement helps employees juggle work and family life, gives them a sense of freedom, and sparks their creativity.

While some experts warned that allowing employees to work outside the office could lead to a decrease in productivity, a sense of alienation, and a detachment from the company, studies suggest that exactly the opposite is true. A well-managed work-from-home program can actually help employees manage their time better, make them feel that they have a more honest relationship with their company, and increase overall job satisfaction.

Think Critically

1. What types of jobs would be better suited for working from home?

2. Could you ever imagine a company with no physical building—just employees working from home? Why or why not?

---

an understanding of business principles, interpersonal and basic work skills, and academic preparation.

Business Principles In companies that apply the marketing concept, marketers work closely with people in other parts of the business such as accountants, production personnel, engineers, and information management specialists. Understanding the fundamental principles of business allows people from across the company to communicate and work effectively together. Important business foundations on which marketing is based are economics, finance and accounting, law, technology, business operations, and management. Marketers do not have to be experts in those areas, but they need to understand basic operations, use business information and reports, and make marketing decisions that support the business's strategy and plans.

Interpersonal and Basic Work Skills Marketers interact with other people. They work with people on their marketing team and with their managers. They often communicate with customers to provide information and solve problems, and they are involved regularly with other people inside and outside of the company. Interpersonal skills including communications, teamwork, human relations, decision making, and problem solving are all important in developing and maintaining effective work relationships.

Businesses need employees who understand and practice basic work skills. Those skills include promptness, courtesy, motivation, self-discipline, honesty, and ethics. Employees who complete work accurately and on time, use resources wisely, and work to contribute to the success of the business will be recognized and rewarded with opportunities for advancement.

Academic Preparation People who choose careers in marketing know that they need strong academic preparation. Today, most career positions in marketing require education beyond high school. Marketers need to have effective mathematics, writing, speaking, and listening skills. Preparation in science, psychology, and technology are helpful in many areas of marketing. Because of the diverse society in which marketers work and the growth of international business, the study of foreign languages and other cultures is also important.

Marketing Functions

Building on their business foundational skills, marketers add other skills in one or more of the marketing functions to prepare for a career. Some marketing jobs are very specialized and are a part of one of the nine marketing functions. For example, a person involved in marketing research is responsible for one aspect of marketing-information management. A person who designs and constructs window displays in a retail mall is performing a specialized promotion activity. In other jobs, the employee must be skilled in several marketing functions. Brand managers for a consumer products manufacturing company need to understand all of the marketing functions. A buyer for a wholesaler or retailer will use skills in finance, pricing, and product management.

Every marketer needs a general understanding of marketing and must be familiar with marketing terms and concepts. In addition, each person will need to develop specialized skills in one or more of the marketing functions.

Market Planning People who work in market planning help identify and understand the markets a company wants to serve. They gather and analyze economic, consumer, and competitive information and recommend appropriate marketing strategies that will be effective in each market. People who work in market planning need expertise in data collection and analysis. They must be both objective and creative as well as effective team members. They will prepare written reports to support their recommendations and discuss the ideas with company executives who make the final decisions.

Product and Service Management Product/service management is responsible for planning new products and services and making improvements to existing products. It requires an understanding of consumer needs and attitudes as well as competitors' products and services. Marketers involved with this function make sure that products are safe and easy-to-use and are perceived as a value by the target market.

Pricing Marketers that specialize in the pricing function are ultimately responsible for the profitability of a product. They need to analyze supply and demand and set a price that will result in the sale of the company's products at a profit. They plan pricing policies and determine how the price will be communicated to the customer. If markdowns are needed, they will determine the amount of the markdown and when it will be offered.

©DIGITAL VISION/GETTY IMAGES

What kinds of tasks might you perform if you had a job in market planning?

Promotion Communication and promotion need to be carefully planned in order to make customers aware of the company's products and services and provide them with the necessary information so that they will make a purchase. Follow-up should be part of the plan to ensure customers are satisfied with the product. There are many skills used in planning promotion, including writing, editing, design, graphics, media, and technology.

Selling When more personal and direct communications are needed to encourage customers to buy, selling is used. A salesperson often has the most direct contact with customers, so he or she is considered the representative of the company. Salespeople must be able to build and maintain successful relationships with their customers. They need skills in oral and written communications, time management, human relations, planning, and budgeting. Today, technology skills are very important because salespeople use computers, projectors, PDAs, cell phones, and the Internet in their work.

Distribution Distribution is a very complex marketing activity. Many marketing jobs are a part of distribution, and distribution specialists need a number of skills. People who plan distribution need to know where customers are located and where they prefer to purchase the products or services. Channels of distribution must be planned including building relationships with other companies involved in the channel. Procedures for order processing, inventory management, packaging, shipping, and customer service need to be developed.

Marketing-Information Management Marketing is scientific and relies on data. Marketers need to be able to instantly obtain and review information. Telemarketers need product information to answer customer

What kind of skills contribute to the success of a salesperson?

questions. Marketing researchers select a sample of consumers to survey. Product managers analyze the daily sales of a brand in an important market.

People involved in marketing information need math, statistics, and computer skills, an understanding of research procedures, and the ability to manage and analyze large amounts of data. They also need communication skills in order to provide reports to other people responsible for decisions that use the information collected.

Financing Financial planning is an important marketing responsibility. Budgets must be prepared, and adequate financial resources must be identified to pay for the company's marketing activities. If customers want or need to purchase on credit, credit plans and policies will need to be developed. Some products will be leased rather than sold, so financial specialists will work with customers to explain the lease terms and complete the necessary paperwork.

Risk Management An increasingly important career area in business is risk management. Businesses face a variety of risks, many of which are a part of marketing activities. Risk management personnel work to provide security for products, personnel, and customers and to reduce the risk associated with marketing decisions and activities. Traditionally, the major risk management activities have been providing insurance for companies so that they can anticipate and manage the cost of possible losses from insurable risks. Insurance companies work with their business clients to identify costly risks and develop operating procedures to reduce them. Security personnel work in all types of businesses to reduce losses from theft, burglary, shoplifting, and other types of crimes.

Checkpoint ▶▶

What are the two types of fundamental knowledge needed for marketing success?

23-2 Assessment

school.cengage.com/marketing/marketing

Key Concepts

Determine the best answer.

1. A series of related jobs with increasing knowledge and skill requirements and greater amounts of responsibility is a
   a. career area
   b. career plan
   c. career path
   d. career choice

2. The marketing employment level in which employees perform very specific work that requires advanced knowledge of a particular area of business operations is
   a. entry level
   b. career level
   c. specialist level
   d. executive/owner level

3. Which of the following is *not* one of the areas of foundational skills needed by marketing personnel?
   a. business principles
   b. interpersonal and basic work skills
   c. academic preparation
   d. all are important foundational skills

4. True or False: In the past, people could learn how to perform marketing on the job, but that is seldom possible today.

Make Academic Connections

5. **Research** Search the employment advertisements in a recent issue of a large newspaper from your state. Identify one marketing job opportunity that you believe fits each of the five levels of employment. Identify the level and the job title and write a two- or three-sentence description of the job duties and qualifications that illustrate why it fits the employment level you selected.

6. **Career Planning** Prepare a table in which you list all of the classes you have completed in high school and those you intend to complete prior to graduation. For each class, list one or more ways it contributes to the knowledge and skills needed for success in a marketing career.

Connect to ◀ DECA *An Association of Marketing Students*

7. Form a marketing research team to study career choices. Survey 25 people and ask them about the primary activity of their employer and get a brief description of their job. Analyze the responses and determine (1) if their employer is a marketing or non-marketing business, (2) if their job is a marketing or non-marketing job, (3) the employment level of their job, and (4) the primary marketing function performed by those with marketing jobs. Prepare charts or graphs and a written summary to report your findings. Present your report to your teacher (judge).

Marketing Education and Career Paths

GOALS

- Describe the importance of marketing education.
- Identify non-management and management career paths in marketing.

KEY TERMS

Marketing Education program, *p. 659*

DECA, *p. 659*

marketing matters

Some people have a career goal of becoming a manager in a business. Others would prefer not to manage other people but to spend all of their time on marketing activities. Companies need effective managers, but they also need people who are experienced and skilled in particular areas of business operations.

In the past, many companies identified the people who were the best performers in each area of the business and made them the managers. Managers were often paid more than other employees. Today, many businesses are providing advanced career opportunities with higher pay for people who do not want to be managers but who are skilled in a particular marketing specialty or function.

List the advantages and disadvantages of selecting the best employees to become managers and paying managers more than other employees. What are reasons why a business might want to let superior employees continue to work in the areas where they are skilled rather than making them managers? Would you ultimately want to be a business manager, or would you prefer to work in a non-management area? Discuss your preference and reasons with other students.

The Benefits of Marketing Education

How do you prepare for a marketing career? When is the best time to begin career planning? Preparing for a career in marketing will require both education and experience. It is never too early to start that preparation even if you are unsure if you want a career in marketing. Marketing skills are useful in many jobs. An understanding of marketing principles and the marketing skills you have will make you a valued employee in most businesses and organizations.

You have already begun your preparation for a marketing career with this course and others you have completed in high school. It is likely that you and many of your classmates have held entry-level

What are the benefits of marketing education?

©PHOTODISC/GETTY IMAGES

Virtual Marketing

The Internet Changes the Job Search

Because of its potential to connect people quickly, the Internet has had a major impact on the way people look for jobs and the way companies search for new employees. The Web has hundreds of sites for linking employers with prospective candidates and thousands of resources by which people can research companies and job openings.

The vastness of the Internet can help or hinder those seeking a job. Job boards on web sites like monster.com allow people to post their resumes for companies around the globe to browse. Whereas job seekers used to have to contact potential employers one at a time, now they can easily and quickly upload a resume that can be viewed by thousands of employers.

However, there is also a downside to this technology. Monster.com alone receives over 35,000 resumes every day. That's a lot for employers to sort through, and it is an enormous amount of competition for the people seeking a job. While job seekers can now easily apply for jobs all over the country, they also have to compete with people from all over the country. In the end, it still comes down to the skills of the person seeking employment, the needs of the employer, and how well the two overlap.

Think Critically

1. What marketing principles might people apply when trying to market themselves to potential employers using the Internet?

2. In addition to those stated above, think of two positive and two negative aspects of using the Internet for a job search.

---

marketing jobs giving you some experience and an opportunity to understand many of the ideas you are studying. You must decide if you want to continue your marketing education and what knowledge and skills you need to develop for the career of your choice.

What Is Marketing Education?

You can learn about marketing and develop marketing skills at almost any point in your education. Marketing education begins in middle schools with career exploration programs, job shadowing experiences, and introductory business courses.

At the high school level, many schools offer business and marketing classes as electives designed to develop general knowledge of marketing principles. Specialized marketing courses may be available to allow study of topics ranging from personal selling and advertising to sports marketing or fashion.

Career programs in marketing education provide the most comprehensive preparation opportunities for high school students considering full-time employment in marketing after graduation or for those considering additional education after high school. A **Marketing Education program** incorporates three types of complementary learning experiences—introductory and advanced courses in marketing, business work experiences, and a student organization called DECA. **DECA** is an international association of high school and college students studying marketing, management, and entrepreneurship in business, finance, hospitality, and marketing sales and service.

The classes offer understanding of marketing principles in an applied academic environment. Work experience gives students the chance to practice and test their marketing skills in a business, interacting with experienced employees, managers, and customers. Participation in DECA complements coursework and job experiences by providing student-led opportunities to build teamwork and leadership skills, participate in professional development experiences such as conferences and seminars, and enhance and test marketing skills through individual and group competitions.

Beyond High School

Marketing education opportunities expand after high school. Two- and four-year colleges offer marketing degrees as well as graduate education programs. Today, most marketers complete additional specialized training offered by their employers or by professional associations to which they belong.

Community College Programs

Community colleges offer business and marketing courses as a part of an academic curriculum through which students can earn an Associate of Arts degree. The courses and degree will qualify graduates for a number of career-level positions in marketing. In addition, the Associate of Arts degree can become a step toward a bachelor's degree for students who transfer to a four-year college or university.

Community colleges also offer shorter certificate programs that provide very specialized study of a specific set of marketing skills (selling, inventory management, small business management) for immediate employment. Two-year career programs that offer an Associate of Applied Science (AAS) degree are structured in a similar way as high school Marketing Education programs. They include coursework in English, math, natural science, and social science. Then students can choose to complete a general marketing curriculum or a specialized program such as Hospitality Marketing, Food Marketing, E-commerce Marketing, Professional Selling, and Fashion Marketing.

Many two-year career programs offered by community colleges include structured part-time or full-time work experiences in marketing jobs and a student organization, Delta Epsilon Chi (ΔEX). Many community colleges now cooperate with high schools to offer college-level courses to students while they are still enrolled in high school. Students who complete those courses successfully can graduate with both a high school diploma and a number of credits toward a two-year degree at the community college.

College Study You can earn a baccalaureate degree in marketing at most colleges and universities. Those programs incorporate study of advanced marketing skills that prepare graduates for career-level and specialist-level positions in business. Popular marketing courses in colleges today include international marketing, entrepreneurship, e-commerce, sports marketing, and marketing management.

Lifelong Learning Marketing education is a lifelong experience. Companies spend thousands of dollars each year to offer training to improve the skills of marketing personnel. Marketers participate in conferences and seminars and read business and marketing magazines to update their knowledge about the best marketing practices. Marketers who want to move into executive management positions will usually complete a graduate program in business such as a Master of Business Administration (MBA). Executive education programs are offered to the

Working in Teams

Have each team member identify a two- or four-year college or university he or she is interested in attending. Visit the web site of each institution and identify the marketing degree programs offered. List them in a two-column table. List those programs that are based on marketing functions in one column and those based on marketing industries in the other.

top marketing managers in companies to improve their understanding of the changing economy, to introduce the latest technology, and to improve decision-making abilities.

Checkpoint ▶▶▶

What are the three types of learning experiences in a Marketing Education program?

Choosing a Career Path

The career opportunities in marketing are so vast that it may be difficult to choose the career path you will follow. However, because of the many opportunities, it is possible to develop a more general career path and make it more specific in the future as you gain experience and complete further education. One of the decisions that will guide career planning is whether you want to prepare for a management or non-management career.

Moving into Management

In the past, it was expected that most people planning a career would prefer to move into a management position if given the opportunity. Businesses were organized as hierarchies with promotions leading to more and more responsibilities and ultimately into supervisory and management positions. While those expectations have changed in many companies,

a management career is still desired by many people.

In marketing, managers are needed for each of the major marketing functions. There will usually be several supervisory positions available in every marketing department. Most companies have one or more executive-level marketing management positions at the top of the company.

Preparing for a management career will require combining the development of marketing skills and management skills. Managers usually have several years of full-time work experience in career-level and specialist-level marketing jobs. They will then become a manager-trainee or supervisor. The career path will lead to an assistant manager position followed by assignments to a series of management jobs with greater and greater responsibilities.

To move into senior management positions, you will want to gain experience in several different marketing jobs, learn as

©DIGITAL VISION/GETTY IMAGES

How can individuals prepare for a management career?

much about business operations as possible, take on important projects for the company, and continue to improve your management skills.

Non-Management Marketing Careers

Businesses have changed a great deal in the past few years. They have reduced the number of levels of management and have given individual employees and employee teams more responsibility and authority. No longer is management viewed as the only way to be successful in your career. Companies are developing non-management career paths and providing rewards and recognition for non-management employees who offer a specific set of important skills to the business.

Companies recognized that an experienced salesperson who enjoys selling might not be happy or effective as a sales manager. That salesperson should have a career opportunity to be a lead account representative rather than having to become a sales manager in order to advance in his or her career. A very creative person who has prepared a number of successful advertising campaigns may be most valuable to the company as a senior copywriter rather than as an advertising manager.

If you choose a non-management career path, you will be able to specialize in one area of marketing if you prefer. You will want to get as much experience as possible in that area to continue to improve your skills. You may be able to move from one company to another to find additional opportunities as you gain experience. You will want to continue your education to ensure that you have expertise in the latest procedures and technology in the area of marketing in which you specialize. You will be considered the expert in that area in your company.

Career Paths in Marketing

A benefit of a career in marketing is that you have many choices of career paths. Also, because marketing is a part of almost every business and industry as well as non-business organizations, you have choices of the types of businesses, locations, and working conditions you want for almost any career path.

A *career path* is a series of related jobs with increasing knowledge and skill requirements and greater amounts of responsibility. You can select a career path in one of two ways—either by industry or by marketing function.

Industry Paths You might decide to select an industry that interests you and consider the marketing opportunities in that industry. For example, you might be interested in automobiles, construction, entertainment, or healthcare. After identifying the industry, you should identify the entry- and career-level job opportunities and the advanced marketing jobs to which they lead.

Marketing Function Paths On the other hand, you might be interested in a specific marketing function such as promotion, distribution, or financing. In that case, career opportunities will exist in a number of specialties and in several industries. You can study the types of increasingly responsible jobs you will hold in advertising, sales, inventory, transportation, or credit services. Each area will have one or more career paths you can follow.

Examples of career paths related to marketing functions can be found in the areas of advertising, marketing research, and retailing. An advertising career might begin with an internship in an advertising agency. Your career could progress to a job in media traffic where you help to place ads in selected media and monitor the media to ensure the advertisements are run as planned. Advancement in advertising might take you through jobs as an account executive, account supervisor, and finally director of advertising.

A career in marketing research starts as an interviewer or data analyst. The next step may be survey planning and design. You can be promoted to a position as a project director and finally to director of marketing research.

A career path with which you may be more familiar is in retailing. Most people start as a cashier, stockperson, or salesperson. By demonstrating initiative, a customer service attitude, and effective job skills, you can quickly become an assistant manager for a department of the business. That job progresses to manager, assistant store manager, and store manager. Beyond that level, retail careers can progress to district and regional management and on to division vice-president.

These are only a few examples of common career paths in marketing. Other choices exist within each of the marketing functions we have examined as well as in the other areas of marketing. You need to review the many available career resources and discuss your interests with experienced marketers to identify the various career possibilities open to you.

Checkpoint ▶▶

What is the difference between management and non-management career paths?

23-3 Assessment

Xtra!
Study Tools
school.cengage.com/marketing/marketing

Key Concepts

Determine the best answer.

1. True or False: Preparing for a career in marketing requires both education and work experience.

2. Which of the following is *not* one of the types of learning experiences that is part of a high school Marketing Education program?
   a. introductory and advanced courses in marketing
   b. business work experience
   c. DECA
   d. all are part of the program

3. A marketing student organization for community college students is _____ .

4. True or False: Because many businesses are reducing the number of levels of management, there are fewer career choices available in marketing today.

5. A marketing career path that offers increasingly responsible jobs in a specialty area such as advertising, sales, transportation, or credit services is a(n) _____ path.
   a. industry
   b. marketing function
   c. management
   d. none of the above

Make Academic Connections

6. **Math** The most recent data from the U.S. Census Bureau compares average yearly earnings based on the level of education completed. Working adults who dropped out of high school had annual earnings of $18,900. Those who completed high school averaged $25,900 a year, and college graduates earned an average of $45,400. What is the percentage increase in earnings that results from earning a high school and college degree?

7. **Decision Making** Prepare a table that compares the advantages and disadvantages of management and non-management career paths. Use the information in the table to develop a three-paragraph statement of which career path you would choose at this time.

Connect to ◆ DECA
An Association of Marketing Students

8. You are interviewing for a job as a salesperson in a new department store opening in your community. The company wants a person with enough business understanding and leadership experience to begin supervising several part-time salespeople within six months. Your teacher (judge) will ask you to describe why you believe you are qualified for the job. Be prepared to convince the interviewer that you are the best person for both the sales and supervisor positions.

GOALS
- Describe the steps in preparing a career plan.
- Discuss how to successfully apply for a job.

KEY TERMS

career portfolio, *p. 666*

electronic portfolio (*e-portfolio*), *p. 667*

marketing matters

How do you prepare for a career in marketing? In addition to the courses you take in high school and college, experience is an important part of your preparation. Some of the experience will be actual work experience in entry- and career-level marketing jobs. But there are many other experiences you and your friends have while in high school that can help to develop skills needed for success in marketing.

Start by making a list of five to eight skills that you believe will be important for people who want a career in marketing. Examples could be human relations and communication skills. For each of the skills you have listed, identify experiences you believe are available in your classes, in student organizations, other extracurricular activities, and in out-of-school and community activities that can contribute to the development of the skills. Be very specific in describing the experiences.

Discuss the experiences with other students and decide which of the experiences seem to be the most useful in preparing for a career in marketing.

Choices and Decisions

Right now you may believe that preparing for a career in business is like trying to assemble a jigsaw puzzle. Hundreds of pieces to the puzzle lay before you, but it is almost impossible to envision how they fit together. You know that marketing careers require a combination of education and experience. It is difficult to decide what types of education and experience you need as well as where and when to obtain them.

You may know right now that you want a career in marketing and even may have decided on the specific job in which you are most interested. On the other hand, you may have decided on a non-marketing career, but you can see how an understanding of marketing will benefit you. Or you may be undecided on a career and are just beginning to consider your choices.

Don't be too concerned if you have not made specific career choices at this time. People change jobs many times during their lifetime and often move into totally different areas of work than they originally planned. Still, it is important to focus on the impact that education and the employment choices you make will have on your career.

Combining Education and Experience

Today, it is less likely that a person will achieve his or her career goal without planning and preparation. A successful business career is more likely for you if you understand the requirements for the job you want and plan to develop the necessary skills. Career planning becomes a process of determining your interests and abilities, exploring the requirements for the job you want, and planning the education and experience you need to qualify for the job. Employers value both education and experience.

You will need strong academic skills (reading, writing, mathematics) as well as knowledge of business and marketing. The courses you have already completed as well as the remaining courses you will take in high school will prepare you for your career choice. College coursework can add to your academic and career preparation.

Experience in business is always an advantage. Employers value experience because it demonstrates your interest in business, your motivation, interpersonal skills, and the ability to apply what you have learned in your classes. It is relatively easy to find an entry-level job in marketing if you are not too concerned about the type of work. Even though those jobs do not always pay as much as you would like and it is difficult to manage a work schedule with school and extracurricular activities, a good work record provides a definite advantage when you apply for other jobs.

If you have successful entry-level experience in high school, you may be able to qualify for more advanced jobs when you seek full-time employment after high school or for jobs you hold while in college. You can add to your work experience by completing internships, working on projects and activities in school

Why are entry-level jobs an important part of a career plan?

organizations, and volunteering in community organizations.

Developing a Career Plan

Planning is an important marketing skill that is necessary to obtain the job you want. Many people do little planning even for things that are important to them. Without a plan, however, you are less likely to achieve your goals. By developing a career plan, you will not only increase the chances of obtaining the job you really want, but you will be practicing an important business skill. Employers will be impressed with the efforts you devote to career planning.

If you want to develop an effective career plan, follow these steps:

1. Complete an assessment of your current knowledge, skills, and interests. Work with teachers, counselors, and others to identify tests and other resources that will improve your self-understanding in order to make the best matches with possible careers.

Fast FACTS

A survey of members of the American Marketing Association revealed that financial compensation was less important in determining their job satisfaction than the culture and ethics of the business for which they worked. Also important were their level of responsibility on the job, having a job that used all of their skills, and receiving professional recognition for their efforts.

2. Study marketing careers in depth to determine the industries and types of marketing jobs available and the work that is required in the jobs of interest to you.

3. Identify the education and experience requirements for the marketing careers that interest you. Interview employees and visit businesses to add to your knowledge. Compare the results with your current education and experience to determine what you need to qualify for jobs in the career area that interests you.

4. Make a list of the knowledge and skills you will need to develop. Meet with experienced people (teachers, counselors, and business people) who are familiar with education and work opportunities to gather advice on the possible choices for additional education and work experience. Share your career plans with them and have them help you make the best matches to achieve your career goals.

5. Prepare a written career plan. The plan may be general at first, but you can make it more specific as you gather more information. The plan should identify the career area of interest to you and possible jobs that make up a career path. You should list the knowledge and skills you will need and the choices of education and experience that you have made to assist you with your career development. You may want to include a timeline that projects how long it will take to complete the experiences listed.

Checkpoint ▶▶

Why do employers value work experience when hiring a new employee?

Obtaining the Job You Want

The importance of career planning will become apparent when you apply for the job you want and are hired because the employer was impressed with your preparation and planning. The information in your career plan will be helpful in completing applications for jobs or for schools.

Preparing a Career Portfolio

A portfolio is a tool used by artists, models, and advertising people to visually demonstrate their abilities and their past work. You may have been asked to develop a portfolio for this or other classes that includes the major projects and activities you complete during the year.

A career portfolio is an excellent resource to help you with career planning and job applications. A **career portfolio** is an organized collection of information and materials developed to represent you, your preparation, and your accomplishments.

©PHOTODISC/GETTY IMAGES

How can a career portfolio help you get the job you want?

Figure This

Changing Job Market

Between 1994 and 2007, the types of jobs in the U.S. economy underwent a great deal of change. The following table shows the number of employees (in thousands) in three job categories. Notice which job types have increased or decreased.

Category	1994	2007
Manufacturing	16,722	14,003
Retail	13,149	15,401
Service	88,851	115,675

Think Critically

1. What is the increase or decrease in employment in each category?

2. What is the percentage increase or decrease in each category?

3. Why do you believe manufacturing employment decreased while employment in retailing and service businesses increased during that time?

Select and organize items for your portfolio that you believe provide the best evidence of your marketing knowledge and skills. Those items can include tests, reports, and projects completed in classes, summaries of aptitude or interest tests you have taken, projects and activities you completed in a club or organization, and even work done for a hobby if it demonstrates important business or marketing skills. For example, you may have developed a personal web site on your computer that demonstrates technology skills. You may have won an award for a marketing research report you prepared and presented for a state or national DECA competition. Both the report and the award are excellent additions to your portfolio.

If you have worked for a business, you may have work reports or performance reviews that can be incorporated into your career portfolio. If you completed a special project on the job and your employer allows you to have a copy, it should be included. Photos of work you have completed provide interesting evidence of skills. Any awards or recognition you have received in school or on the job should be included as well.

Make sure your portfolio is well organized so that you can easily locate items when needed and others can quickly review your work. You will add to the portfolio as you continue your education and work, so design the portfolio so that items can easily be added or removed.

The newest type of career portfolio is an electronic portfolio or *e-portfolio*. An **electronic portfolio** is prepared, maintained, and saved using computer technology. Developing your portfolio electronically not only demonstrates your proficiency with technology but makes it easier to update as well as share your portfolio with others. Scan copies of printed materials you want to include in your portfolio but retain the original versions.

Applying for the Job You Want

Once you have prepared your career plan and portfolio, you are ready to begin your job search and then apply for the marketing job you want.

Identify Jobs The first step in a job search is to identify available positions. Newspapers are one of the best sources for listings of available jobs. They are also usually organized by the type of job or job title.

The Internet has become a very important tool for job searches. Most companies maintain a listing of open positions on their web sites. There are also

How has technology changed the way people search and apply for jobs?

specific web sites where companies can list their job openings. Examples are monster.com and CareerBuilder.com. Many of the web sites allow you to search for jobs by job category, specific job title, company name, or geographic location. Many sites let individuals develop and post their resumes online. Some will even match the resumes to available jobs and send matching resumes to the businesses with job openings. Other sources of job openings are career centers in schools, employment agencies, and recommendations from family members and friends.

Make a Career Match Your career plan will help you identify the companies and select the jobs that most closely match your current interests and abilities and fit your long-term career goal. From the available jobs, select those for which you are qualified and interested.

After you have selected a few jobs, gather information about each of the companies on the list. By learning about the company, you can show the employer how your skills will specifically benefit the company. Businesses want to hire people who will contribute to their operations. By preparing in advance using information

about the company, you will be able to clearly communicate the benefits you can provide as an employee.

Complete Application Materials If you are applying for a job in writing, you will want to send a cover letter and printed resume. The cover letter makes a first impression, so be sure it is well organized, easy to read, and error free. Address it to a specific person if possible. In the letter, highlight your strengths and emphasize why you want to work for the company.

Your resume will outline your preparation and experience. Using a computer, tailor your general resume to the company before you send it. The information in your career portfolio will be useful in completing your resume and cover letter. Select the information that most closely matches the job requirements.

Companies will usually ask you to complete a written application. Have a written copy of all personal information with you when you fill out the application to make sure it is complete and accurate. Print application information carefully to ensure that it is readable and to show that you are careful and accurate in your work.

Virtual Job Applications and Resumes

Seeking a job no longer requires "pounding the pavement." With the assistance of the Internet and a reliable computer, many jobs can be applied for online.

If you have an idea of the company where you would like to work, go directly to the company's web site. Make sure that you are at the official home page of the business.

Look for a navigation bar tab on the web site that refers to employment. Within the employment section of a web site, you may have the option of performing an online job search. Selection criteria might include keyword, location, or department of interest.

Many business web sites provide the opportunity to complete and submit online applications for all levels of employment. Entry-level jobs may require only a completed online application form. Applications for higher-level positions may require the completion of a simplified online form and the submission of a resume, a cover letter, and other written materials as attachments to the application.

Customize resumes and cover letters for specific jobs. Follow the web site's directions regarding how to format the resume for transmission. Simple formatting is best as complex formats and the use of colors and unique fonts may not transmit correctly.

Read all directions and information carefully. Most companies have a policy that inaccurate application information is grounds for dismissal. If you are chosen for an interview, you will need to produce documentation confirming that you are eligible for employment. Personal paperwork may include a driver's license, a Social Security card, a birth certificate, or a U.S. passport. Prior to submitting your application, make sure that all information is accurate and that you have your personal paperwork in order.

Always use caution when submitting information online. You want to avoid revealing personal information on a non-secure web site. If you have concerns, call the company before submitting personal information. Also, before you submit the application, carefully review the information you have entered to make sure that all sections of the application have been completed. Proofread all information to make sure that it is accurate and that there are no spelling errors. Print a copy of the application for your records.

Merely applying for a job online is not sufficient. Personal networking is still among the most effective ways to obtain employment. An interested contact inside a company who knows about your job search efforts can help "pull" your application through the organization by endorsing the value of your credentials to the decision makers.

Unless you are told not to do so in the instructions, you should follow up with a phone call or e-mail to the appropriate decision maker. Always be polite when communicating with prospective employers. Time your follow-up contacts to show your interest but not to be annoying.

Develop Your Skill

Identify a job that you would like to have. Look for online applications for the job at three different companies. Compare the applications for each of the companies. If possible, print a copy of each application and practice completing it.

Work with a teacher or guidance counselor to review your completed applications. Ask for advice to improve each application.

PHOTO: ©PHOTODISC/GETTY IMAGES

Complete a Successful Interview

If you have not had a lot of experience with job interviews, you may be nervous. Once again, the careful and thorough preparation you have completed will help give you confidence if you are selected for an interview. You know a great deal about yourself and the job for which you are applying.

It is important to have a professional appearance in an interview. You want to wear appropriate business apparel that is compatible with what employees in the business normally wear at work.

Make sure you are on time for the interview. If possible, identify in advance the name of the person who will interview you so that you can ask for that person and use his or her name during the interview.

Unless you are told not to do so, you can bring selected items from your portfolio. You will probably be given the opportunity to show and describe them during the interview if you have them. Do not hesitate to refer to examples of your work when answering questions.

Communicate your interest in a marketing career and how the job fits into your career goals. Make sure the employer knows you are interested in working for the company and want to do a good job because of your interests in marketing.

Demonstrate confidence and professionalism during the interview. Do not be afraid to ask questions about the company and the job. In fact, you should prepare several questions in advance and be prepared to ask them.

When the interview is finished, thank the interviewer for the opportunity. Clarify what will happen after the interview and when you can expect to hear from the company. Send a personal note of thanks to the interviewer as soon as possible. Use the note to highlight one or two unique qualities you can offer.

©DIGITAL VISION/GETTY IMAGES

Why is it important for the interviewee to ask questions during the interview?

The Decision

Don't expect that you will be offered every job for which you apply. Your preparation increases the likelihood that you will be hired if you select jobs that are good matches with your interests and qualifications.

You will also need to decide if you will accept the job if it is offered to you. You should use the interview to gather information to be able to make that decision. If the job is not what you expected or does not fit your career plan, you may choose to decline an offer. The person making the offer will probably be impressed if you clearly communicate why you don't believe the job is the best choice for you. If you decide to accept the job, you will do so with the confidence that it is the job that best meets your career plans.

Checkpoint ▶▶

When is it appropriate to decline a job offer?

What tips would you give to a job applicant to help ensure a successful interview?

23-4 Assessment

Xtra! **Study Tools**
school.cengage.com/marketing/marketing

Key Concepts

Determine the best answer.

1. True or False: Work experience in business is always an advantage when applying for a marketing job.

2. The first step in developing an effective career plan is to
   a. complete an assessment of your current knowledge, skills, and interests
   b. identify current job openings
   c. make a list of the knowledge and skills you will need to develop
   d. write a general career plan

3. A _____ is an organized collection of information and materials developed to represent you, your preparation, and your accomplishments.

4. Which of the following statements is *not* true about interviewing for a job?
   a. Wear appropriate business apparel that is similar to what the business's employees normally wear.
   b. Know and use the name of the person who interviews you.
   c. Bring selected items from your portfolio and refer to them when answering questions.
   d. Always accept the job if it is offered to you.

Make Academic Connections

5. **Research** Identify one marketing and one non-marketing job that interest you. Use career information from your school's career center or the Internet to identify the important knowledge, skills, education, and experience required for each job. Prepare a table for each job with the headings, "What I Have" and "What I Need." In each column of the table, describe your current qualifications for that job and what you still need to develop.

6. **Career Planning** Form a team with three other students. Prepare two role-plays of job interviews. The first role-play should illustrate an ineffective job interview, and the second one should illustrate an effective interview. Present both role-plays to other teams and have them identify what was effective and ineffective.

Connect to DECA
An Association of Marketing Students

7. Use a computer to prepare a professional resume you could use to apply for a career-level marketing job of your choice. Carefully edit and print your resume. Present a copy of your resume to your teacher (judge) and explain why you believe it is an effective resume for the job you selected. Be prepared to discuss your resume and answer questions about the information you included.

Chapter 23 Assessment

Check Your Understanding

Now that you have completed the chapter, check your understanding of the lessons with these questions. Record the score that best represents your understanding of each marketing concept.

1 = not at all; 3 = somewhat; 5 = very well

If your score is 42–50, you are ready for the assessment activities that follow. If you score 33–41, you should review the lessons for the items you scored 1–3. If you score 32 or less, you will want to carefully reread the lessons and work with a study partner on the areas you do not understand.

Can you—

— explain why marketing is one of the most important functions in business today?

— provide examples of how marketing jobs improve the economy?

— identify several benefits of working in marketing?

— discuss the benefits of preparing a career plan?

— describe the five employment levels for marketing jobs?

— explain the importance of understanding business foundations and marketing functions when preparing for a marketing career?

— describe the benefits of participation in a high school Marketing Education program?

— explain the difference between management and non-management career paths?

— describe the steps to complete when preparing a career plan?

— explain how a career portfolio can be beneficial in applying for a marketing job and completing a job interview?

Review Marketing Terms

Match the terms listed with the definitions. Some terms may not be used.

1. The type of business or the business function in which you plan to work
2. Any full- or part-time work in a specific position of employment
3. Identifies the progression of jobs in your career path, your plans for education, training, and experience to meet the requirements for those jobs, and a time schedule for accomplishing the plan
4. Career information prepared, maintained, and saved using computer technology
5. A chosen area of work, usually made up of a progression of jobs, that provides personal and professional satisfaction
6. A series of related jobs with increasing knowledge and skill requirements and greater amounts of responsibility
7. The completion of marketing activities is the most important or only job responsibility
8. An organized collection of information and materials developed to represent you, your preparation, and your accomplishments
9. An international association of high school and college students studying marketing, management, and entrepreneurship in business, finance, hospitality, and marketing sales and service
10. An ongoing process involving self assessment, career exploration, and decision making leading to a satisfying career decision

   a. career
   b. career area
   c. career path
   d. career plan
   e. career planning
   f. career portfolio
   g. DECA
   h. electronic portfolio (e-portfolio)
   i. job
   j. Marketing Education program
   k. marketing job

Review Marketing Concepts

11. True or False: While there are a large number of marketing jobs available in our economy, they are generally low paying.

12. True or False: Companies that have non-marketing activities as their primary purpose will usually employ some marketing employees.

13. True or False: If you are interested in a professional career, such as a physician or dentist, an understanding of marketing is useful in your work.

14. True or False: Two types of businesses that are not involved in marketing are manufacturing and farming.

15. True or False: Marketing jobs are found at the lowest and highest levels of a company.

16. True or False: Once you have prepared a career plan, it should not be changed.

17. True or False: Most entry-level marketing jobs require at least a high school diploma.

18. True or False: The people with the greatest amount of authority and responsibility for marketing are executives and business owners.

19. True or False: Marketing education is actually a lifelong experience since you can study marketing from middle school through graduate school and beyond.

20. True or False: To be successful, a career path must end in a management job.

21. True or False: Once you have chosen an industry in which to work, it will be very difficult to switch to a marketing job in another industry.

22. True or False: Career planning is much more important to career success today than it was in the past.

23. True or False: Employers are more likely to hire someone with academic experience and work experience than someone with just academic experience.

24. True or False: A self-assessment of your knowledge, skills, and interests is a good starting point for career planning.

25. True or False: A career plan will not be useful unless it is very specific.

26. True or False: Whenever possible, you should prepare a specific resume for each prospective employer.

27. True or False: Even if a job does not fit your expectations after the interview, you should accept it if it is offered to you.

Marketing Research and Planning

28. Many marketing occupations are among the jobs employing the most people in the U.S. economy. Also, marketing careers are normally among the fastest-growing occupations. Use the Internet to locate employment statistics for the United States or for your state. Identify jobs you believe are marketing occupations that are among those employing the most people or among the fastest-growing occupations. List the jobs and identify those you would be interested in for your future career and those that would not interest you. Provide reasons for your decisions.

29. Using your library or the Internet, locate information on three 2-year or 4-year colleges that offer degrees in marketing. Study the courses you would have to complete to earn the degree.

Prepare a table that identifies the college, the title of the marketing degree, the total number of credits needed to earn the degree, and the total number of marketing credits needed to earn the degree. Now determine the combined total number of credits in the academic subjects of communications (English, writing, speech, and literature), mathematics, and science.

Calculate the percentage of total credits that will be marketing courses, the percentage of credits in the academic subjects, and the percentage of total credits for all other course work. Prepare a pie chart to illustrate your findings. What conclusions can you draw from the table and chart?

30. Select one of the nine marketing functions that interests you as a possible career area. Using career resources in your school's library, career

center, or the Internet, identify three jobs that would make up a career path in the marketing function you selected. One of the jobs should be an entry-level job, one should be a career-level or specialist-level job, and one should be a supervisor/manager-level or executive/owner-level job. Based on your research, prepare a detailed job description for each job and identify the following:

- the amount of education you believe is necessary to obtain the job

- the amount and type of work experience that you believe would be expected of a person hired for the job

- an approximate wage or salary you believe the job would pay

31. Following the instructions of your teacher, form two teams of students and prepare to debate the following issue:

"Companies should select the most skilled employees in each area to become managers."

vs.

"Companies should recognize and reward their most skilled employees but keep them working in the areas where they are the most skilled rather than promoting them to management."

Each team will be assigned one of the two positions for the debate. The team members will work together to develop arguments for their position and against the opposing position. Each team will have five minutes to present the reasons for their positions. Then each team will have five minutes to present reasons against the opposite position or to directly rebut the arguments of the other team.

At the end of the debate, the entire class should discuss the effectiveness of the presentations on each side of the issue. Then other members of the class can present their own views of the debate topic.

Marketing Management and Decision Making

32. You are the manager of a customer service team for a telephone service provider in your city. Your customer service representatives respond to telephoned and e-mailed questions from customers who want to add or change their local services or are experiencing problems and are contacting your business for help. The customer service representatives will have specific training so that they know the information about the services provided, and they can access a computer program that will provide suggested answers to customer problems. If the problem cannot be solved, the representative will schedule an appointment with a technician who can go to the customer's home to make a repair.

You will be hiring 15 new customer service representatives. Based on the information provided, write an advertisement for the position. Include an overview of the position and a description of the qualifications you would require of job applicants. What procedures would you follow and what materials would you require of job applicants in order to select the best new employees?

33. Using an Internet browser and search engine, identify five marketing jobs directly related to

e-commerce. For each job, identify the marketing function or functions that are the focus of the work of the employee. Select at least two of the jobs that interest you. Again using the Internet, locate two companies that are currently attempting to hire a person for the type of jobs you identified. For each company, print the job advertisement that identifies the job title, job description, requirements, and any other information provided. Write a short statement for each position describing how you believe the job would be different if it was part of a business that was not involved in e-commerce.

34. Begin the development of a career portfolio. Prepare a three-ring binder or some other useful means of organizing and maintaining your portfolio materials. Identify the categories of materials that you want to include in your portfolio such as class projects, work products, and others you believe are important as evidence of your career preparation. Begin to add items to the portfolio. Prepare a list of the types of items you would like to develop and include in your portfolio. Use word processing and computer graphics programs to prepare the portfolio materials so that they have a professional look.

Restaurant and Food Service Management Individual Series Event

The Green Lantern Steak House has been a successful family-owned restaurant for many years. The restaurant is famous for delicious steaks, pasta, chicken, fish, and a large fresh salad and homemade soup bar. Loyal customers come from a 50-mile radius to enjoy the excellent food and service offered at the Green Lantern Steak House.

The Green Lantern Steak House has been in business for 40 years in a community with a population of 5,000 people. Fireworks is a new full-service restaurant that has been the first serious source of competition for Green Lantern since it has been in business. The Green Lantern Steakhouse has lost approximately 30 percent of its business since Fireworks opened.

Fireworks offers delicious sandwiches and steaks for higher prices. The restaurant also has live musical entertainment on Friday and Saturday nights.

The manager of the Green Lantern has asked your team to outline marketing and customer service strategies to recapture customers. You will have ten minutes to explain your strategies to the manager (judge). During and after your presentation, the manager can ask questions about your proposed marketing and customer service strategies for sparking new interest in the restaurant.

Performance Indicators Evaluated

- Explain the nature of positive customer/client relations. (Emotional Intelligence)

- Demonstrate a customer-service mindset. (Emotional Intelligence)

- Explain management's role in customer relations. (Emotional Intelligence)

- Develop strategies to position the business. (Product/Service Management)

- Evaluate the customer experience. (Product/Service Management)

Go to the DECA web site for more detailed information.

Think Critically

1. What factors should the Green Lantern Steak House emphasize in its advertising campaign?

2. How can daily specials be used to recapture customers?

3. What is the best means of advertising for the target market?

4. How can competition be good for an existing business that has experienced years of success?

www.deca.org

Glossary

A

account executive the key liaison between the client and the agency

account planner one who talks to the target markets, conducts research, and even travels to see how the target market lives, works, and thinks

accounting and finance the business function that plans and manages financial resources and maintains records and information related to a business's finances

accounts receivable sales for which the company has not yet been paid

advertising any paid form of nonpersonal communication that uses mass media to deliver a marketer's message to an audience

advertising agency a company that specializes in creative advertising

advertising campaign series of related advertisements with a similar look, feel, and theme that centers on a specific product, service, or brand

advertising plan a document that outlines the activities to be completed and resources needed to create advertising

analysis the process of summarizing, combining, or comparing information so that decisions can be made

approach the first contact with the customer when the salesperson gets the customer's attention and creates interest in the product

art director the person responsible for how the ad will look

assets things a business owns

atmospherics elements of the shopping environment that appeal to customers, attract them to a store, and encourage them to buy

attitude a frame of mind developed from a person's values, beliefs, and feelings

attribute-based good products in which a variety of differences exist, and the consumer considers a number of factors to determine the best value

B

B2B business-to-business

B2C business-to-consumer

balance of trade the difference between the amount of a country's imports and exports

balance sheet a description of the type and amount of assets, liabilities, and capital in a business on a specified date

bartering exchanging products or services with others by agreeing on their values without using money

basic stock list identifies the products a store must have available to meet the most important needs of its customers

benefit the advantage provided to a customer as a result of the feature

benefit segmentation divides consumers into groups depending on specific values or benefits they expect or require from the use of a product or service

bidding several suppliers develop specific prices at which they will meet detailed purchase specifications and other criteria prepared by the buyer

boycott an organized effort to influence a company by refusing to purchase its products

brand a unique name, symbol, or design that identifies a product, service, or company

brand advertising builds an image for a brand or company

breakeven point the quantity of a product that must be sold for total revenues to match total costs at a specific price

brick-and-click businesses companies that combine traditional business operations with the use of the Internet

brick-and-mortar businesses companies that complete most of their business activities by means other than the Internet

broadcast media a signal is sent from a central transmitter to receivers in a geographic area

budget a detailed projection of financial performance for a specific time period, usually one year or less

bundling the practice of combining several related services for one price

business blogs regularly updated online journals written by company experts

business consumers those who buy goods and services to produce and market other goods and services or for resale

business cycles recurring changes in an economy

business markets companies and organizations that purchase products for the operation of a business or the completion of a business activity

business plan a written document prepared to guide the development and operation of a new business

business-to-business marketing exchange of products and services between businesses

buying behavior the decision processes and actions of consumers as they buy services and products

buying motives the reasons that people buy

C

capital the difference between the amount of a company's assets and liabilities, or the actual value of the business

capital expenses long-term investments in land, buildings, or equipment

career a chosen area of work, usually made up of a progression of jobs, that provides personal and professional satisfaction

career area the type of business or the business function in which you plan to work

career path a series of related jobs with increasing knowledge and skill requirements and greater amounts of responsibility

career plan identifies the progression of jobs in your career path, your plans for education, training, and experience to meet the requirements for those jobs, and a time schedule for accomplishing the plan

career planning an ongoing process involving self-assessment, career exploration, and decision making leading to a satisfying career decision

career portfolio an organized collection of information and materials developed to represent you, your preparation, and your accomplishments

cease-and-desist order a legal order to discontinue deceptive advertising

central market a location where people bring products to be conveniently exchanged

channel captain a company that takes responsibility to identify channel members, assign distribution activities, help members agree on performance standards, and facilitate communication among channel members

channel members the businesses used to provide many of the marketing functions during the distribution process

channel of distribution all of the businesses involved in completing marketing activities as products move from the producer to the consumer

charter a legal document allowing a corporation to operate as if it were a person

click-only businesses companies that complete almost all of their business activities through the Internet

close the step in the sales process when the customer makes a decision to purchase

closed-ended questions questions that offer two or more choices as answers

code of ethics a set of standards or rules that guide ethical business behavior

cold calling a salesperson contacts a large number of people who are conveniently located without knowing a great deal about each person contacted

communication process the transfer of a message from a sender to a receiver

consumer behavior the study of consumers and how they make decisions

consumer credit credit extended by a retail business to the final consumer

consumer decision-making process the process by which consumers collect information and choose among alternatives

consumer markets individuals or socially related groups who purchase products for personal consumption

consumer perceptions the images consumers have of competing goods and services in the marketplace

consumer price index the change in the cost of a specified set of goods and services over time

consumerism the organized actions of groups of consumers seeking to increase their influence on business practices

controllable risk a risk that can be reduced or even avoided by actions you take

controlled economy an economic system where the government attempts to own and control important resources and to make the decisions about what will be produced and consumed

controlling measuring performance, comparing it with goals and objectives, and making adjustments when necessary

copywriter the person who writes the words in the ad

corporate advertising advertising for a company

corporation a business owned by people who purchase stock in the company

corrective ads ads that companies are required to run to correct any false impressions left by deceptive ads

creative director one who helps guide the creative process and ensures that the creative team's work conveys the right message and is in line with the client's needs

creative strategy how a company positions its brand and product in its advertising

creativity the ability to use imaginative skills to find unique ways to solve problems

culture the history, beliefs, customs, and traditions of a group

D

DECA an international association of high school and college students studying marketing, management, and entrepreneurship in business, finance, hospitality, and marketing sales and service

decision a choice among alternatives

decoding the process by which the receiver interprets the transmitted language and symbols to comprehend the message

demand a relationship between the quantity of a product consumers are willing and able to purchase and the price

demand curve a graph that illustrates the relationship between price and the quantity demanded

demographics the descriptive characteristics of a market such as age, gender, race, income, and educational level

demonstration a personalized presentation of the features of the product in a way that emphasizes the benefits and value to the customer

derived demand the quantity of a product or service needed by a business in order to operate at a level that will meet the demand of its customers

direct channel the producer sells the product to final consumers

direct competition competition in a market with businesses that offer the same type of product or service

direct demand the quantity of a product or service needed to meet the needs of the consumer

direct exporting a company takes complete responsibility for marketing its product in other countries

discounts and allowances reductions in a price given to the customer in exchange for performing certain marketing activities or accepting something other than what would normally be expected in the exchange

discretionary income the amount of income left after paying basic living expenses and taxes

discretionary purchases nonessential purchases that satisfy consumers' wants

distribution (place) the locations and methods used to make the product available to customers

distribution centers a facility used to accumulate products from several sources and then regroup, repackage, and send them as quickly as possible to the locations where they will be used

distribution function determining the best methods and procedures to use so that prospective customers can locate, obtain, and use a business's products and services

E

e-commerce involves business activities, including the exchange of goods, services, and information, completed electronically via the internet

economic market all of the consumers who will purchase a particular product or service

economic resources classified as natural resources, capital, equipment, and labor

economic risk a risk that is caused by the uncertainty of market forces, economic trends, and politics

economic utility the amount of satisfaction a consumer receives from the consumption of a particular product or service

elastic demand market situation in which a price decrease will increase total revenue

elasticity of demand describes the relationship between changes in a product's price and the demand for that product

electronic portfolio (e-portfolio) a career portfolio prepared, maintained, and saved using computer technology

emergency goods products or services that are purchased as a result of an urgent need

emotional motives the forces of love, affection, guilt, fear, or passion that compel consumers to buy

employee empowerment an approach to customer service that gives employees the authority to solve many customer problems

encoding when the sender converts an idea into a message that the receiver can understand

endorsement an advertisement in which a satisfied user publicly expresses approval of a product or service

entrepreneur someone who takes the risk to start a new business

entrepreneurship the process of planning, creating, and managing a new business

ethics moral principles or values based on honesty and fairness

executive summary a short written summary that provides an overview of the business concept and the important points in the business plan

experiments controlled situations in which all factors are the same except the one being studied

exports products and services sold to people in other countries

external information provides an understanding of factors outside of the organization

F

feature a description of a product characteristic

feedback the receiver's response to the message

final consumers those who buy a product or service for personal use

financial forecast a numerical prediction of future performance related to revenue and expenses

financial statement a detailed summary of the financial performance for a business or a part of a business

fine a monetary penalty imposed on an offending company

flexible pricing policy allows customers to negotiate price within a price range

FOB pricing identifies the location from which the buyer pays the transportation costs and takes title to the products purchased

focus group a small number of people brought together to discuss identified elements of an issue or problem

follow-up making contact with the customer after the sale to ensure satisfaction

foreign investment owning all or part of an existing business in another country

foreign production a company owns and operates production facilities in another country

franchising a business relationship in which the developer of a business idea sells others the rights to the business idea and the use of the business name

free economy an economic system in which resources are owned by individuals and decisions are made independently with no attempt at government regulation or control

frequency the number of times a member of the target audience is exposed to the advertising message

G

geographic segmentation dividing consumers into markets based on where they live

green (environmental) marketing marketing activities designed to satisfy customer needs without negatively impacting the environment

gross domestic product (GDP) the total value of goods and services produced within a country during the year

gross margin the difference between the cost of the product and the selling price

gross national product (GNP) the total value of all goods and services produced by a country during the year, including foreign investments

guarantee a general promise or assurance of quality

H

heterogeneous differences between services

human risk a risk that arises because of the potential actions of individuals, groups, or organizations

I

image a unique, memorable quality of a brand

imports products or services purchased from another country

impulse goods items purchased on the spur of the moment without advance planning

income statement a report on the amount and source of revenue and the amount and type of expenses for a specific period of time

indirect channel includes other businesses between the producer and the consumer

indirect competition occurs when a business competes with other companies offering products that are not in the same product category but satisfy similar customer needs

indirect exporting the process in which marketing businesses with exporting experience represent the exporting company and arrange for the sale of products in other countries

industrial economy economy in which the primary business activity is the manufacturing of products

inelastic demand market situation in which a price decrease will decrease total revenue

inflation when prices increase faster than the value of goods and services

input information that goes into the system that is needed for decision making

inseparable the service is produced and consumed at the same time

insurable risk a risk that is faced by a large number of people, is pure rather than speculative, and the amount of the loss can be predicted

intangible incapable of being touched, seen, tasted, heard, or felt

integrated occurs when marketing is considered an essential part of the business and is involved in all important business decisions

internal information information developed from activities that occur within the organization

international trade the sale of products and services to people in other countries

interpersonal communication any person-to-person exchange

inventory the assortment of products maintained by a business

inventory shrinkage a loss of products due to theft, fraud, negligence, or error

invoice an itemized billing statement with terms of payment for the order

J

job any full- or part-time work in a specific position of employment

joint venture business relationship in which independent companies cooperate in common business activities

just-in-time (JIT) inventory level is kept low and resupplied just as it is needed

L

labor intensiveness the amount of human effort required to deliver a service

law of demand when the price of a product is increased, less will be demanded and when the price is decreased, more will be demanded

law of supply when the price of a product is increased, more will be produced and when the price is decreased, less will be produced

lead time the amount of time required to place an ad

leading the ability to communicate the direction of the business and to influence others to successfully carry out the needed work

liabilities the amounts a business owes

liability a legal responsibility for loss or damage

licensed brand a well-known name or symbol established by one company and sold for use by another company to promote its products

lifestyle the way a person lives as reflected by material goods, activities, and relationships

long-range planning analyzing information that can affect the business over a long period of time

M

macroeconomics the study of economic behavior and relationships for the entire society

management involves developing, implementing, and evaluating the plans and activities of a business

managing getting the work of an organization done through its people and resources

markdown a reduction from the original selling price

market the prospective customers a business wants to serve and the location of those customers

market analysis identifies a business's strengths and weaknesses and the opportunities and threats it faces

market intelligence the process of gaining competitive market information

market opportunity an identified market with excellent potential based on careful research

market opportunity analysis studying and prioritizing market segments to locate the best potential based on demand and competition

market position the unique image of a product or service in a consumer's mind relative to similar competitive offerings

market potential the total revenue that can be obtained from the market segment

market price the point where supply and demand for a product are equal

market segmentation the process of dividing a large group of consumers into subgroups based on specific characteristics and common needs

market segments groups of similar consumers within a larger market

market share the portion of the total market potential that each company expects in relation to its competitors

marketing the creation and maintenance of satisfying exchange relationships

marketing concept using the needs of customers as the primary focus during the planning, production, pricing, distribution, and promotion of a product or service

Marketing Education program a career program that incorporates three types of complementary learning experiences—introductory and advanced courses in marketing, business work experiences, and a student organization called DECA

marketing effectiveness both customers and the business are satisfied

marketing information system (MkIS) an organized method of collecting, storing, analyzing, and retrieving information to improve the effectiveness and efficiency of marketing decisions

marketing job a job in which the completion of marketing activities is the most important or only job responsibility

marketing management the process of coordinating resources to plan and implement an efficient marketing strategy

marketing mix blending of the four marketing elements (product, distribution, price, and promotion) by the business

marketing plan a clear written description of the marketing strategies of a business and the way the business will operate to accomplish each strategy

marketing research a procedure to identify solutions to a specific marketing problem

through the use of scientific problem solving

marketing strategy the way marketing activities are planned and coordinated to achieve an organization's goals

markup an amount added to the cost of a product to determine the selling price

mass communication an attempt to reach a wide audience through mass media such as radio, television, magazines, and newspapers

mass marketing directs a company's marketing mix at a large and heterogeneous group of consumers

media plan a detailed listing of where and when ads will run

media planner the person who develops the media plan

merchandise plan identifies the types, assortments, prices, and quantities of products that will be stocked by the business for a specific period of time

merchandising offering products produced or manufactured by others for sale to customers

message what is being communicated

message channel the vehicle by which the message travels

microcredit provides small value loans to people who cannot qualify for traditional bank loans

microeconomics the study of relationships between individual consumers and producers

mission the nature of the business or the reasons the business exists

mixed economy an economic system in which some goods and services are provided by the government and some by private enterprise

mixed merchandise retailers businesses that offer products from several different categories

model stock list the complete assortment of products a store would like to offer to customers

money system the use of currency as a recognized medium of exchange

monopolistic competition the type of market in which there are many firms competing with products that are somewhat different

monopoly the type of market in which there is only one supplier offering a unique product

motivation the set of positive or negative factors that direct individual behavior

multinational companies businesses that have operations throughout the world and that conduct planning for worldwide markets

N

natural risk a risk that is caused by the unpredictability of nature, such as the weather

need anything you require to live

net profit the difference between the selling price and all costs and operating expenses associated with the product sold

netiquette the informal code of conduct regarding acceptable online behavior

new product something that is entirely new or changed in an important and noticeable way

noise any distracting information in the transmission, the message channel, or the receiver's environment that may inhibit or distract from the message

non-business organization has something other than providing products and services for a profit as its primary focus

non-price competition when businesses decide to emphasize factors of their marketing mix other than price

non-store retailing involves selling directly to the consumer at home rather than requiring the consumer to travel to a store

O

observation a way to collect information by recording actions without interacting or communicating with the participant

oligopoly the type of market in which a few businesses offer very similar products or services

one-price policy all customers pay the same price

open-ended questions questions that allow respondents to develop their own answers without information about possible choices

operating expenses all costs associated with business operations

operations the ongoing activities designed to support the primary function of a business and keep it operating efficiently

opportunity the possibility for success

organizing arranging people, activities, and resources in the best way to accomplish the goals of an organization

output the result of analysis that is given to decision makers

P

packing list an itemized listing of all of the products included in the shipment

partnership a business that is owned and operated by two or more people who share in the decision making and profitability of the company

partnership agreement a legal document that specifies the responsibilities and financial relationships of business partners

patronage motives the reasons to buy based on loyalty

penetration price a very low price designed to increase the quantity sold of a product by emphasizing the value

performance standard specifies the minimum level of expected performance for an activity

perishable incapable of being stored for use at a future time

perpetual inventory system determines the amount of a product on hand by maintaining records on purchases and sales

personal identity the characteristics and character that make a person unique

personal selling person-to-person communication with a potential customer in an effort to inform, persuade, or remind the customer to purchase an organization's products or services

personality an enduring pattern of emotions and behavior that define an individual

physical distribution (logistics) the process of efficiently and effectively moving products and materials through the distribution channel

physical inventory system determines the amount of product on hand by visually inspecting and counting the items

planning involves analyzing information, setting goals, and determining how to achieve them

policies rules or guidelines to be used in a company to make consistent decisions

population all of the people in the group that a company is interested in studying

pop-up an advertisement that opens in a new window when a web page is being viewed

positioning statement a specific description of the unique qualities of the marketing mix that make it different from the competition and satisfying to the target market

postindustrial economy economy that is based on a mix of business and consumer products and services produced and marketed in the global marketplace

preapproach gathering preliminary information and preparing a preliminary sales presentation for a customer

preindustrial economy economy that is based on agriculture and raw material development through activities such as mining, oil production, and harvesting timber

price the actual amount customers pay and the methods of increasing the value of the product to the customers

price competition rivalry among businesses on the basis of price and value

price lines distinct categories of prices based ondifferences in product quality and features

price-based goods products that consumers believe are similar but have significant price differences

primary data information collected for the first time to solve the problem being studied

private enterprise an economic system based on independent decisions by businesses and consumers with only a limited government role regulating those relationships

procedures the steps to be followed for consistent performance of important activities

producer the person that facilitates everything that happens after the client agrees to develop an ad or campaign

product anything offered to a market by the business to satisfy needs, including physical products, services, and ideas

product advertising gives the benefits of a specific product or service and relies on rational arguments why a customer should buy it

product assortment the complete set of all products a business offers to its market

product cost includes the cost of parts and raw materials (or the price paid to a supplier for finished products), labor, transportation, insurance, and an amount for damaged, lost, or stolen products

product fulfillment center provides some or all of the activities required to fill customer orders

product liability insurance provides protection from claims arising from the use of the company's products

product life cycle identifies the stages a product goes through from the time it enters the market until it is no longer sold

product line a group of similar products with slight variations

in the marketing mix to satisfy different needs in a market

product usage how frequently consumers use products and the quantity of product used

production the business function that creates or obtains products or services for sale

productivity the average output by workers for a specific period of time

professional liability insurance provides protection against claims of negligent or harmful actions by business professionals

profit motive the use of resources toward the greatest profit for the producer regulating those relationships

promotion any form of communication used to inform, persuade, or remind consumers about a company's products or services

promotional mix the combination of advertising, personal selling, public relations, and sales promotion that marketers use to reach a target market

promotional plan the blueprint for how the elements of the promotional mix will work together to deliver a consistent message

proprietor a person who has sole ownership of a business

proprietorship a business owned and managed by one person

psychographics people's interests and values

public relations (PR) the effort to reach consumers by generating positive publicity

publicity any nonpaid mention of a product, service, company, or cause

purchase order a form listing the variety, quantity, and prices of products ordered

purchase specifications detailed requirements for construction or performance of a product

purchasing determining the products and services needed, identifying the best sources to obtain them, and completing the activities necessary to obtain and use them

purchasing power the amount of goods and services that can be purchased with a specific amount of money

pure competition the type of market in which many suppliers offer very similar products

pure risk a risk that presents the chance of loss but no opportunity for gain

Q

qualifying gathering information to determine which people are most likely to buy

qualitative research research that interprets the why and how of people's opinions

quantitative research collecting data that can be classified into meaningful numerical values

quotas limits on the numbers of specific types of products that foreign companies can sell in the country

R

random sampling a procedure in which everyone in the population has an equal chance of being selected in a sample

rational motives the reasons to buy based on facts or logic

reach the total number of people who see an ad

receiver the person or persons to whom the message is directed, or any person who understands the message that is sent

receiving record a completed listing of all the merchandise received in the shipment and its condition

recession a period of time in which the economy slows resulting in lower production, employment, and income

reciprocal trading a form of bartering in which the products or services of one company are used as payment for the products or services of another company

reference group a group of people or an organization that an individual admires, identifies with, and wants to be a part of

relationship marketing focuses on developing loyal customers who continue to purchase from the business for a long period of time

reorder point level of inventory needed to meet the usage needs of the business until the product can be resupplied

request for proposal (RFP) contains a specific description of the type of product or service needed and the criteria that are important to the buyer

retailer the final business organization in an indirect channel of distribution for consumer products

revenue the money received from the sale of products and services

rich media a variety of digital technologies that provide interactive multimedia experiences for users

risk the possibility that a loss can occur as the result of a decision or activity

risk management includes providing security and safety for products, personnel, and customers as well as reducing the risk associated with marketing decisions and activities

risk-taking a willingness to risk the chance of failure in order to be successful

S

sales promotion an activity or material that offers consumers a direct incentive to buy a product or service

sample a small group selected from the population

scarcity the result of unlimited wants and needs combined with limited resources

secondary data information already collected for another purpose that can be used to solve the current problems

self-concept an individual's belief about his or her identity, image, and capabilities

self-confident a belief in oneself and one's own abilities to be successful

self-directed work team a group of employees who work together toward a common purpose without the usual managerial supervision

self-regulation taking personal responsibility for actions

self-sufficient not relying on others for the things you need to survive

selling direct, personal communications with prospective customers in order to assess needs and satisfy those needs with appropriate products and services

selling price the price charged for a product or service

sender the source of the message being sent

service an activity that is intangible, exchanged directly from producer to consumer, and consumed at the time of production

service quality the degree to which the service meets customers' needs and expectations

service retailers businesses that have services as their primary offering with a limited number of products for sale that complement the services

short-term planning (operational planning) identifies specific objectives and activities for each part of the business for a time period of a year or less

simulations experiments where researchers create the situation to be studied

skimming price a very high price designed to emphasize the quality or uniqueness of the product

social responsibility concern about the consequences of actions on others

specialization of labor concentrating effort on one thing or a few related activities so that they can be done well

specialty goods products that have a strong brand loyalty

specialty or limited-line retailers businesses that offer products from one category of merchandise or closely related items

speculative risk a risk that presents the chance to gain as well as the chance to lose

staffing the activities needed to match individuals with the work to be done

standard of living a measure of the quality of life for a country's citizens

staple goods products that are regular, routine purchases

storage the resources used to maintain information, including equipment and procedures, so that it can be used when needed

strategic brief a short document that defines the target market and articulates the main message of the advertising

strategy a plan that identifies how a company expects to achieve its goals

subsidy money provided to a business to assist in the development and sale of its products

suggestion selling offering additional products and services after an initial sale in order to increase customer satisfaction

supply a relationship between the quantity of a product that producers are willing and able to provide and the price

supply chain flow of products, resources, and information through all of the organizations involved in producing and marketing a company's products

supply curve a graph that illustrates the relationship between price and the quantity supplied

surety bond provides insurance for the failure of a person to perform his or her duties or for losses resulting from employee theft or dishonesty

survey a planned set of questions to which individuals or groups of people respond

T

target market a clearly defined segment of the market to which a business wants to appeal

tariffs taxes placed on imported products to increase the price for which they are sold

test markets specific cities or geographic areas in which marketing experiments are conducted

total quality management (TQM) establishes specific quality standards for all procedures

trade credit credit offered by one business to another business, often because of the time lag between when a sale is negotiated and when the products are actually delivered

trade shows exhibitions where companies associated with an industry gather to showcase their products

trademark the legal protection of the words or symbols for use by a company

trial close providing the customer with the opportunity to buy during the sales presentation

U

uncontrollable risk a risk for which a person's actions do not affect the result

uninsurable risk a risk for which it is not possible to predict if a loss will occur or the amount of the loss

unsought goods products that consumers do not want to buy

V

value an individual view of the worth of a product or service

vendor analysis an objective rating system used by buyers to compare potential suppliers on important purchasing criteria

vendors (suppliers) companies that offer products for sale to other businesses

viral marketing a promotional approach that encourages people to pass along marketing messages though word of mouth, creating a rapid dissemination of information

virtual marketing the completion of marketing activities primarily through the use of computer and Internet technologies

W

want an unfulfilled desire

warehouse a building designed to store large amounts of raw materials or products until they can be used or sold

warranty a specific written statement of the seller's responsibilities related to the guarantee

wholesale member clubs businesses that offer a variety of common consumer products for sale to selected members through a warehouse outlet

wholesalers companies that assist with distribution activities between businesses

Z

zone pricing different product or transportation costs set for specific areas of the seller's market

Index